Sean Egan was born in London. He has contributed to, among others, *Billboard, Book Collector, Classic Rock, Record Collector, Tennis World, Total Film, Uncut* and *RollingStone.com*. He has written or edited seventeen books, including works on The Beatles, Jimi Hendrix, The Rolling Stones, *Coronation Street* and Manchester United. His critically acclaimed novel *Sick of Being Me* was published in 2003, while his 2008 collection of short stories, *Don't Mess with the Best,* carried cover endorsements from Booker Prize winners Stanley Middleton and David Storey.

George Daniell Archive, cover and above photo

Ponies & Rainbows
THE LIFE OF
JAMES KIRKWOOD

Sean Egan

Ponies & Rainbows: The Life of James Kirkwood
© 2012 Sean Egan. All Rights Reserved.

No part of this book may be reproduced in any form or by any means, electronic, mechanical, digital, photocopying or recording, except for the inclusion in a review, without permission in writing from the publisher.

Published in the USA by:
BearManor Media
PO Box 1129
Duncan, Oklahoma 73534-1129
www.bearmanormedia.com

ISBN 978-1-59393-680-8

Printed in the United States of America.
Cover design by Arthur Beckenstein.
Book design by Brian Pearce | Red Jacket Press.

TABLE OF CONTENTS

ACKNOWLEDGMENTS	7
INTRODUCTION	11
ONE	15
TWO	33
THREE	47
FOUR	67
FIVE	79
SIX	111
SEVEN	143
EIGHT	171
NINE	197
TEN	213
ELEVEN	235
TWELVE	259
THIRTEEN	287
FOURTEEN	305
FIFTEEN	331
SIXTEEN	371
SEVENTEEN	383
EIGHTEEN	401
NINETEEN	423
TWENTY	467
TWENTY-ONE	499
TWENTY-TWO	531
EPILOGUE	551
SELECTED BIBLIOGRAPHY	557
INDEX	567

ACKNOWLEDGMENTS

My grateful thanks go to the people who agreed to be interviewed or provide quotes for this book: Gary Beach, Mildred Beach, Arthur Beckenstein, Vasili Bogazianos, Ned Bullock, Ira Cirker, Ross Claiborne, Arthur Cormier, Bob Cromling, Carole DeSanti, John Desmond, Dick Duane, Bruce Eggler, Nick Ellison, Ahmet Ertegun, Trish Garland, Bill Gile, Patti Goldstein, Esther Weber née Hamula, Rupert Hitzig, Matt Hoopes, Louis Ivon, Lucille Macaolino née Jutras, Milton Katselas, Terence Kilburn, T. Michael Kirkwood, Richard Kluger, Larry Kramer, Arthur Laurents, Baayork Lee, Jim Marrs, Vivian Matalon, Donna McKechnie, Terrence McNally, Benjamin Morrison, Andrew Morse, Lila Lee Nichols née Tufford, Donald Oliver, Jerry Paonessa, Jim Piazza, Ronald Plotkin, Homer Price, Donald Roberts, William Russo, Ralph Ruth, Richard Seff, John Shearin, Zachary Sklar, Liz Smith, David Smith, David Spencer, Ben Sprecher, Elaine Stritch, Lomax Study, Dolores Sutton, Jack Sydow, Bob Thixton, Joan Thompson née Kirkwood, Robert Tufford, Sidney Wasserman and Robert C. Wilson.

In addition to speaking to or corresponding with me, the following people kindly provided me with research material and/or answered email queries: Arthur Beckenstein, Vasili Bogazianos, Ross Claiborne, Carole DeSanti, Bruce Eggler, Esther Weber née Hamula, Matt Hoopes, Lucille Macaolino née Jutras, T. Michael Kirkwood, Terrence McNally, Benjamin Morrison, Andrew Morse, Lila Lee Nichols née Tufford, Donald Oliver, Jerry Paonessa, Jim Piazza, Ronald Plotkin, William Russo, Liz Smith, David Spencer, Sidney Wasserman and Robert C. Wilson.

Because this book took over seven years to complete and because of the advanced age group of most of the interviewees, several of the people listed above sadly never lived to see the results of the time they generously gave. Wherever possible, I have kept references to them in the present tense, mainly so as to make it clear that their quotes were ones specifically provided for this book, but perhaps partly so as to exhibit the sort of defiance in the face of the Grim Reaper that was Kirkwood's forte.

I am also grateful for various pieces of assistance to: Yvonne Sorensen Vefik, Herb Sorensen, Karolyn J. Booth, Ray Lembo, Amy Udovich, Marianne Muellerleile, Barbara Bishop, Nancy Hershon Black, Shirley

Richardson, Elisa Lefkowitch, Jennifer Girard and Adam Dixon/the Howard Gotlieb Archival Research Center at Boston University.

Of the all the people listed above, I am particularly indebted to Arthur Beckenstein, who shared the last two decades of James Kirkwood's life. Arthur gave me massive assistance that was selfless on more than one level. He provided me contact information, clippings, DVDs and CDs relating to the subject and granted me the privilege of being the first non-intimate to see Kirkwood's unpublished works and private correspondence. His patient photocopying — page by page for the more fragile manuscripts — wasn't even the half of his sacrifice. Arthur continued to provide assistance to my project even after the point that it became obvious that some of the information I unearthed would be painful and embarrassing to him. A friend of James Kirkwood and Arthur Beckenstein's states in this text that Kirkwood "was very lucky to have Arthur." I consider myself very lucky to have had Arthur's assistance and enthusiasm to count on all through this project. I am delighted that the design Arthur provided for this book's cover carries on a tradition: he devised the covers for most of Kirkwood's published works in the time he knew him.

INTRODUCTION

"He belongs to the new group of major American authors who will dominate American letters — Gardner, Barth, and Brautigan. They describe human beings alive *out there*..."

When *Book World* gave that ecstatic appraisal of his work upon the publication of his fourth novel *Some Kind of Hero* in 1975, it seemed that James Kirkwood was well on his way to permanently sealing his reputation as a literary heavyweight. This impression was only underlined by Kirkwood's ubiquity at that juncture. In recent years, Kirkwood had been working on three ambitious and disparate projects, all of which came to fruition within weeks of each other in 1975. In addition to *Some Kind of Hero*, that year saw the debut of Kirkwood's stage adaptation of his hilarious and critically acclaimed 1972 novel *P.S. Your Cat is Dead!* A hard-edged but compassionate tale of a man who catches a repeat-burglar in his apartment, ties him up and eventually becomes friends with him, the play's then-unusual gay sex references resulted in a reception filtered through the shock of often staid critics. However, it at least achieved the feat of which every playwright dreams in reaching Broadway. The other Kirkwood project to reach fruition that year was *A Chorus Line*, a collaboration between Kirkwood, co-writer Nicholas Dante and director Michael Bennett. Unlike many musicals, this show was no extravaganza but small-scale and fairly naturalistic, especially in the way it focused for once not on the big star or success story but on those earning a crust in the somewhat narrow-horizoned world of the anonymous hoofer. It made a modest entrée just over a week after the *Cat* debut, opening off-Broadway at the Newman Theater (max capacity: 299). Two-and-a-half months later, *A Chorus Line* transferred to Broadway. There was some nervousness among its principals as to whether the power of the play would translate to a large venue. Kirkwood himself, in fact, was one of many who felt that the show lost something when it moved from the intimacy of a smaller space. However, many, many more people thought it just fine in its Broadway incarnation — to such an extent that it remained on the Great White Way three months shy of fifteen years. That record has since been surpassed, but the phenomenon status of *A Chorus Line* is for all time. It wasn't only the public who were enchanted. The play earned Kirkwood a Pulitzer Prize and a Tony Award. It also made him a millionaire.

Some of the tickets for the opening night of *A Chorus Line* had been bought by Thomas J. Crowell for the publisher's staff after Kirkwood's editor there had hit upon the idea of using the show to help publicize Kirkwood's latest novel. *Some Kind of Hero* received some stunning reviews. The *Anniston Star* said that it "…bubbles and rolls with love, meanness, humor and raw life." *Cosmopolitan* declared, "It explodes with cynicism, black humor, sacred and profane sexuality, heartache and humanity." The *Chicago Tribune*'s assessment was, simply, "The best book of the year." All in all, 1975 was an *annus mirabilis* for Kirkwood.

Today, most of James Kirkwood's work is out of print and he is an almost forgotten figure. Although the 2006 reactivations of both *A Chorus Line* and his 1986 play *Legends!* may have sparked some revival of interest in his theatre work, that he wrote five novels in his lifetime, four of them critically acclaimed, now seems destined to remain something resembling a secret. Certainly, the idea of him ever again being spoken about in terms of that *Book World* appraisal are virtually unthinkable.

The critics who loved Kirkwood when he was alive seem to have become embarrassed by their former enthusiasm since his death from AIDS-related cancer in 1989. Kirkwood appears to be viewed with suspicion by the critics who continue to heap praise on the authors with whom he was bracketed by *Book World*. His work is almost perceived as Literature-Lite, mainly due to the fact that his novels did not groan with solemnity but were instead infused with such a humanity and optimism that the prospect of a new Kirkwood book was always heart-lifting to his devotees. This eternal optimism informed the titles of Kirkwood's first and last novels: *There Must Be a Pony!* (the title refers to a boy given a bag of manure for his birthday whose sunny nature leads him to assume it means he has been gifted a foal) and *Hit Me with a Rainbow* (explained Kirkwood, "It means hit me with some of the goodies of life"). Those who sniff at Kirkwood's *joie de vivre* are misguided. The buoyant effect of Kirkwood's prose was not achieved through the irritating deployment of rose tints. Kirkwood was able to make his plots grittily realistic even as he depicted protagonists who refused to succumb to any suggestion that things were unsalvageable.

Kirkwood himself led a life that was as interesting as any of his novels and far more interesting than the slippered life of the average Pulitzer winner. The son of silent screen stars, he grew up in Hollywood surrounded by celebrities and opulence before his parents' ailing fortunes relocated him from Easy Street to just shy of Skid Row. His childhood was littered with divorce, tragedy, sexual confusion and displacement. He spent World War II raising morale on a troop transport and dodging Kamikaze pilots. His professional life encompassed stand-up comedy, acting in film, on stage and on television, and — in a triumphant and personally defining late career change — writing. His private life was equally Catholic, involving loving sexual relationships with both men and women.

Ponies & Rainbows draws upon interviews with over sixty of Kirkwood's family, lovers, colleagues, friends and adversaries as well as Kirkwood's own correspondence and published and unpublished work in order not only to detail the course of a fascinating life but to help confirm once and for all that James Kirkwood was a significant literary talent.

ONE

"…you've had a horrible childhood…You turned out to be an angel anyway."

So says Rita Cydney to her son Josh in James Kirkwood's 1960 debut novel *There Must Be a Pony!* In a book that was largely drawn from its author's own life, that piece of dialogue was one of the most autobiographical passages of all. A glance at Kirkwood's formative years reveals an almost never-ending catalogue of traumas and horrific bad luck: divorced parents, dwindling financial fortunes, debilitating illness within the family, the discovery of a series of dead bodies and endless dislocation. Yet what emerged at the other end of this harrowing rites-of-passage was a man who, though he had a dark and violent side, was preternaturally effervescent, good-natured and humorous. Psychologists, Darwinists and creationists can slug it out as to whether the love of his parents and close family members or some sort of sunny gene saved him from bitterness and self-loathing. Kirkwood himself later said, "Mother says I was a terribly optimistic child…but I think it probably sprang from a certain thick-headed stupidity. Because I certainly saw an awful lot of shit being dumped on the people I loved. Yet, it never occurred to me that it wasn't going to turn out right."

In his non-fiction book *American Grotesque*, Kirkwood describes himself as "a poor kid from the other side of the tracks who never went to college." Some might find such a description surprising considering that not only was Kirkwood originally a true child of Hollywood — both the geographical location and the industry — but would spend much of his formative years with his well-to-do maternal aunt's family. However, the description is not dishonest because, had he wanted to go, there certainly was no money to spend on college for Kirkwood in the twilight of his parents' fading acting careers, something that illustrates just how dramatic was their downwards trajectory.

James Kirkwood Sr. and Lila Lee may not mean much to modern audiences, but in their day Kirkwood's parents were household names, especially in the households of devotees of magazines like *Motion Picture*, *Photoplay* and *Picture-Play*. Though neither of them was in the first rank of Hollywood stars, they were both for a brief while in the middle rank.

Both made their name in silent pictures — Kirkwood Sr. not just as an actor but also director and scriptwriter — and each successfully made the transition to talking pictures. However, their respective successes were relatively fleeting and their son had few particularly glamorous recollections of them professionally and far more images of them enduring unreturned telephone calls and going through the melancholic preparation for auditions that would in all probability not result in a role.

Speaking at a lecture on his mother's career in East Hampton in August 1974, Kirkwood said of Lila Lee, "She had nothing resembling a normal childhood, no family life, no friends her own age, except for co-workers in vaudeville, no schooling, no time with her real parents, until her mother finally came to Hollywood to chaperone her when she was in her late teens." This sad state of affairs was a consequence of Lee being discovered by Gus Edwards at the age of four. Edwards' traveling revue was big box office in an era when cinema was in its infancy and before radio and TV broadcasts existed. One of its attractions was performing children. Audiences lapped up Kirkwood's mother's dancing and singing, but this and the remuneration were scant consolation for rarely seeing her parents or her older sister Pauline (referred to by the family as Peg or Peggy).

Lee was born Augusta Wilhelmina Frederica Appel in 1905. Later, Lee and her employers would cast confusion over her year of birth in an attempt to disguise how young she was, an endeavor in which her son later assisted her for his own reverse purposes. Lila went by the sobriquet "Cuddles" in Edwards' revue. At the age of thirteen, she was told by no less a figure than Charlie Chaplin that she should be in pictures after he had seen her perform at the Orpheum Theatre in Los Angeles. Later that year in New York, Chaplin was proven shrewd when she passed a screen test and was signed up by Jesse Lasky of Famous Players-Lasky Corporation, which later became Paramount Pictures. A change of name was deemed in order and she was given the forename Lila — because Edwards' wife had always liked it — and the surname Lee. She was groomed by her studio, in her opinion, to be the replacement for Mary Pickford, then one of the most famous women on earth as a pioneering superstar of "moving pictures" and planning to decamp to set up what turned out to be United Artists. In 1919, aged just fourteen, Lila Lee appeared in no fewer than ten motion pictures, including *Male and Female*, directed by the legendary Cecil B. DeMille. Though she didn't succeed in assuming Pickford's role of "America's Sweetheart," Lee did make more than 100 films, appearing opposite luminaries like Rudolph Valentino in *Blood and Sand*, Lon Chaney Sr. in *The Unholy Three* and Fatty Arbuckle (four pictures).

Terry Kilburn, an adult friend of Kirkwood's who met Lila Lee, says that although, "she was a very charming woman," Lee "didn't strike me as being overly intelligent." Lee herself wrote in her unpublished and unfinished autobiography that as a consequence of her lack of education, when her son was around ten or eleven, "...he'd come home from school and ask me to help him [and] all I could do was shrug." Not only did Lee attend no classes in a time before mandatory schooling, but she later claimed her childhood was sullied by Edwards kissing and groping her when she was fifteen. She also said that of her $1,000-a-week salary — an incredible amount for the time — Edwards kept the lion's share and her family were sent expenses. A lawsuit ultimately freed her from Edwards' clutches.

Lee did end up in the clutches of another man who had a predilection for young girls — Charlie Chaplin — but she later said that Chaplin — whom she recalled she began dating at around the age of sixteen — was not the lecher of legend but in fact a perfect gentleman. She was less interested in the man with whom she starred in the silent epic *Blood and Sand*, released in 1922. Most women in the Western world would have given their eye teeth to be cast opposite Rudolph Valentino, but Lee preferred blondes to the smoldering Latino looks that had made Valentino the pre-eminent male movie star of the era. In the same year, Lila met her future husband, James Kirkwood.

"She was a slugger, an optimist, a survivor and a true romantic," Kirkwood said of his mother after her death. "And best of all she had an absolutely lovely sense of humor about the world and especially about herself." No doubt all those things were true, but she had a darker side. Homer Price, a friend and neighbor of Kirkwood's for three decades, remembers Lee as "just a delight," but also says she was "a spoilt woman." He recalls being shocked at the treatment to which Lee would subject her now adult son. "He totally, totally adored his mother, who didn't treat him so well actually," he says. "She put him down." He adds that Kirkwood's writer friends Evan Rhodes and James Leo Herlihy expressed similar astonishment at her behavior toward Kirkwood. Price: "In fact, Jamie [Leo Herlihy] got quite disgusted with her."

Kirkwood's description of his father was "charming, crazy, leonine" — a revealing mixture of a superlative, a pejorative and an ambiguity. Kirkwood Sr. (as he will henceforth be referred to in this text) was born in Michigan on February 22, 1876. (Most sources state 1875, but his birth registration paper and World War I draft card show this to be erroneous.) He was one of, it is thought, eight children fathered by an Irish immigrant with two different wives. Terrance (aka Michael) Kirkwood, his second son and half-brother to the subject of this book, says, "In growing up I thought I was Irish. Every time there was an Irish fair I'd always go, and you look up your name and Kirkwood was never there. Once I went to a Scottish fair and sure as hell there's 'Kirkwood,' under another name, as a sub-whatever. Then I came to find out Kirkwood is a Scottish name. But it's all Celtic."

Though both he and Lila Lee were actors, Kirkwood Sr. was much more steeped in the theatre tradition. In fact, he was much more steeped in everything: by the time he met seventeen-year-old Lee, he was in his late-forties. At the start of his acting career, the idea that the nascent cinema medium would become the main outlet for thespian activity was barely imaginable. His film work began in 1909, before the point at which the movie industry was one almost exclusively based in Hollywood. Looking up an old friend in New York named Harry Salter who happened to be an assistant to famous director D. W. Griffith, he found a teenaged Mary Pickford shooting a scene. Griffith noted him observing. Kirkwood later said his father had a face that was "chiseled like the prow of a ship. Women would faint at the sight of him." Griffith certainly seems to have been taken with the striking appearance of this handsome, if slightly lantern-jawed, man. Upon discovering he was a stage actor, the director signed him up for the very picture being made, *The Lonely Villa* (whose eight-minute length was not unusually scant for the era). Kirkwood Sr. quickly became a compelling screen presence and within a few years of his acting debut had begun directing.

Just as Kirkwood Sr.'s acting prowess enabled him to make the transition from stage to film, so his excellent diction and authoritative tones would ensure in the late 1920s that he comfortably handled the passage of films into the age of sound. Recalls Bobby Tufford, Kirkwood Sr.'s nephew, "When he was on a stage — I remember seeing him in *The Life of Edgar Allan Poe* — you could hear a pin drop because he had a voice that would attract your attention and you would listen. He was very, very, very good."

Kirkwood Sr. directed Mary Pickford nine times between 1914 and 1915. He is rumored to have had an affair with America's Sweetheart, but then he is rumored to have carnally known many female stars of the era. His son's friend Evan Rhodes once recalled Kirkwood saying to him, "I never met an actress that he hadn't balled — except for Lillian Gish." Not that this, for Kirkwood's friend William Russo, implied disapproval: "At one point, he said to me, 'Oh my daddy diddled Mary Miles Minter and many others in Hollywood — and so did I.' He sort of associated himself with his father's promiscuity. Like father, like son."

Though he racked up 25 or so movies behind the cameras, Kirkwood Sr.'s directing career began to falter by the turn of the twenties — partly as a result of a drinking problem and a fiery temper, the latter possibly created by a horse-riding accident that briefly put him into a coma shortly after his marriage to Lila Lee. Kirkwood Sr. had to make ends meet through a return to the acting that he had largely abandoned by 1917.

Lila Lee and Kirkwood Sr. met when both were working as actors on the set of the silent shipwreck movie *Ebb Tide* (released in 1922). They were married on June 25, 1923, Lee's eighteenth birthday. According to Kirkwood (interviews) and Lee (her autobiography), it was Kirkwood Sr.'s third marriage. Gertrude Robinson, 1916-1923, was one of his previous wives; details of the other (which may even go back to the nineteenth century) are elusive. In a 1929 article, Lee said that her acquiescence to the marriage proposal was, "…against the advice of all my friends." Indeed. One source, who prefers not to be named, says of Kirkwood Sr., "He had a mania for young women and he would marry them and then drag them down to his level — whatever level that was…Lila Lee's mother told her not to marry James Kirkwood because all you have to do is look to his past experiences and that should pretty well tell you why you shouldn't marry him…I remember they were having cocktails and they asked Kirkwood about his second wife and he couldn't remember her name!"

As if to illustrate that Kirkwood Sr. was a different person to different people, and projected huge charm when he wanted to, Lomax Study — a friend of both Kirkwood *pere* and *fils* — simply remembers him as, "Very, very, very soft spoken, very delightful." Lee, however, saw a vastly more unpleasant side to her new man and her autobiography paints an even worse picture than her horrified relatives imagined. She claimed that Kirkwood Sr. took her virginity before they were married and that she fell pregnant as a result of this first-ever coupling. Kirkwood Sr. arranged an abortion (then illegal). Their relationship continued afterwards, but Lee's autobiography also claimed that the reason it did was that Kirkwood Sr. threatened to tell her mother of their pre-marital carnal relations (then culturally shameful, particularly for women) if it didn't. The implication of this passage is that this is why they got married.

On August 22, 1924, Kirkwood Sr. was working on a scene in his current picture when a studio attendant arrived with the news that Lee had given birth to an 8lb boy at the Good Samaritan Hospital in Los Angeles. Considering the uncertainty in which James Kirkwood would later cloak his sexuality, it's perhaps fitting that a little confusion initially surrounded the new baby's gender. The *Chicago Herald Tribune* reported of the birth: "LILA LEE, FILM STAR, BECOMES MOTHER OF GIRL." Said headline was clearly set before the text below it, which accurately reported that in fact Lee had had a male child, whose name it had already been decided would be James Jr. Some confusion also seems to surround Kirkwood's middle name. His graduation certificate, for instance, renders him as "James Mark Kirkwood Jr." (and he signed those three names in a classmate's yearbook), but the letter "A" is given as his middle initial in newspaper reports from his childhood as well as on a tennis varsity letter certificate awarded at a school he attended prior to the school from which he graduated. On his Notice of Separation from the Coast Guard (1946), it is stated that he has no middle name.

Subsequently, Kirkwood's very date of birth would become a subject of confusion. Like many people in the first profession he chose to pursue, acting, Kirkwood was economical with the truth about his age. The recollection of cousin Bobby Tufford about this is a fairly typical one: "I asked Jimmy how old he was one day and just wanted to make conversation, and he turned [to] me violently and he said, 'You *never* ask an actor how old he is because...' He explained why if you're going to get a part you don't want people to know your age." However, the confusion in which Kirkwood deliberately shrouded his year of birth seems to have stemmed from something more than merely a desire to not prejudice casting directors. Arthur Beckenstein, with whom Kirkwood would share his life from 1969, recalls that when he first met him Kirkwood was still pretending to non-intimates to be six years younger than he was even though by this point he was a full-time writer, a profession in which age is considered to not matter a fig. Jim Piazza, Kirkwood's friend and lover toward the end of his life, says, "Vanity had a lot to do with it and I think because Jim was so puckish... You know: the Peter Pan thing. And he hung around almost invariably with much younger people." Lila Lee Nichols née Tufford, Kirkwood's cousin offers this explanation: "I don't think he really wanted to get old. He thought that would be kinda sad." Whether it be vanity or a deeper-seated primeval fear, Kirkwood more or less continued the pretense up until he died. So assiduous was he in this that many reputable sources — including the Library of Congress — still state his year of birth as 1930. Says adult friend Jack Sydow, "He and his mother made a pact that they would never tell on each other. They both changed their birth dates. I was so mad when I saw his birth date listed when he died. I thought, 'That son of a bitch'...I always thought he was much younger than that."

In Kirkwood's early years, Al Jolson was a neighbor and Gloria Swanson would frequently come over to play cards with his mother. Dolores

Del Rio and Ruby Keeler — actresses whose names have not endured as much as Swanson's but who were almost as famous in their day — were also in the vicinity and social circle. Del Rio was described by Marlene Dietrich as the most beautiful woman in Hollywood and, reveals Beckenstein, "As a young boy, Jimmy had a big crush on her." Lila Nichols says of her own mother, Peggy, Lila Lee's sister, "She met Laurel and Hardy. She used to play golf with Hardy's wife. My father used to play golf with Bing Crosby, Bob Hope and all. Bob Hope offered my father a lot of land in the San Fernando Valley dirt cheap. He said, 'I don't need it.' He made a mistake there." Kirkwood could later recall visits in this period to Pickfair, the home of Douglas Fairbanks and Mary Pickford, then the golden couple of the industry. Jim Piazza: "He used to love to tell me the story about when he went to Pickfair with his mother for a party and they were going upstairs to use the bathroom and he saw Errol Flynn fucking some starlet in the corner and his mother put her hands over his eyes."

As parents, both Kirkwood Sr. and Lee seem to have been a mixture of remarkably affectionate and remarkably negligent. There can be little doubt that Kirkwood was esteemed by his mother and father. Dancer Baayork Lee, who worked with him in the 1970s, sums up the feelings of many about Kirkwood's good nature when she recalls him as a, "Loving, loving, loving, loving, loving person." He is also universally recalled as retaining a twinkle in his eye no matter the tribulations in his life. Says Bobby Tufford, "Jimmy had a very humorous attitude about almost everything and that always used to surprise me." Lila Nichols concurs: "His sense of humor helped him get through all the hurdles in his life, because he just always felt there would be a sunny side coming up." Such a generosity of spirit and optimism does not seem the consequence of formative years spent starved of parental warmth. A glimpse of the love he received from his parents can be seen in a letter sent to four-year-old Kirkwood in 1928 by his father when the latter was abroad in England on acting work. Written on the stationery of the Park Lane Hotel, Piccadilly, London, it reads, "My darling hunny bunny Jimmie boy! I love you and I'm lonesome for you & I'll be so happy when I see you again & can hold you in my arms and tell you stories & love you. I never want to be away from my Jimmie boy again. Tell mama I love her and you must be a good boy and make mama happy. Please tell [indecipherable] to look after my honey bunny boy. All my love to you & to mama. Daddy." At the bottom of the letter, Kirkwood Sr. has drawn a smiling matchstick figure wearing a hat for young Kirkwood's amusement.

Kirkwood himself later said in an interview, "I got a lot of affection from both of them, all the hugging, touching and fondling I could handle." However, in the same interview — and, by the look of it, virtually the same breath — he pointed out profound deficiencies in Lee and Kirkwood Sr.'s attitudes toward being a mom and dad: "I just don't think either of them knew how to be parents. Someone once said of my father, 'He should have had puppies,' because, when you were there with him you got all the attention, but the minute you weren't with him, you never entered his mind. I don't ever remember him talking to me about my thoughts and plans for the future, what I wanted to accomplish, any of that. It was a very of-the-moment relationship." He also said, "And both my parents were fairly heavy drinkers. When you're a kid, seeing your parents drunk does something to you, turns you inward to cope with your embarrassment."

Kirkwood's ambivalent feelings about his parents — which seem to have been as much to do with his displacement and the torn loyalties engendered by their subsequent divorce as the dilettante behavior detailed above — are evidently manifested in a couple of strange sequences in his books. In *There Must Be a Pony!*, narrator Josh tells the reader of his fantasy of being adopted. That that signifies anything could be dismissed were it not for the fact that in *Good Times/Bad Times* — another Kirkwood novel with a teenage protagonist — the narrator has a fantasy about a big limousine pulling up in front of him to spill out a glamorous couple who turn out to be his real parents. Interestingly, Beckenstein reveals, "When Lila was away at a hospital with TB and Jimmy was living with his father, their neighbors and friends Al Jolson and Ruby Keeler wanted to adopt young Jimmy. His father refused the offer."

In 1974, Kirkwood adjudged his parents' marriage "disastrous." There were many monetary problems during it. Lee ceased film work on the insistence, she later claimed, of her traditionalist husband. Kirkwood Sr. clearly had ambitions beyond acting. He was the author of at least two unproduced plays and at least fifty "scenarios," the term in the silent era for what we now call screenplays. Not long after his son was born, he decided to try his hand at producing. He and Lee lost $100,000 — well over a million in today's money — on the play *Edgar Allan Poe*. He and Lee invested another $75,000 in a 110-acre ranch near Hemet, California, but eventually the pair lost that too. That was only the start of it, though. According to an early sixties article by his friend John Griggs in *The Players Bulletin*, publication of an actors' club, Kirkwood Sr. told him that in 1925 his accountant informed him he was worth a million dollars. Kirkwood Sr. declined to take his accountant's advice to let him put a quarter of his fortune away in a trust. Four years later, the famous Wall Street stock market crash ruined Kirkwood Sr. Says Lomax Study of Kirkwood, "He never forgave [him]. His father made a fortune and when he died he was absolutely penniless. Jimmy always, always talked about that and he said what a horrible thing it was to not leave his mother with anything." It should be pointed out that not all of this was Kirkwood Sr.'s fault. Lila Lee admitted in her autobiography that the aforementioned incident where he was thrown by a horse led to a lengthy recuperation period during which MGM terminated her husband's contract of $2500 per week right at the point where he needed that money most to fund the house he was building on Benedict Canyon. Medical bills meant the house-building had to be abandoned.

There exists an enduring monument to what Kirkwood Sr. had and lost. In the Hollywood Hills, directly off Laurel Canyon Boulevard, can be found Kirkwood Drive. The land upon which it sits was once the property of Kirkwood's father. "The father had to give up the property and they named a street after him," explains Jerry Paonessa, another friend of Kirkwood Jr.

Kirkwood wrote of a fire that wrecked his family's Malibu beach house and of a screaming inquest between his parents in front of him as the last strong memory he had of them as a married couple. As an adult, Kirkwood found a poignant letter written by his father to Lee from London, "Pleading with her not to get too involved with John Farrow, the man with whom she was supposed to be having an affair. The news had gotten to my father in London and he was frantic about losing her." Kirkwood presumably means a letter dated June 22, 1928, written on Park Lane Hotel notepaper and probably written around two months before that affectionate note for his son reproduced previously. Kirkwood Sr. penned, "You know the only thing that worries me & that's the thought of losing you. If you have anything to tell me I wish you would do it because it would be better for all concerned." Said his son, "I read that love letter and had such a clutch in my stomach. My God. It was just at the time I lost my family." By late September 1928, the newspapers were reporting the Kirkwoods' formal separation. Lee did not end up marrying Farrow, whom according to her autobiography she discovered was being unfaithful to her. She would marry twice more, however. Kirkwood Sr. also racked up two further marriages.

In Lee's autobiography, she wrote, "I don't think I ever really loved Jim Kirkwood." Lee said that her falling in love with John Farrow was the first time she experienced that sensation and that she wrote to her husband in

London stating her wish for a divorce. Though Lee left Kirkwood Sr. on his return, she did not take her son because her husband, "Threatened to kill me. Threatened to kill Johnny. To kill the baby. To kill himself." Lee returned to the acting career she had abandoned and was paying all the bills for the house in which the two Jimmys lived. She sneaked back to see her son when Kirkwood Sr. was away working.

Kirkwood Sr. divorced Lee in 1930 on the grounds of abandonment. He married actress Beatrice Powers the following year. "She wasn't very nice to my Jimmy," wrote Lee of Powers. "In fact, she was mean…" This seems to be borne out by the recollection of Joan Thompson née Kirkwood, the daughter Powers bore Kirkwood Sr. in 1932. Joan says of her half-brother, "He told me that one time I was taking a nap — I was a couple of months old or something — and he was playing the piano and my mother came in and flopped that thing on the keyboard down on his hands to make him stop." (A version of this incident appeared in *Good Times/Bad Times*.) Initially, ill-health meant that Lee could do nothing about the situation. During shooting on *The Unholy Three* — a 1930 remake of a 1925 film in which she appeared with Lon Chaney Sr. — Lee hemorrhaged. Lila Nichols: "She contracted tuberculosis when she was at the peak of her career and in those days you had to go to a sanatorium." Lee blamed the stress of supporting her ex-husband and the son she rarely saw as the ultimate reason for her contracting what was then called galloping tuberculosis. (Kirkwood Sr. felt it was down to overwork and dieting for a part.) Lee relocated to Flynn's Sanitarium in Prescott, Arizona, where the *modus operandi* was to not allow patients to move. During a bed-ridden year, Lee's stocks and shares were wiped out by the Great Crash. She wasn't able to resume acting for a further six months after leaving the sanitarium. Neither Lee's health nor her career would ever truly recover: when the TB wasn't recurring, she suffered a number of other ailments, progressively so as she got older. This had an inevitable detrimental effect on the roles she was both offered and able to accept.

She did at least manage to get her son back. Lee wrote, "I had a conference with Beatrice and I managed to talk her into giving Jimmy up." In April 1934, Lee formally applied for custody, presumably the source of Kirkwood's recollection of being asked by a judge in court in front of his parents with which one he wanted to live. "This was torture because I loved both of them," he said. Lee was formally granted custody in June '34. However, Kirkwood never seems to have gained the impression that either parent wanted — as opposed to loved — him. Something that would seem to bear out this suspicion is the fact that according to her sister Peggy's own unpublished, unfinished autobiography, when Lee had Kirkwood under her care once more, she placed him in a private boarding school, with her son only coming home on weekends. Kirkwood later spoke of ping-ponging back and forth between parents and, "when fortunes were low" for his parents, his Uncle Leonard and Aunt Peggy's house in Elyria, Ohio. "There was never a time when I was with either of my parents for more than a year-and-a-half," he later recalled. Kirkwood said he attended eighteen different schools, the consequence largely of being brought up wherever one or other of his parents happened to be working. Unfortunately for his parents — and Kirkwood — working was something that began to happen to both of them less and less frequently.

As well as all the moving around, there was the matter of Kirkwood having to get used to his parents' new spouses and paramours. This can be unsettling at the best of times, but an unfortunate trait of his mother's began to emerge when she and Kirkwood Sr. split. Recalled Kirkwood, "My mother was one of those unfortunate women who are only attracted to real bastards. She had a taste for charming scoundrels; a nice man with a profession and his feet on the ground was boring to her…I'd sit back and think, 'Oh God, another lemon.'" A case in point seeming to be Jack R. Peine, a stockbroker whom Lila Lee married on December 8, 1934. By July 2 the next year, they were divorced. In her autobiography, Lee claimed that Peine was a drunk, a gambler and (she suspected) a skirt-chaser. Very shortly into their marriage, with Lila looking for a house for the two, Peine took off to Mexico and didn't return for more than a month. "That was all I needed," wrote Lee, who removed herself to the Beverly Hills Hotel and knuckled down to work on a new picture.

Little wonder that despite his love for his parents, Kirkwood seems to have found it a blessing that he was often dispatched to spend time in Elyria. His four periods of residence with his aunt and uncle — particularly the one in which he concluded his high-school education — were vital stages of stability and security for him in an otherwise chaotic and traumatic childhood. "He came when he was in first grade," says cousin Lila, two years Kirkwood's senior. "He was six years old probably. He only stayed that year and then he went back. Then I think he came back maybe the fourth or fifth grade and then he didn't come back until high school. He adored my mother. My mother was his surrogate mother because she was always there for him." Kirkwood later said of Peggy, "My aunt was very, very dear to me. She treated me just like her other two children. I remember that life with my parents was like being in a kind of crazy film, while life in Ohio was like being in an Andy

Hardy movie. My time in Elyria turned out to be the only really normal schooldays I ever had."

It wasn't just his fondness for Peggy that made Kirkwood glad of his time in Elyria. His cousin Bobby — half-brother of Nichols and eight years older than Kirkwood — says, "It was a very, very nice town to grow up in." He describes it as, "A typical mid-western town of about 30,000 people then, 25 now." Nichols: "We were about twenty miles from Cleveland and about ten miles from Lake Erie…Very, very nice lovely little town." Tufford adds, "Elyria had quite a bit of diversified industry for a small town." In fact, one of the industries in Elyria was that of Tufford's family and the material comforts the Tufford family home was able to offer Kirkwood as a consequence of it must have been another plus-point to his stays in Elyria as both his parents began to fall progressively lower down the income ladder. Explains Tufford, "My grandfather was a famous inventor. He invented the concave, convex rubber heel." Giving flat-slab shoe heels suction quality was as revolutionary for the comfort of the walker as injecting air into automobile tires had been for the driver. "He sold his invention and his patents all over the world," says Tufford. "My grandfather was the second-richest man in the town because of his invention. My grandfather was a millionaire, my father spent it and I'm the third generation." (Nichols, incidentally, was as might be assumed named after her film star aunt. "I was always called Lila Lee, like Mary Anne or Mary Jane or whatever," she explains. "But then as I got older they just called me Lila." "Lila" lives on in the family through the name having been given to one of Nichols' granddaughters.)

Kirkwood's feelings about his second family, however, were complicated, as is illustrated by the recollections of Sidney Wasserman. Wasserman was, like Kirkwood, aged ten when Kirkwood befriended him on his second stay in the town. Wasserman lived near to the Tuffords' house on Park Avenue. The two attended fifth grade at McKinley School. Recalls Wasserman, "He and I would walk home together after school and we became very, very good friends." In contrast to the extraordinarily gregarious person most people would come to know Kirkwood as, Wasserman remembers somebody less forthcoming: "Part of why we became good friends is that I was a shy kid and he was rather shy." Unlike Kirkwood though, Wasserman could at least count himself lucky that he had some stability in his world. "From time to time on Saturday nights he would stay over with me in my parents' home," he says. "One Saturday night, it must have been the middle of the night, I heard sobbing and I looked over to the other side of the room. Jimmy was crying and I got out of bed and I said, 'What's wrong?' and he said that his mother didn't love him. I said, 'What are you talking about? Of course she loves you.' He said, 'No, because if she loved me, she wouldn't be sending me away all the time.' And that was the only time he ever expressed any kind of…Because on the other hand he adored her. She was extremely beautiful. I remember in 1934, Jimmy insisted I meet his mother. She came from Hollywood to Elyria for Christmas and I went over to the Tufford home to meet her and I was absolutely gobsmacked by her beauty. I mean, I couldn't even look directly at her because I was so overwhelmed." Wasserman also recalls Kirkwood's relationship with his cousin Lila as complicated: "I think in a way he was jealous of her because she had a mother and father who if nothing else they were consistent, they were there. I think he envied that and that made it at times difficult where he would lose his temper with Lila. But I think also he admired her and saw in her that she was a very beautiful girl, had this strong attraction to her. That's what I felt when I was ten years old. I don't know whether his attraction to her was so far as to say he wanted to make love to her physically, but that certainly the jealousy that he maybe felt was that he almost wished he could be her, instead of she being she. That he would have liked to have replaced her with her family."

Wasserman suspects that this is something that can't have been easy for Kirkwood's cousin Lila and that the two might have felt they needed to compete for Kirkwood's aunt and uncle's affections. "I know that there were these tensions," he says. "I can recall Jimmy and I were in the Tufford living room and she came in from school or something or other and she saw the two of us sitting there having cookies or milk or something and she walked with her nose up in the air. She walked right by us, like we weren't even around, like there was an odor in the room." Kirkwood's complicated feelings seem to have been reflected in his behavior at the time. "He used to have blow-ups where he'd get very upset," says Wasserman. "He had a very volatile personality and his mood swings were enormous, but it was usually related to he had a fight with Lila his cousin. He stormed out of the house, he'd come over to my place and what have you and he would say how much he hates her, that kind of stuff, and then he'd calm down and the next thing you knew he'd go back home and next time I'd see him he was talking about how he loves his cousin or thinks she's really something."

Bobby Tufford offers this memory: "I used to kid him because sometimes he'd have nightmares and I told Jimmy, 'I was afraid to go to sleep, I was afraid you'd kill me.'"

That Lila Lee was not insensitive to the effects of his unsettled life on her son was illustrated many years later when Wasserman ran into her in the company of Peggy on the main street of Elyria. Wasserman estimates that the incident took place in 1948 or 1949, when he and Kirkwood were now in their mid-twenties. "She said to me, 'Oh, you're just who I want to see,'" says Wasserman. "Except for that ten-year-old experience, I had never seen her or talked to her. We went out to dinner together. Jimmy was already I think living in New York. We had an interesting talk that evening. She wanted to know what I remember about Jimmy as a kid of ten. It took me a lot of maturing and growing up to realize it was pretty sad that she needed to ask me what her son was like at ten." Was she wanting to be reassured that Kirkwood had not been too unhappy? Wasserman: "Right. That's exactly what she gave me the feeling of."

Of Kirkwood's father, Wasserman says, "I don't recall conversations about his dad except to say at that time when we were ten that he never saw him." Kirkwood's relationship with his Uncle Leonard may not have been particularly great either. Wasserman doesn't recall Kirkwood ever referring to Leonard much but does recall an incident when he and Kirkwood were sitting on the Tuffords' front porch and Leonard turned up in a taxi blind drunk. "Leonard Tufford literally flopped out," says Wasserman. "Fell out of the car absolutely three sheets to the wind. Aunt Peg came out and she sort of made very light of it and said, 'Oh, come on now, we got to put you to bed' or something like that. And Jim didn't say a word." In an abandoned outline for his first novel, Kirkwood wrote of the young protagonist living with an aunt and uncle in Ohio. He described the uncle figure as "a chronic drinker plus being a chronic anti- everything: his wife, whom Josh loves, his mother, the Jews, the Catholics, the government, the school system, etc., etc." Kirkwood's cousin Lila admits that her father did have a problem with the bottle. "I wouldn't call him wild but he was a drinker," she says. However, she adds of her cousin, "I don't think he disliked my father because my father wasn't the kind of person who would be the least bit cruel or mean."

While it might be unwise, and unfair on Leonard Tufford, to extrapolate anything particularly from all this — Kirkwood's admitted intolerance of people with drink or drug problems is a more plausible explanation for his reaction to the taxi incident — judging by Wasserman's recollections it does seem fair to say that the most important figures for Kirkwood at this juncture in his life were female. "He thought the world of her," says Wasserman about Kirkwood's feelings about his Aunt Peg. "He really did. He in many ways felt that she was more of a mother to him." Also important to Kirkwood then was his maternal grandmother, who along with her husband lived with the Tuffords. The grandfather and Kirkwood's relationship with him didn't make much of an impression on Wasserman, but he says of Kirkwood's feeling about his grandmother, "He really adored her." He elaborates, "On superficial appearance, she looked grandmotherly. She was a rather large woman, Germanic, didn't speak that much English. Jimmy always talked about what a marvelous cook she was. Frequently when we came home from school she would have made some cookies and milk for us and the cookies were always delicious."

When Kirkwood's maternal grandfather died when he was eleven, Kirkwood's meeting with his mother at Cleveland airport *en route* to the funeral was reported by a newspaper as the first time the two had met in three years. That death, incidentally, would seem to be Kirkwood's inauguration into discovering bodies, although the circumstances surrounding this one were not as out-of-the-ordinary — or indeed debatable — as later incidents. Recalled Kirkwood, "I was playing checkers with him and he was in bed and he asked me to get him a cup of tea. When I came back he didn't want to play checkers anymore. He was just sitting right with the checkerboard on his lap, dead."

Kirkwood and Wasserman's friendship was rudely and unexpectedly interrupted after a year. "He disappeared overnight," Wasserman says. At the insistence of Kirkwood Sr., his son had been sent to St. John's, the only Catholic military school in Los Angeles. Wasserman believes that Kirkwood could have had no prior warning of it: "I definitely feel that he would have said something." To add to the feeling of rupture, Wasserman received no word from his missing friend. "I kept thinking maybe he would write me a letter and he never did," he recalls. Wasserman feels the non-contact was due to Kirkwood's devastation at being taken away from Elyria: "I guess he just wanted to distance himself from any memories of Elyria because he was so hurt." The two were not to see each other again until they were fourteen and it was then that Wasserman got a little more insight into the events: "He kept saying when we met up as teenagers that he wanted to write to me and he never got around to it and he said he hated where he was at and was continuing to be moved around. It was an absolute terrible time of his life."

An extant report card means that it can be stated with certainty that Kirkwood was at St. John's in Grade 4 in the term ending June 1934. He later publicly recalled that he and his schoolmates had to salute their nun teachers and drill with wooden guns. He also said he experienced some brutal discipline there. One particular nun seemed to take intense pleasure in doling out chastisements. Kirkwood claimed though that she met her match one day in the form of a brewery heir called Buddy. When the Sister began hitting young Buddy with a yardstick, she and the on-looking class were astounded when Buddy retaliated, kicking and punching with such fury that the Sister's habit was dislodged. "Of course, we were all horrified by the Sister's getting beaten up," Kirkwood later told the *Cleveland Plain Dealer*, "or as horrified as you can be while you're fervently applauding in your mind…Little Buddy of the right cross? We never saw the dear boy again."

Kirkwood was never impressed by Catholicism — or his father's rather creative attitude towards its supposedly non-negotiable principles. "I think a strong Catholic childhood is something that's warped a lot of people," he said in the same interview. "I was taught that my father would go to Heaven when he died, because he was a Catholic, but my mother, who was a Protestant, would go to Hell and never see my father again. Now, this is just a terrible thing to tell little kids, because they're very attached to their parents…And sure enough, when my Dad died…with five marriages and five divorces, he got the Catholic burial he expected. You figure it out."

Kirkwood's St. John's Grade 4 report card shows him as absent for the last part of the 1934 term. Another report card shows that Kirkwood spent Grade 5, or at least part of it, back in Elyria, again studying at McKinley School. At both schools, he achieved As and Bs in all subjects except penmanship, in which he could only muster Cs and Ds. By 1936, Kirkwood was once again living in California. Lila Lee was trying to edge her way back into contention as what was referred to in those days as a "feminine lead." She and her twelve-year-old son were living at the Manhattan Beach home of Gouverneur Morris, then a well-known novelist, and his wife Ruth. Not only had Lee recently gained a new role, but she had finally alighted upon a prospective partner who apparently did not fit into her usual pattern of, to use her son's choice of word, "bastards."

Reid Russell was a car salesman whom Lee seems to have met through their mutual friends the Morrises. In her autobiography, Lee said she had known Russell for more than a year, that she was "deeply in love" with him and that they planned to marry as soon as he obtained a divorce. Kirkwood would later say of Russell, "She was engaged to a charming guy, one of the few men that actually liked me too, and I was looking very much forward to having him as a step-father…" If Kirkwood's fictionalized portrait of Russell in his novel *There Must Be a Pony!* is accurate, it's easy to understand why. Kirkwood named the Russell character in the book Ben Nichols (the surname of course a reference to the married name of his own cousin Lila). Nichols is a wonderful father figure: handsome, popular, easy-going and, crucially, good with kids. Instead of a "lemon" resentful of his partner's son's presence, he enjoys his company and puts him at his ease. Though Kirkwood felt genuine love for his real father, one suspects that he felt about Russell in relation to Kirkwood Sr. the way he felt about Elyria in contrast to the myriad other places of residence he'd known: a merciful blast of normalcy.

Normalcy though was something that Kirkwood was never destined to know in his childhood. On September 25, 1936, at about 5:30pm, young Kirkwood made his way down the vast garden of the Morrises' house toward a shattering discovery. In a 1980 university lecture, he recalled, "We had a parrot, three dogs and a monkey. I used to let the dogs out to run in the late afternoon. One foggy afternoon, one of the dogs didn't come back. We had a rather large house with a lawn and some citrus trees and a barbecue pit and a barn. I went out looking for the Pekinese… and I found the dead body of this man that my mother was engaged to be married to in a hammock down by the barbecue pit." Kirkwood said on *The Dick Cavett Show* the same year that Russell had, "a bullet hole through his head and a lot of ants crawling around his face. He'd been there for two days."

TWO

It had seemed that Lila Lee, the woman whose career and health setbacks had seen her dubbed the Hard Luck Girl of the Movies and who had been repeatedly maltreated by men, was about to forge a new and better life on every level. With the discovery of Reid Russell's body, she in one blow lost both her professional revitalization and her chance of personal happiness.

In a section of her autobiography handwritten by her collaborator Evan Rhodes, Lee said, "One morning as I was going to work Jimmy said Reid's car is here but I paid no attention. Later that afternoon or early evening, I received a call that J had found Reid's body. And there was a big hullaballoo. I was not able to come right home because we had hundreds of [illegible]. I said to Ruth don't get Jimmy into it. Boy, was he in it…"

Though it was horrifying for a twelve-year-old to discover an already decomposing body, worse was on the horizon. Kirkwood later recalled, "The police came in and really kind of bungled it up because the local police, knowing my mother and being fond of her, immediately assumed that it was suicide and they took the body away and washed the wounds, so consequently there were no powder burns and no fingerprints or anything like that. Then the Los Angeles police said, 'Hey wait a minute — what's going on down there?' It became kind of a *cause celeb* and the Hearst papers picked it up. It was a very nasty affair."

In the September 27, 1936, edition of the *Los Angeles Times*, it was stated that Sheriff's deputies investigating the death were treating the case as suicide. As he would be in several stories reporting the case, Kirkwood was referred to as "James Lee Kirkwood" — i.e., given both his mother and father's surnames. It was explained that a bullet from a .32 caliber had penetrated Russell's head and passed through the other side, but that neither the bullet nor the empty shell had yet been located. Both Morris and his wife were quoted as saying that Russell had recently made suicidal remarks after having lost his job, although Mrs. Morris said she had no idea his state of mind was desperate. Russell's mother had confirmed that the gun found in his hand was one he kept in a bureau drawer at his home. "Deputy Sheriff Coxton and Bright said they will not ask an [sic] autopsy or inquest unless such action is justified by further investigation," the paper stated. With that, and judging things at face value, Lee was left to grieve and contemplate why her fiancé should decide to end it all. Kirkwood, who had lost his long-desired "proper" father-figure, had his own turmoil to address.

Six weeks later, the picture changed dramatically. "THREAT MADE IN DEATH CASE: MOTHER OF RUSSELL WARNED NOT TO PUSH BEACH INVESTIGATION," read the headline in the *Los Angeles Times* of November 11. The story began, "A telephone threat that 'some harm might befall you if you continue to push the investigation into your son's death' was received yesterday by Mrs. Victoria Russell, mother of Reid Russell...While the threat was being made Everett Davis, investigator for the office of Dist. Atty. Fitts, was assigned to the case. He will confer with Mrs. Russell today to learn the details which resulted in the reopening of the investigation. The telephone threat was received by Mrs. Russell at her home yesterday. The voice on the opposite end of the line was that of a woman. 'I've read about the story,' the unidentified voice said, 'and I'm interested in the case as a mother'...Mrs. Russell furnished authorities with information establishing a possible love motive for a slaying...indicating that her 28-year-old son had been carrying on an affair with a wealthy married woman."

The November 13 edition of the same paper carried an article that began, "Prepared to recheck every available but [sic] of evidence in connection with the death of Reid Russell, youthful friend of Gouverneur Morris, the writer, District Attorney's investigators today will visit the scene of the man's demise at Manhattan Beach." It was explained that the decision to reopen the investigation followed a conference between the investigators and Reid's mother. The latter, it was stated, had been caused to doubt the original suicide theory by "numerous clews." Those "clews" were not elaborated upon by the paper, but a possible reason for suspicion being aroused about Russell's death is the conflicting stories supplied by the Morris household about whether he had left a suicide note. In Lila Lee's autobiography, she wrote, "Ruth told me that she had a note from him. But she wasn't going to tell anybody about it so when I went down to the D.A.'s office I said she hadn't received any note. Then Ruth said that she had. But I didn't read the note. She read it to me. Something about he couldn't stand it any longer."

The following day, Mrs. Morris' picture appeared in the paper as questioning got underway at the Hall Of Justice. The 15th saw reportage on the hearing. The *Los Angeles Times* revealed that Morris, his wife and Lila Lee had been questioned by authorities about the destruction of the suicide note that Russell had supposedly written. Mrs. Morris had come across it in a box on her dresser drawer two or three days after the body of Russell had been found. According to Mrs. Morris, the note read, "I told you I was going to do it and now I have done it." Because the case had already been declared a suicide, Mrs. Morris (who it was said informed Lila Lee about the note) decided to burn it. "I wish I had kept the note, as it would have cleared up all of this," Mrs. Morris was reported to have told investigators. Gouverneur Morris said that neither he nor his wife had heard the report of a gun neighbors recalled coming from the Morris home at about 9pm on September 24 (i.e., the day before Kirkwood discovered the body) and added that there had been no quarrel concerning, he, his wife or Russell, who were all good friends. Meanwhile, according to investigator Captain Plummer, Lee had confirmed the Morrises' story that Russell had on occasion threatened to commit suicide. "In fact," she was quoted as saying, "he talked about it incessantly. I had a long talk with him in the kitchen a week before he died and he told me he was in trouble with the automobile company that employed him." Curiously, the newspaper carried what looked like a posed photograph of Lila and Ruth Morris "furnishing information" to Plummer.

The reportage in the *San Francisco Chronicle* of the same day indicated that it was a somewhat more sensationalist publication than the *Times*. Opening with an observation that Gouverneur Morris was finding himself involved in a real-life story that might invite comparisons with the "luscious heroines" and "paradoxical mystery" in which he specialized professionally, it stated that the body of "handsome" Russell had been found on a "gayly colored swing." Lila Lee was charmingly described as a "former beauty," if "willow." In this paper, it was alleged that as Mrs. Morris spoke the words of the suicide note (reported here as "I told you I was going to do it and you see"), she tottered and slumped from her chair in a faint, requiring a matron to hold smelling salts to her face. After a rest to recover her strength, Mrs. Morris explained to the hearing that she had found the note several days after Russell's funeral and had shown it to Lila. She had suggested to Lila that she destroy it because "I didn't want to drag it all out again, and Mrs. Lee agreed with me." Lee said that she had not read the note but had watched Mrs. Morris burn it in an ashtray.

Kirkwood himself made the papers in a big way on the 16th. The *Los Angeles Examiner* carried — under the legend "Russell Death Probe" — the headline "POLICEMEN LOST BULLET, SAYS LAD." The sub-heading was, "CLAIMS HE SAW IT." Beside an incongruous picture of a smiling Kirkwood, the story explained, "Asserting that he saw officers pry a bullet out of a settee and lose it in long grass, Jimmy Kirkwood, 12-year-old son of Lila Lee, gave a new and startling turn yesterday in the probe of Reid Russell's strange death seven weeks ago…Until Jimmy blurted out the statement yesterday to an *Examiner* reporter, police had insisted steadfastly that no trace of a death bullet had ever been found nor of a shell that might have been ejected from the death gun…The bullet, it was declared by the son of the former screen star, was discovered lodged in a settee behind the lawn swing where Russell's body was found. In the process of being pried loose, the missile suddenly plopped out and landed in the high grass growth, the youngster declared, and the officers sought for it in vain." The paper said that Kirkwood's story was corroborated "in part" by Mrs. Morris who, it claimed, told the *Examiner* that "although she herself did not see the bullet, she had been informed of the incident by Jimmy a short time after it occurred."

Contacted about this, what the *Examiner* described as, "startling story," Captain Plummer admitted that an officer named Percy Jones dug a bullet out of a "swing post." The paper continued, "This was a .22 caliber bullet, however, and Jones threw it away, Captain Plummer said, as the pistol believed to be the death pistol was of .32 caliber." The same story featured what Mrs. Morris recalled as the contents of Russell's suicide note "as nearly as possible":

> *Dear Ruth: you thought I would not do it but now you know.*
> *This has been the happiest vacation I have had in a long time. Thanks a lot for everything.*
> *I hope you don't think I didn't keep my chin up.*
> *Good bye. Reid.*

According to William Russo — who became a friend of Kirkwood when the latter was an adult — Kirkwood told him there had been three suicide notes. One of them was in Ruth Morris' jewel box and two were within a newel post on the handrail of a set of stairs in the house, a little hiding place. Russo recalls that Kirkwood told him that the newel-post notes were found after the police investigation into the case was closed. However, in a letter to Russo in which Kirkwood discusses the suicide notes, he does not seem to be talking about fixtures of real life ("…they were handwritten and in my imagination, they would not have been dated.

I don't think anyone who writes a suicide note would particularly care about the formality of dating it"), but rather of the written fiction that Kirkwood later wove the events into.

On the 17th, the *Los Angeles Times* was reporting that Russell's body might be exhumed, depending on the report of a ballistic expert who was attempting to determine whether the .32 caliber revolver found in Russell's hand had been fired recently. If the report concluded that the gun had not been fired in recent weeks, the wound would be examined to determine if a gun of another caliber had caused the wound. The paper reported that the previous day, Plummer, Everett David and Captain Perry [sic] Jones of the Manhattan Beach police department had been at the Morris home where they, among other things, fired several shots from a .32 automatic into a dirt-filled basket in an effort to see which way the shells fell. They reported that they were easily able to find the fired shells. Plummer was quoted as saying, "If Russell shot himself while lying in the swing, it should be an easy matter to find the shell ejected from the automatic. It could not have fallen more than two or three feet from the body, and should have been found easily in the matted grass about the swing." Plummer even went so far as to opine that Russell may not have been killed in the swing: "Another significant thing…is that Russell's arms were folded across his breast when his body was found and one hand was clutching the gun in a position not likely to have been maintained had he shot himself through the head." Plummer also revealed he had questioned the house gardener John Mumolo about the fact that despite working on the premises on the day Russell's body had been found, he had failed to see it lying on the swing. Despite his apparent new skepticism about the suicide theory, Plummer admitted, "We have been unable to establish any motive to indicate a murder." Meanwhile, the paper revealed the police's reaction to young Kirkwood's claim of seeing a detective lose a bullet: "They pointed out many .22 caliber bullet holes are evident on the estate as the result of target practice and rabbit hunting and that several such bullets have been found and thrown away." The paper carried a picture of Davis and Plummer reconstructing the death scene, Davis lying prone on a bench while Plummer examined a picture of the body taken shortly after it was found. That day's *San Francisco Chronicle* even went so far as to claim that Plummer said that Russell's body was carried to the lawn and dumped in the swing to make it look as though he had killed himself there — although the lack of an actual quote to this effect might indicate that this was sensationalist extrapolation from Plummer's more sober direct quotes as reported in the *Los Angeles Times*.

With the following day's edition of the *Los Angeles Times* came the news that Captain Plummer was going to ask for the body of Russell to be exhumed. The previously discussed ballistic test had been unable to determine when the .32 had last been fired because the gun was in such a rusty condition. Though it was stated that Plummer was "emphatically" not advancing a theory of murder, he had been led by circumstances to believe that death may have occurred at some place other than in the swing. A stained pillow found beneath Russell's head had been turned over to police chemists for examination the previous day and Plummer revealed that he was intending to speak to an unnamed life-long friend of Russell's from San Bernardino to see if he could shed light on the case. As was by now the pattern, that day's *San Francisco Chronicle* gave out some intriguing "details" which didn't feature in the *Los Angeles Times*: Plummer was now also of the opinion that Russell may have been the victim of a "love slaying" and that Russell's mother had told him that on a Sunday evening four days before Russell's body was found, a woman had telephoned repeatedly for Russell demanding, "Where is he? Why didn't he come here as he promised?" and saying, "He just can't do this to me." Mrs. Russell said she told the woman that her son was "out with a sweet young lady."

November 19 saw the Kirkwoods and Morrises get a break of sorts when the ex-wife of Russell stepped forward to tell the world through the *Los Angeles Times* that she believed that he had killed himself. Though she hadn't seen him since their divorce in 1929, she said, "He was of moody type and brooded a great deal and would be likely to take his own life if he became too despondent…I think Reid's mother is doing us all an injustice by bringing this up again. I know it is hard for her to believe her son would take his life." This last comment may have been an allusion to the fact that Mrs. Russell was a Catholic, to which religion of course suicide is a damnable sin. The paper also revealed that an eight-year-old son of Mrs. Russell was attending an El Paso grade school but didn't state whether Russell was the father. (Assuming the reportage is correct, Russell either married again subsequently or Lee — waiting for her chance to marry him — was strangely unaware of his divorce.)

The same day, an entirely new theory about Russell's death was introduced. The *Examiner* ran a story headed, "Racketeering Ring Linked to Russell Case." "Reid Russell was murdered because he knew too much" was the dramatic opening sentence. The source for the information was a Detective Lieut. Harry Leslie Hansen of the Georgia Street Division, "an old friend of Russell." The *Los Angeles Times* also carried the story the next day, claiming that Hanson (as they spelt it) had reported to the District

Attorney's office that Russell had told him he was going to quit his automobile salesman's job to smuggle arms and ammunition to a foreign country. Russell had supposedly revealed these plans to Hanson when the two had gone on a weekend party "five days before his death." It was the last time Hanson had seen his friend. The same paper reported that examination of Russell's exhumed body had led a county autopsy to declare that the results of the first autopsy still stood: the wound on Russell's temple was powder-marked and seared, indicating a self-inflicted wound and that the wound was too small to have been made by either .45- or .38-caliber weapons and too big to have resulted from the firing of a .22, thus indicating that the .32 found in Russell's hand was indeed the cause of death. However, it was reported that examination of the stained pillow was going ahead, as was one of a backdrop of the lawn swing in which Russell was found to determine whether there was blood on the fringes of the bullet hole found in it.

The edition of the *Los Angeles Times* on the 21st carried the news that Russell's financial affairs were being looked into and that "other authorities" were beginning a search of automobiles used by Russell and a number of his friends in an effort to find blood stains. District Attorney Fitts emphasized that the authorities were checking every available bit of evidence in the investigation at the request of Russell's mother and that no one was suspected of causing Russell's death. The following day, the paper announced that the clothes Russell had been wearing on the day that his body was found had been retrieved from an undertaker who had taken care of Russell's body. "Both Capt. Plummer and Davis said an important announcement may be made tomorrow as a result of the examination of the clothing," the *Times* reported.

Evidently, no such important announcement was made, for all the *Times* or the *Chronicle* had to report on the 24th after a day in which neither mentioned the case was that Gouverneur Morris was getting sick and tired of the whole business. Having returned with his wife from a stay at a ranch near Fresno, where he had gone because the police investigation was hampering his writing (Lee and Kirkwood had remained in the house), an exasperated Morris branded the entire investigation "ridiculous and foolish." He added, "No matter how much they investigate they'll learn only one thing — that is that the unfortunate young man killed himself. We have given officers the names of five people to whom Russell had declared he intended to commit suicide. I'm sick and tired of being hauled out of bed at all hours to answer questions I've already answered and if this thing continues I'll take legal action to stop the District Attorney's office from making a public show of me."

The 25th saw the *Times* carry a story headed "New Mystery Angles Enter Russell Death Case," although disappointingly the story contained little detail because, "Captain Plummer declined to state the nature of the new information or to state the name of his informant." The authorities did reveal however that the status of Russell's bank account and the reason for him being discharged from his job were being investigated. In addition, the gun was due to undergo tests to find out the atmospheric conditions to which it had been subjected. The authorities were interested in finding out where the gun had been from the time of Reid's death to the re-opening of the investigation into it.

On December 12, 1936, District Attorney Buron Fitts closed the case on the grounds that "blood tests" had confirmed there was no foul play. Fitts, it should be noted, has subsequently (and posthumously) been accused of being in the pocket of movie studios. Prior to the Reid Russell case, he had allegedly helped cover up the reasons for the death of a husband of actress Jean Harlow. He had also been involved in a decision to drop a statutory rape charge against a wealthy man, a decision which was subsequently exposed as possibly influenced by bribery. Fitts would also be responsible for closing down another celebrity-associated case involving potential murder, this one of director William Desmond Taylor, who died in 1922. (In the year following the Reid Russell controversy, James Kirkwood Sr., lover of suspect Mary Miles Minter, was questioned in the reopened, inconclusive Taylor investigation.)

Naturally none of this proves anything regarding the Russell case, nor does the fact that in a précis of events Mrs. Morris gave to the *Los Angeles Examiner* she claimed it was she, not young Kirkwood, who found the body, espying it in the swing from the balcony of the house after returning from a trip to look in the house's barn with Kirkwood after he had alerted her to the presence of Russell's car. Nor does the fact that in Lila Lee's autobiography she notes that with three particular men with whom she broke up, one committed suicide, one attempted suicide and one threatened suicide — and this tally does not include Russell. Nor does the fact that that autobiography had a working title of *All My Lovers are Dead*. There again, said autobiography contains a bizarre passage about the storm that engulfed Lee after Russell's death which opens up another possibility, although precisely what is not clear: "They started digging around the place & they found out that our gardener had had relations with a sheep, had buried it. It was too silly to make the papers. The gardener had made a pass at Jimmy when he was alone in the house in the afternoon. He was gotten rid of but fast."

Few were left unscathed by the case. Even if we can discount as an appalling but impermanent ordeal the fact that Kirkwood had to try to go about his daily business, including schooling, with this media sensation raging around him, some damage was irreparable. The bad publicity ensured that Lila Lee lost her career — again. Though she had made a reputation for bouncing back from professional troughs before, this was a bridge too far. Kirkwood later said that when the Russell death occurred his mother was "working on a very bad picture at Old Republic Studio." Now even bad pictures would become hard to obtain: the records reveal no motion picture releases featuring Lee after 1938 — except her finale in 1967's *Cottonpickin' Chickenpickers*, considered one of the worst films ever made. Lee had also lost, judging by her subsequent marriage record, possibly the only man who could have ever made her happy. Though there is no evidence that it is related to the Russell case, it is arresting that in April 1939 Ruth Morris committed suicide. The following month, Gouverneur Morris was involved in a car crash, though survived and lived on until 1953. If we are to infer that Gouverneur Morris was the prototype for the camp author Merwin in Kirkwood's *There Must Be a Pony!*, it hardly seems likely that the relationship with his wife was a physical one (although they did have a daughter), which makes one wonder whether Mrs. Morris was the "wealthy married woman" with whom Reid Russell's mother claimed her son was having an affair.

"I think he committed suicide," Lee said of Reid Russell in her autobiography. However, Evan Rhodes wrote in his handwritten notes that Lee had said to him, "Do you want to know about the killing?…not the killing — the suicide," a passage that the suspicious might interpret as Lee correcting herself after letting her guard slip. Kirkwood opined that the case was suicide, the result of pressures piling up on Russell that he couldn't handle. Others are not so sure. Some even feel that Kirkwood himself had something to do with Russell's death.

In his book *Diary of a Mad Playwright*, Kirkwood spoke of toying with the idea of hiring a hitman to kill Kevin Eggers, one of the producers of his play *Legends!*, and of actually telling Eggers this to forestall his execution plan. He doesn't entirely convince the reader that he is joking, nor even entirely give the impression that he wants to convey that he is joking. In a 1986 interview, Kirkwood said, "I'm forever surprised that I'm allowed out in public. I really ought to be in a rubber room." This can all be dismissed as humor, but knowledge of Kirkwood's more extreme behavior suggests it might just as easily be Kirkwood leaving clues to a psychotic nature. As an adult, Kirkwood had a propensity for violence which was child-like in being the brattish response to not getting his own way but was nonetheless extreme. His 1940s and 1950s stand-up comedy partner and sometimes lover Lee Goodman publicly noted that he was often on the receiving end of it, and Kirkwood acknowledged this as true in print. Jim Piazza, another Kirkwood lover, this one from the eighties, was also a recipient of and witness to Kirkwood's capacity for physical abuse and found it highly disturbing. "I don't know why the subject came up," Piazza recalls, "but I said to him, 'Jimmy, did you ever kill anybody?' He just looked at me and said, 'Yes.' I said, 'During the war?' And he was very vague about it. He said, 'Never mind.' I always had a theory about Jimmy. I always wondered in the back of my mind if he had actually killed his mother's lover because I think he and his mother were so, really, really, almost unnaturally together in a way. I wouldn't have been surprised if they had had sex. That whole scenario seemed a little strange to me that the body would be in the back yard for so many days without being found and all that kind of stuff and the suicide note not being found until much later. And Jimmy could go off and be very volatile at times. He could be scary."

Arthur Beckenstein says that Piazza's supposition about incestuous relations between Kirkwood and his mother are "absurd, offensive and disgusting." He also points out that Lee was someone Piazza "never met or ever witnessed together with Jim." Beckenstein says of the Reid Russell case, "I never questioned the fact that it [was] a suicide," and also says of Kirkwood that apart from one incident involving producer Joe Papp, "I never witnessed him being physically violent with people." Yet William Russo also became suspicious about Kirkwood, in his case through intellectual avenues. A college professor who taught his students Kirkwood's writing and who says he considered himself "James Kirkwood's Boswell," he found the characters of Josh Cydney and Peter Kilburn from Kirkwood's first two novels — in both of which books premature deaths of friends of the relator of events occur — to be deliberately unreliable narrators. "It's interesting the motifs that crop up in the death scenes in his books where the narrator in particular cannot tell the real from a dream," Russo observes. "I think that there are a number of writers out there who think a book is a game of chess with the reader. It's that Nabokov viewpoint and I think that's what Kirkwood was doing." This may sound like an over-theorizing professor finding meanings the author did not intend to convey, but Russo had many conversations and exchanged many letters with Kirkwood over the years, ones in which he says Kirkwood seemed to be suggesting that he had left a trail of clues in

There Must Be a Pony! and *Good Times/Bad Times* hinting that the deaths in them — and implicitly the real-life counterparts of those deaths — were not as innocent as they seemed: "And when I pushed him too hard [he'd] back away." With regard to Reid Russell, Russo says, "I think everybody found something strange about the story. The police certainly did. All we have to go by in fact is Jim's version and I just think even he raised a couple of issues about the suicide note or notes and suggested that they were incredible. I raised that with him a couple of times and he got very upset." Russo says he asked Kirkwood directly whether he had something to do with Russell's death. Russo: "He said, 'I can't talk about that now. I'll talk about it later when I get my hands around your throat.' He was always playing that way…He certainly didn't like to hear that sort of line. Talk about coy. Every time I would bring up the Reid Russell issue he would certainly dance away."

Kirkwood had such a troubled childhood that it is academically easy to find a motive for murder. As well as Piazza's Oedipal theory, we could also surmise a rootless boy who feels he has finally found a stable family unit courtesy of a mother who is at last spending time with him and a father figure of whom he is genuinely fond devastated beyond imagination and reason by news that the adult pair are to split up. We can also surmise that there is something suspicious about Lee's very strange claim not to have bothered reading Russell's suicide note. However, the evidence against Kirkwood — if we can even call it that — is far from unambiguous. For instance, Russo has also observed that Kirkwood was angry about Russell not taking himself off to a secret place to kill himself, rather than doing it in a place where he would, and his mother potentially might, find his body. Why would he be angry at Russell for doing this if he knew he or Lila Lee had murdered him?

Unless Kirkwood — by now a trained actor — was putting it on. He certainly seemed to get over the death quickly at the time, displaying a cavalier and mercenary attitude by Halloween of '36. Lila Lee wrote, "There was a little bit of blood left on the swing & Jimmy used to charge .25 a head [to see it]. Jimmy was the hero of the school." (In 1986, Kirkwood claimed to the *Los Angeles Times* that this was revenge on Russell for committing suicide: "That was my way of getting back at him.") Additionally, Russo had other reasons to be suspicious. "Jim was fascinated with killers," he reveals. "He mentioned to me he wanted to talk to Ted Bundy and I always thought that was curious." Russo found the details Kirkwood related to him of his discoveries of various dead bodies throughout his childhood rather inconsistent. Russo says in *Riding James*

Kirkwood's Pony, "As years passed, I became more and more concerned about our cat-and-mouse games. At first I was challenging a celebrity author, but I began to suspect that I was playing games with a potential serial killer."

THREE

Following the Russell investigation, Kirkwood was once again uprooted.

He later recalled that to escape the publicity surrounding the death, he was sent to live on a cattle ranch in the foothills of the Sierra Nevadas. (This sounds like it may in fact have been the previously mentioned ranch at which Gouverneur Morris and his wife stayed.) While there, he attended a public school in Friant, California, commuting the nine miles to it via the unusual method of horseback. The school consisted of one room and he graduated from the eighth grade in a class of four, two of whom were Native Americans, the other a white girl. Kirkwood said he had ringworm the entire year he was there. On the ranch, he worked for his room and board by milking cows, serving food and washing dishes. He later told the *Los Angeles Times* that it was a happy time. "What 15-year-old [sic] doesn't want to be a cowboy?" he reasoned. When Kirkwood returned to California, he was enrolled in the very different environs of Beverly Hills High School. Though the name Beverly Hills drips with associations of stardom and wealth, Kirkwood recalled of his six months at the school, "There was no money at all by then and everyone else there had cars."

While his mother had suffered setbacks for reasons that were mainly not of her making, Kirkwood's father was facing a career in a freefall due not only to the dwindling parts available to thespians in their sixties but things more karmic. "When he began to get older, my father couldn't have gotten a job other than acting," Kirkwood told *After Dark* magazine in 1972. "He was from the old school and he was an actor. Period. He had a Christ-awful, maniacal temper, and maybe that's fine when you're dealing cards, but once they take the deck away from you, you suffer from it. When his career started downhill, it came to the point where people said, 'Oh, we remember that old sonofabitch and this or that awful outburst.' And he paid for it. And it was sad because he was a good actor."

The subject of the humiliations faced by the once-famous, now has-been actor is something that clearly made Kirkwood melancholic. "It's very sad to see an actor and an actress who have been terribly successful but whose careers have gone past their peaks," he told the same magazine. "It's sad to see them try to work in the business, to make a living, to achieve a dignity to their lives when a lot of people won't even answer the phone when they call, when they can't get an agent. In a way, it's heartbreaking." Yet though he learnt early that an actor's fortunes could go rapidly into reverse, by the age of at least eleven Kirkwood had his heart set on following the career paths of his parents. Writing in *Playbill* magazine many years later, with his acting career having been superseded by writing, Kirkwood tried to explain why it is that somebody is prepared to put up with the humiliations, rejections, fear of failure and periods of unemployment that go hand-in-hand with the life of a thespian: "Like a virus, it's something you cannot not do. There is no cure. The urge to entertain, to play for the bug that lurks within. To make-believe, to feel and hear the approval from an audience is congenital, endemic, incurable and a few other adjectives." When Kirkwood was eleven, his father mentioned his son's thespian ambitions in an interview, saying, "He must follow his own inclinations in the matter. It is only natural that he should have that ambition, since both his mother, Lila Lee, and his father are of the theatre. But if he becomes an actor I shall insist that he be thoroughly prepared for it, the same as for any other profession, such as law, medicine or engineering."

Kirkwood spent another period in Elyria, moving back in with the Tuffords at the age of fourteen. It is possibly immediately prior to this that an extraordinary incident occurred between Kirkwood and his father. Says Jim Piazza, "He told me a story about his father coming home drunk one night when he was living with him in New York at this Bachelors Club. He was always hitting Jimmy and he just took his belt and he just beat the shit out of his father and took his money and left. I think he maybe was fourteen." Though in a taped conversation between Kirkwood Sr. and his son dating from circa 1959, his father claims to recall spanking Kirkwood only once when he was "a baby," there seems little doubt that the retaliatory belt incident happened, judging by the fact that Kirkwood brings it up with his father therein, even if by now, the 35-year-old Kirkwood can laugh about it. Kirkwood later wrote of this incident in which he exacted his revenge on his drunken, near comatose old man in his heavily autobiographical unfinished novel *I Teach Flying*. Following the scene, the son character uses the stolen money to return to Corain, Ohio, the fictional equivalent of Elyria. This pretty much ties in with Bobby Tufford's observation, "When he came to us, my recollection is that he wanted to get away from his father. I don't know whether he was mistreated or what. He was not happy living with his father."

Considering his recent devastating experiences — and the general displacement in his young life — one might assume that Kirkwood had by now withdrawn into a shell. Almost inexplicably, however, the reverse seems to be true. Though his old Elyria buddy Sid Wasserman found him to be a very different person to the one he was before, it was in a positive sense: "He was tall. He was a good-looking kid. He was very personable. Friendly to people. I don't know of anybody that really didn't like him." In fact, the popularity of the newly gregarious Kirkwood caused some friction between he and Wasserman that meant their friendship was never quite the same again: "I saw that he was extremely popular and very, very in demand by all the popular kids in high school and I was feeling somewhat rejected. I remember having a couple of talks with him and we blew up at one another and I don't remember any further contact with him until he came back before graduation." Kirkwood's newfound gregariousness seems to have been a legacy of his mother's relationship with Jack R. Peine (whom Lee wrote that her son liked) or Reid Russell or both. In *There Must Be a Pony!*, where protagonist Josh had been "some little, furry, woodland creature that was scared of its own shadow" he, through the aegis of Ben Nichols — based on Russell and possibly Peine — suddenly becomes so talkative that on one occasion his mother suspects he is running a temperature.

It was probably during this stay in Elyria that Kirkwood made the second and possibly third discoveries of dead bodies in his life (if we discount his grandfather). "I was riding home from school with a friend of mine in Ohio," said Kirkwood on *The Dick Cavett Show* in 1980, elsewhere naming the friend as "Don." "It started to rain and he said, 'Listen, why don't I go in the house and start making some peanut butter and jelly sandwiches? You take the bikes and put them in the garage…So I took his bike and I swung the garage door up…and this boy's mother had hanged herself and she was hanging in the garage." As if bearing out William Russo's perceptions of inconsistencies in Kirkwood's body-finding recollections, in a 1980 lecture Kirkwood said, "Through the garage door, his mother had hanged herself. She was hanging from a beam in the garage." This suggestion that he had not swung up the garage door and found the body but seen it through the window chimes with his cousin Lila's knowledge of the incident — although, having said that, she herself remembers the death as that of a man. None of the other Elyrians questioned for this book remember the incident. Esther Hamula, Kirkwood's teenage Elyrian sweetheart, says, "I looked through our yearbook for the Dons and talked to a couple of men students I know and we couldn't come up with any memories of this happening, nor connecting a Don with it."

Recalls Tufford, "Jimmy said he was afraid to go out for a walk because every time he went out for a walk, he either found a body or something."

In a college address in 1987, Kirkwood said, "After a while, people used to call me The Body Finder. If a kid came over to the house and asked my mother or father or an aunt and uncle I used to be shipped off to live with, 'Can Jimmy go hiking in the woods? We'll be back before dark,' the answer would be a resounding: 'No: he'll find another one. No hiking in the woods, no hiking anywhere. You go swimming right here, in the river behind the house.' So, of course you know what I found floating in the river, don't you?" In a 1980 lecture, he gave more detail: "A friend of mine drowned in a river called Black River. Nobody found him for a couple of days and they dragged the river for him but they didn't find him and we just imagined that his body washed down the river toward Loraine and into Lake Erie. Well, guess who went swimming about a week later and bumped into him?" Black River ran behind a grander house to which the Tuffords had moved on Elyria's Grafton Road. Yet Esther Hamula doesn't remember the incident. She offers, "Both Lila [Nichols] and I came to the same conclusion that Jimmy always had a compulsion to exaggerate many, many facts, and sometimes if things were not popping around him, he would make them up. I know for a fact, he…embellished an event that we all were involved in and we all knew nothing happened as he told it. It was all part of his personality. We all took what he said with a grain of salt." Regarding the dead body in the river specifically, Hamula says, "Lila said for sure if that had happened to Jimmy, she would have known about it because he'd have bounded into the house screaming and laughing or reacting with hysteria." Though Elyrian newspapers of the period record local hangings and drownings that correspond in some respects with Kirkwood's recollections above, none have come to light that feature his name.

Even if the body finding was true, Kirkwood's now extroverted personality meant he almost certainly enjoyed Elyria more this time around. "He got to date a lovely girl," says Nichols of Hamula. The latter was the daughter of Hungarian immigrants who lived in the poorer part of town. She was the same age as Kirkwood. "I was just very friendly to everybody, didn't matter what side of the town they were from," says Hamula of a romance that straddled the tracks. "He and I quickly became an item. He was very, very unpretentious. Money or status didn't mean anything to him at all." It was Kirkwood's cousin Lila who drove Kirkwood and Hamula to their first date, a movie. Hamula: "The movie was either *Phantom of the Opera* or *Frankenstein* but it was a scary movie. I didn't like scary movies and he loved that because that meant I could just hang all over him and scream. He just loved to tease that way. And then we went next door for ice cream sundaes and then she appropriately picked us up and drove me home. She doesn't remember that at all but it was a big event in my life." Kirkwood didn't mind the five-mile trek to the Hamulas' house, nor its modesty compared to the Tuffords' home. "He just loved coming to our house," Hamula recalls. "Our house was quite well-furnished and it was a pretty house [on] the edge of a park and he was just very comfortable." What did the two have in common? "I liked literature and he did too and we liked to go to the movies together."

It was while Kirkwood was on this extended stay in Elyria that his father came to nearby Cleveland with the play *Tobacco Road*. *Tobacco Road* — in which Kirkwood Sr. played Jeeter Lester, a role which would in some respects come to be his signature one — was a notorious production at the time for its sexual frankness, bad language and unflinching depiction of the conditions in which poor whites lived in Georgia. Kirkwood later said, "One day after my father had opened in the first national company of *Tobacco Road* in Chicago…there was this great pall over the household and I wondered what it was. It turned out that the whole cast had been arrested and dragged to the police station." By the time it reached Ohio, the play had been banned in Chicago and Detroit. Though the Mayor of Cleveland had undertaken not to act as censor but to listen to the feedback from the citizenry about the play, there were four police observers at its debut performance in the town's Masonic Auditorium. There was also, perhaps needless to say, a record first-night crowd. Among it were Kirkwood and Hamula, presumably transported there by either Kirkwood's Aunt Peggy or his cousin Lila. "He was very eager for me to meet his father," Hamula recalls. It was a somewhat bittersweet experience for young Jimmy, for his father's famous temper was mortifyingly on display. Kirkwood recalled in a 1982 home movie, "It was the first time I'd seen my father on the stage. One of his first lines was 'Those sons of bitches' and there were two little women in about the fifth row and when he said it they both went, '*Ohh!*' He just stopped the play and he walked right down to the footlights and he said — voice like a lion — 'What's the matter, ladies? Didn't you know there were sons of bitches in the world?' Then he turned around and he went right back into the scene. Well, I was so embarrassed."

Kirkwood Sr. was nicer after the curtain fell when he received his son and his beau backstage. Says Hamula, "He was very cordial and Jimmy was proud to introduce me to him. I had a feeling he hadn't seen him for a while." A picture of Kirkwood Sr. and Jr. subsequently appeared in the local paper *Cleveland Plain Dealer*. Beneath a staged shot of the two supposedly enjoying breakfast together, it was explained that this visit was the first time the two had seen each other in two years.

The journey back to Elyria seems to have occasioned some serious necking, if Kirkwood and Hamula's snickering on a radio show many years later is anything to go by.

Naturally, Kirkwood Sr. utilized the presence of the play to visit his son at the Tuffords. "I remember him coming out to the house," says Nichols of Kirkwood Sr.'s stay in '38. "He loved to make Irish stew and we had a big party. He was very charismatic, very handsome and had a beautiful singing voice." Clearly, this man with a "Christ-awful, maniacal temper" could charm the birds out of the trees when he felt like it. Not so charming was what was presumably his decision to uproot his son yet again for pedagogical reasons. Kirkwood was now packed off to Brewster Academy, a school in distant Wolfeboro, New Hampshire. Certainly that it was Kirkwood Sr.'s decision is implied in *Good Times/Bad Times*, the novel in which Kirkwood fictionalizes his time at the school.

Brewster Academy was a curious amalgam of public high school for the "townie" pupils who made up about eighty percent of its enrollment and private prep school for boarding students from all over the country. When Kirkwood enrolled, the school was on the cusp of a change that would eventually see it go completely private and very exclusive. Mildred Beach, a Brewster contemporary of Kirkwood's, says that many of the "dorm students" "were sons of wealthy families that did not have time for their young people." Asked if she felt Kirkwood was one of those students, she replies in the affirmative.

Brewster Academy was set in an idyllic locale. Those questioned for this book have confirmed that Kirkwood's description of the school in *Good Times/Bad Times* — sitting on a lake, surrounded by flat woodland, with wooded foothills and rugged mountains making up the horizon — is spot-on. Yet the peaceful natural surroundings were at odds with the school's situation. Kirkwood himself said of Brewster, "It was a very strange, rag-ass, run-down, sad school at the time." Rag-ass it may have been but it seems unlikely that Kirkwood's parents could have afforded to pay its fees. In *Good Times/Bad Times*, one of the actors' club friends of the father of the protagonist pays for his time there as a gift. In the original outline for *There Must Be a Pony!* (which initially featured a Brewster counterpart) the fees are paid for by an effeminate novelist friend of the family named Merwin, who as mentioned could have been a fictionalized Gouverneur Morris. Whoever stumped up, Kirkwood recalled that he spent around two cumulative years at Brewster Academy, living in a dorm called The Estabrook on the third floor. He appears to have broadly hated it but, as with the circumstances surrounding the death of Reid Russell, was later able to use his bad experiences to positive effect in his writing.

In *Good Times/Bad Times* — where the school is called Gilford Academy — Kirkwood portrays a pupil named Peter Kilburn being sexually pestered by headmaster Mr. Hoyt, who is in denial about his sexuality (most notably when an alcohol rubdown scene turns sinister). Kirkwood would later recall, "The headmaster was rather sadistic. He was also a latent homosexual. He took a shine to me and we had a very unhealthy time of it for a while. I was terrified of him and I disliked him intensely." Unlike in the book, the shine said head took to Kirkwood/Kilburn would seem not to have been made manifest. Though there seems a consensus that Walter G. Greenall Jr., the Brewster headmaster on whom Kirkwood based Hoyt, left the school abruptly and unexpectedly in 1942, neither Beach nor fellow Brewster contemporaries Ned Bullock, Lucille Jutras Macolino or Donald Roberts recall him being sexually interested in his pupils, male or female. (Kirkwood may also still have been at the school when Vincent Rogers took over from Greenall, but Rogers doesn't seem to have served as the headmaster template. When Kirkwood visited Wolfeboro while researching *Good Times/Bad Times*, his conversation with Bullock about the school focused only on Greenall.) "As far as I know, Jimmy was never a victim of sexual abuse," says Arthur Beckenstein. He attributes the alcohol rubdown scene to "a vivid sexual imagination."

Said imagination seems to stem from Kirkwood's desire to portray Greenall in as villainous a light as possible. Kirkwood's severe dislike for the man the pupils called (though certainly not to his face) "Stretch" is not entirely understandable. Says Bullock, "He wasn't everybody's buddy. I guess you could say he was fair. Stretch wasn't that bad a guy." Roberts says of Greenall, "A wretched human being. Right out of Dickens. He was very insensitive. He was cold, indifferent, harsh. I thought he was awful." However, even he admits that on the one occasion he can recall being scolded by Greenall, "He was justified for reprimanding me." Though Greenall was fairly strict (the "townies" had to be in their homes by 7pm as a condition of their free education; pupils were addressed by their surname, with the female ones afforded the prefix "Miss"), his regime was certainly not brutal: there was no corporal punishment, nor even a formal uniform. Perhaps it's simply the case that Kirkwood took one of the irrational, disproportionate dislikes to people for which he became known to be prone. Or perhaps he was doing something else of which he appears to have made a habit: conflating different people. "He said to me he wanted to kill that person," says William Russo. "Whether it was actually the headmaster or someone else at the college may be an interesting question. I think it was an instructor. That was my sense: it was a person in authority." For what it's worth, Kirkwood made the Brewster honor roll in at least one semester under Greenall.

In *Good Times/Bad Times*, there is an element of joy in Peter Kilburn's unhappy stay at Brewster in the form of an extremely close friendship that he strikes up with a fellow pupil, Jordan Legier. (Kirkwood originally planned to call him Ted, which would seem to be the real name of the boy Jordan was based on.) Legier is a rich but sickly young man from a New Orleans family whose ill-health — and the physical violence of the headmaster — eventually leads to his premature death. It is Kilburn who discovers his body. In this case, art didn't mirror life exactly, according to comments Kirkwood made at Northern Illinois University in 1980: "Did I have a friend like Jordan? Yeah. I did have a friend and he did die. But he didn't die at school, he died at home — he had a bad heart…He was my closest friend. That made a profound impression upon [me]. I think friendship is such an important thing. I've had a few close friends who have died and I feel very strongly about losing them and that's usually why in almost every one of my books, the protagonist has a close friend that dies." William Russo says, "My theory — because I have nothing to go by it — is that somehow Jim has merged two stories here to throw us off. I think he was with Ted in New Orleans when he died, not in New Hampshire as happens in the book. There's enough of a difference to make me wonder when was Jim in New Orleans, and under what reason would he be there. He did not die at Brewster. I have that directly from Jim. He told me that probably in 1979 or 1980. I kicked myself for not keeping notes after my conversations with him. I swear he gave me the last name of Ted and I don't remember it." Beckenstein semi-supports this idea when he says of the possible real-life Jordan, "I got a feeling that maybe there was somebody, although he might have put someone else from another part of his life into that situation." In his *Esquire* article on Clay Shaw, reprinted in his book *American Grotesque*, Kirkwood revealed that he had visited New Orleans once prior to his 1968 trip there to interview Shaw. However, there seems to have been no New Orleanian on the Brewster Academy rolls during Kirkwood's time there, nor a Theodore. There was one Edward. Eddie Coughlin, a resident of nearby Ossipee, died at his home of shotgun wounds on April 8, 1942, a death that according to his friend Ned Bullock was almost certainly a suicide. Coughlin may have known Kirkwood but it's unclear whether the latter was still at the school at this point. (The protagonist of Kirkwood's 1975 novel *Some Kind Of Hero* was named Eddie.) Almost exactly a month after Coughlin's death, another seventeen-year-old Ossipee resident and Brewster Academy student — Alfred Libby — died. Kirkwood almost certainly wasn't at Brewster by then — he appeared in a play mounted by students of Elyria High School in mid-May — but the fact that Libby's death came "after a year of illness" according to a newspaper report is intriguing in light of Jordan Legier's sickliness. Yet as both these pupils were "townies," they don't fit other aspects of Kirkwood's description of Jordan. A Wolfeboro boy named Phillip D. Wiggin died in November 1940. As he was fifteen years and four months old, he would have been in Kirkwood's sophomore class if he went to Brewster, but there is no record that he did. In terms of pupils actually dying at the school as Jordan does in the book, Mildred Beach says that a boy killed himself at Brewster in her time there, though is not certain it was during Kirkwood's own shorter stay. She reveals, "There was a...dormitory student who took his life. I do not remember the details. We all were concerned to lose an acquaintance, in that manner. At that time schools did not have counseling to accept a situation of that type. We all felt it was unfortunate that if he had a problem that there was not someone he could talk with. I do not remember that Jim lived in the same dorm as this chap." Beach told a third party that the boy hanged himself in Brown Hall, arrived in September and was dead by Christmas. He was from a very wealthy family and was unhappy about being moved from school to school. (That last sentence — apart from the wealthy part — perfectly summarized Kirkwood, so it would be understandable if the two were friends.) Beach adds, "The school closed the case as quickly as possible to avoid bad publicity." If this is the case, they were certainly successful: neither police records, school records nor local newspapers turn up the death and no surviving pupils contacted — either directly by this author or on my behalf by Matt Hoopes, Alumni Officer of Brewster Academy — recall it. Hoopes, a teacher at Brewster starting in 1975, himself heard rumors about a pupil suicide on campus before his time but only vague and confused ones.

A reason for the disinformation Russo suggests on Kirkwood's part could be that the death of Ted was not a natural one. For Russo, the motive for Peter/Kirkwood to murder Jordan/Ted is suggested in *Good Times/ Bad Times* when Peter Kilburn finds out that his friend has jotted down notes on him. When he put this to Kirkwood, it seemed to touch a nerve: "I asked him at one point how could Peter trust Jordan when he discovered that Jordan was writing a book about him, maybe a psychological study, and Jim jumped up out of his seat and started pacing and started rewriting the book before me. He could get very passionate. I think he was rewriting the book so that I was picking up on things he didn't want to admit to." For those inclined to Russo's discernment of clues, in *Good Times/Bad Times*, Peter Kilburn is reading a book on the Boston Strangler.

In 1986, Kirkwood told reporter Steve Warren he had been sexually active since he was twelve, although as was typical with his interviews declined to specify the gender(s) of his sexual partners. When Peter arrives at Gilford, he declares in his first-person narrative, "If I'm a fanatic about one thing, it's having one particular best friend that I can really connect with." Peter certainly finds that in the shape of Jordan. Kirkwood's depiction of their closeness in *Good Times/Bad Times* led more than one critic to question the assertion that Peter makes that the relationship is not sexual. For instance, Kirkwood's (gay) friend Benjamin Morrison recalls, "Jim and I talked...about the real-life boy who was the basis for Jordan. At the time, I'd insisted that the relationship should have been consummated sexually, that it wasn't likely-logical that it wasn't. Jim said that in real life the desire had not been expressed." (Morrison also says, "It was clear to me that he discovered the body of his friend, the Jordan prototype.") The gay magazine *Mandate* said in a November 1975 article on Kirkwood, "*Good Times/Bad Times*...does seem to beg the reader's credulity in those episodes dealing with the question of whether or not there was any actual sexual relationship between Peter and Jordan. The affection between them was so overwhelming that it's somewhat difficult to believe that nothing other than snoring went on beneath the bedcovers." "Well, they *didn't — because* they *didn't!*" Kirkwood is reported to have responded to *Mandate*'s interviewer. "Because *I* didn't at that time in my life with this guy who was my best friend in prep school. The Jordan I knew was more or less *asexual*. But the fact is they didn't. Not only were they not what you would actually call homosexuals, but even if they *had* been, they wouldn't have been attracted to each other. They were just terribly close friends, and if there had been a physical attraction between them, I would have put that in. I wouldn't have shied away from it." William Russo is not so sure. "I don't think two boys of ages sixteen or eighteen in the 1940s — or even in the 1960s or in the 1990s — hop into bed together because they're cold," he says, referring to Peter and Jordan's nighttime discussions under the bedcovers, rendered as innocent by Kirkwood in the novel. "In *Good Times/Bad Times*, there's a major lecture given by Mr. Hoyt on Sodom and Gomorrah, and in fact that turns out to be a very big motif in the book. I asked Jim, 'What country would archaeologists find Sodom and

Gomorrah?' And he gave me all kinds of strange answers except the correct one, and when I mentioned it to him he just laughed. The correct answer for Sodom and Gomorrah is Jordan."

Another Brewster student of the time, Barbara Bishop, who was a year behind Kirkwood, says, "I am quite certain he was not 'attached' to any student, male or female." For Bullock, though he didn't find Kirkwood effeminate, he saw him as plainly homosexual, an impression he picked up in the sole conversation he can recall having with him. Bullock: "Jim I think was more of a lonely boy. I guess I was out back waiting for my father to come and get me and Jim all of a sudden was there and we were talking. In my life I've been talked to by many gay males because my actions are not effeminate but they're not [very] male. I think Jim thought maybe there might be somebody there that he could be close to. We didn't have much more than fifteen minutes of conversation." Did he think Kirkwood was making a pass at him? "No, I think he was just looking — just to see what my reactions would be or is there a chance of some sort of friendship or something and to find out whether we might be two of a kind."

Yet despite this, Kirkwood seems to have had a girlfriend at this juncture. Her name was Nancy Martin and she lived on East 10th Street, New York. Her place of learning was the exclusive (accommodation for each girl's horse and a man-servant) Hewlett School, Cedarhurst, Long Island. While one might assume that such a long-distance relationship was rather insubstantial by definition, Miss Martin's schoolmates didn't seem to think so, judging by comments in Hewlett's 1941 yearbook. Under the heading "Song Titles" in a section in which popular songs of the day are humorously employed to sum up pupils' traits, "One Melody For Two" is printed as appropriate for "Nancy and Jimmy." Elsewhere, it seems to be implied that Martin receives a letter every day from Kirkwood.

The fact that a March 1941 letter to Martin, complete with postmarked envelope, is in Kirkwood's papers implies that the relationship ended acrimoniously, as though Martin returned it to him. Said letter provides some interesting insights into the development of Kirkwood's professional ambitions. "The glee club has me for one of its numbers — I just about killed myself trying out but now I'm in," he revealed. Donald Roberts confirms the exclusivity of the Brewster vocal group to which Kirkwood refers: "Every male student was invited by a man called Bertus Vaughan, who was the Latin teacher, to sing for him in an audition. It was probably, of the whole school, no more than a dozen, eighteen male individuals. It was a highly coveted thing to be part of that Glee Club."

Of Kirkwood's abilities, Roberts recalls, "He was an excellent singer, and he had a tremendous ability to sing a falsetto. He did not sound like a counter-tenor. He sounded like a high-pitched female. I suppose we might say he sounded like a castrato." He adds, "Occasionally — and this was pretty damn stupid — they would dress him up *a la* transvestite and make him sing like a woman. It was silly and we all laughed at it and he went along with it."

An even sillier scenario with the Glee Club was enacted at Greenall's insistence. Kirkwood said, "There was a program in which you had to compete against other schools for points. You did it in tennis and basketball and football and this and that and we did it in Glee Club. The headmaster, because my parents had been in the theatre and been actors, recruited me to do Hamlet's soliloquy 'To Be or Not to Be' in front of the Glee Club as they hummed behind me. Can you imagine how I felt? To come out in front of my peers. He also wanted me to wear black tights and a black thing that his wife made, a shmatte, to wear on top. I was forced to come out and recite 'To Be or Not to Be' in hopes that our school would pick up some extra points. He had heard that one of the other schools had a magician, so it got started that way." Kirkwood aficionados will recognize the scenario from a scene in *Good Times/Bad Times*, which fictionalized account according to Kirkwood was "more or less the way it happened."

In the letter to Nancy Martin, Kirkwood also revealed the persistence of his thespian ambitions when he said, "Don't you think we both should appear in a play on Broadway together — I do — it would be lots of fun. We could go out every night after the play and all sorts of things." A more interesting revelation in the letter, considering Kirkwood's long-term professional development, is this passage: "Have you ever written a play or tried it? I'll not answer that question. (I'm trying to write one now.)"

Kirkwood got one of his wishes fulfilled a mere eight months after writing that letter. Bobby Tufford's memory is that his cousin's first professional role in the acting career that would take up the first two decades of his adult life came at a point in time when Kirkwood was staying in New York with his mother. Tufford: "The war had just started I believe and *Junior Miss* was a play and they needed someone to fill in for a part because they had been drafted to go into service. His mother said, 'Why don't you try out for that, Jimmy?'"

Junior Miss, written by Joseph Fields and Jerome Chodorov, revolves around a well-meaning teenager who causes havoc with her matchmaking. Kirkwood recalled how he got the part to the *Corpus Christi*

Caller-Times in 1971. "I told my mother that I wanted to be an actor," he said. "And she said I was crazy…and too young. She had a cocktail party one night and I met my first Broadway agent. He told me they were having auditions to replace young actors in *Junior Miss*, which was one of the biggest hits in the '40s. I went over there and lined up with about 40 other boys. I was so nervous I dropped the script and parctically [sic] stuttered. At the end of the auditions, I turned to go and Moss Hart… imagine Moss Hart, himself…said: 'Young man. You.' Naturally, I thought he meant another kid and kept walking. Finally he said: 'No. The nervous one. You.' I got the job and worked for four or five months. And nobody knew that both my parents were movie stars."

Kirkwood was drafted in to play the character Joe in September 1941 and stayed with the show — which premiered in November — until March the following year, during which time the play switched venues from the Lyceum Theatre to the 46th Street Theatre. There is — as with so much of Kirkwood's life — some confusion surrounding the chronology here. In one later résumé, he said this role happened when he was fourteen, in another fifteen. Standard enough when someone is shaving some years off his age, but a *New York Times* snippet from January 1943 states that Kirkwood had taken on the role that month. However, the fact that in his Coast Guard Notice of Separation, Kirkwood's Name and Address of Last Employer is stated as "Max Gordon" (*Junior Miss* producer) at "Lyceum Theatre, New York, New York" and gives September 1941-March 1942 as the period of employment seems to indicate that if the 1943 stint did happen (which would place it between his enlisting in the Coast Guard and his date of entry into active service), it was a brief return engagement.

Kirkwood recalled that following his Broadway debut he returned to Brewster Academy. It was to be a short stay. "I kept running away from that place and after about two years I flatly refused to go back," he later said. "It's the only smart thing I ever did." His school records show that he was present at Elyria High School for some, possibly all, of his graduation year. There, he spent probably the happiest period of his life so far.

"Those were my college days and that's when I was gone, but I think he liked that because then he was the only child in the house," says Lila Lee Nichols. "Not only that, we had moved to a new home just on the outskirts of Elyria that was very pretty and he loved being there and loved being able to drive a car, and having a normal American life…He was popular, he was well-liked…He loved it. He said he felt like Andy Hardy because everything was so much fun…He was a good student, well-liked, had many friends and was a handsome kid." Another pleasing aspect of life in Elyria for a man who loved animals was the fact that, according to Bobby Tufford, "We had about fourteen dogs." Kirkwood befriended a terrier in particular, who slept on his bed.

At Elyria High School, Kirkwood, naturally, chose drama as one of his activities. Tufford: "I think he had a photographic memory because he was in the class play in high school and he brought home the book one day and asked me to cue him on his lines. He just went through it once and he knew everything — and he had a lot of lines in this play." Esther Hamula, Lila Lee Nichols, Sidney Wasserman and Arthur Beckenstein concur on Kirkwood's preternatural powers of retention. Wasserman says that although he doesn't recall the specifics, "As a kid, he could remember so many things about his life and what was happening to him."

Completing this picture-book white-picket-fenced environment in which Kirkwood exulted was dating. Whatever gay vibes he may have given off to Brewster schoolmate Ned Bullock, to apparently everyone else he seemed "normal." Esther Hamula says, "We just picked up where he had left off." However, she adds, "I was not interested in going steady, not at all. I was more interested in what they called playing the field." Kirkwood seemed more amused than annoyed by this. Elyria schoolmate Ralph Ruth recalls Kirkwood himself was not exactly a one-woman man: "I think she feels that she was probably his number one girlfriend for at least part of the time that we were seniors, and that may be true, but Jim was interested in more than just Esther in that high-school class." Ralph Ruth recalls Kirkwood possessing a maturity that the opposite sex found appealing: "In general he was a year or two ahead of us in social behavior." Dating in the early forties was all very innocent. Hamula: "There were occasions when we were alone of course, but during that era people double-dated all the time. We always went around with groups. We really weren't alone together that much. Beyond kissing, nothing ever happened." Whatever Hamula and Kirkwood's lack of romantic exclusivity, they were very close. Hamula: "We really were good friends. My mother was an excellent cook and she always had cookies. He used to come to our house every day. Sometimes he'd come through the door with a somersault: 'Well here I am, and where are the cookies?'"

Nobody would have been able to infer from this wholesome lifestyle the traumatic events Kirkwood had experienced, whether they be his fractured and dysfunctional family or discovering the body of Reid Russell. (Or whether they be more questionable traumatic events like his body finding or the death of "Jordan.") He simply never spoke of any of them, at least to his peers. News of the Manhattan Beach tragedy had of course reached Elyria and would have been a source of immense interest for children his age, but Kirkwood never satisfied curiosity. Bob Cromling, another pupil at Elyria High School, recalls, "That did come up in passing conversation, but Jim never dwelled on it. Apparently he wanted to keep that part of his life separate from the life he was leading in Elyria. He didn't want to face up to his past. He wanted to let it go." Kirkwood's list of politely prohibited subjects included his parents. Ruth: "He was very reluctant to discuss his parents, the experience and the very existence of the careers of his parents." He adds though, "Certainly I didn't ever detect any rancor or any strong bitter feelings." Kirkwood practiced what he preached. Ruth says, "He was respectful of the rights of others to their privacy and their own business. More so than most other kids his age."

It has to be said that living in denial about his past — which by any standard he was — does not seem to have done the teenage Kirkwood any harm at all. Cromling's assessment of him as a "happy-go-lucky kind of fella" seems to be the view of all his contemporaries who knew him at this juncture. In fact, the only difficulty caused to Kirkwood by this buoyant personality he had strangely acquired was when he got too happy-go-lucky for the liking of his elders. Ruth: "Jim was always sort of 'onstage.' Even in situations at school, he would tend to be light-hearted and sometimes perhaps incur the annoyance of a teacher."

Kirkwood's Aunt Peg didn't necessarily completely fit into the wholesome Doris Day-movie mold of Kirkwood's life. Kirkwood later revealed, "I'd come home from a date and she'd ask what movie I saw. I'd tell her, then she'd say, 'And did you fiddle around a little?' I'd say, 'Peggy!' To which she'd reply, 'Well, you have to have a little fun, don't you?'"

Kirkwood's report card for his senior year, Grade 12, at Elyria High School, shows him achieving consistent As in all his subjects: English, sociology, biology, American history and (second semester only) Civica. Only once did he get anything below this, mustering just a B in English in the first term of the second semester. Perhaps this was because Kirkwood missed four days of schooling that semester, as opposed to none the previous one. He was "tardy" on a total of one occasion the entire year. He finished with 32 credits, precisely the number required for graduation. Kirkwood, along with Hamula, made the National Honors Society, experiencing the tapping ceremony at a special school assembly where a touch on the shoulder told you that your excellent academic record had afforded you the privilege of being one of only about eight to ten pupils out of a class of more than 300 brought up onto the stage to be recognized.

Kirkwood graduated on June 3, 1942. In the Elyria High School graduation yearbook, the legend beneath Kirkwood's picture read, "Intelligent, actor and very good looking/He'll always be after that theatre booking." That the graduation tradition of signing each other's pictures in the yearbook can be bittersweet is underlined by what Kirkwood, in reference to their stormy relationship, wrote beneath Wasserman's photo: "Thru thick & thin — mostly thin!" Meanwhile, on the last page of Hamula's yearbook, Kirkwood appended her initials followed by the initials of all the boys he thought were interested in or connected to her. "He just loved that," she says. "I was not interested in going steady with anybody so he just thought that was hilarious. As long as I was spending time with him, that was okay." In said yearbook, Kirkwood, with his pompadour and sensual eyes, is easily among the most attractive faces on view. An indication of the unsettled nature of the childhood Kirkwood was leaving behind is provided by the fact that where everyone else lists extra-curricular activities at the start of their entries, Kirkwood lists Beverly Hills High and Brewster Academy, two of his other schools.

The fact that he did not go to college was something that would give Kirkwood a slight inferiority complex throughout the course of his life. That he did not further his education seems to be down to either a lack of funds and the scarcity of scholarships in the era or a desire to resume the acting career that had begun so conspicuously the previous year, or both. Says Nichols, "I suppose my parents would have helped him, but I don't know that he wanted to." Conceivably, of course, he might have wanted to enter the Tuffords' family business but Bobby Tufford doesn't recall any discussion of this: "When Jimmy came to live with us, the family business was still going but it wasn't as prosperous as it had been in the 1920s." Elaborates Nichols, "By that time there were other patents and other heels were being made because a patent only lasts so many years, so there was a lot of competition. There wasn't as much money so there wouldn't have been a place there." In any case, of course, a young man who had already smelt the greasepaint and heard the roar of the crowd was probably not going to be excited by the thought of shifting rubber heels. Another career possibility was tennis, the sport that would be a passion throughout his life. "He thought of becoming a professional player when he was a young man," says Beckenstein. However, Homer Price, Kirkwood's friend and tennis partner in adult life, laughs at the idea, remarking, "We didn't look great on the court — but we got the ball back." Additionally, in those days of "shamateurism," a professional tennis career was only achievable after slogging through and making a name in Grand Slam events that awarded no prize money.

Nichols: "He wanted to be in the theatre, wanted to be either in Hollywood or New York or someplace where it was going on." Hamula: "Yes. Oh, definitely. He was going to Hollywood first. He was headed for Hollywood out of high school to become somebody." Wasserman points out, though, that the specter of the draft hanging over the country made every youngster's career plans tentative: "The war had broken out and none of us knew exactly what's going to happen. None of us talked that much beyond the war."

Kirkwood later said, "I know why I became an actor — I think, because my parents were actors. I became an actor for the wrong reasons. Then when I got into it I realized that the whole purpose of being an actor is to really do work that makes people sit up and say, 'Wow, look at that, look what he can do.'" He also said of following in his parents' footsteps, "I think at first it hindered me because I thought it might be too easy for me to get into the business. But I think it gave me a good perspective about the business. It made me see it without looking at it through prisms or colored glasses."

There does not seem to have been any great trauma attached to Kirkwood's July 1942 departure to Hollywood (by way of New York to visit his mother), with him not taking particularly great pains to keep in touch with his old friends. This includes Hamula, who received no letters from him until he was in the service, which would have been a minimum of five months later. Nonetheless, Kirkwood would always remain fond of his days in Elyria and his home-away-from-home with the Tuffords, which provided a mercifully calm note on which to end a childhood that Kirkwood said made him, "to put it conservatively, an agitated child." Tufford says, "When he pursued his career and became famous, if you want to call it famous, he never forgot my mother. Jimmy had a residence in Key West and he wanted my mother to stay in that apartment and take care of things and of course he paid for everything." Another acknowledgement of the good times he had in Ohio was the fact that from 1975 Kirkwood copyrighted his works to "Elyria Productions."

In a résumé sent out to the media in around 1960, Kirkwood explained his perspective on a childhood that had reached a state of awfulness more times than do most complete lives: "I prefer to think of it as an unusual childhood, albeit not a happy one. Christ only knows, it wasn't boring." By now, of course, his reinvention of himself as an author meant that he was able to grab a solace from his childhood traumas that he previously had not. They were now that boon of all creative writers: Raw Material — and great Raw Material at that. He continued, "If I hadn't been through these bizarre experiences I doubt if I'd have ended up writing a long letter, let alone novels and plays. Also, at this stage of my life I'm enjoying a relatively happy adulthood, so there's no use brooding about an unhappy childhood. I think we must press on, not sit around in the puddles of our past. Then, too, a well-known author once said: 'Writing is turning one's worst moments into art — and sometimes money!'"

FOUR

"I always felt alienated there, even as a kid."

Those were Kirkwood's words about California in an interview with *The New York Times* in 1982. He elaborated on his reasons in a 1976 interview. "I still get a strange, sometimes panicky feeling, in California," he said, "especially about sundown. I get taken straight back to childhood. All those divorces. Seems like somebody was always leaving somebody and fighting for your custody." Unfortunately for Kirkwood, he had no real choice but to go back to this alienating environment with its extremely bad memories if he was going to make it in his chosen career. Kirkwood had clearly decided, despite his Broadway experience and his father's extensive stage work, that it wasn't the theatre in which he wanted to ply his trade, at least at this point. He headed out to Hollywoodland because he was aiming for the movies. Initially, Kirkwood was probably staying at his father's Argyle Avenue apartment.

Since his divorce from Lila Lee, Kirkwood Sr. had had two further families. His marriage to Beatrice Powers had ended in 1934. Asked if Kirkwood Sr.'s marriage to her mother was troubled, Joan Thompson says, "They all were. All five of 'em. He simply was not a man who was meant to be with one woman. I guess it was loss of interest." When Joan was three, her divorced mother decided to move with her daughter to New Jersey to live with Joan's maternal grandmother. "I only saw him a few times after we left California," Joan says of her father. "I don't think I really felt like a daughter. He's just someone I knew and of course my mother didn't speak well of him. I'd get letters from him sometimes: 'My darling daughter' or whatever." She estimates that the last time she saw her father was when she was twelve.

Despite his failings as a father, Kirkwood Sr. did not cease to have children. (Lila Lee's only child was Kirkwood.) Kirkwood Sr.'s marriage to Marjorie Davidson, to whom he was betrothed in 1940, produced Terrance Michael Kirkwood. The latter — who began to go by "T. Michael Kirkwood" in his late twenties after majoring in Theatre Arts at LACC because his agent thought Terrance sounded too British and its abbreviation was unisex — was born in January 1941. (Beckenstein: "Jim always referred to him as Terry.") He obviously doesn't have this memory about his half-brother first-hand but has had it related to him: "He wanted Dad to kind of hook him up with some producers, directors, and Dad didn't want to do it. So Jimmy made a call saying he was James Kirkwood and of course they took the call because they knew Dad and when it turned out to be *him*, it was fine. But anyway [it] got back to my dad and he got very pissed off about it and chased him out of the house." This incident was another of those fictionalized in *I Teach Flying* and therein segues into another bizarre scene which would also seem to stem from real life. Jim Piazza: "They were living in this horrible circumstance and they had a huge fight and the father came after him to beat him up and they were running down the street and his father's bathrobe opened up. He said he had the biggest dick he'd ever seen in his life." Also instantly privy to that fact — at least according to the way it is rendered in *Flying* — were numerous pedestrians and drivers, of whose presence Kirkwood Sr. seemed heedless as he continued pursuing his son in a blind rage.

Kirkwood took his first apartment, presumably due to having been thrown out of Argyle Avenue by his father following the incidents detailed above. This would seem to be the one at the Ojai Apartments on Whitley Avenue that he shared with Tom Hammond. Both worked as doormen at Grauman's Chinese Theatre, the movie house famous as the venue whose forecourt was graced by the handprints in cement of all the top motion picture actors. Hammond would later become a theatrical agent and the manager of actress Bernadette Peters.

During his time at Grauman's, Kirkwood secured a break, one that seemed to have more to do with gossip columnist Louella Parsons — a friend of his mother's — than luck or perspiration. Parsons trailed Kirkwood's imminent arrival in her syndicated column ("I can hardly realize Lila Lee's son is 18 years old. He is on his way out here from New York to try his luck in pictures. His dad, James Kirkwood, is a great actor"). That Parsons failed to mention the name of Lee's son was an error for which she made up by announcing his gig on the door at Grauman's as though it were some sort of career milestone. Before long, she was crowing in print, "Bill Pine and Bill Thomas saw our little note… They went up and took a look at him with the result that he makes his movie debut." The gentlemen concerned ran the Pine-Thomas Organization which would ultimately produce approaching a hundred pictures for Paramount. Contemporaneous reports state that young Kirkwood was first cast by them in *High Explosive*, also known as *You Can't Live Forever* (1943). Kirkwood tended not to mention this film in his later résumés and career synopses, giving the impression that *Aerial Gunner* was his entrée. Released in 1943, the latter was one of a spate of morale-building pictures that were put into production upon America's entry into the Second World War. Kirkwood's role was only a small one and he himself described it as a "quickie film." He also wryly observed of it, "It led to a return engagement at Grauman's." In reality, he is immediately visible in neither film, a mere extra. Kirkwood did at least make a discernible appearance in *Hollywood Canteen* (1944), another morale booster involving the real-life titular venue where on-leave servicemen could rub shoulders with movie stars who were doing their patriotic bit. Bob Cromling: "He called or he wrote back to some of his school mates to go see the show, because he played a serviceman just outside the Hollywood Canteen and the camera swept the servicemen as they were watching and waiting for the stars to come in. I saw the movie and it was, 'Oh there he is and there he's gone' type of thing." Kirkwood's acting roles saw him billed as "James Kirkwood, Jr.," a necessary distinction in light of the fact that his father was still a jobbing thesp.

Times were rather tough for Kirkwood in Hollywood. "I remember Jimmy's early days," recalls his cousin Bobby Tufford, who had travelled with him from Elyria — partly to visit his Aunt Lila in New York — and ended up staying in California and obtaining work there. "I was out in California and Jimmy was just beginning to come into his own, or trying to, and one afternoon I went over to his place to see him and he was sitting on the floor eating cereal. [Laughs.] I said, 'Why didn't you tell me you don't have any food, then I would have gotten you some?'" In fact, times were so hard that Kirkwood recalled he was compelled to take a job in addition to the Grauman's work. He started as a sheet metal cowler at Lockheed Aircraft in Burbank, working the "graveyard shift" of midnight-to-7 a.m. The strain of this overwork brought about the end of his nascent motion picture career. Kirkwood suffered what he described as a "breakdown." In a late sixties résumé, Kirkwood said as a consequence of this, he had to spend some time "recuperating" in Tucson, Arizona. He later disclosed that he was, in fact admitted to a mental hospital. Many years later (1980), he was toying with the idea of writing a novel about his experiences called *For Inmates Only*.

It may even have been the case that Kirkwood worked as a prostitute in this period. The often very autobiographical *I Teach Flying* depicts a protagonist being recruited by a madam when working the door at Grauman's. In a seventies letter to William Russo, Kirkwood jokingly wrote that he might "go back to hustling." However, nobody spoken to for this book has expressed even when prompted any recollection of Kirkwood mentioning having done gigolo work.

Kirkwood claimed that his period spent recuperating before returning to Hollywood amounted to six months, but this seems an overestimate: his departure from Elyria was in July '42 and by December 11 that year he had enlisted in the Coast Guard. Thoughts of entering the service had been in his head even back at Brewster Academy. Ned Bullock says the subject was discussed in their brief conversation there. "We knew we were going into the service," he recalls. "He thought that he'd like to go into the ambulance corps." Either the conversation was prompted by Kirkwood still being at the school in December 1941 when the Japanese bombed Pearl Harbor or by the posturing of Hitler before that which had convinced many that conflagration was coming. Kirkwood described his decision to enlist as "a moment of wild abandon, group spirit and nutty-ism." Such moments had affected quite a few young American men since December '41. As Lila Nichols recalls, "We were all very patriotic in our country and everybody wanted to go." Kirkwood's decision to make his war effort on the seas may have been the result of seeing other family members taking that route: both Bobby Tufford and Lila Lee Nichols' husband Harris had joined the Navy.

Following his time in boot camp, which presumably encompassed the six weeks records show he spent at radar school, Kirkwood started active duty on March 23, 1943. As with so many other young men, the Second World War could have been the point at which James Kirkwood's life story came to an end. He had the good fortune, however, to run into one Lomax Study. Study (pronounced "Stoo-dee") was stationed with the US Coast Guard Barracks in San Francisco as morale officer, preparing to head up a morale office on the *USS Admiral H.T. Mayo*, one of the Navy's troop transports. One of his additional extra duties was to oversee the groups of young recruits who would arrive from boot camp and then be sent to the South Pacific. Recalls Study, "One particular group of about fifteen men arrived on a very rainy Wednesday afternoon and instead of calling them to attention I said, 'At ease and let's get out of the rain and come inside.' I wasn't very military, as you can see. I had a reason to do this because I knew these kids were scared to death, at least most of them were. Went down the line when I could and shook hands with each and every one of them and said hello, which was not very military, but that was my way of doing it. As I came up to one very young man who was good-looking I asked him his name and he replied, 'James Kirkwood, sir.' 'Oh,' I said, 'To hell with that "sir," you are at ease, but, by the way — James Kirkwood? Are you any relation to the great James Kirkwood, the actor? The one who made the Jeeter Lester of *Tobacco Road?*' Jimmy replied,

'He's my father and my mother is Lila Lee.' I might just add here that in St. Louis, Missouri, where I was brought up, I was quite well-known in my young teenage and early twenties as an actor doing radio and considerable theatre, such as *Private Lives, French without Tears, Topaz* and various musicals. 'Well,' I said, 'Jimmy, I wish we were in New York as Wednesday is matinée day.'" Study dismissed the group and departed. About twenty minutes later, he realized that Kirkwood had something unusual about him and was perhaps someone who would be an asset to his morale office on the *Mayo*. Study: "I started to look for him and found him washing his clothes. I asked him what his orders were and he said with kind of a fear and trepidation, 'I'm going to some island in the South Pacific'... I asked him if he could type and he replied, 'Yeah, I can do about fifty words a minute.' Well I asked him, 'Would you consider working on a troop transport instead of your present assignment?' 'Oh gee — you bet I would,' he replied. I went to my commanding officer in charge and asked him if he would consider changing James Kirkwood's orders. I elaborated on who Jimmy was and he was rather impressed. I told them that he could type and that I had ideas of a newspaper in the morale office on board ship." Whatever his parents' dwindling fortunes, the allure of their names on this occasion possibly saved Kirkwood's life: his orders were changed and he was welcomed aboard the *Mayo*.

As his career in the Coast Guard began, by his account another of Kirkwood's careers — if one can call it that — came to a merciful end. The Body Finder was about to discover his final corpse. "I was on beach patrol, which is what they did at first before they put you on the ship," Kirkwood recalled in 1980 on *The Dick Cavett Show*. "I was patrolling in Half Moon Bay, California, and I had a dog. He was like a pit-bull. He kept pulling and pulling. It was very dark and I thought it was just a clump of seaweed and so I kept pulling him away. Finally, I just went over and I jumped on the seaweed to say to the dog, 'Yes, here we are, there's the seaweed' and it was the body of man who had jumped off the Golden Gate Bridge and committed suicide and floated in. My foot went right through his stomach. It was just horrible." Kirkwood also told Cavett, "I'm actually going to write a book sometime called *The Body Finder* about a kid that just happens to go through these experiences."

Following its "shakedown cruise" (test run), the *Admiral Mayo* departed from its home port of San Francisco to Le Havre, France, to pick up American GIs who had been prisoners of the Germans. The *Mayo* was a mighty vessel. Seven hundred feet long and weighing more than 30,000 tons, it carried a crew of 700 coast guardsmen and often well over 7,000 troops. The logistics for a vessel of such a size were mind-boggling. Study recalls, "Our chow line when we were going with seven or eight thousand people used to start at 5.30 in the morning and go 'til about eight o'clock at night without stopping." Kirkwood later recalled that on board the *Mayo* he visited Southampton, Le Harve, Marseilles, Portugal, the West Indies, Panama, the Philippines and Korea.

After Le Havre, the *Mayo* sailed to Boston. Remembers Study of that latter city, "The whole town went crazy and gave us a reception like I have never experienced before in my life. Jimmy had called his mother who at that time lived in New York and she insisted that he come down to a special party that his mother knew was being planned for him, 'And by the way, bring that man Lomax Study who had your orders changed'… Well, we arrived at her apartment the next day and she immediately called a taxi to take us to the party. When we arrived, the door was opened and there she stood, Gloria Swanson, a close friend of Lila's. Well, the apartment was filled with showbiz people and it was fun, fun, fun and a night to be remembered."

Lee's relief at her son's change of orders may have been a little misplaced. It is undeniable that Kirkwood was safer than the average soldier on a battlefield. "We had it pretty easy," is Study's summation of life for the crew of the *Mayo* during the war. In addition to their dry berth and three guaranteed square meals per day, "We were also under escort, because that's the way it is when you have a troop transport. There were only four of them in the whole Navy and the *Admiral Mayo* was the biggest, I think." The morale office probably had it easier than most of the crew. "The morale office was a separate unit onboard ship," says Study. "It was like a little office and off of that office there was a place for Jimmy. Now it wasn't a private room or anything, but he shared I think with three other guys [in] bunk beds." In contrast, "The troops were six in a row up to the top of the ceiling and in about a 30-foot-square cabin, you had like 25 or 30 people. That was pretty tight." However, during the worst period of armed conflict in the history of the human race things were never going to be a bowl of cherries even for the Coast Guard. "The guys that were sent to these various islands were troops protecting them, that's what the Coast Guards did," says Study. "A lot of guys got in the Coast Guards thinking they were just going to be guarding the US shores and the Mississippi River. Well, [laughs] bullshit. The Coast Guard boys were the ones that took the troops across the British Channel on the invasion and there were more of them killed there than any other place because they were so numerous and the Germans were ready for them to come ashore anyway." Study says that life aboard the *Admiral Mayo* could be "hectic and somewhat scary." A ship carrying 7,000-plus troops intended to be deployed on the various battlefields of the world was a prime target. Enemy submarines and war planes were a constant, even if background, fear. Though Study estimates that the *Mayo* suffered only 25 airplane attacks during the remaining two-and-a-half years of war, when they happened they were naturally nerve-wracking, especially when they involved Japanese Kamikaze pilots, the prototypical suicide bombers. This must have been especially so for Kirkwood, whose duty in this eventuality was to assist the anti-aircraft in one of the ship's dozen gunnery turrets as a loader. Says Study, "I must say he carried out his duties with courage and exceptional guts. You have to be very quick with the loading because after you have shot one you shoot another and shoot another. Anti-aircraft has a loader to load the ammunition into the next guy who will put it in. These kids were four and five in a group. Jimmy all through his career as a sailor, he was a gutsy guy. He wasn't afraid to get up in the gunnery. Of course he was, but he didn't show it. Jimmy could be the sweetest, nicest guy and yet when he was on board ship and he would see the planes were coming or there would be an alert, he got tough as hell. To me this was kind of interesting. He was tougher than I was. You've got to be pretty goddamn brave to see these goddamn Japanese guys who were just committing suicide. I mean they fell in the water more than they did on the ship, thank God — they only hit us once the whole time we were under fire — but that's because we had good-and-plenty-of-it men."

Kirkwood's Coast Guard Notice of Separation states that he was a "Radarman Third Class (Reserve)," but Study doesn't recall him ever being called upon in that capacity on board the *Mayo* ("The radar job was already filled"). When not loading anti-aircraft or understudying the radarmen, Kirkwood had a role to which this perennial optimist was superbly suited: keeping people's peckers up. Study: "There was always somebody that heard that his mother was dead, and here we were out in the middle of the Atlantic or down in Panama Canal or wherever the hell we were and when you have that many people aboard there are all kinds of problems. A twelve-hour day was nothing. I mean, what the hell else are you going to do? You're all aboard ship and you got to take care of people. We had no medical responsibility at all, just a human responsibility. It was really a marvelous experience for him, and for me too… And he did all kinds of things in the morale office. For example at one point we picked up a group of troops in Marseilles. I think there were six or seven thousand of them that had already been at the Battle of the Bulge in Germany and they thought they were going home and our orders were to take them to Okinawa. When they realized that, there was almost a revolt. I remember Jimmy saying, 'Jesus Christ, what are we going to do now?' I said, 'Let's get them all to do an art exhibit.' And you'd be surprised at the horrible things that these boys wrote!"

One of the morale office's functions was to put out a daily newspaper. Study had the idea to call it *A.M.*, a reference to the New York newspaper *P.M.* Credits on surviving copies of the paper list Study as the "managing editor" and Kirkwood the "assistant editor." However, Study readily admits, "I can't write worth a damn. It was Jimmy's newspaper. Jimmy Kirkwood was the editor and wrote a gossipy, newsy and humorous — very, very humorous — [account] of all the events that happened on board ship, and there were many. We had an old electrical copy machine that knocked out as many as two-to-three-thousand copies in an hour each day and it was Jimmy Kirkwood's writing and humor that made it a worthy daily paper. It was a one-sheet newspaper on both sides and he would fill that up with what so-and-so did, some guy broke his toe or fell down or some guy got in a fight on board ship with another guy because they weren't getting along."

"Sometimes he went overboard," Study says of Kirkwood's stewardship of *A.M.* "He criticized the captain once for something that he had done and put it right in the paper. Well, holy shit, he was called up on the bridge and chewed out and the guy said, 'How dare you do this?' and he said, 'Well, what are you talking about, it's a free country, isn't it?' Here was this kid talking to the captain who could throw him in the brig if he wanted to. He would make statements against the principle or the rules or whatever. But that's what made the paper what it was." Asked if when reading *A.M.* he remembers thinking that Kirkwood could become a professional writer, Study unhesitatingly says, "Yes. Yes, I did, because he wrote so well."

His writing talent aside, Study says of Kirkwood as a person, "I would say he was just a regular kid." Study remained friends with Kirkwood throughout his life and later found himself bewildered by Kirkwood's un-regular lifestyle: "One thing I will tell you, the part of his life that he spent with me, he was not interested in men. He was as straight as an arrow. He had a girlfriend in San Francisco and when we put into port he was off that ship so quick that you couldn't see straight. And likewise in Boston or any other place… I don't remember her name. This girl was a San Francisco girl. He met her when he was in the service. I know that whenever we would come to port he would make a beeline for her apartment and stay there." Study also recalls, "During the war, if you were a homosexual, they didn't want you around. That was kind of a law and there were several boys who pretended to be that way so they could get out, they were scared to go, and he always thought that was terrible."

At one point, one of the *Mayo*'s chief petty officers was actor Victor Mature, whose movie career was a couple of years old. When the *Mayo* docked in Marseilles for a three-day layover, Mature was selected to be the main attraction of a show mounted for a contingent of army nurses stationed just outside that French city. Such shows were normally of quite a professional standard. Study: "We had a regular jazz band on board that I had recruited by going through the archives and picking… [bandleader, violinist and singer] Carl Ravazza. I used to MC the thing. Jimmy was kind of the stage manager whenever we put something on, whether it was on board ship or ashore." Study took the opportunity the Marseilles layover afforded him to fly up to Paris to visit his mother. Upon his return, a worried-looking Kirkwood met him at the airport. He said, 'Study, I don't know what the hell we're going to do. I can't find Victor Mature anyplace — he's out getting drunk. He's been away, he had leave.' I said, 'He knows we're doing the show, he'll show up — you wait and see. He's a trooper.' Well, no Victor Mature and three or four thousand nurses, probably all girls. We started the show and then Mature arrived and he was just as dead drunk as he could be. I said, 'Victor — wait a minute.' He said, 'Don't worry about me, I'm all right'… So I foolishly let him get on. His patter wasn't to sing or dance — just tell jokes and talk. He had a pretty good patter and it lasts for maybe seven or eight minutes." This day, Mature deviated from his normal routine: "He said, 'I know what you girls are coming to see' — and he unzipped his pants and took out his pecker and waved it at the audience. I screamed at Kirkwood. Kirkwood pulled the curtain and got him off, got him in the jeep, took him back to the [ship]. He should have been thrown in the brig but he wasn't. Jimmy Kirkwood really saved the day." Mature's "insult" of the nurses made headlines in services newspaper *Stars and Stripes*.

When in the second quarter of 1945, the *Mayo* delivered troops for the Allies' invasion of Okinawa; the ship experienced some of its fiercest assaults. "We were under attack by numerous Japanese aircraft for several hours, one of which hit the fan tail and killed two of the US marines that were manning that particular gunnery station," recalls Study. "We were under real pressure." It was the last action the crew of the *Mayo* would see in World War II. The Japanese surrender in September that year meant that the ship could return to its home port of San Francisco.

Kirkwood was anxious to get back to civilian life and his acting career. Study recalls, "He knew that he had a chance to do something in New York through his mother. I can't remember exactly the details, but he wanted to get out. They wouldn't let him out because they needed him and he didn't have enough points. He was screaming and yelling about this and upset: 'What the hell — the war's over'...So Jimmy stayed in for another month or two and then finally he did wangle his way out."

Kirkwood's recalled his best friend on the *Mayo* as a man by the name of Vin. Having got through so much action unscathed, it was a grotesque irony that Vin and several others should perish in a non-combat situation when hostilities had ceased. "It was a ridiculous accident," Kirkwood later recalled. "They were laying a new floor in the head... and they used some kind of tar and you're not supposed to smoke or light a match. Some guy got up in the middle of the night to go to the john and sat down and lit a cigarette and the whole thing blew up, combusted. About thirteen or fourteen men were just fried in their bunks and my best friend was one of them. So that was a very bad kind of send-off as far as getting out of the service." It was also the second time in less than five years that Kirkwood had lost a best friend to the Reaper.

That is if we are to believe Kirkwood about either Jordan or Vin. Though a Vin Morin is listed in copies of *AM* as the magazine's production manager, naval records do not show any such accident happening on the *Mayo*. When told about Kirkwood's recollection of this accident, Lomax Study was bewildered, pointing out that he would have heard about it. William Russo says, "It wouldn't surprise me that he took two incidents. Maybe there was someone he knew in another situation — I mean, he was a body finder — and he transposed it, put in a military setting, or said that that's where it happened... I think interviews are the places where his disinformation would be most evident."

Kirkwood was given an honorable discharge from the U.S. Naval Service on January 24, 1946, though remained a reservist until January 1952. He left active service with the American Area Campaign ribbon, the Adriatic/Pacific Area Campaign ribbon, the World War II Victory ribbon and the ETO Area Campaign ribbon. Though Kirkwood had undoubtedly shown bravery in his term of service, Study points out of the honors, "We all got the same. Every guy on that crew that was under fire was entitled to those kinds of things." Interestingly, Kirkwood's Authority For Discharge for his term as an apprentice seaman (which lasted for three years from December 11, 1948) — stamped, like his Notice of Separation, as "Recorded" on August 5, 1947 — lists his year of birth as

1930. One wonders whether this apparent administrative error is what later gave him the idea to begin stating his age as six years younger than what it really was.

In the Christmas season of 1945, with his ship back in the States, the war behind him and his discharge imminent, Kirkwood would have been forgiven for imagining that calm lay ahead. In fact, some of the most extraordinary and traumatic experiences of his entire life were about to befall him.

FIVE

When his ship docked in San Francisco, Kirkwood paid a visit to his father's Los Angeles apartment. T. Michael Kirkwood was now aged around five. One of his only significant memories of Kirkwood as a child stems from it. Says T. Michael, "He was coming home from the Coast Guard and Dad said, 'Now look out for him and come and tell me when he's coming'…When he saw me waiting for him, he started hiding behind trees and playing little games and stuff."

"My mother was much younger," T. Michael says of Marjorie Davidson. "I think she did small theatre, maybe with him at some point, and that's when they met. Jimmy is really my half-brother, although we didn't even think about that, we just said 'brother.'" Kirkwood Sr.'s parenting skills would seem to have improved by the time he was on his third child, for T. Michael harbors far fewer ambivalent feelings about his father than did Kirkwood and none of Joan's negative feelings. "To me, my dad was fantastic," he says. However, he does point out, "He was 65 when I was born. I'm 63 *now* and I have *grandkids*." He says, "Jimmy was sixteen years older than me so he had a different experience. I'm sure there were a lot of things he didn't like but he never told that to me. He always seemed to really enjoy Dad when he came out to California." T. Michael would, though, occasionally pick up mixed feelings, especially from the forewarnings Kirkwood later gave him about the novel he was writing about their dad, but only realized the full extent of how much Kirkwood may have badmouthed Kirkwood Sr. (or at least his bad aspects) at his brother's memorial service, where he says, "This asshole got up and was saying how great Jimmy was and it was too bad he had a drunken father and a drunken mother."

T. Michael remembers Kirkwood getting on "very well" with his own mother, though thinks he might have been slightly discomforted by her, possibly due to sexual attraction on his part. "I read a diary Jimmy kept at one point," he says, "and part of it had been in the service and I guess he just left it at Dad's place and I went through it once and he said something like, 'Not sure how to take Dad's wife' — which was my mother — because they were close to the same age, I guess."

Kirkwood Sr. and Marjorie Davidson separated when T. Michael was young. T. Michael: "He got custody of me and I lived with him 'til about the second grade, which is about seven…He wanted me to go to Catholic school. My mother lived closer to the Catholic school so I guess they had an agreement I could go live with her as long as I went to Catholic school. Then I would see him in mid-summers. I would stay with him, I'd meet him for church on Sundays (she didn't go to church) and we'd go to have Orange Julius and maybe go to a John Wayne movie."

Going by Kirkwood's recollections, the family visit to Argyle was just about the only happy occurrence at this juncture of his life. As well as (supposedly) the death of his best friend, Kirkwood had two further pieces of devastating news with which to deal as he prepared to return to civilian life. Firstly, his fiancée dropped a bombshell. Said Kirkwood in a 1976 radio interview, "The ship docked in San Francisco and I got right to a phone and called her up and I said, 'Hey, I'm back, isn't that great, I'll be out in three weeks, blah blah blah.' And she said, 'Oh, Jimmy, gee I meant to write you something in our last letter.' I said, 'What was that?' She said, 'I got married last month.'" The fiancée was a girl Kirkwood identified as "Eleanor" who either hailed from or was living in Philadelphia. Kirkwood also said that he had been to school with her. As he was a veteran of so many, it's difficult to work out to which pedagogical institution Kirkwood is referring. There was an Eleanor D. Moore in Kirkwood's class at Brewster Academy, although her biography in Brewster's Fall 2006 newsletter following her death doesn't mention her ever living in Philadelphia. She also never married. There were three Eleanors at Elyria High School in Kirkwood's last period there but Esther Hamula says of Eleanor Catherine Kavalecz, "She…lived in the same neighborhood I did, and [I] knew her personality well. Definitely, for sure, I know Jimmy would not have dated her, at any time." (Additionally, Kavalecz's daughter reports that her parents married in November 1946, way past Kirkwood's mustering-out date and therefore not consistent with his story.) Of Eleanor Groffen, Weber admits "I had to find my high-school yearbook, peer into her face, etc., and even then I had no recollection of ever seeing her in any of my classes or activities." For Kirkwood to have associated with this Eleanor unnoticed by someone so close to him seems inconceivable. Hamula adds, "But I didn't want to just say this to you, so I called three of my classmates…and they made almost exactly the same remarks as I have: that he would never have dated the first Eleanor, and no one recalls the second." Hamula also conferred with classmates about Eleanor Kelly: "All of us knew Eleanor Kelly, and we all felt while Jimmy certainly knew Eleanor Kelly, he was not involved with her in any way. At that time, we all had our little groups or cliques, but we also *all* were acquainted with each other, went to the same events…" In the lengthy résumés Kirkwood wrote as a young man, some of them designed to provide discussion topics for interviewers, he mentions the traumatic stories of neither Vin nor Eleanor, despite detailing many other incidents in his life, both tragic and comedic.

Kirkwood claimed a third hammer blow in this period in the shape of the badly deteriorated health of his mother, who had gamely attempted to mount yet another comeback in her movie career. Her dormant tuberculosis had returned and she had been found to have a cavity in her right lung. This was something that had been hitherto kept from Kirkwood, it being services policy to try to maintain the morale of the men by suppressing bad news from home wherever feasible. Because medical records exist confirming Lee's state, this is the one part of the triptych of misfortune Kirkwood alleged that can be confirmed to be true. Naturally, Kirkwood was distraught. Recalls Study, "He loved his father but he really was a momma's boy more than anything else. I don't mean that in a sissy way, I mean in a good, strong way of love."

Kirkwood recalled that, given leave, he reached New York but that he didn't have any money to go to see his mother in the sanatorium in upstate Saranac Lake nor to buy her a Christmas present. Unable to get a loan from a bank because he had no collateral, he turned for help to his stepfather, whom he didn't name but would have been John E. Murphy, Lila Lee's husband since 1944. Though said stepfather was at the time experiencing difficulties in his relationship with Lee — Kirkwood felt that he thought she wasn't being a wife to him, due to her illness — Kirkwood assumed that Murphy would at least agree to a loan. He later said, "I asked my stepfather, who was a millionaire, I think for $150 and he said, 'Gee, Jim, I don't know about that. Have you read *The New York Times* today? Well the market's down a couple of points. So if you could scatter round and get it elsewhere I'd appreciate it'…He really had a lot of money. It would have meant nothing to him." Kirkwood also found that his stepfather had changed the locks on the family apartment. He was reduced to living in a hotel called the Broadway Central, of which he said, "This real fleabag. My first encounter with bedbugs."

The merry Yuletide spirit of the people he passed in the street naturally only rubbed salt into his rapidly multiplying wounds. He said, "It was two weeks before Christmas and I thought, 'Hey, this isn't the way it's supposed to be when you get out of the service!'" A solution to his troubles materialized when he passed the toy store F.A.O. Schwartz on Fifth Avenue and saw a window display of stuffed chimpanzees holding squirt guns. Kirkwood: "I had about ten dollars to my name. I didn't have enough money to buy a gun. I don't think I really wanted to buy a real gun, but I did buy a squirt gun for $4.95." Because the gun he purchased was not of the bright or luminous hue one normally associates with a water pistol, it was a fairly convincing facsimile of a genuine firearm. Kirkwood spent the next five to ten days (his estimation varied) going "around stores and banks like a madman!…I was trying to hold up some kind of a store. It never occurred to me to hold up a person but to hold up a store and not a big store and not a store where I was going to get caught…Then I did the cowardly thing: I picked a store run entirely by women."

The store in question was a lingerie shop and the hold-up was farcical. Kirkwood: "I was terrified, absolutely terrified, and I was so terrified that when I made my big announcement, 'This is a hold-up,' it came out like [whispers] 'This is a hold-up.' And the woman looked at me and smiled and she said, 'Pardon me, what was that?' I said, 'This is a hold-up' and she said, 'I don't think I heard you'…And I said it a third time and she reached across the counter and she put her hand on my shoulder and she said, 'Why, I have a son about your age.' And I thought, 'What does that have to do with it?' Then when she understood that I meant business, she turned into steel and she said, 'Get out of here! You get out of here.' I said, 'No, this is a hold-up.' She said, 'Get out of the store'…The other people in the store got a little hysterical when I took out my squirt gun because it looked like a real gun and there was a lot of screaming and chattering and I finally got her backed away from the cash register and then I couldn't open it. By then I was so nervous that my voice was cracking and I was screaming and I said, 'How do you open this thing?' And she just looked at me. I said, 'I'll kill you if you don't tell me how to open this.' And she just kept looking at me. She wasn't going to help me. I liked her. She was a great lady." Kirkwood finally managed to gain entry to the cash register. "I got six hundred and some dollars," he said. The next day he visited upscale Fifth Avenue department store Lord & Taylor: "I bought my mother a gold quilted hostess gown and a bed jacket and slippers (things that you could wear in a sanatorium) and I got a train ticket and I went up and spent Christmas with her."

That Kirkwood's confession was not restricted to interviewers suggests that the squirt-gun stick-up did actually happen. T. Michael Kirkwood says, "He told me that, that he actually did that. I said, 'You shitting me.' He said, 'No, I swear it.'" Also testament to its probable truth is the heart-stopping verisimilitude of Kirkwood's account of it in the novel *Some Kind of Hero*.

Asked by an interviewer in 1976 whether if he'd had a real gun he would have used it, Kirkwood said, "No. The whole thing was so alien to me as it was. No, I never could've. The clue to that is I certainly never did anything like that again — because I was terrified. I look back on it now really in a kind of loving horror. I don't really believe I did that — yet I know I did it…I think that in order to do something like that, you've got to be a little momentarily deranged. A normal person doesn't do that." Kirkwood said he told his mother what he'd done about two years after the incident. "Oh, God, I thought she was going to have a heart attack," he recalled. "And I also didn't rat on my stepfather. I knew that he married her and not me." (Murphy and Lee were divorced in 1949.)

The robbery continued to tug at Kirkwood's conscience. He even seemed to think that by mentioning the incident in interviews it might lead the way to some sort of reparation. Speaking in 1976, he said, "The statute of limitations is up now, but I've talked about it an awful lot. I told Barbara Walters on the *Today Show* and I thought, 'Well, why don't they call up?'" The alternative of going back to the store and giving the money back under his own steam was no longer a viable option: "I used to go by it often. It occurred to me to give the money back, but by that time it was no longer a lingerie shop. The front of the store was now a camera shop and I thought, 'Well, I'm not going to walk into a totally strange place and say, 'I held this store up, here's the money.'"

Somewhere in this post-war chronology in Kirkwood's life came a return visit to Elyria. While in Ohio, Kirkwood made a proposal of marriage to his old sweetheart. Esther Hamula recalls Kirkwood turning up in his white sailor's uniform and the two of them sitting on the swing on the front porch of her family's home. Says Hamula, "[He] said, 'Would you marry me?' I said, 'What? Jimmy, remember years ago you said you didn't think you could stay with one woman when you got married?' So I said, no, when I got married it would be for life." Hamula interprets Kirkwood's previously stated antipathy toward matrimony as being the result of seeing the endless failures of his parents' sequence of betrothals. Was he serious in his proposal? Hamula: "He was sincere. He wasn't joking around." Nonetheless, she says of the rejection, "Oh, I don't think he was heartbroken." It wasn't until 1976 when Kirkwood mentioned "Eleanor" on a radio show that Hamula suspected that he made the proposal on the rebound. "That's okay," she says now. "I was writing to several boys [in the service]. Maybe they thought that I was in love with them." Or there's another possibility. The paucity of evidence about his engagement to "Eleanor" suggests that not only was she an invention for publicity purposes but was an invention rooted in Kirkwood's real-life (if in slightly different circumstances) rejection by Hamula. Once again, Kirkwood seems to have been spinning reality to his own promotional ends.

A marriage proposal in 1946 had a somewhat different significance than it would have now. In an era before reliable contraception, wedlock was considered by many a way of simply accepting the inevitable: a sex life was almost certainly going to lead to children, so those children may as well be borne by someone who you liked rather than be the result of a casual encounter which might lead to the stigma of bastardization. Perhaps it is her generation's often rather prosaic attitude to the convention of marriage that leads Hamula to state that she thinks the union might have actually worked had she accepted Kirkwood's proposal. "You know, I do think about that," she says. "I truly do. I think it would have been okay because of the type of personality I am. I would have put up with a lot of things. I would have been very encouraging and if he didn't succeed in whatever he was trying, I'm sure I would have stayed by him." In fact, Hamula ultimately got wed for genuine love to a man she met when she was 22. She says, "He has a personality something like Jimmy's. He has a terrific sense of humor. I love men with humor. He just made a game out of everything." Something else Hamula's husband has in common with his predecessor in her affections is a love of tennis: "He was Ohio state tennis champion."

Come his discharge, Kirkwood naturally wanted to pick up the thread of his acting career. He chose to do so, however, not in California but in New York. Though in those days that city was the home of what television production there was, it seems unlikely that Kirkwood had lowered his original sights from movie stardom. More likely is that he wanted to be near to Saranac Lake, where his mother was so unfortunately obliged to be located.

Kirkwood's payment upon discharge had been $85.48, with initial mustering-out pay of $100. He obtained a job as night clerk at the Waldorf Astoria Hotel and began auditioning. A card he or his agent prepared in July '46 declared that he played leads, character, straight and comedy in the "juvenile" field (not as peculiar a word for a 21-year-old who said his voice range was "15-25" as it would be now). His dialects were given as "Brooklyn, Midwestern, Southern, New England, English, Irish, French." Said card fills in some detail about his early professional thespian activities, noting 28 unnamed radio shows recorded on the West Coast when in the service, three unnamed television shows made in Boston, a stint in *Janie* in New York and stock work in California, Deer Lake, Cragsmoor and

Martha's Vineyard. His filmography doesn't mention *Hollywood Canteen* but does list — as well as *Aerial Gunner* — *You Can't Live Forever, No Hands on the Clock, March of Time* and *A Yank at Eton*, plus the *This is America* series and "Commercial pictures." A Lexington telephone number is provided.

Upon his relocation to the Big Apple, Kirkwood looked up his little sister. Though she had stayed with her grandmother in New Jersey when her mother remarried when she was eleven or twelve, Joan would spend weekends with her mother and stepfather in New York. Of Kirkwood, she says, "I saw him a lot during my teenage years." However, though he was clearly keen to establish a sibling relationship with Joan, the latter reveals that at no point did Kirkwood try to engineer a rapprochement between Joan and the father she had already, unbeknownst to her, seen for the final time. "Why should he?" she says. "He was a responsible person. My father was not. And that must have grated at Jimmy, because he probably did nothing for him the whole time he was growing up. It fell to Lila and her family."

Eventually Kirkwood secured several jobs in summer stock, that staple of the American theatre whose title derives from the fact that it operates in the sunny months and its fixed repertoire of alternating productions enables the re-use of scenery and costumes, "stock." He appeared in *Joan of Lorraine* with Diana Barrymore and was subsequently signed for the same part in a six-month tour, this production starring Sylvia Sidney. Kirkwood also recalled in this period, "Closing out of town in several plays," actors' parlance for a production not moving to the prestigious setting of Broadway, which outcome — the hoped-for culmination for any new play — is referred to in the trade as "coming in."

Under the G.I. Bill, Kirkwood studied under Sanford Meisner, one of the first proponents of Method acting. He also began studying voice under one Harold Fonville. Another of Fonville's G.I. Bill students was the late Lee Goodman. Born in 1923, Goodman was, like Kirkwood, showbiz through and through. Ronald Plotkin, Goodman's lover for twenty years beginning in 1960, says, "He was a child actor…Lee was a natural talent. He was a boy tap dancer. His first Broadway show was *Conversation Piece* with Noël Coward and then he went on the road with *Dead End* and was in the business until he had to go into the army at age of eighteen or nineteen."

In the 1991 book *Intimate Nights: The Golden Age of New York Cabaret* by James Gavin, Goodman revealed that Fonville had encouraged him to stick around after a lesson one day to see a pupil who was unable to sing in key but had remarkable enthusiasm. "You're gonna scream with laughter," Fonville, perhaps rather unprofessionally, promised. Kirkwood arrived and complained when he saw Goodman present but was told not to worry. However, when he noticed Goodman shaking his head at his singing efforts he asked him what the matter was. "Well, God, you're way off-key!" Goodman replied. He tried to help Kirkwood stay in tune by singing a number with him. At this point, Fonville noticed what might be called a chemistry between them: the juxtaposition of Goodman's solemn, quasi-weary and slightly jug-eared countenance and Kirkwood's undisciplined, youthful energy was funny.

"When I met him he was literally starving," Gavin quoted Goodman as saying of Kirkwood. "He was a bright, cute kid, and he could always get somebody to take him to dinner. He was very ambitious and desperate to accomplish something." The two moved into a cold-water flat on West 48th Street — the heart of New York City's tough Hell's Kitchen — whose rent was $28 per month and which Kirkwood would later describe as, "Five rooms, all of them bilious green — it was a railroad flat, more like a bowling alley, with the john in the hall that you shared with the tenants of the next apartment, no heat except a kerosene burner, and every kind of insect, rodent, or 'the little people' as we called them." Recalls Joan, "Most of the furnishings were ones that he would walk off with from hotel lobbies…chairs and lamps and all that kind of stuff." An item in the *Joplin Globe* from December '48 seems to contradict Kirkwood's estimation of the rent but not of the apartment's squalor: "Jim has knocked out walls and made a few large rooms out of a lot of small ones. The landlords don't care. They're glad to be getting approximately a hundred dollars a month for quarters that were unrentable. Jim doesn't want to move. He likes the home he has made for himself. If you offered him a modern apartment in midtown at $400 a month, he'd look the other way." At some point, Lila Lee also lived at the apartment.

It was Kirkwood who suggested that he and Goodman team up in a comedy act. Goodman later admitted he was reluctant. Fonville happened to be pianist at the well-known Fifth Avenue nightclub Number One and it was he who arranged for Kirkwood & Goodman to enter the club's weekly talent contest in April 1948. The pair did so, "…more as a dare than anything," Kirkwood said. Ronald Plotkin explains, "It was a period when nightclub and cabaret performance was very hot and they saw something in each other [they] felt could work." The stand-up routines they'd cooked up won them the contest and the prize of a week's engagement.

Kirkwood later said, "The first night that I ever worked in a nightclub was at Number One, Fifth Avenue in New York and I was *scared*. I thought, 'My God, I'm gonna be running out there in front of a lot of drunks, they're going to start throwing swizzle sticks at me…'" It's not clear whether he is referring here to the talent show night or the start of the pair's engagement proper on May 14, but either way there was an interesting upshot to Kirkwood's terror. He recalled, "There was a comedienne on the bill, Nancy Andrews. She was an old pro and she saw me shaking and I was pale and nervous and frightened and everything and she said to the waiter, 'Get the kid a martini.' I said no, I couldn't have a drink. Drinking then just put me right under the table. But anyhow, she got me a martini and she started telling a joke." One of the funny stories Andrews told Kirkwood was about a psychiatrist with two sons which would feature in, and provide a title for, his first novel.

So well did Kirkwood & Goodman's engagement go down that it stretched to six months. A highly successful partnership was underway. This new career was something Kirkwood later said was, "Something I'd never imagined until it happened by fluke." As both were broke, Kirkwood and Goodman had to scrabble around for material. Goodman wrote a parody of "Tea for Two" in hipster lingo and found some comedic props. Kirkwood brought into the act what Goodman described to Gavin as "some terrible old art songs. One of them, 'Downy Little Brownie Man,' was unbelievably racist." However, the main attraction of the team was the perennial contrast between their appearances and demeanors, whose big-brother-little-brother nature even extended to Goodman being two inches taller than his partner. (Kirkwood found himself being referred to as "the little one" because he measured "only" six feet.)

In the different world of the 1940s, Kirkwood's sister was able to attend nightclubs despite her tender years. Consequently, Joan was privileged to be an eyewitness at many of the pair's engagements including Number One, of which she makes the interesting observation, "It kind of catered to a gay crowd." It was a crowd in which Kirkwood and Goodman would not have felt out of place, for the two were partners in more ways than one. Plotkin says, "I think it was the first serious relationship that they both had," but adds that though he thinks this was not Kirkwood's first relationship with a male, it was for Goodman, who had hitherto been living a heterosexual life. Plotkin: "Then it became a problem because Lee was the one that never had to rehearse and Jim was the one that [started] the vacuum cleaner very early in the morning and Lee was trying to sleep. They were doing that and working clubs and not getting home until four or five o'clock in the morning and Jim was manic about 'Rehearse, rehearse, rehearse'...Lee felt it wasn't really necessary to rehearse as much as Jim wanted to rehearse. I think they were lovers for two years or maybe a little longer than that and then they decided it was not good for the act for them to continue to do this."

Though not aware of Kirkwood's sexual relationship with Goodman, Joan was beginning to realize there was something different about her half-brother. She recalls, "My stepfather made a remark. At the time the big word was 'pansy' and he made that reference to Jimmy and I was so upset my mother made him tell me that he was kidding. He could tell he was gay." Not only had Ned Bullock thought he detected something alternative in Kirkwood's sexuality back at Brewster Academy, but *I Teach Flying* suggests Kirkwood had had sexual encounters with more than one male during his teens. (William Russo believes that there may have been something sexual between Kirkwood and Reid Russell and that this was related in a camping scene flashback in his novel *Some Kind of Hero*.) However, only recently Kirkwood had been enthusiastically intimate with a woman in San Francisco and before that had lived an almost preposterously all-American if probably chaste life in Elyria. This was a dramatic change of lifestyle. Though Kirkwood would continue to have sexual relationships with women as well as men for at least the next seven or eight years, he was now set on the path to the full-blown homosexuality that would characterize his private life from the age of around thirty onwards. Arthur Beckenstein asserts, "He was gay. He played the game of avoiding sexual definition and was a product of his time. He did have a few affairs with women when he was younger, but I would question whether he was emotionally committed."

"Lee Goodman...was the straight guy — in a comedic sense, I mean," says Patti Goldstein, lifelong friend of Kirkwood's, of the comedy style of Kirkwood & Goodman.

"The two of them were foils of one another," says John Desmond, a director and friend of Kirkwood's. "Lee was the put-down kind of character and Jimmy was the bright-eyed, bushy-tailed kind of 'Let's go for it' [character] with all the energy and excitement...I saw Jimmy a number of times on stage and he was really a delight to see. He had a magnetism to him." Says another of Kirkwood's long-term friends, journalist Liz Smith, "They never made it big like Martin & Lewis or Rowan & Martin, but they were exactly that same kind of act: one serious guy and one comic guy. And Jimmy was so *cute* then. He was so adorable. And Lee Goodman was an ordinary-looking kind of guy — not cute and losing his hair.

He was the serious one and Jimmy was the crazy one…They were the forerunners of a lot of people who made it, really even Dean Martin & Jerry Lewis…Lee Goodman would be standing up there delivering some little monologue that was serious about something and then Jimmy would be bouncing up and down beside him saying, 'Oh, let's all tell about the first time.' It was very shocking and funny in those days. They were real forerunners of Rowan & Martin, who were big deals on American television. They did it first. They just never hit it commercially big." Jack Sydow, a director who saw the act in 1951 and who became a friend of Kirkwood's in the sixties, concurs about the Martin & Lewis comparison, saying, "But it was the intellectual version of that." Dolores Sutton, an actress who would work with Kirkwood, demurs: "Jimmy and Lee were not playing a dopey one and a smarter one. It wasn't that inane a kind of a character and Jimmy didn't use his body in that way. It was sharper, more satiric comedy. They lampooned and they had points to make." Richard Seff, a friend of Kirkwood's from '53 or '54 and his sometime agent says, "It was really charming, contemporary. They made fun of things that were of the moment." Famed musical librettist and director and close Kirkwood friend Arthur Laurents offers, "[Kirkwood] had a beanie. So there you get the tenor of the act." He denies that they could have been as successful as Martin & Lewis: "They did fine for what they were. Martin & Lewis were classic comedians and Jimmy and Lee Goodman were cute. They were like naughty boys. Very endearing, I thought."

Plotkin explains, "They wrote most of their own material, both contributing to it. They both had very sharp funny minds and the skits would come out of them and from experiences or from things that were said to them or whatever the timely topic might be." Sketches that Kirkwood and Goodman performed in their seven-year career included a satire on the cornball writing style and exclamatory titles of articles in the *Reader's Digest* ("Is Russia Building a Tunnel under Idaho?"; "I Did Not Live Through Menopause"; "Are America's Tennis Balls Underfuzzed?"; "Let's Face It — Honeymoons Are Dirty!") and "Buck and Bobby," a take-off on a Jack Armstrong-type radio show. Sydow recalls another sketch: "There was one part of the act where they went through the audience and they were on a bird walk, and they would point out women and they would make up names for [them]. If there was a gray-haired woman in a fancy dress, either Lee or [Jimmy] would say, 'Oh, look, there's a gray-haired pouter, but she's got such an unusual pattern."

This style made Kirkwood and Goodman a hot act very quickly and they became regulars at New York establishments like Blue Angel, the

Bon Soir, Café Society Downtown, Number One and Le Ruban Bleu. The stage act naturally grew in sophistication as their partnership thrived. Plotkin: "They did musical numbers as well. It was not strictly a stand-up comic duo. They had songs and they had writers that wrote songs for them. Lee had a wonderful baritone voice and Jim had more of a tenor voice. They sang very well together. There was generally a piano player as I recall, or when they were appearing at the Bon Soir there was a trio there and they used to accompany them."

It wasn't just the nightclub circuit on which Kirkwood & Goodman operated. In January to February 1950, Kirkwood & Goodman were recruited for a Broadway revue, *Dance Me a Song*, a show that featured Bob Fosse, Donald Sadler and Wally Cox. Kirkwood & Goodman performed three sketches. As early as 1948, they landed a notable television spot, appearing on the very first edition of Ed Sullivan's show (then called *Toast of the Town*) on Sunday, June 20. Plotkin: "They said it was very exciting because it was the first live variety show." The theme of the show was show business teams. Sharing the bill were Rodgers & Hammerstein and fellow up-and-coming comedic duo Dean Martin & Jerry Lewis. On *The Joe Franklin Show* in 1980, Kirkwood reminisced, "We were looking down the backstage list of who was going to be on and: Martin & Lewis live. I looked at Lee and I said, 'Oh, my God, what terrible luck.' We were doing very inside, sophisticated stuff and they were very broad and popular and a marvelous comedy team. Rough competition first time out." Goodman later claimed that Jerry Lewis offered to buy a Kirkwood & Goodman sketch, "The Sabre Dance," a duel with swords and soup strainers. When the pair complained that that was their biggest number, Lewis suggested they come and see him and Martin perform. Goodman told Gavin he and Kirkwood "hated" what they saw: "They were a symbol of the broad humor we were fighting against. Television was just beginning, and they all were going back to seltzer-squirting and pie-in-the-face. So all our efforts to be sophisticated were against the time."

In the coming years, the Kirkwood & Goodman duo would become familiar within the environs of broadcasting studios, both radio and TV. In fact, such excursions provide the only recorded testaments to their professional partnership, for, sadly, there seems to be no surviving film or tape of Kirkwood and Goodman on stage. In addition to one-offs on TV variety programs, they appeared on Sullivan's show a total of eight times and on the *Garry Moore Daytime Show* twice a week for two years. They were also regulars on *The Kate Smith Show*. Radio-wise, they had their own Kirkwood & Goodman program on WOR five nights a week for two years (the two would intersperse records between sketches) and a Saturday morning show for Mutual Network called *Teenagers Unlimited* that ran for 26 weeks.

The latter, live, show occasioned an incident that underlined the greater professionalism of Goodman. "They were interviewing these students," explains Plotkin. "There was a little Asian-American boy who was being interviewed and Jim said, 'And what is your name?' And he said, 'My name is Harry Dong.' He looked at Lee and he said, 'I can't!' and he started laughing and Lee had to take over and finish the interview, and he could hear Jim howling in the background…Jim would break up and Lee was always the one that was able to carry things on."

This, though, wasn't anything like the main source of conflict between Kirkwood and Goodman. The impetus for Kirkwood to constantly rehearse that Plotkin mentions above stemmed from what Kirkwood later admitted to Gavin was his insecurity about being the weaker partner, him knowing his singing, dancing and comedic timing were not in the same league as Goodman's, who, infuriatingly, didn't even have to work at his gifts. Additionally, Kirkwood was irritated by the way that his onstage "fuck-up" persona was assumed by people to apply to real-life when in fact he oversaw most of the pair's business affairs. The manifestations of Kirkwood's frustrations could be ugly indeed, especially when he was drunk. Goodman was the target of his rage. "I had a terrible, terrible temper," Kirkwood admitted. "I used to beat the shit out of him." One particularly unpleasant incident in 1949 saw Kirkwood physically throw Goodman out of a cab during a post-mortem over a supposedly spoiled sketch in a Number One set from which the pair were riding home. The following evening, Goodman's scratched face had to be passed off to the audience as the result of a car accident. Less violent but still disturbing was an incident backstage at a club when a late and drunk Kirkwood demanded some of Goodman's shortcake. When Goodman pointed out that the club would give him shortcake of his own, Kirkwood replied that he wanted some of Goodman's. When he finally realized he wasn't going to get any, Kirkwood put his hand in his partner's plate and rubbed the cake all over him. "He was like a mean little kid," Goodman said.

Liz Smith's apparent suggestion that Kirkwood & Goodman alluded to their sexual relationship on stage was theoretically very dangerous. At the time, homosexuality was illegal in all American states and (Illinois excepted) would continue to be so for nearly a quarter-century. The punishment for sodomy in New York itself was imprisonment. Plotkin, though, echoes many interviewed for this book in asserting that Kirkwood sailed serenely above the dangers associated with being gay. "Their attitude was it was not an issue," Plotkin says. "They weren't flag wavers, they didn't hide anything. The people that they knew in the business were aware of it but it was never an issue." Says Richard Seff, "Frankly, the way we thought of being gay was like we were born left-handed. Most people are right-handed. That's about as traumatic as it was for all of us. It wasn't a big deal. It was just the way we came out…We lived a kind of subterranean life where we had to keep this secret — and the secret was that we were some of the brightest and the best-looking people in town."

Certainly, an attitude of tolerance seems to have characterized the circles in which Kirkwood and Goodman plied their trade. Liz Smith met Kirkwood through one of their regular gigs, the Bon Soir. She was a young wannabe at the time, her jobs working for *Modern Screen* magazine and as Kay Ballard's road manager being staging posts to the status of queen of the syndicated gossip columnists that she enjoys today. She says, "The Bon Soir was one of those Mafia-owned nightclubs. It was funded by a lot of tough guys and had a big gay clientele and they protected everybody. Nothing bad ever happened to you if you were in one of these Mafia nightclubs. There were a lot of them in New York, really all of the ones that were sort of offbeat and had about a half-gay clientele were usually owned by the Mafia or dominated by them or they paid protection to them or something." She adds, "But I don't know how much Jimmy and Lee knew about that. They were just performing there."

Kirkwood certainly seems to have known about it. In a 1968 résumé he wrote that the Mafia, "owned several of the clubs the team worked in." In point of fact, the pair could have used the protection of the New York Mafia in their first out-of-town engagement, in what Kirkwood described as a "huge club" in Montreal, Canada. The contract was for eight weeks on "great money." The duo dispatched a luggage trunk to Montreal and followed it by plane. Their opening night dinner show was, said Kirkwood, "a major disaster." It transpired that the club orchestra spoke only French. Kirkwood's adequate ability in that language was not sufficient for him to communicate their musical arrangement requirements. In addition, said Kirkwood, "The club was too big for us." Though the clientele were English speakers, they might as well have been only versed in French judging by Kirkwood's comment that, "Our humor was alien to the audience." Unfortunately for Kirkwood & Goodman, the establishment was run by the caliber of people who owned most of the venues they played in the Big Apple. Kirkwood recalled that the team were quickly summoned to the front office where sat four disgruntled hoods. One of them was already on the telephone to the local radio station booking a replacement singer for the late supper show. Another was writing out a release from their contract for the pair to sign, waiving salary and giving them only plane fare back to New York. The contract was shoved at them. When Kirkwood and Goodman complained that they had a firm eight-week contract and would rather not sign but wait until morning when they would call their agents, two of the men stood up, took off their jackets and displayed "a couple of impressive shoulder holsters." The pair signed the contract. They were then escorted to the delivery alley where they had to stand in the snow until two bus boys opened the rear door and tossed their clothes, props and music arrangements out onto the ground. They were told to get out of town and to never mention being forced to sign the release. More misery was piled upon this. The duo had beaten their trunk to Montreal so had to hide out in a hotel for three days in order to wait for it and ship it back home. "I have a hard spot in my heart for Montreal," said Kirkwood nearly two decades later.

Kirkwood recalled other hairy incidents in the career of Kirkwood & Goodman, if none as frightening as that. On their first night at the Ruban Bleu in New York City — a show covered by the press, including the prestigious *Variety* — things were going very well until a six-foot tall man suddenly jumped up from his table and hurled a full bottle of champagne at the pair. It smashed against the piano, narrowly missing Kirkwood's head. The club owners did not want the man booked for reasons of the hassle and bad publicity involved. However, Kirkwood insisted the man be taken to a police station. When he was, it was discovered that he had escaped from a mental institution. He'd picked up a girl, taken her to the club and had become upset when after the wining and dining she had declined to go back to his hotel and told him the act was great and that Kirkwood & Goodman were "cute" — hence the flying champagne bottle. Inconveniences more comical than disturbing occurred when the duo performed a show at a hay fever sufferers' convention in Duluth over a Labor Day weekend. Kirkwood later reported, "The audience won out — much more noise from their end in the wheezing and sneezing department than from the act up on stage."

The pair traveled to the UK at one point to play at the Embassy Club in London. Another out-of-town appearance in California at the Macombo, the leading nightclub on Los Angeles' Sunset Strip, gave Kirkwood the chance to catch up with Lomax Study, whom he hadn't seen since the *Admiral Mayo* days. Though Study didn't know at this point that Kirkwood had become bisexual, he recalls a rather heated discussion with the comedy pair on the issue of homosexuality. Study: "They were at the house one night for dinner and we were talking and they brought up the subject and I just told them how I felt about it. I could see that they were not in accord with me and so I said, 'God damn it — that's no way to do...' I don't know what I said. Maybe I was rude because I felt rather strongly about it...I've never understood that part of life...They didn't make anything of it. They didn't say, 'Well, we're a pair,' or anything like that...They were just discussing it." Study didn't get the impression that they were lovers, even in retrospect: "Lee Goodman, there's no question he had a black man that was following him around every show he did and I think they were lovers. Maybe [Kirkwood & Goodman] were a pair for a while, but...you never saw anything: holding hands or love or anything. Quite the contrary. They were a couple of men together who if they got mad with each other said, 'What the hell are you talking about, you damn fool?' and that kind of an attitude, just like regular men do."

Though Study changed with the times (he says, "Now, you know, that was then and now is now and things have changed, people have changed... Look, I've been in the business so long that half of our friends here in Hollywood [are gay], not half but, well...They're charming, loving, wonderful people and they're good friends. I just don't happen to agree with their sex preference, that's all"), it is perhaps Lomax's type of bewilderment and hostility that ensured that long after homosexuality had ceased to be something for which the state could persecute an individual in America, Kirkwood continued to be coy in his art and even to a certain extent his private life about his proclivities.

As the years progressed, Kirkwood and Goodman began acquiring steady fans. "They had set routines and set skits they did and they became very well known for," says Plotkin. "People used to go back and see the same things over and over again, because they were funnier and also they would ad lib certain things." The loyalty of some devotees, however, could be wearying. Kirkwood later lamented those fans "who would come night after night until they knew the act backwards and would eventually start saying the punchlines out loud two seconds before the performers." He also remembered a fan the pair nicknamed "Our Lady of the Finger Cymbals," who would show up every so often and provide musical accompaniment for the act from a ringside table. (He later co-opted the phrase for his fiction — a character nicknamed "Our Lady of the Poppies" appears in *Good Times/Bad Times*.)

No matter how successful their joint act, Kirkwood and Goodman each maintained parallel solo careers. Virtually right at the partnership's inception, Kirkwood was offered and accepted a role in the Broadway revue *Small Wonder* alongside Tom Ewell, Mary McCarthy and Joan Diener. As well as continuing to work in summer stock, Kirkwood secured radio acting work, appearing as Toby Smith in the long-running teenage sitcom *The Aldrich Family*. (At some point in his acting career, Kirkwood's mellifluous tones were employed to record books for the blind.) Goodman, meanwhile, was using his goofy personality to obtain commercials work, which would one day become his main source of income. This extracurricular activity was a matter of necessity. Of the remuneration the two were receiving from stand-up, Plotkin says, "It was never enough…I don't think they were paid what comedians are paid now, the top comedians." (He adds, "Jim was the one that was really adamant about being paid fairly and of course on a couple of occasions they ran into Mafia types that said, 'No, this is what you're getting and nothing more.'")

Come 1953, Kirkwood was offered a major television role of his own. *Valiant Lady* was a new CBS live daily soap opera. Richard Seff, who'd recently given up acting for agency work, got him the part. Such were the times that competition was not stiff. "When I first began my life as an agent I was stuck in the brand-new field of television," recalls Seff. "I was young and it was young and I was able to open doors because my competitors were young too, so it wasn't like I was fighting the titans. I was just beginning my client list. Frankly, I was calling up all the actors I knew personally. Jimmy was never signed to the agency I was with, but he was an actor I knew who was freelancing and so I could call and get permission to submit him." The part Kirkwood obtained was that of nineteen-year-old Mickey Emerson. This meant that he would be playing a character a decade his junior. John Desmond, a director on the program, laughingly observes, "Well, Jimmy always looked like a prep school graduate…"

From the way Kirkwood told it, it was the pressure of both working on *Valiant Lady* in the daytime and continuing the nighttime club dates of Kirkwood & Goodman that caused the rupture of the latter pair's professional relationship. He later spoke of an exhausting full year in which he was averaging only three or four hours sleep per night, causing him to oversleep, commit on-screen fluffs and on one occasion actually fall asleep on camera. "The strain was too much," Kirkwood said, but added, "By that time, the glamour of appearing in nightclubs had worn off."

Though Kirkwood's claim of lack of sleep is confirmed by others and though his disdain for superficially glamorous nightclubs seems to have been sincere (in 1978 in Lorain's *The Journal*, he would memorably describe the type of comedy nightclubs in which he had worked as "upholstered sewers"), the end of the Kirkwood & Goodman comedy act came about — according to Goodman — for a different and far more dramatic and ugly reason. In the sketch "Downy Little Brownie Man," Goodman played the narrator Mrs. Stanley and Kirkwood her son who accompanied her on the glockenspiel. One night in 1954, Goodman was trying to set up the number but suddenly found Kirkwood engaging in one of his not-uncommon, not-quite-benign pranks, doing his best to put him off with birdcalls from backstage. Goodman had had enough. Plotkin: "[Lee] just pulled the curtain aside and he popped him one in the face and all [the audience] heard was this glockenspiel clinking all over the floor. Lee was finally getting even. That's the kind of thing that Jim used to just torment him with." The audience was roaring with laughter, but Kirkwood's face was black. Goodman daren't turn his back on him as the two finished their set. Afterwards, Kirkwood grabbed hold of a wooden hanger and proceeded to hit Goodman over the head with it. "I had double vision for a week," Goodman told Gavin. "That's when I decided we had to break it up. He was very hurt when I decided to break up the act."

Initially, the two both struck out on their own and opened on the same night, Goodman at Le Ruban Bleu, Kirkwood at Number One. Plotkin: "Lee being — this sounds terrible — the more talented of the two and the more musical of the two had a little bit of a following. That's how the job came for Checkerboard Square, because there was a talent agent that saw him." Seff, though, is of the opinion that Kirkwood's heart was not in a comedy career. "Jimmy was attempting to be an actor," he says. "That was his primary interest."

Despite everything that had passed between them, Kirkwood and Goodman would be lifelong friends. In fact, Goodman would play a major part in Kirkwood's crucial decision to become a novelist. In the meantime, the Checkerboard Square gig Plotkin mentions — spokesman for Ralston Purina, who manufactured cereals Rice Chex and Wheat Chex — was hugely lucrative for Goodman. "He was their spokesperson for nine years," says Plotkin. However, commercials were just the start of Goodman's success. Plotkin: "He was doing movies and also off-season he would do road companies of shows. Lee was in *A Bachelor in Paradise* with Bob Hope and Lana Turner, he was in *Imitation of Life* with Lana Turner and Sandra Dee, he was in *Music Man*. He was a very rounded performer and always sought-after to play these wonderful parts." He adds, "Never really liked being in Los Angeles. Any chance he could get to go back to New York he went back to New York, and most times he stayed with Jim."

It's rather surprising that Kirkwood never used the wonderful raw material his stand-up comedy days constituted in a novel. "I think the closest he came to that was *Hit Me with a Rainbow*," says Plotkin, referring to the comedy-aspiring character Stosh in Kirkwood's final work of fiction. (Vito in *P.S. Your Cat Is Dead!* also does a little stand-up, albeit combined with striptease, though as with Stosh the reader doesn't see him perform it.) Goodman certainly suggested a book of some sort based on the pair's stand-up days when Kirkwood had established himself as a writer. Plotkin: "He would say, 'One of these days we should write a book about what we went through establishing the act and all that.' I heard that many times."

Perhaps, though, the stand-up days did have a writing-related legacy. One of Kirkwood's résumés records that in the early 1950s, during a full year's run at the Bon Soir in Greenwich Village, he enrolled in a short story writing class at nearby New York University. It didn't immediately lead to much. Kirkwood's self-confessed Boswell recalls Kirkwood telling him of his dissatisfaction with the short story format. "He said it didn't suit him and I think he liked the bigger canvas," William Russo says. "The sense I had was that he had, in his early career, tried some short stories but he didn't really find they worked for him. I think they were autobiographical. In fact, I wouldn't be a bit surprised that they were tidbits that would show up in a greater novel." The above-mentioned résumé said, "But his urge to write…was interrupted when he was offered the part of the 'son' of Valiant Lady on the now defunct television soap opera of that name."

In the long-term, though, the class led to big things. Kirkwood later claimed that before beginning *There Must be a Pony!*, it had "never" occurred to him to try writing. He cultivated a myth that his decision to try his hand at literature was the spontaneous result of a period of unemployment several years after the Kirkwood & Goodman days, but the NYU enrollment clearly indicates an earlier hankering to be a wordsmith. Discounting the suggestions of such a bent revealed in his letter to Nancy Martin back in the Brewster Academy days (lots of schoolchildren think they have ambitions that are really passing fancy), this hankering seems to have directly resulted from being part of the Kirkwood & Goodman act. Despite acknowledging that Goodman was the superior showman, Kirkwood wrote in the résumé that he "began writing much of the team's material." In doing so, he found that, to use his own words, "The writing bug began to nibble" at him. He enrolled in the short story class to satisfy his "urge to write things of a more serious nature." That urge took time to be completely fulfilled, but the foundation-stone of a literary career had now been laid.

Parents Lila Lee and James Kirkwood Sr. in movie Ebb Tide, *1922, made before they were married.* COURTESY OF ARTHUR BECKENSTEIN

Kirkwood's mother Lila Lee, movie star. COURTESY OF ARTHUR BECKENSTEIN

LILA LEE, FILM STAR, BECOMES MOTHER OF GIRL

(Picture on Page 3.)

Los Angeles, Calif., Aug. 22.—[Special.]—James Kirkwood, film actor, was working on a scene today when a studio attendant arrived with the news that James Kirkwood Jr., eight pounds heavy, had put in an appearance at the Good Samaritan hospital. Lila Lee, Chicago's star, who is Mrs. Kirkwood, had been rushed to the hospital this morning. Mother and baby are doing well.

Some confusion attended Kirkwood's birth! Chicago Daily Tribune *edition of August 23 1924.*

With his parents. COURTESY OF ARTHUR BECKENSTEIN

James, Rex

And His Most Loyal Subjects

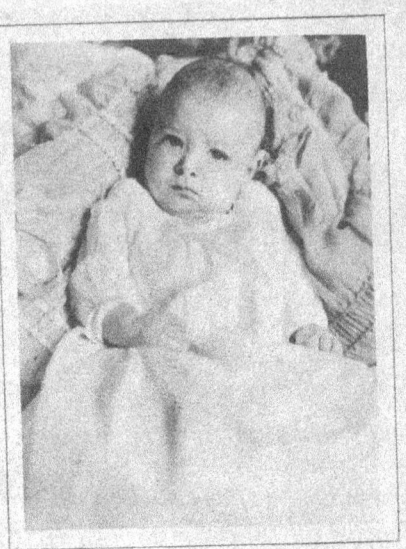

James, Junior, is, verily, a king in the Kirkwood domain. He rules like a true autocrat, his baby curls his crown and his tiny dimpled hand his sceptre. Among his subjects are a score or more of motion picture celebrities, friends of his mother and father. But his parents, Lila Lee and James Kirkwood are, of course, his most devoted and loyal subjects.

And since he cut his first two teeth the other day, at the age of five months, they think him more wonderful than ever.

Lila admits that she finds it hard to leave him to his nurse when she is called to the studios to appear before the cameras in "The Midnight Girl." And James, Senior, experiences a similar difficulty when he has to leave the nursery to portray his role of an artist in the Broadway stage play, "Ladies of the Evening."

Photographs taken for Movie Weekly by Russell Ball

MOVIE WEEKLY
Page Five

"James, Rex and his most Loyal Subjects" — a 1925 newspaper clipping giving an idea of what a notable family Kirkwood had been born into.

Beloved Aunt Peg, who provided Kirkwood the only stable family life he ever knew. COURTESY OF ARTHUR BECKENSTEIN

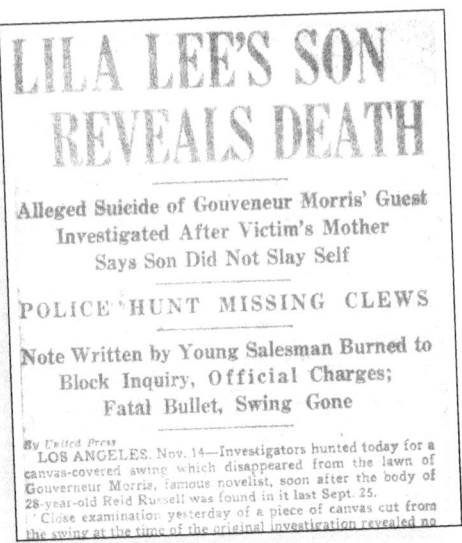

Aged 12, Kirkwood makes national headlines as he is embroiled in a potential murder investigation.

Flanked by Ruth Morris and his mother, 1936. Did one or all of them murder Reid Russell?

Lila Lee in court. This picture is believed to be from Halls of Justice questioning about the death of her lover Reid Russell in 1936. COURTESY OF ARTHUR BECKENSTEIN

Alma mater Brewster Academy. Kirkwood fictionalized it as Gilford Academy.

Walter G. Greenall Jr., Kirkwood's hated headmaster at Brewster Academy. He may have been the inspiration for the villainous Mr. Hoyt in the novel Good Times/Bad Times.

Teenage sweetheart and penpal Nancy Martin.

With his cousin Lila Lee Nichols née Tufford. COURTESY OF ARTHUR BECKENSTEIN

Kirkwood's high school graduation photo, 1942. COURTESY OF ARTHUR BECKENSTEIN

High school girlfriend Esther Hamula. COURTESY OF ESTHER WEBER

With Esther Hamula. COURTESY OF ESTHER WEBER

SIX

Valiant Lady was originally created by Frank and Nancy Hummert for radio, on which it ran from 1938-46 and 1951-52. However, the new TV version in which Kirkwood was cast bore little resemblance to its antecedent.

In its television incarnation, which started on October 12, 1953, *Valiant Lady* charted the ups and downs of a white, clean-cut, wholesome American family who lived in the town of — ahem — Middlebury. The conventions of the time, naturally, dictated that the head of that family was the father, Frank Emerson, played by Jerome Cowan. However, soap operas were aimed at women (the very colloquialism "soap opera" an allusion to the fact that detergent manufacturers targeted the shows' female demographics with their commercials between or around the action), hence the "Lady" in the title, which actually began to make more sense when Frank died of a heart attack. The titular lady was Helen Emerson. Kirkwood later said, "When they were first casting *Valiant Lady*, I was signed for the part of the son before they had set the mother part. An agent sent my mother up for the part and they didn't know at the office that she was my real mother and they looked at her and read her and they said no, there wasn't a family resemblance." Instead of Lila Lee, Helen was played (originally) by Nancy Coleman. In addition to son Mickey, the Emersons had two other children, Diane (originally aged seventeen and played by Anne Pearson) and Kim (originally nine years old and played by Lydia Reed).

The creation of the TV show has been credited to one Allan Chase but Ira Cirker says, "I put the whole thing together. I cast the whole thing and put it on the air and I stayed with it about a year." The *Valiant Lady* television show was broadcast live at noon, Monday to Friday, all year round. Cirker was the show's main director but had two days off, on which occasions the directing tasks were undertaken by John Desmond. Desmond explains, "It was only fifteen minutes long, which in those days was the ordinary length." Cirker explains that part of the reason that the television version of *Valiant Lady* was similar to the radio incarnation in name only is not just because of the prerequisites of the differing mediums but his interest in exploring the then relatively unknown possibilities of

TV: "When a show is on the air which is for the ear, it's very different than something that is going to be on television, which is very visual. I wanted it not to be static. This was very early television. I had built a whole house for this family, where you could go from one room to another room, to another room, to another room and then outside, all within the confines of the studio, which allowed for much more action and movement. I also in casting went for non-radio actors. I went for theatre and motion picture actors. That's why the leading lady that I selected was from Hollywood, and then people like Dolores [Sutton] who was mainly from the theatre. Jimmy came from all areas, theatre as well as radio and film."

"I don't think he auditioned," says Cirker of Kirkwood. Instead, the actor was hired, "…on the strength of the body of work that he had done and recommendations from Dolores and other people that were on the show…which was unusual. But then again Nancy Coleman was from Hollywood and I didn't audition her either. She was rather a big name then." Cirker was aware of Kirkwood's stand-up work when he engaged his services. Asked if knowledge of this played a part in his hiring of Kirkwood, he says, "Well, it might have in the sense that I knew that he was more than a radio actor. A radio actor could be very good and I did use several, but they were crossovers from one medium to another so I figured since he was working as he did prior in several media that he is more than just a stand-up-in-front-of-a-mic actor." Did that the fact that Kirkwood was actually considerably older than the part he played not worry Cirker? "No, it didn't because Jimmy had an eternally young quality, and without having to play at it, he was mischievous, he had a zany quality." Dolores Sutton, who played Diane Emerson from 1954 to1955, concurs: "He used to come off like this kind of innocent little boy, adorable-looking and wonderful and sweet. Multi-talented guy and yet could sit around in a studio with me and get more fun out of trying to make me laugh while I'm acting a scene and think nothing of it. He'd put on costumes, he'd make faces, he'd do everything, and so there was a kind of eternal young kid there."

It's difficult to imagine that a man of Kirkwood's intelligence and ambition was going to think *Valiant Lady* was anything more than a stepping stone, something that seems borne out by his later comments on the program: "The pay was good, the work was steady, I was learning my craft." He would later sometimes wryly note that his role as Son of *Valiant Lady* made him sound like a racehorse. He also poked fun at the unlikely succession of crises that a daily drama requires its protagonists to go through, the implausibility factor increasing the longer the show runs: "Pick one tragedy from Column A and two from Column B. 'Gee, Mom, who's suffering from cancer, heart disease, tuberculosis, terminal hickies, amnesia or dull, dingy, under-par hair today?'" A glance at the show's storylines over its run confirms that Kirkwood was not exaggerating here. Frank Emerson ignored his heart problems and worked himself to death. Helen ultimately took up with an airplane pilot named Chris Kendall who was separated. Following the latter's divorce, Helen found herself in the middle of a bitter custody battle between Kendall and his ex-wife. After all that, the relationship with Kemble foundered and Helen ended up getting married to a Governor Walker. The Diane character had most of the best storylines. Originally so clean-cut that she constantly badgered her mother to send her to expensive college Briarmount, she soon became a bad girl, abandoning her college ambitions to elope with older divorcée Hal Soames. However, it was another of her lovers, Joey Gordon, who came to the rescue of the Emersons when they were taken hostage by an ex-partner of Helen's. The Diane role seemed to exhaust the actresses who secured it, the program getting through a new one, on average, each year. Though the character of Kim was too young to be involved in many dramatic storylines, this was more than made up for by the escapades of her screen brother, even though originally Mickey was quite a white-bread character. "The 'Hi, Mom' type I played wasn't interesting enough, so they made me into a neurotic who tried to strangle his college roommate," Kirkwood said. Mickey went through quite a bit of heartbreak. His widowed mother took in a lodger to keep a roof over the family's heads. Said lodger was a pretty girl named Bonnie Withers, who had been married to a man sentenced to prison. Mickey fell in love with her. Although at one point she ran away to Bloomfield to escape Mickey's attentions, in her last will and testament she nominated Mickey to look after the baby she had borne by her jailbird husband — which was quite lucky for the baby as she then experienced a sudden death requiring the enactment of this provision. Needless to say, when the husband was released from prison, he had his sights set on getting back his child.

"We rehearsed in the mornings before we went to the studio in a rehearsal hall," explains Desmond, "then went to the studio about hour-and-a-half, two hours before air." The rehearsal studio was on 110th and 5th Avenue, Harlem, then as now a notorious part of New York City. Desmond: "Occasionally we were called for evening rehearsals. It was scary." Not quite as scary but still often nerve-wracking was the live nature of the broadcast show. Though to some in the mid-1950s television still seemed akin to science-fiction technology, it was still quaintly broadcasting much of its drama as it happened. Needless to say, many mistakes would occur in front of the nation's housewives. Desmond: "Stagehands would cross in through the set and so on. It happened occasionally but it did happen. People did forget their lines and the stage manager would show it to them. We'd just cut the audio in the control room and throw the line out and they would carry on." Cirker: "Usually the fellow actor helped them out of the mess. They clued them into it by a certain line and then they could pick up again. They didn't freeze in other words, they just went up." Cirker disputes Desmond's recollection of being able to cut the sound in this eventuality: "There was no way that you could cut out of it. You had to improvise. Depending on how clever we all were, you wouldn't know it."

Says Sutton, "To actually have a large amount of acting rehearsal, it didn't happen because the cameras, they were setting them up and moving them and then you would do a scene and you would have to close your mind to all the other stuff that was going on. In addition to which there were live commercials. I think about two or three. It would open with one. I remember Proctor and Gamble had a table of goodies or something that they were displaying. It was one of the big baking companies that sponsored this thing. It was a rather arduous thing because you would do the reading, you would do the set-up with the camera, then there would be a dress, and then you would go right on the air. It was very stressful and that's why a lot of people kind of caved in...I know we would all stagger out of there exhausted. It was a studio on 109th Street, way up for all of us because we lived downtown."

"The beginnings of the television soaps were kind of interesting," says Cirker, "because it brought out the people who had been in all the other media, and they had to work much faster. It wasn't like a movie where you learn one little scene and then you shoot it all day. People had to adjust, people had to work faster — God knows, I did — and it was both challenging and sometimes frustrating." This innately rapid pace was exacerbated by Cirker's style: "I got more challenging in my work. I had them always in action, doing things." Little wonder that the combination of this and the nightclub gigs made Kirkwood reach a state of exhaustion. Sutton confirms that Kirkwood did indeed fall asleep when the show was on the air: "It happened. One of the times it happened, it was a scene that we were doing together and he was so exhausted he fell asleep before the scene. During the broadcast, but as his scene was coming up."

Desmond's comments about *Valiant Lady*'s place in the global scheme of things echoes Kirkwood's: "It paid well. Not like a show would pay today, not at all, but what it was really was [was] a proving ground for actors to earn their stripes. It was a good job." Cirker also points out, "It was steady. Show business was not a great place for making a living unless you became a star, and also very [little] longevity's involved in the work because you could do a play on Broadway, it could close in two days, it could close out of town, a movie could be a flop, all kinds of things. The soaps were the longest-running enterprises on television so that there got to be a sense of security to the actors. They knew they wouldn't starve." How popular was the program? Desmond: "Oh, I think on a scale of one-to-ten, it was probably eight or nine." The litmus test of which, of course, was whether its actors would be recognized walking down the street. Desmond says Kirkwood was.

Despite the privileges attached to the show and a perseverance with it that eventually made him the sole mainstay, Kirkwood couldn't bring himself to take it completely seriously. Desmond recalls that he and Kirkwood would travel in to work together in a four-door Buick convertible that had once belonged to Lila Lee's husband John Murphy but which Lee had given to her son. Desmond: "He was a very quick study and so he wouldn't memorize his lines until the morning of the show. We lived on the same street in the Village on 11th Street. We used to take this touring sedan and ride up 8th Avenue and he would be zooming in and out of traffic — at that hour in the morning it's very rough traffic — and memorizing his lines. I would be cueing him [laughs] as we were dodging cars and motorcycles and vans and so on. It was a wild way to get to work."

That Kirkwood had not yet decided that he no longer desired carnal relations with females is demonstrated by the fact that he was seen out and about with various young women at this stage. Beckenstein says that Kirkwood was dating one Dee-Dee Dixon for a short period probably at some point in his thirties. Dixon was possibly a costume designer and Kirkwood, his mother and Lee Goodman later attended her wedding. Another of Kirkwood's beaus was actress Elaine Stritch. "Elaine was adorable, wonderful and lots of fun and a straight-from-the-shoulder kind of lady," says Desmond. "No bullshit there. They went out together frequently." He adds that Stritch was seeing another man: "She had an affair with him at the same time as she was dating Jimmy, so who knows what the actual story was." "Well he always used to brag that he deflowered Elaine Stritch," says Jim Piazza. "He was her first boyfriend." "No, that is not true," Stritch says. She does confirm, though, "I slept with Jimmy Kirkwood. It wasn't serious at all. I had had very little experience in that department and Jimmy was a loving person that was very sweet to me and gentle. Nothing ever came of it. We're not in love, didn't have a real romance. I don't know anything about his love affairs but I know he was bisexual. I know it now. I'm not so sure when I became aware of it. I don't think anything about it. I don't concentrate on those kinds of things and I'm not surprised about anything. I've known Jimmy for all my life and he's singularly one of the funniest human beings I've ever known in my life. And extremely talented. But his mainstay is humor. He is singularly, genuinely humor-ish [sic]. He has real humor that flies above an awful lot of people who do not have it."

Asked if Kirkwood was living a straight life when he first knew him, Desmond replies, "Yes, he was, but straight with a lot of curves." So curved, in fact, that even Desmond got confused. Muriel Bentley (1917-1999) was a well-regarded ballerina who would ultimately be most famous for her roles as The Woman with the Red Pocketbook in Jerome Robbins's *Fancy Free* (written, like all the major roles in that show, for the dancer who played it) and — considerably later — the Stepmother in Agnes de Mille's *Fall River Legend*. She was another woman with whom Kirkwood was seen out-and-about during the fifties. There was a fairly big age gap between the two, Bentley being seven years Kirkwood's senior. Asked if there was anything going on between Kirkwood and Bentley, Desmond says, "They were very close and she was an adorable lady...Yes, they were together. I use the word 'together' — they weren't really...It was always that hidden agenda." Richard Seff agrees, scoffing, "I don't know about 'going out' with Muriel Bentley. They were good friends. There are many relationships that are very friendly and even loving but they were never lovers that I know of. You're either gay or you're not gay. I don't even believe in this bisexual stuff." Kirkwood's sister is also skeptical on this point, saying, "I doubt it seriously. I thought she was like a good friend. Somebody to do things with and so on." However, Joan also says, "She was in love with him...I know she wanted to marry him. She told me." As is his wont, Arthur Laurents is the most caustic of the lot in his dismissal of the notion of Kirkwood having sex with women ("You've taken my breath away!") and Bentley in particular ("She's a lesbian"). "I think that maybe Muriel Bentley was an attempt at trying something that was not going to work out," offers Jack Sydow, though admits he didn't know about the relationship. Interestingly, as Laurents alludes, it may have been Bentley who was "trying something that was not going to work out": she never married and in later years lived with ballet manager Betty Farrell.

Ronald Plotkin, though, is emphatic that Kirkwood and Bentley's relationship was sexual: "Oh God, was it ever," he says. "They were hot and heavy. They were having a mad love affair...They were very physical with each other. Muriel was a ballet dancer. A lot of those ladies in those days were very, very physical and very sexual and I guess maybe in a gay man's eyes, it's almost like being with a boy dancer." Plotkin admits he never knew the pair when they were a couple but says, "I knew her very well. We were very close…They definitely were [lovers]. That I know from history and being told and being around both of them." Even Beckenstein, he of the doubt that Kirkwood was ever "emotionally committed" to women, concurs: "They had a torrid sexual affair." Referring to Kirkwood's final novel, Beckenstein says, "Jimmy imagined Maggie in *Hit Me with a Rainbow* as based on a chance one-night-meeting with Ava Gardner, who he met with Frank Sinatra. But the sexual chemistry of the affair with Maggie was based upon the chemistry of his affair with Muriel. I'm pretty sure they had a hot sexual relationship at the time. I'm not sure I understand it, but I don't doubt it." He also says, "There was talk of his marrying Muriel Bentley," though points out that a reference to Bentley as Kirkwood's wife in *Who's Who in American Writers* was a Kirkwood prank. He adds, "They remained good friends all their lives."

Plotkin says it is his understanding that Bentley was given an engagement ring by Kirkwood. He also reveals, "Muriel's mother never approved of Jim. She just didn't like him. I guess because he wasn't doing the right thing. He wasn't marrying her daughter." However, exasperation on the part of Bentley herself does not seem to have precipitated a relationship crisis, the type of which might lead to a split-up. Plotkin: "They both had careers. She was busy with the ballet and he was busy doing his thing. It didn't sound like she was frustrated."

As a friend of Bentley both at the time and throughout the rest of her life, Dolores Sutton knew quite a lot about the relationship. "She was crazy about him and he would talk about her all the time," she says. "There was talk, but they never got to the point of even being engaged or letting people know anything like that." She estimates that they were an item for over a year: "…and then I do not know what happened, but suddenly it was no more." Asked if the couple were similar personalities, Sutton laughingly replies, "No, they weren't. She was a very volatile, hot-headed, passionate New York creature and he was not." Asked if she — Sutton — knew that Kirkwood and Lee Goodman had been lovers, Sutton says, "Yes. He made no bones about that, really." This would indicate that Bentley, therefore, also knew. Sutton is unsure about how she herself got to come by this information: "While he didn't conceal anything very much, he behaved always in the most proper manner about those things. He didn't really discuss that with me. I knew what I knew, and he didn't hide anything, but he didn't flaunt anything."

In the issue of magazine *Radio-TV Mirror* cover-dated July 1954, Kirkwood's romance with Bentley was explored in a fairly substantial feature running across a couple of pages titled "Jimmy Kirkwood — his love story." Considering the skeptical attitudes of some of Kirkwood's friends and family about the authenticity of the relationship, no doubt some in his circle assumed it was in a then-prevalent tradition: stories planted by the entertainment industry that were designed to throw reporters and/or the public off the lavender scent. From what he said in the article, it would seem that Kirkwood first started to notice the dark-haired, long-lashed, slightly Italian-looking Bentley when she would visit ballet dancer John Kriza, who lived in the apartment above his. "I thought she would probably laugh if I asked her to go out with me," Kirkwood said. "After all, she was a well-known dancer, a star of the Ballet Theatre." The magazine suggested that this insecurity was attributable to the fact that he was "as shy and young and eager as Mickey Emerson himself." Eager he may have been, but as young as Mickey Emerson we know he certainly wasn't, nor did shyness ever seem to have been a part of Kirkwood's make-up as an adult. In any event, Kirkwood didn't pluck up the nerve to ask Bentley for a date "…for a long time. Lee and I were working and Muriel would come into the club with this escort one week and another one the next, and I would see her and be conscious of her all evening but I was still a little shy of her. Then, when I was doing the role of Toby Smith in *The Aldrich Family* on radio, some of us were invited to a party for one of the cast members of the stage hit *Wonderful Town*…I can't even remember now who the actor was or anything about the occasion. I only remember that there was Muriel, at the party, and that I must have been feeling particularly pepped up after our show. Muriel had on a big picture hat. Her long black hair was up under it, with just a fringe of careless bangs across her forehead. Her eyes looked even bigger and darker and more beautiful than I remembered them…I suddenly walked up to her and bent over and kissed her. Just like that. Without a word of warning to her or myself. She didn't slap my face, as I deserved, and she didn't say anything. She just looked appalled, as well she might. Not to be routed again by my fears, I grasped the advantage. 'What are you doing for dinner tonight?' I demanded." The article — which indicated that this romance started prior to the summer of 1953 — went on to say that Bentley felt that the reason for Kirkwood's initial maintenance of interest in her was his fondness for her black miniature French poodle. Interestingly, the name of that poodle was Too Much aka TM. This name — and abbreviation — would be used by Kirkwood for his protagonist in his novel *Some Kind of Hero* more than twenty years later. Kirkwood said that in fact it was their similar sense of humor that created a bond. The bond had to be strong to survive their mutually exclusive work patterns. Kirkwood would often be starting his act with Goodman in a club at ten-thirty or eleven at night just when Bentley was finishing her work at the Ballet Theatre. This situation was exacerbated when Kirkwood landed the *Valiant Lady* role, with Kirkwood suffering from the exhaustion mentioned previously and Bentley finding that she was cueing him in her leisure time. Kirkwood's mother would often come over to help in that department and Lila and "Moo" — Kirkwood's nickname for Bentley — "got along famously." The article revealed that the couple wore matching rings (though presumably not engagement rings, as it's difficult to imagine that this would not be mentioned), that Kirkwood was a better cook than Bentley, that they would bicker when she would interrupt his conversational train of thought with a comment *a propos* of nothing, that though Kirkwood wasn't the bossy type he did insist that she keep her hair long when she was toying with the idea of cutting it short and that Kirkwood had incorporated some dancing into the Kirkwood & Goodman stage act as a consequence of having become confident about his hoofing since he and Bentley had danced together for the first time at the annual Ballet Ball. (A photograph of the pair dancing — or pretending to — in their stockinged feet was one of those that accompanied the article.)

It's difficult to know how seriously to take the contents of such a puff piece, but it's also difficult to imagine that the more banal details of the romance are anything anyone would have had the patience to invent. In fact, the only truly unconvincing note in the article is Kirkwood's improbably poetic and mannered turn of phrase. When he did one day prove his literary abilities, it was emphatically not with lines like, "Her long black hair was up under it, with just a fringe of careless bangs across her forehead."

In 1955, John Desmond hit upon a neat idea. He was due to direct an edition of *Lamp Unto My Feet*, a live Sunday morning religious show that dramatized a moral dilemma in a section that was followed by a panel discussion of the emotional and ethical ramifications of what had just been portrayed. Presented with a script for a three-hander called "Something for Bernice," the thought occurred to Desmond that its cast of father, adult daughter and adult son provided an ideal opportunity to recruit the Kirkwoods *en masse*. Because of the age gap between Kirkwood Sr. and his ex-wife, they could easily play father and daughter, while Kirkwood Jr. could just about plausibly play Lila Lee's younger brother.

Though times had been lean recently for Kirkwood Sr., when contacted on the West Coast by the show's producers, he didn't, as might have been expected, bite their hands off. Perhaps this was due to the contrariness of which his oldest son often spoke or perhaps it was merely the realism of a man now pushing eighty who realized that no new acting role was going to make a significant difference to his life. Somebody with nothing to lose often has an advantage in negotiations. Recalls the then-teenaged T. Michael Kirkwood, "I knew Dad didn't want to go because they didn't want to pay for the transportation and everything. We were sitting at the club having lunch and they must have called him about ten times in a row. They finally agreed to do whatever it was he wanted." With contracts signed, Kirkwood and Lila Lee went to meet the flight for which Kirkwood Sr. had declined to pay. Lee later wrote that "it broke my heart" when she saw her ex-husband's dilapidated suitcase: when the two were married in 1923, her present to him was a set of leather luggage with silver sterling fittings that cost around $2,000.

Desmond's neat idea soon began to seem like gross naiveté. Firstly, there was no love lost between the ex-spouses. Kirkwood later recalled, "My mother and father had not seen one another in quite a few years and although they didn't have an outright feud, they weren't all that fond of each other after they got divorced. They put up with each other because they had a child in common I suppose." The rehearsal was disastrous. Kirkwood: "My father couldn't remember his lines, had a violent temper and it was a religious show and we had priests in attendance as technical advisors, so when my father would go off on a line, he'd say…you know. And my mother would think, 'Oh my God, I wish he'd stop that'…It was a terrible time. My mother was so nervous that she acted like a silent screen star: there was an awful lot of eye work because she was petrified that he would go off on his lines." Desmond recalls, "They were just so beside themselves with fear because the old guy, wonderful actor, could not remember word one and so Lila and Jimmy decided that, 'When he goes up here, I'll say X-Y-Z and you…' So they figured out how they would save the show." When airtime came, the salvage job proved unnecessary. "He sailed through like a fire engine would," marvels Desmond of Kirkwood Sr. "And that wonderful voice, like the purr of a lion — he was just incredible. We got off the air and Lila came over to him and said,

'You son of a bitch!'" Kirkwood: "Of course, he came though letter-perfect and we were like gibbering idiots."

Such was the stress induced by the show that Kirkwood and Desmond felt compelled to retire for some alcoholic relief. "I was attending at the bar and I suddenly just went 'Arrgh! My God!'" recalled Kirkwood, "and I came down with acute appendicitis and I know it was the experience of doing the show with the two of them. Something had to blow up and it just happened to be my appendix." Kirkwood and his father acted together at least one other time, sharing top billing in September 1959 in an episode of the courtroom drama series *Accused*.

T. Michael never saw "Something for Bernice" because his father didn't possess a television. By this time, he had begun to get to know his brother a little better: "In the fifties, I saw Jimmy more. He and Lee lived out here for a while off Laurel Canyon, and they played all the places out here like Ciro's, Mocambo and all these places that are no longer there. The time I went to see him I was very young but he was on a program called *The Spade Cooley Show*. It was a big show." When Kirkwood moved back east after the stint with Goodman in California, T. Michael saw Kirkwood "very infrequently," though adds, "Whenever he was coming out here to have a meeting with somebody about a script or whatever, he would always call us." In addition, the Kirkwood brothers wrote to each other. T. Michael recalls corresponding with Kirkwood about his *Valiant Lady* role: "I used to write him as a joke and say, 'Okay, this is what happened when you left the room.' He used to write back to me and say, 'Are you mentally stable?'…One of his lines was, 'How is our father who art in Hollywood?' which is a Catholic thing. It was just part of his humor."

It was around the point of the *Lamp Unto My Feet* program that the other component of the Kirkwood sibling triumvirate rather dropped out of the picture. Joan Kirkwood had, like Lila Lee before her, developed TB and also like Lee spent time — in her case a year — in Saranac to take advantage of its supposedly beneficial mountain air. (Kirkwood visited her there.) Luckily, Joan was of the first generation able to avail itself of effective drug treatment for the disease. Having recovered, she left New York in 1954 for Brazil, where she was married. Though she returned to the States a year later, she moved with her husband to Dallas. "I was married to an alcoholic and it was an all-time consuming situation," says Joan of the petering-out of her relationship with her half-brother. "He was always drying out or whatever and I was just totally wrapped up, so it would be a sporadic Christmas or a once-in-a-while phone call and that was it." She had no relationship at all with her other half-brother, only meeting T. Michael after Kirkwood's death. "He's always been out in California," she reasons. "We were just never in the same place."

As the *Valiant Lady* role continued, year-in, year-out, it would be a remarkably inefficient actor who did not pick up some tips on perfecting his craft. Kirkwood certainly felt that he did that, although his improvement, from his recollection, was more like an epiphany than an incremental accumulation of technique. As he recalled, "When I started out, I was not a good actor. I had all the externals, knowing the lines and all that, but I never knew quite how to listen. Then one day on *Valiant Lady* I had a scene in a hospital with my girlfriend on the show, who was a wonderful actress. I just sat there listening to her reacting as if I was visiting someone I loved in a hospital. Afterwards, she came up to me, gave me a hug and said, 'Today, you learned how to act.' 'What do you mean?' 'Why, you were no more conscious of your next line than of the ceiling above you.' She was right. For the first time, I was rid of nerves, comfortable in the part, and with the cameras — this was months after I'd started on the show — and I didn't feel that I had to 'act.'"

Kirkwood spoke about his acting abilities in *Equity*, the journal of the actors' union, in an interview published in October 1963, a period following publication of his first novel but one in which he still had a foot in the acting profession. "I believe I'm a good actor and I would hope to be a fine one, if I were allowed to work seriously at it often enough," he said. However, he would in later years seem to contradict himself when he stated, "It took me until I was in my early thirties before I knew I was not going to be one of the best actors in the world." (He was pushing forty when the *Equity* piece was published.) In the aforementioned interview in which he discussed his then-eleven-year-old son's thespian ambitions, Kirkwood Sr. had said, "Amongst many of our young stage aspirants of today there is a notion that success can be won and the top reached without any of the drudgery that the old-timers tell about. That notion is an utter folly. There are occasional and accidental instances of youthful players suddenly shot to stardom. But you will notice that they are also the ones who quickly drop from sight. It always has required long hard work to succeed on the stage and it always will. All the talent in the world will not suffice if it is not polished by constant study and application." This might sound like a rather staid worldview expressed in somewhat pompous tones, but the comments Kirkwood gave to *After Dark* magazine in 1972 suggest that he himself thought he could have been a better actor had he paid his dues. Kirkwood conceded that he didn't know what it was like to be the son of someone really big like Dean Martin, Bing Crosby,

Frank Sinatra or Judy Garland ("That must be an entirely different bag") but did know that being the offspring of two famous people could be an incentive to going into show business and that this could cause someone to join those ranks before they were ready. He said, "You see the result of your parents — whether it's talent or chemistry or personality or whatever — and you don't really see the years of work that led up to success. You think it's an easy thing to step, not necessarily into their shoes, but in their business." He noted that there were advantages in the form of doors being opened to you that ordinarily wouldn't be, but that in his case those doors were "open all too early." He continued, "I started acting at 15 [sic] and I shouldn't have exposed myself at that age because I just didn't know. I was going for the end result rather than working at my craft. I was concentrating on making a name for myself because being the son of famous parents makes you competitive…to achieve some kind of success."

He also told *Equity*, "I don't think I started out with an overabundance of native talent; I'd say I had to learn what proficiency I now possess. Probably, I entered the profession with the idea it was not all that difficult to be a good actor. Also, my mind was teased by the end results, of becoming a celebrity of sorts, instead of achieving a deep knowledge of my craft. I wanted to gallop instead of learning how to walk. But I've grown to love acting for the right reasons." Kirkwood said he loved the rehearsal period, the investigatory process of creating a character, the joy in performing a part well and in feeling the response from another actor and from the audience. "Oh, I'm hooked," he said. "Walking out onto the stage is like stepping into the sun."

Cirker opines, "He was facile, which was not necessarily a bad thing in that form. It was glib, which came obviously from his nightclub work, but not necessarily in great depth. But he got better as he went on, in terms of trying to get below the surface of a character. I would say that his nightclub work in the short haul stood him in good stead, but not necessarily in the long haul." "I don't want to put him down, but he wasn't a very good actor," says Desmond, "but he was a personality in spades and he was a delight to be in the studio with." Seff: "He wasn't an actor. He couldn't have played Hamlet. He was a personality. He would fit nicely into a revue because in revues you simply had to be an engaging sketch actor, meaning a light comedian, and maybe sing a song or two." Sutton: "I think he had talent, but I don't think it was his major talent." Was Kirkwood one of those actors who simply play themselves? Desmond: "Yes, I think that's safe to say." Sutton: "Yes, that's what he did. And it was a very charming self." Desmond does add that Kirkwood made up in professionalism what he might have lacked in technique, always reliable when it came to memorizing his lines. "He was a quick study and remembered well," he says. "And remembered a million other things that actors have to remember."

Though he certainly wasn't wooden, *Valiant Lady* footage doesn't contain Kirkwood performances that leap off the screen — but then he was hardly delivering inspirational material. Furthermore, it was material that we know from Desmond he wasn't inclined to hone to whatever level of perfection it could reach. However, a performance in TV drama *Divorce Court* (recorded during the *Valiant Lady* stint) suggests greater depths to Kirkwood's talent. The role — as a man attempting to get custody of his children — is a little meatier than the *Valiant Lady* material. Kirkwood rises to the occasion well. He also improvises impressively when his fellow actors clearly wander off-script.

However, whether or not Kirkwood was a great actor is actually irrelevant to the issue of why he never became a big star. There have been plenty of actors — both in Kirkwood's era and subsequently — who became box-office icons without being outstanding at their craft. Looks have been more crucial than talent in more than one movie star's success story. Though very slightly beaky in profile, Kirkwood in all other respects most certainly had the matinée-idol looks associated with movie stardom, right down to twinkling blue eyes. (Sutton: "He was adorable-looking, really. I once used that word to describe him and he got so mad at me.") He also had a clear, deep speaking voice handily unidentifiable with any particular region or social caste. If we are to believe his estimate of having clocked up over 500 appearances on television, and his claims of having attended more auditions than was good for his mental well-being, it also can't be said that he lacked application. Joan Kirkwood says, "He just never could make it big-time in acting. He was effeminate and I don't know if he could be believable as, say, a leading man." However, it's doubtful that film and TV audiences not so *au fait* with the minutiae of Kirkwood's life would see him as anything other than conventionally masculine. It simply seems that Kirkwood was not a beneficiary of the crapshoot that acting, like so many artistic professions, constitutes. Consequently, *Valiant Lady* was the pinnacle of his success in the field.

Ira Cirker left the show he had done so much to bring to the airwaves to work on a new soap, *Another World*. Into his shoes as director stepped Herbert Kenwith, who had hitherto been associate director for Cirker. Kenwith now alternated with Desmond. His elevation exacerbated a clash of personalities between him and Kirkwood.

Patti Goldstein, who worked on publicity for the program, recalls Kenwith as a "funny little guy" who "Jimmy did everything in his life to make miserable. He thought Herb was kind of a pretentious little guy. He was very prissy, and that's all Jimmy had to see. Of course, we all thought it was hilarious. I wouldn't want to be on the butt end of Jimmy's humor." "Herb was a talented guy," says Sutton, who lived in the same building as both Kenwith and Cirker, "but he was nervous — and he had a right to be because he had five minutes of acting rehearsal — and Jimmy used to like to tease him and drive him cuckoo, mix up the props, do all kinds of things." Cirker: "I heard that! It was outrageous, some of the bitchery that went on between those two. Herbie was very uptight all the time and Jimmy was playful and Herbert couldn't stand his playfulness so he got so uptight he would scream at him over the talkback all the time."

This mischievousness and inability to take the show too seriously is something that it seems Kirkwood and Sutton shared and partly led the latter to leave the show after two years. "Jimmy and I wrote a kind of sketch about it," Sutton says. Sutton had a house on Fire Island, a theatre community, where she put on a show every Saturday: "So one night we wrote a sketch about ourselves, Mickey Emerson and Diane Emerson. We ended it with a song and the last lyrics of the song were: 'But don't be scared/ Don't be afraid/It may be *merde*/But we get paid.' We look out and our producers are sitting right there, and the director. Boy, there was trouble. I was the one who got in more trouble really…Well, I got other offers and also I was laughing, I was getting silly with the whole thing, and so I kind of wanted to get out and of course that funny little song didn't help my situation there. Jimmy got away with it, but I'd made fun of the whole thing. They were wonderful times, they really were, but I couldn't have stood it for the full length of time, and I don't think they could have stood me either!"

"*Valiant Lady* was hilarious and everybody laughed and carried on at the expense of all the people who produced it and directed it and wrote it," says Patti Goldstein. "There was a woman who wrote it whose name was Martha Alexander who was, oh how shall I put it, not the most creative creature that ever drew breath. And I think that Jimmy and Dolores and Earl Hammond [Hal Soames, Helen's new love] and people like that, the actors who were in it, thought they could do much better fixing lines as they went along. Jimmy in particular."

John Desmond's decision to cast Kirkwood in *Lamp Unto My Feet* despite his misgivings about his acting abilities was possibly due to the fact that he had become a friend of Kirkwood's. As with so many people who got close to Kirkwood, he remained that way for life. "He was such a delight," says Desmond. "Everybody — *everybody* — loved Jimmy. They just did because he [had] such a winning and out-of-the-ordinary humor. He was crazy and we all appreciated it enormously. He was a real ice-breaker. At any big party he was like the star...The parties that we went to, it was long before smut [became] part of the American vocabulary and Jimmy would say the most outrageous things and people adored it. Somehow he could say, 'Crap,' 'Shit,' whatever and it was funny...He could get away with anything. He had some unique charm — this halo — that followed him about."

It was presumably because he was so fond of his adored colleague that Desmond agreed to go along with a criminal plan Kirkwood hatched one day. Unlike the squirt gun stick-up, this would be a victimless one. Desmond: "Alfred Hitchcock made *Rope*. It was the story of an upgraded New York boy who murdered a friend and I think that Jimmy was obsessed — obsessed is a pretty strong word, but completely overwhelmed — with the story of two guys collaborating in the disastrous events...I think that Jimmy was enamored with getting by with crimes. He offered me the enhancement of a coconspirator."

The caper Kirkwood had in mind was hardly of the nature of events depicted in that famous 1948 motion picture. His idea was that he and Desmond would go to the New York deli Rubens following a *Valiant Lady* broadcast, order and consume some food and walk out without paying for it. When the pair got to Rubens, however, they were unable to put this dastardly plan into operation because the venue was virtually empty, thus ensuring that their exit would be too conspicuous. "So he said, 'Let's go to the Plaza,'" says Desmond. "The Oak Room is a very chic watering hole at the Plaza Hotel in New York. We went and we ordered scotches and steak and the whole schmegeggy. We had a plan that we would get up and leave the table — like, go to the men's room, make a phone call, etc., etc. — and then one of us would stay and be the anchor while the other one skipped off. Jimmy decided that he would be the anchor. Well, he got so fucking nervous I said, 'You go and I'll be the anchor.' After making some forays to the men's room so that we established that we could leave the table, he went and I stayed. Then after a certain amount of time, I left. I [went to] the Greta Garbo entrance and as I was going through the Oak Room I hear this voice holler, 'Oh, John, John, Jo-ohn.' I thought, 'Oh, my God'...It was a friend of mine called David King-Wood. He's an English actor. I ran out of the Greta Garbo entrance and David pursued me outside and said, 'We're having some drinks and blah blah

blah.' I said, 'David–get the fuck away from here, I'm running out on a check!' And David — Oxford graduate and once played Vivien Leigh's leading man in *Romeo and Juliet* when they were kids — he was appalled at my behavior of running out on a check at the Plaza."

Clearly, Kirkwood was never fated to live a life of crime.

Kirkwood saw a high turnover of colleagues at *Valiant Lady*. Nancy Coleman bailed out of the title role in 1954. "She got a play but she also was not feeling well from the whole thing," says Sutton. "Even for people as young as I was then, it was a very exhausting schedule and Nancy Coleman was just falling apart under the pressure." Coleman was replaced by Flora Campbell. The role of Bonnie Withers also saw two different actresses play it. Lydia Reed was replaced as Kim Emerson by Bonnie Sawyer. The attrition rate for Dianes, meanwhile, was massive, Anne Pearson being replaced by Dolores Sutton who was replaced by Sue Randall who was replaced by Leila Martin.

Kirkwood's ambiguous accomplishment of being the only unchanging face in the main cast throughout the show's four-year run was apparently narrowly obtained, for at one point Kirkwood said he came perilously close to being written out. He later noted, "Writers on soaps change every six months or so because they tend to burn out on story ideas. A new writer came on and suddenly I, Mickey Emerson…only just out of college, was considering taking an engineering job way up at the head of the Amazon River. It was a secret project and as my Mom, Valiant Lady herself, warned: 'Mickey, I don't think you should take that job, it's extremely dangerous.'" Kirkwood began to realize just how dangerous as he watched the show when he wasn't on it for continuity's sake and found himself observing scenes in which his prospective employer was telling other people that the job was so hazardous that whoever took it would be facing dangers ranging from disease to deadly snakes to tribes of head-hunters and might possibly not be coming back alive. Kirkwood: "I finally went to one of the producers and said: 'Hey, doesn't really look like such a good job up there in Brazil, does it?' He assured me I would not exactly be doing the cha-cha-cha; the new writer was not all that fond of me or my character and had decided that Valiant Lady, already being a widow and thus valiant, would be even valianter if she lost a son — me." Kirkwood found himself getting gloomy at the impending loss of work and steady income and it was hard for him to smile in what were to be his last few weeks in the role. Then, just as Mickey was packing to go to the airport, the script had him experiencing a change of heart and deciding to stay in Middlebury after all. Naturally, he enquired why this sudden *volte face*. Kirkwood: "I...was told that the writer himself had been fired and the new writer liked me and had spared my life in the nick of time."

Despite his relief at his job being saved, Kirkwood continued to harbor ambitions for roles of a more substantial nature. In 1956, he received a call from agent-producer Gus Schirmer Jr., who informed him that screen legend Tallulah Bankhead was planning a three-month summer tour of a revue that would be a spin-off of her previous such enterprise, *Follies*. Needing a young comic, she had expressed interest in Kirkwood because she'd been told about his work with Goodman and had seen him on *Valiant Lady*. Curiosity seems to have played some part, too: Kirkwood later recalled that having observed him "weeping and wailing" on a television soap, she couldn't quite believe the comedy part of him. In addition (and almost inevitably), when Kirkwood went to Bankhead's east sixties townhouse for his audition at 1:30 one afternoon after a *Valiant Lady* broadcast, it was to discover that she was yet another screen goddess of whom his father had had carnal knowledge. Or as she put it, after shaking hands and stepping back as though to get a better look at him, "I knew your father..." (Significant pause) "Very well." (This was Kirkwood's printed version. Jim Piazza recalls Kirkwood said she stated she had "fucked" his father.) Bankhead also knew Kirkwood's mother, if not quite so intimately. Back when Lila Lee was still in vaudeville, Bankhead had invited her out to lunch after being impressed by her stage presence. The actress was visibly taken aback to find such a young girl bouncing into the restaurant and bored at having to lunch with a baby. Lee reminded her of this when their paths crossed later down the line. Lee wrote in her autobiography of her suspicions that Kirkwood Sr. and Bankhead had an affair when she and Kirkwood Sr. were married, but admitted she "couldn't swear to it."

Kirkwood was extremely apprehensive about the audition. As he put it, "I was nervous enough auditioning for industrial shows, singing ballads to Buicks, for God's sake." In fact, he was so shaky during the *Valiant Lady* rehearsals that Joy Ails, one of the production assistants, asked him if there was some problem. When Kirkwood explained for whom he was auditioning later on, Ails immediately opened her purse and provided him with his very first Valium. Kirkwood said he took her advice and swallowed it as soon as they got off the air. One wonders what would have happened if he hadn't, for the audition turned out to be probably the most bizarre of his life. Kirkwood dressed in his best gray flannels, sport jacket and freshly shined shoes and armed himself with a selection of skits from the Kirkwood & Goodman act. He circled Bankhead's house for ten minutes before ringing the doorbell at 1:30 on the nose. A textbook butler opened the door and told him, "Upstairs to the living room, Miss Bankhead will be down soon." Once there, Kirkwood took a seat and nervously awaited the star. Kirkwood could hear Bankhead screaming at her Pekingese ("No, goddamn! Dolores — get out of the way!") and her dresser ("Chris, I said the beige one, that's yellow — are you blind!") This only made Kirkwood more nervous and he was thinking of going home when a voice called down, "Are you there?…I'll be right down!" Kirkwood rose as he heard Bankhead descending the stairs. Bankhead was wearing a beige slack suit, her hair as "gorgeous" and face as "incredible" as Kirkwood and so many others recollected from cinema sightings, although she somewhat undercut the vision she presented by picking at her eyelashes on her descent and saying to him, without a greeting, "I always wake up with all this shit sticking to my eyes, you know, all this sleep gook, do you do that, darling?" (Kirkwood replied in the affirmative.) After imparting the news of how well she had known his dad, Bankhead explained to the son of her former lover, "I need a comedian, but I don't want an old dirty one, like David Burns. I want a young fresh cast and that includes a young comic. Now, darling, I've seen you on your soap and I think you're absolutely adorable, but what sort of comedy do you do?"

This was a question Kirkwood said he never really got to answer fully, let alone demonstrate, for the rest of the rather lengthy "audition" was characterized by interruption. From Kirkwood's description of her behavior, Bankhead seems to have been rather similar to how Homer Price remembers Kirkwood's own mother: a delight but spoilt. She would ask Kirkwood to tell her about his comedy routines and his soap work and to perform something for her, but Kirkwood would usually get only as far as a first sentence before Bankhead would butt in with an anecdote from her brilliant career or an observation centering around what was clearly her favorite subject — herself — or be interrupted herself by a telephone call from a friend which she declined to cut short even though it clearly concerned trivia. She did at least listen to Kirkwood when she asked him about his parents and his childhood.

After a couple of hours, the telephone interrupted them again. It was Gus Schirmer calling to see how the audition had gone, him probably assuming Kirkwood was long gone. Kirkwood heard Bankhead tell Schirmer that he, Kirkwood, was "just perfect." The reasons were the fact that he was "young and attractive and looks like he has — well, breeding. He's a gentleman." Bizarrely — for she had not seen Kirkwood perform anything — she then told Schirmer, "His comedy is marvelous, just what

I'm looking for. None of that baggy pants stuff. Yes, I'm delighted." When Bankhead got off the phone, it was to offer Kirkwood the job. She sat beside him and after a lengthy period complimenting him for all the qualities about which she had gushed to Schirmer on the telephone, swung her legs up onto his lap and asked, "Did you ever see such beautiful ankles?"

The first time Bankhead was to hear the *Reader's Digest* sketch Kirkwood had been intending to perform for her was two weeks later when rehearsals for the show — titled *Welcome Darlings* — began. "It was a glorious summer," Kirkwood later said. "I loved working with the legendary lady...A woman that I absolutely adored and was marvelous to work with, as opposed to the many legends and rumors about what a terror she was." To tour with Bankhead, Kirkwood had to ask the producers of *Valiant Lady* to temporarily write him out of the storylines. Desmond says, "Generally speaking, the television producers were permissive when people got good parts because it was good for them as well."

Welcome Darlings also featured Sheila Smith, Donovan Crichton, Burnell Dietsch and The Martins. Kirkwood got second billing for his role, which constituted master of ceremonies, comedian and song-and-dance man. He received some great notices. Richard Seff: "He was the kind of innocent pretty boy that worked so well against her because she was the sophisticated, *demi-monde* lady." *Variety* described Kirkwood as "a fine vis a vis." The *Cranston Herald* proclaimed that he "just about stole the show with his zany ability to make a lot out of very little. Young and endowed with a million dollar personality, Kirkwood has all it takes to make him one of our future 'tops' in the word of natural comics."

There were similar raves in other publications which can't be easily identified because Kirkwood put together a notice sheet on which he neglected to attribute quotes:

"One of the most pleasant surprises was to find young James Kirkwood of NBC's [sic] *Valiant Lady* fame in the cast singing, dancing, and joking his way through the program with a boyish freshness that belongs only to him. Just how he is going to explain this cavorting with such a delightfully wicked lady to his mother, Helen Emerson, will be a problem only he can solve. Here is a musical comedy side to Kirkwood that you must see."

"An ingenuous sort, Mr. Kirkwood sets up a neat contrast to Tallulah's ultra-sophistication, and gives the show a set of laughs quite in keeping with but never stepping into her domain."

"Kirkwood is a bright young comedian of the Johnny Carson mold who should be a big hit in the movies or on TV not too long hence."

"James Kirkwood, Jr., an ingratiating juvenile man, is a very pleasant master of ceremonies, sings agreeably and is especially funny in a solo bit which ribs *The Readers Digest*."

"Kirkwood, a most personable chap, begins to take over through the revue and projects himself into an admirable leading role in which he sings, acts and helps to brighten up an already illuminated evening."

"He achieves a few deliriously funny moments…"

"Several of the top moments of the revue are in the hands of James Kirkwood, Jr., a very clever young actor and entertainer."

"…a company starred with James Kirkwood's absurdly youthful rendering of most sophisticated adult humor. TV addicts know this guileless face well. In person he is much, much better than on the screen, with his feigned terror for his boss-lady and his cleverly nonsensical solo skits."

"'Get Back in the Trunk' will give you James Kirkwood in a wonderfully different role. 'Love and Thimbles Petered' is a takeoff on Peter Pan: and it flies high with fun. But when you hear Kirkwood in the 'Reader's Digest' bit you'll probably stop the show yourself with your own laughter. This reviewer did."

It's remarkable how frequently in these notices "youthful" and variant words crop up: Kirkwood turned 32 at around this juncture. The better-informed *Variety* had added a somewhat backhanded comment to its praise, describing him as a "veteran café youthful," but clearly he was a man who (especially in dimly-lit theatres) came across — courtesy of his fresh face, effervescence and enthusiasm — as much, much younger than he was. The other remarkable fact is how much Kirkwood seemed a comic or variety star-in-the-making to so many who saw him in *Welcome Darlings*. While the dramatic superficialities and inanities of *Valiant Lady* were the things for which Kirkwood became best known in the entertainment field before his writing career, he clearly had a considerable talent in a very different and much more significant area. Going by those raves, it certainly sounds as though he deserved his own television variety show. If anything, his failure to effect a breakthrough to TV or even film in this light entertainment department is even more mystifying than his failure to make it into the big time as a straight actor.

Kirkwood and Bankhead remained good friends and Kirkwood would later, when times were hard, be her "caddy," the term she used for the attractive (and usually red-headed) young men she would employ to do menial tasks about the house. Beckenstein: "He always said to me, 'You would have loved Tallulah'…She used to play a game with people: she'd say, 'Tell me, darling — who is it you would like to meet?' They would tell her and then she would try and arrange it. Jimmy said he would love to meet Eleanor Roosevelt and one day he got a call from Tallulah Bankhead and she said, 'Darling, come over on Thursday at four. Mrs. Roosevelt is coming over for tea.' He was all excited and went over to Tallulah's house. They were having a wonderful time chatting and suddenly Tallulah got up and said, 'Now keep talking, darlings, I'm just going into the bathroom, I'll be right back.' And she went down the hall into the bathroom and opened the door and sat on the toilet and started peeing and somehow didn't shut the door. After Mrs. Roosevelt left, Jimmy said, 'Tallulah! I can't believe your behavior. How could you do that?' She said, 'Don't be silly, darling — Mrs. Roosevelt pees, too.'"

One of the notices for *Welcome Darlings* threw up this interesting nugget: "In his spare time Mr. Kirkwood has collaborated on a three-act comedy, *The Marriage Habit*, which producers are now nuzzling." It's another piece of evidence that the story that Kirkwood had an almost Damascene conversion to the idea of writing just before beginning his first novel *There Must Be a Pony!* was a myth of his own devising.

Not only does *The Marriage Habit* precede *Pony* by at least a couple of years, but so does the step outline for a work called *Nothing but the Night*. Unfortunately, a side-effect of this apparent myth-making is that the role of Edwin "Ed" Duerr in Kirkwood's literary development has been rather airbrushed from history. Duerr seems to have been as pivotal in the writing-oriented course Kirkwood's life took as Robert R. Kirsch, the *Los Angeles Times* literary editor and writing tutor who he always made pains to credit, possibly even more so. Beckenstein says of Duerr, "I didn't meet him. I talked to him on the phone once." Though he says, "I don't think they were close," Beckenstein also says, "He was an older man who I think Jimmy may have had an affair with who kind of mentored him. He was very cultured and I think was a very good influence on Jimmy."

Duerr (1904-1985) was the director of the University of California Little Theatre and went on to become Radio and Television Supervisor for Young & Rubicon Inc. In 1950, he published *Radio and Television Acting: Criticism, Theory, and Practice* (Rinehart & Company). The copy Duerr presented to Kirkwood carried the inscription, "For Jim — this book is especially yours because all the while I was writing it you helped by arguing with me." (Kirkwood sort of repaid the compliment when he named a school sports coach Duerr in his first book.) It was Duerr with whom Kirkwood was collaborating on *The Marriage Habit* in '56 and as this seems to be Kirkwood's first major or serious attempt at trying to write something with a view to selling it commercially it could very well be the case that it was Duerr who made Kirkwood think of turning his hand properly to writing in the first instance.

A copy of *The Marriage Habit* exists in Kirkwood's files, a fragile document on onion-skin paper. It is a 159-page play revolving around the desire of people to permanently pair off and the clashes it causes. The main characters are Nancy Welles, a movie star (retired) in her forties from Elyria, and her son Kevin, a twenty-something newspaper employee. Kevin, who lives in a West 48th St cold-water walk-up flat whose bathroom is shared with other residents in the building, is courting a young lady named Dorothy. Nancy is toying with the idea of marrying an Elyria businessman whom she doesn't love but who is decent and well-off and of whom Kevin approves. Nancy's plans are thrown awry when she meets an unreliable but charismatic entrepreneur called Steve, who is trying to fund a new play in a way not too dissimilar to the manner in which Max Bialystock in Mel Brooks' later film *The Producers* did: flattering ladies of a certain age and a certain degree of sexual starvation. Kevin most certainly does not approve of Steve. Thrown into this pot are perpetually bickering couple Jay and Sylvia, who seem a perfect advertisement for not getting betrothed, and Mr. Dowd, a cantankerous neighbor (and bathroom-sharer) of Kevin's. Ultimately, Nancy rejects Steve and congratulates herself — and is congratulated by Kevin and his new fiancée — on her resolve. She then suddenly decides that it is naïve to try to deny your true nature and goes off in search of Steve, asserting that she probably will marry him.

It's impossible to know which of the authors is responsible for which components of what is a rather enjoyable play, especially as both are now deceased, but it would seem a logical assumption that Kirkwood mainly supplied the life experience and Duerr primarily the technique. Certainly, much of the milieu seems mined from Kirkwood's life: the ageing movie-star mother, the Hell's Kitchen flat and the fact that it is stated that Kevin's mom has a propensity for marrying "lemons." Meanwhile, the sure pace and smooth structure of the play are things for which Kirkwood's own later theatre projects — whatever merits they may have had — were not renowned.

It was presumably Duerr and Kirkwood who were behind the placing of mentions of their collaboration in various parts of the media during mid-1957. On June 3, *The New York Times* carried a short item headlined "Kirkwood Jr. Writes Play," which reported that "James Kirkwood Jr. is branching out" with a work written in conjunction with "Edwin Duerr, a radio and TV director." Nine days later (and five days before the authors registered the work at the Library of Congress Copyright Office), the

Chicago Tribune also mentioned *The Marriage Habit*. Whitney Bolton went one better in his gossip column in August. Bolton said Kirkwood had "done what most actors dream of doing: he has written a play which has been described as excellent and probably will be seen on Broadway this winter." Alas, though it certainly seems a stagable play and despite the best efforts of amenable journalists (Bolton would admit when recommending *There Must Be a Pony!* in print that he and Kirkwood were friends), there is no record of any production of *The Marriage Habit* ever being mounted.

Nothing but the Night, written by Kirkwood alone, would seem to date from the around the same period as *The Marriage Habit* simply because the only copy in existence is typed on the same type of onionskin paper as the surviving copy of that last work. It would seem safe to assume that *The Marriage Habit* predates *Nothing but the Night* because if Duerr was Kirkwood's non-prose writing mentor at this stage in his life, that logically precludes Kirkwood having struck out on his own, writing-wise, before their collaboration. A step outline is a description of a movie screenplay rather than a screenplay itself, although as reading experiences the two formats are not dissimilar. *Nothing but the Night*'s step outline — typed in capital letters and running to 152 pages, plus eleven pages of preceding character description — features a fading female movie star (Mira Burgess) and her devoted teenage son (Paul), who goes to a Brewster Academy-type prep school called Baird Academy, albeit as a day pupil. There are other elements familiar from Kirkwood's life, most notably the fact that Paul and his friend Barry run out on a check at the Oak Room. The murder plot that Paul hatches with Barry against his hated stepfather might also indicate an autobiographical element if we are to believe the supposition regarding Reid Russell floated by at least one person earlier in this text. Said murder plot is something with which Barry — the joint lead character along with Paul — agrees to go along because he essentially wants to be Paul. Paul is everything the bookish, would-be writer Barry, is not: confident, handsome and popular. The murder plot has an ironic and tragic end when Paul and Barry return from the apartment in which the stepfather is staying without having done the deed — he turns out to be "entertaining" his ex-girlfriend — only to find that Paul's mother has been burned to death in a fire at the country hotel at which the three are lodging. Because of the alibi that Paul and Barry have carefully plotted, she has fatally rushed into the flaming cabin in which she is certain Paul is trapped.

The story is reasonably convincing and the plot development broadly plausible. There is, though, an overall feeling of blandness and a sense of nothing not previously seen before, even in the late 1950s. Its very vintage and necessary adherence to the prevailing moral codes also gives it a patina of age. In his character notes, Kirkwood states that Barry is "a latent homosexual but would never dream of engaging in any overt form of sexual activity unless he were led into it." Leaving aside that this is the type of coyness about homosexuality that would become tiresomely familiar in Kirkwood's novels, this latent homosexuality is not really made explicit within Kirkwood's step outline. Meanwhile, the worst epithet heard is "Crazy!," which might well be accurate for the era but helps embed an overall feeling of almost comical tameness and all-American corn. As does the rather privileged backdrop. Paul, Barry and their Baird classmates are not the type of underprivileged delinquents depicted in the contemporaneous movie *Blackboard Jungle*, but well-bred, well-off young men and women who are already driving and booking their own restaurant tables. Again, not necessarily sociologically inaccurate, but it harkens back to a time when the American media only portrayed to the country a rose-tinted, clean-cut view of itself.

Despite its blandness, one can discern some interesting things in the step outline, albeit ones that suggest the story might have worked better as a novel. The milieu might be uninteresting in this skeletal form, but fleshed out with the unique turn of phrase and likeable writing persona Kirkwood would later display as a prose writer, it could have ended up as something rather more substantial than the ten-a-penny celluloid morality tale it is.

"It sounds suspiciously like *Rope*," says William Russo of *Nothing but the Night* when told its plot. "Might have been something inspired by that. It is his classic theme: murder, and murder involving parents."

"He was always talking about writing," says Dolores Sutton, referring to 1954 and 1955, the years on which she worked on *Valiant Lady*. "Plays, then. He once talked to me about a play he wanted to work [on], an idea he had, so it was always in his mind." She also says, "This was a guy who… had other objectives all the way. We used to talk about it. He never saw himself just doing [stand-up], any more than he saw himself being on a soap opera for the rest of his life."

Following his happy experience working with Bankhead, Kirkwood's theatrical career seemed to be going from strength to strength when, approaching the end of the *Welcome Darlings* tour, he was awarded the role of Patrick (As a Young Man) in the Broadway show *Auntie Mame*, due to start at the Broadhurst Theatre at the end of October '56. Patrick is the nephew of the titular Mame, a woman who wants to prevent her young charge becoming stuffy and to instead grow up as hedonistic and carefree as she is. The Mame role was to be played by Rosalind Russell, who was also very influential backstage. Kirkwood: "Rosalind Russell had called me up and sent me flowers and said how marvelous it was that I was going to play her nephew…I couldn't get out of the Bankhead show because I was doing a couple of monologues and I didn't have an understudy and I was a week late. Then by the time I got to rehearsals, they had been rehearsing for about ten days." Kirkwood also returned to *Valiant Lady* at this point, making once again for a somewhat onerous workload.

It was at this time that Kirkwood's old Elyria school pal Bob Cromling hooked up with him. Cromling was now resident in Cleveland but visiting the Big Apple with a group to take in some stage shows. Kirkwood took Cromling to see him perform in a broadcast of *Valiant Lady*. Cromling: "He took me up to the booth and of course nobody should be in the booth other than the lead people who run the show, but he said, 'This is a friend of mine, it'll be okay' and all that sort of stuff. He went downstairs and we saw the whole show from the booth and through a large window… He did well, he had a lot of following, a lot of letters would come into the station for Jim, because this went out in the afternoon where all the women would have a little time to watch TV. He felt very comfortable in the role from what I saw, and of course the letters from all the women helped a lot." Following the show, Kirkwood gave Cromling his phone number and the two arranged to talk about old times over a beer after Kirkwood had finished rehearsing *Auntie Mame* for the day. Cromling: "I was to call him and he would tell me just where we would meet. I called and I called and I called and there was no answer." A puzzled Cromling had to leave New York to return home the next day. "About two months later I got a letter from him stating why we didn't make connections," he says. "He had just learned that he was not going to be in *Auntie Mame*… It was undoubtedly an evening where he would be with his friends and kind of a sorrowful drinking party probably ensued just to get over the fact." "It was a very cruel way in which I was fired," Kirkwood said. "In the Bankhead show, Tallulah had to fire a couple of people but she faced them and she said, 'Darling, it's just a matter or chemistry and I know it's heartbreaking and I know it's terrible and dreadful but you're just too tall' or 'too short' or whatever and I think that's what [Russell] could have done with me. She avoided seeing me. I was kind of treated like a leper."

Kirkwood recalled showing up a couple of hours late for *Mame* rehearsals on what he estimated was the fifth day of rehearsals, presumably meaning rehearsals for him. Russell was rather frosty. Kirkwood: "It had always been 'Jimmy' and this day she looked at me and she said, 'Well, Mr. Kirkwood. I'm so glad you could find time to join us.'…I rehearsed a scene before they broke for lunch in which I had about five lines. And that was it. After lunch, I was told I could go home for the rest of the day because they were going back to work on previous scenes in which I was not involved."

Kirkwood said he had made a date for dinner with a girl who was in the Bankhead show and told her to meet him at the theatre. Unable to get her on the phone to rearrange their meeting place, he returned to the theatre at around six or seven that evening. As he turned the corner, he was confronted with an amazing and appalling sight: "Twenty guys all about my size, general type, weight, age, standing out there with scripts." His instinctive thought was, "My God, they all look like Patricks!" Kirkwood's disbelieving hunch that these were all auditionees for the role of Patrick (As a Young Man) turned out to be correct. When Kirkwood unexpectedly entered the theatre, it was somewhat to Russell's discomfort. He recalled, "I was put into one room and I could see that she saw that I was backstage and she was saying, 'What's he doing here, he's not supposed to be there!'" Kirkwood was informed that Miss Russell was displeased that he had been a week late (not two in this recounting) for rehearsals. Kirkwood pointed out it was known this would be the case when he was hired. He also pointed out that he had a contract. Kirkwood was also informed by a third party that Russell had thought he was too "funny." He wasn't informed whether this meant funny hah-hah or funny-strange. In desperation, Kirkwood asked if he could read for Russell again. Permission was "reluctantly" granted and Kirkwood turned up at the theatre the next morning. He waited for an hour ("trying to hide the humiliation burning inside") before he was told that Russell had phoned to say she'd been "delayed" and — farcically — to go ahead and read without her present. Even more farcically, Kirkwood did, later acknowledging, "It was like making a screen test without film in the camera." Kirkwood was let go. "I think that everyone was very nervous about the show…" he said. "But it was a cruel way to find out about it."

Kirkwood's letter to Cromling, written much closer to the time than his later published reminiscences, almost makes the matter sound more of a resignation than a dismissal: "Miss Russell wouldn't stand for the few remaining conflicts I had because of 'Valiant Lady.' And I could not get out of them as I had an iron-bound contract. So I had to bow out. I was terribly unhappy but there was nothing to do." For her part, Russell denied that she had had Kirkwood fired. Upon seeing his April 1969 *Playbill* article in which he related the events of his dismissal, she sent him a letter care-of his current publishers Simon & Schuster declaring, "I have never fired anyone in my entire life" and claimed that the producers and the director Tec DaCosta "made all casting decisions." She signed off, "All the best from that mean, unkind 'Auntie Mame'" (but, in hand, "Rosalind Russell"). Richard Seff, who was then assistant to Russell's agent David Hocker, disputes Russell's denial. "I don't know what it was that she didn't think was right but she did and she had control and he was let go," he says. "All I know is what David Hocker told me. She may not have been alone in the dismissal. I'm sure she talked it over with Tec DaCosta, but I know David told me she wasn't happy with Jim's quality for the role. It was probably mutually agreed that she deny any involvement in it."

Cromling's assumption that Kirkwood immediately went out and got smashed following the news seems plausible, although it's difficult to work out how the next day's farcical new reading for a Russell who didn't show fits into the chronology. John Desmond reports, "We were close friends at that [time]. They just shuffled him off and it was a very distressing and difficult time for him emotionally." This incident may actually have been far more significant than a humiliating dismissal. It may conceivably have been the point at which Kirkwood lost his best chance for stardom. Not only did *Auntie Mame* rack up 639 Broadway performances over the next year-and-a-half, but in 1958 it was turned into a feature film that was one of the biggest-grossing hits of the year and was nominated for six Academy Awards, including Best Picture. Although the movie didn't retain much of the cast of the Broadway production, had Kirkwood bagged the film role of Patrick (As a Young Man) it would have been his first truly significant Hollywood job and might have opened the door to bigger celluloid things.

Kirkwood had asked CBS to allow him more leave from *Valiant Lady* so that he could accommodate the *Auntie Mame* role. Now an unfortunate necessity presented itself. "I quickly phoned the soap opera and asked them not to write me out," he recalled. "It had already been done and by the time I was written back in, the show itself had been written off by CBS and we'd been replaced by a gameshow."

April 24, 1957, saw Lila Lee become the subject of *This Is Your Life*, the NBC television program that took a celebrity down memory lane in the company of people from his or her past. Lee Goodman (introduced on it as Lila's "son's best friend") had a pivotal role in the program. Skullduggery was always necessitated by the fact that the featured celebrity never had any idea the show was going to happen. "Lee was responsible for getting her to the studio," says Plotkin.

During the program it was revealed that the one-time Hollywood star was now reduced to menial office jobs to make ends meet and was sometimes unable to obtain employment at all. One of the reasons for the latter turned out to be, in her son's stated opinion, that she would fetch up to interviews for such humble posts grandly clad in a fur coat. The Reid Russell case was touched on, or perhaps glossed over. In the program's distinctive second-person, present-tense vernacular, compere Ralph Edwards said, "He has no connection with you whatsoever."

This Is Your Life subjects never had any idea who the guests — produced from backstage, usually chronologically and individually — were going to be. In having Kirkwood Sr. appear on Lila Lee's *This Is Your Life*, the program provided a guest who was even more of a surprise than usual. Kirkwood later said, "It was the first time they had ever had an ex-husband or wife on. There was a policy, but I gave my permission. I thought it might be amusing." When Kirkwood Sr. materialized and, rather hammily, said to his ex, "Lila — those lips I've kissed so many times, may I have one more?" Lila acquiesced, but her son later reported she was not amused. In fairness to Kirkwood Sr., he was gracious to Lee, praising her for her patience over his failed business ventures. Not that this impressed her. Kirkwood: "I said to my mother at the party they had at the Hollywood Roosevelt where you got your charm bracelet and your camera for embarrassing yourself to death, 'I'm taking dad to lunch tomorrow — would you like to join us?' My mother said, 'No, dear. As your father's so charming, I just might throw up.'"

After the broadcast, Kirkwood wrote to Bob Cromling, "I thought my mother carried the whole thing off beautifully and I only hope it will mean a new career for her." No fewer than five producers came on at the program's end, one by one, to promise Lee that she had roles in named television shows of theirs. Although one of them at least seems to have been as good as his word, there would be no new career. Some will infer tragedy for a woman who had known nothing but stardom from the age of four to her early thirties, but in fact contemporaneous interviews show Lee admitting that she was less interested in a revitalization of her acting career than her friends and family were for her. "I wasn't a dedicated actress to begin with," she said. "I'm not a young girl anymore and I know I'm not going to set the world on fire." Kirkwood would admiringly comment in a lecture he later gave on his mother how unblemished by ambition she was.

The final broadcast of *Valiant Lady* took place on August 16, 1957 (suggesting that Kirkwood's recollection of it coming off the air almost as soon as he was written back in after the *Auntie Mame* interlude was an example of his penchant for dramatic telescoping of event). The newly unemployed Kirkwood decided to try out for commercials. He'd pragmatically done a "fair share" before. (Even more pragmatically, he said he'd once done a V.D. film for the Army Signal Corps.) He recalled that the first audition he attended for this line of work in this period was bizarre and humiliating. As with so many other bizarre and humiliating incidents in his life, it would later transpire to be great Raw Material. As he wasn't yet an author, this consolation did not exist at the time but the incident was eventually profitably used in his novel and play *P.S. Your Cat is Dead!*

Kirkwood claimed that the audition in reality was more humiliating than rendered in *Cat*. This would be remarkable. The commercial was for a new soft drink and the audition took place at an advertising agency. Kirkwood said he was confronted with a massive conference table around which sat at least a dozen men and women, all of whom had the air of casting for some motion picture extravaganza rather than a one-minute TV slot and all of whom spoke in solemn tones about the artistic integrity of the scene, motivation, etc. The director explained to Kirkwood that the part for which he was auditioning was a man who dives into a swimming pool, swims its length, climbs out, shakes off the water and is handed a can of the new soft drink. "You take a sip, say, 'Oh, boy, that's the greatest taste — what is it?'" the director informed him. The director waited for that to sink in before asking Kirkwood, "Think you can handle it?" Kirkwood refrained from sarcastically observing that it might be a bit much to ask of someone who had only been in the business ten years, and replied in the affirmative. He did the same when the director asked, "You do swim, don't you?" The director glanced around the table, pointed to the floor, and said, "Then — dive in!" Kirkwood later said, "He wanted me to dive into a non-existent pool, swim the length, jump out, shake off the water, take a non-existent can from a non-existent spokesperson and…I couldn't believe it." But the people around the table were beaming back at Kirkwood as though there was nothing strange about this request and he found himself slipping off his shoes, stepping up onto a sofa and jumping onto the carpet, where he proceeded to pantomime swimming the length. As he was reaching for the invisible can, the director's voice broke in: "Wait a minute, Mr. Kirkwood, you didn't look as if you were enjoying the swim!" Something snapped in Kirkwood. "No," he said. "Actually, I didn't." "Ah-hah," the director said, glancing around the table with a smile. "See, I could tell, now let's try it again and this time—-""No, no," Kirkwood interrupted, "You see, I really didn't enjoy it." The eyes of the entire room were now on Kirkwood as he pointed to the floor. "There's too much chlorine in that pool, it hurts my eyes." Kirkwood turned and left the room. It might have made for an admirably contemptuous exit except for one unfortunate fact: he had forgotten his shoes. Red-faced, he walked back to the door to retrieve them. "A hand reached out," he recalled, "dropped them on the floor and the door closed."

Kirkwood decamped to the West Coast not long afterwards, although not to escape the ridicule of the New York acting fraternity. In recent years, the East Coast had begun to lose its status as the home of the small screen. Kirkwood later wrote, "I looked around to find all of television had moved to the land of paradox, enigma and ennui, California. Westward ho was the cry and I heeded it." Kirkwood's move was also motivated by other ambitions. "I think I thought I was going to be a movie star," he said.

He thought very wrong.

SEVEN

John Desmond might recall him being recognized in the street, Bob Cromling might recollect that he received adoring letters from the nation's housewives and the critics might have been enamored of his performances in *Welcome Darlings*, but in Hollywood James Kirkwood found that he couldn't get arrested.

According to a 1960 article by his journalist friend Whitney Bolton, Kirkwood arrived in California with a "handsome bundle of savings," with which he proceeded to buy "a little house above the Sunset Strip." He would be somewhat confined to that house. His first real prolonged period of unemployment was a situation with which Kirkwood found it rather difficult to deal. Though he was enjoying the California sun (he later spoke of having stayed around the pool a lot at this time) and though no doubt being in close proximity to his father was also a boon, he recalled "frustrating days spent driving from Fox to Warners to Screen Gems, to the agents' offices lining the Sunset Strip, feeling all the while like an entry in the livestock show at a county fair, not always a prize entry either."

Kirkwood said he obtained neither an agent nor a single day's work in his first six months in California. Finally, after dozens of auditions and interviews he signed with what he described as a "good" and "respected" agent who was "enthusiastic" about his abilities. The agent asked his new client to come to dinner the following Friday and to bring with him another of his clients, the actress and singer Patricia Morison. That Friday morning, he phoned his new agent to discuss the time of the dinner and mode of dress. The agent's houseman answered. Kirkwood could barely understand him because the houseman was in tears. A different voice came on the line, that of a policeman who proceeded to explain to Kirkwood that his agent had committed suicide that morning. "Now, when your agent kills himself — are they trying to tell you something?" wrote Kirkwood of the incident in *Playbill* magazine. After the recent jubilation of finding someone to represent him and notwithstanding that the agent had clearly been suffering problems more profound than his own, it must have been sickening for Kirkwood, particularly as it was yet another example of the kind of thing he had almost become used to: violent death unexpectedly bludgeoning its way into his life. If all this is true, that is. Newspaper reports of a suicide by Miss Morison's agent are not readily in evidence.

Because Kirkwood was liable to inject both myth-making and his wry, sometimes flippant, humor into his writing and interviews, it is difficult to disentangle truth from contrived anecdote or poetic juxtaposition of event in the sequence of what happened next in his life, which period ultimately led him to embark on his career as a novelist. For instance, following that "Are they trying to tell you something?" comment in *Playbill*, Kirkwood's next sentences are, "I decided to write a novel. And did." However, this decision seems from everything else he ever said and wrote about it to have been a more gradual thing.

He wrote in a 1972 *Playbill* article: "I got to thinking: a composer can compose, a writer can write, a painter can paint every day but an actor cannot give performances by himself without attracting unfavorable comment from friends and neighbors and a reputation for being a certified ding-a-ling. So there was the problem of why to get up in the morning." Kirkwood knew he couldn't compose or paint. "My handwriting was embarrassingly scruffy but I could always buy a type-writer. I did and that same day enrolled in a writing course at the UCLA. The first evening session was devoted to a lecture by our professor on the do's and don'ts." The foremost "don't," he was informed was, "Don't try to write a novel." Kirkwood continued, "I came close to wrapping myself around a telephone pole speeding home that night in order to slam a piece of paper in the typewriter and spell out: '*There Must Be a Pony!* — a Novel by James Kirkwood...'" It's a nice story but it doesn't quite gel with — even if it doesn't clearly contradict — the one above about how his agent's suicide was the immediate catalyst for his decision to write. It also itself doesn't correspond with occasions he wrote or verbally recalled that *There Must Be a Pony!* was started before he enrolled in the University of California writing course. For instance, this passage from a résumé circa 1968: "Despite all the work I'd done in New York on the stage, in nightclubs and on TV, it was like starting all over again on the West Coast...I was getting edgy to say the least. I decided I must do something with my time outside of waiting for the phone to ring, going on interviews, or lying on the beach letting the sun bore a hole through my brain...Finally I awakened one morning at 2.00 a.m. in a cold sweat and started right then to write a book about the experience I'd been through finding that body when I was twelve and the resulting trauma." Even the "I could always buy a type-writer" comment presents a problem: elsewhere he said that the typewriter was brought as part of his luggage in his move from New

York. We can assume that Kirkwood did indeed bring the typewriter with him over from the East Coast, simply because he was very specific when talking about it in an article for *Playbill* magazine, even despite the fact that this article — published in 1983 — was written from a greater distance from the events than was the '72 *Playbill* piece. In the '83 article, Kirkwood actually stated, "I began writing, oddly enough, because I fell I love with an electric typewriter while playing the son of *Valiant Lady*." Said machine belonged to the current writer of the show: "It was an imposing blue monster of an IBM and I asked permission once to try it out." Kirkwood merely used the typewriter to knock off a brief letter but "…I was so impressed by the heft of the thing and its raw striking power that, although I had no idea of becoming a writer, I zipped out a few days later and plunked down five hundred and some dollars for one of my own." Five hundred and some dollars was of course a staggering sum of money to spend on anything in the mid-1950s. Kirkwood: "Well I wasn't going to leave a typewriter that cost that much out on the street with an old mattress, a lamp and some unused kitty litter, so I dragged it out to la-la land." (As well as the fifty words per minute of which he was capable, according to Lomax Study's recollection, when he enlisted, Kirkwood went on at least one typing course in the Coast Guard.)

The story of getting out of bed at 2am to begin writing a novel was elaborated on by Kirkwood in a 1963 *Equity* interview feature. In this account, Kirkwood estimated the time as "about 3 a.m." and put a cinema superstar in the thick of the action. He said, "I remember it clearly because I started screaming. Liz Taylor, who lived down the hall from me at the Montecito, must have heard me because she came to see what was the matter, and I told her, 'I'm going to write a book'…So I got out of bed, unveiled a typewriter and started banging away." Leaving aside the discrepancies with other stories, it's not as unlikely a scenario as it might first appear: Taylor was someone with whom Kirkwood had a connection, if loose, throughout most of his life. Beckenstein: "He knew her when he was growing up in Hollywood and he had a very close friend, Arthur Loew Jr., who was dating Elizabeth Taylor." Taylor eventually ended up effectively playing Kirkwood's own mother when she appeared as Rita Cydney in the 1986 TV movie of *There Must Be a Pony!* (Taylor declined to be interviewed for this book on the grounds that it was her policy not to speak publicly about deceased friends.)

Muddying the waters a little more, Ron Plotkin says that Kirkwood's old comedy partner was a font of inspiration. "My recollection is that Jim started to write *There Must Be a Pony!* after he started the classes at

UCLA," says Plotkin. "He lived downstairs at Lee's [Goodman] house and Lee was a source of encouragement during this process." However, he does add, "This was before I met either of them so I am going on what I was told by Lee and Jim." Certainly, Goodman was to some extent in the picture. Speaking in the *Los Angeles Times* in 1976, Kirkwood said, "So I rented the lower portion of my old partner Lee Goodman's house and set up an office: I had decided to write a novel." (One wonders though what happened to the house Kirkwood was supposed to have bought.) Not necessarily contradicting any of the preceding, William Russo says that Kirkwood was inspired to write *Pony!* when he caught a television broadcast of the 1955 Hitchcock movie *The Trouble With Harry*, which begins with a boy discovering a body which his mother recognizes as her ex-husband, and suspected that it had been based on the Reid Russell affair.

One thing Kirkwood never changed his mind or gave contradictory details about was the downside of acting, much of which he hadn't seen in his career prior to his move to the West Coast. In a 1968 résumé, Kirkwood wrote of acting, "As much as I love the actual work, I despise the life of constant insecurity — more of not being able to practice and improve in your chosen craft during periods of inactivity between jobs. You can study in schools and with acting teachers for a century but you can learn only so much that way. One must be able to act with a certain amount of regularity, or else you stand still." He also said, "You are continually in the position of being allowed to work. There is a singular lack of dignity in the acting profession. You always have your hand out for a job."

Kirkwood reported in that *LA Times* interview that the reaction of people who knew him to his proposed career change was, "You're gonna *what*?!" In a 1987 college address he elaborated, "Almost all of my friends, even my close ones, greeted this news with utmost derision, with laughter, with comments like 'Look who's writing a novel.' 'Hey, you never even went to college, did you?' A few people even suggested they doubted I'd *read* a novel." Kirkwood said he was part of a Friday night poker game at the time and when asking for cards would find himself on the receiving end of witticisms like, "Ernest Hemingway wants a pair."

As people grow older — especially if they have become successful — once distressing scenarios tend to evolve in their brains into funny stories. Though Kirkwood made comparative light of this derision at a point in his life where it no longer mattered — i.e., when he had proven his mettle as a wordsmith — it possibly hurt him more than he let on at the time. He told the *Los Angeles Times* in 1976, "Never went to college. Always wished I had." Homer Price confirms that Kirkwood had a slight complex about not having attended university that lasted all his life. Kirkwood went on in that college address, "The more I heard that, the more determined I was to write my book…I used all that negativity as fuel in my tank. The more kidding, the more I got up every morning and faced those blank pages." A tone of bitterness is detectable in those comments even three decades removed from the events to which they refer. Kirkwood's revenge — and for all his qualities he was a man who exulted in revenge — might be considered to be the fact that in years to come his books would be taught on campuses. William Russo, one of the professors who taught Kirkwood's books, says, "I've met people who are in show business [with] very high IQs. He was incredibly bright and clever and I think he was doing very sophisticated things in his texts." Just about the only encouragement Kirkwood seems to have received in those early days of literary aspiration was Goodman's, which Plotkin summarizes as, "'What do you have to lose? Go ahead and do it.'"

To be fair to Kirkwood's skeptical friends, on the surface they may have looked right. Arthur Beckenstein says of Kirkwood, "Jimmy loved to snuggle in and read every night when he went to bed. He was a fast reader and would get through a book rather quickly. Jim read all sorts of books: fiction, non-fiction, psychology, self-help, etc. He was often raving about someone he had just discovered. He had a keen interest in meeting an author he enjoyed reading and picking his brain. In his home, he had an extensive library with a few thousand books he had read. His library was not lined with classics, though he had a fair share. He was unpretentious as a person and his reading tastes varied greatly. He read for his enjoyment and his curiosity about whatever." Yet though Kirkwood was a reader in the time Beckenstein knew him — and presumably was before that — he seems to have been a strangely indiscriminate one. Beckenstein is unable to provide the name of a single author of whose work Kirkwood was a devotee. Neither was any other friend of Kirkwood to whom this author spoke. Kirkwood also didn't have a writer's mien: his utterly extroverted and playful personality was not in keeping with the fairly studious manner that goes hand-in-hand with the role of novelist. Even Terrence McNally, the acclaimed playwright who would later become a good friend of his, says, "Jimmy seemed more to be someone in show business and entertainment than a novelist…We didn't talk about literature much. We talked about having fun and our friends and good meals and things to [do]."

However, Kirkwood was in possession of several of the things necessary to be a great writer. The first was that Raw Material frequently mentioned previously. Happy it may not have been for much of the time, but he truly had had an amazing and intriguing life. He had already found himself going through in his 34 years more trauma, heartbreak, elation, tragedy and unusual or noteworthy situations (domestic and professional) than most people might experience in literally half a dozen lifetimes. Kirkwood had a second pre-requisite for good writing. "He was a born storyteller," says Beckenstein. "He could tell a story and fascinate people."

Not that any of this was enough on its own. The adage "Everyone has a book in them" is as well-known as it is untrue. It overlooks the fact that while the raw material that might make for an interesting narrative resides in all human beings, the capability of regurgitating that material and then shaping it into readable prose emphatically does not. Meanwhile, the transcribed anecdotes of a man considered a good raconteur by his friends or dinner party companions would most certainly not make easy reading: on paper, their repetitions, grammatical errors, gaps in logic and trail-offs would be glaringly apparent in a way they would not when enjoying that person's physical company. There has to be a genuine ability to string a sentence together — and string strings of sentences together — while side-stepping phrases and sometimes words previously deployed and even close proximity of words that happen to rhyme. In addition, one has to possess the ability to carefully place and dovetail the incremental revelations and strands of event that make up a plot. Kirkwood, it transpired, had that way with written words.

Finally, Kirkwood had one other attribute that a great novelist needs. Good, natural-sounding speech patterns are as essential to a novel's greatness as compelling and slick prose. In a 1982 lecture, he explained that his ear for dialogue stemmed from his thespian years: "You've played a lot of parts and you've had a lot of lines to say and you can feel whether the dialogue is sayable or not, or if it's readable. Sometimes you read dialogue in novels and if you really stop and think about it, you say, 'No, people couldn't actually talk like that, or they'd be the head of Parliament, or they'd be the President.'" (He also mentioned in that lecture another benefit of his years as a thesp: "Actors tend to be very introspective at times and very observant because they're always looking at other people to see what they can snitch from them.")

Kirkwood had his pick of compelling raw material for his first novel. He could have opted to write the remarkable life story of his mother, the just-as-remarkable life story of his father, of his time at St. John's military school, his stints at Brewster Academy, his spell in a mental institution, his days dodging Kamikazes and U-boats on the *Admiral Mayo*, his squirt-gun stick up, his time as a soap opera star, his remarkable experiences in the theatre like the Tallulah Bankhead audition or the *Auntie Mame* firing or a host of other things that would make for interesting dramatic scenarios and narratives. Only someone who had lived the remarkable life that Kirkwood had could ignore all of these things to tell the story of the circumstances surrounding the death of Reid Russell.

Tallulah Bankhead was the inspiration for this decision. Like many others, she was highly impressed by his verbal storytelling skills. Kirkwood later said, "She would always try to get me to tell people about my discovery of the body of my mother's fiancé. She would never let me get away with telling a condensed version. And everyone always seemed fascinated to hear the story the way I was telling it." When he decided to write some sort of book, "Since that particular story had always gone over so well verbally, I figured that's where I should start."

"I'd always had a compulsion to tell of this bizarre event, of the effect it had on a young boy," Kirkwood said elsewhere. He also said, "The impetus for the novel had always been with me...I have always wanted to 'tell about' what happened, to explain what it felt like at that age to lead an entirely abnormal life and to have tragedy strike in one's own backyard..." Once he began — and his story of a rough first chapter emerging from him in a torrent of enthusiasm and therapeutic unburdening is a convincing one — he kept going. "The fever hit me immediately," he said. "I could hardly wait to awaken and get on with it. So it went, day by day, splashing out of me."

If he didn't apprehend it already, Kirkwood learned during the writing of *Pony* that no matter how naturalistic a writer's style, novels differ from real life in a very significant way: they require a second act. However interesting the Russell events would be to prospective readers, especially if well-rendered, those events would still leave them unsatisfied, for there had never been a proper resolution to them. If we are to assume they played no sinister part in his death, Kirkwood and his mother had never really found out why Russell did what he did. In story terms, this was a significant problem. Kirkwood could — and did — convincingly portray the circumstances leading up to and immediately following the discovery of Russell's body — including an element that was not even considered by the media as they engulfed Kirkwood's family, namely the fact that Kirkwood had lost a prospective stepfather of whom he was very fond — but he needed something in addition to that, a conclusion that would not leave the reader thinking that the piece of art he had just read had simply petered out. In the absence of a real-life ending, Kirkwood had to invent one. As Kirkwood put it, "*Pony* was certainly autobiographical, but heightened and imagined on."

The writing style Kirkwood employed for this book was one that had lately become fashionable: that of the colloquialism of the adolescent. This fashionability had started in 1951 with the publication of J D Salinger's novel *The Catcher in the Rye*. Rapidly anointed a modern classic, *The Catcher in the Rye* featured a first-person narrative that brilliantly conveyed the grammatical sloppiness and repetitiveness of an adolescent's speech patterns, thereby also helping to demonstrate teenagers' spiritual callowness and emotional vulnerability. At the same time, it was not as natural as it appeared. The speech patterns of Salinger's protagonist Holden Caulfield were nowhere near as repetitive or stop-start as they would be in reality, a necessary artistic license to sustain readability. An additional license is the fact that Salinger makes his character's internal dialogue — his thoughts — resemble his external dialogue — his speech — when the two are not necessarily the same, or even similar, at all (although some believe Caulfield's narrative is actually him speaking to a psychiatrist). Another book of the era that featured a teenage milieu and adolescent colloquialism (though not nearly so well-rendered) was *I'm Owen Harrison Harding* by James Whitfield Ellison, published in 1955. Ellison's stepson Nick would work as Kirkwood's editor in the seventies and Kirkwood revealed to him that he had read *I'm Owen Harrison Harding*, though it's not sure at which point in his life. Interestingly, in *Pony*, Kirkwood names the Ohio town in which the protagonist sometimes stays not Elyria but Ellison.

Asked in approximately 1979 by TV host Jim Whaley which author had influenced him most, Kirkwood said, "I suppose early on Salinger, because when I read *Catcher In The Rye*, I thought, 'Uh-oh, that sounds like the way I would write if I could write.'" Those who detect from that quote a certain competitiveness tempering Kirkwood's admiration for Salinger's artistic achievement would, judging by the recollection of William Russo, be correct. Kirkwood apparently felt almost as though he had been beaten to the punch. Russo, speaking without prompting about the issue, says, "I think he was taken aback by Salinger, maybe that was part of [his] inspiration: that if J D Salinger was writing in [a] James Kirkwood voice, then he ought to start writing it himself."

In *Pony*, Kirkwood actually made his fictional counterpart — whom he named Josh Cydney — fifteen, as opposed to the twelve he himself had been when he had made that horrific discovery in Manhattan Beach. His original intention had been to make Josh a seventeen-year-old narrator relating an experience that occurred to him at the age of thirteen, but he abandoned that plan following complications caused by him shedding much of his original plot.

The first-person point of view Kirkwood employed in *Pony* may have been simply a logical consequence of him writing about events in his own life but he stuck with it long-term, using the subjective narrative voice in all his novels except his last one. Kirkwood later explained, "I always tend to write in the first person because I think I have much more of a connection as far as telling a story to somebody than if you write in the third person. Then I feel like I'm telling it to one person." Whether it was accidental genius or literary *nous* that led him to adopt the writing method that best conveyed his yarn-spinning abilities, Kirkwood's prose style certainly had the immediacy and informality of conversation. Plotkin says, "Reading one of his books is like sitting in a room listening to him tell the story. That's what I loved about his books. And I told him that one time."

Despite the invented resolution and the tweaking with his counterpart's age, *Pony* was always destined to be fundamentally a novel drawn from Kirkwood's own life and by extension the lives of his loved ones. Chief among the latter, of course, was his mother. Not only would the book be bringing back extremely painful memories for Lila Lee, but it inevitably would not portray her in too great a light, what with its detailing of her penchant for feckless men and her dilettante attitude to parenthood. Kirkwood wasn't affected by many qualms about this as he wrote *Pony*. "I've never felt shy about using that material," he later said. "I know a lot of writers who have felt hesitant about exposing that part of their lives, but not me." One of the reasons in this instance is that a certain vindictiveness attended the early stages of the manuscript. "As a matter of fact, when I began the book it was out of anger at my mother," he later revealed. "*There Must Be a Pony!* was a harangue against my mother." He added here his frequently-aired parental grievance: "She should have had puppies or kittens, not a kid." However, his anger quickly dissipated: "After forty pages, I got bored with my anger…and it turned into a love letter to…her." Kirkwood began to apprehend Lee's own difficulties caused by, among other things, being a junior actress in the days before child labor laws: "I realized what a tragic, awful life she had had and I thought, 'My God, who am I to ring the bell on her?'" This led to a genuine breakthrough in Kirkwood's relationship with Lee. "For the first time I felt a real compassion and tenderness for her, as opposed to the obligatory love a son has to feel for his mother," he said.

Unfortunately, the book actually caused a slight setback in his relationship with his father. "My father was very offended by *There Must Be a Pony!*" Kirkwood revealed. "Mostly because I'd written a book about my mother and not about him." A counterpart for Kirkwood's real-life dad doesn't appear in the book at all. Josh's father is handily dismissed as a ne'er-do-well Canadian whom his mother married in wartime and whom he has not met in his sentient life, thus neatly jettisoning a problem Kirkwood had foreseen. As he put it, "My mother and father were both such incredibly colorful characters that I would never have been able, at that stage of my writing, to juggle the two in one book. I had to choose one, or else everything would have gone splat. And besides, nobody would have believed it anyway." The only truthful element in the scant details about the fictional father seems to be Josh's comment that he himself is a Catholic because his father wanted him to be one.

At some point in this process, Kirkwood decided that though he had storytelling and writing skills and raw material, in order to ramp up the effect of his efforts he should attend a writing class. Some prospective writers are resistant to such a course of action on the grounds that writing can't be taught but is a natural ability of which one is either in possession or not. Kirkwood, though, was not from a writing background and perhaps it is the fact that in the acting profession taking classes is standard that motivated his move. Initially, Kirkwood signed up for a course in an extension division of UCLA. He said he was utterly depressed by the first class, at which somebody stood up and proceeded to read a substantial list of all the things the students were not to write about. "It seemed to me the wrong way to go about writing," he recalled. "Luckily, someone told me about Robert Kirsch's creative writing seminar, so next week I transferred into it. My first question to him was: 'What can't you write about?' And I was elated when he said the question was irrelevant."

One of Kirkwood's classmates was Terry Kilburn, a former child actor "increasingly disenchanted" with acting. Kirsch was the *Los Angeles Times* book editor and critic and a novelist himself (sometimes under pseudonyms Robert Dundee and Robert Bancroft). "He had quite a reputation as a teacher and I felt lucky to get accepted into the class," says Kilburn, who calculates his enrollment as taking place in 1958. Kilburn and Kirkwood had actually known each other back in New York, first meeting, in Kilburn's estimation, in 1953 or '54. Of the fees for the class, Kilburn says, "It was minimal. UCLA, at that time, it's a state school and if you lived in Los Angeles…" Kirkwood later spoke in interviews of him and Kilburn being placed together in Kirsch's class, along with Anne Kramer, the wife of movie producer Stanley Kramer, because seating was arranged alphabetically. Also according to Kirkwood, the class was comprised of sixty to seventy pupils, took place once a week in the evening and lasted for three hours each time, with a coffee break. Like all those about which Kirkwood had enquired, Kirsch's course was not for novel writing but short story composition. Kirkwood later said, "Professor Kirsch said at the beginning, 'Don't anyone turn in part of a novel, you don't know how, it's a waste of your time and a waste of mine. I only want short stories.'" Kirkwood added, in a comment which reinforces the evidence that he had begun *Pony* before beginning to attend writing classes, "I, of course, went home and worked even harder on my novel…"

Kirkwood recalled that two students' work would be assessed at a time. It would be turned in one week, photocopied and passed out to the class the next and publicly evaluated by Kirsch the one after that. This type of examination of one's efforts would be nerve-wracking in the best of circumstances, but Kirsch did not take prisoners. "I was completely intimidated by Kirsch," Kirkwood said. "He would storm in every week like a football coach and slam this mysterious big black briefcase down on the desk and tear into everything everybody had written the week before — in a helpful way." When after two semesters it came Kirkwood's turn to hand in some writing, he was extremely nervous, not least because while the other student that week had submitted the customary two short stories, he had done what no student had before and defied Kirsch by submitting part of a novel — the first fifty pages of what would become *There Must Be a Pony!* "The night I was up at a bar I was so terrified, I stopped and had two Scotch-and-waters on the way to UCLA," Kirkwood said. "He arrived late for class, seemed to be highly agitated, paced around, slammed his briefcase on his desk, and announced, 'We will not have class the regular way tonight.' I thought: 'Oh-oh, I'm going to be a whipped in public.' He went on to say he didn't know why he taught this class; he said he made a good salary on the *LA Times* and did we realize 'the crap I'm forced to read week after simply week?'" Kirkwood's heart was now thumping in his throat. Kirsch continued, "But this week I suddenly realized why I teach: because every once in a blue moon someone turns in something so exciting, so original, so — I'm going to say it — brilliant, that it makes it all worthwhile. Now who in this class is named Kirkwood?"

Though he had been his tutor for two semesters, Kirkwood claimed that Kirsch had failed thus far to learn his name, despite the fact that pupils were seated alphabetically and despite learning the names of Kilburn and Kramer. When Kirkwood would raise his hand to comment on someone's work, Kirsch would nod in his direction and say, "Um-hmnnn — you." This evening would embed itself irrevocably into Kirkwood's memory as much as, now, his name would be indelibly imprinted on Kirsch's brain. "I was elated," Kirkwood recalled. "I just floated while he read from *There Must Be a Pony!* and discussed what I had done. It was the most exciting night of my life."

The excitement, though, wasn't merely due to Kirsch's praise, ego-gratifying though that was. Kirkwood, as requested, went to see Kirsch during the class coffee break. The two shook hands. Kirsch said he hoped Kirkwood didn't mind but he'd shown the writing to his wife. His wife "loved it too." Kirsch invited Kirkwood back to his house after class, where he met said wife and had a drink. Kirsch wanted to know how much more Kirkwood had written of the book. The answer was about 200 pages (although Kirkwood's estimation varied slightly with recountings of the conversation). According to Kirkwood, Kirsch also asked the surely unnecessary question if he wanted to have it published when it was finished. Additionally, he asked if Kirkwood had an agent. When his pupil revealed that he hadn't, Kirsch said he would be happy to send it to his own agent and to his publisher, Little, Brown. "I was more flattered by this suggestion than filled with any hope of publication," Kirkwood said.

All of this sounds like classic Kirkwoodian myth-making, but Kilburn says, "I do remember that" of the I–suddenly-realized-why-I-teach incident. The only spin committed seems to be in the form of Kirkwood slightly truncating events. Says Kilburn of his and Kirkwood's tutelage under Kirsch, "We were both invited at the end of the first semester to join his advanced class, and that was quite an honor and it was during that time that he was working on *There Must Be a Pony!*" Kirkwood never mentioned this select class (which Kilburn recalls as about fifteen-strong) in his reminiscences. Kilburn also says, "The advanced class was not necessarily just short stories," thus calling slightly into question Kirkwood's boasting of a maverick disregard for a no-novels edict. Kirkwood and anyone else, of course, would only have been invited into the advanced class if their work had impressed the tutor, so the suggestion in Kirkwood's anecdotes that the section of *Pony* that made Kirsch realize why he taught was the first piece of his writing the tutor had seen cannot be true if Kilburn is remembering correctly. One thing seems not in doubt, though. Kilburn: "Jimmy was the star pupil." He adds, "Bob Kirsch was very, very encouraging to both of us, actually, but more so to Jimmy…advising him and repeating many, many times, 'Write about your own experience, write about what you know'…Jimmy liked working with him a lot and felt very encouraged." Describing Kirkwood as a "born writer," Kilburn says, "He was always so witty that it didn't surprise me. I thought right from the beginning that he would probably follow through. The value of taking that class for me was that I found that I'm not a writer."

Kirsch's approval was a piece of good news that would have been welcome for Kirkwood in any circumstances, but was particularly so now. In early August 1958, his mother was involved in a terrible accident in her Manhattan apartment. As told by Whitney Bolton in his syndicated column, Lila Lee was steaming some velvet garments when she fainted and fell into a tub of near-boiling water. In the hour before she regained consciousness, awful damage was done to her body. She pulled herself from the bath in agony to ring her doctor. The doctor turned out to be away for the weekend. Lee fainted again and was alone for a full day before being discovered. Joan Kirkwood Thompson reveals a detail about Lee's accident that would seem to have been discreetly omitted by Bolton: "She was drunk."

Kirkwood flew back across the country. "When he went to see her in the hospital, he didn't recognize her," says Joan. After what Bolton estimated were "weeks" in hospital, Lee travelled to Ohio to be nursed by her sister Peggy. Kilburn says of the accident, "I do remember talking with him about that and how concerned he was for his mother." Kilburn was yet another person who noticed there was something "off" about Kirkwood's childhood recollections. "I got the feeling that he had a very sort of sadness about his parents," he says. "Whenever he spoke about his mother, it was always with a slight melancholy tinge. He didn't talk about her making cookies or cooking his favorite dinner or anything like that."

As a consequence of being championed by Kirsch, Kirkwood signed terms with literary agent Phyllis Jackson of MCA Artists Ltd, who remained his book agent until her death in 1977. On February 13, 1959, Jackson sent Kirkwood a letter in which she reminded him that they had previously met in the Barberry Room when he arrived to pick up his mother. She wrote, "At that time, I thought of you as an actor. Now, after reading the first 150 pages of THERE MUST BE A PONY, I think of you as a writer. You very definitely are that, Jim. The manuscript shows far more than promise. It has some fine writing and excellent character delineations. I have only a few minor reservations, but I won't go into that now for the simple reason that it isn't fair to talk about changes, cuts and possible reconstruction of some of the parts until I have read it all. I did want to get word to you quickly and to tell you how pleased I am to be representing you on this project. Hurry and get the rest of the book to me for personal as well as business reasons. I simply must know how it all works out."

"I am pleased to know that you are pleased," wrote Kirkwood in his reply, dated February 18, 1959. "I am working away as fast as I can to finish the book. Unless I am deluged with acting jobs and family problems I should have it completed in about two months. Bob mentioned Little Brown & Co. and the possibility of an advance from them in the event they were interested in it. At this particular point in my financial life this would be most welcome."

However, though Kirkwood was excited about the turn of events and the possibility of an injection of capital on the horizon, he didn't get carried away. With his head clearly screwed firmly on, if exhibiting a first-time writer's naiveté, he continued, "What I am writing is very close and dear to me and cliché: something I've felt for a long time I had to get out of me! However, in the event I never write another thing, I would like it to be as commercially rewarding as possible. Therefore I would want a publisher, if one wants me, to be of a mind to exploit and publicize the book with endless amounts of money and energy. If a publisher didn't feel that strongly about it I would rather look elsewhere. I would also prefer to retain all other rights outside of the original novel rights."

On March 9, 1959, less than a month after her original letter, Jackson sent Kirkwood a Western Union telegram reading, "LITTLE BROWN OFFERING CONTRACT SEVEN HUNDRED FIFTY DOLLARS NOW ANOTHER SEVEN FIFTY ON COMPLETION. LETTER FOLLOWING. CONGRATULATIONS." Kirkwood later said of the telegram, "I was struck dumb with joy." He replied to Jackson on the 12th. Although he said, "I'm very excited and will pound on my typewriter every day, faithfully," he was still anxious about what he felt might be his one and only literary excursion making a sufficient splash. He wrote, "There is one thing I would like to be sure of. And that is the fact that we have some agreement as to the amount Little, Brown & Co will allot for publicity and exploitation. I feel very strongly about this and hope you will be able to work something out along this line." Additionally, he took pains to point out that he already had an idea for the not-yet-completed book's front cover. Kirkwood also revealed that he was even anxious that his forthcoming advance might jeopardize his qualification for the $40 per week California State Unemployment he drew when he was between roles.

Kirkwood recalled that at this juncture, bizarrely, his résumé suddenly began finding favor with Californian casting directors and just as he was moving on from acting, he started being offered roles. At first, he was happy with this situation. Most first-time novelists, after all, are either squeezing in writing in a schedule dominated by a day-job or else are subsisting on the pittance that part-time employment generates. Kirkwood recalled that in this period he was, "…appearing in most of the filmed series being shot in Hollywood." *G.E. Summer Theatre, Kraft Theatre, Odyssey, Perry Mason, Day in Court, December Bride, I-Spy, Alfred Hitchcock Presents, One Step Beyond, Phillip Marlowe, Lock-Up, Studio One, This Man Dawson, Shotgun Slade, Accused, Verdict Is Yours* and *Court-Martial* were just some of the television programs that Kirkwood now became entitled to feature on his résumés. Ironically, however, he began to feel less and less inclined to send those résumés out: so much acting meant he was only able to work on his manuscript when he had a few days off. He felt he wasn't devoting as much attention to his developing narrative as it needed. He also felt he wasn't even giving his best to his acting. It being the case that the first instinct for a jobbing actor is to bite off the hand of anyone offering him a role, initially Kirkwood was torn. "It's a miserable task for an actor to turn down work," he later said. He recalled he felt compelled to remove himself from temptation's way and relocated from California to a ranch in Imado, Arizona, near the Mexican border, where he was in the vicinity of only a gas station, a general store and post office, numerous cows and no thespian activity whatsoever.

Though his acting career would be revived, by necessity, in the early 1960s and, for fun only, the 1980s, it was something of the end of a chapter in Kirkwood's life. He would later sum up that chapter by saying, "I always worked but I never got that part that would have made people say, 'My God, look what he can do.'" Some might unkindly suggest (and Kirkwood, as previously detailed, hinted himself) that what he could do was not particularly extraordinary. However, for *Valiant Lady* staffer Patti Goldstein, Kirkwood — whatever his later success with prose — was always a thespian dabbling in writing. "You're an actor, you're an actor, and that's it," she says. "[It] doesn't matter whether he had a role or he didn't have a role. You never stop. [Theatre] really was the essence of him. What happened to him afterwards or how he transmuted it or transmigrated his soul or whatever — that's swell. But basically, get down to it, scratch the surface, you have an actor." Terrence McNally offers similar comments: "He loved acting. He was thrilled when he got the part of a moderator in that Joan Crawford movie, *Mommie Dearest* [1981]. He was so excited. Some people say, 'Once an actor always an actor.' He always, I thought, would have given everything up to be in a play."

"I worked night and day in a trance-like state," Kirkwood said of his manuscript. "Until I finally looked at the number on top of a page and found it to be 893." Kirkwood contacted Little, Brown to see whether the word limit in his contract was negotiable and found it wasn't. He then had to settle down to cutting, something many writers find more difficult than the business of writing itself, it involving the jettisoning of scenes, dialogue and clever phrases over which the author has labored and with which he has previously been pleased, something especially difficult if the deletion is required not because of any intrinsic fault but simply because something has to go in order to make the published book's page count cost-effective. Even dispensing with sub-standard or repetitious prose can be painful, it rarely being easy to cut one's losses on material originally felt worthwhile. However, the main reason that *There Must Be a Pony!* changed considerably — massively even — before it reached print is because Kirkwood ultimately turned it into two separate novels.

Initially, main character Josh was writing his narrative as a sequence of letters from a prison cell where he was being held for the murder of his headmaster at his prep school. The prep school was a thinly disguised Brewster Academy and the story took in the death of the protagonist's best friend there (whom Kirkwood at this point was calling Ted). The tumultuous events surrounding the death of the fictionalized Reid Russell occurred prior to the Brewster section, when Josh was four years younger. When he had written around 250 (not 893) pages, however, Kirkwood stalled. In an undated letter to his editors at Little, Brown, he said, "A copy of your letter arrived yesterday and the timing couldn't have been better. I had reached a point of not writing during the last week. I felt something was wrong and I knew way down deep inside of me that it was undoubtedly because I had bit off too much for my typewriter to chew up. Although I have always had the end in mind which I outlined to you, during the last few weeks I had begun to think, myself, that maybe the book should only be about Ben, Josh, Rita, and the effect on them of Ben's death. That maybe going on to the other story is another book entirely. Your suggestion confirmed my doubts."

In his letter, Kirkwood revealed what he thought to be a solution to his artistic impasse. Instead of having Josh murder his headmaster, he would have him assault him when trying to run away to be with friends of Rita, his mother, currently in a mental institution after a breakdown caused by the strain of the investigation into the death of Ben, the fictional counterpart of Reid Russell. Kirkwood actually wrote a detailed outline of what would happen following the death of Ben but decided not to show it to Little, Brown ("I would rather just go ahead and do it. I think it will work out fine"). The outline included time spent in Ohio following his mother's breakdown in which Josh was unhappy due to an alcoholic, bigoted uncle.

This rethinking of the plot necessitated some significant changes to the narrative style. Now that Josh was no longer being held on a murder charge, Kirkwood felt it wouldn't be suitable for the narrative to consist of his letters to his lawyer. He added, "I don't want him to tell it to a psychiatrist because (chemically) enough of everybody always blabbing everything to THEM. Also, and mainly, he is able to cope with his situation, although the time may be near when he cannot. I would like to avoid making him the typical, crazy, mixed-up kid. In spite of the fact that he has every reason to be." (Kirkwood could have added that telling the story to a psychiatrist — which from his words sounds like it might be a suggestion by his publisher — would have made it just too similar to *The Catcher in The Rye*, if you accept the fairly widely-held belief that Holden Caulfield is speaking from an analyst's couch.) Additionally, Kirkwood had decided to shorten the timeline. "As it is now he's a seventeen year old boy telling of an experience that happened when he was thirteen," he wrote. "The way that I've figured it out now, in my mind, he will be telling of the Ben story approximately a year after it happened. I believe there cannot be a time lapse of four or five years without an awful lot of filling in. Too, one year makes it more compelling. So I will have Josh be fifteen, nearly sixteen, when Ben's death occurs. I don't think a boy thirteen would be conversant enough with the language to enable him to relate a story that could possibly turn into a 350 page book, Ann [sic] Frank's Diary not-withstanding."

Kirkwood concluded, "I shall work like a demon now that I have made up my mind where I'm going. At this point Josh is just about to find the [suicide] notes. His mother's breakdown follows within a month or so. Then to Ohio. Thence on to New Hampshire and Brewster Academy where I spent two years. The end. Hope this meets with your general ideas. Of course, I will be ready and willing to work on any suggested changes after I have completed the first draft."

However, though both Kirkwood and his publishers had clearly and independently reached the conclusion that the novel as it was progressing was not working, there were still huge changes to come, if not to the manuscript as it was then Kirkwood's plans for it. Those familiar with Kirkwood's *oeuvre* will recognize from the above plan that the parts that don't revolve around the Reid/Ben death and its immediate aftermath are largely elements of the story that would constitute his second published novel, *Good Times/Bad Times*. In other words, he went further than what he mused in the letter about making some of the second part of the manuscript another book and lopped off the Ohio/New Hampshire parts of the story completely. Either way, it's noteworthy that only someone who had experienced Kirkwood's incident-packed adolescence would be able to get two substantial books out of it.

Perhaps Kirkwood did actually write, not merely plan, the Ohio and New Hampshire sections. Certainly, in January 1960, correspondence shows that he was still being asked to make cuts by Little, Brown, and this despite having already eliminated approximately 100 pages from the first draft of his own volition. At this point, he was informed by his editor that the book needed to be shortened by around 5,000 words in order to facilitate a cover price of $3.50. In addition, his editor had suggested eliminating risqué words and passages to make it more suitable for magazine serialization. Also — although Kirkwood admitted that he might have "made this up" — all of this was to be done in nine days or less. Kirkwood was distraught, partly because he was under the impression that the editor had told him when they'd last met that he couldn't see how the book could be cut further without harming it. Kirkwood's letter to his editor, dated January 30, 1960, was strong stuff, as can be gleaned from these extracts: "It's bad enough to be awakened out of a sick, sweaty, 103 degree temperature sleep for any phone call — let alone one from you regards further cutting of my child…I am upset…I can't believe if the book is as good as we all hope that 50 cents is going to be its downfall… I firmly believe that any more major trimming will damage the book considerably…I hate to think of altering the book for reading purposes to the tastes of people at whom I would only want to *throw* the book…If I feel I want to write for magazines then I will aim my writing so that it will fall within the margins of what they feel they can print…You must admit that this further idea of cutting springs not from artistic reasons but rather to achieve a desired result in the cost of the book…" Kirkwood then engaged in what can only be described as brinkmanship, threatening to withdraw the manuscript from Little, Brown completely: "*There Must Be A Pony!* is very near and dear and close and personal to me and when it comes to pounding it in shape to fit certain standards and costs as one would in marketing a lamp, a bottle of cologne or a shirt — then I become upset, dismayed, disillusioned and come near to the conclusion that maybe the main thing was to have written the book as honestly and as well as I was able. And that if it turns out that it is not feasible to produce it for others to read — that is unfortunate but maybe a fact…I hope I am not going to be forced into a cooling off period." Kirkwood even signed the letter "Yours, at the moment." He also added a sarcastic postscript: "Maybe it will help if we shorten the title, too."

A couple of days later, Kirkwood sent a letter to Phyllis Jackson, enclosing a copy of his letter to Little, Brown. Jackson was in London at the time, something that no doubt added to his slightly frenzied state of mind: an agent can act as a valuable buffer between author and publisher and soother of artistic temperaments. Kirkwood was angry that Jackson had left the country without telling him of his publisher's latest intentions ("I broke an ashtray," he revealed). He wrote, "It would be a shame to set back the publishing date, but I wouldn't be surprised if that happens. If we come to a real stand-off — what are my rights, I wonder?" In this letter Kirkwood also revealed that he had been introduced to the film director Alan Pakula by friend Stewart Stern and that Pakula, having read the manuscript of *Pony*, was "terribly enthusiastic" about making a motion picture of it.

Judging by the fact that Kirkwood was able to send galleys to his mother of what was presumably the final version of the manuscript on April 6 that year (there seems little reason for him to wait two months and then send her an out-of-date version), it would seem that the whole issue had been resolved by then. The Little, Brown first edition of *There Must Be a Pony!* came in at 311 pages. The fact that its price was $4 rather than the $3.50 that had been discussed suggested that this was Kirkwood's preferred page count and that the dispute with his publishers had been resolved by the publisher backing down.

As well as his mother, Kirkwood allowed other eyes to see the manuscript before it went into print, possibly before it went to the publisher. Lomax Study — who was living near him in California — recalls Kirkwood getting a second opinion from Study's mother-in-law. Study: "She typed like terrifically, so Jimmy asked her if she wanted to look the script over and maybe do a little revising or changing and when she read the whole thing she was shocked because of the language and so forth [laughs]. But she typed out a bunch of things for him. Of course he could have done that himself, but he was just anxious to hear what somebody else thought of it. I never read any of it then, don't ask me why."

As for the other opinion Kirkwood canvassed before print, that of the woman whose partial biography *There Must Be a Pony!* effectively constituted, he said, "I sent my mother the galleys for *There Must Be a Pony!* because I thought she ought to read them, just in case there was anything that might offend her. I was really nervous waiting for her reaction." Part of the letter he enclosed read, "I am finally getting off a set of galleys to you in the mail today. Of course, I am dying for you to read it. I will say nothing about it (except one thing) because the book will speak for itself. Only know that the character of the mother, although certainly based on you, is not actually you. When I first started writing the book I believe I was worried about how the character might appear in print, about what comment I was making on the mother. Now, I am not worried. Everyone that has read the book loves the mother, is sympathetic toward her, and roots for her. As, in the book, her son does without fail throughout. She is his only concern. Mainly, I hope you will read the book for entertainment, in spite of having lived through parts of it in life. I believe it is highly fictionalized. Certainly it contains no message (except HOPE) and it was written solely to provide a reading experience. Most of all, I hope you enjoy it, like it and, of course, will want to recommend it to strangers in super markets, standing on street corners, and taxi drivers, stray cats and dogs and all our friends. Naturally, I want your honest opinion. We will still be friends no matter how you feel about it."

Kirkwood later recalled the telephone call in which his mother gave her verdict: "I had three lighted cigarettes there — one in my mouth and one in each hand. She said it made her laugh and it made her cry. And then she said, 'Jimmy, the boy is you. You've just written yourself perfectly. And the character of 'The Mother' is very well-written, too.' Now, that just tickled the hell out of me. The boy was me, but the character of the mother was well-written. She wasn't offended at all until some of her lady friends began saying things like, 'How could Jimmy do a thing like this?' But what they ignored was the fact that the boy had great empathy and love for his mother."

There Must Be a Pony! was published by Little, Brown on September 6, 1960, as a hardcover. Unlike all Kirkwood's subsequent works, it was not credited to "James Kirkwood" but to "Jim Kirkwood" to avoid confusion with his father. (His father died before publication of his second work, the play *UTBU*.) *Pony* was dedicated to "Lila Lee and James Kirkwood Sr. — with love and shingles." The latter phrase seems to be a reference to a Kirkwood comedy sketch called "Love and Thimbles Petered."

The first sentence of *Pony!* lends one to believe that we are about to embark on a journey into *Catcher In The Rye*-type teenage colloquialism and conversationalism: "If you want to know the truth — it just about kills me to go over the whole thing." At this stage of his career, though, Kirkwood was no Salinger. Although Kirkwood's first-person narrator

Josh Cydney uses a discursive style, at least in the beginning, which does resemble the disordered, rambling mind of the adolescent and although he does occasionally pay lip service to a direct, formal address to the reader ("I don't think I've told you about her two other marriages"), the prose drifts toward a conventional narrative rather quickly, and furthermore an inappropriately conventional narrative. Josh uses words that simply do not sit convincingly in the mouth of a fifteen-year-old ("promontory," "vacillated," "*bon mots*"). Also jarring is the employment of literary sentences like, "There was an unmistakable elegance about her" and "For the first time in my life I felt like a real person instead of some little furry woodland creature that was scared of its own shadow." Meanwhile, a line of dialogue from a girl of around thirteen — "May both my parents — and my grandparents — be run over by the longest, heaviest freight train in existence if I divulge one syllable!" — is the kind of speech that no adult, let alone child, would be heard enunciating outside of the set of a bad soap opera.

Not that Kirkwood has forgotten what it is like to be a child. When Josh begins to idolize his mother's beau Ben Nichols and perceive him as a surrogate father, it is a genuinely moving section which will provoke dormant memories for every reader about unconditional childhood worship of glamorous adult relatives or family friends. A similar verisimilitude — for men, anyway — is attached to Josh's anxiety about being considered a "sissy."

Kirkwood's decision to make his fictional counterpart fifteen instead of the twelve he was when the Russell suicide occurred means that certain aspects of Josh's behavior — his hero worship of Ben, his lack of rebelliousness — strike one as being unusually innocent for a kid of his age, but it is nonetheless still plausible, even despite the fact that the era has been updated: although the year in which the story takes place is not specified, the narrative mentions that Nixon is foreign minister — by which is presumably meant Vice President — which would place events between 1952-1960.

There are a couple of pieces of what would come to be vintage Kirkwood. Chapter eight features a laugh-out-loud moment arising from classic observation prowess when Josh sits next to a boy on a school bus who proceeds to exasperate him by insisting he can swim in a pool but not in an ocean and asking him the nonsensical question, "Do *they* have sharks in the ocean?" Overall, though, the moments of twinkle-eyed zest that would characterize Kirkwood's three middle novels are few and far between. What is most remarkable about *Pony* is how Kirkwood fails to make gripping prose out of what is superb subject matter. The scene where Josh finds Ben's body is well-done and eerie (albeit very slightly undermined by an unnecessary foreboding) but things rather sag after that. The scenes at the house after the arrival of friends and the police following the discovery of the body are almost boring, while the crucial chapter eighteen, in which suspicions start to be aroused about whether Ben Nichols' death was in fact suicide, leading to Rita Cydney being suspected of murder, is actually slightly soporific.

In chapter 26, Josh says despairingly of Ben's death, "There had to be some explanation for what happened. It couldn't go on being a mystery for the rest of our lives." As mentioned previously, in reality it did, but Kirkwood's fictional resolution is ingenious. Josh checks out the space beneath a loose newel post — a hiding place of which Ben and Josh are aware but Rita isn't — and there discovers two suicide notes, one to his mother, one to Josh. In them, Nichols admits he is unable to find a way out of his complicated personal life (it has been posthumously exposed that he had a wife of whom Rita and Josh had not been aware). Rita Cydney is off the hook, while also gaining a certain emotional closure. The note to Josh tells the parable of a boy who is such an eternal optimist that when gifted a bag of horse manure for his birthday by his psychiatrist father in an experiment, he starts digging at it with the cry, "I figure with all this horse shit — there must be a pony!" (The profanity was daring for the era.) Ben's note advises Josh to hunt for the pony he himself could never quite locate.

The book ends — as did, to a greater or lesser degree, all Kirkwood fiction — on a determinedly optimistic note. Josh makes a pledge that he'll keep looking for the pony: "When you really figure it out — that's the only way to go on living." This passage is again what would come to be vintage Kirkwood and is genuinely endearing, but a pleasing finale can't disguise the fact that *Pony* is a slight and overrated work.

The most interesting elements of the book for a Kirkwood aficionado are the insights it affords into the author's own life. Like so many first novels, at times it is almost sheer autobiography. Kirkwood later said of the way Josh/Kirkwood is depicted discovering Ben's/Reid's body, "… it's exactly what happened." *Pony* helps make Lila Lee's traumas real rather than the bland stuff of newspaper reportage, with passages like, "Although she's a movie star, she hasn't made a real picture — I mean a good one — in about a century. Some people call her a 'has-been,' but she's only forty-one years old. What they don't realize is she was practically a kid when she started." Following Ben's suicide, Josh remarks of his mother, "After all the misery she'd been through in her life — now this!" Josh makes a comment about his sensitive face that puts one in mind of John Desmond's observation about why Kirkwood seemed to be able to get away with his foul language: "It's this sensitive face that makes me talk the way I do sometimes…when you look one way and talk another it has a certain shock value." There are more playful autobiographical nods. In chapter twenty, Kirkwood gives one character the name of his *Valiant Lady* alter-ego Mickey Emerson. Not only does he give Ben the married surname of his cousin Lila Lee Nichols, but the latter observes, "He used a lot of names from Elyria. The football coach's name was Clymer and he used his name in the book. "

Pony begins a tradition in Kirkwood books in the way the author alludes to his homosexuality but in a rather awkward and confused way. Though Josh is depicted as straight, he is, as John Desmond might term it, straight with a lot of curves. Josh is considered a sissy by his mother's pre-Ben boyfriend Lee. Josh observes, "You turn out that way because the only men you're ever exposed to are such big-mouthed, crude, ball-clankers that you automatically don't want to be like them. You don't want to be like a woman but you don't want to be like them either. So you just sort of remain in a void for a while until you figure out what the hell the score is." Josh also reveals, "I've also been exposed to a lot of weird stuff because of the way I look. I mean if there's a *bona fide* homosexual within a thousand miles, you can bet he'll find me and make a pass." Meanwhile, one of the book's central characters is a screenwriter called Merwin who refers to everybody as "sweetie." "He's really very effeminate but somehow it doesn't bother people because he's so completely effeminate that what can you do?" says Josh, He adds, "And thank God he never runs around with a lot of other effeminate people. It's miserable when they travel in packs."

Anyone reading all this would assume that Kirkwood in real life was a.) not gay and b.) had a slight antipathy toward gays, or at least camp ones (or at least camp ones who traveled in packs). None of this of course necessarily made Kirkwood a hypocrite: this is a work of fiction and it is his job to portray characters and tell a story, not espouse his own views on every subject touched on in the text. There is also the possibility that Kirkwood was actually accurately reflecting his own feelings about homosexuality at Josh's age: it's not unusual for fifteen-year-olds to feel queasy about homosexuality — even the ones who are beginning to suspect they might be gay themselves. Nonetheless, these were the first signs of a difficulty Kirkwood would create for himself in his fiction: he clearly wanted to refer to homosexuality, but felt unable to address it in a direct or sometimes even non-pejorative way.

There Must Be a Pony! was previewed in the June 1960 edition of *Library Journal*, wherein Kirkwood said, "I hope I have written a story about several specific people as opposed to a book with a message in it. I will be gratified if people are moved, feel sympathy for the main characters, experience suspense, are made to laugh at times and brought close to tears at others." "Wouldn't we all?" most writers might be forgiven for retorting to these banalities, but there were some interesting revelations further on in the piece. "Any day in which I am kept from writing for reasons beyond my control is a miserable day," Kirkwood said. "An unfulfilled day. It's not even a day; it's half a day. So maybe I have been hit by this fever. I certainly hope so. Because with all its occupational miseries, writing leaves me with a sense of satisfaction that cannot be duplicated. I think I am hooked!" The article also disclosed, "He types standing up: 'Then I can pace around easier.'" The article added that Kirkwood was working on a dramatization of *Pony* and that he wrote every day in his Los Angeles domicile.

Interestingly, right below this *Library Journal* piece was an item on James Leo Herlihy. Herlihy was also just about to have his own debut novel — *All Fall Down* — published (although Herlihy was already an established playwright and short story writer — and indeed revealed in the piece that he had written several other novels which he would not allow to be published because he was dissatisfied with them). It was absolutely fitting that Herlihy and Kirkwood should feature in adjacent profiles. The two would be friends throughout the rest of Kirkwood's life. According to William Russo, the two men met through Tallulah Bankhead, who optioned Herlihy's play *Crazy October* at around the same time as Kirkwood and Bankhead were appearing in *Welcome Darlings* together. Some of the similarities between the pair were quite uncanny. As well as both having connections to Bankhead, they were both actors-turned-writers and the debut novels of both featured teenaged protagonists (indeed, one wonders whether one might have inspired the other to begin his). They also both had sexual relationships with men. As with the friendships of many gay men, it was not a platonic relationship but neither was it one in which they could be defined as an "item." Inevitably, they would one day collaborate, though the combination of two of the finest writers of their generation was not to produce the joint *meisterwerk* one might assume. Mutual friends referred to them as "Jamie" (Herlihy) and "Jimmy" (almost nobody seems to have addressed Kirkwood by his preferred "Jim").

The alliteration of the phrase "Jamie and Jimmy" frequently heard from their friends only serves to heighten the idea of them as two parts of a whole or of bookends.

Fortunately for the new writing career on which Kirkwood was so hooked, *There Must Be a Pony!* actually got better reviews than it merited, not least the one provided by Robert Kirsch for the *Los Angeles Times*. That Kirsch was reviewing a book he had seen at such an early stage and helped into print was sort of inevitable, but that doesn't quite make it right. One doesn't have to be too much of a curmudgeon to question the propriety of somebody passing public judgment on a book that he has partly molded (unless we are to make the illogical assumption that Kirkwood employed none of the technique in which he had been instructed in Kirsch's class) and whose slating might offend people to whom he is close (Kirsch's own publisher, his own agent, his own wife and of course Kirkwood himself) and potentially call into question his own skills as a writing tutor (although Kirsch doesn't mention he taught Kirkwood and had an intimate involvement with the novel — another eyebrow-raising matter in itself). Nonetheless, Kirsch was not alone in pouring praise on *Pony* so it would be unfair to dismiss his review. "*There Must Be a Pony!* by James Kirkwood Jr. is far and away the best first novel of the year" was how Kirsch's critique started. (Actually, Herlihy's first novel — for one — was better.) He found it "…filled with compassion and a depth of feeling, yet never self-pitying or maudlin." He quickly addressed the comparisons that would predictably be made between Kirkwood and Salinger: "…there are some superficial resemblances between his work and *Catcher in the Rye*…I venture to say that in many ways *There Must Be a Pony!* is a better novel. Not only does it give us access to the mind and experience of a young boy facing the battering rites of passage, but it goes deeper into motivation and forces and it illuminates a theme never stated or implied in Salinger's work…The youth faces not only the injustice of his own experience but an injustice deepened by the essential persecution of authority." Fair enough, but when Kirsch says of this slight novel with a glitzy backdrop and often superficial and vain characters, "These are not ordinary people in ordinary circumstances: these are characters out of Kafka or Proust," he is blowing smoke up the reader's backside.

The New York Times said of *Pony*, "Vigorous, sensitive, compelling. It makes the step to that area of universality which is at the core of all great fiction." The *Los Angeles Examiner* asserted it was "an unusual and compelling book, can easily be called exceptional." In the UK where it was published in 1961, *The Observer* (a national Sunday paper) said, "The boy's narrative is brilliant; the dialogue has an electric sparkle; there is no taint of the meretricious…Mr. Kirkwood has constructed his novel with the greatest skill and justifies every step in his moving drama."

Somewhat less gushing superlatives were forthcoming from Kirkwood's father. So upset was Kirkwood by his dad's nebulous, disinterested praise and his disinclination to discuss his novel that he banged out a quite extraordinary letter to him that started out complaining about this but ended up seeming to bring forth all of Kirkwood's frustrations about his father's faults as both parent and human being:

Dear Father,

I just think you ought to know how terribly disappointed I was with you. Of course I suppose I was a fool to expect anything but your usual vague reaction. But to shrug off a book that has taken your son two years to write, that I have poured everything into, with one of your charming words "glorious," and then only after you have been pumped for it — is really a little discouraging.

And as if that weren't bad enough — when you knew I was upset about it you still showed not the slightest interest in discussing it with me.

Or do you think it is abnormal of me or too demanding to hope that my own father might spend five or ten or, yes, maybe even a half hour talking about the book? About what he liked or didn't like or remembered or anything about it for Christ's sake!

Of course, you've never really given a damn for people's feelings — if it meant you had to do anything about them, if it meant making an effort. It's just too bad that you can't turn all this marvelous energy in religion you've suddenly acquired toward people that are close to you.

If this hurts you I am sorry, but you have hurt me and I can't let it go by unspoken. I only hope the book makes some money as others think it will so I can help you toward a few comfortable years.

[Signed: Jim]

Arthur Beckenstein found this letter amongst Kirkwood's papers. As did many in pre-computer days, Kirkwood made carbon copies of his typewritten letters. There is no way of knowing whether in this instance Kirkwood sent the letter and kept a copy or whether he lost his nerve and didn't send it or whether he simply wrote the letter as a form of catharsis with no intention of putting it in the mail, but the fact that Kirkwood seems to have kept copies of all his dispatched correspondence makes it likely that he did send it. The letter exhibits amazing bitterness and, if indeed it was received by its addressee, must have been a very uncomfortable read for Kirkwood Sr.

Of course, Kirkwood Sr.'s reticence about the book becomes understandable when considering the dubious character of the deceased father of Josh Cydney: without the prior knowledge that Kirkwood needed the convenient device of making the father a deadbeat dad in order not to have to accommodate a second larger-than-life parent in the text, Kirkwood Sr. might conceivably have thought that this reflected his son's genuine feelings about him. Kirkwood, though, seemed to think his father's grievances were all about being left out. "As it turned out, he later told someone he was very hurt because he wasn't in the book," Kirkwood subsequently said. "He was upset because it was about my mother and, goddammit, where was he?"…When I heard about it, I told him, 'Don't worry, Dad. You're going to be in one…'"

It's unlikely that this promise to revolve a novel around Kirkwood Sr. was simply an appeasement gesture. Despite the tone and contents of the above letter, Kirkwood was plainly fond of his old man. This fondness is quite evident in the previously mentioned private tape recording of the two conversing circa 1959 (a third, male party seems to be present in the room, possibly T. Michael Kirkwood). On it, a laughing Kirkwood goads his dad into reciting dirty jokes, filthy limericks and unprintable anecdotes, all delivered in that elegant, stentorian voice. However, while Kirkwood did attempt what he came to call his "daddy book," his efforts were desultory. Not only did his father never live to a point where the novel was complete, neither did Kirkwood.

EIGHT

Though Kirkwood had told his publisher that Alan J. Pakula was "terribly enthusiastic" about making a motion picture of *Pony*, it was in the end the famous director who was effectively responsible for Kirkwood's debut novel never reaching the big screen.

When the galleys of *Pony* were sent around to the movie studios before it was published, Pakula took the author to dinner. The two then retired to Pakula's Beverly Hills hotel room to finish their discussion about a movie version. Kirkwood recalled, "…about midnight I had my hand on the doorknob and was leaving when he suddenly asked, 'Did you ever think about doing it on the stage first?' I said I didn't think it was feasible. He agreed, but asked me, 'Would you like a nightcap?' That was my mistake. By 4:00 a.m. we were jumping around the room over chairs and tables acting out the way certain scenes might be done on the stage. By the time I left it was agreed I would do my damndest to dramatize it and he would produce it on the stage. Two weeks later I turned down $50,000 from MGM for the movie rights." In a resume that was distributed to the media shortly before the publication of *There Must Be a Pony!*, Kirkwood wrote that he had, "already turned down several movie offers for *There Must Be a Pony!* in order to dramatize it himself for the stage. Plans call for a Broadway production at the end of the current season or during the fall of 1961." In the 1963 *Equity* interview, Kirkwood explained how "…being an actor, my fondest dream was to see it come to life on the stage."

Adapting a play from one's own novel may immediately sound like an easy task, merely a matter of decanting a novel's narrative into the page layout of a different medium. However, while the lifting of pre-existing dialogue from the original source material is an easy part of the process (though not exactly effortless a full generation or more before the advent of the highlight-and-paste technology of the home computer) and while the deployment of many of the same tableaux is possible, dramatization also involves significant rethinking and reworking. The theatre play imposes limitations on the writer relating to budget, logistics and tradition that don't apply to the novel. The physical impossibility of a stage company having more than a few sets on hand cuts down the number of scene locations possible. Financial restrictions impose a ceiling on the number of actors, hence characters. The time taken to dismantle sets and limited space for split sets is an impediment to the rapid switching between scenes common in novels. Related to all these things is a requirement for less action and more dialogue, including the insertion of conversations solely in order to explain the occurrence of events problematical to depict. Little wonder then that Kirkwood later said, "I spent a year-and-a-half writing the novel and about the same time working on the play."

Of course, once that hard work is done, there is then the delay while the logistics of the pre-Broadway tryout tour — booking of theatres, casting, hiring — are sorted out. The fall of 1961 turned out to be a wildly optimistic guess for when *There Must Be a Pony!* would hit the stage. In the interim Kirkwood busied himself with acting roles.

It was presumably the *Pony!* play and the attendant need to be near Broadway that prompted Kirkwood's move back to the East Coast after the publication of the play's parent book. Robert Kirsch — who had already been the engineer of profound and welcome change in Kirkwood's life — must have seemed like a fairy godmother yet again when he told Kirkwood that he knew of an apartment available in New York. The apartment belonged to a friend of Kirsch's named Howard Rubin — whom Kirkwood never actually met — and was located on the top floor of a building on W 58th Street, the same street on which Kirkwood had lived in the forties and fifties. "It was the strangest apartment one could conceive," Kirkwood said. Ron Plotkin, who stayed in it with Lee Goodman at one point, says, "It was a five-floor walk-up in an old building right next to the Plaza Hotel. It was what we referred to as a studio or efficiency. It was one huge room with a bathroom and a Pullman kitchen where you can prepare a breakfast or whatever, no elaborate meals." Plotkin also remembers it having a butcher block. Some will recognize this layout as that of the apartment that featured in Kirkwood's novel and play(s), *P.S. Your Cat is Dead!* Plotkin: "He pretty much described it as it was."

Opinions among friends who visited it are divided as to its merits. Jack Sydow says, "It was a wonderful apartment. It juts out like a garret apartment. It had heightened ceilings with a peaked roof." However, Elyria school pal Sidney Wasserman, who bumped into Kirkwood on Broadway in 1964, was shocked at what he felt to be its shabbiness. Wasserman: "He said, 'I'm in a cold water flat it's dreadful.' I remember it was very drab and going up those steps to the top floor was really depressing." However, it wasn't the merits or demerits of the apartment that would cause Kirkwood so much distress and which would cause him to immortalize it in his art.

Rather it was the fact that from the moment he began living in it, he was subjected to burglary. The apartment, he recalled, had "dozens of locks on a steel door. It didn't matter, I kept getting robbed week after week from the day I moved in." "Dozens of locks" is clearly an exaggeration. The frequency of break-ins stated here would seem to be too. Elsewhere, Kirkwood put the break-in figure at three times in fourteen months and noted that his burglar(s) would wait until a point when he had managed to replace everything before striking again, the latter itself suggesting far longer gaps between burglaries than a week. However, repeat burglary certainly occurred. Plotkin: "He was always calling us in California: 'Dammit — guess what happened again?' I think it was just easier to do the top floor and either get out through the roof or look out the door and see if somebody was there and just run down the stairs." He adds, "Apartment buildings like that, they were very trusting in those days — people would buzz downstairs and they would just buzz them in. Or they would get on the next building and go through the skylight to get into the building."

Kirkwood recalled that he had a burglar alarm installed when he had to leave the city for a while. Unfortunately, when workers installing a similar system on the floor below slammed a door to test it, it triggered Kirkwood's own alarm, causing all the residents to be evacuated until the alarm could be fixed a day later. When the other residents later moved out of the building one by one, Kirkwood's lot worsened. It gave burglars the run of the place. Nothing seemed to impede or deter the burglar(s) and his/their methods became incrementally more audacious. First merely upset, with each invasion of his private space, Kirkwood got angrier and angrier. He recalled that finally one evening he sat in the darkness clutching a steel bar *hoping* that the intruder would make another appearance. He only snapped out of it when he got a third eye image of his quasi-maniacal self.

As with so many awful events in Kirkwood's life, distressing as it was at the time, it constituted excellent raw material. "I even developed a kind of relationship with the burglar and began to fantasize about meeting him," he said. Thus was born the idea for what would be Kirkwood's masterpiece.

While promoting his first book in 1960, Kirkwood said, "I'll never give up acting. I love the work when I'm working, but I loathe what you have to go through to get employment. Maybe the book will help because it's got my name in print and people don't know where they've seen the name — they just know it." The latter is sort of what happened when director Jack Sydow cast him in the Lerner & Loewe musical *Brigadoon* in the summer of 1962.

Sydow had met Kirkwood in 1951 through Pat Carroll, a fellow Ruban Bleu performer. After reading *There Must Be a Pony!*, Sydow realized he shared an agent with him. He got in touch in February '62 — Kirkwood had no memory of their previous meeting — and asked if he would be interested in the non-singing role of Jeff Douglas. Sydow says he doesn't recall Kirkwood taking the part through any particular need of money. "I thought he would do an acting job as a lark because he enjoyed doing it," he says. Of the decision to cast Kirkwood, Sydow says, "I had never seen him act except at the Ruban, but I knew the kind of vitality that he had and the kind of sincerity that he had and the kind of sweetness, really, that came across. Because the part of Jeff Douglas can be really terribly sarcastic and come off not good if you have the wrong person in it. I knew that he would be wonderful, and he was. He had a marvelous energy and he enjoyed working on the stage and the enjoyment came out in the seriousness with which he attacked the role. He was the perfect comedian because he always attacked everything seriously. It was not as if he was making a joke, the way so many comedians work today. They're so aware of their jokiness." Kirkwood got some good reviews for his performance in Sydow's production. One paper described him as "this delightful trouper who deftly handles his witty and humorous role."

Kirkwood and Sydow became close. Sydow: "From the time we first met we became good friends. Never lovers, unfortunately." While they were in *Brigadoon*, the whole cast went for dinner at a restaurant in Palm Beach. Sydow: "It was a cafeteria but they had martinis and Manhattans already mixed sitting in beds of ice in the line. Jimmy came back with his food and he was such a strange combination of joy and displeasure. I said, 'What's the matter?' He said, 'They won't give me a drink.' I said, 'Why not?' And he said, 'She says I'm not old enough!' He was thrilled to death that somebody said he wasn't old enough to have a drink but he was probably in his early thirties, [in fact, he was 38], but yet he wanted a drink. It was so funny."

Sydow was a good friend of Farley Granger, one of the principal actors in Hitchcock's *Rope*, the film that had led to Kirkwood's inept check-walking crime in the *Valiant Lady* days. "Farley was getting rid of some clothes and we were approximately the same size then," says Sydow. "He gave me a really nice green sweater. Jimmy saw me wearing it one day and he said, 'That's my sweater!' I said, 'What do you mean?' He said, 'I want that sweater, it's a perfect sweater.' I said, 'Jimmy, I just got this from Farley. I love this sweater.' 'Oh no, no, it's mine. It's me.' Then he kept going on about this sweater. At one time I went up to his apartment to meet him — we were going out for dinner — and there were sweaters laid all over the apartment. He said, 'You can have any two of these sweaters if you give me the green sweater.'" As a matter of fact, Sydow had the green sweater tucked under his raincoat, having been planning on giving it to Kirkwood anyway. Sydow: "I pulled out the green sweater and I threw it and I said, 'Take the fucking thing, stop bothering me!' A few days after that he was wearing the sweater and he got out of a taxi and Farley Granger saw him and he said, 'That's my sweater!' I think I probably laughed more with Jimmy Kirkwood than I've ever laughed with anybody."

Come July of 1962, it was time for Kirkwood to devote himself to his own play as *There Must Be a Pony!* made its pre-Broadway debut at Ogunquit Playhouse, Maine. The play, initially, at least, had twelve scenes, divided into two acts. Its set was relatively intricate, consisting of a split-level box showing a cross section of the hall, the game room and a bedroom of the home of Rita and Josh Cydney. The action — set in the then-present — covered a period of a year. The version of this incarnation of the play amongst Kirkwood's papers is dated January 1962. Though the story being told is essentially the same as that of the book, the novel's events are condensed and rearranged and we see points of view other than Josh's. There are also differences in emphasis: for instance, Josh is far bitterer toward Ben and there is more recrimination about Ben and his motivations. A key difference — and probably an astute change, considering the heightened requirement for action in an acted story — is that Josh finds Ben's note when he lifts the newel post to brain what he thinks is an intruder. A less clever tweak is making Josh intrigued by stockbroker Ben because — implausibly — Josh is a whiz with shares. An alteration that seems unwise for a different reason is the flip Josh does over Ben's head with the assistance of Ben's interlinked hands — a risky maneuver on a nightly basis. The exposition is usually competent, although a device whereby Josh is given monologues in which he speaks directly to the audience is lazy. Though it has a spot or two of melodrama, though patches of it are boring — especially the prattling show-business gossip of Rita and her friends — and though it has a feeble finale in which Josh chides pet parrot Chauncey for not being able to speak, this adaptation of *There Must Be a Pony!* is a pretty good play, certainly more dynamic and more interesting in subject than most theatre productions.

Myrna Loy played Rita, Donald Woods had the role of Ben Nichols, Peter Helm was Josh and Josh G. Wood depicted Merwin. An unknown paper said of the Maine premiere, "The play is a remarkable character study of a film star on the rocks after a successful career and several less rewarding romances. Myrna Loy is equal to every twist that fate and the rising momentum of the play supply...Peter Helm richly and naturally depicts her son...*Pony* drags talkatively until mother and son meet Ben Nichols, played to perfection by Donald Woods...No script of recent memory has offered such variety of emotions to the star as in the Rita Cydney role. Myrna Loy wins attention, affection and concern and continuously holds the audience, in spite of a few wavering spots, which will doubtlessly be smoothed out during the other summer showings. Individual scenes stand out too: Mary Patton, as Ben's wife enacts a thrilling tirade; Adelaide Klein is bitterly sardonic as a scandal-seeking film columnist." It concluded, "If tightened up in the first act...and if the scope of some of the minor characters is enlarged...*There Must Be a Pony!* seems definitely headed for Broadway success."

Like all plays, *Pony!* was subjected to what is these days called "finessing." By the time the play moved to the Westport Country Playhouse a couple of weeks later, director John Stix had streamlined things a little. Lines referring to male birds in the house trying to escape from their cages were cut, as was a scene where Rita exposed herself. The opening scenes where Josh talked directly to the audience and explained his life and recent events at his home had been changed to an opening where Merwin and Rita's friend Sally Knapp were groping around the darkened set. This meant that some of the crucial events were relegated to a flashback, which — as if to prove that amending a play can cause as many problems as it solves — at least one critic thought might confuse the audience. The role of Merwin had been expanded. The set had also been tweaked, with Rita being provided a walk-in closet — thus explaining to the audience some of her disappearances — and the covers of her bed were now pointedly turned down in some scenes.

Reviews for the Westport performances were mixed. One unknown paper said, "The cast has not done their reading, or, if they have, have not been able to give life to a fine novel which is suffering the usual maladies in its transition to a play. Both the novel and the play are Mr. Kirkwood's first efforts and although the choice of a tragic-comedy may have been more courageous than wise, he has succeeded more than some others in breaking down that thin but stubborn line that divides the two spirits." The same paper felt that the first act was too long by some fifteen or twenty minutes and that Loy did not make her part come alive, partly because of maladroit acting and partly because of the writing: "The so-called wild goings on that she is relating sound less exciting than a night around the swimming pool of Bob Kennedy." The paper concluded of the play's story, "It is a better plot than scores of Broadway plays start out with. But it needs sharpening of the storyline, and the acting clarification of the characters and confusing changes in time and some good trimming all round." If this were done, the paper stated that it stood a good chance of running on Broadway but that, "As it stands, it's heading towards the slaughterhouse." Loy got a better review from the *New Haven Evening Register* (the other actors also got plaudits) but similar reservations were made about the script: "Viewed as a whole, the play certainly is entertaining and does have a moral. But it does need tightening up, especially in the first act. And the first scene is confusing." *The Norwalk Hour* reported that the play was at least well-received by the audience ("Curtain call after curtain call brought the stars and entire cast back for bows"). It also praised Loy whom it said, "is the key to the success of the play and her command of the stage is complete all the time she is on." Of the script, the paper opined, "…this play…combines drama, humor, heartbreak and tenderness." The impartiality of this suspiciously gushing reviewer is brought into question when it emerges that he/she is *au fait* with the fact that the audience included "Miss Leatrice Joy of Riverside, who is a long-time friend of Lila Lee." *The Darien Review* carried a long and thoughtful critique. The reviewer Ray Yates had the advantage of having seen a Maine performance. He approved of some of the changes and disagreed with others. He was impressed by both Helm as Josh ("turns in an outstanding job") and Loy as Rita ("She combines the quicksilver and lightning of vanished joy with the gossamer delight of true happiness…she is wonderful to behold…") Yates' summary was that *Pony!* "…richly deserves showing in New York as one of the future 'best plays' of the coming season."

A review of a *Pony!* performance at the Falmouth Playhouse — in between the Maine and Westport showings — in the *Cape Cod Standard Times* carried a rather amusing line: "It does seem that the actress played so well by Miss Loy gets one hard knock too many." In point of fact, real life is sometimes more merciless than can be plausibly depicted in fiction: Lila Lee had already suffered far more traumas than was portrayed in *Pony!* and sadly would suffer more in the coming years. *The Cape Cod Standard Times* also stated that the play would make its Broadway debut on September 27 at the Cort Theater. This opening never, in fact, happened. Not only did Kirkwood's estimation of the fall of 1961 turn out to be an optimistic guess for when *There Must Be a Pony!* would make its debut, but his very postulation that it would reach Broadway transpired to be presumptuous. *There Must Be a Pony!* — after all the hard work in writing, casting, rehearsing and then amending the script to address the deficiencies that came to light in the tryouts — shortly became just another play that failed to come in.

In her autobiography, Loy wrote, "Things began to deteriorate as we neared New York. Out-of-town critics attacked me and the play. There was still that hangover from films; they were punishing me for having been a movie star." However, she admitted, "Lila, as depicted by her son, had a drinking problem, a flamboyant temperament, and a mean streak. The kind of vulnerability that made her palatable was hardly my forte." Loy also asserted that Kirkwood began his changes to the script because he was "intimidated by the critics." She said, "I don't think that many of the changes were as effective as his original script. And he's so quick the actors couldn't catch up with him." Additionally, she felt that Pakula was distracted by the time he had to spend in Hollywood to oversee the movie *To Kill a Mockingbird*. She said, "As I recall, another producer got into it and I began hearing rumors that he wanted to replace me with Kim Stanley."

The way Kirkwood later told it was that Loy announced that she would not be playing Rita in the play's planned New York run and that Kim Stanley, who had actually been his first choice for Rita but had turned down the role, saw it in Westport and decided that she now did want to take it. Whatever the truth, though Stanley was widely considered a great thespian, she was also considered unreliable. "The greatest tragedy in American theatre," Kirkwood later said of her. "A supremely, divinely gifted actress. I think about her a lot because I worked with her in a play one time. She always had emotional crises and was born with a huge streak of self-destruction…She agreed to do the part after it turned out Myrna wasn't going to come into the city with it. But Kim hadn't racked up a very good track record in *A Far Country*…Everybody involved with *Pony* wanted some insurance, just in case she didn't show up and all, and Lloyds of London wouldn't touch it. That was one of my biggest heartbreaks in the business because I could just taste her in that part, and feel her and see her." This version of events leaves open the possibility that casting problems were responsible for the play not making it to Broadway rather than the response to the tryouts, but in any case things had been seriously undermined seven weeks into the tryouts when the show's producers, Alan Pakula — the man, remember, who had persuaded Kirkwood to turn his novel into a play in the first place — and Joel Schenker, sold their interests in the project.

Jack Sydow feels Loy could never have been believable as a cinema queen like Rita Cydney. He says, "I thought Miss Loy was very nice, but she didn't have that indescribable thing that movie stars have. She didn't have the 'It.' It's a chemical thing that you can't learn, it's just there." But for Sydow there were more fundamental problems: "I think the stage version always needed work. It didn't have the impact that the novel had because you're able to get into the inside of people's minds in the novel… It's so difficult to do on the stage what you can do in a novel. You can take your time doing it and the emotions are built up. I just think it's very difficult to condense it. I don't think that that particular work lends itself."

The following year Kirkwood was opining in print that the summer circuit tryout tradition created a false sense of ample time in which to work out problems. Though the cast and crew are relaxed because of the month of rehearsal, eight playing weeks and a couple of weeks for rewriting and recasting that process involves, "…once you go into rehearsal the gong rings and it's a hundred-yard dash with maybe three days' stopover in New Haven, a couple of weeks in Philly, and, if you're lucky, two more in Boston. You'll either come in or close, and you know it. With a summer tour in stock it's too easy to postpone decisions, to rationalize the trouble spots not only in writing but in the casting, directing, producing — everything. Therefore the commitment is not that total."

At least one good thing for Kirkwood came out of the experience of trying to stage his novel, namely sweet revenge on Rosalind Russell. Prior to the play's premiere, Kirkwood and Loy were invited to a party at the Hollywood home of film producer Ross Hunter. Loy spotted Russell and, unaware of the *contres temp* between Kirkwood and her several years previously, took him over to meet her. Kirkwood recalled, "They embraced and Ros said to her, 'I hear you're going to do a play — isn't that marvelous?' And Myrna Loy said, 'Yes, and have you met the author, James Kirkwood?' And she went like that [mimed offering outstretched hand]. I must say I looked at Rosalind Russell for a long time and then I took her hand and I shook it and I said, 'How could I ever forget your kindness to me? I'll never forget the beautiful way you treated me a few years ago in New York'…Myrna said later that she had never seen Rosalind Russell blanche quite as much. She almost backed into the swimming pool and then she suddenly saw, I think Van Johnson, and said, 'Oh there's Van — hi dear!' and away she went."

The real-life prototype of the play's lead female character was not in attendance at any of its performances. From May to September, Lila Lee was on a round-the-world cruise paid for by her son following one of the painful hospital stays that would pock her life. Kirkwood mentioned in a letter to Lee a cost of around $3,000 for the cruise, a very considerable sum of money for the time. Kirkwood suggested to his mother that the money might be better spent on a down payment on a house in California for her ("Because you can't live like a gypsey [sic] any more, bouncing about from one tiny apartment to another"). Lee evidently disagreed about the priorities. It was perhaps fortunate that she did not see the play: the Rita character was drawn more haughty and petulant and less sympathetic than in the novel.

Asked in 1963 whether he was fonder of the novel or the play of *There Must Be a Pony!*, Kirkwood said, "Each one has qualities near and dear to me." Unfortunately for him, only one of them could be termed a commercial or critical success. Shortly afterwards, Kirkwood relented and sold the movie rights to *There Must Be a Pony!* However, its moment was now gone. The property bounced around Hollywood for many years but in the end an adaptation only made it to the small screen, and that very belatedly.

Asked in that 1963 *Equity* interview whether he planned to write for the theatre again, Kirkwood said, "Yes. But the theatre has become such a luxury. Everything has reached the point of absurdity. Why should a star…march home every week with a guarantee of $3,500 against ten per cent of the gross, or about $10,000?…He's making it hard for the show to payoff." Referring to an apparently fictional actress named Adeline Van Opstal, whom he kept mentioning in the interview in conjunction with an apparently fictional actor called Ben Sugarman, he said, "He should be like Adeline who only took a straight $4,200 for her last play and thereby kept the nut down." Additionally, he opined, "I fear the theatre *is* terribly over-unionized. Quickly let me add that I believe in unions, specially for talented craftsmen, but not when they are running the show, not when they become dictators." He pointed out that Equity (the actors' union rather than the magazine) didn't tell a playwright or a producer how many actors he must have in his play but that a producer was informed by union dictate how many people he must employ backstage. "It's frightening…I would like to see apprentice actors, would-be playwrights, producers and directors employed as stagehands, curtain pullers, stage door men, prop men…Because many unskilled laborers backstage in the theatre I believe are overpaid and underdedicated. I've been in shows with a cast of five and yet had to fight my way through a mob of sixteen stagehands having a bull session in the wings to make an entrance. It's wrong, it's disgusting, and it's sick…I feel strongly about anything which causes the number of plays produced to dwindle year by year."

In that 1963 *Equity* interview, Kirkwood had spoken of being "in the throes of" writing a new novel called *Sting, Stang, Stung*. This title may have been a joke: it is a quite extraordinary interview in which, though Kirkwood makes several serious points, he seems unable to keep a straight face for long. (His talk of actors Ben Sugarman and Adeline Van Opstal — all-time greats of international stature although probably not currently paid-up members of Equity whom he claims to know well and keeps finding excuses to bring into the discussion before admitting in mock shame that he has barely met either — is a hilarious piece of verbal riffing. He later used the Van Opstal name fleetingly in the unproduced musical *Murder at the Vanities*.) Possibly the novel itself was fictional. In 1975, he stated, "I wish I had just stuck to writing after the first book; instead I went back to acting and pissed away a lot of time, as it were."

Nineteen sixty-three certainly saw a lot of acting activity from Kirkwood. In February, he appeared in a City Center, New York, revival of the Irving Berlin musical *Wonderful Town*. Kaye Ballard starred and Kirkwood took the role of Frank Lippincott. Kirkwood's description of the character demonstrates his facility with language, especially a sparkling colloquialism: "A terribly naïve soda jerk who doesn't know which-a-way anyone went." Kirkwood recalls of the reception to the play, "I was rewarded by an exciting set of reviews, which hardly anyone saw. They were posted on the bulletin board backstage in letter-form from the critics. That was during the newspaper strike." This was not to be the last time that a strike — at least in Kirkwood's eyes — adversely affected a play with which he was associated.

Kirkwood wasn't amused when the casting director of a television series complimented him on his *Wonderful Town* performance but then added that it was too bad she was a casting director for a show having to do with lawyers and courtroom trials. Speaking in 1963, Kirkwood observed, "I wanted to shout, 'I'm not really a dumb soda jerk. I'm a good actor who *pretended* to be one. I could even pretend to be a murderer, in spite of the fact that I'm freshly shaved, don't have a facial tick, and am not wagging a Thompson submachine gun in your face.'" Clearly the irritations of the acting profession were getting to Kirkwood once more.

The summer of '63 saw Kirkwood renew his professional relationship with Jack Sydow when the latter directed him in the role of Kenneth Gibson in a production of *Call Me Madam*. Martha Raye was in the lead role in the show's six-week tour on the Music Fairs circuit. Sydow recollects of Kirkwood's performance, "He knew he would be good with Martha Raye and indeed he was. They developed a very good friendship, off the stage as well." This role involved some trilling from Kirkwood. The latter's voice had clearly improved since the days when Harold Fonville had told Lee Goodman he would scream with laughter when he heard it. Sydow reveals, "In *Call Me Madam* he does 'You're Just in Love,' the double chorus. He was fine. I don't recall that it was a pretty voice, but it was a perfectly good musical comedy voice for that kind of material." However, "It wouldn't hold up with a serious ballad."

Kirkwood's run in the play was interrupted on August 24, 1963, when — two days after his own 39th birthday — he received the news that his father had died at the age — he thought, for he was as unaware as everyone else that his father was born a year later than people realized — of 88. The gregarious man who had once been rich enough to be able to lose more than a million dollars in the 1920s and who had been married five times had experienced sad twilight years of poverty and singledom. Says Lomax Study, "I remember going to see the old man when he was living on Argyle Street [sic] in a miserable little one-bedroom apartment having newspapers stacked up in the living room and that kind of thing. Here was a man who was a big star and a big showman and his last days of his life were a misery." Kirkwood's own recollections chime with Study's: "Mostly, in later years…he just existed — and ended his days flat broke." Kirkwood also said, "My stomach turned over when I saw *Day of the Locust* because that's the way my father ended up, in one of those little Spanish courts with that awful furniture that achieves a smell and never loses it." Kirkwood did also say, however, that right up to his death, "he was still pinching waitresses, running a hand up and down the arm of any female he came across and murmuring, 'Good Christ, what a delicious morsel you are!'"

T. Michael Kirkwood was in the service in West Germany when he received the news. "I only had thirty days left before I was coming home anyway," he says. "So they sent me home for the funeral and then they're not going to bring me back because by that time they were just going to let me go. I'm sitting home within a couple of weeks of getting back watching the news and there is my unit in Vietnam. They had to have packaged them up and flown them over there in no time after I left and I just thought, 'My *God.*' I just had the strangest feeling my father passed away so I wouldn't have to go to Vietnam. It was the same month that Kennedy was assassinated so it was a real shit year!"

Kirkwood's own more ambiguous feelings about his father were possibly reflected in the fact that Jack Sydow, like several others spoken to for this book, can barely remember a conversation with his friend in which he mentioned his dad. "It was odd how little I heard Jimmy talk about his father," he says. "I heard a great deal about his mother, on the other hand."

T. Michael: "I guess when you get a telegram (in those days, everything was telegrams) the stage manager holds it 'til the show's over 'cause you don't want to give somebody bad news that their family has just been wiped out in a tornado or something then they have to go on stage. So after the show they called him aside and said, 'Your father passed' and whoever the actress was said to him, 'You take as much time as you want, go out there and get things done that you have to get done.' So he got to California before I did and then I got held up." Joan Thompson née Kirkwood, pregnant in Dallas and not easily able to obtain care for her small child, decided not to attend the funeral of a man she describes as a stranger to her.

T. Michael had a shock with which to contend in addition to the death of his father once he reached Los Angeles. He had for a while "kind of suspected" the true nature of his brother's sexuality, though, "He never just came out and said anything necessarily." When Kirkwood picked T. Michael up at the airport, it would be for T. Michael the "first time it kind of exploded in my mind." He explains, "He's with three or four guys that are much older and obviously very gay. Not being splashy or anything, it's just this is the way they are and you just take one look and you say, 'Oh yes they are.' So I was a little shocked about that. But I was also just beat up about Dad dying and so on…" T. Michael didn't feel particularly beat up about the revelation of his brother's true leanings. "I didn't know much about homosexuality or anything except it creeped me out as a child because adults had come onto me a couple of times and it was scary," he says. "I was not judgmental about it and I never really thought about it one way or another and Jimmy was open about [it] in front of me later. Like once I had to go pick him up at some house in West LA above Sunset Boulevard. The other guy came down, said, 'Okay, I'm leaving first, I'll see ya,' and they went into a big embrace and everything and I just walked away and walked over to the window and didn't pay attention. It was a big kiss and all that stuff. It's family. It's your brother. You don't hate somebody because they have a different lifestyle than you."

Lomax Study happened to be in Los Angeles and was invited to the funeral. He recalls, "The old man was laid out in an open coffin and there were like four people there. It was kind of sad, really." Even so, there were elements of high comedy to the service. One was provided by the by-now septuagenarian Mary Pickford, who walked in, according to Study, "…a little tipsy." Study recalls, "She had this little bottle and she said it was holy water from the River Jordan. She went up and she said, 'Oh, Jimmy, you were so wonderful to me when you directed me.'" Pickford then proceeded to pour the water over the body before her. T. Michael: "Jimmy told me that Mary Pickford went up to our dad's coffin in the church, after most everyone had gone, and with much crying and muttering she suddenly slapped our dead father. Then she left." He adds, "My father had told me she could have been my mother if they had gotten married."

Kirkwood himself recalled the funeral home being filled with "those odd California people whose full-time occupation it is to attend funerals. Some young misfits, but mostly elderly, be-wigged, be-hatted over-rouged ladies of death whose bible is the obituary page." As Kirkwood entered the room containing his father's casket, one of these apparitions stopped him with a claw-like hand and — as though to provide one final confirmation of his dad's famed cocksmanship — informed him, "I was just an extra player in early talkies but I knew your father well. I did, really well." Said lady proceeded to blush, batting her over-mascara eyes like a (very) superannuated schoolgirl.

Finally, Kirkwood asked the undertaker in charge to clear the room of people with flash-cameras, as well as the young man who had proffered a copy of the paperback of *There Must Be a Pony!* for him to sign. He then pulled up a chair and sat down next to the coffin for a final talk. "I told him what an extraordinary creature he was, how I always loved him, despite the lack of normalcy provided by him," Kirkwood said. "After a while I had a strong, compelling, burning urge to pee." Telling his father he'd be right back, Kirkwood stood, noticing an extremely uncomfortable sensation in his crotch area. He recalled that he went to the men's room, unzipped his fly and examined himself, whereupon he discovered something that initially dismayed him — but then made him laugh until tears ran down his cheeks. Seated next to his father again, he reached into the coffin, took his father's lifeless hand and squeezed it. "Well, old dear," he said. "In honor of your funeral, I've come down with the clap!" Kirkwood noted later that it seemed terribly appropriate.

Despite their very different experiences of him as a paternal figure, the funeral of their father seems to have cemented a bond between the half-siblings, who also found that as they were both now adults they could communicate on a different level. On the evening of the funeral, the two went to dinner together. T. Michael: "Went out to Malibu. Went to a restaurant right on the ocean and talked a lot about life in general. After that, any time he had to come into town he would always call me and ask me if I could take him to the airport and pick him up or whatever, so we kept in touch and we were always friends."

T. Michael received a surprise from his brother the following day, one at odds with Kirkwood's later public assertion that his father "ended his days flat broke." "We were driving around," he recalls, "and we were going to lunch or something and he handed me a savings account book and said, 'This was Dad's and this should be yours, 'cause I'm fine and you need the money.' And it was like three thousand dollars. I was shocked. That was '63 so it was a goodly sum." T. Michael also recalls of his brother in this conversation, "He said to me, 'And don't worry about Joan, I've taken care of her.' I had the opinion that Joan had asked him for help over the years at various times."

The surprisingly healthy state of Kirkwood Sr.'s finances was down to the fact that, though he had found work hard to obtain for many years and in spite of his advanced age, in the period immediately preceding his death he had secured a late run of work. T. Michael: "It's funny because he did three films between '61 and '63 and he was edited out of two of them… One was that super film with Gregory Peck, *To Kill a Mockingbird*. I don't know what the hell happened in it, but he wasn't in it. The other one was a film called *Two Rode Together*, Jimmy Stewart and Richard Widmark, and he was edited out of that." The prong of this cinematic trident from which Kirkwood Sr. was not excised was the Marlon Brando vehicle *The Ugly American*. T. Michael: "Where [Brando] becomes the representative of the United States in that country…Dad was one of the senators that interviewed him ahead of time. It's in the first fifteen minutes of the film and I used to get to see that every now and again, which was great for me just to remember him."

What with the failure of the *Pony* play and the loss of his father, Kirkwood had not had an easy time of it of late. However, things were going to get worse, professionally and emotionally, in the near future.

Kirkwood in the Coast Guard, mid-1940s. COURTESY OF ARTHUR BECKENSTEIN

AM, *magazine of the USS Admiral H.T. Mayo, edited by Kirkwood, 1945.*
COURTESY OF ARTHUR BECKENSTEIN

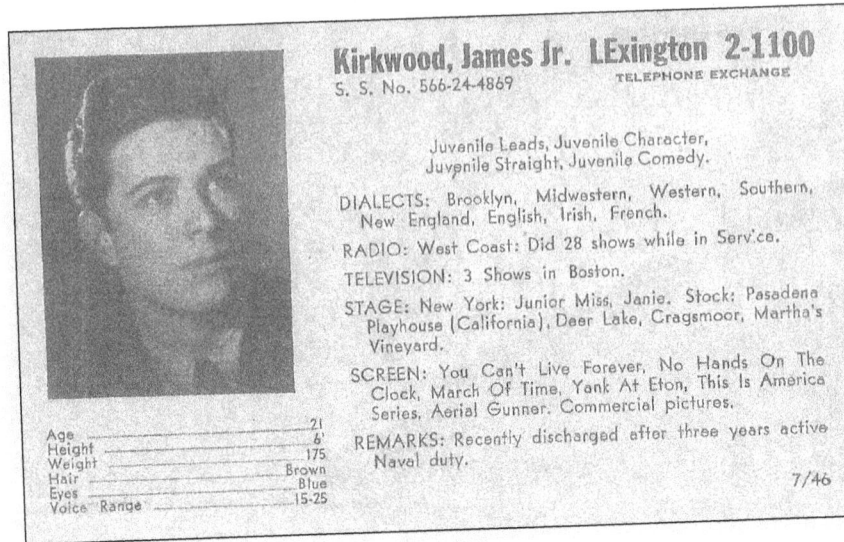

Kirkwood resumed his acting career after the Second World War. This résumé dates from July 1946. COURTESY OF ARTHUR BECKENSTEIN

Kirkwood with his half-brother Terrance. COURTESY OF ARTHUR BECKENSTEIN

The comedy duo of Jim Kirkwood & Lee Goodman. COURTESY OF ARTHUR BECKENSTEIN

Kirkwood with his Valiant Lady *screen mother, actress Nancy Coleman, 1954.*

Kirkwood in the Fifties with Muriel Bentley, the major female love of his life.

Kirkwood and his parents gathered together in 1958 to film an episode of Lamp Unto my Feet. COURTESY OF ARTHUR BECKENSTEIN

Kirkwood and his parents in Lamp Unto my Feet.

Kirkwood with screen legend Tallulah Bankhead in Welcome Darlings, *1956.*
COURTESY OF ARTHUR BECKENSTEIN

Kirkwood and his mother on Lila's Lee's This Is Your Life, *1957.*

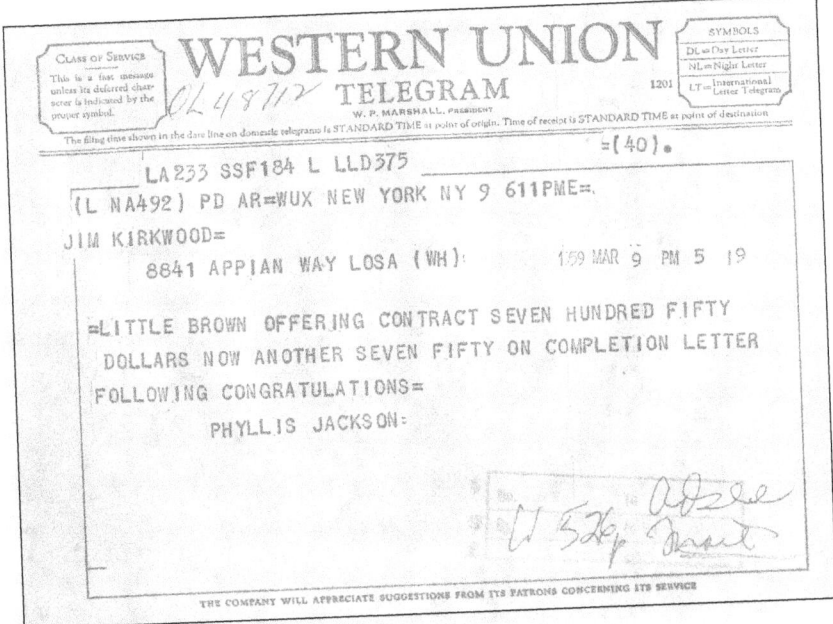

Life-changing news for Kirkwood as his agent telegrams him to let him know that his first novel has been accepted for publication. COURTESY OF ARTHUR BECKENSTEIN

Kirkwood outside the court where Clay Shaw was tried, 1969.
COURTESY OF ARTHUR BECKENSTEIN

Kirkwood's aunt Peg and mother flanking...the only man prosecuted over the murder of President Kennedy, Clay Shaw. COURTESY OF ARTHUR BECKENSTEIN

NINE

In 1964, Kirkwood's childhood Elyria friend Sidney Wasserman ran into him on Broadway.

"I happened to be in New York City on my work with students from a social agency, and I see this guy coming toward me and I thought to myself, 'That's Jimmy,'" says Wasserman. "I had lost my hair and I definitely didn't have that youthful look, but he looked like I remembered him always. I went up to him and I said, 'Excuse me, are you Jimmy Kirkwood?' He said, 'Yes.' I said, 'Do you know who I am?' and [he] looked and he said, 'No.' I told him who I was and he sort of staggered backwards. He said, 'Look, I'm on my way to audition. I want to talk with you, I want to see you, can you come to my flat at five o'clock this afternoon for a cocktail?' I went and we had an hour's talk or an-hour-and-a-half. I asked him, 'How is your mother?' and he said, 'Well, I bought her a house in Key West and she is staggering along, not doing great.'" Despite the large poster of Lila Lee that Kirkwood had on display in the W 58th St. apartment, the wounds of his childhood obviously still ran deep. Wasserman: "And then he paused and he said, 'You know, when I needed her the most, she wasn't there for me…'"

Kirkwood may have told his brother he needed his father's savings more than he, but Wasserman did not get the impression his old friend was doing well. Though he did not know and Kirkwood did not volunteer that he had had a novel published, Wasserman was shocked at the poverty he saw. "It gave me a picture that he was really struggling," he says. "I think those were tough years for Jimmy," says Homer Price of the span of time between Kirkwood's first and second published novels, if not necessarily the exact point Kirkwood met Wasserman. The financial burden imposed on Kirkwood by having to pay the rent on his mother's Key West apartment (not mortgage on a house as Wasserman remembers, though that would occur later) and the rent on his apartment in the city would seem to have led him to take quasi-humiliating employment. "He did odd jobs," says Price. "For instance, he read to Brooke Astor's mother. He would read to her for twenty bucks an hour or something like that. He and Jamie [Leo Herlihy] used to do that and then Freddie Bradlee, Ben Bradlee's only brother, took over Jamie's place I think doing this little reading duo for rich ladies. They would go and read to these rich ladies and being both actors, they really put on a show, I am sure."

Though Lee's incredible bad luck with her health would mean medical bills throughout her life, in that year, she — and by extension her son — got some financial respite. Her third husband John Murphy died in January 1964 and though in his will he understandably left the bulk of his $1.2m fortune to his wife Mary, he also made provision for his previous spouse, leaving Lee a trust fund of $30,000 from which it was stipulated she receive not less than $250 per month until she remarried (which she never did). It was a nice gesture, and an uncommon one in the experience of Lee, who had not had much luck with men. Behind it seems to have laid a tangled set of relationships. Explains Beckenstein, "Jack Murphy had a mistress at the time that he was married to Lila named Mary who became a good friend of Jimmy's and Lee Goodman's, and I knew her well. Jack divorced Lila and married Mary. When he died, Mary got all of his money and I think she felt a little bit guilty about that and sent Lila a little bit of money when she was ill." Beckenstein adds, "Mary was like family to us in those days and when she had a stroke, we always looked in on her. Jimmy felt a responsibility toward her. But in the way that the aunt in *P.S.* had some control over Jimmy Zoole, Mary had control to a degree over money due Lila." Beckenstein is here referring to the *P.S. Your Cat is Dead!* character Aunt Claire, who has her nephew Jimmy Zoole dancing on a string via the long-term prospect of an inheritance. Beckenstein and Plotkin concur that Kirkwood based Claire on Mary Murphy and her financial power over Lila Lee.

Perhaps it was poverty that led Kirkwood in '64 to make what many thought a strange choice (and some a despicable one) in his acting career. Giving over (free of charge despite his poverty) his West 58th Street apartment to NYC-visiting Lee Goodman and Ronald Plotkin, he embarked on a five-month tour of South Africa as Charlie in a production of *Never Too Late*. He admitted that even his friends raised their eyebrows at his willingness to perform in a country in which apartheid held sway. His co-stars were Nancy Donahue and Roland Winters, with his ex-*Valiant Lady* colleague Nancy Coleman in a supporting role. Not that this could be construed as meaning Kirkwood was dismissive about the suffering of non-whites in that country. Donahue said at one of Kirkwood's memorials, "Jim played my husband in this tour, which included a stint in Cape Town for mixed-race audiences. We got into some trouble there because we hooked up with a young radical who was living on the edge of detention." Kirkwood himself claimed he "…was almost deported from South Africa for speaking to a meeting of South African Negro actors and artists."

In Johannesburg on the second or third night of the run (his accounts varied), Kirkwood broke his leg onstage at the beginning of the third act. He had no understudy. Kirkwood: "The people that had produced the play had brought over all Americans and it would have been a great loss to them if I had just gotten on a plane and gone home." Kirkwood's leg was set and put in a cast and he would take to the stage like that every evening. When the cast came off three months later, he was strapped up and literally limped the rest of the tour. Donahue (who said the break occurred on the second night) recalled, "He kept right on going and he worked on crutches and he would sometimes flail them around in the air to make his point. He'd pound on the floor. Sometimes he'd even throw them at people."

Kirkwood: "I didn't miss a performance but the leg used to swell up and it was very, very painful." Kirkwood said that he had to have a morphine shot half an hour before each performance, then another one in between scenes one and two of the second act. It wasn't until the doctors began taking him off the medication that he realized he had built up an addiction. "I did the most terrible scenes," he recalled. "I don't think Bette Davis or Joan Crawford would have equaled them. Was crawling around the floor crying, saying that I couldn't go on and they would have to bring the curtain down unless I got my shot." Though he didn't say it explicitly, it may have been at this point that Kirkwood began to understand, even forgive, the addictions of his parents, especially his father's. He put it in more general terms: "I had had no tolerance for people that were addicted to anything, including alcohol I suppose, until that time and then I realized that it was purely a physical addiction. It was a very, very difficult thing to break. I had to go to psychiatrists and I was put on different drugs, tranquillizers and everything."

T. Michael, incidentally, remembers his brother telling him of Nancy Donahue, "I almost married her." If Kirkwood was referring in this context to the period in which he and Donahue worked together on this play, it would suggest that he was still a little schizophrenic about his sexuality and continued to have hankerings for conventional heterosexual coupledom.

While in South Africa, Kirkwood took part in a radio play version of *There Must Be a Pony!* A one-hour affair written by Kirkwood for a Durban production company, it saw Kirkwood take on the role of the boy Josh. Considering he was now middle-aged, this may seem to have required a suspension of the audience's disbelief even for radio, but at least it was a more credible scenario than the one depicted in the *Pasadena Star News* in September 1964 in which it was claimed that Columbia Pictures wanted Ringo Starr of The Beatles to play Josh in a movie version of *There Must Be a Pony!*, although this does have the smack of a publicity stunt. After seeing the *Never Too Late* run to its completion, Kirkwood paid a visit to his old friend Lomax Study, then living in France, before returning home.

Towards the end of 1965 (but prior to November 8) Kirkwood wrote a long, impassioned letter to his mother about her alcoholism. That terrible accident in the late fifties had not put Lila Lee off the bottle. Says Joan Kirkwood Thompson, "After she recuperated from that, she was out at his house in East Hampton and he got so mad at her about drinking that he took all his liquor and he threw it offshore." She describes her half-brother's relationship with Lila Lee as, "Like a parent and child, but reversed." Joan also says, "During the later teenage years, I probably saw her a half-dozen times. I spent the weekend with her a couple of times… When I was in my very late teens, Lila came to New York and I think she had just come back from Saranac then. She was living with friends when their apartment was vacant. She went from one place to another for a while and then as Jimmy became more successful, he got her her own place. She was a very heavy drinker. He really never talked about things that bothered him deeply except for Lila's drinking."

In what looks like a rough draft of the letter — written in shock after he had found out through a mutual acquaintance that his mother had been hospitalized — Kirkwood says, "I'm convinced that all of your health problems have resulted from drinking, from having your resistance lowered, and although you will deny it naturally I attribute the accidents you've had, the broken shoulder, the burns, the ankle, etc. to the same problem…" Referring in part to the surgical excision of her right upper lobe in 1961, Kirkwood continued, "It seems so foolish that with barely more than one lung and emphysema and diabetes that you should purposely set about weakening your system." Sadly, this was not to be the last impassioned letter Kirkwood would find himself writing to the woman he called "Mama" about her self-destruction. Perhaps a clue as to why can be found in a doctor's report on her death, which rather tragically revealed, "When I first met Miss Lee (September, 1961) she had visited many clinics, seen many doctors, known many disappointments, and was not quick to trust again." Said report noted recurrences of TB after Lee's initial 1929 "cure" in 1945, 1948 and 1960, as well as the sometimes brutal treatments for the disease that were employed in the era in which she first contracted it. Also noted were a hysterectomy and an appendectomy in 1944, a collar bone operation in 1950 and "extensive" skin grafts necessitated by the scalding caused by the 1958 bathtub fall. It would seem that Lee was trapped in a vicious circle, driven by her health problems to a hedonism that only worsened those health problems.

One of the ways Kirkwood tried in his letter to persuade Lee that it was worth coming off the bottle was by stating, "There seems to be a good chance for me finally to achieve some measure of success with this play…and if I do I would certainly want you around to enjoy it…" The play to which he referred was *UTBU*, set to begin rehearsals on November 8, a collaboration with James Leo Herlihy. As touched on previously, it must have seemed natural for the pair to join forces. Not only were they relatively newly emergent and acclaimed writers (the most recent of Herlihy's novels, *Midnight Cowboy*, was published in 1965 and quickly moved toward being recognized as a modern classic), but they were extremely close. Homer Price: "His probably most intimate relationship, the one he confided in most, was James Lee Herlihy." Price feels that Herlihy remained Kirkwood's greatest confidant even when Kirkwood embarked on his two-decade relationship with Arthur Beckenstein. "Well, it was a very different relationship," he says. "I mean, it was one of peers — they were the same age. They had known each other for a long, long time. They met in the fifties if I'm not mistaken and had been through a lot together and they were both would-be actors and then became writers. Arthur was much, much younger and I think Jimmy and Jamie were lovers way back probably, but I don't think it was ever serious. At any rate they developed a very close relationship and there's a couple of pieces of evidence that would lead me to conclude that Jimmy really confided in Jamie even more so than with me. I was on the peer level, of course. Arthur was a lover and the relationship was not the same at all. Arthur was not tapped into that same world, really." For his part, Beckenstein says of Herlihy, "Jimmy always considered him his best friend, although he didn't really see him very often — talks on the phone — because of the distance. Jamie lived in California or Key West. They just felt a kinship. They talked for hours and had a great correspondence back and forth. He would talk to Jamie and bounce things off of him. Ideas and philosophies. They were an influence on each other." Kirkwood himself refers to Herlihy as his best friend throughout his 1989 book *Diary of a Mad Playwright*.

John Desmond, Kirkwood's old friend from the *Valiant Lady* days, ran into Kirkwood and Herlihy when they were writing what would transpire to be *UTBU* in Torremolinos. He knew both well and is not so sure that collaboration between the pair, even though each was so immensely talented, would have ever been a good idea. "They were both strong personalities and Herlihy was outspoken and sometimes rude," he says. "I adored him, mind you, but still he was difficult and Jimmy was a pussycat — sometimes!" Beckenstein says, "Jamie Herlihy was a bit mystical. I always found him difficult whereas Jimmy Kirkwood was very, very down-to-earth and fun to be around. He could relate to anybody." Certainly the traumas involved in writing the play tested the pair's opposites-attract friendship.

UTBU is essentially a farce, or as Kirkwood himself put it in a letter to a friend, "It's a nasty comedy, and the meaner it's played — the better." It centers around a blind man named William Uggins and his organization Unhealthy to be Unpleasant (the UTBU of the title), which is dedicated to killing people of which it disapproves — a rather broad category, as Valerie Rogers, a pushy mother of a daughter she is mercilessly grooming for stardom, fatally discovers. Uggins presents such people with what he claims are awards, wrapped up like a present, and instructs them to open them only when alone. The award is a bomb. His latest would-be victim is a more deserving case for extermination: J. Francis Amber, who has decided to poison his mother in order to inherit enough money to mount a stage play. When Amber realizes that he has been rumbled by Uggins, he turns the tables and attempts to bump off his would-be assassin. William Russo reveals that Kirkwood told him that *UTBU* was the least personal of all his works, which he says he found an odd statement: "It deals with parents, it deals with all of his favorite themes, it deals with murder incorporated, unpleasant people who deserve to be done away with — a very common theme in his work."

"*UTBU* was really a be-fucked production from start to finish," Kirkwood later said. There is a certain exaggeration here: unlike the play of *Pony*, *UTBU* did achieve the feat of "coming in" after its tryouts. Additionally, a quite spectacular cast was assembled for it, including Constance Ford, Margaret Hamilton (the Wicked Witch of the West in *The Wizard of Oz*), Tony Randall, Thelma Ritter and Alan Webb. Richard Seff marvels, "What a great cast. My God. All names, almost every role." Nonetheless, many things did go wrong with it.

Problems started with the attempt to acquire a director. Kirkwood: "Jose Ferrer had agreed to do *UTBU*, but then he thought about it too long and said he couldn't afford a failure. He said, 'Why don't you send it to [theatre critic] Walter Kerr first and see if he likes it. Then we can talk more.' Can you believe that?" John Desmond: "I thought it was a good play and Jimmy loved Nancy Walker and he hired her, he and Herlihy, to be the director and she fucked it up. She made a lot of sight gags and it was disjointed." Walker was better known as an actress, having been a Broadway star since she appeared in the original productions of *Best Foot Forward* and *On the Town* in the early 1940s. "Jimmy knew her and her work and she was a friend of the producer," explains Jack Sydow. Kirkwood later lamented of Walker's work on *UTBU*, "She's a brilliant comedienne, but I think, because of the personalities involved, that she was stunned by their fear and demands. Also, she was gripped by that same awful fear. I guess she thought: 'My God, this is going to be a whole new career and away we go; it's got to work, it's gotta be!'…Besides, Nancy should have been directing non-stars…When you start fooling around with Alan Webb and Tony Randall and Thelma Ritter…you're dealing with people who have had lengthy careers and who've built up complex little iggies, and they have whole bagsful of areas that are trouble spots."

In fact, and unpublicized at the time, Walker was taken off the job of directing as Kirkwood and Herlihy began to get worried about the production. A reflection of the panic that had set in is that Kirkwood and producer Lyn Austin called Kirkwood's old friend Jack Sydow to come and rescue the production at no less a stage than Christmas Day. This was two days before its first Broadway preview with the play just finishing its tryout in Philadelphia (December 13-25, 1965), having been in Boston (November 8-December 1) before that. Sydow recalls, "I only saw one performance in Philadelphia. It was amazing to me that the play was not doing better because the cast was extraordinary." Sydow had a conference with Austin and agreed to take on the work. Sydow: "We drove back up in a limousine on Saturday night. It was Lyn and Jimmy and me and we talked about a rewrite that he did during the day. We gave it to the cast that night and then I worked on the play for about ten days." There had been a hiccup when Sydow indicated he wanted a percentage as well as his fee. Austin was reluctant and Sydow decided to engage in brinkmanship over the issue. Sydow: "I told Jimmy I was going to do that and I asked him if it was all right with him and he said, 'Of course, don't let them screw you.'" Sydow's demands were met, although the victory would be rendered moot by what transpired.

Two strange things occurred as Sydow began to try to rescue the situation: Herlihy departed the scene and Walker remained on it. Of Herlihy, Sydow says, "I think that he felt that he didn't want to be involved in all the mess anymore. There had been terrible fights with Nancy Walker and she had brought in Ira Wallach, who was a friend of hers and who was a comedy writer, to do work on it without talking to Jimmy. There'd been a big blow-up about that. Jamie didn't like the way the direction was going. Jimmy wanted to push it through, get it done, even if he didn't like it very much. There was a bit of a rift over that." Herlihy insisted that his name be taken off the credits. "He was firm on that," recalls Homer Price, adding, "Jamie was a little miffed at how the arrangement turned out, financially. But they smoothed that over. Certainly didn't ruin their relationship." As for Nancy Walker, the fact that she and Lyn Austin were old friends probably explains why she failed to make her exit. "She hung around," recalls Sydow, "and she eventually started to become a problem because she started to give notes to the actors on the sly and that was really irritating, but it wasn't major so I didn't make a fuss about it. It was understood from the time that I came there that she was going to be around. It was terrible. It was something that I shouldn't have agreed to and that the producer should have taken care of."

In unpicking the problems with the play in the short time that he had, Sydow came to the conclusion that Walker had put too much of her stamp on it: "Nancy Walker did a lot of business in the play that was wonderful business, marvelous comedy business, and it was the kind of thing that she could do, but all of the actors couldn't do it. And she had loaded the play with too much and not paid enough attention to the text." As well-known and celebrated as the cast was, there were also problems there. Kirkwood later said, "We had three stars — all talented and temperamental and terribly afraid of failure." For Sydow, the chief problem was Tony Randall, who played J. Francis Amber. In the climactic scene, Randall's character attempts to murder his on-stage nemesis William Uggims (Alan Webb) via a series of different methods that all end in a comedic failure. "He was giving away the joke all the time when I first saw the play," Sydow explains, "and I finally got him to the point where when he picked up the axe from the wall and raised it over his head there was something diabolical in his eyes and you really thought he was going to do it — and then of course the top falls off, when he pulls it back…I finally convinced Tony Randall that he should approach all of them as if they were going to work."

Though Kirkwood had been understandably miffed about the discourtesy of Walker involving Ira Wallach in writing without his consent, he wasn't too proud to call in a script doctor himself. "After I was working on it, Goodman Ace gave us a few lines," recalls Sydow. "He was the writer of *The Easy Aces*…He was a very well-known comedy writer. Jimmy talked with Goodman Ace and got a couple of very funny lines. It happens all the time." Sydow also recalls, "Tony Randall did become terribly obstreperous. One of the lines that Goodman Ace suggested was when in a confrontation with his niece he said, 'Me, me, me — I'm surrounded by egocentrics.' Which was a very funny line and he didn't think it was funny. I convinced him finally to say it."

The New York previews began on December 27. Despite illness, Lila Lee flew up from Florida to see her son's play on its official opening night, January 4, 1966. The mink she wore was borrowed but — somewhat to the amazement of Evan Rhodes, whom Kirkwood had asked to accompany her — she was treated like a huge star by teenaged autograph hunters at the theatre entrance. "She's the last of a breed," one explained to Rhodes. Things went less well for her son on an opening night Sydow describes as "a disaster." Once again, Randall was a major problem. Although he performed the "Me, me, me" line faithfully and had the good grace to admit his mistake about it (Sydow: "It got a huge scream and a couple of nights later he told me that a very good friend of his told him it was the funniest line in the play"), he reneged on the other change on which he had agreed. Sydow explains, "What happens is the star falls back on what they feel is right even though it's wrong and they've been rehearsed to do it a different way. The opening night jitters comes. He went right back to where we were, before I started working on the show… He handled the attempts at killing as if they were a joke and so nobody believed him, so it took the whole edge of the thing off." Kirkwood himself said, "Tony let himself get trapped into that actor's thing of, 'Yes, I'm playing the bastard, but I don't want the audience to hate me.' So, instead of being the meanest sonofabitch on earth, he kinda gave the audience a little wink after about twenty minutes as if to say, 'Well, I know I'm playing this monster, but I'm really cute. I really don't want to kill her, but we'll have a little fun about it.' And the moment he telegraphed this to the audience, the play went out the window." He added, "The same thing with Alan Webb. He wanted to be a blind bomber, but didn't really want to break anything flailing his cane, and he didn't really want to hit Margaret Hamilton on the ankle. Mostly, stars have so many things to protect that they can't be entirely open and honest. They can't go with the creative flow of the work."

However, it has to be pointed out that that work had its own problems. *UTBU* is perfectly respectable but essentially slight. The gags are often reasonably clever but with one exception never funny. (That exception comes when child prodigy Miss Blank delivers a cacophonous song for her audition. When in the silence afterwards someone points out that the telephone is ringing, Amber responds, "I thought it was my ears.") Meanwhile, the warmth and vivacity that are the strengths of Kirkwood's writing style are not suited to the cold-eyed medium of satire and therefore absent. Though it's not mean-spirited, *UTBU* is as black a work as *There Must Be a Pony!* was ultimately sunny. The analysis above, it should be pointed out, is of the commercially available edition as published by Samuel French, which is different in some ways to what the audiences saw in 1965/66. As Sydow explains, "The first scene in *UTBU*, the office that slides offstage, was cut before I got there. The published version is what Jimmy wanted them to see."

The reviews of *UTBU* were mixed. *New York World Telegram and Sun* reviewer Norman Nadel called it "…a moderately up and down comedy, with the emphasis on the ups." He continued, "Once you realize that the mad UTBU bomber and the nastiest man in New York are out to do each other in — a fact unfolded early in the play — the suspense lies only in the way they might accomplish it. Playwright James Kirkwood has striven diligently to build that but only toward the end of the play does this particular contest come up to expectations. Meanwhile you are pleasantly occupied because Kirkwood has created some exotic oddballs… The trouble is that once you meet each character and discover his or her entertaining eccentricities, said eccentricities thereafter repeat, usually with progressively less effect…As the mad bomber, Webb is at his best when he enters a room, swinging his white cane, cracking his greeter on the shin and knocking vases about. We're not supposed to laugh at blindness but his portrayal of a pious killer who cannot see is macabre humor at its best…The one role which actually builds is that of Randall's niece…I do recommend *UTBU* because there is a lot of treasurable humor in it." *The New York Times* was not impressed by how derivative the piece seemed, claiming that the director "…quite rightly sensed the necessity to liven up the script with action but necessity has only been the mother of inventory. We spend two hours seemingly taking stock of a lot of old shows and slapstick films…We suffer with two genuinely funny performers who are trapped in a creaky vehicle." The *Herald Tribune*'s verdict was: "Some accounting must be made of the fact that this is the friendliest unsatisfactory play to invade the city in some months…author hasn't had a solid comic idea to see him home and so has had to pick up strays…A hopeful farce becomes a wistful one." *Daily News* called it, "A cheerfully manufactured comedy with a highly companionable cast…Script does wander a little far now and then but it isn't anything to get mad at and it has some imaginative conceits and constructively funny lines."

Other reviews: United Press International: "Everyone has tried so hard to make it a madcap comedy romp that this little fantasy has been overwhelmed by an avalanche of directing and acting clichés. There are some excellent actors trapped in this charade." Associated Press: "A bunch of nimble performers make it the password to a good deal of zany, offbeat amusement…farcical satire delivers a beguiling amount of fun." *Wall Street Journal*: "*UTBU* is a lot of things, farce, black comedy, regular comedy, satire but principally entertainment, for it is more notable for its variety than its consistency…much of the time the play bubbles along pretty well keeping the customers happy…an enlivening if unimportant evening." *New York Journal American*: "It has overtones of *You Can't Take it With You* compounded with the most flagrant insanity of Olsen and Johnson, it is vociferously cornball and contrived but there are many times when it is impossible not to bust out laughing. I believe it will attract a certain zany following but I doubt that it has enough substance in situation and character to become a popular success."

Kirkwood always felt that the sort of sentiment in that last line was wrong and that what stopped *UTBU* becoming a popular success was a combination of three other things. One was the cast problems already mentioned. The second was the supposedly hidden agenda of the *New York Times* reviewer. Kirkwood said, "We were in the position of having Stanley Kauffmann out there writing his first review as official critic for *The New York Times*. And I think he was just saying, 'I'm going to show those fuckers that they've got somebody around who won't let anybody get away with anything!'" Kirkwood averred that Kauffmann was a frustrated writer, the author of many unpublished novels and unproduced plays. "Those things have got to show in a man like that," he said. "Not that it was a great play. But it was a funny play." However, Kirkwood maintained that the primary reason for *UTBU*'s failure was the New York transit strike that began on New Year's Day, 1966. People stayed away from the theatre, he felt, not so much because of poor reviews or word of mouth but because there was no easy means of getting in and out of the city. There does seem to be some evidence to support this. The January 6, 1966, edition of *New York Herald Tribune* carried a story headlined, "Theaters Hurt on First Matinée of the Strike." It began, "Broadway's usually full Wednesday matinée was hurt yesterday by the transit crisis. Long-run plays and shows in the less-than-hit category were most severely hit…" It stated that two plays were probably closing due to the strike — *The Right Honorable Gentleman* and *Any Wednesday* — and one definitely was, *The Devils*. It added, "Playing to only a quarter house at the matinée, the comedy *UTBU*, which opened Tuesday to mixed notices, will close Saturday." *UTBU* disappeared after fifteen previews and seven performances.

Sydow is not so sure about the transit crisis theory. Though he says, "I hate to talk about Tony Randall when he's gone and can't defend himself," the director pins the blame on the star: "If Tony Randall had given the performance that he should have given, I think the reviews would have been much stronger." Sydow summarizes *UTBU* as having, "a very funny idea, but it gets lost along the way."

Judging by other comments Sydow makes, the transit strike may have been highly useful to the author psychologically. "He always had a rationalization that covered him," says Sydow of Kirkwood. "He had a rationalization that it wasn't the fault of the material, it was something else. I'm sure that his rationalization with *UTBU* was that it was fucked up by the original director and then there was the transit strike." Sydow seems to suspect that it is this very ability to rationalize that led to Kirkwood's buoyant personality: "I'm sure that he had ways of avoiding any depression that would hang over people. I never was affected by his depressions and I think it's because he covered it up. He was a master at that…Jimmy always had a *modus operandi* of how to handle things." Sydow agrees that this mentality may have stemmed from Kirkwood's traumatic childhood: "Well, golly, he *had* to learn how to handle things. And handle it so it wouldn't rub off on other people." He further speculates, "Jimmy loved to be loved and I don't think he would want to upset people with his depression."

James Leo Herlihy could well have used Kirkwood's purported ability to rationalize away failure. Demanding his name be removed from *UTBU*'s credits was only the tip of the iceberg of Herlihy's complexes about his art, ones which would eventually lead to him turning his back on his own remarkable talent. This was something that Homer Price saw first-hand. "Jamie and I were together, let's say, for a year, 1966, and so I knew Jamie very well and he was sort of my guru, even though he was only about five years older than I," he explains. "The difference between Jamie and Jimmy was that Jimmy would put anything out there he could possibly get published, didn't matter, and Jamie was very self-critical and he ended up with a whole bunch of stuff in a trunk that he wouldn't even let anybody see, much less try to publish." After 1971 — and despite the fact that *Midnight Cowboy* was not only acclaimed but a bestseller, helped by a famous film version — Herlihy didn't publish another word of fiction. Price: "I saw his working habits. He was tormented, really, and finished up a book of short stories called *The Sleep of Baby Philbertson* that summer and that didn't have much success and the very next thing he attempted was *Season of the Witch*." The latter was a novel featuring two young runaway hippies written from a female protagonist's point of view. Though superficially modish, it felt slight and forced, especially after the gritty depth and verisimilitude of *Midnight Cowboy*. This was something noted by the critics. "It wasn't as good as his earlier stuff," says Price. "He was very disappointed in *Season of the Witch*. It was a flop. He found it very difficult and at the time of *Season of the Witch* got discouraged and didn't want to write anymore."

"Oh, but it's not quite that simple!" demurs Jerry Paonessa, a friend from the mid-1970s of both Kirkwood and Herlihy. "Jamie is a very complicated man, and that was not really the intellectual, emotional evolution of that at all. I spent hours at Jamie's foot trying to learn about life and the film business and writing and he had pretty much decided that he wasn't going to write anymore. He felt he didn't have anything to say that hadn't been said before and better. He also had a very difficult time with aging, a very, very difficult time, and that was as much of it as the writing was. Jamie was not the kind of guy who relied on the critics. He pulled out of *UTBU* because he didn't think it was good and he pulled out of life because it wasn't very good for him." (Herlihy committed suicide in 1993.) It should be noted, however, that another person to whom the author spoke for this book — Jim Piazza — says that Herlihy told him personally that the reception to *Season of the Witch* was the reason for him ceasing to publish his work while another — Benjamin Morrison — says he got the same story through Kirkwood.

As well as friendship, Kirkwood kept up a correspondence with Herlihy. Though his letters to Herlihy are often misspelled and ungrammatical, as well as stuffed with in-jokes impenetrable to anyone but sender and receiver, they provide a valuable insight into how Kirkwood really thought and acted behind his public façade. This especially applies to his sexuality: the letters are almost shockingly frank about gay life, or at least Kirkwood's gay life — its promiscuity, its bitchiness and its mechanics (from around 1980: "The Greekling drove all the way out here for five hours of Passionate Leave yesterday and three orgasms took place which is not bad for an old man of 80 — me. One anal, one oral and the other whacking off. Weeeeeee. SHOOTING SPERM starring Baby Jim Kirkwood"). In almost every letter, Kirkwood refers to his friend by a new effeminate nickname (Dolly Dearheart, Flossie Nightentits…), tells Herlihy how much he loves him (this expression of affection usually involving an obscene simile) and imparts gossip about whom he is having sex with or wants to and/or about which mutual acquaintances are fornicating. He also frequently attempts to nudge him into resuming writing, either on his own or in collaboration with him. Beckenstein: "He always felt it was such a waste that he stopped writing, that there was so much more in him." From the endless obscenities and familiarity, it seems clear that Kirkwood and Herlihy continued to be lovers. The letters also indicate that Herlihy collaborated to a small extent with Kirkwood on the latter's work, not just as a sounding board but even via physical writing, however limited.

Despite *UTBU*'s initial failure, it was not a complete disaster. A Kirkwood letter of February 1966 to a former colleague on the South African tour named Hymie pointed out that publishers Samuel French had bought *UTBU* for stock and amateur, that it was being submitted for foreign productions and that there were even "film nibbles." Meanwhile, the same letter stated that Kirkwood had "just this week sold the novel" that "I began in South Africa," a turn of events that had left him "delighted."

By the time of that letter, Kirkwood had alighted on the title *The Angels or Whoever* for his latest prose effort. His delighted state, though, was not to last. He later spoke of the manuscript having gone "from publisher to publisher." It would be a decade-and-a-half before the novel achieved publication, rewritten, with the new title *Hit Me with a Rainbow*. On January 24, 1967, nearly a year after Kirkwood's delight at having sold the book, Herlihy was writing him a letter commiserating over his treatment at the hands of publishers Putnam, culminating in the big turd they had dropped down his chimney the previous week — the latter presumably notification of the decision that they would not after all be publishing his second novel. (If Putnam was not the publisher that had bought the book in February '66, then Kirkwood must have been even more devastated.) In a missive in which he is very careful to heap praise on Kirkwood as a writer and a person, Herlihy concludes that *Pony* gave readers less opportunity to catch Kirkwood inventing and that *The Angels or Whoever*, because it strayed from personal experience, lacked the personable Kirkwoodian qualities of the debut.

That the published version of *Hit Me with a Rainbow* was easily the least of all Kirkwood's books and that it took substantial revisions suggested by his editor to even reach that level of sub-mediocrity indicates that *The Angels or Whoever* was rejected for solid aesthetic reasons. However, no author deliberately sets out to write badly and every author utterly believes in his latest work.

Kirkwood's devastation must have been made all the worse by the fact that only a few years before he had astounded a jaded figure like Robert Kirsch with his talent and that he had been, upon publication of his debut, the darling of the literary season.

TEN

"Licking my wounds…I decided to try the boards again," Kirkwood said of the unexpected stalling of his literary career.

These days, he at least had somewhere more salubrious in which to tend to his lesions than the West 58th St. apartment. On September 13, 1966, Kirkwood purchased a home on Barry Avenue in the Springs area of East Hampton, Long Island, New York. "At the time, he was looking for a house on the water in the Hamptons and just walked up to the door of a small little waterfront cottage," says Arthur Beckenstein. "Jim asked if the owners would be interested in selling. It was a matter of timing and good luck and he bought the house for a steal" ("steal" equating in this instance to $29,000). Barry Avenue was an unpaved and probably private dirt road at the time. Its name changed along with its profile at some point in the sixties, becoming Squaw Road. However, Kirkwood's abode was always lovely. "The house was on a beautiful property that jutted out into the channel of Three Mile Harbor, a picture postcard bay," says Beckenstein. "Jim added a living room facing the water with big windows to take advantage of the beautiful view." A deck was added across the front to further facilitate that objective. As it faced due west, the house was afforded a spectacular sunset whenever the sky was clear. Also beautiful were the bay's parades of motor boats and graceful, classic sailboats with their masts silhouetted against the sunset on busy summer weekends.

One wonders whether his new mortgage is what led Kirkwood to pursue acting with renewed vigor. Regardless of his financial commitments, though, unlike James Leo Herlihy Kirkwood wasn't going to give up his writing because of rejection, whether it be by the public, critics or publishers. When he turned his attention to a new novel, the result was a spectacular return to form.

If we are to assume that his plans in a letter to his mother dated January 18, 1967, were fulfilled, Kirkwood formally began writing *Good Times/Bad Times* on January 19 that year. Therein he says he will "…dive right into the next book" on the morrow and not "let time go by." (Said letter incidentally was written in dismay at hearing Lila Lee had been hospitalized again and that her doctors had discovered "spinal nerve damage due to liquor.") Of course, to some extent Kirkwood had already written some of *Good Times/Bad Times* because the framing device of letters to his lawyer from a boy in a prison cell after killing his headmaster, which would provide the structure of *Good Times/Bad Times*, had originally formed the structure of *There Must Be a Pony!* before he'd changed his mind about including his Brewster Academy days in that narrative. Additionally, in his previously mentioned undated letter to Little, Brown, Kirkwood had mentioned a new outline he had devised for his first novel, one eventually partly abandoned. Although Kirkwood did not follow it to the letter, the abandoned parts of this outline would to a large extent form the plot of *Good Times/Bad Times*. It read: "…the book would follow up with Josh's finding the suicide notes, his mother's eventual nervous breakdown, and the boy's loneliness. He goes to Ohio for the first half [of] the next school year but life with his uncle is impossible. The man is a chronic drinker plus being a chronic anti-everything: his wife, whom Josh loves, his mother, the Jews, the Catholics, the government, the school system, etc. etc. The constant upheaval in their household, after Josh' s recent experiences, is too much for the boy to take so he prevails upon Merwin to help him. Merwin sends him to a prep-school in New Hampshire that he, Merwin, had attended some twenty-five years earlier when it was a good school. By this time the school is seedy, filled with more town-students than boarding students, and run by a man with a Lincoln complex. A stern, disciplinarian who frowns upon 'show folk,' has a cowed wife and a brilliant and precocious 13 year old daughter. The prep school is no fun for Josh. The New Englanders are cold, the boarding students, except for one frail boy, are not interested in Josh and he is not intrigued by them. They are alien people to him. The one boy, Ted, comes from a very wealthy family and has a bad heart condition. They become great friends. The boy should never be in school in his physical condition but his parents are ashamed of having sired a sickling and bored with the idea of having a son who cannot keep up with the other boys. They send him great lumps of money which he often shares with Josh because he cannot use it and it means nothing to him. Their friendship is the one thing that keep [sic] Josh at the school. When the boy dies of an attack one night he is heartbroken, then furious at the attitude of the headmaster. He takes a sum of money from the boy's room, packs, and leaves the school. He has had enough of abnormal living. He wants only one thing. He will not return to his uncle, living with Merwin, although it would provide laughs would be as abnormal as staying at prep school, his mother is out of the question because she is still in a rest home and although her eventual recovery is in sight it is not a fact yet. He wants only one thing. To go to the ranch and live with Andy and Midge until his mother is well. Although he is not out of his mind he knows damn well he can't go on the way he has. He wants to be in a quiet place with two people that love him, and not only love him but one another. He's had a letter from Midge and she and Andy have returned to the ranch so he knows they're there. He isn't even going to call them, he's just going to fly out there and appear and he knows it will be all right with them.

"One of the teachers sees him leaving the campus. He walks the few blocks to the heart of the small town the school is situated in, takes a taxi to a nearby town 12 miles away from which he can get the train to Boston. He is intercepted at the station by the headmaster. He tries to sneak on the train but the headmaster grabs him. He fights like a tiger to get away. He pulls no punches, he kicks, smashes the headmaster in the head with his suitcase and it turns into a knock-down drag out. He is taken into custody and brought to the police station where all sorts of charges are lodged against him by the headmaster, stealing the money, being neurotic, a trouble-maker etc. etc."

Considering the misgivings Little, Brown still had about the length of *Pony* even when everything but the story revolving around the Ben-Rita-Josh triangle had been jettisoned, Kirkwood took the correct — perhaps only — course of action in turning the Brewster Academy material into a separate book. Some might suggest that he took the wrong — and rather puzzling, considering how developed was the story — course of action in then not going ahead after publication of *Pony* and writing *Good Times/Bad Times* but turning his attention instead to *The Angels or Whoever*. One suspects that Kirkwood would have felt that writing another novel with a teenage protagonist would seem — to him and to critics — like repeating himself. In the end, of course, he did repeat himself as far as the public — who had no knowledge of the abortive second novel and its adult milieu — were concerned, but it transpired not to matter: following one book about an adolescent with another feels less desperate after an eight-year gap rather than a one- or two-year gap. The quality of that second published book is another consideration, of course, and in this sense things panned out perfectly for Kirkwood, for it's doubtful that *Good Times/Bad Times* would have been as good a novel as it is had Kirkwood plunged straight into it after *Pony*. Though *The Angels or Whoever/Hit Me with a Rainbow* was never going to be a great book, the very act of writing it meant that Kirkwood picked up more technique and understanding of the novel form — particularly what *not* to do — which he was then able to put to good use in *Good Times/Bad Times*. He also obtained for himself a distance of time from the person he was when he wrote *Pony*, thus cutting down further potential for stylistic and philosophical similarity.

Perhaps surprisingly for such an autobiographical novel, Kirkwood put some research into *Good Times/Bad Times*. Ex-Brewster schoolmate Mildred Beach recalls that Kirkwood exploited the opportunity of appearing in the play *A Country Girl* at the Lakes Region Playhouse in Gilford, the small town directly across (and visible over the lake) from the grounds of Brewster Academy, to refresh his memory of his alma mater. "That was some time in the 1950s," she says. "We visited with him between the matinée and evening performances. He spoke of *Good Times/Bad Times* and planned a trip to Wolfeboro to re-establish buildings, locale, etc., in his mind." If her dating of the visit is accurate, then Kirkwood paid another visit to New Hampshire to research the book, for Ned Bullock, another Brewster alumnus, recalls a meeting with Kirkwood in Wolfeboro that he seems certain was in the second half of the sixties. (A photo Kirkwood took of Brewster Academy with the year 1966 written on it bears him out.) Bullock: "I had a photographer's studio up on North Main Street and he showed [up] and talked to me: what did I remember of the time of being in Brewster? He arrived in the afternoon and we spent an hour or two shooting the breeze. We discussed Greenall quite a bit: did I feel the same way [as him] about Greenall? And I sure did. At that time I wasn't as mellow as I am now."

From his abandoned outline for the second part of the *Pony* novel, Kirkwood retained in *Good Times/Bad Times* the setting, the doomed, sickly best friend, the unpleasant headmaster and the blow-up with the latter. Several elements, minor and major, were altered. Kirkwood elected not to make the book *There Must Be a Pony! Part Two* by simply giving his protagonist a different name, having a friend of the protagonist's father obtain the school placing, not Merwin (who isn't a character in the book) and rendering the protagonist's mother deceased. The Ohio sequence doesn't appear. Though Ted — renamed Jordan — does die and though Peter is disgusted by the headmaster's attitude about the death, it is not this that primarily causes the bust-up that results in imprisonment but rather attempted sexual abuse by the headmaster. The bust-up becomes something more profound than the "knock-down drag out" but instead a killing in self-defense (the original plan anyway when writing *Pony*). The name Kirkwood chose for his protagonist was Peter Kilburn. Says Kirkwood's old writing classmate Terry Kilburn, "I was very flattered when I hadn't seen Jimmy in a long time, he named one of his leading characters Peter Kilburn. That was kind of nice. I just assumed it was either a compliment or an unconscious memory."

Unlike *The Angels or Whoever*, this book was deemed fit to print by a publisher, specifically Simon and Schuster.

On January 30, 1968, Kirkwood was one of the 447 signatories of an advertisement that took up two full pages of the *New York Post* headed "If a thousand men were not to pay their tax bills this year." It put him among people who believed "that American involvement in Vietnam is morally wrong" and who pledged that they would not "voluntarily" pay the "proposed 10% income tax surcharge or any war-designated tax increase." The ad also declared that "Many of us will not pay that 23% of our current income tax which is being used to finance the war in Vietnam." Kirkwood's name sat alongside those of writers like Nelson Algren, Noam Chomsky, Thomas Pynchon and Gloria Steinem. Kirkwood had agreed to take part at the behest of James Leo Herlihy, another signatory, who had written to him about it on June 20, 1967.

However, Kirkwood could not always be relied upon to be what was then called "right-on" and is now termed "politically correct." Not only had he toured in South Africa, but in his February 1966 letter to his *Never Too Late* colleague "Hymie," he wrote — presumably in reference to one of the calls for a boycott of apartheid South Africa very common at the time — "I have not signed that silly thing about South Africa and will not, because I know that it's only depriving fine liberal people from theatre and hasn't a goddam thing to do with punishing Dr. Werewolf and his government." Kirkwood was also not averse to seeking tax breaks that some might find inconsistent with his Democrat leanings. Kirkwood was certainly no racist (Piazza: "I never heard Jimmy make a racist remark, in fact, among his dearest hearts were his longtime [black] housekeepers in both the city and in the Hamptons, though he wasn't above teasing them"). However, his correspondence with Herlihy occasionally throws up joking references to "niggers."

Kirkwood collaborated at this juncture with his friend Evan Rhodes on a proposed stage musical called *The Boys on the Hill*, a step outline for which existed by April 1968, presumably the 42-page document in Kirkwood's papers. Rhodes met Kirkwood at Bon Soir in the Kirkwood & Goodman days when Kirkwood singled him out in the audience to banter with. He was reintroduced to him a dozen years later by James Leo Herlihy. (Kirkwood didn't recognize Rhodes.) Though Rhodes was a widower, he became homosexual. Kirkwood and Rhodes were long-term friends but Beckenstein says it is his belief that they were never lovers. Though Rhodes would go on to literary acclaim with *The Prince of Central Park* and also produce more populist fare like men's adventure novel *Safari*, at this point the sole book bearing his name was *Only You, Dick Daring! or, How to Write One Television Script and Make $50,000,000*, a non-fiction collaboration with Merle Miller.

The Boys on the Hill ("working title," the synopsis is anxious to point out) is a comedy about an interesting group of people: Congressional page boys. These teenagers acted as Boy-Fridays to the men who ran America. According to Kirkwood and Rhodes' script, the boys (nicknamed "the legs of Congress") hailed from every state in the union as well as every social, economic and ethnic background. They had an unusual degree of personal freedom for their age, earning as they were a then-healthy $345 to $405 per month and domiciled in lodgings far from parental reach. The world they inhabited was naturally a highly exciting and glamorous one that made them privy to the secrets of the rich and powerful. The job didn't come without its penalties: the boys had an onerous workload that saw them attending high school from 6:30am to 9:30 am before doing a full day's work on Capitol Hill.

The musical centers around two page boys who start as friends and end up in bitter political and moral opposition, Josh (that name again) Wilder from Montana being the bumbling heart-of-gold Democrat and Vic Grainger the manipulative, smooth Republican. Like the other boys, they are billeted at the boarding house of Maggie Cummings, an octogenarian who acts as a mother figure to — and in reality lives for — the boys. Her house happens to be on a prime development property. Her refusal to sell up to the developers makes her enemies, including ones on Congress. Whereas Josh and the other pages are prepared to fight for her cause, Vic is ready to betray her in order to effect his own societal advance.

Because the surviving story is in broad form, it's difficult to tell whether *The Boys on the Hill* would have made a good show. The setting and situation certainly is interesting and, fleshed out and (naturally) given some good songs, it might make for compelling and moving material. It certainly attempts to touch all the bases: the authors state in a preamble that the microcosm of the pages' daily lives reflects the macrocosm of American government and society. Human interest is covered both by the Maggie Cummings/land development situation and a romantic subplot. However, that this is a mere outline can't excuse the fact that the resolution is rather undramatically arrived at (Maggie's home is saved by various rather casually rendered acts of negotiation, brinkmanship, deception and blackmail at a ball). This inability to come up with a thrilling finale is something that would be a feature of most of Kirkwood's scriptwriting, whether it be for stage or screen. Even at this point, it should have been clear to Kirkwood that he was always uncertain beyond the parameters of first person, semi-autobiographical prose which is not so reliant on climax.

Another way Kirkwood kept busy at this juncture was in starting work on another novel, although he admitted it was "haltingly on little cat feet…" This tentative approach would seem to have permanently characterized his approach to the book, the aforementioned, never-finished novel about his father, *I Teach Flying*.

While editing *Good Times/Bad Times*, Kirkwood had noticed that the fuel bills in his East Hampton house were unusually high. Suspecting that there was something awry with the new thermostat in his office, he called in a plumber. The plumber was Joe McAree Jr. of Sag Harbor, Long Island, who came over to his house on February 8, 1968. McAree gave Kirkwood a paid invoice for $29.27 for his work, dated March 1, 1968. It's not known if McAree by that date had informed on Kirkwood to the police for growing marijuana plants in his guest bedroom.

"Jim went to a party where everyone was given some marijuana seeds," says Beckenstein. "Jim was the only one who was successful at getting the seeds to grow — in five terra cotta flower pots, under a grow-light in a spare bedroom. The plumber got $100 to turn Jim in." On March 11, 1968, at around 10:45 am, Kirkwood was arrested at his home on suspicion of drug possession. He was freed on $500 bail. Local newspaper reports revealed that McAree — then an unnamed informant — had been responsible for the busts of several students at nearby Southampton College as well as a trio of arrests at a separate 1965 local raid. One small glimmer of good news for Kirkwood was the fact that his age was rendered as 37 and 38 by the papers that carried the story, instead of the 43 he actually was.

Kirkwood was in a grim situation. Although America in 1968 raged with debate about whether people committing the allegedly victimless crime of smoking marijuana should even be subject to prosecution, such right-on rhetoric didn't go down well in courtrooms, nor with much of the public: it was that very year that presidential candidate Richard Nixon successfully campaigned on a promise to crack down on drug use. Kirkwood theoretically faced five years imprisonment.

The bust disrupted his long-term schedule. He had intended renting his house out for the summer, but could make no plans until he found out whether a grand jury would accept his defense (presumably the claim that he grew the plants out of curiosity that he would later publicly make) or indict him. As the case dragged on into May, it caused problems with a trip he was planning on making to New Orleans for a feature assignment he had obtained from *Esquire* magazine. Kirkwood's rather frightened state of mind is illustrated by some notes he typed up on Saturday, May 4. He headlined the notes, "Thoughts about lawyer and our casual conversation the day before Fri May 3," although it's not known whether he sent these notes to his lawyer or merely bashed them out to vent frustration. They read, "I must be a little crazy. The casualness of our not knowing about the Grand Jury date has really upset me. I'd called you over a week ago and you were going to find out then. Then it took me six calls to get you yesterday. Is the defendant's lawyer notified about the date or the calendar or does he always have to inquire. You had originally said if it wasn't in April it would be in early May you thought and here it is early May and nothing's been ascertained. I can't possibly take off and spend a week in New Orleans where my energies are supposed to be directed-to writing an article on a very tricky case — not having any idea of what's happening to mine. Is there a possibility it's already gone before the Grand Jury and we don't know about it. Like this last week. Then I must phone you as early as possible and find out." Matters dragged into the following month. Kirkwood was informed via telegram on June 3 that the grand jury had indicted him and that he was to attend court on June 7 for arraignment. Ultimately, Kirkwood pleaded guilty and received a suspended sentence of a year and a $500 fine.

His stated motivation of curiosity may have been true but Kirkwood was an enthusiastic recreational drug user, something which became more pronounced the older he got. A literary agent recalled sitting next to Kirkwood at a dinner many years later and being amazed when Kirkwood lit up an after-meal joint. T. Michael Kirkwood recalls an incident when *A Chorus Line* opened in Los Angeles in 1976: "He invited me. We were downstairs at the Shubert and he comes over to me and says, 'Hey!' and Florence Henderson is coming down the stairs of the escalator and says 'Jimmy!' and he says, 'Oh shit I've got to go talk to her. Here take this.' And he hands me a cigarette and I look and it's a fucking joint! Here we are with people all around. I was shocked. I had smoked before but I thought it was kind of funny." Terrence McNally says, "Jimmy smoked a lot of pot, which is very much part of his story. I wouldn't say he was a pot head, but he was very uninhibited." His drug intake wasn't restricted to marijuana. When Kirkwood did make it to New Orleans, local Benjamin Morrison recalls, "We smoked dope together and [took] poppers together too while he was here and it was the first time that I had ever heard of poppers." Kirkwood would also acquire a taste for another drug. "Jimmy certainly liked his cocaine," Homer Price says. However, he adds, "Jimmy was definitely not a coke addict. I mean, when he was working, he didn't indulge. He was a recreational cocaine user." Others dispute the latter assessment of Kirkwood's use of cocaine during the 1980s.

The "very tricky case" in New Orleans to which Kirkwood referred in that aforementioned note to his lawyer was that of Clay Shaw.

Shaw at that point was one of the most famous men in America. On March 1, 1967, he had been charged with conspiracy to assassinate President John F. Kennedy. It would make him the first person to ever be put on trial for that nation-shattering death (Lee Harvey Oswald, of course, having been murdered before he could be put in the dock.) The charges had been brought by Jim Garrison, the District Attorney of Shaw's native New Orleans. Kirkwood had met Shaw after Shaw had been charged, their encounter taking place at the East 7th Street New York apartment of James Leo Herlihy when Kirkwood was working on the last chapter of *Good Times/Bad Times*. Kirkwood later explained that Shaw and Herlihy had mutual friends and that Herlihy had suggested Shaw call him, Herlihy, if he was ever in the city. When Shaw did so in November 1967, Herlihy invited him to dinner. Knowing his best friend would also be intrigued, Herlihy then invited Kirkwood. Homer Price is fairly certain he was also there that evening. Like Herlihy, Kirkwood and Price, Shaw was gay, although as a hulking man of six-foot-four few people's idea of a "pansy."

Benjamin Morrison — although he would only come to be acquainted with either Kirkwood or Shaw at a later point — thinks that it is possibly Shaw's sexuality that led to Shaw agreeing to speak about his situation to Kirkwood on the evening of Herlihy's dinner party. Morrison: "He sort of sat at Clay Shaw's knee and said, 'How did you find yourself in' — and the words still stay with me — 'in this predicament?' Clay would have been fascinated to have this cute guy as his audience and sort of instant party companion." Price says of Shaw, "[We] were so impressed with him as an honorable and interesting man." Shaw was certainly an urbane and elegant individual. A decorated soldier, businessman and published playwright, he had been wealthy enough to retire in 1965 when only in his early fifties. He had been managing director of New Orleans' International Trade Mart from 1946 until that retirement. Subsequently, he had dedicated his time to restoration projects in New Orleans' French Quarter. On the surface, the suggestion of him plotting to kill anyone, let alone the president, seemed incongruous to say the least.

The way Shaw told it to Kirkwood, just before Christmas, 1966, he was requested to come into the offices of the District Attorney, where he was asked by assistant D.A. Andrew Sciambra if he had ever met Lee Harvey Oswald, who was known to have been in New Orleans in 1963. Sciambra explained that their investigations had shown Oswald had associated with a Clay Bertrand and wondered if this might be him. From there, things snowballed, if slowly. At the time of Kirkwood's meeting with Shaw, the New Orleanian was still waiting to go to trial, something that would not happen until February 6, 1969, the two-year gap a result of Shaw appealing the decision to prosecute him.

Following his meeting with Shaw, Kirkwood asked his agent to get him a commission from a magazine to write about it. Though Kirkwood had never written a magazine article before, his agent was successful in persuading men's glossy *Esquire* to agree to run the proposed piece, hence Kirkwood's trip to the "Big Easy." When it eventually appeared in the magazine's December 1968 issue, Kirkwood's article was ridiculously partisan. In it, he stated that the transcript of the preliminary hearing of the state of Louisiana against Clay Shaw "without too much of a stretch…brings to mind the Spanish inquisition." This would be an absurd statement even if we are to accept his assertion that "Hearsay was freely allowed, dead men spoke…" Meanwhile, his contention that we can read anything about bias in the court from the alleged fact that "objections by the defense were mostly overruled, those of the prosecution were mostly sustained" is muddle-headed — surely the quality or relevance of the objections are the issue, not the quantity either way?

In the article, Shaw comes across as a plausible and convincing man, and this is not simply because he is not up against any opposition from his interviewer. He talks sagely of people in positions of power abusing that power, of power hardening "into a privileged cast of nobles…" Shaw is also convincing when he talks of living "moment to moment" with the trial hanging over his head: "I…try to enjoy each and every moment to the fullest, whatever it is, a book I'm reading, the birds in the patio out there, a sunset, an enjoyable meal, the companionship of friends, a game of bridge. Perhaps with the sword of Damocles hanging over me, I'm even made more aware of the simpler pleasures of life." Even despite its partisanship and leaps in logic, the *Esquire* article was a good one, well-written, punchy and moving — with the caveat that Shaw's emotional speech about the small pleasures of life would have seemed sickening phony lip-quivering should he have been guilty of what he was accused, which many still believe he was.

"There's no doubt that the District Attorney has dedicated himself to getting a conviction but the scapegoat is being stubbornly resistant about playing the villainous part assigned him," Kirkwood wrote in the final paragraph. This sympathy for Shaw characterized *American Grotesque*, the book Kirkwood would ultimately write about Shaw's trial. It might be instinctively concluded by some that Kirkwood's partiality was either caused by him liking Shaw on a personal level (which he apparently did) or even him being irrationally swayed by some sense of solidarity or kinship with a fellow homosexual. This is not to suggest that Kirkwood did not genuinely believe Shaw was innocent: nothing in Kirkwood's make-up seems to suggest the despicable qualities it would have required to knowingly cover up the facts of an assassination. However, if nothing else, Kirkwood was an emotional man.

Yet a recollection of Sid Wasserman casts an entirely different light on Kirkwood's thinking. When the pair had met in New York in '64 and gone back to Kirkwood's apartment to reminisce, the talk had turned — as it did with so many Americans at that juncture in history — to the still-recent violent death of their head of state. Wasserman was surprised, even dismayed, at the attitude his old friend revealed about the theories that were beginning to grow in answer to the many unexplained questions about the assassination. "It was just about four or five months after the assassination that we met up and there was a lot of turmoil going on in the United States about who did it and was it more than one assassin and all this kind of stuff," says Wasserman. "I was so convinced that this is a CIA conspiracy and friends of mine at the time, we all agreed on that. I thought that anybody that accepts that one assassin explanation is naïve… We started to exchange ideas and finally Jim said to me, 'Oh, I don't agree with you at *all*.' He totally bought the Lee Harvey Oswald story, that it was one guy." Though Kirkwood seemed sad about Kennedy's death, he was so adamant in his feelings that Wasserman assumed that it resulted from dogma: "I realized in talking to him that politically we weren't necessarily on the same wavelength. That I wasn't sure that his being in New York made him as liberal as I was in the sense in politics." Told by this author that in fact Kirkwood was a Democrat and campaigned in a small way for Democratic presidential candidate George McGovern in '72, Wasserman said, "That's great news, I'm glad to hear that."

Toward the end of 1968, Kirkwood secured an advertising feature in *Esquire* — presumably as a consequence of the connections made via the Clay Shaw feature — called "My Bazaar." In a double-page spread, Kirkwood was seen posing in a Jordan Marsh walking coat, a Cladyknit

Irish fisherman pullover and an Irish cottage robe. A giant bottle of Brut and a similarly oversized Nero watch framed the pictures on the vertical plane. "Author James Kirkwood lives a very different life from yours and mine — which is why he dresses with such casual care," the advertisement declared. A quarter of the copy was dedicated to puffing *Good Times/Bad Times*, published according to the ad in October, though the first week of December seems a more likely timeframe.

Good Times/Bad Times was dedicated "To Lila Lee and Mary Murphy with love." The book carried some impressive cover endorsements, including ones from authors Nathaniel Benchley, James Leo Herlihy, Gore Vidal and Tennessee Williams. The publishers were so spoilt for garlands that they could even decide not to print an endorsement from Noël Coward, whose proffered comment of, "A finely written book; very funny and also very moving" was only used on publicity sheets. Though there might be a suggestion of a gay network and a coterie of friends at work with some of these people, the book certainly deserved their accolades.

At eighteen, Peter Kilburn, the protagonist of *Good Times/Bad Times*, is older than Josh Cydney from *There Must Be a Pony!*, but not by much. Like Josh, he endures traumas that no one of his age should ever be required to.

Although *Good Times/Bad Times* attempts to capture the argot and mindset of the young, the conceit of the book — that it is a journal designed to aid the lawyer who has been engaged to defend Peter in his forthcoming murder trial — rules out any attempt at the conversational narrative of *The Catcher in the Rye*. From his prison cell, Peter recounts the events that have led him, a relatively ordinary individual, to take actions that have plunged him into the surreal and barely believable situation of facing life behind bars.

Peter is the son of an ageing, alcoholic father with a faltering thespian career, modeled of course on Kirkwood's own father. The father is a widower. A friend of his father's from the actor's club at which he spends most of his time has bought Peter his senior high-school year at Gilford Academy, a New Hampshire prep school struggling to overcome the trauma and bad publicity of a recent homosexual scandal involving two pupils. That the establishment is a disguised Brewster Academy is something at which Kirkwood hints by calling the town in which it is located "Brewster." (Gilford itself is, as previously touched upon, named after a town across the lake from Brewster Academy.) Though based on Kirkwood's schooldays in the forties, the book is set contemporaneously, Kirkwood including a couple of references to the Vietnam War (one of which is somewhat contrived).

Kirkwood is merciless in his depiction of both the acting profession and his father. The former he describes as the "saddest profession in the entire world" even more than "whoring." His father is "usually insolvent and I'm afraid always will be." He and Peter are living in a "tacky apartment" on Argyle Avenue, the Hollywood street of course that in fact Kirkwood Sr. did call home during the last decades of his life. The early cameo appearance of Peter's father is superbly done, managing to be compassionate but devastating. Scrubbed up and bewildered, he turns up to see Peter in prison after having used his son's unfortunate situation to chisel more money from the habitually generous friends at his club. After promising to get Peter some treats, he disappears on a drinking binge — to Peter's complete lack of surprise.

After this, we are taken back to Peter's arrival at the school. The cast of characters at Gilford is well-drawn, Kirkwood believably portraying a wide variety of social types, intellects and temperaments among Peter's fellow pupils. Particularly convincing though is Mr. Hoyt, the demonic, tilting-walked headmaster who just barely keeps his irrational temper and unnatural sexual proclivities beneath a civilized exterior. The story is a sort of love triangle between these two and Jordan Legier (pronounced Luh-zhay), who arrives at the school after Peter has given up his dream of acquiring a best friend there (a convincing teenage hankering). Jordan is a twenty-year-old from a rich New Orleans family. Though a couple of years the senior of the school's oldest pupils, his heart condition makes him slightly below average in height and very below average in health. He is aloof but not snobbish, sarcastic but compassionate. He is also the only pupil not intimidated by Mr. Hoyt: the headmaster has been promised much needed money for the school if Jordan graduates, so can't afford to alienate him for fear he will decide to leave. Aspects of Jordan's character are not quite convincing — for instance his ability to coolly remain above the fray of his schoolmates and his verbal humiliation of the school bully. *Completely* implausible is his comment about Cary Grant: "Any man who says he wouldn't whack off with Cary Grant is either a liar or can't get it up." Boys and young men simply did not speak like this to their peers in the sixties, and don't do so now unless they are both gay and courageous. What is certainly believable is the friendship that develops between the new recruit and Peter. The unique and slightly idiotic relationship between adolescent best buds is captured perfectly, complete with petty bitchiness, insanely reasonless laughing hysterics and in-jokes repeated again and again until wrung dry.

It is this closeness that infuriates Mr. Hoyt, a would-be pederast who can never admit it, especially not to himself. Hoyt is attracted to the good-looking Peter and after Peter sustains a back injury uses the alcohol rubdown prescribed by a doctor — plus the fortification of alcohol he has partaken of by the conventional means — to attempt to sexually assault his charge. This massage scene — in which a bewildered and scared Peter pretends to be asleep — is half-comedic, half-chilling. When Hoyt catches Jordan and Peter in bed together — the explanation is an innocent one — his jealously is transmuted into righteous rage and he assaults Jordan, whose sickly metabolism cannot withstand the attack and packs up within a couple of days. Peter is naturally devastated by his friend's death and tries to run away. A furious and out-of-control Hoyt fetches him back. When Peter tries to run away again the same evening, a climax ensues where Peter is pursued through a night-time snowstorm by his drunken, lecherous and by now psychotic headmaster. Ultimately, Peter kills Hoyt with a boat hook in self-defense. This denouement is not actually as interesting or satisfying as what has preceded it. Though we feel Peter's disgust when Hoyt on one of the occasions he catches him presses cold, rubbery lips to his unwilling face, the chase is not particularly nerve-wracking.

Author John Knowles was kind enough to give Kirkwood an endorsement for his later work *P.S. Your Cat is Dead!* (albeit one not ultimately used, at least on or in the book itself), but he was a bad luck charm for Kirkwood in one sense. *Good Times/Bad Times* was always dogged by comparison to Knowles' novel *A Separate Peace*, published nine years before it. There are definitely similarities between the two works: the prep school backdrop and the fact that they revolve around two best friends, one of whom is both preternaturally wise and doomed. (In Knowles' book, the spite of one of the friends dooms the other, not psychological wretchedness on the part of the headmaster). Ironically, *Good Times/Bad Times* is easily the superior of the two books. Where *A Separate Peace* is rather cold, pat and uninvolving, *Good Times/Bad Times* is warm, funny and moving. Its plot and characterization furthermore are convincing whereas *A Separate Peace* feels contrived, except for the boy's death, which is shocking and credible. *Good Times/Bad Times* also compares favorably to the daddy of all contemporary coming-of-age novels. Though *The Catcher in the Rye* is thoroughly enjoyable, its relentless colloquialism makes it ultimately feel slightly insubstantial: the argot might be impressively sustained but doesn't provide the narrator quite enough of a palette, vocabulary-wise, to confer gravitas.

It is ironic then that the flaw that prevents *Good Times/Bad Times* from being a truly great novel is its vocabulary. Notwithstanding the fact that Peter is an articulate, intelligent, thoughtful middle-class eighteen-year-old — and despite the fact that Kirkwood seems to try to cover himself by having Hoyt state that he has a high IQ — the prose he writes is too eloquent. No matter how intelligent an eighteen-year-old might be, he would not use the little stylistic devices and flourishes of a seasoned author the way Kilburn does. For instance, this passage in chapter three: "That September day was beautiful, warm and cloudless, and the view looking across the lake from the school was exceptionally peaceful, flat wooded lands bordering the lake with a few scattered summer lodges and cottages and then beyond, wooded foothills leading up to rugged mountains, thick with trees themselves." It's not as if Kirkwood doesn't have the ability to depict less articulate and ordered thought (or in this case writing) processes. Immediately afterwards, comes: "My impression of the campus and surrounding country that morning could be summed up by two words — clean and, somehow, innocent. Innocent sounds odd, maybe unspoiled would be more like it."

Although all first-person narratives betray artistic license in their deployment of streamlined, eloquent prose that nobody (except perhaps a professional author) would use in his diary, journal or any other written account — and readers know this and are willing to suspend disbelief about it — it becomes a problem with a protagonist as young and relatively unlearned as Peter, and that's even leaving aside the fact that we are asked to believe that this story is scribbled down in a cell with little or no revision. For that reason, *Good Times/Bad Times* would have been a considerably better book had Kirkwood taken the decision to make it a retrospective account, allowing him the sophistication of adult reflection and language. Had he done that, *Good Times/Bad Times* would have truly gone down in the history of American letters as a great work, for its author has a knack for capturing little aspects of being young that most people have forgotten by the time they are in their forties. For instance, when he is given a lawyer whom he immediately doesn't like and is told by him he is in a heap of trouble, Peter responds with the type of guilelessness of which no adult is in possession: "Don't! Don't scare me! I'm scared enough already!" Similarly memory-jolting are Peter confiding he is usually shy around people, his nervousness in front of the headmaster, his quest for a best — as opposed to bog-standard — friend, his squeamishness over certain thoughts or words (he refuses to enunciate "fart") and his endless vulnerability.

Though not a great book, *Good Times/Bad Times*' disarming tenderness and compelling (if quasi-claustrophobic) narrative sees it through to the status of a very good one and makes it the type of book one looks forward to resuming reading, the last an achievement that is by no means common.

As ever for Kirkwood, the book ends with an optimistic sign-off — literally so in this case: Peter Kilburn's signature is placed at the end of this rather massive missive to his lawyer.

Some gay activists were irritated by the book, feeling its depiction of a repressed headmaster pursuing a boy reinforced assumptions about an association between homosexuality and pedophilia of which they were tired (and which were prevalent then to a degree barely imaginable today). This can arguably be dismissed in the same way as can the assertion that depictions of heterosexual child sexual abuse slanders straights. However, there is little denying that an unfortunate aspect to this book is the fact that there creeps into it a suggestion that homosexuality is "wrong." Peter, for instance, is very anxious to point out to the reader that he and Jordan did not have sex. He shrugs off his admission to dalliances with homosexuality in his early teens by saying that at that age boys are ready to copulate with anything that moves. He is also hoping to find witnesses for his trial who can attest to his heterosexuality, thus undermining a prosecution case which will probably posit Peter murdering Hoyt as punishment for "exposing" his affair with Jordan in school assembly. Of course, this is a work of fiction and the character of Peter Kilburn can't be reasonably expected to have Kirkwood's exact viewpoint on life — but we have been here before with his nervous comments on homosexuality and almost pejorative descriptions of gays in his first novel. One gets the feeling that between Kirkwood's insistence on planting clues to his sexuality, his determination to not definitively reveal his sexuality and his decision to tackle the subject matter of sexual abuse, he finds himself fighting with dirty tactics his way out of a corner he never intended to back himself into in the first place.

By the way, great quote from the book: "I think it's far more preferable to use the word 'cock' instead of 'penis.' Cock is clean, forthright and sort of jaunty. Penis sounds like something you'd only touch with a pair of tweezers."

Writing in the *Sunday Los Angeles Times*, Marjorie Driscoll said of *Good Times/Bad Times*, "Kirkwood has chosen an unusually effective form for his novel." Referring to the framing device of Peter's letters to his lawyer, she asserted, "…he has had time to think, time to search for an explanation, and that, too, is there. Still a third purpose is served.

The reader, aware of the inevitable approach of tragedy, can sense the significance of small happenings — as they point toward disaster. Bit by bit the story tightens, tenses, and comes to the climax…" Driscoll adjudged it "a profoundly searching, brilliantly written novel." Richard Bradford of *The New York Times Book Review* called the work "hilarious and terrifying" and asserted that Gilford and Mr. Hoyt would become classics of the prep school genre in literature. If the latter sounds a somewhat easy achievement in a narrow field, there was no ambiguity about his effusive conclusion about Peter Kilburn: "His loose-jointed but lucid narrative and his point of view — sometimes sophisticated, sometimes naïve but always crisp — are what makes the novel such a joyful taste of Heaven and a shattering glimpse of Hell." "An engrossing…Salinger-esque novel…Recommended," was the verdict of the *San Francisco Examiner*. "A warm, interesting and readable novel," opined *Chicago Sun-Times Book Week*. "Makes absorbing reading," said *Library Journal*. *Publishers' Weekly* offered, "James Kirkwood's new novel offers solid reading."

Probably the most positive review was that provided by Cleveland Amory for *Cosmopolitan*, although the fact that he somehow managed to get an extract from his review on the front of the jacket of the first edition of *Good Times/Bad Times* indicates he was not a completely impartial figure. Grandly using the Royal We, Amory declared, "We have the pleasant task of recommending to you the best young novel by the best young novelist we've read in many a moon: in fact, since 1951 when a then-young man named J.D. Salinger wrote a young novel called *The Catcher in the Rye*…he has done what very few highly praised first novelists have done in all literary history: written a second novel that is even better than the first…*Good Times/Bad Times* is as sensitive as *The Catcher in the Rye*, one of our all-time favorites, and yet sensational too." With its eye on *Cosmopolitan*'s young, free, single and female demographic, Amory also said, "At first you may think it's too *boyish* for you. It isn't…and Mr. Kirkwood writes so well that we would recommend his novel even if there were not a single girl in it." Amory concluded, in reference to Peter Kilburn's habit of saying "Spending a lot of time," "This is a book you *will* want to spend a lot of time with!"

An uncommon bad review came from *The New York Times*, whose Eliot Fremont-Smith had fun with Amory's description of Kirkwood as young, pointing out that the same had been said about Kirkwood nearly a decade previously upon his literary entrée. Though he found the book "well-written" and "controlled, amusing, sensitive, suspenseful, touching,"

Fremont-Smith also found it full of "expertly copied stereotypes" and "smooth, white." He additionally wrote: "Although Boy and Boy Prime often share the latter's bed, nothing happens. At the same time, however, it transpires that Boy Prime…is active on the side with both sexes. The Boy shows us how to feel about this, which is respectfully, tolerantly, charitably and calmly. In the meantime, there has been ample opportunity for prurience to be transformed into superior disgust at that terrible headmaster. Very neat and tidy…" Fremont-Smith adjudged the book to be "a not quite homosexual novel" aimed at "not quite heterosexual male readers" and "the wives of men who graduated from prep school a quarter-of-a-century ago." Though there is the whiff of sexual disgust in the review, he seems more than anything to be raising an eyebrow at Kirkwood's twisting himself into knots about what he is or isn't endorsing. Fremont-Smith adjudged *Good Times/Bad Times* a "good/bad" book that was flawed by that thing hated by *The Catcher in the Rye*'s Holden Caulfield: "phoniness."

When asked what his favorite of his own books was, Kirkwood would always cite *Good Times/Bad Times*. He explained to Jim Whaley in approximately 1979, "Only because I get so much mail from readers who say it has touched them, mostly on the basis of friendship and the importance of having a good friend." In 1971, Kirkwood said, "I get between six to eight letters a week about *Good Times/Bad Times*, mostly from girls between the ages of sixteen and the early twenties, who ask me if the marvelous close friendship between the two boys Peter and Jordan is really possible." That such a close, if unconsummated, friendship was depicted as possible also made the book appeal to boys and young men who found that their sexual thoughts were not of the mainstream variety. Jim Piazza: "Because gay people were so desperate for any kind of role model, *Good Times/ Bad Times* became like the bible for gay teenagers in the sixties." In fact, this stature in life and literature was reflected back from reality in 1972 via a novel called *Shockproof Sydney Skate* by Marijane Meaker. A then-controversial story of a teenage boy with a lesbian parent (they fall for the same girl), its very well-read protagonist is impressed by the Paintbox Theory that Jordan laid on Peter in *Good Times/Bad Times* — essentially that we are all given a paintbox of variable quality and potential to paint our way through life by the "Big Joker in the Sky."

Good Times/Bad Times was the first Kirkwood work read by his future Boswell William Russo. He was astounded by the novel and thought it contained far more than even the friendliest critics saw in it. "I think it was extremely complex," he says. "I saw things in it that amazed me, and I thought, 'This is an interesting writer.' His use of the unreliable narrator, the motifs that kept cropping in and out of the book and the use of names in the text…" With all Kirkwood's books, Russo feels Kirkwood was smarter than the unobservant critics: "Playing with the truth and the veracity of the characters was some of the things that I'd have debates with him about. And he would say to me, 'I don't lie in my writing, I might lie in life just not to hurt people,' but I think that there's a game of chess going on in his books."

Discounting the drug bust and its associated problems, the period surrounding the publication of *Good Times/Bad Times* was clearly a very agreeable one for its author. Not only were the reviews generally highly favorable, but other revenue streams were coming in as a consequence of his sophomore prose effort. In *Playbill*, Kirkwood's writing veritably shone with his delight as he stated that this time his acting career truly was something with which he was dispensing: "Add to this reception a good paperback deal, Book-of-the-Month Club, and a most salubrious movie sale and…yes, I think it's writing and writing novels at that."

That salubrious movie sale may have brought Kirkwood some handy ready cash but it, of course, did not guarantee a motion picture would be made, and indeed one never was. Not only would comparisons with *A Separate Peace* haunt the *Good Times/Bad Times* book, but they would dog attempts to bring it to the screen. Beckenstein: "*Good Times/Bad Times* was optioned immediately and it seemed a sure thing that it would be made into [a] movie. There was a married couple who were writing the script and they suddenly got divorced and that fell through. There were a number of other times when there was great interest in it, it seemed like it was gonna happen, and it just never did. Then *A Separate Peace* became a movie. At the time it was seriously being considered for a production and they felt they didn't want to do it because *Separate Peace* was similar subject matter." By 1972, Kirkwood was lamenting to *After Dark* magazine about the *Good Times/Bad Times* movie, "Warner Brothers says they have close to $300,000 tied up with the project, what with the purchase and two screenplays. And they say they're not going to make the movie, but they won't let anybody else make it…It's because it might be a big success and then they'd look like fools." Kirkwood intimated he was kicking himself for not insisting on a reversion clause in the book's film rights as he had with the film option taken on his first book. He was persuaded not to rock the boat over reversion rights by his agent, who pointed out that *To Kill a Mockingbird* director Robert Mulligan had been recruited, offices had been assigned, a script had been commissioned and casting had begun. Kirkwood: "Nobody foresaw that Mulligan was going to hate the script and walk off the picture, or that the studio was going to be sold." He claimed that the previous year the studio was planning to revive the project, but balked when they found out that Paramount was intending to shoot *A Separate Peace*, worrying about the market for films about prep schools being flooded. He said, "If *Separate Peace* is a good movie, then Warners will immediately say, 'Ahh, quick. Let's do another story about two guys in a prep school. Let's make *Good Times/Bad Times*.' But it will then be a pallid imitation, like the films which came out after *Easy Rider*." In fact, the move version of *A Separate Peace*, directed by Larry Peerce and written by Fred Segal, was a box-office flop upon its September 1972 release. Kirkwood friend and sometime editor Nick Ellison says, "That kept *Good Times/Bad Times* from becoming a movie. Every time somebody would say, 'This is a masterpiece,' the studios would keep saying, 'Yeah, but look what happened to *A Separate Peace*.' And we'd say, 'Yeah, but look at *A Separate Peace*, look at the movie it was, and look at the tenor of it.'"

Kirkwood was touched that upon publication of *Good Times/Bad Times*, Clay Shaw took time away from his own predicament to send him a good-luck telegram. In fact, it was only a few days later that Shaw received the news that after his long battles through the legal system to have his proposed trial be declared invalid, the Supreme Court had turned down his appeal. By this point, Kirkwood was, in his own words, "some two hundred pages" into his novel about his father (something that makes it all the more extraordinary that he never finished it in his lifetime). Despite this — or perhaps partly because of it, what with his evident reluctance to work on *I Teach Flying* — he contacted Roberta Pryor at his agency and asked her to see if she could secure him an assignment from a national magazine to cover the Shaw trial. In fact, Kirkwood ended up getting himself the assignment. Jim Goode, articles editor of *Playboy*, was an acquaintance. Kirkwood rang him with the idea and it was agreed he would send Goode an outline. Goode hemmed and hawed about commissioning it, concerned about the pro-Shaw stance that Kirkwood had taken in the *Esquire* article. (*Playboy* had published a fairly sympathetic and lengthy interview with Shaw's prosecutor Jim Garrison in October '67.) Yet when Kirkwood was given the nod, he — judging by his later published account — did not even have to actually promise to be impartial. Kirkwood was to receive $200 for the feature plus $1500 expenses, regardless of how long the trial went on. In the event, Kirkwood was to get an entire book out of the trial, although it's doubtful that the stress and grind — professional and personal — involved in covering it was something for which he ever felt he was appropriately remunerated.

ELEVEN

Benjamin Morrison wrote James Kirkwood a fan letter after the publication of *Good Times/Bad Times*, which he had enjoyed even more than he had *There Must Be a Pony!* Morrison: "I think it was probably a P.S. down at the bottom of the fan letter but I just said, 'If you're ever in New Orleans please give me a call' and I gave my phone number and had no anticipation in the universe that he was ever going to have a reason to be here."

No doubt neither did Kirkwood, but upon his return to New Orleans to cover the Shaw trial, he made contact with Morrison, who was then a first-jobber copy editor at the city's daily paper the *Times-Picayune*. Kirkwood himself had no reason to know that Morrison was homosexual, but Morrison sort of knew Kirkwood was. "I presumed he was gay virtually before I met him," he explains. "He didn't like this, but *Good Times/Bad Times* in hardback edition, the background color or secondary color on the cover was lavender and the edges of the paper were all done in lavender and I think that was a kind of secret code back then for identifying gay books for the gay reader but the straight reader isn't going to notice that at all and is not going to be scared off by that. He got sort of upset about that when I told him that. It's not anything that I read, but I instantly saw the cover of the book and I thought it was a gay book. He said he'd had no idea and additionally talked about the original cover motif, a box of Good & Plentys, a candy mentioned in the text." Richard Kluger, Kirkwood's line editor at Simon & Schuster for *Good Times/Bad Times*, thinks this theory about the dye is urban myth. "I'd be astonished," he says. "Our production department would not have known that Jim Kirkwood was gay. I knew it, but I certainly didn't ask them to put a topstain. I would not have known that a purple topstain would have been a signal to the gay community."

Morrison says he also picked up a hint from the effeminate Merwin: "Here's a gay uncle who is probably, next to the boy, the most well-thought of character in the [book]. Straight people didn't write about gay people then except to ridicule them or to make villains out of them." Though that might be a less disputable clue to Kirkwood's leanings, it also seems rather subtle to the modern mind. However, in a day and age when homosexuals did not have any formal meeting places or communications networks, the antennae were necessarily more sensitive. Morrison: "[It] was sort of like scrabble, or a picture puzzle, and you just had to put things together on your own." Morrison adds, "Jim was very sweet and very seductive toward me. We had a little affair while he was here, and actually I think once in New York. One of the things that I most remember about him was that he touched people while he talked, and I'd never been with anyone who did that before."

Kirkwood rented a New Orleans apartment for two months and hired a young man named Bruce Eggler to be his researcher. Eggler had been recommended to Kirkwood by someone at Tulane University who knew he both needed work and had some experience in journalism through being a writer and editor on a student newspaper. "I ended up doing very little real research," recalls Eggler. "But I think he wanted me to help him with local background, customs, etc. One specific question I remember was how the fact Louisiana law was to some extent based on the Napoleonic Code would affect the course of the trial. I think I said I didn't know." Lest some jump to the conclusion that there was an ulterior motive to Kirkwood employing but not using Eggler much, Eggler says, "I don't recall ever being aware of Kirkwood's sexual orientation."

In January 1969, locals found virtually the entire world descending on New Orleans. The trial was the hottest ticket not just in town but on the planet and Kirkwood was lucky enough to be there. Morrison: "They were tough about credentials at the trial and the reason Jim could get in every day and sit in the press section was he was representing a major national publication. This is kind of crucial too: *Playboy* was paying the bills at that time. He would have had zero, no source of money in the universe then. I mean nothing." *Playboy* would ultimately decide it didn't want Kirkwood's prospective article, but this may have mattered less than might be imagined, for Morrison says, "My idea is that he definitely planned on making a book out of the trial before he arrived in New Orleans."

In her very pro-Garrison book *A Farewell to Justice,* Joan Mellen claimed that in March 1968 Shaw decided to commission a book about the case, to be written from his point of view. "It would attack Garrison as a homophobe and assert that he was being victimized because he was a homosexual," she wrote. Mellen claims that after Shaw sounded out a friend named Stuart Timmons (a gay author), who declined, he turned to another homosexual scribe in the shape of James Leo Herlihy and that though the latter also turned him down, Herlihy recommended Kirkwood. Mellen: "Kirkwood would pretend to be 'objective.' Kirkwood's editor at Simon & Schuster, Richard Kluger, says he would never have signed up *American Grotesque* had he known of Kirkwood's special relationship with Clay Shaw." Mellen cites as her sources an interview with Timmons and a conversation with Kluger. Later on in her book, Mellen again ridicules the idea that Kirkwood and Shaw met by chance. While it doesn't necessarily bear out Mellen's claim, this line from the form letters Kirkwood sent to magazines soliciting a commission to cover the Shaw trial certainly bears thinking about: "On the phone [Shaw] said that since meeting me, he'd read my first novel *There Must Be a Pony!*, that he'd enjoyed it thoroughly…and would I be interested in writing a book he'd been approached about with him?" Having said that, Mellen's assertion that the book Shaw wanted written would claim that he was being victimized because he was a homosexual instinctively strikes one as extremely unlikely: gay men did not out themselves in late sixties America, even under duress.

"Yeah, I think that's accurate," says Richard Kluger of Mellen's claim that he would never have signed up *American Grotesque* had he known of Kirkwood's special relationship with Clay Shaw. Though clearly knowing nothing of any deal between Kirkwood and Shaw of the type claimed by Mellen, he says a relationship between Kirkwood and his subject "…undercut credibility. It would have sent a signal to me that he was compromised to some extent by his connection." Kluger recalls of his decision to sign *American Grotesque*, "I worked with him on *Good Times/Bad Times*. I edited that with him and I knew Jim a bit. I thought it would be an interesting book." He admits, "I'm sure I understood that he thought Shaw was getting screwed and it was a set-up…I'm sure I must have seen the *Esquire* piece. He was coming to do a book that was an exposé against Garrison." However, asked if he would have signed the book if he'd known it was going to be quite as partisan as it ultimately was, Kluger says, "No. It's one thing to be partisan, but you have to make a case and you have to make it based on factual stuff or opinions that are well fortified." From other comments he makes, it almost seems as though he and the publisher considered *American Grotesque* the bait they would have to swallow in pursuit of Kirkwood's follow-up novel to *Good Times/Bad Times*. Kluger: "I have a vague memory that…he came to me with a two-book proposal, one of which was *American Grotesque* and the second may have been another novel. He did not get much of an advance for *American Grotesque* and I had resistance from my colleagues to do the book. I had to bull it through because I thought Kirkwood was an author we should keep publishing and we'd done well with *Good Times/Bad Times*, but even so it looked like a questionable project. I do think that he had to agree to present us a two-book deal to sweeten the project."

Benjamin Morrison had also read Kirkwood's *Esquire* article but that didn't necessarily make him sympathetic to Kirkwood's view on the subject of Shaw (whom at that point he didn't know). "I just couldn't imagine anybody wanting to have anything to do with somebody who was accused of conspiring to kill the president, and at that time I was naïve enough to think that Clay probably had something to do with it," he says. Morrison recalls that this was not an uncommon thought in his hometown at the time: "'He must be onto something' was the thing you tended to hear over and over and over again." Though Morrison had initially begun to form the same point of view, over the forthcoming months and years, he began to perceive things very differently, coming to the belief — partly through his friendship with Kirkwood — that the decision to prosecute Shaw was literally arbitrary. He says, "Garrison had decided there was a conspiracy which went on in New Orleans and that somebody would have been the ringleader of it and was trying to find someone to charge that with. Then, somebody mentioned the word 'clay' — it would be like somebody saying that they had to pick up a clay pot at Woolworth — and suddenly Clay Shaw was the prime suspect. That's the way Jim [Kirkwood] wrote it and that's the best explanation of it." Asked in 1970, the year after the trial, if he felt Garrison genuinely thought Shaw was part of a conspiracy to assassinate Kennedy, Kirkwood said, "I think he might have wanted to believe that at the beginning and just was stuck with this one defendant and so he did everything to make it appear that he *was* guilty." Zachary Sklar, editor of Jim Garrison's 1988 book on the case *On the Trail of the Assassins* and co-author of the screenplay of the Oliver Stone film *JFK*, which was partly based on Garrison's book, unsurprisingly doesn't agree with that assessment of the impetus for prosecution. However, he does admit something that may come as a surprise to many: "I don't know if Clay Shaw was innocent or guilty. I don't think Garrison even knew." However, he adds, "What he said to me was, 'I had this conspiracy by the little toe. I didn't think that Shaw was running a conspiracy.' He just thought he had a little toe. And he said, 'I'll be damned if I'm gonna let go of it.'"

Shaw's trial began on January 29, 1969. Morrison: "Jim was writing the book on a daily basis. He would go to trial every day, he would write his version of the highlights of the trial that day. He would also go through the paper to see what the local papers were seeing as being the lead or the important thing or whatever was going on that day." Garrison was relying on the testimony of witnesses who asserted that a very tall, white-haired figure with whom they had seen Lee Harvey Oswald and/or one David Ferrie in New Orleans was in fact Clay Shaw, a man who claimed he heard a conversation of Ferrie, Oswald and Shaw's about bumping off Kennedy and people who said that Shaw and Clay (or Clem) Bertrand were the same people.

The verdict came in on March 1, 1969. In a 1970 radio interview, Kirkwood agreed that many felt that the jury would return a guilty verdict, himself included: "The jury was very hard to read. They were a very stoic bunch of men." The other reason that he felt a guilty verdict was coming was "the Zapruder film being showed over and over." If the trial of Shaw achieved one thing of value, it was to prise from the vaults the only visual record of the assassination of President Kennedy. Shot by local clothing manufacturer Abraham Zapruder, it captured the sight of Kennedy's demise with dispassionate bloody precision. Though familiar and iconic today, at the time the public had never seen it. Zapruder sold the footage to the Time-Life company, which published selected stills from it in its magazines, but did not allow it to be screened. The entire courtroom gasped as it was unveiled, the awful end of their head of state turned instantly from a mental abstract into a stomach churning reality in which a terrified wife chases part of her husband's brain across a car trunk. Leaving aside the fact that the action the film revealed seemed to many to instantly render absurd the insistence by the authorities that Kennedy had been killed by bullets fired by a cumbersome bolt-action Manlicher Carcano rifle from the Texas Book Depository to his rear, it was possible that it had had an emotive effect on the jury that left them determined to make somebody pay for what they had just seen, with Shaw the only obvious target for their supposed wrath.

In fact, the verdict was a unanimous Not Guilty. Garrison took some consolation from the fact that the jury also observed that — contrary to the conclusions of the Warren Commission investigation of the assassination — they thought there had been a conspiracy to assassinate the President. It was strange that he did so: opinion polls amongst Americans going as far back as '63 showed that a majority of them shared that conspiracy view, although there is some evidence that the numbers went up considerably as a result of the Shaw arraignment. Even Morrison scoffs at the lone-gunman viewpoint, saying, "I don't think anybody thinks that the *Life* magazine version of that is the whole truth."

Following the verdict, Kirkwood went about interviewing everybody connected with the trial that he could. This included jurors, witnesses, the judge and defense and prosecution teams. Naturally, he wanted to interview Garrison and — eventually — got his wish. Bizarrely, considering that Kirkwood would later describe Garrison as "one of the most dangerous men I've ever encountered," the two Jims got along famously, finding common ground on such things as their enthusiasm for the play *The Glass Menagerie* by local legend Tennessee Williams and their belief that Robert Kennedy would have made a good president had he also not been slain. Kirkwood was later asked by a journalist if he found Garrison "oily." He replied, "Not at all. He was charming. Bright, personable, with a good sense of humor." He then added, "He was absolutely terrifying. It was as if Hitler had the personality of Cary Grant or Jack Lemmon."

Kirkwood did not, however, confront Garrison with his suspicion that he had authorized the interception of his mail and the tapping of his telephone. "Jim showed me his mail box on the day after it had been broken open and he felt very paranoid," says Morrison. "I think I even heard a couple of clicks on the phone. I'm from a political family and my father's phone had been tapped and you could hear people clicking and even talking in the background on my father's phone. It was a little more sophisticated in Jim's case, but you did just hear that a conversation started and there'd always be a click." "That's the kind of thing I think is total bullshit," says Sklar. "If that kind of stuff was happening, I don't think that was coming from Garrison's office. I think that's the kind of stuff that was being done by what we call Black Operations. That's exactly the kind of stuff that they do. Garrison's office never did stuff like that. They didn't have time to do that. They were under siege. [Kirkwood] was totally naive, and didn't know a thing that he had walked into. Just was totally in over his head."

Garrison's career certainly didn't seem to suffer from the verdict. In 1969, he was re-elected as District Attorney for the second time. While Garrison was gearing up for the poll, Kirkwood left town to knuckle down to writing his book. Richard Kluger left Simon & Schuster in early 1970, with Michael Korda replacing him as the book's line editor. (Korda did not respond to an interview request for this book.) What he did see of *American Grotesque* before his departure left Kluger rather disappointed, particularly considering the "clean" manuscript of *Good Times/Bad Times* he'd had the pleasure of editing. "I do remember that I had issues with him about the book, in terms of the overall quality of the writing," he says of *American Grotesque*. "It was a problematical book for us. I was not pleased with some of it. I know he was doing revising. It needed work. It was hopelessly long and the partisanship of the book was still more troubling." Kirkwood's friend Evan Rhodes helped him pare down a massive manuscript that even in its published form constituted a 661-page book.

During the process of writing and editing *American Grotesque*, Kirkwood found that non-fiction was not his métier for a few reasons. The first was that he initially had a stumbling block in deciding upon a style. It was something that James Leo Herlihy helped him overcome. A friend of both men, Jerry Paonessa, explains, "He said, 'I'm doing this but don't know how to do it.' He started to panic. Herlihy said, 'You sit down and you say Jamie Herlihy, have I got a story for you.' Pretty much that, and that's what emancipated him from his inability do to it." Another impediment sprang from Kirkwood's emotional involvement in what he was dealing with. "Writing it was not a happy time for me," he later said. "I was immersed in what I felt was a pot full of injustice. I wasn't dealing with some hypothetical trauma. I was dealing with someone who was really suffering — Clay Shaw. And with a man, Garrison, who I thought was a real monster." Then there was the kind of hard labor that he had not encountered when writing novels. For someone who had always been able to draw upon a handy well of personal experience, having to schlep to libraries and archives to look up or double-check facts was a culture shock, or as he put it, "…all that bloody research." Even when the book was physically written, it was still far from finished. Kirkwood: "It took much more time because of all those lawyers having to [go] over it. Everyone was worrying about libel suits…I feel much freer with my imagination, so I don't think I'll ever write non-fiction again…But I'm not sorry I wrote it…I got hooked on the subject. It became a cause."

Kirkwood was hardly in a position to complain about alterations being requested by publisher's lawyers. He had made his own tweaks with the facts. In the original *Esquire* article that he reproduced at the front of *American Grotesque*, Kirkwood had quoted a woman anonymously but whom Morrison identifies as Muriel Frances (a Mrs. Muriel Bultman Frances Bognor is cited as a friend of Shaw in the testimony of one Goldie Moore and thanked by Kirkwood in his acknowledgments) as saying, "Clay 'shacked up'…with me…" It was a line that Morrison admits was "used to mislead people. That was calculated." Also calculated was Kirkwood's refusal to directly discuss the nature of Shaw's sexuality throughout the book. "Clay just said that he did not want that mentioned," says Morrison. "I think Jim may have told me that some years afterwards." Morrison adds, "But it was on the checklist of things that had to be in the book" and that he feels that Kirkwood attempted to at least suggest Shaw's sexuality via a reference to sado-masochistic costumes seized by the D.A.'s office which Shaw passed off as Mardi Gras garb. The moral dilemma in which Kirkwood found himself here may have been another reason why he largely stayed away from non-fiction after *American Grotesque*. On an emotional — even to a certain extent intellectual — level, one can understand why Kirkwood did not want to state in his book that Shaw was gay in an age when that revelation could cause social ostracism. However, having taken on a journalistic job, he also had a duty to act in a professional manner and to present to the reader all the facts so that the reader could decide whether or not they impacted on Shaw's behavior or defense in any way. To be fair to Kirkwood, this dilemma did not only afflict those on Shaw's side. Zachary Sklar found himself in a similar position when collaborating with Oliver Stone on the screenplay of *JFK*. "The only thing that I feel slightly uncomfortable with in [the] *JFK* film is the depiction of Clay Shaw's homosexuality," Sklar says. "I took the position that Garrison did: that it was irrelevant and shouldn't be shown. But Oliver felt that it was important to show that this was a motive for Shaw to be covering stuff up. That it would give some explanation for that."

American Grotesque, subtitled "An Account of the Clay Shaw-Jim Garrison Affair in the City of New Orleans," was published by Simon and Schuster in December 1970. It was dedicated to James Leo Herlihy. Explained Kirkwood of the title, "My editor thought of the word 'grotesque' after reading the manuscript. The word is a fascinating word to me: if somebody says something or someone is grotesque I immediately want to know 'Who,' 'Why,' 'What,' 'How?' My first working title was *Adventure in New Orleans* but that seemed very tame. I thought of the whole trial as an adventure. I got into it by a fluke and it became an adventure that I had to see the end of. I think we were just all sitting round and someone finally said '*American* Grotesque' because it does have all of the elements of the most grotesque side of our society."

"...subjectivity sticks out all over me like so many porcupine quills," says Kirkwood in the preface to *American Grotesque*. He is at least being upfront about his bias and, arguably, his candor on this point makes it acceptable: the reader knows what he is getting. Except where it comes to Shaw's sexuality. The discretion/deception on this matter that starts right at the beginning of the book with the reproduction of his *Esquire* article continues throughout. In chapter two, Kirkwood notes that Shaw sounded happy to hear that he, Kirkwood, was hoping to come to New Orleans to attend the trial and attributes it to him welcoming a friend and supporter. Kirkwood must have known that Shaw was possibly happier Kirkwood was coming because he was an attractive younger man. Harmless enough so far, one might think, but the avoidance of this issue leads to sometimes ludicrous omissions. Kirkwood reveals in chapter twelve that he noticed a pact existed between defense and prosecution to ensure obvious homosexuals did not get on the jury. The fact that Kirkwood was doing his level best to completely avoid the subject of Shaw's sexuality presumably explains why Kirkwood doesn't try to offer a reason for what is a puzzling unanimity of purpose. Ultimately, Kirkwood's circumspection even leads him to harm Shaw's case: whereas Kirkwood could plausibly cite Shaw's sexuality and the fear of its exposure as a reason for Shaw denying association with David Ferrie — a homosexual suspect in the assassination who was found dead within hours of a New Orleans newspaper breaking the story that a JFK death probe was being conducted in the city — he instead clings to a position that Shaw did not know Ferrie that is increasingly absurd in the face of a slew of eyewitness linking the two. This is particularly absurd considering Ferrie and Shaw's respective singular appearances. Not only was Shaw a memorable sight with his hulking physique and albino-esque features (in his form letters written to magazines from whom he was hoping to get a commission to cover the trial, Kirkwood himself said of Shaw, "Because of his physical appearance and his face, he's a man easily recognized"), but Ferrie was pretty much unforgettable: he suffered from alopecia, the condition which causes the loss of all bodily hair, and compensated for this by pasting on utterly unconvincing eyebrows and head hair.

Though the manuscript of *American Grotesque* had been cut down substantially, the book in fact could have been considerably shorter. At the very least, some of its blather could have been replaced by more pertinent passages. In chapter three, Kirkwood spends a full page waffling about his rented New Orleans apartment (three very large lamps in the living room, apparently). The question of why he thinks people will be interested in this detail more than evidence that he did not include in the book — many witnesses in Dealey Plaza where Kennedy met his fate, with testimony relevant to the inconsistencies in the lone-gunman theory, are not mentioned, for instance — is a perplexing one. Far worse discursiveness and skewing of priorities is to come. It's not until nearly the 200th page that the trial proper gets underway, mainly due to Kirkwood's insistence on detailing the jury selection process in massive depth. Although the court processes of Louisiana in the sixties can now be mildly interesting on a historical level and at the time could have been on a procedural level, at this length they are ultimately tedious. It's a surprise that Kirkwood didn't realize this: he relates how bored all the journalists sitting beside him are by the selection process.

Kirkwood reveals that he is not approaching the trial from a right-wing angle. Chapter three yields the fact that he is a liberal (or at least incredulous at the thought of the impending Nixon presidency). In chapter ten, he underlines his non-right-wing credentials further when he fulminates about the informal racial segregation in New Orleans.

Once the trial gets underway, the book actually begins to zip along, the details of the murky world inhabited by David Ferrie, his friend Lee Harvey Oswald and their friend Clay Bertrand aka (allegedly) Shaw strange and fascinating. Those of the Dealey Plaza witnesses who are represented also have a compelling and disturbing tale to tell. All of this is helped by Kirkwood's easy-rolling and frequently humorous writing style. Unfortunately, Kirkwood's partisanship keeps weakening the proceedings. He displays a propensity to reach conclusions about the evidence — or to explain away the evidence — in ways that are simply, and sometimes embarrassingly, illogical. For instance, early on he has problems with the prosecution objecting to a defense request to have a witness named Sandra Moffitt MacMaines granted immunity from prosecution if she comes to town to testify. The prosecution lawyer points out that if the witness came to the city and committed an offence, "we would not only charge her, we would be guilty of malfeasance in office if we did not charge her." This is surely reasonable but Kirkwood scornfully concludes, "I could not help thinking, 'Well that takes care of Sandra.'" Later on, Kirkwood writes of Aaron Kohn, managing director of the Metropolitan Crime Commission and an opponent of the Shaw trial, "…Garrison had gone so far as to have Kohn thrown in jail on occasion." According to Joan Mellen in *Jim Garrison: His Life and Times*, Kohn was imprisoned for falsely accusing a grand jury member of frequenting a bordello, but that is perhaps not the point: does Kirkwood really imagine that a D.A. can peremptorily imprison somebody without due process?

Moffitt MacMaines (in some sources spelt Moffett) was named by witness Perry Russo as one of the people who had been at a party where he heard Ferrie, Shaw and Oswald conspiring murderously. Chapter 24 relates a bizarre exchange on the witness box where the defense counsel expresses amazement that despite "going" with Moffitt MacMaines for five years, Russo couldn't cite her address. As both the defense and Kirkwood knew but which Kirkwood doesn't point out, Russo was gay.

One would hope that if Kirkwood had known of the FBI informant status of *Newsweek* journalist Hugh Aynesworth, he would not have given over some of chapter nineteen to him, reproducing parts of a written account he asked Aynesworth to provide of his and one William Gurvich's investigation of the witnesses from the sleepy town of Clinton, several of whose inhabitants testified that Oswald had come to register to vote there in the company of Shaw and Ferrie. One of them was John Manchester, the town Marshall, who said that he had spoken to a white-haired man who had told him he was the director of the International Trade Mart in New Orleans. (Aynesworth's account purports to highlight inaccuracies and inconsistencies in their claims.) Kirkwood, incidentally, doesn't seem to have been particularly bothered by the fact he relates that Aynesworth approached Russo during the trial and made a comment to him whose details were disputed but whose aggression wasn't. Chapter six is where Kirkwood introduces us to journalist James Phelan. Phelan had come to report the trial but was obliged to wait outside the courtroom because he was called to appear as a witness for the defense over alleged inconsistencies in a memo about the recollections of Perry Russo. Kirkwood reports that Phelan was badgering people coming out of the courtroom and asking, "What's going on in there? What's happening? What did so-and-so say?" Far from wondering about the propriety of this, Kirkwood says, "There was something immediately likeable about Phelan."

In chapter nine, Kirkwood reports the defense asking whether the state can get into the subject of the events at Dealey Plaza and that trial judge Edward A. Haggerty gives an ambiguous answer. "If you could not hear the groan in court, you could feel it," Kirkwood writes. To which the reader is entitled to answer, "What on earth does that mean?"

Kirkwood is justified when he has fun with two of the prosecution's strangest witnesses. On the witness stand, Perry Russo was almost comically discursive, unable to give a concise or at times proper answer to a simple question about his claim to have heard the assassination discussed by Ferrie, Oswald and Shaw. He was nothing, though, compared to Charles Spiesel, a New York accountant who claimed that he had met Ferrie and Shaw when in New Orleans and had heard them discussing assassinating the President. After giving his evidence, Spiesel was asked by the defense whether he had a history of believing that people were hypnotizing him, whether he thought he was the victim of a communist plot and whether he fingerprinted his daughter on her return home at the end of each university semester to make sure that she was the same girl who had left. He replied in the affirmative each time.

Yet while Kirkwood is merciless in his depiction of the weakness of those witnesses, it is one-way traffic. He makes massive allowances for the performance on the witness stand of Lt. Col. Pierre A. Finck, one of the pathologists who performed the military autopsy on Kennedy's body. "Witness and questioner were completely mismatched chemically," Kirkwood wrote of Finck's cross-examination by Alvin Oser. "Dr. Finck neither seemed able, nor did he care, to respond to the questions. He was not hostile, however, but his concentration and meticulous attention to detail had deserted him." This is frankly a pathetic way to try to account for the fact that manifold contradictions and inconsistencies revealed themselves under the cross-examination, as did a disturbing state of affairs in the autopsy room, with people ranked higher than the colonel for reasons unknown obstructing the paths that any autopsy should rightly take. It also raises the point of why Kirkwood is possessed of such an anxiety over this subject. We can understand to some degree the defense wanting to discredit allegations of a conspiracy regardless of whether Shaw was involved in it (without rebuttal, the prosecution witnesses to this alleged conspiracy might have had an emotive effect on the jury which could impact on their client), but Kirkwood personally seems almost desperate for the reader to believe the lone-gunman Warren Commission Report conclusion that Finck endorses. Meanwhile, Kirkwood seems to find amusing rather than reprehensible the buffoonish stonewalling of Dean Andrews. A bizarre, portly character who used hipster lingo, Andrews was a local lawyer whom Garrison's investigations had supposedly found had been asked by a man named Clay Bertrand to arrange for legal representation for Lee Harvey Oswald after the latter's arrest. As well as being bombastic and pugnacious, Andrews declined to answer questions for fear of self-incrimination, a state of affairs that was unfortunate to say the least, let alone suspicious. Kirkwood, though, found him "peppy."

Kirkwood seems to believe in a conspiracy of his own that is far more implausible than the one the prosecution posited. At the end of Chapter 33, he wonders how it is that the name Clay Shaw and his employing the *nom de guerre* Clay Bertrand and/or his associating with Ferrie and Oswald could make a jump from a conversation with Andrews which Andrews was now denying to the witnesses of the sleepy town of Clinton to the mailman who said he delivered letters to a house at which Shaw was staying addressed to "Clem Bertrand" to Perry Russo to a middle-aged woman who claimed Shaw had signed a guest register as "Bertrand." The explanation for these many and various witnesses — nothing like all of whom could be posited as having a hidden interest in saying what they were saying — is, for Kirkwood, sinister: "The questions were as fascinating as the possibilities were frightening," he writes in a statement that impugns the integrity of every witness to take the stand for the prosecution. Compounding this silliness, on the very page previous to his grand conspiracy theory, Kirkwood accuses supporters of Garrison who attend court of his own sin. "...their persistence in maintaining total belief in the state's case, no matter the evidence, was beginning to turn rancid," he complains without a shred of irony.

All this is even before the Tadins take the stand. Nicholas M. Tadin, who linked Shaw and Ferrie, did not just seem plausible because he was from a "respectable" background (unlike many of Garrison's witnesses, he was neither a convicted criminal nor — just as bad in many people's eyes then — gay, but a married middle-aged business agent for a musician's union). Significantly, he was not one of Garrison's scheduled witnesses, but had stepped forward during the trial after reading in newspaper reports of Shaw's denial of any involvement with Ferrie. Tadin was the father of a deaf boy who had been taking flying lessons from Ferrie in the summer of 1964 and was concerned about his sixteen-year-old son's safety around the latter. Tadin testified that on one occasion that summer, he had seen Ferrie with a tall, white-haired man of whom Ferrie had himself volunteered the information that he was named Clay Shaw, was in charge of the International Trade Mart and was "a friend of mine." Tadin's wife gave evidence virtually identical to her husband's. Kirkwood acknowledges that these were powerful witnesses, but has no explanation for their testimony.

The Tadins had expressed a distaste for Ferrie and Shaw. Though not explicitly stated, it would have been clear to the observant amongst both those following the trial and those reading Kirkwood's book that their distaste stemmed from their feelings about the pair's apparent homosexuality. This was not played up by Garrison or his team. Garrison could easily have opted then or at any point to turn the jury against the defendant to bolster a clearly flagging case by exploiting a revulsion about homosexuality common in 1969. Even Kirkwood acknowledged in *American Grotesque*, "The trial had remained relatively clean in that respect." Kirkwood could be accused of being less clean in his own tactics. At one point in the book he refers to a little fun had by some pro-Shaw trial attendees teasing a well-known but unnamed conspiracy theorist reporting on the trial over an incriminating photograph that supposedly suggested he has sadomasochistic sexual preferences. Mischievously implying that somebody has something to hide about his sex life that would make the public think less of him if they knew of it is a bit rich coming from Kirkwood.

The ludicrous nadir of Kirkwood's subjectivity comes when he posits a *cordon bleu* like Shaw having to contend with inadequate fast food during the trial as yet another example of his suffering. He describes him "bravely chewing his way through his sandwich."

Kirkwood's interviews with people associated with the case are presented in a lengthy coda. The Perry Russo interview often has little to do with the Shaw trial but is a fascinating portrayal of a man who clearly has "issues" and who prevaricates in conversation about whether it was definitely Shaw he saw conspiring as much as he had in the witness box. The unexpected bonhomie between Garrison and Kirkwood is also interestingly rendered. Kirkwood's interview with Judge Edward A. Haggerty Jr. is that too, as well as mind-boggling. Haggerty proved quite a good judge, with the notable exception being his apparently arbitrary exclusion of the testimony of police officer Aloysius Habighorst, who claimed that Shaw admitted during his arrest booking-in to sometimes using the pseudonym Bertrand. Kirkwood presents a hilarious pen portrait of a man who miraculously managed to do his job well during the trial while secretly pulsing with an epic distaste for what he repeatedly and repetitively calls "queers." However, Kirkwood cancels out the points he scores in these well-written and humorous sections with his bewilderment at the conviction of the jurors he speaks to that Shaw knew Ferrie and/or Oswald. As John Leonard sardonically said of Kirkwood's refusal to believe the many witnesses linking this trio in his *New York Times* review of *American Grotesque*, "Were they all mistaken or lying?"

Having said all of this, there is actually an upside to Kirkwood's bias. When relating the cross-examination of state witnesses, he gives us information about ambiguities and inconsistencies in their evidence rarely found in Kennedy assassination literature sympathetic to Jim Garrison. For instance, not many pro-conspiracy theorists have mentioned that Russo — according to Kirkwood, anyway — incredibly seemed to be taking nips of alcohol from a flask during his testimony. Also on the positive side, Kirkwood scores a shed-load of brownie points for a remark in Chapter 40. Commenting on yet another repeat of an overplayed and barely comprehensible prosecution attorney's point about the trajectory of the assassin's bullets, he says, "This earned a ripple of snickers and would have earned him a custard pie had the ammunition been available." The image is sidesplitting. We should also point out that Kirkwood claims that he invited Garrison to make a statement about his political and assassination theories which he would include, uncut, in his book and that Garrison declined. Though this appears to be true — a copy of a letter to Garrison dated May 11, 1969, containing this offer exists in Kirkwood's files — the generosity doesn't mitigate the self-deception that ruins this book.

By chapter four, incidentally, Kirkwood has made the first of many references to how "attractive" is the woman to whom he is talking. This adjective is repeated so often, about so many different women — essentially, all of the females he relates encountering — that it becomes a motif of almost surreal levels, as though he is gauchely trying to convince the world that he is hetero. The crescendo of this surrealism is reached when he has his post-trial meeting with Garrison. When Kirkwood reports that he said to the D.A., "Give my best to your wife. I spoke with her during the trial several times. She's extremely attractive," the reader wants to deliver Kirkwood a custard pie of his own.

In that bias-acknowledging preface, Kirkwood asserts that the book would be inferior if it were impartial, likening an objectivity that he gives a human pronoun to a "stalking automaton" crushing people and things because "all he knows is he has to get from point A to point B and bugger the consequences." In actual fact, such is the skill Kirkwood reveals in *American Grotesque* at engrossingly relating courtroom drama and such is the complete lack of skill he displays in allowing his emotions to enable him to make logical conclusions about what he is seeing and hearing, it's clear that the opposite is the case. *American Grotesque* is a potentially good and historical book — to this day, the only one solely dedicated to one of the most important trials of the twentieth century — made in many places nothing less than laughable by Kirkwood's mediation.

It so transpired that *American Grotesque* was released at around the same time as *A Heritage of Stone*, Garrison's own book on the alleged conspiracy. (Kirkwood: "I think it's a well-written book. He's a facile man with words. I don't happen to agree with his theories. Also, he didn't tell me in the book anything that I had not known before of his theories.") *The New York Times* was one of several publications that reviewed both books together. Though John Leonard asserted that "the state embarrassed itself with surreal incompetence" in the Shaw trial, he was scathing about the way Kirkwood seemed to bend over backwards to dismiss the idea of Shaw's associations: "Unfortunately, Mr. Kirkwood is so conscientious in his reportage that one wonders *why* so many people claimed to have seen Mr. Shaw with Oswald and Ferrie…We have only Mr. Kirkland's [sic] emotional word on innocence to go by. Such a word isn't conclusive, not even in a book reviewer's court. Mr. Kirkwood's loyalty to a friend is admirable; his taped interviews with all the principals in the…Shaw trial are fascinating; his attention to trivia is in the best parajournalistic tradition — the little boy who cried Tom Wolfe. But legitimate questions about John Kennedy's assassination aren't answered according to the buddy system." *Life* magazine complained about *American Grotesque* of "too many transcripts of courtroom testimony, too many documents reproduced in their entirety, too few insights, flashes of color or character portraits." *The Los Angeles Times* was a lot kinder. "A single large and splendid book on the subject," it said in reference to the Shaw trial, "has now arrived and I suspect that it will stand unrivalled." Noting that it had been mentioned in the same breath as Truman Capote's 1966 tome *In Cold Blood*, which effectively invented "New Journalism" (reportage with a structure more common to novels), it found this not altogether accurate but stated, "The comparison however gives you an idea of its merit." In the *Village Voice*, Faubion Bowers — who it should be noted was a huge fan of Kirkwood's writing in general — called it a "gripping, appalling, shocking, frightening book."

Reaction to the book amongst Kirkwood's friends was, for what it's worth, enthusiastic. Homer Price says of *American Grotesque*, "That book is very solid, and really a piece of American history that was extremely well-researched." Paonessa thinks it "an amazing, wonderful piece of writing," and even goes so far as to opine, "It was his best book. Oh my God, I think it's just phenomenal." Benjamin Morrison reviewed the book at the time. "I wrote about it in an extremely positive sense and had a little bit of second feelings about it, but I felt so much, not just because of Jim, but because of what was in the book, that the book really needed to be supported," he says, "and the reason was that at that time, in New Orleans, 'den of thieves' comes to mind and I can't necessarily say anything bad about the Mayor at the time or anybody else at the time, but it was a dangerous time to be on the planet. This is the Vietnam War and I mean if you complained about the war you got drafted. This is [the] era that we are talking about and so it was easy and accurate to be paranoid about the authorities, both national and local. The paper that I worked for, almost nothing negative appeared in the paper about New Orleans except if it was a scandal. The best writer at the paper came up to me, he was working on the desk that my review was going through, and he said, 'I just want to congratulate you, your review is really good and it's really good somebody can tell the truth.'"

Perry Russo was not happy with the book and the way the interview he granted Kirkwood was presented. In *American Grotesque*, Kirkwood wrote that he had asked Russo if he had a message for Shaw and that, in part, Russo had replied, "…what would Judas Iscariot tell Jesus Christ?" Interviewed in 1993 by William Matson Law, Russo scathingly said, "That's a great line but…I didn't say it." He added, "I gave him an interview with Garrison's awareness of it. The guy was way off the fucking beam…He's lost his sense of reality somewhere. And for what reason? He propositioned me for sex. I told him, 'I don't get turned on by you.'" Asked what he thought of *American Grotesque*, Zachary Sklar says, "I think it's a very one-sided, vitriolic view of the case. I don't think it's a mistake to say, 'I have a view of this case and I'm gonna write it that way'…That's upfront and I think he was honest. I got the impression that he thought Shaw was being persecuted because he *was* gay, and I know that that was a popular theory around gay circles of New Orleans for a while." "I haven't read his book," says Louis Ivon, Garrison's chief investigator. "When it was going on, I read so much about it and I figured I wanted to have a clear mind on everything I did or said and I just didn't believe in all these book writers. I really didn't have no confidence, because I think everybody had a motive behind their book writing. I really haven't read Jim's [Garrison] book either, you know."

It was logical that *American Grotesque* and Garrison's book be reviewed together, but Kirkwood felt that this harmed sales of his tome. Not long after its appearance, Kirkwood said, "I thought *American Grotesque*, would be well-received, but it wasn't as far as sales were concerned. And after that I was very bruised and sore. But I couldn't very well stop. Especially then." He lamented elsewhere, "The *Life* review, which was bad for both books, concluded that neither Kirkwood nor Garrison had actually solved the riddle of the Kennedy assassination. Well, Jesus Christ! That wasn't the point of my book. I never purported to solve any riddle. But Jim Garrison did! And so many times the waters got muddied." He also felt that the unusually high price of his book — $11.95 — harmed its impact: "If I had it to do over, I'd omit the pictures and cut a lot of the copy to reduce production costs. I have a tendency to overwrite as it is. I always have to cut and cut. What I'd really like to do is write a book about 223 pages. I like short books." "That book really went nowhere at the bookstores," says Terrence McNally, "and it was a tough read, I must say, and it's big too. It looked like a phone book practically. He was very disappointed that it did not fare better. Truman Capote had covered that market, the factoid sort of book, and I think people were just tired of the Kennedy assassination and anything about it. I know he cared about that book a lot. We used to laugh because he was always giving it to people, like he had a lot of copies to get rid of. I had a neighbor in Bridgehampton and she was like a Jimmy Kirkwood groupie. She was a widow and she was a good twenty, thirty years older than me, but she was just so thrilled to meet Jimmy and she said, 'Oh, I would love an autographed book.' I knew he was going to give her that one. I think she wanted *P.S. Your Cat is Dead!* or *There Must Be a Pony!*, and instead she got the big one."

"Clay Shaw was finally acquitted, but he had to spend all of the money he'd saved for his retirement to be acquitted," Kirkwood later said. Says

Bruce Eggler of Shaw, "I had no personal contact with him, but from everything I've heard or read, he was financially ruined, emotionally exhausted and never able to get back close to normal." "I'm a little bit skeptical of that, frankly," responds Sklar. "Because I know that the guy got help from the CIA, and those lawyers that were working for him were being paid by somebody." Whether or not Shaw was ruined by the case, Ivon says he got the impression that Shaw became almost reclusive afterwards. Certainly, his alleged old French Quarter gay haunts were now out of bounds. Ivon: "Just my routine work and that there with the District Attorney's office and investigations, I really don't know if I ever seen him anymore in the Quarters." For Sklar, it was Garrison who was put through the wringer: "They attacked him so viciously from so many directions, with so many preposterous stories. Including the story that he was gay himself, and that he had fondled a little boy...[It was] thrown out. It never got anywhere. That was a CIA leak. Jack Anderson...was a very reputable syndicated columnist, but he also happened to have been a CIA asset and that was a leaked story in his column, which had no merit whatsoever. Garrison was also brought up later on charges of taking bribes. And that was thrown out as well. I know that Kirkwood thinks that Shaw is the great victim in this case, but Garrison went through an awful lot too. Believe me, he was unfairly treated, and still is, by almost everyone in the media."

"I was with him right up until the time that he died," says Ivon of Garrison, "and no, he never did regret [bringing the case] and he often spoke about it." Sklar says, "Garrison was amazingly not bitter. He really paid no attention to his critics. His only interest was in getting to the truth, and he kept at it over a period of more than 25 years when he was already long gone from the District Attorney's office and could easily have dropped the whole thing and said, 'Well, this is a bad part of my life. It was a nightmare. Goodbye, I'm gonna have a nice life as a state appeals court judge,' which he was very popularly elected to. He kept digging, he kept searching and he kept trying to find the truth. Basically the number that the CIA had done on him had worked. He was dismissed as a reckless politician and a crazy man. He was really considered by everyone to be the lowest of the low. His reputation in this country was terrible. Certainly not in New Orleans, where they actually knew him. He was still enormously popular there, and ironically, in the gay community, his biggest supporters, because he was, as a judge, the strongest supporter of gay rights there was in New Orleans."

Garrison died in 1992, but not before executing an acting role as Earl Warren — the Chief Justice the deficiencies of whose Commission

Report on the assassination had first made Garrison sense a cover-up over the President's death — in the film that was partly based on his investigations. "He never got to see it in a movie theatre," says Sklar of *JFK*. "He was quite sick by then. He saw it on video in his bed, and he was quite pleased. I think his attitude was that sooner or later, truth does have a way of coming out. He didn't feel embittered that he hadn't gotten the answer. I think [that] he was genuinely outraged that so many people didn't share his sense of outrage."

As for any misgivings on Kirkwood's part, though he had them about *American Grotesque*, he never had any about its subject. "Jimmy and Clay stayed in contact for as long Clay lived," says Morrison. Asked if Kirkwood ever acquired a glimmer of doubt about Shaw, Homer Price says flatly, "No, and neither did I." He adds, "I think we all asked him questions, but my memory is that he was very forthright and dispelled all doubts. He's just a man of integrity, and you could tell that. One never knows for sure but, boy, you could have fooled me if Clay wasn't really on the up-and-up. He was a very charming man and a very decent man. Just all of the vibes were good. And this was not just me, this was Jamie and Jimmy."

Homer is talking of three intelligent, humane and liberal men, who would certainly have no truck with someone whom they considered to be a member of a secret far-right cabal that had helped murder their democratically elected head of state. If Clay Shaw was what Garrison posited him as, surely he would have had to be one of history's finest actors to pull off such a persuasive and lifelong performance. Sklar responds, "People who live in the world of intelligence have cover stories that are totally persuasive to people. Kirkwood, or anyone who is not familiar with how sophisticated intelligence works, could easily be fooled by a cover story. Believe me, intelligence operatives do not announce who they are, what they believe in, and what they actually do. They tell you things that are exactly the opposite, and they make you believe it."

As well as being intelligent, humane and liberal men, Herlihy, Kirkwood and Price have another thing in common, with each other and with Shaw — their sexuality. Could this have conceivably impaired their judgment about Shaw? Homer Price concedes, "Gay people, being a minority that's been discriminated against, tend to stick up for one another." However, he scoffs at the idea that shared sexual orientation would make them overlook signals that indicated Shaw was not what he claimed. "C'mon, of course not," he says. "No sensible person would say that all gays are wonderful. In fact, I'm rather anti-gay in some ways myself. I mean, this gay marriage thing, lost us the [2004 presidential] election."

And yet the passage of time has proven that Clay Shaw was not all he seemed. During his trial, Shaw swore under oath that he had never worked for the Central Intelligence Agency. This assertion was untrue. Sklar: "Victor Marquetti was a very high CIA operative who was in on the meetings at the highest level. Richard Helms was CIA director at the time when Shaw was being tried. Victor Marquetti reported later, after he left the Agency, that during the Shaw trial, but regularly, Helms was asking, in meetings, 'Are we giving Shaw enough help?' This is the director of the CIA." In 1979, Helms gave evidence in a libel case in which he confirmed an association between Shaw and the Agency. "The explanation that Richard Helms gave when he was forced to testify under oath and actually acknowledged that Shaw had worked for the Agency was that he was in this program of businessmen who supplied information to the Agency," says Sklar. "He made it sound like it was a routine kind of thing. However, the clearance that Shaw had was called 'QKENCHANT.' 'Q' usually indicates the highest level of clearance." Sklar continues, "That Shaw was simply a guy who was reporting as a businessman to the CIA is not a plausible explanation. If it were, why didn't Shaw just say that on the witness stand? And then he would not have been perjuring himself." In 1970, Clay Shaw filed a suit against Garrison and five others for acting in bad faith in bringing charges against him, but passed away before the case was resolved. One wonders whether Shaw's August 1974 death was a blessing in disguise for Kirkwood: it meant that he would never have to confront his friend about facts that gradually emerged over the years that proved he had looked him in the eye and told him mistruths.

There were mysterious circumstances surrounding that death. A neighbor called the local coroner's office after seeing a group of men carrying a covered body on a stretcher *into* Shaw's house. The house was empty when people from the office came to investigate. Within a day it had emerged that Shaw had already been buried. A coroner had cited the cause of death as natural causes due to lung cancer. The New Orleans coroner expressed concern. Sklar: "I did talk to the coroner at the time, Frank Minyard. He wanted to do an autopsy on Clay Shaw, and was in fact intending to." However, an exhumation did not take place. "He was told not to," says Sklar. "The local press, of course, took Kirkwood's view of this whole thing and thought that Shaw had been violated enough, and I think there were editorials and so forth saying, 'Hasn't this man suffered enough?' Minyard basically caved to that and agreed not to do the autopsy."

Up until 1991, Americans who either had a vague unease about the conclusions of the Warren Commission Report or who were convinced that it was spurious were living in the shadow of what might be termed the establishment point of view on the subject. Although there had been much debate, investigative journalism and scores of books (including three by Garrison, one a novel) on the topic, there had not really been a mass-market media event articulating the non-establishment or alternative point of view on the issue of Kennedy's assassination. With the release of Oliver Stone's film *JFK*, the alternative version of events came into focus with a huge cultural splash. Stone was the director of the moment, riding high on the success of, amongst other films, *Platoon*, which 1986 picture was groundbreaking in its unflinching depiction of the sense of chaos and purposelessness that was the experience of many American soldiers in the Vietnam War. *JFK*, whose screenplay was initially solely written by Sklar before becoming a Sklar-Stone collaboration, was based on two of the most important of the alternative-theory Kennedy books, Jim Marrs' *Crossfire* and Garrison's third book, *On the Trail of the Assassins*. In the latter tome, Garrison refined his theories about the alleged conspiracy, partly because of the declassification of previously secret documents. Jim Marrs' book was more of a compendium of information about the actual assassination. Marrs discussed the prospective film with Stone. "He wanted something with dramatic effect and so he wanted to personalize it and he settled on the person of Jim Garrison," Marrs explains. "At that point he had Garrison's book, which gave him a lot of details about the Clay Shaw case in New Orleans but not very much detail at all about the actual assassination and I just happened to be at the right place at the right time: I had just published *Crossfire*." Screen heartthrob Kevin Costner was cast by Stone as Garrison and Tommy Lee Jones as Shaw. The two most impressive performances were probably Joe Pesci as a manic Ferrie and Gary Oldman as a brooding Oswald. The result of all this was a movie lasting over three hours which not only put on celluloid the theories of Warren Commission doubters, but exposed them to millions of people throughout the world, in the process introducing a new generation of Americans to the idea that their own president was subjected to what Garrison termed "a *coup d'etat*." It was a persuasive and powerful cinematic experience.

Benjamin Morrison caustically observes that the same adjectives could be used to describe the Nazi propaganda films of Leni Riefenstahl. "A lie," he says of the film. "There's almost not a single truth in there. If Clay were alive today the only thing he would like was what he looked like as Tommy Lee Jones, virtually naked and sprayed gold. It's like my sense of what Jim Garrison's prosecution was: that you have an idea of what you are going to do and you do it and you don't let the facts stand in your way." "I was outraged at that Oliver Stone movie," says Homer Price. "It was just so, so biased and fictional, really. He should have read *American Grotesque* to get the facts straight." Bruce Eggler says, "I swore to myself that Oliver Stone wouldn't get any of my money so I didn't go to see it in a theatre. From what I've seen of it in TV airings, it is very well-made — and totally dishonest in its depiction of Garrison, his case and the whole assassination controversy. I'd put it squarely in the tradition of *Birth of a Nation* and *Triumph of the Will*: cinematic excellence in the service of a big lie. One tiny example: Stone cast a lot of local people in small roles, including [someone] who worked here at the *Times-Picayune* as a copy boy and in other mentally non-challenging jobs. He has since died. He was grossly overweight and it was difficult to understand him when he spoke. What role did Stone give him? Foreman of the jury. Gee, do you think he was trying to convey the impression that a jury capable of acquitting Shaw had to be made up of mental defectives?" Beckenstein: "A total fabrication. I totally believe Jimmy's account was a truthful account. I met Clay Shaw and I stayed in his house and he was a cultured, bright gentleman who was kind of a civic leader of New Orleans and not at all like what he was portrayed in the movie." Kirkwood died two years before *JFK*'s theatrical release. Beckenstein says that had Kirkwood been alive then, he would have been debating its merits with Stone on chat shows.

In 1992, an extremely belated paperback edition of *American Grotesque* was published by Perennial, officially to coincide with the 20th anniversary of Kennedy's assassination but surely partly prompted by the *JFK* movie. It constituted a certain counterweight to Stone's vision, but Kirkwood could conceivably have also helped create a movie that put up the opposite argument to *JFK*. Director Milton Katselas reveals that during the late 1980s he and Kirkwood discussed turning *American Grotesque* (which he calls "a great book") into a motion picture. He says, "We didn't go into it in any depth, but we talked about it on a couple of different occasions."

Jim Marrs has actually begun to change his mind about a crucial aspect of the case. He explains, "I'm not convinced this conspiracy resulted in the assassination, but there seems to be no question in my mind that there was a conspiracy to kill the president centered in New Orleans…I think Clay Shaw was a handler. He was a cultivated man, sophisticated man. I think he was mostly mixed up in all of that because of his sexual proclivities and he ended up partying with some of these people." Sklar adds a technical point: "As far as Clay Shaw goes there's nothing to connect him to Dallas except his connection to Lee Oswald. But, again, Lee Oswald was a low-level intelligence agent being moved around by forces greater than himself and in many instances incriminating himself, not realizing that he was going to be the patsy in the assassination. I am personally of the opinion that Lee Oswald did not fire a rifle that day. If Oswald didn't do it then that certainly would exonerate Clay Shaw, whose only connection to the whole thing was his connection to Oswald." Marrs poses a question: "Then why is it so obvious that the government, the mass media, any number of people, took extraordinary lengths to try to discredit Jim Garrison?" He provides a long answer to his own question that revolves around a theory about the US government trying to cover up a botched attempt to cure polio with an adulterated vaccine that caused an epidemic of cancer in the country. He says, "As a result of all this, they began a covert, hasty and dangerous attempt to try to come up with an anti-cancer vaccine primarily centered in New Orleans." Marrs says that Ferrie was "associated" with a pair of doctors attempting to create this vaccine and "was running a covert government cancer lab in his apartment, which by some reports included Lee Harvey Oswald. The more that Garrison investigated, the more that they ran the risk of all this coming out."

One final twist comes from Benjamin Morrison. Referring to information that subsequently came to light that Shaw worked in some capacity for the CIA, he describes it as, "The only time that I really got a sense that Clay was anything different than what he presented himself as…" When this author suggests that this revelation slightly undermines the assumption that Clay Shaw was innocent, Morrison has this to say: "I'm going to tell you a story, and I don't think I am going to be happy giving you the name of the friend of mine who told me this, but a contemporary and longtime friend of Clay's — they were not like bosom buddies or anything — went to see Clay in the hospital when Clay was literally on his deathbed and what my friend told me after he got back from that was that Clay told him something along the lines of, 'Garrison may have had the right idea, he just had the wrong man.'"

TWELVE

The back cover of the jacket of *American Grotesque* carried a photograph of a bearded Kirkwood (Benjamin Morrison: "He said he grew his beard and moustache so that he wouldn't have to try out for commercials anymore — to force him to stop being an actor") on the steps of the trial's courtroom.

The photograph carried the credit "Arthur Beckenstein." The book's copyright page bore the credit "Designed by Arthur Beckenstein" in reference to the typography and layout. Beckenstein would be a fixture of Kirkwood's book jackets. His following novel would also have a Beckenstein photograph on the back and all of Kirkwood's first editions from *Some Kind of Hero* onwards would carry Beckenstein's credit as jacket designer. More importantly, he would be a fixture in Kirkwood's life.

Beckenstein was at the time 26 years old and working for a design studio devising corporate communications and identity. He later became Art Director of Dow Jones and throughout the eighties was promotion art director for *People* magazine. He and Kirkwood met at a party, probably in 1968. Beckenstein was part of a large group and the two didn't make a connection that day. They first connected properly on Saturday, August 9, 1969, at a dance bar in the Hamptons called the Millstone. "It was in the middle of nowhere, on what seemed at the time like an endless road through cornfields," says Beckenstein. However, there was a particular reason why the trek was worth it, the Millstone being one of the few outlets in the era (especially in that locale) that catered to the sexually unconventional. Beckenstein: "It was a gay bar that was a very popular social watering hole for all the young gay men and women who came out to the Hamptons on summer weekends." Despite the two-decade age gap, the pair hit it off immediately. "He asked me if I wanted to come home and see his first editions — whatever that meant," Beckenstein wryly recalls. At the time, Beckenstein had a share in a house on Three Mile Harbor with two women and three other men, all of around his age, who had all come with him in his Firebird convertible, so he told Kirkwood he had to find rides for his housemates before he could take up his offer. This accomplished, "I followed Jim home to his house on the other side of the harbor and spent the night." Beckenstein points out, "There was no talk that night about what we did in real life, during the week, but I knew who he was. One of my housemates had given me a copy of *Good Times/Bad Times* for Christmas and I absolutely loved it. Jimmy wrote in the first person and it always seemed like he was telling a story directly to you." As with other gay men who read the book, Beckenstein found no problem with what might be argued to be its ambiguity about homosexuality, but quite the reverse: he felt he was reading the work of a kindred spirit. He says of the appeal of *Good Times/Bad Times* to gay people, "I think he, as narrator, felt a bit like an outsider."

The next morning, Beckenstein turned to Kirkwood and said, "Balled anyone lately?" His smart quip initially fell a little flat. Beckenstein: "He said, 'What?' I repeated, 'Balled anyone lately?' He said, 'What did you say?'" "Balled anyone lately?" is in fact the first thing, aside from at their introduction, Jordan says to Peter in *Good Times/Bad Times*, a sardonic echoing of a question asked of new boy Jordan by the school's self-professed lothario Wiley Bevan. When Kirkwood didn't seem to recognize his own work, Beckenstein squirmed. "It just seemed so out of context and out of character, coming from me," he recalls. "I suddenly felt very uncomfortable and thought maybe I made a mistake. Jimmy didn't know that I knew he was a writer." However, just as that question cemented the friendship between Jordan and Peter, so too it created a bond between Kirkwood and Beckenstein. The latter says, "When Jimmy suddenly realized that the line was his own and where it came from, he was deeply touched. After that we talked about his writing, his parents, etc."

The two were almost immediately a couple. "I saw him every weekend after that pretty much," says Beckenstein. That the sexually rampant Kirkwood should be attracted to the extraordinarily handsome Beckenstein was a given, but the fascination was more than physical. He would be a huge part of Kirkwood's life right up until the latter's death.

"I really felt I was in over my head," Beckenstein admits of their early days together. "I was only 26 and very inexperienced, quiet, shy and not terribly worldly. Jimmy was a successful writer and his parents were movie stars. I wasn't really familiar with them, because they were silent screen stars, before my time, but movie stars, nonetheless. His friends were all successful writers and actors. I felt out of my element. I had no great accomplishments. But I was very taken with this handsome, charming, charismatic wonderful guy I had met."

Though Beckenstein shared the East Hampton house with Kirkwood, he and Kirkwood never formally lived together as most people would define the term." I went out to East Hampton every weekend starting in

1969," explains Beckenstein. "I worked in NYC during the week…The Hamptons weren't a place where you could really pursue a career. It's larger now but it's a resort community and everybody naturally wanted to live there but unless you were in real estate or an antique dealer there weren't too many careers that you could at that time pursue." He adds, though, "Even if he was away with a show on the road, I considered East Hampton home…I loved our life in the Hamptons. It was exciting and beautiful. There were always fascinating people from all walks of life, interesting dinners and wonderful parties. During the days, our life was simple, rewarding and fulfilling." There were other benefits to Kirkwood's company: "I got to go places and meet people I never would have had the opportunity to on my own, attend all sorts of events and always had house seats at the theatre. We saw everything, did everything." Beckenstein found that this social whirlwind was something that Kirkwood's preternatural social skills made him superbly equipped to handle: "He was interested in everything and could discuss it with anyone." As a consequence of his "sense of humor" and "unpretentious demeanor," Kirkwood was trusted and confided in by "people from all walks of life — intellectuals, politicians, plumbers."

Kirkwood may have played hard but Beckenstein found he worked hard, too. "He had an amazing drive to write," he says. "He loved writing. He would get up in the morning and just start typing and working. He was enormously productive…He also answered every bit of mail that came his way and had very regular correspondences with a number of readers. I don't know how he accomplished as much as he did in a day." Though as the years advanced Kirkwood had understandably ceased typing while on his feet, Beckenstein recalls, "He did have a stand made so that he could type standing up so he could switch back and forth." Kirkwood would be "locked upstairs and he would not want any disturbance. He would write first drafts in longhand…and then he would type his drafts." Beckenstein also points out, "He read all the time. He was very smart. He didn't go to college but he was up on everything, on history and current events."

By this time, Kirkwood had let go of that ill-fated City apartment on West 58th Street. Beckenstein: "When Jim came into New York City, he stayed with me. I had [a] small one-bedroom apartment in a brownstone building on West 74th Street." Beckenstein says the city was "exciting and full of adventure" for a pair who considered themselves to some extent a young couple: "I was 26 and Jimmy was a very youthful 45, but he looked ten years younger and certainly had the spirit of someone years younger. He never lost that childlike delight and excitement within."

"I think it took right away," says Homer Price of the romance. "I wasn't there. I was away for the summer or whatever, but I think it was a very strong physical attraction at the beginning. And Jimmy liked to have somebody who was around and available — how shall I say it? — to help take care of him. Arthur was terrific. Arthur really knocked himself out in taking care of Jimmy…Jimmy would call up on a Friday and say, 'Arthur, go pick up that on your way out,' or something like that and Arthur was very obliging." Says *Valiant Lady* days friend Patti Goldstein, "Arthur first of all was very, very handsome and there was a sweetness about him and I think Jimmy was just captivated, couldn't help but be. Jimmy was smote." Goldstein recollects that this was the hardest she had ever seen her friend fall for anybody. Richard Seff offers, "Arthur represented a kind of calm. Arthur is really more of a civilian, as we call them in the theatre if they're not in show business. I think he just had such a completely grounding personality." Asked if he got the impression that Arthur made Kirkwood happy, Seff says, "I know he did because he told me he did."

Liz Smith offers: "Arthur Beckenstein, the 'Little Dark Angel' as Jimmy always called him." Those inferring a certain intensity, or at least sobriety, about Arthur from that description, would be correct. Kirkwood had found a partner as reserved as he was himself gregarious. "Arthur was never warm and gooey and funny and giggly," says Kirkwood's director friend Bill Gile. "He was a very strong, supportive partner. He always stayed out of things he didn't think were his business like the creative process. I cannot say anything bad about Arthur. I can't even say anything good about Arthur because Arthur was just there and he was never intrusive." Arthur Laurents says, "Arthur worshipped Jimmy and it was — not physically but mentally — an S/M relationship. He was Jimmy's slave." However, Laurents also admits, "[Kirkwood] wasn't taking advantage of him…Anything Jimmy did was fine."

"They were incredibly different and the whole thing about opposites attract or whatever, that's for sure," says Kirkwood friend Andrew Morse. "Arthur is the sweetest person on the planet. Very gentle, very sweet. It's funny — they were different in some ways and they were similar in some ways. They both had very, very good senses of humor, incredibly funny. I went out for dinner one night with Arthur, Jimmy, Jed (Jimmy's agent). I maybe said two words the whole time. Between the three of them, I was just dying of laughter. Arthur has a subtle, quiet way about him, but he's very sharp and he has a wonderful soul, he's got a wonderful heart. I don't know if he understood Jimmy so well as he accepted him and just loved him. It was very nice. Jimmy was very lucky to have Arthur."

Some have inferred — incorrectly — that there was a financial benefit for Kirkwood to Beckenstein's presence in his life. "His family is extraordinarily wealthy," says Piazza of Beckenstein. "I mean beyond rich, and I think Jimmy was always very impressed by that." Piazza is talking about the thrill for Kirkwood of proximity to affluence, but Arthur Laurents goes further by saying, "Arthur paid for everything. Jimmy didn't have to ask. Arthur gave." "No, I wasn't helping him out," says Beckenstein. "He wasn't poor." He also says, "Yes, my family was well-off, but in those days when I was with Jimmy, my salary was my total source of income." However, this assumption that Beckenstein was a financial boon for Kirkwood seems to have taken hold in their circle. For instance, Laurents is not the only person interviewed for this book who erroneously believes that one or both of the houses Kirkwood would own in East Hampton was the property of Beckenstein.

Beckenstein's happy memories of his early years with Kirkwood at their shared Barry Avenue/Squaw Road weekend abode are almost Disneyesque: "Jim took delight in seeing the birds and chipmunks outside his home and often would patiently stand outside, offering a handful of sunflower seeds to any brave chickadee that would land in his hand. Or to the resident chipmunks. There was one brave, tame chipmunk who lived under the front porch and would eat out of Jim's hand when offered sunflower seeds. Spike, as he became known, would come in the house when Jim left the door open a few inches and run over to a wing chair, where Jim would sit patiently holding a handful of seeds up near his chest. Spike would climb up his leg and up his arm to his shoulder. He would fill his jowls with seeds and run out the door to deposit the catch in his burrow, then come running back for more. Spike the chipmunk eventually became the mouse that Eddie shared his cell with in *Some Kind of Hero*. That same summer Jim took in a little brown baby bird that had been abandoned." Kirkwood christened the feathered newcomer Mia Sparrow, a reference to actress Mia Farrow, daughter of actress Maureen O'Sullivan and John Farrow, the actor whom his mother had left his father for. When let out of her cage, the bird would amuse the residents by landing on their heads. The next year, a feline who appeared at the door one day was also given residency rights, and what name could Kirkwood bestow on it but that of another sleek black cat Bobby Seale, charismatic chairman of the revolutionary party the Black Panthers? A trip to a vet unearthed the information that Kirkwood's Bobby Seale was a girl, but she already had her name. Says Beckenstein, "Spike disappeared a year before Bobby Seale arrived at the door and Mia Sparrow flew away one day and never came home."

With a relationship as long-lasting as Kirkwood and Beckenstein's, the law of averages means that things were not always so blissful. "There were bumpy spots there," says Price. Kirkwood — a disciplined writer — would get particularly irritated if Beckenstein interrupted his chain of thought. Price: "He used to get awfully annoyed at Arthur because Arthur sometimes would invade his privacy over silly little things. He built a special door to the upstairs in East Hampton to keep Arthur out and Arthur would come in anyway and say, 'Where's the shovel?' or 'When are we having dinner?' and Jimmy would say, 'Arthur, I'm trying to work!' Oh God, Arthur is very headstrong."

As with many male gay relationships, true love did not preclude outside sexual partners, at least on Kirkwood's part. Price: "Arthur's not very promiscuous and Jimmy certainly had other interests and never talked about it to Arthur. In fact, one of his most repeated phrases to me was, 'Don't tell Arthur!' Arthur knew all along, but it was never enunciated, never verbalized." "I wasn't happy about that," Beckenstein says of Kirkwood's promiscuity. "Being as we weren't together all during the week, I knew that he might have seen other people. But I knew that we were together every weekend. It was something that wasn't really talked about. He didn't want me to know about anything…Times were different also. It was a more promiscuous time…I just took our relationship day-to-day in the beginning, thinking, 'What does he see in me? What have I accomplished?' I decided to just enjoy it while it lasts. I think with that attitude, it really helped our relationship." He insists that while Kirkwood spurned the notion of faithfulness, "Jimmy adored me and treated me as very special."

Whatever the number of Kirkwood's partners, it seems safe to say that from hereon in, they were all men. Not necessarily related to this, Kirkwood seems to have had something of a shock in a relationship with a woman whose identity is not known. "He always said that he had this brief affair with a woman who claimed that she had a son by him," says Jim Piazza. "There was supposed to be an illegitimate child out there. I knew that he was very concerned about that and thought that she was lying to him or something, but then people said they had seen the kid and he looked just like Jimmy. There were all those stories. I never met her personally and I never knew the name." Piazza estimates that the child was born sometime in the 1960s.

If Kirkwood's previous sexual relationships with women had indeed been an attempt on his part to stifle the sexual urges that in his heart of hearts he knew were the strongest, it would seem that by the turn of the seventies that kind of denial had ceased to be part of Kirkwood's makeup. And yet Kirkwood's attitude toward his own sexuality would always remain at the very least complicated. "He was open in the way he lived his life," insists Beckenstein. Certainly the fact that as far back as the mid-fifties his fellow *Valiant Lady* star Dolores Sutton knew of his leanings indicates that Kirkwood wasn't putting up a false front. Such a false front would have been far easier for Kirkwood to maintain than it would for many gay men. As Price points out, "In public he was always very masculine. My observation is that even very masculine-looking men, if they're gay you can tell. But Jimmy had none of that. You just never would have thought meeting him, or being around him even, that he was a homosexual." (Price adds, "He could be a real camp. He could really lisp and put on the fag drawl and he was very funny among intimates.") Beckenstein says that archetypal macho man author Norman Mailer was an "old friend" of Kirkwood's.

Yet Price admits, "Jimmy, to the outside world, certainly gave the impression of being straight and did not like any insinuation to the contrary. In fact, Leonard Bernstein once made a terribly slighting remark down in Miami, and said, 'Oh, that's the Kirkwood Crowd over there' — as though that was the Faggot Crowd. (He was not a nice man, Leonard Bernstein.) Anyway, Jimmy took great umbrage at that." Price offers in explanation: "This was still the days when you did hide that kind of thing. We've made progress since then."

Naturally, part of this nervousness comes from being a product of his times (a phrase that several of Kirkwood's friends use to describe him regarding this issue). After all, as Jack Sydow points out, "The cops could come in and arrest everybody and finally the gay boys rebelled in Stonewall, but up until then…When you get used to covering all the time… even as you get older it's not the easiest thing in the world to come right out and be blatant about the gayness." "He may have enjoyed the sexual ambiguity of it," says Benjamin Morrison. "Jim was of a generation in which no one knew anyone who was gay. It was just not done. Not much of anybody was out then. There wasn't a place [for] us then, we just didn't know where we fit in or anything else and so we just tried to get along with everybody else and not be noticed for the wrong reasons and Jim may have stuck to that virtually through his entire life."

Yet Kirkwood continued to display ambivalence about his sexuality that isn't easily explained by habit. After all, Kirkwood's lifetime saw massive advances in social tolerance that were themselves bolstered by legislation. Between 1970 and his death in '89, state after American state either decriminalized homosexuality or stopped prosecuting it and, probably more importantly, homosexuality rapidly ceased to be for many the taboo or cause for revulsion that it had been throughout the nation's history. Yet Kirkwood almost aggressively continued the process of giving "the impression of being straight" to "the outside world" that Price detected. He declined to discuss his sexuality in interviews and he steadfastly featured main protagonists in his art who were heterosexual. Though he would always ensure that there was a gay incident or sexually alternative supporting character in his novels and plays (Benjamin Morrison: "The breadcrumbs are sort of spread out there [in his work]"), not once did his works have a leading character who was unequivocally homosexual. "I myself lived openly with a man but he was leery of that," says Laurents, adding that this leeriness applied to both Kirkwood's life and art. As for why, Laurents has an interesting idea slightly different to the man-of-his-time theory offered by several: "It was about wanting to be part of what I call 'that world' — celebrities...Jimmy cared a lot [about] the newspapers and the gossip columns and all that...You have to realize where Jimmy was born and what kind of world. He was born in a Hollywood world of those values...and that's what he kept. He always lived in that silent screen world, not consciously but he did. Glamour, celebrity, don't tell."

"He never wanted to be known as a 'gay writer,'" offers Beckenstein. "By that, I mean he wanted his appeal to be more universal...I don't think he wanted to be pigeon-holed...I don't think of him as being semi-secretive... He thought he was a writer that just happened to have gay characters in the book. He felt that sexuality didn't have a lot to do with what he was writing about. He wasn't making a gay statement. He was telling a story...Yes, he was a product of his times, but if he were alive today he would not be out marching in any parades." Without wishing to patronize Beckenstein — who knew Kirkwood better than anyone — there seems to have been a nervousness about Kirkwood attached to his sexuality that doesn't quite gel with a mere disinclination to jeopardize his sales figures. Jim Piazza recalls Kirkwood as late as the 1980s even going to slightly ludicrous lengths to dispel suspicions about which way he swung: "If he was going to some place, he would have a woman somewhere in the mix." William Russo reveals that Kirkwood was horrified when he approached a gay magazine in the 1970s about writing a piece on Kirkwood. (It transpired that Kirkwood's hostility toward appearing in the magazine was reciprocated. "The editor really didn't want to do a Kirkwood piece because he wasn't an activist," says Russo. "He wasn't out, he was too coy.")

Was there an element of self-loathing? Laurents: "I don't think so. In his private life he was a fuck-meister." Jim Piazza thinks otherwise. A gay man who was 23 years younger than Kirkwood, perhaps significantly he of Kirkwood's friends is the most disinclined to make excuses for him. He in fact thinks Kirkwood "probably hated being gay. That pre-liberation generation, it was so much closeting and so much hiding and so much lying that it infects someone. I think it's hard. Obviously his success and money shielded him from the real world so he never really was confronted by homophobia. I don't think that ever came into play. But there was a part of him that was very closet-ey and I think being closeted implies a certain self-loathing. I mean, you wouldn't hide who you were unless you were embarrassed by who you were. That's all part of it and it's complex. Homophobia is not confined to straight people. I think a lot of gay people are homophobic."

There may have been an additional psychological layer that interfered with Kirkwood's rational thought here, namely the specter of his father. Kirkwood never actually formally "came out" to his family about his sexuality but they all ultimately became aware of it by a process of osmosis (casually introducing people to Beckenstein seems to have been one way Kirkwood had of communicating this fact about himself). Lila Lee Nichols: "I don't think it was ever discussed. It was just accepted. You knew and it was okay." Joan Kirkwood: "He never discussed it…He'd say things in jest…One time he bought me a very pretty robe. It was a deep pink and it was quilted and it had a jeweled collar. It was in a box and when he took me where I was going, it was a side street, he pulled the robe out of the box and he put it on and he started swirling around and dancing in the street. He would do things like that. No straight man would ever do that. But as far as talking, no." That T. Michael Kirkwood doesn't mention his father discussing his half-brother's homosexuality suggests that his father was not aware of it or perhaps was not admitting it to himself. T. Michael accepts that his father would probably have been the kind of person who disapproved of homosexuality. Kirkwood himself would presumably have been aware of this fact. Bearing in mind Kirkwood's description of Kirkwood Sr. as a man with "a Christ-awful, maniacal temper" and a relationship with him that was if not quite love-hate than nuanced, one wonders whether Kirkwood refrained from fully declaring his sexuality to the whole world even after his father's death because there was some small part of him subliminally cringing at the thunderous denunciation that he could imagine would have emerged from the ship's-prow face of his fearsome dad.

For her part, Joan feels her father knew of his eldest's sexuality. "I'm sure he did," she says. "He was a little on the effeminate side and just his life. He would have to be stupid not to know." She also opines, "I'm sure that distressed him no end, because he was hyper-masculine." Of course, this may all be a bum rap on Kirkwood Sr.: actors are very used to meeting gays in their industry and working cheek-by-jowl with them often engenders a tolerance and even fondness in the most unlikely of macho men.

Theorizing is not so necessary with Kirkwood's mother. Beckenstein says Lee "certainly was" aware of her son's homosexuality and that it was not a problem for her. Friend and sometime Kirkwood publisher Ross Claiborne recalls, "Jimmy and his mother came to a party that my partner and I had in the Hamptons probably in the early sixties. She may have been the only straight person there and seemed to be able to handle that with great aplomb."

One should add a couple of caveats here. One is that in a sense Kirkwood has a cast-iron defense to the accusation of hypocrisy about the veiling of his sexuality in his art, namely the fact of his sexual relationships with women. He wasn't — unlike several gay writers of his generation — someone writing about a heterosexual life of which he had no direct or intimate knowledge. More importantly, all of this discussion and analysis would probably be considered laughably irrelevant by all of Kirkwood's friends, Piazza perhaps excepted. His public reticence doesn't seem to have caused any problems with his gay pals, even militant ones. "It was not an issue," is a phrase heard frequently and independently from those spoken to for this book on this point. Openly gay playwright Terrence McNally was a friend of Kirkwood's from the 1970s onwards. He says, "Jimmy could get away with anything he chose to do because he was so charming. I guess if he was on a talk show acting like he wasn't gay, that wouldn't bother me because he was trying to sell a book or something." Shrugs Laurents, "He wasn't that kind of person." Laurents reserves his disdain for "people in government who are gay and promoting anti-gay legislation. That's horrible."

Whatever the cartwheels he might have performed to maintain a certain façade for some elements of the community, Price does point out that Kirkwood drew the line somewhere: "Although he certainly had a history of some heterosexual activity…he didn't push it. He didn't try and throw that up at you as some other people I have known have: you know, 'Oh, I used to fuck girls.'"

As to the attitude of Kirkwood's relatives to their gradual realization that he was now unequivocally not the marrying kind, cousin Lila says,

"It's no one's business what they do with their private life as long as they're happy and not doing anything criminal. I see nothing wrong with that. He liked my husband, my husband liked him. Some men who are not gay aren't always too receptive, but my husband liked him very, very much. It was never a problem. Never." Cousin Bobby Tufford wryly says, "Jimmy was a homosexual and the girls used to look at him and say, 'Jeez, what a thing,'" but he also had no problems with Kirkwood's lifestyle ("I knew that Jimmy was homosexual, but I didn't question about it or anything of that nature").

Tufford says of Kirkwood as a teenager, "Jimmy was a fine-looking man and the girls really thought well of him. I had no inkling at that time that there was any indication toward him becoming homosexual. None whatsoever." Yet strangely, he also says that he wasn't surprised when he found out he'd become a full-blown homosexual. This lack of surprise is something he shares with Kirkwood's high-school friends. Bob Cromling: "I guess I had the feeling that if you're in the acting profession it's very easy to be homosexual. There is a preponderance of gays in the arts." Cromling didn't see any "signs" in the time he knew Kirkwood. Ditto for Ralph Ruth, although for him too it makes sense retrospectively. Ruth: "The acting and entertainment and the Hollywood-New York scene would have encouraged that kind of personality trait if the makings of it were there. And I felt with Jim, the makings of it were there from the beginning. I certainly, at the time, never labeled his personality as someone who was destined to someday come out as being gay. I just considered Jim to have a personality that was quite different from that of any of the other guys that I associated with in high school, and the best word that I can find for it is effeminate. He certainly was always very comfortable in the company of either girls or boys in high school, but his manner of dealing with either kids of the same sex or kids of the opposite sex was a little different from that of most high-school boys. So I felt not at all surprised when I learned that he had decided he was gay. I found that I was not the only one with that reaction." Sidney Wasserman offers, "I felt that he had a lot of unhappiness, he was mixed-up in a lot of ways, but also that he had an enormous need to be loved. Where that took him I don't know, but my feeling was that I wasn't totally surprised." Any signs? "He didn't show to me that he was interested in boys as a sexual object, but that he was looking to women, mother figures, grandmother figures, for the love that he was seeking." Esther Hamula, the woman who could have ended up as Kirkwood's wife, says, "It didn't surprise me, not at all." She then, however, seems to contradict herself, saying, "Maybe it surprised me because I did not ever feel he had that orientation when he was around in Elyria."

His novel about his father was not immediately resurrected by Kirkwood following the completion of *American Grotesque*. Instead, he embarked on writing a play that would ultimately be called *P.S. Your Cat Is Dead!* born out of those paranoid days he had experienced when he was robbed three times in fourteen months at the West 58th Street apartment.

"I never did meet my burglar friend in life," he later said. Kirkwood instead invented a personality for his tormentor as he placed him center-stage in his new work. As well as a bisexual, Kirkwood made the burglar a man with a singular way of speaking, his Bronx gutter argot speckled with clumsy philosophy. Kirkwood named this man Vito. He was based on a real person, the splendidly titled Gino Marino. "Gino was a waiter at a restaurant called the Bull's Head Inn in Bridgehampton probably in the early sixties," says Beckenstein. Homer Price, who knew Gino, says, "Punk is not quite the right word — a lower middle-class, kind of street guy that we all were seeing out there in the late sixties." Price is here clearly using the phrase "lower middle-class" in the way it has come to be employed in the United States in modern times: as a euphemism for the unmentionable term "working class." Price: "He had a real New York accent, talked like a street guy and *was* up until a certain point." Beckenstein, who met Gino once, found him, "Kind of scrappy and good-hearted." "He was a character," says Price. "Sumner Lock Elliott was among our crowd out there — the Australian author — and he would call him 'Summer' instead of 'Sumner.' We all adored him. I don't know whatever happened to him. I haven't heard about Gino for so long. I think he's not with us anymore." Were Gino and Kirkwood lovers? "Oh, I don't think you'd call it lover but I'm pretty sure they fooled around," says Price. Beckenstein estimates Gino to have been ten-to-fifteen years younger than Kirkwood. "The guy who he later turned into the robber in *P.S. Your Cat is Dead!* was someone he had met who kind of stalked him for a couple of years afterwards," is Piazza's recollection of what Kirkwood told him of Gino, adding that being stalked was not something that Kirkwood would necessarily find a negative thing: "I think Jimmy loved any bit of drama that came his way. I think he made his life purposely exciting. I think he would go out of his way to create drama." Kirkwood himself said of Gino, "…a real hustler-hooker, into everything wrong and a real pussycat. A soft touch. A chronic liar. You could give him $50,000 and next month someone would have taken him for it. But tough on the outside. Rugged." As to whether Gino knew that Kirkwood had immortalized him, Beckenstein says, "I think he probably found out. I don't think he told him at the time." Though in Vito Kirkwood was inserting another sexually alternative character into his *oeuvre*, he at the same time attempted to hold onto his own privacy regarding his proclivities by making central character Jimmy Zoole — who lives in the apartment Gino/Vito burgles — straight.

Another character in the play had a prototype from Kirkwood's real life, namely Kate, the assertive common-law wife of Zoole who throws him over on New Year's Eve. Kirkwood said, "The girlfriend in the play is an old girlfriend of mine who read it and didn't find it at all amusing." Director of a version of the *Cat* stage play Vivian Matalon recalls Kirkwood telling him that the character's mixture of ballsiness and vulnerability was based on Elaine Stritch. "There was a rumor about that," says Stritch. "I never talked to him intimately about it. I think probably [I] had something to do with it." Kirkwood — exhibiting the defensiveness that he seemed to acquire over this work in general — insisted, "The girl is not a bitch. She walks out on Jimmy because their relationship is at a point of diminishing returns. She leaves him because she cares. She knows he's not going to marry her. He's too unstable — a boy-man, not a man. And an actor besides!"

There was a real-life prototype for Jimmy Zoole as well. Zoole has appeared in a soap opera but has never secured the big, breakout role. He lives in a New York apartment that is repeatedly burgled by incrementally more audacious methods. Out of the sheer boredom of waiting for roles to materialize, he has begun writing a novel. Sound familiar? "I wrote *P.S.* as an entertainment," said Kirkwood, "and to tell how I felt about acting, how rough it is when you devote twenty years of your life to [it] and don't quite make it. The constant rejection. Day after day. Week after week. I've always been amazed at the resiliency of actors." He also said, "We all feel at one time in our lives that we're losers. That's what I wanted to…capture."

It may be the case that if *P.S. Your Cat is Dead!* had been staged quickly then Kirkwood would never have turned the play into a novel. Kirkwood spoke about the problems of getting an idea from the page to the stage in that interview in *After Dark* magazine whose cover date of February 1972 was probably not long after his completion of the play. "The trouble with the theatre is that everybody is so goddamned afraid to jump into the pool," he lamented. "They're afraid of failure…Of course, part of it is the terrible cost. A simple three-act comedy can go as high as $200,000 just to get it open. That's why more things should be done in regional theatre. When my friends ask me what I'm working on, I say I'm writing a play. And they look at me like I've lost my mind. They know how scared everybody is."

Kirkwood may not have lost his mind, but he does seem to have forgotten what he had been through hitherto in his life. When Kirkwood had switched to writing, he was liberated by the fact of a profession that had no logistics attached to it. He could just sit at a typewriter and do it. Getting his work to the public required no more than persuading a publishing house that it was commercial — not necessarily guaranteed, as he had painfully learned with *The Angels or Whoever*, but at least a whole universe removed from the auditions meat-market and the high ratio of rejection inherent in thespian life. So why, having alighted on this salvation of his peace of mind in the shape of novel-writing, did Kirkwood allow himself to be sidetracked into playwriting? The mountains to climb involved in putting on a play bear a huge resemblance to the obstacles littering the path to success in the career he had left behind. Richard Seff recalls, "He did say to me once he liked writing because it was something he didn't have to get permission to do. With an actor, you can't work unless someone asks you to." The same applies to mounting a play, insofar as willing financiers have to be found. Even if one succeeds in putting on a play, circumstances beyond one's control can make the whole exercise futile — as with (if we are to believe Kirkwood's theory) *UTBU* and the transit strike. One is tempted to assume that Kirkwood's thinking was muddled by the cultural and psychological tugs he still felt from his former profession.

Kirkwood made his own attempt at self-analysis on this issue in an article in *Paterson News* in March 1975, at which point he had two plays in rehearsal. Referring to his stung feelings after the failure of *UTBU*, he said, "As much as I loved the theater, I suppose I had made a tacit rule that if I couldn't win all the marbles — well, then, I wouldn't play. I told myself I had lost all ambition to be a playwright. Wrong. I didn't lose it, I only misplaced it." Acknowledging that putting on a play involved one's work and original vision being tampered with by "producers, directors,…actors, dancers and singers, not to mention backers, theater-owners and anyone else into whose mitts a script happens to fall" he returned to a theme of loneliness that he had mentioned earlier in the article in relation to novel-writing. "Suddenly you're thrust into a family, instant adoption, enveloped by those intense and incredibly intimate friendships that bloom between theater folk in a matter of days, if not hours," he said of the advantages of putting on a play. Kirkwood proceeded to veritably drool over the raucousness of a coffee break, the stunned silence when a scene is going well, the enthusiasm and inspiration of actors and dancers, the pure excitement of witnessing cold words on paper being brought to life and the myriad component parts of a production being assembled. This most gregarious of men — and proven prose stylist — was almost admitting that he wasn't cut out for the life of the novelist. It's a quasi-confession that might go some way toward explaining why he would by the late seventies virtually abandon it in preference for one spent collaborating with others in devising — usually futilely — play scripts and film scripts, something that would adversely affect his literary legacy. In the early 1970s he, thankfully, at least showed the presence of mind to hedge his bets. With the play of *P.S. Your Cat is Dead!* completed, he — perhaps fearing its story, dialogue and ideas would be lost if it was not produced — decided to turn it into a novel. In doing the reverse of what he had done with the novel of *There Must Be a Pony!*, he created a work of art that was far superior to the *Cat* play (in any of its three incarnations) and indeed his overall *meisterwerk*.

The novel — dedicated to Arthur Beckenstein — was published by Stein & Day in November 1972. It came to be acquired by that house via an unusual route. In late 1971, George Caldwell, a senior Stein & Day editor, opened a bookstore in East Hampton called Book Hampton with his partner George Castello. Kirkwood attended the store's opening party and became a customer. He would sometimes stop to chat. Eventually, he suggested that Caldwell meet his agent. Caldwell agreed and a day later the manuscript of *P.S. Your Cat is Dead!* was on his desk. One wonders, though, why the name of Little, Brown, Simon & Schuster or a similar house did not end up on the book's spine. "Stein & Day was not a leading publisher," says Richard Kluger, editor of the last work of fiction Kirkwood had published. "It was a second-tier publisher. If he was still represented by [Phyllis] Jackson, she wouldn't have taken it there until the leading publishers had passed on it." If this is the case, those leading publishers were spectacularly wrong in their rejection.

P.S. Your Cat Is Dead! is James Kirkwood's first (published) novel about an adult. His protagonist is different to his previous protagonists not only in being well past the age of majority, but in not being completely likeable. James Zoole is a more cynical, argumentative and profane individual than either Josh Cydney or Peter Kilburn. He is also of a parlous mental state. His repeated burglaries and his permanently sputtering acting career (though he enjoys acting, he hates the humiliations of auditions, such as the one for a soda commercial which entailed miming swimming the length of a boardroom table) have driven him to paranoia, anger and fear. The fact that he is hurtling towards forty is not helping. (His résumé claims he is

32 rather than 38: "I rationalized it was because I looked younger, always played young parts. This was true but the prime reason was this: lopping off a few years gave me more time in which to succeed.") The book feels very streetwise and contemporary, both again departures: the Hollywood movie circle and prep school backdrops of Kirkwood's previous books are relatively cloistered and in some senses old-fashioned atmospheres.

Zoole comes home on a snowy New Year's Eve to find Kate, the woman with whom he has a stormy and decaying relationship, packing her bags. After she has left, he discovers in his apartment the burglar who has been repeatedly looting him and who even stole the sole copy of the manuscript of his novel. Infuriated, Zoole overpowers the burglar and ties him up to a standalone butcher block. Some minor sadism takes place. Zoole torments Vito when he tells him he's hungry. When the burglar complains he needs to urinate, Zoole cuts off his trousers and underwear and indicates he should do it in the butcher block's sink over which his groin area happens to be placed.

Then something strange begins to happen. While Zoole dithers as he tries to work out an appropriate punishment for the thief, their banter causes a mutual respect and admiration to build up. The burglar — a low-born but thoughtful man who imparts the fact that he is bisexual as casually as he does that his name is Vito Antenucci — engages Zoole in conversation which before long has him questioning how he lives his life. Their rambling discussion — punctuated by sullen pauses and barbed exchanges as Zoole remembers precisely what this man entered his apartment to do — is in turns moving, intriguing and hilarious. By the book's end, the two are firm friends and both have experienced epiphanies: Zoole has an improved perspective on his problematic life and the burglar is brought around to a genuine realization that it is time he did something more conducive to self-respect.

That the chapters are very short and dialogue-heavy and that this is the slimmest of Kirkwood's novels (212 pages in its first edition) perhaps betrays the book's origins as the script for a stage play, ditto its minimal cast of characters, brief time span (essentially one evening) and mostly single-venue setting. Yet the book never has a static or stultifying feel. This is not particularly because Kirkwood opens the story out with a handful of exterior scenes, but because the characters are so endlessly fascinating. The one time the novel feels limited by its origins is a lazy piece of exposition upon Zoole's discovery of Vito's presence a quarter of the way through the book. Amazed to find Vito appearing fearfully from under the bed when he accidentally fires his gun, Zoole is, immediately and unprompted, given by Vito a *précis* of how he came to be here: "Take it easy, it's a draw, no harm done, I didn't take nothin'. Right after I — down through there…she came, surprised me, I left the gun by the TV. Ducked under the bed. Then you come. I didn't take nothin'. My mother's grave." Though the lines show the brilliant ear for dialogue Kirkwood displays throughout, the speech itself is the kind of bringing-the-consumer-up-to-speed device that is essential in an art form of which interior dialogue is not a component but which is completely unnecessary in a novel.

Because the faults in *P.S. Your Cat Is Dead!* are minor, it seems fairer to tackle the rest of them before dealing with its triumphs. Near the start of the book, Zoole reproduces his acting résumé. It is remarkable for its resemblance to Kirkwood's own *curriculum vitae*. Although he pays lip service to fictionalizing the titles of shows in which he has appeared (including one called *The Angels or Whoever*), in places Kirkwood simply reproduces parts of his own career chronology verbatim, including references to appearing in *Wonderful Town* with Kaye Ballard and *Never Too Late* in South Africa, *Lamp Unto My Feet* and *Divorce Court* on TV and his *Teenagers Unlimited* radio show with Lee Goodman. It's a rather strange strategy. Kirkwood was surely intelligent and — by this stage — experienced enough to know that an essential element of fiction is the maintenance of artifice. Many writers use the kind of true life experience that underpins this book — indeed, it would be foolhardy of a writer not to exploit such raw material — but when, for instance, it is noted that Zoole appeared for four years as Mickey Emerson in a TV soap called *Valiant Lady* and had performed with Tallulah Bankhead in *Welcome Darlings*, the reader is in danger of being distracted from the story he is being told and becoming jarringly conscious of the "real" world. Another small fault is that familiar awkward place into which the combination of his reticence about his own sexuality and his simultaneous determination to address alternative sexuality puts the author. Kirkwood's heterosexual protagonist is depicted as bewildered (if slightly intrigued) by the (surprisingly numerous) gay characters he meets in his life. Making his leading character "red-blooded" but surrounding him with gay incident is a tired Kirkwood device by now and the cumulative effect of his having used the same approach in his previous works is that it stretches plausibility, let alone annoys us in its coyness.

However, this is the first Kirkwood book where any faults are not major. The book is the epitome of Kirkwood's "storyteller" prose style, his penchant for writing as he might speak, with of course the massive artistic license all novelists employ for a smooth-flowing read. He immediately buttonholes the reader with a second-person first line ("Did things ever get so outlandishly rock bottom rotten that you went around muttering… I don't believe it!") and makes occasional asides to him. Stuff like this, the sparklingly realistic dialogue and the nugget-sized chapters make the book incredibly accessible, even with a sexual subtext that would have been rather shocking in its time.

The book is brilliantly plotted and paced. Vito's unloading of his life story — which takes in a bizarre mixture of hoodlum activity and unconventional employment like stand-up comedy and striptease — does not feel false despite the prone and tied position in which Vito spends the vast majority of the book. Kirkwood adroitly portrays a natural, incremental opening up by Vito and a growing friendliness between two people who start out as utter opposites and, indeed, opponents. The only really false note comes when Zoole tells the reader that he never thought of simply ringing the police to arrest Vito, but doesn't really explain why. Of course, had he done so there would be no storyline, but Kirkwood could surely have thought of some plausible reason, especially when he has the advantage of a character in such an irrational and fevered state of mind as Zoole.

Vito is really the star of the book, his personality exhilaratingly well-drawn. That his past is told in his vernacular only adds to the charm: Vito's rough "Bronx," peppered with fancy words he has learnt from a literate lover, his wisecracking delivery and his singular turn of phrase are wonderful and endearing. It's tempting to say that Vito would make for a great book himself, but it probably isn't true: his amusing way of expressing himself and streetwise wisdom work when framed within the bemused viewpoint and powers of expression of Jimmy Zoole, but his small vocabulary and limited knowledge would probably become wearing spread across the course of a novel seen exclusively from his perspective.

The most delicious moment in the story occurs when Kate returns to the apartment because Vito's shouts for help during an earlier phone call had gotten her worried. Zoole has agreed to Vito's request for a cigarette, though not to untying him. Kate comes through the door to find the half-naked Vito being fed drags on the smoke by Zoole. The astounded state to which she is reduced by the tableau is utterly hilarious. Vito — who has already adjudged her a "ballbreaker," partly because of her callous postscript to her goodbye note in which she had informed Zoole of the demise of his beloved kitty (named Bobby Seale) in the wording of the play's title — instantaneously decides to have some fun with her. There is a flash of understanding between he and Zoole, and they proceed to make Kate believe that they have been having an affair, and have been doing so for quite a while. Vito knows Kate and Zoole's pet word for their sex sessions and knocks her sideways by saying, "…did you think you was the only one gettin' in on those great — Hugglebunnyburgers?…We call ours Bang-arama-thons, but what's the diff? Bang-arama-thons — Hugglebunnyburgers, six of one, half dozen of the other. What you lose on the peanuts, you make up on the bananas, right?"

The denouement to *P.S. Your Cat Is Dead!* is an honest-to-goodness happy ending. Vito saves Zoole from a bunch of sado-masochistic homosexuals who have invaded his apartment and turned nasty. (Zoole called them up to scare Vito before the relations between them thawed.) Zoole then lets Vito go. Over the next couple of days, Zoole finds that he misses him. Vito returns. He has gotten involved in a dispute with a Mafioso type of his acquaintance, but has emerged the victor with $3,600 in cash and cocaine with a street value of $5,000 — enough to finance keeping Zoole afloat for a year in Mexico while he starts again on the book Vito now feels guilty about having destroyed the only copy of. The book Zoole writes is…*P.S. Your Cat Is Dead!* It's verging on the pat and the corny but it works, and sweetly so. Kirkwood truly does have a knack for a gorgeously mellow and life-affirming conclusion.

The tidy ending, the Christmassy time-frame and atmosphere and the morality-tale elements make this Kirkwood's modern-day, streetwise, alternative-outlooked equivalent of *A Christmas Carol* — sort of. *P.S. Your Cat is Dead!* is Kirkwood's greatest book because it is the apotheosis of what his future editor Nick Ellison describes as his "velvet fist" prose style: the ability to deal with hard-hitting subject matter without sacrificing utter readability.

William Russo disagrees with the idea that Kirkwood's dropping-in of real facts about his life is a stylistic minus. "I think that it lends credence to his story," he says, "because he is telling the story as if this is what happened and that's what good fiction writers do. They're very convincing and his books are convincing."

Film critic Rex Reed supplied an endorsement that arrived too late to be used on the hardcover edition. It read, "James Kirkwood's new novel, *P.S. Your Cat Is Dead!* is both sadistic and tender. Among its highlights are one of the strangest New Year's Eves ever created in print and one of the most unusual friendships since Joe Buck met Ratso Rizzo in *Midnight Cowboy*. I found it riveting, unique and extremely imaginative…a gratifying work by one of our most gifted young writers." Though he was a friend of Kirkwood's, Reed's dutiful supply of a rave was in only one way inaccurate — describing the author as young.

There were many good reviews, probably the most important to Kirkwood — he is on record virtually as saying so — being that of *The New York Times*, which declared, "Kirkwood is a fine writer, and keeps the suspense taut all the way." Strangely, *The New York Times Book Review* treated *Cat* as a crime novel, appraising it alongside — among others — Agatha Christie's latest. "A curious offbeat fantasy, perhaps more a psychological story than a mystery novel proper..." it conceded. Its conclusion was, "Kirkwood is a fine writer and keeps the suspense taut all the way." Faubion Bowers wrote in *The Village Voice*, "Reading it, I have not laughed out loud (and all alone) so much since I was introduced to *Cold Comfort Farm* by another very off-beat writer. In every Kirkwood book there is an undercurrent of eroticism which makes the loins twitch, although I can't cite a single porno passage. Similarly, touches of the macabre give an eerie coloration to his work...The fact is Kirkwood with three novels, one play and a book of reportage proves himself a master of his craft. He knows how to tell a story, hold the reader's attention, and delight with the surprising nuance or shocking situation. I further suspect that everything Kirkwood writes has actually happened, although this may simply be the legerdemain of a magician who makes you believe what couldn't possibly be, let alone be believed." Mentioning that both *Playboy* and the Book Find book clubs had picked *Cat* as their selection this season, Bowers continued, "...it pleases me to record Kirkwood's ever-increasing acceptance. Any writer as special as he is prone to being overlooked by a hoi polloi. When that happens it means writers can't afford to write what they want to and should. Similarly, when an author is too widely popular he gives his readership what it demands. Kirkwood at the moment is at that wonderful point between enough recognition to keep on going and so overly much he won't have to. I hope he stays there, for he is far too good, too important to the literary scene, either to be neglected or lionized."

The first line of Bowers review was, "Some people wait all year for Christmas. I personally wait for James Kirkwood's novels." An impressive encomium, to which this author will only add that *P.S. Your Cat is Dead!* is a far more important fixture of both the Kirkwood and the literary canon than it has ever been given credit for, including by Kirkwood himself. It is simply one of the greatest novels of the twentieth century.

Nineteen seventy-two saw a brief revival of the Kirkwood & Goodman comedy act.

The occasion was a fundraising show in East Hampton for Democratic presidential candidate George McGovern. At this point, Goodman and his partner Ronald Plotkin spent weekends in a one-bedroom apartment above a two-car garage Kirkwood had added to his East Hampton home in the early seventies. Goodman and Plotkin had gone in as financial partners with Kirkwood on the addition. The reunion gig took place at the American Legion Hall in East Hampton. Though the Kirkwood & Goodman act was quite a long way in the past by this time, Ron Plotkin says, "There were still a lot of people in the Hamptons that knew them and so there was kind of a buzz and everybody was saying, 'Oh my God, are they really going to do this?'" The resurrection of the act brought about a revival of old conflicts. Plotkin: "Jim kept saying, 'We got to rehearse, we got to rehearse' and Lee kept saying, 'We don't have to rehearse every twenty minutes. We'll go over it once. We're not getting paid to do this. We're gonna do it for the fun.'" Plotkin reports that Kirkwood "tormented" Goodman enough that he would grudgingly make the trek down into Kirkwood's quarters to practice. "Lee said, 'This is the reason we broke up the act,'" Plotkin recalls.

The night of the performance (which Mr. McGovern did not attend) was the first time that Plotkin had seen the pair's act. "They did just one of their well-known skits from the act, The Fickle Finger of Fate or Bucky and Bobby," he explains, adding, "It went over very well." In the interests of completism, it should be reported for those who aren't aware that the well-received performance of Kirkwood & Goodman did not swing the '72 presidential election for the Democratic candidate and that Richard Nixon was re-elected by a landslide.

So elongated was the process of getting *P.S. Your Cat is Dead!* to the stage that Kirkwood had completed yet another novel by the time of its premiere. In fact, the two works appeared almost simultaneously. The new novel was not the one about his father, despite the fact that in the February '72 *After Dark* interview he had indicated his intention of getting back to the book that had been put on the back-burner in '69 for the Clay Shaw trial. "It also has to do with my half-brother," he told the magazine. "I had a working title, *The Most Expensive Acre*, but I don't like that. It'll just have to come to me. It's about an eighty-something-year-old actor who raises a young boy and the great disparity between their ages and their whole worlds. The boy loves his father and fears his dreadful temper, but he sees a great decline in the old man's career. The boy becomes a hooker, a hustler, in order to support his father."

The newer novel was to be one based on Kirkwood's terrible experiences at the close of World War II when he (supposedly) came out of the service to find that his life was in tatters: his best friend dead, his fiancée married to another man, his mother gravely ill and his financial state so parlous that he had to stoop to a store robbery. "The robbery is what made me write that book," Kirkwood later said. "I always wanted to tell what it was like to do something like that." He decided not to make the conflict from which the protagonist emerged the Second World War, however. Possibly this was through a desire to remain contemporary: the '41-'45 struggle was already ancient history to young Americans. However, a possibly subliminal motivation was the fact that setting such an autobiographical novel in the aftermath of that war would practically constitute announcing his true age. It seems significant that promoting the published book, he came out with falsehoods like this one: "I had been in the Korean war" (*Roy Leonard Show*). Though Kirkwood said he considered setting the book at the time of the Korean War (1950-1953), at some point he opted for the war in which his country had effectively been engaged since 1965 and which would not truly conclude until 1975. As well as serving to disguise his age, using the Vietnam War as a backdrop would certainly engender a contemporary feel. Kirkwood also decided that he would make his protagonist a returning prisoner of war.

In late 1973, Kirkwood was having trouble finding an ex-POW to provide him with the sort of personal experience that he hoped would give his book verisimilitude. At this point, very few Vietnam POWs had been released. One day, chatting to a librarian in East Hampton, he mentioned his problem. The woman to whom he was speaking turned out to be a friend and ex-roommate of a woman who was married to Arthur Cormier, one of the very first Vietnam POWs to return to America.

Cormier, born in Maine but raised in New Jersey, was 31 years old when he was captured by the Vietnamese in 1965. "I was flying a rescue mission," he explains. "I was really a medic on back of a rescue helicopter. We flew within thirty miles of Hanoi and when we were shot down, I bailed out of the helicopter. I made it eight days before I got captured and they tried to rescue me twice while I was trying to evade and then got captured and taken to Hanoi and spent a couple of weeks at the Hanoi Hilton." The latter is the sardonic title given by American troops to the Hoa Lo prisoner of war camp. From there Cormier was transferred to another POW camp on the outskirts of Hanoi which the American inhabitants had also given a sardonic nickname — The Zoo — where he estimates he spent "the next five or six years," before going back to the Hanoi Hilton and thence freedom. In all, he was a Vietnam POW for seven years and three months. Cormier was billeted with one other person for a period of time, then two others and, towards the end, large groups.

He also spent six months in solitary confinement and was tortured in an effort to force him to sign statements denouncing his home country. "I went four years without receiving any letters and I was able to write about once a year," he says. "But my pilot and co-pilot were not able to write for the first four years."

In the time he was away, Cormier's homeland had changed, in some ways beyond recognition. "We were stuck in a time warp," he says. "Some of the guys I lived with got magazines at the very end and saw these ball players with long hair and all that, and some of the guys would say, 'My son better not have long hair — as soon as I get home I'll make sure he cuts it'…Well, long hair was in at that time and a lot of them had a great difficulty with the hair and all that sort of stuff. Just couldn't realize that's the way it was." The returning POWs also had difficulty with their marriages. Cormier describes reunited husbands and wives having problems in their newly revived relationships as, "Very common. I got a divorce. She wanted a divorce the third day after I got back, but it took us three years to get divorced."

It was these and other problems about which Cormier spoke with Kirkwood when the two met for the first time in either September or October of 1973. "We had about two sessions about a month apart," Cormier says. "The first one, I think lasted about half a day and the other one a couple of hours. He had an outline, but that's about all. I had no idea what he was going to use it for. He had the questions and I just answered the questions the best that I could, in diagrams — some of the compound and all that — so he had a good idea. I made a diagram of the camp, but he changed it a little bit to suit his needs. I gave him some of the stories that went on in the camp, but I didn't name anybody, just general information basically and some of the ups-and-downs we had." Cormier was surprised to find Kirkwood inordinately interested in one particular area: "Having a homosexual relationship and that sort of stuff. I can remember him kind of pressing me on that point too a couple of times. I didn't live in every cell, but the cells I lived in, I didn't see any of that going on." Like many who met Kirkwood for the first time, Cormier initially had no inkling that he was gay: "Until I went over to his house and he introduced me to his friend that was living with him at the time. Then I realized that he was gay. But that didn't put me off from him. He was a nice person, I thought."

On November 13, 1973, Lila Lee died at Saranac Lake, aged 68. She had been in hospital since June 25 with progressive shortness of breath and coughing. (Her TB, as it had recently, remained inactive.) She suffered while there what seemed to be her fourth major stroke of recent years. The medical records show that when her son visited, her mood brightened, but by October 22 she was refusing food and telling doctors she wanted to die. Though her health turned around sufficiently for her condition to be described as "good," she abruptly developed congestive heart failure and new circulatory damage to the brain, became stuporous and comatose and died quietly at 12:30 pm on the seventh post-operative day following surgical gastrostomy for feeding.

It was the close of a life that, in its later years at least, had been marked by a quite incredible catalogue of suffering. Beckenstein recalls, "When I met her in the seventies, she had already had a couple of strokes and she had trouble speaking and walking and she was very bright red all the time." He adds, "She still carried herself with the stature of a movie star." As Kirkwood himself recounted in his 1974 lecture on his mother, "She was almost burned to death in a freak accident and spent two years in hospitals having skin grafts over a fourth of her body — thank God her face was not burned. When she recovered from this, TB struck again and she finally had to have a lung removed. She recovered from this operation against all odds and was rewarded for her spunk by whoever pulls the strings with emphysema, diabetes and cataracts." In 1986, Kirkwood said, "That she lived to age 68 was really incredible." He added, "But her death was a real loss for me, no matter how much I used to try to rehearse it to prepare myself."

This eulogy doesn't touch on the massively ambivalent relationship Kirkwood and his mother had. His comment to Wasserman that she was never there for him as a child more than a decade after their schooldays is a startling illustration of this ambivalence, as is possibly a recollection by his old *Valiant Lady* colleague John Desmond. The latter had a house near Woodstock and Kirkwood spent the night there with Beckenstein on the day of Lila Lee's death. "I hugged him when they drove into the lane," says Desmond. "And he didn't cry. I thought he would dissolve into tears but he didn't." However, there may have been another reason for Kirkwood's stoicism. As Desmond also says, "He really was a survivor."

On August 25 the following year, Kirkwood appeared at the John Drew Theatre in East Hampton in a presentation called *Life with My Movie Star Mother*. With the assistance of slides, clips from her films and extracts from the autobiography she had begun to write with Evan Rhodes the previous summer, Kirkwood told the story of his mother's never-quite-happy life. His skillful blending of Rhodes' uncompleted manuscript — basically, Lee's verbatim anecdotes — and his own memories made for an enlightening and moving lecture which, lengthened, could have made for an excellent biography and a non-fiction work on which he, unlike with *American Grotesque*, was on sure ground.

Following his mother's death, Kirkwood sold the house in Key West's South Street in which she and her sister Peg had lived in recent years. Kirkwood was clearly now doing a little better than he had been between his first and second books, having paid $16,000 in the early seventies for the three-bedroom house, even if it did come furnished. He had probably installed Lila Lee in Key West because the warm climate was good for her long-suffering respiratory system, but he had clearly taken to the area himself. In early 1973, he paid $7,000 for his own house on Key West's Catherine Street. The house was within a compound of thirteen Cuban cigar-makers' cottages built around a common swimming pool in a landscaped park-like setting. Kirkwood built a second story on this house. When his mother passed away, he gave the ground floor over to Peg. "He was very loyal to his aunt," says friend Bill Gile. "He had offers on that house that were all the money in the world and he wouldn't sell it because that's where she wanted to live." Bobby Tufford, Peg's son, says, "He was so good to my mother. He'd send her money. 'Jimmy — you just *sent* me money.' He forgot."

"He split his time between Key West and New York, heading south as soon as the weather turned cold," explains Beckenstein. Located at land's end, ninety miles from Miami down the Florida Keys, the isle of Key West was almost always sunny. It also had a significant artistic community (even if some of the writers, etc., only "wintered" there), as well as much alternative culture. "It was a lively, vibrant place," says Beckenstein. One of the many gay writers who would either live or winter in Key West was the great Tennessee Williams. The author of *Cat on a Hot Tin Roof* and several other classics of the American stage was a friend of Kirkwood's and an admirer of his art (the feeling was mutual), but he was also a fan and friend of Lila Lee. "Tennessee always treated her like the movie star she had been," says Beckenstein.

In late 1974, Kirkwood was in a New York theatre lobby during the intermission of a play. Informed by a director under whom he had once worked that Michael Bennett was present, Kirkwood acidly retorted, "Say hello to the little bastard for me." Bennett was a stage director who had prevaricated about helming the play version of *P.S. Your Cat Is Dead!* before finally declining it. Eventually, it was Bennett who made the first move, coming over to Kirkwood, snapping his fingers at him and telling him he'd been trying to get hold of him. Kirkwood recalled the director saying, "Have you ever thought about writing a musical?" Kirkwood responded that he'd given the matter thought but had no idea how to go about it. (Presumably he wasn't counting *The Boys on the Hill*.) Bennett's thoughts on that were that this figured — if it was easy, people would be turning out musicals left and right. Bennett suggested they meet the next day. When they did, he explained to Kirkwood that he wanted to do a show about chorus dancers auditioning for a Broadway musical. Bennett was a former dancer himself. As a veteran of more auditions, if not dancing ones, than he cared to remember and as someone who had often been inordinately upset by them, Kirkwood was immediately intrigued by the idea. He signed on immediately for a project that he recalled all the principals at the time referring to as "this little musical about chorus dancers."

Jack Sydow recalls seeing an interview with Kirkwood in which the latter said of the theatre lobby meeting and the agreement to do the show, "The reason I did was because I had my Fig Newton that day. If I hadn't had my Fig Newton I don't know what I would have said." Kirkwood could thank his lucky stars for his fix of the fruity soft cookie in question, references to his love of which recurred in his work and interviews. Said little musical about chorus dancers would become the biggest phenomenon in the history of Broadway and make Kirkwood a multi-millionaire.

THIRTEEN

The "little musical about chorus dancers" did not have a title until very late in its life but for the sake of convenience the one plumped for just weeks before the show's first preview is what it will henceforth be referred to as: *A Chorus Line*. Some wanted it called simply *Chorus Line* but the non-definite article was considered crucial because it meant it would appear first in the "*Times* listing" — the Theater Directory of *The New York Times*. Deciding on the structure and content of the show was as torturous as alighting on a title was relatively easy. Had it not been so, Kirkwood would probably not have been asked to come aboard the project.

Michael Bennett was born Michael DiFiglia in 1943 in Buffalo, New York. Though Bennett had his share of being a "gypsy" — an anonymous hoofer in the chorus — he was one dancer whom his contemporaries and colleagues recognized as someone who would not have to return to the depressing reality of ordinary life when his limbs were no longer young and nimble enough to pound the boards. This at least is the recollection of Donna McKechnie, a dancer and friend of Bennett's who would be a star of *A Chorus Line* and ultimately Bennett's wife. "Everyone knew he was going to be a choreographer one day that would be important," she says, "so he always had this group of people kind of following him everywhere he went, or if they had a question they would go to Michael. He was always the beacon for everyone." Bennett choreographed *A Joyful Noise* (1966) and *Henry, Sweet Henry* (1967). Both shows were flops but come 1968 he had his first hit with *Promises, Promises*. *Coco* (1969) saw him choreographing Katharine Hepburn and in the following two years he worked on Stephen Sondheim shows *Company* and *Follies*. He also directed a non-musical in the shape of 1971's *Twigs*. He graduated to the roles of director and librettist for musical *Seesaw* (1973), although his Tony award for that show was for his choreography.

According to friends and associates, Bennett had the idea of a show that made stars out of those cast members of musicals who are necessarily anonymous as far back as 1972. These ideas seem to have been crystallized by politics, with Bennett speaking of the proposed show as a work of honesty that might act as some sort of antidote to the general sense of disillusion the 1973 Watergate saga had created. Subsequently, Bennett merged his concept to some degree with that of two dancers who had appeared in *See Saw*, Michon Peacock and Tony Stevens. By coincidence, the latter pair had had a similar idea, although it was a little vaguer than Bennett's. The trio decided to make their first step a research project in the form of a marathon rap session at which dancers would talk about their lives and their careers. It took place in mid-January 1974 in two rooms at an exercise center in Manhattan. Eighteen dancers attended, among them Donna McKechnie.

McKechnie recalls of Bennett, "He said, 'I don't know what this will be, if it's a book, if it's a movie, if it's a workshop, if it just ends here, if it's a play, a musical. I don't know, but it's something that I want to explore.' That's how he set it up and we went around with [four] questions: tell me your name, your age, where you were born and why did you start dancing." Those questions would, in fact, ultimately be the questions asked of the dancers by Zach, the director figure in *A Chorus Line*. The dancers' responses were taped. Some of the stories that emerged were quite extraordinary, featuring dysfunctional childhoods, aching ambition and sexual confusion. People in the room, many of whom had naturally worked together many times before, suddenly found out how little they knew about one another. Bennett was particularly moved by the story recounted by Nicholas Dante who at the age of 33 was facing the twilight days of his dancing career. It was a career that he had gone through terrible traumas to follow. Born Conrado Morales in 1941, he had endured the stigma of growing up gay in a macho Puerto Rican culture. He only became a dancer because his ambition to major in journalism was stymied by his homosexuality. Some sources say mocking of his effeminacy forced him out of school, others that the authorities there asked him to leave because of his sexuality. Either way, complicated feelings about his proclivities ran like a seam through his subsequent dancing career. As a predominantly gay man and a former dancer, Bennett saw much of his own story in Dante's. Dante's story would ultimately form the monologue of the character Paul in *A Chorus Line*, just as many of the stories heard that night would find their way, in some way, into the show's finished script.

There was another tape-recorded rap session in the second week of February but then the project — if that's not too strong a word for what was such an inchoate idea at this point — stalled while Bennett worked on other shows. Eventually, Bennett returned to the idea and bought out Peacock and Stevens, who had continued to make tape recordings of dancers' memories and thoughts in the interim. Bennett, meanwhile, had been approached by Joseph Papp, director of the theatrical producers the New York Shakespeare Festival. Though said organization had started out promoting the Bard's works, it had become something bigger than that with the hippie musical *Hair*, the international success of which meant that this not-for-profit concern could put on minority taste and experimental productions at its location at the Public Theater in Lower Manhattan. Papp had actually approached Bennett about a show he wanted to put on at the Vivian Beaumont Theatre in Lincoln Center, *Knickerbocker Holiday*. Bennett was amused by the idea that he should mount a revival of a Kurt Weill Broadway musical dating from 1938. He responded with a *non sequitur*, telling Papp of his vision of a musical about chorus dancers. Papp listened to the idea and to some of the dancers' tapes. He gave the go-ahead for the project to be developed at the Shakespeare Festival's expense. The dancers would be paid $100 per week and a rehearsal space and a skeleton crew would be made available at the Public Theater.

It was on the surface an inauspicious formal beginning. The August-September 1974 rehearsals at the Public took place in the day precisely so that dancers would be free to take jobs in shows that might become available to them, $100 being a somewhat meager weekly remuneration even for 1974. Bennett would later admit that the only reason some of the dancers stayed with the show is because they didn't have alternative employment. "No one's that noble," he observed. Bennett himself was more familiar with Broadway extravaganzas than the environs of non-profit theatre. Yet it is unanimously agreed by those involved in *A Chorus Line* that the Shakespeare Festival picking up this show was the best thing that could have possibly happened to it. The static rehearsal process — or "workshop," as it came to be called — gave everybody the luxury of time. As McKechnie puts it, "It...rarely happens and may never happen again. We were allowed to make all of the wrong choices in order to find the right choice." Even though Kirkwood came late to the proceedings, he recognized the importance of this process. In 1980, he spoke of the conventional route for plays of "rehearsing for four or five weeks and then...right into the theatres whether on the coast or out of town and then come right into Broadway." This comment is reminiscent of his talk in 1963 of the "hundred-yard dash" that tryouts constituted. He also said, "One reason for the success of *A Chorus Line* was a very, very long time in rehearsal and workshop, so that we were allowed to make all of the terrible mistakes that anyone makes putting any show together with all of those egos and different personalities...I remember we had a first run-through of *A Chorus Line* in a rehearsal hall down on 19th Street and, without an intermission, it was something like four hours and twenty minutes…We were all depressed. But the fact is, we didn't have to raise a curtain that evening in front of a paying audience. Consequently, we could perform major surgery instead of doing patchwork. We didn't have to please an audience; we only had to please ourselves. We had such a long time in which to do it."

In September 1974, however, the run-through to which Kirkwood refers — as well as Kirkwood joining the company — was quite a way off. Initially, Bennett was working on the show's script — even before his meeting with Papp — with Nicholas Dante. Like several of the dancers who attended the rap sessions, Dante would not be cast in the role to which his life story had given rise. "I don't think he was right for it," says McKechnie, fully aware of the irony of the statement. "I think Michael knew that he wouldn't be this sympathetic character. I'm guessing — I didn't get that from Michael." For Dante there was a consolation not available to the other dancers who had seen their life stories appropriated for the project but failed to obtain a part. McKechnie recalls, "Nicholas always told me, 'I want to be a writer' and I thought, 'Well, that worked out great.'" Dante later revealed in a playbill for a Los Angeles production of *A Chorus Line*, "I'd been writing for about ten years, but nothing had been produced." Despite his lack of writing credits, Dante possessed some brilliant raw material to which Bennett wanted access. McKechnie again: "I think he was moved to the point where he wanted that monologue so badly he started having great ideas about how to have this breakthrough, because at that point in time no one had ever talked about homosexuality in that way and that was always a crisis in his life. I think at that point in time that's when everything started to form in his mind. He was a great editor anyway. If he wanted that monologue, he was going to give Nicholas his opportunity." Not that McKechnie sees it as simple manipulation of Dante by the director to gain access to his story: "I think that was part of it, but I think he was more generous than that. I think there was a much more emotional connection Michael had with it and it was about *his* opportunity: he was on the line as much as anybody else was." McKechnie's feeling is that Dante was never destined to be the sole writer of the project. "I think he always felt that he would be able to work it out in one way or another with bringing another writer in," she says of Bennett. "I think he was that smart and savvy. Because he had done it. He had been in experiences before where that's what happens…In other words I don't think it was ever all of a sudden, 'Well, I got to get a writer for this….'"

McKechnie's recollections are of wobbly early days. When the cast assembled — including herself and Baayork Lee, the latter of whom had not attended the rap sessions — the result was so dire that she and several friends in the cast referred to it as *The Towering Inferno*, title of the disaster movie about a burning building that had been big box office that year. "It was like the first part of the workshop where we had put our stories to memory and we just went one after the other down the line, just to get Michael a sense of where he could go with it," she explains. "We were all sitting in a semi-circle and, right down the line, one person to the next to the next, talked about their horrible childhood and of course with the sense of competition in the air everybody tried to make it worse and worse. It was so deadly and there was no music yet. It was horrible." She recalls that the person displaying the most equanimity in the room was — perhaps surprisingly — Joe Papp: "The thing that makes him kind of great, he just understood the process and he'd seen enough things be so awful, he allowed for all that creative change. Most people would have just run screaming out of the room and said, 'What have I gotten myself into?'"

McKechnie also says, "Out of that horror of a day, he discovered how he had to go down the line, but one person would be the seven-year-old and the next person would [be] adolescence and then getting to Cassie where she was an adult. They would kind of hit him in the face, the character Zach [who] was dealing with his own personal life. So out of that horribleness came this discovery of where he had to go. That's the kind of thing that was going on because he wanted the book to be on the right track before he brought the music in." Baayork Lee explains, "When you're a pilgrim and pioneer, you're just putting one foot in front of the other. We didn't know what we were doing. Now you have a word: a workshop, a work-in-progress. We didn't have any title for it. We were working on a show — that's all everybody knew, and we went in every day and we danced 'til we couldn't walk and then we would sit around and we would talk about ourselves and then Nicholas and Michael would put some structure to it. But basically they were our words…He just went through different stages of our life and that's how the show is structured. It starts at four and then the next character goes onto twelve and then the next character and the next character, and it ends up at seventeen years old and when you come to New York." Some might assume from the finished show that dancers generally have tragic existences over and above even the universal sadness attending careers that necessarily end when people are not even halfway through their lives. However, there were plenty of dancers interviewed who were perfectly happy with their lot. "And he didn't use their stories," says Lee. "Because he really didn't think they were interesting enough." She does add of the stories that did make the cut, "They're not all sad: [the character] Mike, he wanted to dance and his sister went and then his mother took him, so that's not a sad story."

The Zach character fulfills much the same function in the show as Bennett did in real life, auditioning and directing people in a manner that might be termed manipulative. Were they the same person? Lee: "Well, Michael says no, that he's not Zach, but there are a lot of elements that I believe are: controlling the audition and the way Zach does it. Michael also has his story in two of the characters — Don Kerr is some of Michael's story, so elements of him are up there as a teenager, and then of course his relationship with Cassie, I believe Michael took some of his experience and put it in there."

Trish Garland, who played Judy, says, "Those were our stories so there was a partial fear that people were going to go, 'Oh, my God, who cares about that?' Or you're telling your life story and they go, 'Well that sucks'… When you're performing your own material, it's really hard to be objective about what's going on and the thing that you fear the most is that someone is going to reject your life, because it was a little bit different than in most cases. Jimmy and Nicholas Dante didn't really write all the material. It was there and they finessed it. Did they write things? Of course they did, but the meat of the material existed."

With some idea of where he was now going, Bennett took the step of bringing in the score providers. He chose Marvin Hamlisch to compose the music and Edward Kleban to devise the lyrics. Hamlisch had written the music for a dozen movies including *The Swimmer*, *Bananas*, *The Way We Were* and *The Sting* (the latter two pictures garnering him three Academy Awards on the same evening between them). Theatrically, he had scored the dance arrangements for Bennett's show *Seesaw*. Kleban was far less well-known. However, the fact that, aside from record productions, the only professional works he had to his name were club revue material and the musical *Gallery* did not mean he was completely obscure: Hamlisch knew of him through having heard Barbra Streisand perform his song "Better." For *A Chorus Line*, Kleban was using only half his gifts, as he normally wrote melody too. For McKechnie, it was at this point that things started to gel. Hearing the song "At The Ballet" — where Sheila tells of how she escaped the misery of a cold, unloving childhood home via dancing — she was very moved: "I thought, 'This is going to be a remarkable piece of theatre' because of that song, because it was so authentic and real and beautiful and touching and all the metaphors were just so accurate."

However, though things began turning from a Towering Inferno into something that looked as though it could have a genuine resonance, Bennett still thought that the show needed what might be termed a real writer. It was in the four-month gap between what became known as the first and second workshops that Bennett and Kirkwood's meeting in a New York theatre lobby occurred and Kirkwood was immediately grabbed by the idea of a musical that was based around auditioning for a show (at that point, it was still undecided whether this would be a series of auditions or — as would eventually be settled on — a single audition). It might be significant that at the time *P.S. Your Cat is Dead!* — with its denunciations of the humiliations actors face in trying to land jobs — was churning in his head, as the play was by now working its way to a Broadway opening. He later said, "All of us involved with putting *Chorus Line* together, except for Edward Kleban, have been performers and we all felt so strongly about the show, having been through the constant auditions, having been up on that line." In the same vein, he said elsewhere, "Having been a performer, I know that terror that comes with standing on a bare stage auditioning when you can't see really who's out in the theatre and you have nobody to bounce off of and you want the job so badly and that terrible, god-awful rejection that you feel when they say, 'Thank you.'" He also said, "I was hooked...I felt the essence of the show in my guts."

"He called me and told me they had offered him to be co-author and he told me what they wanted to pay him," recalls Arthur Laurents. "I said, 'Grab it. Because you have no experience, you don't know, and I think it's going to work.' He didn't really know much of what he was doing about that." Kirkwood signed on in December 1974. He was promptly surprised when Bennett told him he would be working in collaboration with Dante. The latter was also surprised. Dante later recalled Bennett presenting the fact that he now had a new collaborator as a *fait accompli*, and a not very polite one at that, Bennett informing him over the phone and then hanging up. However, the news was bittersweet: *Good Times/Bad Times* was Dante's favorite book. When Dante informed Kirkwood of this at their first meeting, Kirkwood turned to Bennett and said, "There will be no problem here." Dante and Kirkwood took to each other. Dante told Ken Mandelbaum, author of *A Chorus Line and the Musicals of Michael Bennett*, "I know that Marvin and Ed had their difficult moments, but Jimmy and I never did." Kirkwood himself said, "Nicholas was a joy to work with; our main quarrel was over punctuation. That's a happy collaboration, believe me."

Considering how late he was coming into the project, when Kirkwood was introduced by Bennett to the cast and crew, it would have been understandable if they felt or even exhibited resentment at his unexpected arrival, either because the implication was that he was coming in to correct shortcomings or simply because he was an outsider (and a non-dancing one) in a tight-knit bunch. However, this doesn't seem to have raised its head at all. Both McKechnie and Lee indicate that this was partly due to the trust the cast invested in their director. Lee: "If he felt that that was what we needed…I mean, we had been in workshop for almost a year and especially coming from me because I was his assistant… I trusted him with my life…I was just a dancer, I'd never spoken on stage, I had never really sung on stage alone and here was someone giving me the opportunity and the show was in his head." McKechnie actually says she was "relieved" by Kirkwood's arrival. Though not doubting the project's worth, she says of this point in its development, "Static's a good word. There would be like this little bubble of something and then it didn't go anywhere. As good as Michael was, the talent of him is also to recognize that he is not a writer. All the work was valid and important, but we needed someone and we were lucky to get Jimmy Kirkwood, because he knew the vernacular, he knew the feeling, he could get emotionally involved in it in a split second. He understood that world." McKechnie says the news of Kirkwood coming on board was "handled well. He introduced him to us, and Nicholas was up on stage with him, I believe. The tone was that there was excitement about someone coming in to make it better. Every step of the way with Michael's leadership and creative directorship we were taken to these better places, so there was a sense of, 'We're going in the right direction.' I didn't hear anybody saying, 'Oh dear, now we're in trouble.' Which is what happens in a show: when they start bringing people in, you go, 'Oh dear.'" In fact, it may have been beneficial merely that an outsider came into an atmosphere that sounds like it was becoming claustrophobic, even stultifying. McKechnie: "This was a community of people who were supportive, but [there was] also like a lot of sibling rivalry going on. Because of the nature of the work — when you're in the process of dredging up all of this kind of past and trying to be forthcoming in our feelings — everybody was in their angst most of the time. A lot of the dancers weren't psychologically adept to what was going on and so a lot of friction was happening. It wasn't always a big, friendly, huggy group."

That initial positive reaction to the principle of Kirkwood's arrival, for McKechnie, was only underlined when the cast got to know the newcomer. "The thing that I loved about James so much was that he was coming in as like a big brother," she says. "He had such respect and admiration for what we were doing. He was very successful in his own right and he wanted to be a part of it. I think he felt very excited about it, but he kind of stayed in the background, stayed in the shadows, was always supportive, never acted out in front of anybody. He was just a sweetheart and always was very sensitive to Nicholas' feelings. Nicholas could be the diva. I'm not saying anything out of school. He could be mean, he could loving and he could [be] erratic, all these things. But he just totally loved James so much because he felt respected and he felt taken care of." McKechnie also picked up a continuing affinity on the part of Kirkwood with the non-backstage side of the arts: "He wasn't a writer who removed himself from that performing experience." Further down the line, the show's press agent Bob Ullman had his own reasons to be thankful for Kirkwood — whose gregariousness and personableness made him the archetypal most popular man in town — coming aboard. Ullman said, "Before *A Chorus Line* opened at the Public, I couldn't get any media interested. The only person the press was interested in was — not Marvin Hamlisch, who had already written music for Streisand — but Jimmy Kirkwood. Everybody adored Jimmy Kirkwood."

Kirkwood recalled Bennett introducing him on an individual basis to various dancers who had attended his rap sessions so as to "inhale the essence" of their experiences and attitudes. (It's unclear whether Kirkwood was referring to just the cast members of *A Chorus Line* or to other dancers whose memories had been recorded as well.) How much Kirkwood got from the tapes of the rap sessions would become a bone of contention for him in future years. In a 1980 interview, Kirkwood said, "Ed Kleban, who was in on the project before I was, knows that I never heard those tapes. Michael played me about five minutes of them one time just to get the sound of all those people talking…I did get a transcript of it, but what you get from that is some characters, and you get a diversity of personalities to pick up on, but then the writer has to put that together." Elsewhere he said of the transcripts, "I would check off a line here and there that I found particularly touching or funny. But you can't expect to put 25 dancers or travel agents or stockbrokers in a room, let them talk and come up with a Broadway play."

"Once we started working on the show we put in very long days," Kirkwood said. "Nick Dante…Marvin…and the lyricist, we all worked on our own in the morning, got together in the afternoon and worked till two in the morning, then went over to Michael's apartment for an overview of what we'd done so far...Basically, we just started talking about dancers we'd all known. There was the one we called Sheila, who's a little over-the-hill, there was the one who almost became a star, the one who was never really pretty, the dancer who couldn't sing, the new kid who's trying out for his first show. Just people that we all knew. Then we started dividing up the characters amongst ourselves and enriching them; if a character struck a particularly responsive chord among one of us, he would be in charge of writing it." Kirkwood also recalled what-if sessions at Bennett's apartment: "What if there's a dancer who has stopped a few shows in featured spots, but is now down on her luck and back auditioning for the chorus? What if she and the director had lived together years before and now they meet again on another level? What if there's a boy who thinks he can charm his way through the audition by making jokes? Playing what-if can be fun and exhilarating: it can produce spin-offs you never imagined when you began the game." Kirkwood and Dante were also asked to help Hamlisch and Kleban overcome a difficulty they were having in devising the song about adolescence that Bennett felt was needed. Dante and Kirkwood wrote a one-act mini-play encapsulating everything they could think of about adolescence for Hamlisch and Kleban to raid for lines. The result was the number "Hello Twelve, Hello Thirteen, Hello Love."

Kirkwood also said, "The other joy of working on that show and having three months of rehearsals was that as the show evolved, you got to know all the people in the cast so well that you could almost not write for them. What you wrote for them *had* to almost sound good because you'd had birthdays with them and Christmas and parties and dinners, gone to see other shows, and they became friends. I think it makes it easier because you use what is there to be used and the rest you forget about. For instance, when Paul hurts his ankle, and someone says 'Get him this,' 'Get him a glass of water,' we felt that somebody ought to say, 'Get him a valium. Has anybody got a valium?' Well, getting to know Kelly Bishop, the obvious one to say, 'I've got one — I've had three already today' was Kelly. So you got to know people's sense of humors too."

There was also some of Kirkwood himself in the emerging script. Homer Price says, "Knowing Jimmy so well, I saw exactly where Jimmy was. There were many lines there that you knew very well that came right from Jimmy. For instance, when one of the people said, 'Yeah, I got off the bus, I had on white shoes, a white dress, I looked like a goddamn nurse!' I can hear Jimmy *saying* it, that was so Jimmy. And a line about Buffalo ["To commit suicide in Buffalo is redundant"]. That was another Jimmy line."

There is a line in the show that if it was not Kirkwood's is quite a coincidence. The character Bobby says at one point, "Well actually, I don't know how I turned out as heavenly as I did.'" This is extremely reminiscent of Rita Cydney's comment to Josh in *There Must Be a Pony!*, "…you've had a horrible childhood…You turned out to be an angel anyway." Interestingly, asked later if any of the characters in *A Chorus Line* were him, Kirkwood said, "I probably identify with Bobby, who is the one that does a comedy routine at first and is kind of flip. He says, 'Do you want to know about all the wonderful and exciting things that have happened in my life — or do you want the truth?'" One character revealed that his real name was Beckenstein. Reid Russell also made an oblique appearance in a song where a character mentions seeing her first dead body. A remark Lila Lee once made to her son about Kirkwood Sr. — "Your father went through life with an open fly" — also ended up in *A Chorus Line*.

What Kirkwood would no doubt not consider publicly admitting re the which-one-is-you question is that he identified with some of the characters because they were gay. In co-writing *A Chorus Line*, Kirkwood was finally free to be instrumental in putting gay characters center-stage — as opposed to in supporting roles — in a way he could never bring himself to in work that was solely his own.

Baayork Lee might feel that "Nicholas and Michael would put some structure to it. But basically they were our words" and Trish Garland might assert "Those were our stories," but there is a leap from that sort of sentiment to the belief of some critics that *A Chorus Line* was not written in the conventional sense, a point of view even held by a friend of Kirkwood's like Liz Smith, who says, "Well, you know that was an improvisation, the whole book. Seems to me, Michael deserves the credit." Smith is clearly alluding to the tapes that began the whole project. Kirkwood was infuriated by the assumptions that the play consisted almost of a series of transcriptions and the consequent lack of credit he felt he and Dante received in some quarters, including ones close to home. In June 1980, he dispatched a tart telegram to Hamlisch after the latter had appeared on Phil Donahue's chat show and had stated how anxious he was that his contribution be acknowledged yet didn't mention the book writers, a "lack of generosity and graciousness" Kirkwood told the composer he found "appalling and disheartening." In November 1975, Kirkwood wrote a letter of complaint to *New York News* reporter Douglas Watt about the fact that nowhere in his rave review of the show had he mentioned the book writers. Watt responded that he had been confused as to how much of the book to attribute to Bennett or he and Dante. Kirkwood responded, "…the book itself was written from beginning to end by Nick and me. With of course assistance from the many meetings and the general collaboration…" He gave examples of his and Dante's work: "…we wrote the entire middle section about adolescence and growing up and high school as if it were a play and then Marvin Hamlisch and Ed Kleban musicalized it. Sometimes I wrote a scene — the Cassie/Zach relationship — and Nick went over it for possible cuts or polishing. Sometimes he wrote a monologue — Paul's — and I went over it." Beckenstein confirms this. He recalls, "I remember sitting in Jimmy's sublet apartment on Bank Street many afternoons when he and Nick were working on dialogue, creating the dancer's characters, saying to each other, 'What if she says…,' 'And he would say….'" Kirkwood would later recite Paul's and Bobby's monologues from *A Chorus Line* in lectures about his career and did not even have to use notes to do so, which implies both intimate familiarity and a proprietorial feeling.

Kirkwood's points are completely valid, of course — with the caveat that he was being handed raw material on a plate, the kind of which he was lucky enough to have in abundance himself and had been able to draw on for his art. Some of the dancers — especially those whose stories appear in *A Chorus Line* but who saw the parts based on their lives go to other actors/dancers — could be forgiven for thinking they deserved a certain credit on the playbill and/or financial remuneration. An indication of how intertwined were those life stories with the plot of *A Chorus Line* is an observation of Baayork Lee, whose experiences gave rise to the character of Connie Wong, whom she also originally played. Lee has subsequently directed productions of *A Chorus Line* and says, "I've now detached myself from that character and I can treat her like another character in the show, whereas in the beginning I would practically torture the actress playing my role because I wanted it to be me." Some of the dancers have expressed their bitterness at being almost coerced into signing a release that gave Bennett *et al.* the right to use their stories and likenesses for a pittance.

Probably the most important contribution Kirkwood made was adding a more general human interest element. Baayork Lee says, "I don't know if it was Jimmy's idea or Michael's, but they felt that you just couldn't get up for three hours and tell these sad stories, that you needed some kind of hook, some kind of love interest or some other element, and I'm sure that's how Jimmy got aboard. Donna was pulled out of her role which was

Maggie and they created this name Cassie and then we find out their back story…Everybody's role had been fleshed out. Everyone was taken care of except the role of Cassie and so it was her turn." The character Cassie is the only one of the seventeen dancers who is truly over-the-hill. She is a failed movie actress who is having to return — almost with her tail between her legs — to the anonymity of dancing in the chorus to make ends meet. Zach is reluctant to allow her to do so, possibly because of his stated reason — that it is too undignified — but as likely because of his complicated feelings about a woman whom it emerges is also his former lover. The Cassie character had great resonance for the woman who played her. Kirkwood: "Donna McKechnie really almost did become a star. She got great notices in hit shows like *Promises, Promises* and *Company*, went out to Hollywood, sat for two years and had a nervous breakdown. She went back to New York, but if she wanted to work, she either had to go back to the chorus or stay unemployed while she tried out for featured parts. If you're 35 years old, that's a very difficult decision."

McKechnie says, "I think James was the most important influence at that point in time. I had enough experience to know that if you don't have a story that goes forward…It's like everybody doing their little separate monologues in the beginning — it was interesting and riveting for the first three and then you saw it all coming down the pike. The real craft of writing was apparent to me when Jimmy Kirkwood came in and worked with us improvisationally. I mean he didn't just go away and write it and then give us the pages. It was very collaborative, the whole experience with him. And there were times when he and Nick would just go off and write together and I'm sure there were times when he just went off and wrote and then brought it in to Nick and then to Michael. I don't know about that, but I just assume that because that's the way it felt. But I do know that things were turned around and that part of the show was the last to be set in place and the most important part in terms of getting it right, to not lose the point of view of what the play is about."

Cassie and Zach have a heart-to-heart in which the audience learns something of their respective and mutual pasts. For McKechnie, this section — to which she refers as the Second Act of *A Chorus Line*, which doesn't formally have one — marked the point at which the show really began to seem special. She says it was a section requiring much subtlety in composition: "They found a way to write it so it wasn't the forefront interesting part of the story or the most important part of the story. There's a point in the musical when the dancers have come back onstage after Paul's monologue and they are getting ready to learn the tap combination and winding down to the end of the audition and now Zach is trying to justify his reason to kick her out, or not give her the job, because he doesn't want her there. So at the top of that scene he starts criticizing her: 'Don't pop the head, you don't look like anybody else, stay in line,' and it builds to this angry outburst and then they have this fight as if they went in the wings or out in the hall, so it's this kind of cinematic thing where everybody in the background is doing this kind of precision [singing], 'One, one, singular…,' or they're counting, they are doing numbers and then the lights change and they're in the background but it's very dramatic as Cassie and Zach are on the line in their own lights, one at each side of the proscenium, and having finally the argument they never had when they broke up. It was written in a way where it wasn't all detail, detail, detail that you would in a play. It was written with enough specifics but enough general idea. It was really minimal; so that the audience would get a sense of it, but not be pulled into their story that much so that it could get back to the chorus line again after that."

Not that Kirkwood could take anything like sole credit for the poignancy here. In this scene the very worth of the genre of the musical is encapsulated and affirmed via the incredibly intricate interweaving of the dialogue, the lighting and the Hamlisch-Kleban song "One," overall credit for which must go to Bennett, whom Lee states flatly was a "genius." Lee: "The scenes with Cassie are very isolated from the rest of the show because we are not on the stage at all when they do their first scenes, but their second scene, this is where Michael Bennett's genius comes in. It's with three characters, meaning Zach, Cassie and the Line. We participate in that scene and it's absolutely brilliant because throughout their conversation we interject. We are dancing in the back and very softly and all of a sudden, we're doing 'Right and left and right and left and *right*' and then she's right into her dialogue with him, finishing off what we said — 'right.' It's just brilliantly put together."

Lee is as convinced as McKechnie of just how crucial the Cassie-Zach scene was to the show. Lee's recollection, in fact, is that this scene was Kirkwood's only real involvement in the show. From what we have seen, this can't be the case, but when asked if the fact that what she imagines was his sole contribution to *A Chorus Line* made Kirkwood a multi-millionaire was disproportionate remuneration, Lee says, "I don't think so, because that's a big part of the show." Despite her earlier comments about Kirkwood and Dante only "finessing" the raw experience of the dancers, Trish Garland says she noticed things improving when Kirkwood came on board: "He brought that incredible wit that he had, and he had his own genius." Garland also disputes the idea that Kirkwood's only real input was the Cassie and Zach scene. "I think that whoever said that, that's totally inaccurate," she says. "A lot of people aren't on board from the very initial [moment] but what they bring to the table is so wonderful that it just brings everything up. I think that's what Jimmy had."

McKechnie emphasizes that at some point in some sections attribution of contribution becomes impossible. She says, "Ed [Kleban] had a lot to do with the show that he never gets credit for, because he was so shy. He was hiding himself away at times. I think that Ed had a lot to do with 'Hello Twelve…' In the interviews with Michael and with Ed, we would talk about our adolescence. I remember sitting in the theatre in the orchestra and we were just sitting around on chairs in the orchestra seats and just talking about experiences when we were twelve and my true life experiences as an adolescent ended up in six different characters. It was a *potpourri* of all these different things. The one-liners would come out, so it was a combination of all of us." Of the writing, she says, "Michael, too, by the way. It's hard to separate at a certain point in time, in the process, because everybody gets on the same wavelength almost and you are finishing each other's sentences."

In February 1975 the company performed that run-through referred to by Kirkwood that revealed that the play ran to four hours and twenty minutes. This was over twice the length for which they were aiming. Or as Kelly Bishop — who played the character of Sheila — remarked to Kirkwood, "Honey, we got *War and Peace* meets *Ben-Hur* as a musical." It was at this point that Joe Papp told Bennett he could not allocate any more of the Shakespeare Festival's money to the project. Before this could engender a crisis, a fairy godmother arrived in the form of LuEsther Mertz, chairwoman of the Shakespeare Festival's board of directors. She was present at the run-through and enjoyed it. Even more luckily, she was very wealthy. She wrote a check to cover the seven weeks' work Bennett told her the show still needed. It was by the skin of their teeth, but the company still had the luxury of time.

"It was glorious having the time to tear it apart and put it together again," Kirkwood wrote. "Instead of making cosmetic Band Aid changes, we could perform major surgery. Whole subplots were eliminated." Glorious it may have been, but naturally it was still something of a labor, as Kirkwood acknowledged: "That was the hardest part — paring it down until it was tight and clean."

In order to help invigorate the now slightly jaded cast, the company performed the show at the Newman Theatre at the Public in early April

1975 before an invited audience comprised of, by Kirkwood's estimation, no more than 45 people. Ron Plotkin: "We got a phone call on I guess it was a Sunday morning and he said to Lee, 'Would you and Ron come down and like to see this thing that we're doing?'" Plotkin and Kirkwood's old comedy partner Lee Goodman did not know what to expect. "It was a full run-through at the Public Theater with lighting and costumes," says Plotkin. "Besides the creative people I believe there were maybe ten to fifteen invited guests…Lee was going through a period in his life when the jobs were fewer and far between. When they sang, 'Oh God — I need this job,' he just started bawling and at the end of it, we were just so stunned. Jim looked at us, [and said], 'Well, what did you think?' We said, 'What did we *think*? My God.'"

However powerful what they had seen, length was still a problem. "The run-through that we saw lasted approximately four hours," recalls Plotkin. He says that Paul's monologue that Sunday, "…went on forever…I can't remember how long it was but it was a good 25 minutes or half-hour, which is a long time for a monologue in the middle of a musical… Michael went to Jim and said, 'You've got to talk to Nick. We've got to cut that down…' And Nick said, 'That's my life up there and I don't want to do it, blah blah blah.' Jim calmed him down and said, 'Look, we have to do this. We're going to keep it up there, but it's not going to be to the detail.' Jim had Nick's respect, so it worked out well." Plotkin also recollects, "On that day the show had an intermission which was eventually cut." Asked by Jim Whaley in approximately 1979 what was the most difficult part of writing *A Chorus Line*, Kirkwood said, "It was keeping it succinct and stripping it down to a two-hour-and-ten-minute show so that we could do it without an intermission. What we wanted to do by not having an intermission was to keep the tension of the audience the same as the performers. To get those people on that stage for a final two-hour major audition at the end of which some were going to get the job and some were not going to get the job. So the suspense and tension and emotion built up. We thought if we let the audience out of the theatre for an intermission and they could light up a cigarette and buy some orange juice and say, 'Well, isn't this an interesting musical?' that that would break that tension."

The honing process seems to have engendered a certain weariness in Kirkwood. "My office was in the Village," explains Plotkin. "He would call me when he was sitting through performances before they officially opened [and say], 'Could you come here and sit through this turd with me?' It's like, 'I can't sit through this anymore.' And of course I would jump at it because I loved it. He used that terminology because he didn't want to make any more changes and he wanted Michael to freeze it. So I would go there and sit with him and help him with notes and stuff like that. He just needed the moral support. It was fun for me and it was work and torture for him because he wanted to get it frozen so they could officially open." Recalls Homer Price, "He worked his ass off, day and night…He was just working himself into a frenzy." People like Goodman, Plotkin, Beckenstein and Price were in a privileged minority, for Kirkwood didn't speak too much about what he was doing to friends at this point. He later explained to a TV interviewer, "I [was] so secretive about it when I was working on it. People would say, 'What are you doing?' I'd say, 'I'm working on this little musical down in the Village.' I was superstitious about pumping it up too much."

Lest it be thought that Kirkwood did not generally enjoy the process, Arthur Beckenstein's recollection should be mentioned. "*A Chorus Line* was a wonderful collaboration," he says. "I haven't had that much experience in theatre, but I know it was just a joyous time. I think the collaborators all felt so much like a team and a family, and the cast members. I know he really enjoyed that time and was very proud of what he was doing and really felt from the beginning that it was going to be successful. They felt they had a hit on their hands." Homer Price recollects, "Two or three weeks before it opened, he said, 'This is gonna be a *huge* success, and everybody knows it.' And I said, 'Can you put some money in it for me?' And he says, 'They won't even let *me* have much of a share.'"

Kirkwood was a busy man at this juncture. On April 3, the play of *P.S. Your Cat is Dead!* — following a tryout in Buffalo, Michael Bennett's New York State hometown — had its first preview at the John Golden Theatre on West 45th Street. Though the John Golden Theatre was just a short cab ride from the Public Theater, the reception that greeted *P.S. Your Cat is Dead!* was a universe away from the eventual response to *A Chorus Line*.

FOURTEEN

Curiously, though there is no reason to doubt Kirkwood's claim that he put in "long days" on *A Chorus Line*, Vivian Matalon, director of *P.S. Your Cat is Dead!*, says Kirkwood was spending most of his time at the John Golden Theatre — although, admittedly, flitting back and forth between the two shows would have been easy.

Matalon came on board the project after two different directors had bailed out. In addition to Michael Bennett, Clifford Williams, who worked for the Robert Stigwood Organization, came close to directing. As with Bennett, Kirkwood would work with him on a far more successful show. "I went into rehearsal with that, February or so '75," Matalon recalls of *Cat*. He says he was aware of the work Kirkwood had already started and was continuing on *A Chorus Line*: "Because he even told me that he was trying to work out a number for *A Chorus Line* which sounded like a wonderful idea, when people would sing, 'This is the knee that Carol Channing sat on when she sang, "Hello, Dolly," etc.'" Matalon says he never got worried that Kirkwood might become distracted by his dual role: "I never had any kind of lack of contact with Jimmy."

Matalon was offered *P.S. Your Cat is Dead!* after getting on well with Richard Barr and Charles Woodward, co-producers along with Terry Spiegel of the new *Cat*, on a production of two Noël Coward plays the year before. "I thought it was extremely funny," he says of the Kirkwood play. "A marvelous piece of comic writing. I didn't think it was about anything particularly important, but I thought that the character of Vito was very, very interesting and Jimmy Zoole was very, very interesting." He adds, "I had read the novel and loved it."

Jack Sydow recalls that when he read the play version of *P.S. Your Cat is Dead!* he wrote Kirkwood a note: "I said, 'When this play is done, be sure that what you have written is done,' because the first version of the play that I read was excellent. Now Jimmy had a tendency to be very malleable with the directors and make all sorts of changes and what I was telling him then was to stick to his guns and do what he had written." Judging by the recollections of Matalon, Kirkwood stuck to his guns on some points and not on others. Regardless, the result was one of the most controversial plays seen on Broadway to that point and a commercial disaster.

Matalon recalls, "What I did want in that first production and I could not persuade Jimmy, I wanted him to cut the scene where the people invade his apartment. I thought it did nothing for the play and I thought it was an unpleasant scene. I didn't believe it for a minute, but I tried to make it work and I had very, very good actors doing it, but I thought the play should have remained only between Vito and Jimmy. I felt that very, very strongly. I thought he was very stubborn about it." He adds, "He was always sweet and we never had any significant disagreements." If that goes some way to refuting Sydow's theory about his friend being "malleable" in the hands of directors, Matalon also says, "We did make a lot of cuts." He gives some examples of changes made: "When the woman said, 'Well what is that — the "Fuck You Clause?"' That was in the original script and I said to him, 'You know, I don't think it's right that she would say that. Why doesn't she just say, "What kind of clause is that?"' and Jimmy [Zoole] said, "We call it the Fuck You Clause"…Also, nobody in the play appeared not to have had a homosexual experience…I don't think *everybody* in the world is gay. It was giving the wrong impression that everybody in the world at a certain time can be had…I said, 'You can't do this. I don't think that makes any sense.' In the original script there is a great friend of his who is straight but once or twice they went to bed together. Jimmy was very, very easy about cutting those references." Kirkwood's willingness on the latter point, however, may have had deep-seated psychological reasons that went beyond a mere desire for dramatic plausibility and may have informed his startled reaction to the tone of the reviews.

There was a significant structural difference in the play compared to the novel. Whereas in the book, the revelation of Vito's presence in the apartment comes as much as a surprise to the reader as it does Zoole and only occurs quite a way into proceedings, in the play the viewer is aware of Vito being there right from the start whereas Zoole is not. Did Matalon not think of suggesting this be changed, on the grounds that there is no reason why the viewer needs to know Vito is present at the beginning — and indeed it would add to the drama if he suddenly and unexpectedly appeared from under the bed as he does in the novel? "I didn't. I mean I did what I thought was right. It may not have been right, but it began with [Vito] being seen on a skylight and I think the first words in the play were he dropped down and said, 'Shit.'" The fact of that first word — a fairly shocking way to open proceedings in a play on Broadway in the mid-seventies — may possibly be why Kirkwood decided to make this change from the novel.

Tony Musante took on the role of Vito and Keir Dullea (one of the astronauts in the film *2001: A Space Odyssey*) was Jimmy. Matalon: "[They] were, as it were, both given to me because I was in England. I did not want Keir Dullea, something which I really regretted thinking because I later did many plays with Keir and he is a much underrated actor. Tony I did not know and effectively what I got on the phone from Dick [Barr] was, 'Listen you either accept Keir Dullea or we are going to have to go elsewhere'…I think because they had sent it to various other people and everybody had turned it down…So I went along with it. It proved to be a marvelous piece of casting. Then when I came over, I did cast and we had auditions for the role of the girlfriend who was played by Jennifer Warren and her boyfriend who was played by Peter [White], and Jimmy didn't want Jennifer. Jimmy wanted an actress called Holland Taylor. I thought Jennifer had a marvelous kind of New York look and he went along with that."

Matalon reveals something that subsequent events made ironic: "Sal Mineo, according to Jimmy, had wanted to do it and Jimmy did not want him." Mineo got the thumbs-down from the author in his quest to play Vito because, Matalon says, "He just didn't think he was good enough." Mineo would later play Vito in a West Coast production of the play and would be described by Kirkwood as "a perfect Vito." It is the director of that West Coast production, Milton Katselas, who reveals that a young Robert De Niro read for the role of Vito in New York. "My friend Mike Shurtleff helped to cast in New York and [said] that Bobby De Niro read for it," says Katselas. "He couldn't do it, there was some problem, but he was hilarious." "That I never heard of," says Matalon. "This is completely new to me. If I could have had the talent of Robert De Niro in that role I would have grabbed him. I mean, Tony was lovely to work with, [but] as good a performance as he gave — and it was very, very good — he did not really register as a street kid."

Matalon reports that Musante didn't seem to have a problem with the fact that he was bare-assed throughout most of the play but did have an issue with something unexpected: "You never know about actors' quirks. The only line Tony objected to — and Tony is, as is Keir, evidently heterosexual — was when he said, 'Listen, I have to take a pee.' He did not want to say that word. He wanted, 'I have to take a piss.' And my suspicion was that he thought that the word 'pee' sounded effeminate."

The play's tryouts in upstate Buffalo spanned a (Matalon recalls) four-week period. There, Matalon says, "It went wonderfully." Final tweaks were made in preparation to *Cat* coming in. "We made cuts," says Matalon. "We structured the waiting time between laughs, etc., etc. It was a very, very pleasurable experience…I mean they went absolutely wonderfully all the way through Buffalo, through previews in New York." Audiences in New York City seemed to be as appreciative as the Buffalo crowds. Matalon says, "Opening night went really well." However, on that opening night — April 7 — there was a huge cloud on the horizon. Matalon: "I actually knew prior to the end of the play that the reviews were not going to be what we had hoped for and I will never, never want to go through anything like that again, because knowing before the curtain rose that you were not going to get well reviewed…Not that they were going to be bad, but they were not going to be good. I knew because the critics come to previews and you can get ahead of them if you have a knowledgeable press agent. Our press agent had let me know that she'd seen Clive's review."

The Clive referred to is Clive Barnes, theatre critic for *The New York Times* and then by common consensus the most powerful man on Broadway, able to make or break a show with a critique. His review — published on Tuesday, April 8, 1975 — was headed: P.S. YOUR CAT IS DEAD! IS RAUNCHILY FUNNY: KIRKWOOD USES FARCE FOR SERIOUS PURPOSE. On the face of it, this didn't suggest anything particularly devastating, nor did his opening paragraph, where he described the work as, "raunchily funny and oddly unhealthy all at once," and also said that despite its lack of dramatic credibility, "only the very up-tight will fail to get a few raucous chuckles from the wonderful showbiz dialogue that crackles with bitchery like a campfire." However, some of his other comments struck a nerve — both with critics and Kirkwood himself. "Personally," said Barnes, "I found the strong suggestions of sado-masochism distasteful (this is the one theatre in town where no one should wear leather unless he is certain he cannot be misconstrued) and I note that this is the first public-public [sic] play that appears to be actually proselytizing for homosexuality." However, even this didn't seem too damning and Barnes continued with some more kind-ish comments: "…Mr. Kirkwood has a downright wicked way with words and a perversely droll taste of the outrageous. This is by no means a brilliant piece of playwriting but it has some shrewd commercial insights. The situation is not unlike Shaw's *Arms and the Man* in its own strange way." For Matalon and Kirkwood, though, the conclusion of the review summed up the tone of the critical reception generally: "This is not the kind of play to take your aunt to, unless she is in show business or the kind of aunt you can't take anywhere else."

John Simon of *New York* magazine was far more vituperative. His review began, "There are dishonest plays and then there are ultra-dishonest plays such as *P.S. Your Cat is Dead!* by James Kirkwood." He continued, "The current play is made up of not so much two acts as two homosexual wish-fulfillment fantasies." Of Vito's face-down bondage, Simon said, "This is the fantasy of the middle aged homosexual in which 'a piece of rough trade' — the kind that often brutalizes and sometimes kills the client — is overwhelmed, immobilized and tormented in turn. It is in other words a Steigian dream of glory infantile, homosexual style." Simon opined of Vito trying to use his wiles and his charm to talk his way into Zoole's bed in "Act — or Fantasy — Two," "Since this is a Broadway show in need of heterosexual patronage — though its primary purpose is clearly the delectation of homosexuals, as the vociferously responding, largely homosexual opening night audience made manifest — it stops short of having him succeed. But the play is, if you'll pardon the word, open-ended: it concludes with Vito…spending the night on upright Jimmy's couch, and since Vito's acumen is inexhaustible, members of the audience who yearn for an unconventional happy ending are encouraged to assume one while others leave without their sense of decorum explicitly assaulted." He complained of the "ever-popular homosexual fantasy that any heterosexual is ultimately available for homosexual purposes…It is voiced repeatedly by Vito, who assures us that everybody swings a little…A bigger [dishonesty] is the portrayal of Jimmy, the supposed archetypal straight, as someone who acts and talks like, at the very least, a latent homosexual." Simon complained that the "unsavory proceedings" — he also mentioned the point when Jimmy says to Kate that he may castrate Vito while brandishing a pair of scissors — might make for a study in pathology or campy farce but that the way they are turned into jolly parlor comedy is "an even greater dishonesty."

Simon also didn't like the way the play treated its female characters, from which he extrapolated a viewpoint of women on the part of the author. He talked of Jimmy's dialogue with Kate as displaying "deep-rooted hatred" for Kate. The depiction of Kate, Janie (one of the interlopers) and Vito's unseen but badmouthed ex-wife moves Simon to note, "I hope the women's movement take note of how its brother-in-arms, gay liberation, portrays women onstage."

Simon did praise Matalon's slick staging, conceded that Kirkwood could write some funny lines and singled out Tony Musante for praise amongst the actors. But he closed with, "In one of his most applauded lines, Kirkwood compares life to a shit sandwich: if so, what need to go to his play just to get a triple-decker?"

It should be pointed out that not only is Simon noted for vituperative critiques but he has often been mired in controversy over allegedly homophobic comments. Nonetheless, at that point in history, such reviews as his put the spotlight not on what may have been the personal bigotries of the critic but on the play he was lambasting. Additionally, one can only imagine the discomfort caused Kirkwood by the blatant assumption throughout Simon's review that the author of the play was — to use his rather clinical if grammatically correct term — homosexual. Matalon: "It was a time when the love that dared not speak its name was beginning to refuse to shut up. And it was at the beginning of the militant gay movement and so there was a lot of political resistance to it. It had not been all that long since the American Psychiatric Association had declared that homosexuality was not an illness." "That was John Simon's agenda in those days," says Terrence McNally. "He was obsessed that there were always gay men writing plays who were not out, and he knew that Edward Albee was gay, that Tennessee Williams [was] gay, Jimmy Kirkwood was gay. My first play was very gay and I got the opposite: 'Oh God, why don't they shut up,' so there's no winning with that man. John Simon could do that because who's going to sue him for libel? His review of [*Who's Afraid of*] *Virginia Wolfe?* was the same way: 'We all know that it's about four men and that there's no way they're real women'…It was a form of gay-baiting homophobia that writers in America had to deal with in those days and that's long gone. You could be homophobic then in a way you can't anymore."

"We tried the play out in Buffalo," Kirkwood later said (or, more accurately, ranted) in *Mandate*. "Buffalo, for God's sakes! Middle America, middle-aged to elderly people — and we sold out every performance for a month. Part of the reason is that they had been warned it might offend them. I think it served as an incentive." Kirkwood was taken aback by the reaction of the New York critics: "I don't understand it. I don't think I'm a tacky writer. I may not be funny enough, or serious, or bright, or intellectual enough, but I know I don't write junk. Some of them said I was proselytizing for bisexuality. What's that? If I wanted to proselytize I'd come out with banners flying!…All I know is that the audiences liked it. Of course every author says that when his play closes…The critics seemed to take a personal affront to the idea that two more-or-less 'normal' men start talking about homosexuality, instead of my presenting gays as a minority group that runs around screaming things like 'Get her,

Mary!,' and presenting them as freaks…Wouldn't you think that in 1975 the critics in our largest city would be sophisticated enough so that sort of thing wouldn't pose any threat to them?"

Matalon remembers an emergency meeting in an advertising agency after publication of the notices. "They were trying to work out some kind of campaign and Jimmy looked like a terrified child and he could barely speak," he says. "It was because he had expected really very, very positive reviews." In 1972, Kirkwood had told *After Dark* magazine that for the play of *P.S. Your Cat is Dead!* he wanted a tough producer and a youngish, very 'head' director "because the play is somewhat perverse, dirty and now." That being the case, why was he so taken aback by some of the Broadway reviewers' comments? Kirkwood's *Mandate* quotes indicate something of a sensitivity, to say the least, about the response to the homosexual content. Asked if he thinks part of Kirkwood's "terrified child" reaction was due to the fact that he was shaken a little by the attention directed to a sexuality he was guarded about in his art, Matalon responds simply, "Yes, I do."

The upshot of the advertising agency meeting was, for Matalon, an attempt to almost disguise the play's theme. "The producers had been expecting a huge kind of response — as had Jimmy, because the audience reaction was wonderful," he says. "The notices really were not terrible, but they were much less than they had thought and they got afraid of the content. They devised an advertising campaign which avoided for the most part the homosexuality…I really thought the producers became ashamed of the show. They became ashamed of its sexual content and that they were being called faggots. I think if they had not, if they had ignored that and really done a campaign about how amusing it was, how witty it was, there would not have been a problem and it would have been able to run."

Long-time Kirkwood champion Rex Reed attempted to come to the play's rescue with a column in the April 18 edition of the *Daily News* in which he lambasted the "ignorant, lethal and completely unjustified bad reviews." It was to no avail, not least because the edition of the *New Yorker* magazine three days later applauded Kirkwood's alleged message of "Bother gender!" in sexual matters, objected to his "preaching on the subject of sex" only because it made for an incongruously serious second act after a riotous first one and stated that the play was one whose script attempted "the reform of unthinking heterosexuals."

His half-brother had sent Kirkwood a box of candy by Western Union to wish him good luck for the opening of *P.S. Your Cat is Dead!* T. Michael: "He said, 'Well, it was too late, the show closed but I brought it over to

Chorus Line and of course the dancers devoured it in ten seconds.'" There is a metaphor of some sort to be extracted from that.

P.S. Your Cat is Dead! closed on April 20 after five previews and sixteen performances, leaving Kirkwood clearly smarting with a sense of injustice. "The New York producers had two other shows besides mine running on Broadway and decided to sacrifice mine when their money ran out, although we'd played a month in Buffalo to sold-out performances and the New York audiences liked the show," Kirkwood asserted the following July. However, he had the therapeutic advantage of having something else on which to concentrate. In a short space of time, that something else would become far more than therapeutic but rather — without any exaggeration — life-changing.

Of the invited-guest preview of *A Chorus Line* that had taken place in early April, Kirkwood later wrote, "Even with such a small group, electricity filled the air…but there were those who wondered if it might be *too* special. Would the problems of chorus dancers auditioning for a Broadway show be universal enough to grab a lay audience? Would they care? We prayed to God they would." They did. By the time *A Chorus Line* had its first preview on the 16th, Kirkwood would have been aware that the plug was being pulled on *Cat*, making for an overlap for him of extraordinarily conflicting emotions.

Previews are strange beasts, a way of presenting a show to a paying public while simultaneously saying, "Not really." Professional critics are not supposed to attend, their presence not required by the producers until the formal opening night, by which time the show's wrinkles will have been — supposedly — ironed out. The audiences for the previews know that though they are paying for the privilege of witnessing the show, what they are seeing is not actually the finished article and that their reaction (or more usually lack of reaction) may bring about changes designed to improve it. The whole concept can sound weird for the non-theatre-goer, but is par for the course for the performers. Except, in this case, for one thing. The generation of performers in *A Chorus Line* were familiar with out-of-town tryouts in (usually) Boston, Philadelphia and New Haven. The *A Chorus Line* tryouts were stationary and this may have assisted the incredible buzz that the show began to generate: people who heard others raving about it did not have to hunt around or wait for it. McKechnie recalls the show becoming a word-of-mouth sensation "Right away."

The audience were seeing a show with no conventional star, no lead character, little in the way of costumes (it was exclusively naturalistic grungy dance rehearsal clothes up until a sort of ironic glitzy finale of a dance sequence), no more than a minimalist setting — mirrors and a white line was basically the set — no intermission and no formal second act. On all counts, they could not care less. Lengthy standing ovations and floorboard-rattling cheers were the norm after every performance. McKechnie recalls, "There was no money for publicity and all of a sudden the buzz was so potent that people were flying in from all over the world… Ruth Gordon was there like five times. Groucho Marx was there. He brought us a big cake, with a big axe in it on a foot — you know: break a leg. Diana Ross came in and was sitting on the steps next to Dick Cavett. Paul Newman leaning against the wall. It was unbelievable." Recalls Beckenstein, "I was there at one of those early previews with Jimmy and someone from the producers' group pulled him into the lobby because Ingrid Bergman and Raquel Welch wanted to meet him. Can you imagine? It was so exciting because of the buzz." With a maximum capacity of 299 at the Newman Public Theater, the celebrities who attended were extremely conspicuous.

Yet even despite the show being the sensation of the moment before it had even formally opened, Bennett saw room for improvement. A big dance scene featuring Cassie was pared back. The heart-to-heart between Cassie and Zach was streamlined. The most significant change, though, was to jettison an ending that seemed to be leaving — notwithstanding their ecstatic reaction to the show overall — a sour taste in the audience's collective mouth. As originally written, Cassie was not one of the eight dancers whom Zach finally gave a job. Robert LuPone, the actor who played Zach, shouted at the dancers onstage from out in the audience, just as a director would at an audition. LuPone found that he was being heckled by audience members, many of whom seemed angry that his character would not choose Cassie. (On one occasion at the Newman he was deliberately tripped, although wasn't sure whether this was because of Cassie's rejection or Zach's general nastiness.) Even for audience members mature enough to be able to separate fiction from reality, the rejection of Cassie — already humiliating herself by returning from Hollywood to the meat market of chorus auditions — was upsetting. In this, Bennett was — depending on to whom you talked — striving for realism (McKechnie) or poignancy (Kirkwood). "It wasn't working," says McKechnie. "Symbolically, when Cassie doesn't get the job, that means that everybody loses so the audience would leave so depressed." Kirkwood wanted Cassie to get the job on the grounds that a director can hardly not pick the best dancer. Dante was in favor of the *status quo*. However, it was Marsha Mason, actress and wife of celebrated playwright Neil

Simon, who effectively had the final say, or at least decided Bennett's final say. McKechnie: "Even though we were in previews, my character was flailing out there. [Mason] followed, beat to beat, my through-line throughout the entire show and was able to give Michael some intelligent feedback about where I was going. I owe her a lot of thanks because she said, 'She's got to get the job.'"

Though not unwelcome, Mason's contribution seems to have been unsolicited. She was presumably on the scene because of the fact that her husband had been asked, in a shroud of secrecy, to add one last bit of sweetening to the show. Some directors would have been swept away by the euphoria of nightly standing ovations from celebrity-packed audiences, but Bennett was the epitome of the perfectionist. Anxious to beef up the show's laugh quotient, Bennett employed Simon to act as a script doctor. Judging by an interview granted to Gary Stevens and Alan George for the book *The Longest Line*, initially nobody involved in *A Chorus Line* knew of Simon's contribution except Bennett, Bernard Jacobs, president of the Shubert Organization, and choreographer Bob Avian. Simon's involvement was presumably secret because Bennett was assuming that Dante and Kirkwood would not be happy about the doctoring. Beckenstein says that when he found out about Simon's role much later, Kirkwood was "annoyed." This may have been simply because he wasn't consulted. After all, Kirkwood had been happy for Goodman Ace to similarly augment *UTBU*. It's probably partly because of this secrecy that memories conflict about precisely what Simon contributed to the show (although the endless rewrites and editing that had already happened no doubt played its part in the confusion).

Simon initially disagreed with Bennett's feeling that the show needed to be funnier. As well as considering *A Chorus Line* to be working as it was, he was additionally reluctant to get involved because of a Dramatists Guild rule that prohibited such action without the consent of the show's official authors. Simon said in his autobiography that Bennett sent round a copy of the script and rang him to say, "It's okay with Jim and Nick. They just wouldn't want it to get around. But they would welcome your help." Under the impression therefore that Dante and Kirkwood had acquiesced to his doctoring, Simon agreed to provide some funny lines. Script doctors understand they will receive no credit, but neither did Simon ask for payment. "I...picked my spots to add or change lines," he wrote in his autobiography."Five, ten, twenty of them, maybe more, were interspersed throughout the script. I gave most of them to the character played by Kelly Bishop [Sheila Bryant] because Kelly could deliver a funny line better than anyone in the show." Simon also said, "I have no idea…how much actually went in and when I went to see the show weeks later, I never knew what of it I wrote. I never remember what I write…" Just to illustrate how confusing is the issue of attribution, McKechnie — contradicting Homer Price's conviction of it being Kirkwood's — says that the "suicide in Buffalo was redundant" line was Simon's, yet Simon himself wasn't sure and thought the line might have been in the show already — adding that it was probably lifted from Mark Twain in any case. Bernard Jacobs, meanwhile, recalled standing with Bennett and Kirkwood at a preview and Bennett poking him when Kirkwood joined in the audience's laughter at the valium reference and saying to him, "You know, he thinks he wrote that line!" What is not in dispute is that Bennett proceeded to pass off the new lines as his own — although this may have been in order not to alert Kirkwood and Dante to the fact of the outside contribution.

"Very necessary," says McKechnie of the script doctoring. "Michael was enough of a skilled showman that he knew that there had to be more humor so [the audience] could find the release so that they could stay focused on it. Otherwise, it's too hard, it's too harsh. The humor makes it palatable."

Sitting on the steps in the Newman one day, unable to get a proper seat now that everyone in town wanted one, Kirkwood suddenly found himself experiencing a strange emotion while watching the ensemble number "Hello Twelve, Hello Thirteen, Hello Love." "They're dancing like crazy and it's a very upbeat number," he recalled. "I suddenly started to cry and cry and cry. And I thought, 'What am I crying about?' And I thought, 'Dammit — I wish my mother was here. She'd get such a kick out of it.'" Nonetheless, Richard Seff, who attended one of the previews at the Public, discerned a profound ambivalence on the part of Kirkwood about the show. "He looked kind of gloomy," he says. "It hadn't even been reviewed yet but you could tell from seeing it this was going to be something special. I hugged him and said, 'My God, you've done it in your first musical.' He was very unhappy and I said, 'What's wrong with you, are you crazed? Are you the kind that only likes failure?' He said, 'No, it's not that. It's that I get so pissed because I've written all these books.'" Seff appears to feel that on some level Kirkwood was contrasting his new success with the fate of *American Grotesque*: "He had spent so much time on it and he believed in it implicitly and it wasn't a success at all in terms of sales. And he said, 'I spend three weeks [sic] of my life on this musical…' — it didn't come from his guts the way the book did — and he says, 'It looks like this is the thing I'm going to be remembered for [for] the rest of my life.' For some reason that deeply bothered him."

The official opening night of *A Chorus Line* took place on May 21. Naturally, demand for tickets was strong. So strong that Kirkwood and the rest of the creative staff couldn't get into the theatre and — dressed in their dinner clothes — had to simply listen to it in neighboring theatre The Other Stage via the piped sound that Papp had arranged. The reaction they heard over the PA was an ecstatic one. Every so often one of the party would nip over to take a peek through the back door of the Newman. The reviews came in around midnight and were as positive as the crowd reaction had been.

Some of the lucky people who got to see history in the making at the Public Theater on opening night were more than two dozen sales, marketing, editorial, publicity and other key employees (including the president) of the publishers Thomas Y Crowell. They had been taken there by Nick Ellison, Kirkwood's editor for his forthcoming book with that publisher, *Some Kind of Hero*, which would appear in September. "It would excite the sales staff as to Jim's 'fame,'" Ellison explains of the rationale. "It was at Jim's invitation also. It was also a way to tell booksellers around the country that Jimmy was the author of this new hit which helped us get more books into stores — the advance sale before customers bought even one copy."

Even better was to come for the show. On July 21, 1975, *A Chorus Line* moved to Broadway. Where it had been playing in a theatre that didn't quite fit 300, it was now at the Shubert Theatre, whose capacity was nearly 1500. In addition came the unquantifiable degree of upgrading involved in being on the street that is the Mecca of American theatre in a venue that has played host to some of history's most famous and celebrated shows. The spotlight of the world was now on the company. Not that this made McKechnie, for one, nervous. "I never like openings because it's just too much and the critics are there," she says. "This opening was for all of us. I could honestly say we were so happy. That's when we started loving each other again like good sisters and brothers because the opening night at the Shubert was a glorious success. It was like a love-in. The audience had seen it many times before. The critics already loved it. It was just like, 'Oh let's see it in this new house' and it was totally beautiful. I always have stage fright. No stage fright. I thought, 'God, this is the ideal, this is the way it's supposed to be every opening night' but it never is. And if there was any cynicism about the move, it was, 'Oh my God, now that it was so wonderful down at the Public how is it ever going to move to a bigger house? It's not going to be the same'…That was quieted immediately because it was even better." Not everybody agrees on the latter point. Says Ellison, "It played so much better in a small theatre, in spite of all the efforts to compensate for the lack of intimacy when on Broadway. That's what Jim told me, and I agree."" I agree with that on a level," McKechnie concedes. "Because there was nothing like that experience. It's so raw it's upfront and personal. You could never recapture that."

Patti Goldstein was one of several of Kirkwood's friends who had followed the project from first stumblings through Newman previews to Broadway. As with just about everybody, she was bowled over. "When you go to the theatre there comes every once in a while you'll be sitting there and you realize that you're seeing something really special and you know it almost at once," she says. "There's a thing that comes from the stage and it bounces back from the audience and that's what *A Chorus Line* was. I'm talking about a kind of electricity that happens."

Mainstream success had not been inhibited in any way by the fact that homosexuality was a theme in *A Chorus Line*. McKechnie has a theory as to why the subject didn't present an impediment whereas in *P.S. Your Cat is Dead!* (which she admits she hasn't seen) it so recently had: "The material is so powerful it makes you cry and it's all served up in this heightened reality of music. That's Michael's genius: to serve it up in this great silver platter."

Some Kind of Hero continued Kirkwood's roll.

The book was dedicated, "For Lee Goodman in fond memory of the nightclub years." Plotkin: "Lee was very emotional about it and very surprised." The dedication page also featured the line, "With special thanks to former POW Arthur John Cormier." Though largely set in 1973, the book was published in August 1975, four months after the United States' involvement in Vietnam ended.

Some Kind of Hero is a novel in three parts/acts. Part one takes place in a Vietnamese prison camp nicknamed by its inhabitants the Bel Air Country Club. The inhabitants number protagonist/narrator Eddie Keller, who serves five years there after being captured in the Tet offensive in February 1968. Part two details Keller's return to civilian life in 1973 following a mass release of POWs. The third part details the criminal measures Eddie takes to deal with the devastating financial and emotional problems he faces upon his return to his homeland.

The book starts with Eddie telling the reader he has a secret of which he wants to unburden himself. Though brief, it is a very unpromising section containing some remarkably bad writing. Chapter two features an awful, meaningless metaphor: "Now the enemy is — all around, like a plate of spilled soup in the sky." This is followed by a couple of lines that are almost as bad: "Last one who says he isn't confused gets his tonsils ripped out. And *then* tossed in the pool."

Part one of *Some Kind of Hero* is interesting but not great. Set almost entirely in Eddie's cell, it is naturally limited in scope, boasting the sort of static quality to be found in a play. Eddie Keller is a likable character. He objects to a cellmate's scurrilous comments about Marilyn Monroe on the grounds that she is dead. Said cellmate isn't with him long and Eddie's only companion until the arrival of a new cellmate is a visiting mouse that he names Spike. A new cellmate is put in with Eddie in late 1970. The newcomer is in a purple rage at having been captured just before a leave period of thirty days in which he intended to marry his girlfriend Ginger. He remains in this rage for a week. The atmosphere is tense in the confines of the cell. Eventually, Eddie and the new arrival become firm friends. Kirkwood calls him Vin Poirier, the first name at least being that of his friend supposedly incinerated onboard the *Admiral Mayo*.

The two hatch plans to go into real estate on the day of their much hoped-for, ever-distant release. Eddie's interest in real estate is surprisingly convincing from someone like Kirkwood who really knew only about artistic circles. Eddie is married and Vin has Ginger but the two become lovers. It is the first time gay sex is depicted in a Kirkwood novel without being dismissed as a youthful experiment or abuse and the development of the intimacy — which starts out with the two watching each other masturbate and eventually becomes fairly infrequent but violent full intercourse — strikes a true note. Even so, those readers familiar with Kirkwood's writing might be forgiven for groaning at this line: "During those days, I thought that when the time came to look back on it, I would be ashamed to speak of sex. Now that the time has come, I find I'm not." By now we're wearily used to this kind of "I've-never-done-this-kind-of-thing-before-honest" semi-apologeticness. We're also used to a flashback appearance of a friend from the protagonist's teens called Boots with whom he had dabbled in gay sex. This is the second Kirkwood novel in which a Boots is mentioned in such circumstances (the other being *Good Times/Bad Times*). Kirkwood also seems to slip in an allusion to his unpublished novel *The Angels or Whoever* when Eddie offers up a prayer to "God — or whoever, the man in the moon, the goddamn angels, whoever was up there." Like (supposedly) the real one, the fictional Vin dies just as a return to civvy street is on the horizon. In *Hero*, he succumbs to a disease not specified but which seems to be dysentery.

Though Kirkwood has clearly done his research and asked pertinent questions of Arthur Cormier, there is no real verisimilitude in this section: Kirkwood doesn't furnish the dense, matter-of-fact detail that would make us half-believe he had really been through the POW experience. Nor is there much feeling of danger or fear on the part of the POWs and never really any true sense of the aching sadness of being forcibly kept from home. Kirkwood's attempts to convey the latter are sometimes surprisingly incompetent for a writer of his abilities. In chapter three, he commits the cardinal writer's sin: Telling, Not Showing: "…loneliness was the worst. It left my mind too much to itself. The mind is a tricky clown to deal with. Stubborn. Tell it not to think of certain things — sex, baked spare ribs, snuggling warm and safe in bed with Lisa until noon on Sundays — and it won't do anything but flash them on in mile-high letters." This, however, is not nearly as inadequate a passage as the one in the same chapter in which he says, "The endless drag-ass hours stretched out on my bed started to get to me." Rather than being held incommunicado thousands of miles from his loved ones, he could be talking about a boring weekend in Montana. There are some good scenes in part one, though. The best and funniest occurs when an irritated Eddie tells the newly arrived, bad-tempered Vin not to scare off Spike and receives a reply in the form of "a rather substantial fart," causing Eddie to have to suppress his giggles.

The 'Nam section is not boring but is slight, coming over more like a rather lengthy curtain-raiser (it takes up a third of the book). The POW scenes, or at least some of them, might have worked better as flashbacks, with Kirkwood using the most vivid 'Nam episodes to heighten the drama in the sections set in the States.

Part two is the weakest section of *Hero*, especially the scenes involving Eddie's wife Lisa, which are very superficial and never convincing or moving. Because she had not received a single letter from Eddie in his five years away (he was never allowed permission to write one), Lisa has understandably taken up with a new man. She has also lost all of Eddie's army pay in a failed business venture with her lover. Eddie's reunion with Lisa depicted in chapter 25 in what are Kirkwood's first real adult love scenes in his fiction (discounting the end-of-the-affair bickering of Zoole and Kate in *Cat*) is strangely unengaging. By chapter 27, Kirkwood has descended into badly-paced soap opera writing, replete with some awful dialogue (when Lisa tells Eddie during copulation that she has recently had an abortion, he responds, "It's one spectacular turn-off. Especially announced during flagrant not-so-delecto"). Additionally, Eddie's harshness toward Lisa doesn't chime with the compassionate and warm person we have come to know him as. These faults are at least slightly redeemed by the pithy and believable way that shortly afterwards Eddie sadly concludes that the marriage he'd clung to for solace during his incarceration has gone in a puff of smoke.

Eddie's meeting with high-class hooker Fritzi Donovan gets off to a promising start with some good dialogue, but his interlude with her outstays its welcome, not least because of some truly tedious (and frankly vainglorious on Kirkwood's part, assuming they are drawn from real life) sex scenes. It's not so much bad writing as authorial sloppiness that afflicts chapter 32 when Kirkwood has Eddie explaining to suspicious army brass that the reason he signed a statement in 'Nam condemning his own country was because Vin had been stricken with the illness that seems to have ultimately killed him. In fact, Eddie had signed the statement in order to get Vin out of the solitary confinement to which he had been consigned for insubordination. (Kirkwood repeats this error in chapter 34.) There is more soap opera stuff in chapter 33 when Eddie goes to visit his child for the first time. Conveniently, he is able to get into his wife's building when a departing resident holds open the door for him. When he approaches her front door, even more conveniently a plot-advancing (and somewhat mawkish) scene between Lisa and her new partner takes place within easy earshot.

Neither of the first two parts of *Hero* feel like Kirkwood writing. In the case of part one, it is due to a game but failed attempt to step outside of the autobiographical writing style that it was now obvious was Kirkwood's main strength. With part two, it is simply because of bad writing and poor characterization. Though this section is, again, an approximate third of the book, it feels as flimsy as a wheat cracker. Things aren't helped by the prose continuing, as it has from the start, to show occasional laziness. Almost disturbingly frequently in *Hero*, Kirkwood's colloquialism seems more like slapdash writing ("I simmered down but not really") or shorthand notes he hasn't bothered to turn into proper prose ("Bought civilian clothes, no more walking around a certified hero").

One can't help but feel that the real Kirkwood book starts with part three. This is the section where all the positive characteristics of Kirkwood's previous novels finally appear: the writing is warm-hearted and sprightly, the characterizations and tableaux true-to-life and the dialogue sparklingly believable. Things pick up almost immediately when Eddie departs his San

Francisco army base to travel to New York to see his mother, who is in a nursing home after recently suffering a stroke. His reunion with his slowly recovering, speech-impaired mother — his estrangement from whom had led him to join the army in the first place — is utterly convincing. A couple of chapters later, Eddie meets his real father for the first time in eighteen years in another good, convincing scene. The man turns out to be half-affable — proud of his war hero son — and half-monstrous — treating waiters like dirt and contemptuous of his sick ex-wife. When his father turns down Eddie's embarrassed request for a loan to pay his mother's medical bills and to find her an apartment, they part on bad terms.

Now desperate for money (his army pay is being withheld because of the allegedly traitorous statement he signed in the Bel Air Country Club), Eddie over the course of three chapters plans and executes a store hold-up with a squirt gun. Everything about this section rings true, partly because we follow Eddie's endless dithering, fear, losses of nerve, impatience with himself for his hesitation and then finally his execution of the gut-wrenching deed almost in real time. This is the kind of verisimilitude that the prison camp scenes lacked, the sort of stuff that can only come from the author having lived every second of what he is describing. The robbery scene is rendered just about exactly as Kirkwood described its apparently real-life antecedent in interviews and our stomachs churn and hearts race as Eddie goes through a hold-up that bears no resemblance to cool-dude movie scenarios and every relation to the ambiguous emotions and human clumsiness of reality.

Flushed with elation at the success of his crime, Eddie resolves to commit another, deciding to rob an unattractive woman whom he sees putting stacks of bills into a briefcase at a bank. As he follows her, he realizes she is an even easier target than a female would normally be: she has an elevated shoe. Her disability means that when she realizes she is being followed, all the woman can do is make "the most pitiful attempt to run." She promptly falls flat on her face and can only watch helplessly as Eddie makes for the briefcase that has flown from her grip. But Eddie has been moved by her physical ugliness, her handicap and her helplessness and merely sets the case upright and departs. This beautiful scene is suffused with humanity.

Eddie then decides to target someone who is ugly in a different way: a reptilian character called Tank whom he sees in another bank queue and whose vulgarity and callousness — all communicated in loud conversations with bank staff — make Eddie conclude he is a more deserving robbery victim. As luck would have it (and the luck doesn't strike the reader as implausible), Tank is not only collecting a lot of cash bills but has a friend who is carrying $185,000 in negotiable securities. After a robbery in a men's room in the financial sector, Eddie decides to sell these on, and here the one unconvincing turn of this part of the book occurs. He visits the stock exchange and *by sight* identifies somebody dishonest enough to buy the securities for a reduced price. Said person — by remarkable coincidence — happens to have an uncle in the Mafia. This isn't a major fault, because everything that happens afterwards — Eddie striking a deal to sell the securities, a nerve-wracking preamble to the exchange, an ingenious getaway after the man and his uncle try to double-cross him — is perfectly persuasive, not least because of some more Kirkwood dialogue that simply sounds like faithfully reported speech. The newly rich Eddie dispenses his money generously; not only assisting his mother as planned but helping out both his newly estranged wife and Ginger, Vin's devastated girlfriend.

As with his two previous novels, Kirkwood gives his protagonist a pretext to write his story down. Bursting to tell someone of what he has pulled off but knowing it would not be prudent to do so, Eddie commits it all to paper. The last chapter is a beautiful meditative piece in which Eddie ruminates on his life and his philosophy about how to live it. One paragraph in particular truly captures the *joie de vivre* of Kirkwood as a person and the qualities of his best writing as he gushingly lists things he loves: "…like the circus or the lobster I cooked last night or seeing *Gone With The Wind* or thighs or kelly green and deep blue or a great snug sleep during a rainstorm or the stray cat that's begun taking meals with me out on the deck or the two sea gulls that are trying to incite me to jealousy with their feats of soaring or Bette Midler's recording of 'Do You Wanna Dance?' or the third cup of coffee that tasted so sensational five minutes ago." He almost tops that on the following page: "Today I'm dedicating myself not only to the pursuit of happiness but the catching by the tail and dragging down into clover of it." It is a lovely ending that leaves a glow in the reader's heart.

It can't, however, quite disguise the fact that it caps a closing third act that has saved the book from mediocrity. It's tempting to suggest that Kirkwood should simply have lopped off parts one and two, leaving us with a high-quality novella. This instinctive thought, of course, is illogical: without the context provided by the first two parts, we wouldn't understand what motivates and drives Eddie to such extremes in the end section.

It would be irrational to assume that where Kirkwood's writing falls down in *Hero* is only where he disobeys the write-about-what-you-know rule he dictated to, amongst others, his brother when asked for advice on the profession (and which Terry Kilburn's recollection suggests he picked up from Robert Kirsch). After all, the scene in which Eddie tries robbing the deformed woman and the scenes in which he engages with the Mafia in order to unload his securities are believable and gripping despite not coming (as far as we know) from experience. However, it can't be denied that the most transcendent scene in this novel derives from Kirkwood's own life: the one with the squirt gun stick-up. For this reason, one can't help but feel when reading the relatively thin Vietnam scenes that their replacement by Kirkwood's own real-life war story — dodging kamikazes and U-boats on the *Mayo* in between keeping people's peckers up and trying to control drunken stage performers — would have made this a much better book. His paranoia about his vintage becoming widespread knowledge was normally a harmless, even amusing, little vanity but here it has conceivably damaged Kirkwood's art.

Nonetheless, wildly uneven as it is, the book contains some of James Kirkwood's best writing. The Book of the Year accolade bestowed on it by at least two reviewers was overdoing it somewhat, but where it is good, *Some Kind of Hero* is magnificent. The comparisons by *Book World*, *Chicago Tribune* and others with some of the most celebrated voices in contemporary American letters — Barth, Bellow, Brautigan, Gardner and Heller — was not isolated praise, as a glance at extracts from other reviews proves:

Washington Star: "What America may be discovering is that Kirkwood is one of its most entertaining storytellers — snappy without being wise-ass, kinky without being perverse, tender without being schmaltzy. Above all, he is gloriously and energetically funny."

Boston Globe: "…marvelous book, of great energy, wit and passion. A lasting success, I predict…I was in love with this drastic clown, completely hooked by the whole brilliant story that kept me up all night."

Western Review of Books: 'In his worm's-eye view of America in 1972 [sic], the author manages to avoid being trite or superfluous by filtering it all through the tragicomic mind of his 'hero,' Eddie. Love, death, sexuality, in Eddie's words, 'the whole shooting works,' are freshly and deeply experienced. Like Saul Bellow's Augie March, with all his troubles he still refused to lead a disappointed life…Warning: You could get high on this book!"

Worcester Telegram: "There is enough sex of most varieties to win the heart, the characters are vivid, the situations and dialogue dramatic, and a skillfully manipulated theme of heroism runs through the novel."

Washington Post: "A portrait of modern heroism, of Some Kind of Hero, our American, contemporary kind: caught in a war, ambiguous about himself, close to crime, yet never far from compassion and deep love…"

The two most perceptive reviews, in the way they capture the essence of Kirkwood's writing — a streetwise grittiness counterpointed by an unexpected warmth and loving nature — were those of *Cosmopolitan* and — of all periodicals — the *Anniston Star*. The former said, "Kirkwood's novel explodes with cynicism, black humor, sacred and profane sexuality, heartache and humanity." The latter observed of the book: "...bubbles and rolls with love, meanness, humor and raw life."

Kirkwood's POW source, Arthur Cormier, was also pleased by what he read. "The story was basically a pretty good story and he depicted the camp life pretty realistically and then the aftermath," he says. "I thought it was a very ingenious way of ending the story."

There were, of course, negative reviews. Harlan Ellison covered *Hero* for the *Los Angeles Times*. Clearly unaware of how much it owed to Kirkwood's own experiences on leaving the service, he found the plot suspiciously similar to the 1931 James Cagney film *The Public Enemy*, in which a soldier "...mustered out...finds hard times and turns to crime because society has dumped on him and owes him something. With the singular difference that sin is ultimately rewarded by death and dishonor in the Cagney flick and Kirkwood's 'hero' gets clean away and with a boodle..." He went on, "...the film makes the point that even when the feces hit the fan and the returning hero gets bad-rapped by a society too quick to forget its debts to those who served, only an essentially weak man resorts to crime, while Kirkwood's novel asserts vigilante action is acceptable when the going gets rough." Of the writing, he said it was "in the usual breezy Kirkwood mode, no less readable and no more mature than his excellent *There Must Be a Pony!*" Ellison made a valid point about Kirkwood's protagonists being cut from the same pattern: "The character of Eddie is the same first person narrator named Josh Cydney in *Pony*, Peter Kilburn in *Good Times/Bad Times*...and James Zoole in *P.S. Your Cat Is Dead*...the same superficial, dimpling, toe-scuffer." However, Ellison was just about on his own when he adjudged this, "A character who grows extremely wearisome with repetition." Suggesting the reader wait for the paperback instead of spending hard-earned on a hardcover, he said, "This is by no means a bad book; it just isn't a very good one." Raymond A. Sokolov opened his slating in *The New York Times* with the admission that he had read none of Kirkwood's previous fiction, or *American Grotesque* or seen *A Chorus Line*. "...after forcing my way through this shapeless, artless saga of a Vietnam POW, I am quite happy to have missed out on all those earlier opportunities," he said. He described Eddie's suffering in his Vietcong cell as "textbook degradation" and said of the prison section that it was "painfully long and reveals only that a conventional character will react conventionally to conventional bad treatment." He complained of limp and lazy sentences, observing of passages like, "I've fought and lost the battle about when and how to put down that, on top of everything else, I'm a POW," "This is not the stuff of popular fiction nor, certainly, of lasting literature. It falls in between, on its face." Despite the fact that Sokolov seemed to be ignoring the book's many merits, it can't be denied there was at least a glimmer of truth in his criticisms. He also raised a valid point when he asked, "…why is Keller justified in blaming his wife for adultery when he himself had done as much with Vin? You could say that Kirkwood is applying the old double standard in a new way."

Kirkwood was infuriated by Sokolov's review. He said, "I got all good reviews around the country except of course for the *Sunday New York Times* which is the most important prestigious review that you can get. It was really an overkill. It was a very, very bad review and the reviewer was also the ex-food editor and consequently highly qualified…It was such a bad review that of course I wanted to kill him." Kirkwood decided against murder but determined to get revenge. Walking past the offices of *Variety* magazine one day, the idea hit him that if he couldn't kill Sokolov physically he could do it metaphorically. "So I went into *Variety*," he recalled. "The men that work there are really sweet, usually ex-actors, elderly gentlemen. I said, 'I would like to take out an obituary.' And the man said, 'Ohh' and took my arm. He said, 'What do you have in mind?' I said, 'Well, something rather large, trimmed in black.' So he sat me down and said, 'You know, they're rather expensive.' I said, 'That's alright, money is no object'…And he showed me some samples. So I finally took an obit out. I just prayed to God that nobody would know of him and know that he had not left us."

The obituary appeared in the *Variety* of Wednesday, October 1, 1975. It was the largest ad on page 120 — bigger even than the one taken out to commemorate the 16th anniversary of the death of singer and actor Mario Lanza or the three on the same page for the clearly much-loved recently deceased thesp Archie Robbins. It read:

IN MEMORIAM
RAYMOND A. SOKOLOV
NEVER TO BE FORGOTTEN
FOR HIS LITERARY CRITICISM
                      JAMES KIRKWOOD

In eager anticipation, Kirkwood went down to Times Square that very Wednesday morning and feverishly opened the publication. "There was the bit, trimmed in heavy black, and my heart leapt like a fawn," he said. "My agent scored me for lacking in class by doing that and I said, 'Oh, Phyllis — I never pretended to have class but I hope I have a sense of humor, although it might be a little perverse'…I felt good about it because I got rid of the anger, 'cause to me it was a very unfair review. I heard a story — I don't know whether it's apocryphal or not — that he also worked at *Newsweek* and only came in once every couple of weeks and that on this Wednesday he happened to come in and there were two men standing in the men's room at the urinal talking about his death, saying 'Gee, I didn't even know he was sick, did you?' The other guy said, 'No.' At which point they heard the door open and they turned around and here was this man. I hear one man got rather damp."

When Kirkwood recounted that story on *The Dick Cavett Show*, the audience dutifully laughed but one wonders whether we — or they — should. In one sense, Kirkwood was right: Sokolov mentioned most of the book's bad points and, unlike even Harlan Ellison (of whose negative review, incidentally, Kirkwood doesn't seem to have been aware if he thought the *Sunday New York Times* one was the only bad notice), couldn't find anything good whatsoever to print. But aside from this "overkill" — as Kirkwood correctly termed it — why was Kirkwood affronted that a mere food writer should presume to pass judgment on fiction? Had someone who was normally a food writer given the book a rave, would he have similarly dismissed the very idea that such a person should have been commissioned to write the review in the first instance? Had a restaurant reviewer come up to him at a party or in the street and told him how much he loved *Some Kind of Hero*, would Kirkwood have refused to accept the compliment on the grounds that he wasn't qualified to give it?

Kirkwood's inordinate and irrational fury seems all the more remarkable considering that he had spent much of the previous few months on cloud nine over the success of *A Chorus Line* and — of course — the generally ecstatic reception to *Some Kind of Hero*, which according to a feature on Kirkwood in February 1976 had racked up the best hardcover sales of any book he'd written so far. That Kirkwood managed to find the time, energy and willpower at this happy juncture to be both inordinately furious and incredibly petty illustrates something that several of his friends — as much as they adored him — implicitly or explicitly acknowledge: that he had a nasty streak. Not a huge one and not one seen more than infrequently, but there nevertheless. Lila Lee Nichols recalls,

"If he didn't like somebody he *really* didn't like somebody." Homer Price says, "He had strong likes and dislikes. If he didn't hit it off with somebody you knew it right away. I introduced him to one of my very best friends and he took an instant dislike to him. They almost had a fight, in fact." Jerry Paonessa admits, "Despite his extraordinary humor and talent, he had a very dark side which he carried to his death." Ron Plotkin: "He had sometimes this vindictive quality to him: 'Do me wrong, I'm going to get even with you.' Even with his success." There would actually be far more ugly incidents than the Sokolov one involving physical violence when Kirkwood didn't feel he was getting the artistic credit he deserved. One wonders whether these occasional flashes of steel and displays of petulance were the inevitable downside to the good-humored persona he virtually admitted in a college address in 1987 to having adopted . "If there is one thing you should cultivate, it's a sense of humor," he told the students of Suffolk Community College, Southampton. "If you don't have a sense of humor, buy one, borrow one, observe people who have one, *steal* one. Do anything to develop a sense of humor. That's the springboard that will get you over the hurdles. Life does have its share of surprises and not all of them come with party hats and confetti, but if you can treat the bummers with a sense of humor you'll be way ahead of the game and you're guaranteed not to develop ulcers." Certainly, if one remembers the contrast between the bewildered, lonely boy who had gone to live in Elyria as a ten-year-old and the endlessly jocular fellow he had become by the time of his return to Ohio just a few years later, it does seem that Kirkwood had practiced exactly as he preached. Nothing wrong with that approach to life, one might respond — especially if that development of humor had effected such a positive change in his personality — but being outwardly humorous does not necessarily mean that one is happy inside and being determined to always show a positive public face — the covering up that Jack Sydow has recollected — inevitably carries a mental penalty. Where and how did Kirkwood give vent to the frustrations that affect every human life? It's not difficult to imagine that Kirkwood's exaggeratedly sunny, optimistic character — the one that made him such a joy to be around and which acquired him more loving friends and fond acquaintances than any biographer could possibly find the time to interview — is what caused him to blow his top so disproportionately. His occasional meanness and even violence prove the point that every pressure cooker must have a safety valve. The irony is that such displays slightly besmirch the good name that his determinedly maintained good humor served — perhaps were partly designed — to build up.

A footnote regarding Kirkwood's recurring bit-part player Boots from William Russo: "Boots may well have been a real person. Jim used to occasionally call himself Sly Boots…He said to me once, when I questioned him about names in books, 'Oh, I just pull them out of the air,' and I thought, 'Yeah, right.'…I asked him what was the Latin translation of the word 'Boots' and he had all kinds of interesting responses but not the right one. I presume you know what the translation of 'boots' is in Latin? It's Caligula."

Nineteen seventy-five had been Kirkwood's year. Even the failure of the *Cat* play had been an ambiguous one. His name had been very prominent as an author of two groundbreaking shows which virtually overlapped on Broadway and the fact that one had failed commercially and the other succeeded did not completely diminish that. Meanwhile, *Some Kind of Hero* placed him for many critics in the front rank of American novelists.

"*Chorus Line* was like some sort of miracle," says Terry Kilburn, the man who had seen Kirkwood's writing flower back at UCLA nearly two decades before. "I was going to send an opening night telegram and I forgot. So I thought, 'Well, I'll wait 'til the show closes and I'll send him a closing night telegram.' But it never closed." Whatever the intensity of the acclaim for *A Chorus Line* — and despite the fact that by 1976 Michael Bennett was simultaneously overseeing three companies as they geared up to perform the show in three different cities: New York, LA by way of San Francisco and London by way of Toronto — nobody at that point could have predicted that it would stay at the Shubert for almost fifteen years, breaking the record for the longest continuous Broadway run in the process. Kirkwood told author Ken Mandelbaum, "I turned down a very lucrative book offer to work on the show because I was convinced it was going to be a big success." Kirkwood made life-changing amounts of money from *A Chorus Line* even though he had been unable to invest in it. Ellison recalls that Kirkwood almost walked away from the project at one stage because — notwithstanding that there were no investment opportunities left in the show — he felt the remuneration was inadequate. "The whole thing almost fell apart," he says. "He almost stopped because Michael Bennett — close as they were — was very tough with a nickel and negotiating and Jimmy said, 'I'm not going to finish this damn thing unless I get a point.' There was a last-minute brinkmanship negotiating but it all worked out. We celebrated one night with a couple of drinks when it was resolved." (Arthur Beckenstein demurs slightly: "I don't remember Jimmy almost bailing out of *A Chorus Line*.

I do remember him fighting with his agent for the point.") Kirkwood's negotiations resulted in him securing one percent of the show's gross receipts. "It represented a substantial amount of money," says Ellison. "Obviously the play on Broadway, but the ancillary rights. The film [went for] six million dollars, the national touring show, the merchandising, the revenue streams combined was a phenomenal amount of money. And it kept going on and on and growing. It didn't diminish after a few months."

Then there were the intangible but undeniable benefits of having co-authored the show. Never again would a Kirkwood book jacket appear without a mention somewhere on it — often the front cover — of his role in this Broadway sensation. Never again, either, would anybody in American theatre say "James *who*?" Offers to write stage shows now arrived regularly. This new recognizability crossed over to the moves: Hollywood also came a-calling.

Yet, though it made him financially secure for life and he found himself in-demand because of it, the success of *A Chorus Line* would, artistically, prove to be the worst thing ever to happen to James Kirkwood.

FIFTEEN

In 1976, art and life overlapped in Kirkwood-world when Matt Hoopes, a teacher in his mid-thirties at Kirkwood's alma mater Brewster Academy, assigned *Good Times/Bad Times*, the Kirkwood novel that took place in a thinly disguised Brewster, for his sophomore English students.

Hoopes had first discovered the book five years previously. He is not sure whether he read somewhere about Kirkwood basing Gilford Academy on Brewster, but having been a summer visitor to Wolfeboro in his youth and now owning a small summer home in the area he was very familiar with the Brewster Academy campus and could spot the architectural parallels in the text. It wasn't generally known by Brewster staff or pupils at the time that their school had been immortalized in fiction. "I don't remember that coming to my attention for maybe four or five years," says David Smith, who obtained his first Brewster teaching post in 1969. Smith became headmaster of Brewster the year before Hoopes took up a teaching post there in '75.

Hoopes thought the book would fit in well with other boarding school-related books he had been teaching such as *The Catcher in the Rye* and *A Separate Peace*. Of course, the fact that the book was recognizably set in his pupils' own school was a God-send for someone faced with the often tough task of getting kids enthusiastic about reading. Hoopes also says that the fact that he was gay "possibly" played a part in his keenness to teach the book. He recalls, "I wasn't sure at first whether it would go over well with the students and there was the gay element that in those days was tricky for the classroom, but my department head was a very liberal fellow and he said, 'Well go, give it a shot.'" Of the book's evasions and semi-apologias for homosexuality, Hoopes says, "I did notice it but…I kind of was doing the same thing myself. In the seventies it was difficult, especially in a school, so I was on my guard a bit. It didn't offend me." Does it now? "I've only been out about twenty years. Yeah, probably more so now, but at the same time I can see why. I probably might have tried to throw people off the scent."

By the mid-seventies, Brewster Academy had changed quite a lot since Kirkwood's spells there over thirty years previously. Recalls David Smith, "The school had gone strictly private again in 1964/65 with a regional high school being built in Wolfeboro. Going into the recession, the early seventies, it almost ceased to exist. I became headmaster of a school that only had 74 students in it. But then it grew over the years and now has close to 400 students." Though private, the school wasn't closed off from the Wolfeboro community, maintaining a percentage of roughly twenty percent "townies" to this day.

Of the assigned book, Hoopes says, "It was extremely well-received. The kids actually tore through the thing just to find out what happened. They were extremely happy that the headmaster was done away with and felt that was only just. They had assignments each night of maybe two or three chapters. We'd have a discussion the following day. Unfortunately, some of them raced through it and I had to slow them down because they'd start talking about things that the other students wouldn't know about. The younger kids were in love with the school — as they got older they got more bored and what have you — but the tenth-graders were so fresh and so interested. They were extremely pleased that a book had been written about their school. They all wanted to know which building was which. I thought it was a fabulously well-written book. You could visualize what he was describing. He gives us all those hints throughout of what lies ahead. We had great discussions. He does a great job of the camaraderie and all the individual personalities."

A work like *Good Times/Bad Times* was inevitably going to throw up some awkward, even inappropriate, discussion in a classroom. The passage in which Peter Kilburn says he prefers the word "cock" to "penis" was certainly one of those. "I think mostly giggling," Hoopes recalls of the reaction. "Being a gay guy I would try to move along. I guess I was a little nervous." Of the alcohol rubdown, he says, "Some of my students, they felt that was too detailed and too sexual." He remembers this reaction coming in particular from female students: "You have to remember the period of time and everything else. They didn't think that a headmaster would even think about doing something like that. Girls in that period of time didn't know anything about homosexual activity, especially between men."

Hoopes wound up teaching the book at Brewster for around eighteen years. He says, "I think the reaction did change from the first time I started as society had changed. Students were not shocked or anything. Some would [say], 'Well, that's gay' or 'Why do we have to read this?' But overall they did enjoy it." Though Hoopes once got an "earful" for assigning a book of Stephen King short stories for summer reading, remarkably neither Hoopes nor Smith recall any adverse reaction from parents over the assignment of *Good Times/Bad Times*, a book that would usually be considered rather risqué for fifteen-year-olds, especially in the seventies.

In the early eighties, Hoopes decided to contact Kirkwood. After obtaining his address, he bundled up letters of comment and query from his pupils along with a covering letter. "Nothing happened for a while," says Hoopes. "But then he finally responded…He didn't reply to each and every one and he shied away from some of the questions — and I can understand why — but over the years he enjoyed that. One of the criticisms the kids had which they wrote several times to him about was why he chose to do the flashback to already let us know at the very beginning of the novel what had happened and that the headmaster had been killed. They thought it would have been more dramatic if it unfolded as a series of events leading up to that. We kicked it back and forth a number of times." Hoopes wanted to take the exchanges one step further: "We had all-school assemblies once a week where different people would come and speak, but he said that he couldn't make the trip." It was very unusual for the gregarious Kirkwood to decline an opportunity to appear before an interested audience. Hoopes has a theory as to his reticence: "It probably had to do with the questions the kids asked. They didn't ask whether he was gay [but] they asked why did he do such-and-such with this character and that character and maybe he picked [that up]. He didn't answer some of those questions. Ones about was it necessary to have four, five pages of the headmaster rubbing the kid's back or whatever." Hoopes says he eventually guessed Kirkwood was gay, principally from reading material about him. He recalls, "In our correspondence back and forth I just assumed that he also assumed that I was gay. I didn't ask directly." He did not speak about Kirkwood's sexuality with his pupils: "I just let them assume what they assumed."

It was also in the early eighties that a couple of representatives of a major Hollywood studio that had purchased the film rights to *Good Times/Bad Times* visited Brewster Academy. David Smith recalls that they "came to the school very early in the process, considering whether they were gonna make the movie or not make the movie or rewrite the book or whatever. They came to look at the campus and then the question was asked of me would you allow for this book to be filmed on this campus and by doing so associate it with the school." Smith replied that he would have to ask the board of trustees, but says that for his part, "I probably would have given a thumbs-down. It's one thing to have one of your teachers using a book like that and using it in a way that you trust the teacher, it's another thing to put this thing out there in somebody's else's hands." Hoopes, meanwhile, was given the job of providing a guided tour of the campus and demonstrating how its landscape matched up with that in the novel. He says, "I could even point out, 'This is where James smoked' and tennis courts where the headmaster looked out of the window." However, the filmmakers revealed at the end of the tour that they did not see potential in the school as a shooting location beyond the "unspoiled" air that Kirkwood talked about in *Good Times/Bad Times*. Recalls Hoopes, "He ended up by saying that the campus was far too pretty to make the film." Understandable enough, perhaps, as was the filmmaker's remark that he didn't think the world was ready for a film with homosexual themes, but these remarks were accompanied by a bizarre comment indeed. Hoopes: "He thought that he would change the plot and the headmaster was a serial killer and he killed the students and [buried] the bodies in his wife's garden. I thought, 'How in hell is *that* better than the gay theme?'" All these issues were moot, however, for the school never heard from the studio again.

Though Kirkwood did not take up the offer to visit Brewster, he did at the end of the decade invite Hoopes to visit him. Unfortunately, it was too late. Reveals Hoopes, "I was planning to head that way for spring break. I was hoping to be able to learn a whole lot more. But then he passed away."

In 1975/76, Kirkwood participated in a revival of *P.S. Your Cat is Dead!* Despite its disastrous Broadway run, producer Arthur Whitelaw picked up *Cat* for a West Coast staging. Though Kirkwood would appear to have to some extent stuck to his guns for the first production, he apparently had no intention of doing so now that he was being given a second chance with it. "No matter what, I do not consider this a critic's play," he later wrote of *Cat*, but he certainly seems to have been stung into a major rethink of the play by the critics' reception to it. The West Coast production would see what he himself admitted were "extensive rewrites." There would be even more rewrites a couple of years later for another New York production. This insistence on reworking his previous efforts over and again when he could have been devoting his energies to new novels would be one of the things that would mar the rest of his writing career.

The West Coast production of *Cat* — originally staged in San Francisco starting on July 22, 1975 (i.e., even before *A Chorus Line* had graduated to Broadway), later transferring to Los Angeles — was directed by Milton Katselas, who was chosen by Whitelaw because he had previously directed the play *Butterflies Are Free* for him. He also happened to have a connection to Kirkwood: James Leo Herlihy was a close friend. In fact, Katselas has a feeling that he first met Kirkwood at a party at Herlihy's home. Katselas had not seen the original New York production, but liked what he read when he was given that production's play script. "I thought it was daring and funny as hell," he says. However, he also had ideas about how the play could be improved. Kirkwood would later say that the extensive rewrites were something Katselas "nudged me into."

"I just told him that I thought we should go in somewhat different directions with it," recalls Katselas. The director found the author to be a receptive audience for his ideas. "My opinion was that he was dissatisfied with what was put on," says Katselas. "Not that he was feeling that it was like inferior, but he just wasn't satisfied quite with what happened and always with a writer the reviews don't help. I think Jimmy was a little bit bent out of shape about those reviews and a bit angry." Katselas says he could understand Kirkwood being stung by the comments about proselytizing for homosexuality, but for dramatic rather than psychological reasons: "Although it had serious elements to it, it was a comedy and when you come in with that kind of comment you start to get the audience thinking that they're coming to see something of significance or some propaganda and not just to have fun. Jimmy, being ironic as he was and humorous as he was, was looking for the humor." Katselas thought one of the main problems was the tone of the scene involving the kinky intruders: "There were these wild gay guys and I thought that that was part of the reason that the thing got turned and that the humor should be found above and beyond the gayness of it. I thought that the play could be just leaned a little bit differently." Though he doesn't specifically say it, it would seem Katselas wanted to bring more of the flavor of the novel of *P.S. Your Cat is Dead!* to the stage: "As I recall, I liked the book better than I liked the play. It's deeper and it's like it can happen to any of us and the play I think headed it a little bit toward the homosexual scene."

Even so, Katselas was not insistent on his suggestions: "I assured him that if he didn't want to do this it was fine with me, and I would understand that. He liked what we talked about and we proceeded and worked on it quite strenuously, not just before, but during the production." "I did a whole rewrite for the San Francisco production that makes the play work better," Kirkwood said at the time. "It's a much better play now, tougher and stronger." (Elsewhere, he defined the strength of the new production "rewriting for reality rather than for Neil Simonish comedy.") He added, "Even so, as much better as this new production is, I still really do think that the New York critics would have attacked it on the same grounds they did before." The rewrites, incidentally, did not include transplanting the action to the new venue of the play: *P.S. Your Cat is Dead!* remained a New York story. Kirkwood dispensed with his idea of acting in the play himself — he mentioned that he "might" appear in it in *Mandate in* November 1975 — and Robert Foxworth was cast as Zoole, with Jeff Druce taking the role of Vito. The first commercially published version of the play was the West Coast version.

The problems with the play start in the first few seconds when Vito descends into Zoole's apartment through a skylight and then has to take cover when Kate appears: as with the New York version, this causes to be lost the wonderful moment in the book where — to the bewilderment of both Zoole and the reader — a startled Vito appears from under the bed after Zoole accidentally fires his gun.

Kirkwood is consistently tweaking and amending the lines with which we are familiar from the novel, and adding others. Some of the changes improve, some detract and some seem pointless. On the improvement side, Kirkwood actually gives Zoole a plausible reason for his not having called the cops. As Vito points out to him, Zoole has no evidence against him — plus, "How are you gonna explain the bare-ass bit?" On the debit side, the manner in which Vito persuades Zoole to give him a cigarette is not as natural as in the book, seeming like what it really is: a plot device to provide a bizarre sight for Kate and resultant comedy. Similarly, whereas Vito unburdening himself of his life-story to the man who holds him captive doesn't seem at all implausible in the novel, in this play Kirkwood seems to lose his nerve over this and decides to have Zoole force Vito to tell him his story so that he will have raw material for a new novel to replace the one Vito threw out and which he doesn't have the heart to start again from scratch. Vito's occasional fancy words are less natural than in the book because for some reason Kirkwood decides to make his ex-lover Ben an architect, not a writer. On the other hand, the way that the subject turns to Zoole's failed acting career is smooth-flowing, the consequence of Vito remarking that Zoole should be on Broadway when Zoole starts improvising on a conversational theme.

As in the first version of the play but not the novel, the three interlopers are mixed sex. The inclusion of Janie is a mistake, reducing the feeling of Zoole being in real danger that exclusively male interlopers provided. Vito's intervention to save Zoole from the intruders is correspondingly less important and in any case less dramatic than in the novel. The wonderful resolution to the novel — Vito miraculously able to offer Zoole an escape from his cul-de-sac after coming into some money — is replaced by no salvation greater than Vito offering Zoole a chance to share a good, cheap apartment with him because "I'm with the minor Mafia," hardly a life-changing offer. In any case, we can't believe that Zoole would be interested in it (not that he exactly accepts it) because he hasn't made the deep bond with Vito he does in the novel. The ending is rather weak: Vito pretends to leave and minutes later comes back in through the skylight. Zoole lets him stay. The kiss-off line (Zoole playfully to Vito: "Blow it out your ass!") is puny and smacks of Kirkwood attempting to be trendy in a day and age where such street language — especially at the close of a play — was rare in the theatre. On top of all this is the fact that overall the characters simply aren't as likable as they are in the book.

Naturally, the caveat must be raised that if we had never read the novel of *P.S. Your Cat Is Dead!* we might consider this play a perfectly fine piece of work. Additionally, the very newness of the milieu would have almost conferred quality by default in 1975/1976. Another caveat is that this is the sort of play that comes to life in the flesh, with the zingers provoking the kind of laughter that makes for a warm and happy theatre atmosphere. However, though it can't be denied that the dialogue crackles with energy and has a real zip and vitality, this play is vastly inferior to the novel.

Nonetheless, this critic seems to be in a minority about its shortcomings. "There were laughs like I've never heard in the theatre in that play," says Katselas of a reception that he recalls as "tremendous." Such was the reception, says Katselas, that there was soon "a demand by various theatres to bring it to Los Angeles." For the run of *P.S. Your Cat is Dead!* that was to start at the Westwood Playhouse, Los Angeles, on February 25, 1976, some decisions were made that were more than a little ironic for a play that is partly concerned with the brutality of the acting profession. Robert Foxworth was dispensed with, Keir Dullea being brought in to reprise the role of Zoole he had taken in the New York production. There was also heartbreak for Jeff Druce, who "was hilarious and very, very likeable," according to Katselas. The director explains, "This is a commercial world and…we were looking to guarantee ourselves a little better box office here." Sal Mineo — who had read for the role but who had been rejected by Katselas, and who had also been rejected by Kirkwood himself, according to Vivian Matalon, for the New York production — was considered a stronger marquee name than Druce and was asked to play Vito. Katselas admits that Druce was, "Very, *very* unhappy."

Mineo took over the role toward the end of its San Francisco run. Originally a street tough of Italian extraction from the Bronx, his acting career had started illustriously with Broadway roles in Tennessee Williams' *The Rose Tattoo* and — opposite Yul Brynner — in *The King and I*. He also appeared in some highly notable movies: *Rebel Without a Cause* (which earned him an Academy Award nomination), *Giant, Somebody Up There Likes Me, The Gene Kupra Story, Exodus* (another Oscar nomination), *The Longest Day* and *The Greatest Story Ever Told*. He additionally had a brief career as a pop singer, securing two *Billboard* top thirty hits (one a top ten) in 1957. As well as being from the same background as Vito, Mineo shared something else with the *Cat* character in the form of his bisexuality. Perhaps not unsurprisingly, then, that Kirkwood changed his mind about Mineo and described him as the "perfect Vito" in the published version of the second version of the play (which he dedicated to the actor). Not that similar characteristics and background were all that mattered, of course. There was also the issue of talent, which despite the recent lull in Mineo's career — *P.S. Your Cat is Dead!* was something of a comeback for a man whose last major film role had been a decade previously — Katselas was left in no doubt Mineo possessed in abundance, something that made a mockery of his initial rejection(s).

Katselas was also taken with Mineo as a person. "He was a fabulous guy," he recalls. "Just fabulous. He was a kind of a hustler and humorous. We were walking in San Francisco about three o'clock in the morning and there was a drunk, and the drunk looked up and said, 'Hey, Sal baby, how you doin'?' Like — everybody knew him. We became very close during the production and went to lunch almost every day and even though I am not homosexual, we joked always about homosexuality and kidded each other about it and had just the greatest time. I used to call him a Persian Prince, because that's what he reminded me of: a sort of very dignified Persian Prince. I think he would have really knocked 'em dead, because he was just great in the part." Demonstrating the validity of that belief, Mineo attracted some raves for his San Francisco appearances. Critic Bob Kiggins said, "…Mineo all but steals the show with his outlandish, marvelously antic gestures, his facile facial contortions and his robust delivery. Mineo's nimble, engaging performance calls for a visit to the Montgomery Playhouse."

On February 12, 1976, during the rehearsal period for the LA production, Katselas was so impressed by Mineo's performance in a run-through of the play that he effectively prostrated himself before the actor over his previous rejection of him: "I went up on the stage and I told Sal how great he was in the part and, as good as Jeff Druce was, I was stupid not to take him to play the part. I said, 'This is your part, nobody else should play this part' and he wept." At around 9:30 that evening, Mineo was stabbed to death outside his West Hollywood apartment building. He was 37. Kirkwood later recalled to Roy Leonard, "The spooky thing about that…I had gotten to know Sal just through the play and he and I were going to do it off-Broadway. I was going to play Jimmy. The day before he was killed, he called me up. He said, 'You know the only thing I'm worried about? I think the woman that owns the Westwood Playhouse doesn't know how to promote this play. I wish we could do something really splashy to put it on the map. Let's see if we can't come up with some real publicity gimmick.' That was about four o'clock one afternoon and about seven o'clock the next morning somebody called me and said, 'My God — I just heard the news on the *Today* show. Sal was killed last night.' And you know for a split instant I thought — because he was a crazy guy — 'Oh God, wouldn't it be terrific if that was just some kind of a joke or publicity gimmick?'"

In 1979, one Lionel Williams was jailed for the killing, apparently a bungled robbery. In 1976, a devastated cast and crew — less than a fortnight away from the play's opening — were not even able to mourn properly. For Kirkwood, the *déjà vu* of unexpected violent death in his life must have made it cumulatively more devastating. "At that point Jimmy was ready to throw in the towel," recalls T. Michael Kirkwood. "He didn't even care if the show opened or not." However, with so many financial and emotional interests in it, the play, one way or another, had to be staged. "It was extremely difficult for all of us," says Katselas. "But, you know, not that bullshit about the show goes on, it's just what else you gonna do? You got to do it and you get yourself up and you get your actors and you proceed." The major difficulty was naturally who to get in to play Vito. The obvious candidate was the person who had most recently played him but who had been rather ruthlessly dispatched from the frame by Mineo's appointment. "It took some persuading for him to come and do it," admits Katselas of Jeff Druce, "but he did come and do it and ended up in a friendly way and ended up studying with me after that production closed." Katselas remembers the rehearsals continuing in an atmosphere partly comprised of "comic surrealism," referring to "detectives that kept coming around who were not the brightest and just asking questions again and again that didn't seem to me to be leading anywhere."

Cat opened at the Westwood to, Katselas says, "A great response and you know we had a very, very decent and good run here." Asked if he felt that some of the response may have been due to a sympathy vote, he says, "Well, I honestly believe that as good as Jeff was, and he was very good in the part, sympathy or not, we would have done better if Sal was in the part." "It was very eerie to have to see him replaced and have the play open on time," said Kirkwood. "It really made me sick to my stomach and kind of took my heart away from that play for a while."

The death of Mineo arguably proved true a phrase with which Kirkwood was apt to come out and which possibly revealed the darker side of this ostensibly sunny man. It was a phrase of which Katselas (who remained close friends with him after *Cat* finished its Westwood run on March 28) and their mutual friend Herlihy always tried to convince him the falsity. "He used to say, 'Life is a shit sandwich and every day you take another bite,'" says the director. The line, of course, appears in *P.S. Your Cat is Dead!* Katselas: "We tried to talk him out of that, that just wasn't the way it was and it was up to you to eat whatever it is you wanted to eat and serve whatever it is that you wanted to serve."

There was cause for Kirkwood's optimism to return in April '76 when he and Nicholas Dante shared a Tony Award for Best Book of a Musical ("book" being slightly confusing theatre-world parlance for script). *A Chorus Line* garnered another award the following month, one even more prestigious. Kirkwood later recalled for TV interviewer Merv Griffin the moment he heard the news: "I was in Toronto. It was the opening night of the international company, which was the company that was going to London. I had done a radio show plugging *Some Kind of Hero* and I got back to the hotel and I thought, 'Well, I've got about fifty minutes before the opening night.' So I turned on the television set and I whipped into the shower. I came out of the shower very naked and I was drying off and the news was on, Walter Cronkite. He said something about Beirut and then he said, 'The Pulitzer Prizes were awarded today. Saul Bellow for fiction.' I said, 'Oh, wouldn't he get that' and I turned away and the next name I heard was mine. I was naked but I wanted to run out into the hall and yell, 'We won, we won!' It was very exciting because the Pulitzer Prizes, you don't know you're nominated like the Tony Awards. The Pulitzer thing is very private and secret and they just come out some day and say, 'Well, these are the people that won it.'" It was the first time the Pulitzer Prize for Drama had gone to a musical since 1962. Kirkwood revealed of the award he shared with Bennett, Dante, Hamlisch and Kleban, "It looks like a college diploma."

Though he had expressed ambivalent feelings about the position occupied by *A Chorus Line* in his career — and would do in future — Kirkwood would have to be a real sourpuss not to obtain some pleasure from the show's success, and a sourpuss was one thing he could never be accused of being. That year, he spoke of his joy "to know that that show is going to be running at the Shubert Theatre in New York three or four Christmases from now. You walk by and you see the marquee — and now we have one of those electric things going around like the Times Square building used to have — and I saw my name on it for the first time: 'Winner of Best Book, Tony Award' or something, and when you see your name go around in big lights…I stood there, I wanted to stop taxi cabs and say, 'Hey, look at that!'"

In June '76, Kirkwood completed the first draft of a screenplay titled *Poland My Poland*, a rewrite of the 1942 film *To Be or Not To Be*. Screenplays were a new medium for him but he was soon veritably churning them out. He revealed to Roy Leonard in January 1978, "I was a little intimidated by writing them because of the technique. All of the POV, NIGHT, DAY, REVERSE ANGLE, CLOSE-UP, MEDIUM SHOT, TRAVELING TRUCK. All of those terms. I thought, 'Oh God, I don't know if I want to get into all of that.' But I found it a very easy form to slip into." A couple of years later, he admitted to Jim Whaley that he was "probably at home more with the novel" but said, "Since I've gotten into screenwriting…I rather like it. Screenwriting is like putting a jigsaw puzzle together because you have the freedom of going so many places, as opposed to the theatre where you have to think, 'Well, it's got to be one set, five characters and you have to worry about how to get people on and off stage. But a movie you can take a scene right up to the crucial point you want to make and then you jump to the next scene. It's a messy way to work too for me. In about the middle of a screenplay, I think, 'This is like a jigsaw puzzle and I can't get it together.' But then suddenly it starts taking shape."

To Be or Not To Be was set in occupied Poland and starred Jack Benny and Carole Lombard. It comedically but affectionately depicted the heroic struggles of the Polish resistance to the Nazi occupiers. The main characters were Joseph and Maria Tura, well-known Polish actors, the former pompous, the latter faithful but flirtatious. The pair and their friends in the resistance seek to intercept Siletsky, a traitor who has arrived back in Poland to betray the names of resistance fighters to the Germans. In this they are assisted by Sobinski, a handsome air force pilot with whom Joseph Tura erroneously believes his wife is having an affair. The movie was reasonably entertaining, though never laugh-out-loud funny. Considering the mediocrity of his later film scripts, Kirkwood's new version *Poland My Poland* is surprisingly adroit, although he, of course, has his work made a lot easier for him by the existence of a template, to which he broadly adheres. A change he does make is an update of the script for modern sensibilities. Somewhat predictably one of the ways he does this is via the introduction of a gay character. Whether one thinks this is a mark of societal progress is dependent on one's opinion of lisping drag queens (much merriment is sought from an inability to pronounce the letter "s"). A somewhat wittier piece of modernization — or rather post-modernization — is provided by the fact that the movie turns America's traditional Polish ethnic jokes on their head by portraying as an element of the Poles' national character a propensity to make Czechs the butt of their humor. Not that the gags themselves are exactly, to use a phrase of Vito Antenucci's, "weepers," and in any event Kirkwood sees nothing wrong in repeatedly employing that hackneyed ethnic joke where words are Polish-ised by shoving an "i" onto the end.

The script unimaginatively retains the feeble conclusion of the original, which is based around a running gag about someone walking out in the middle of a Joseph Tura performance, but perhaps Mel Brooks dictated this rather than Kirkwood. It's also rather surprising that Brooks chose to remake a movie so of its time that it was as much a propaganda exercise as a piece of entertainment. Nonetheless, Kirkwood acquits himself reasonably well.

Recalls Paonessa, who wasn't involved in the project but heard about its development through Kirkwood, "Mel Brooks is the most somber person in the world and Jimmy wrote this really wonderful line. I think the Mel Brooks character says, 'Oh him — I wouldn't touch him with a ten-foot Czech.' As opposed to a ten-foot Pole, right? Jimmy and I thought that was hysterical…Mel Brooks did not get it and [Kirkwood] said 'Czech, Pole,' and he said, 'No, I still don't get it.'" Beckenstein's recollection seems to indicate that Brooks understood but had other misgivings: "He told Jimmy, 'I think that's in bad taste.' Jimmy responded, 'You have a scene with cowboys sitting around a campfire farting [in *Blazing Saddles*] and you think Poles telling Czech jokes is in bad taste?'" Nonetheless, Beckenstein's memory is that Brooks seemed happy with what was delivered. "That was something that was a sure thing," he says. "[Brooks' wife] Anne Bancroft was going to be starring in it. Suddenly she got a Broadway show — *Golda* — so that shelved it for a few years. When it came out again it was rewritten with another writer." Kirkwood's script is not appreciably inferior to the Ronny Graham- and Thomas Meehan-written exercise that made the screen (as — again — *To Be or Not To Be*) in 1983. There was some consolation for Kirkwood. "I think he was paid a hundred thousand dollars for that," says Beckenstein.

This process of working hard on a project that he had no reason to think would not make the big screen and having to content himself with high remuneration when it didn't would be the almost invariable pattern in Kirkwood's association with Tinseltown. By the end of that association, his outlook was bitter. In 1976, though, Kirkwood had no way of knowing that *Poland My Poland* would be the first of several of his screenplays not to make it to celluloid and that his screenwriting career would constitute, like his revisits to his old material, a deadly distraction from novel-writing. In 1976, he was probably happy in the conviction that his Hollywood time had come. "After *A Chorus Line* there were so many offers that came in, one after another," says Beckenstein. "There was an offer to write an opera for Beverly Sills and I remember him having a meeting with her. He had a meeting with Goldie Hawn about writing a movie. He had a meeting with Carol Burnett about writing something." Kirkwood himself said in a radio interview that November, "It's strange. Sometimes it makes you a little bit sad too because I have the same talent that I did three years ago and nobody ever asked me to write a screenplay. If you're associated with something that is almost a super-hit, which *A Chorus Line* turned out to be, then everybody wants you. I think that they think you have that touch." Did he feel used? "Not really, no, because I'm delighted to be part of that success. I can't not admit that it's a thrill…It's fun."

Says Beckenstein, "After the success of *A Chorus Line*, there were endless invitations to all sorts of interesting people's houses, dinners and entertaining evenings. Jimmy was tremendously entertaining. Everyone wanted to be his friend." "You don't feel used professionally as much as you do socially," Kirkwood said in '76. "Suddenly you get invited to an awful lot of parties and affairs and functions and opening and closings that you never were invited to before and you're treated in a way that sometimes you feel used by people who are trying to impress other people by having you on hand. But actually it's a great old time." Perhaps too great a time in the eyes of those who would have wished for more novels than the single one Kirkwood produced during the rest of the course of his life and for which the largely unrealized film and stage projects Kirkwood embarked on in their stead were hardly consolation. Beckenstein doesn't feel that the socializing particularly ate into Kirkwood's work hours but Jim Piazza says, "It made him very rich, it made him very independent, it made him a lot of money afterwards because he could demand a lot of money for screenplays and things, it got him access to everybody, made him famous and he got all the invitations, which in a way for a writer probably has a certain kind of doom…I think a huge success like that just catapults you into a whole other area…I don't think Jimmy was particularly grounded. I don't think he was one of these guys who had a real base of strength. As a person he was kind of lost."

November of '76 saw Kirkwood traveling to the West Coast to start editing work on his script for the movie of *Some Kind of Hero*, which was to be produced by Jerry Paonessa, who was then running the feature film and television production company of rock star Neil Diamond and was to be an enduring and close friend.

While in California, Kirkwood appeared on KABC radio on the 23rd, the guest on a talk show with a call-in element. His old flame Esther Hamula, now Esther Weber, rang the show at the urging of her sixteen-year-old daughter and Kirkwood and Hamula spoke for the first time since Kirkwood's marriage proposal in 1946. Kirkwood's initial reaction to the announcement that he was about to hear a voice from the past was an anxiety attack about the fact that his true age might emerge. Told the caller was a friend from his high-school days, he said, "Oh my God! If you tell *when* I'll find you and shoot you!" However, upon hearing that it was Hamula, he evinced what seemed genuine pleasure at a call from what he called "One of my first great loves." Kirkwood also spoke to Hamula's daughter after the show and had a brief correspondence with her, responding to her letters requesting advice on becoming a writer.

The interview — conducted by Carole Hemingway — produced some interesting insights into Kirkwood's life and state of mind at the time. He trotted out his usual type of homily about optimism ("I think if we're not optimists, there's no point in getting up in the morning — 'cause we're gonna get the bad news anyhow") but added some layers to that: "I think the older I get, and I hope the more mellow I become, I learn to savor almost every day — as opposed to when I was younger, like in my teens and twenties. I used to negate every day because the success that I was looking for hadn't been achieved. Like today, I had a good day working with Jerry Paonessa who's producing the picture of *Some Kind of Hero* and we worked all day cutting and trimming and it was good work… and we had a good Mexican dinner." Asked what do you do when it's a bad day, Kirkwood said, "I think when you have a bad day — a really bad day, I'm talking about a bone-crusher — then you ought to be very honest and just admit it and have it fully and say, 'I am really in hell today, I'm having a terrible time, I don't know why everything's crashed down around my head, but I'm going to give into it and not fight it.' Because I think if you give in for a whole day and just say, 'Well, this is it, I'm not going to work,' what are you gonna do? 'Well, I'm going to eat hot fudge sundaes and go to a movie' or whatever you want to do. And just get rid of that day. Exorcise it. I used to say, 'I'm not going to be depressed, I'm not going to be depressed' and then I'd fight it off and string it out into a week. Now when I have a real bummer, I just have it fully and get over it."

On his newfound success, he said, "Well, I have to admit that [things] in the last year-and-a-half have been pretty wild. You know, it's funny. I've written five or six books and I've made fairly good money from them. I made a good living. I have a nice house in East Hampton. I live well, I'm relatively happy and I thought I was doing fairly well. Then after *A Chorus Line*, I can't tell you the people that said, 'Oh boy, Jim, God, it's so good to see you finally make it. I mean, we were all so worried about you'…And a couple of times I said, 'Gee, I didn't know I was having it all that bad, I sold a couple of books to the movies, which didn't happen to be made (I think they're going to be made now), but I made a fairly good income and at least I didn't have to work for somebody else. I was able to write on my own.'" Of those previous books, he said, "They had a cult readership. *Good Bad/Bad Times* is taught in a lot of high schools and universities. It comes after *Catcher in the Rye*, after *A Separate Peace*. But I never had that huge bestseller, like say Tommy Tyron does or Jacqueline Susann or Leonard [sic] Uris. I just had a good steady readership."

It was in 1976, that Kirkwood moved to the East Hampton house in which he would reside for the rest of his life, albeit punctuated by his usual forays into a city apartment and his stays at his home in Key West.

Kirkwood's writing studio at Barry Avenue/Squaw Road was attached to the house but had a separate entrance. It was cool (possessing a sunken floor), well-lit (boasting a wall of stacked awning windows) and convenient (it had its own bathroom). Unfortunately, it was built very close to the property line. The next-door neighbors in Squaw Road added a swimming pool on the edge of their property closest to Kirkwood's writing studio. Though Kirkwood was fond of his neighbors, the shrieking and splashing of their grandchildren took its toll on his patience and concentration and he began to look for a more private abode. His insistence on another waterfront home with a view ostensibly limited his options, but ultimately he found the perfect house for his needs. It was in Oyster Shores Road, also on Three Mile Harbor. Built in 1950, tall oak trees shaded the property, which boasted lush, mature landscaping, affording an ideal place to write. That was by no means its only plus-point. Situated on a bluff about forty feet above the water level, it provided a spectacular view of the whole bay. The rocky shoreline was natural and fresh water springs along it fed into the salt water bay all year round. Wildlife and birds would come to drink from the springs. Local fauna included swans, seagulls, ducks, egrets, ospreys and herons, and — on-shore — numerous songbirds, chipmunks, pheasants, raccoons and occasional foxes and owls. There was a little dock in front of the house enabling the keeping of a small boat or a swim in the clean water. Kirkwood could even take advantage of the bay's abundance of fresh clams, scallops and oysters. "I missed the sunsets," says Beckenstein of a building that faced north-east, "but the house on Oyster Shores Road would surprise you with a glorious sunrise." Kirkwood's studio with its roll-top desk was on the second floor with a magnificent view over the bay. "In this place, Jimmy's creative juices flowed," Beckenstein notes.

Meanwhile, Kirkwood obtained a new base in the city, either in '75 or '76. He had rented an 8th Avenue apartment for a short while in the early seventies after having given up the lease at West 58th Street in the second half of the 1960s. Beckenstein says the 8th Ave place was "small" and "dreary" and that Kirkwood "rarely spent time there." After that, he sublet a furnished apartment for about a year on Bank Street in Greenwich Village, which is where he was staying when he was co-writing *A Chorus Line*. However, Kirkwood had set his sights on Manhattan Plaza on 43rd Street and 10th Avenue, within walking distance of the theatre district. Manhattan Plaza was a federally-subsidized residential complex seventy percent of whose apartments were originally reserved for "people in the performing arts." "You had to get on a list to get into that building," says Beckenstein. Kirkwood obtained a 45th-floor Plaza apartment which he adored. There was a boon for the tennis-mad Kirkwood in addition to his new city apartment being a handy place to meet collaborators in simpatico surroundings: Manhattan Plaza boasted five weather-protected courts of sufficiently high quality that Billie Jean King could sometimes be seen playing there.

Nineteen seventy-six was the year that Kirkwood and his Boswell first met. "I had been teaching his books in my college courses and students were constantly asking me questions about the books and about James Kirkwood," recalls William Russo. "So I put together a little multiple-choice test for him and I sent it to him. I had questions about his books and I wasn't quite sure what he would do, but he answered them all and sent them back with every answer incorrect or about as odd as you could get and some very strange marginal comments and after that I guess we were friends." Over the years Russo taught his students all Kirkwood's novels except *Hit Me with a Rainbow*. "I thought he was greatly underestimated," he says citing writers loved by academic critics such as John Updike, Norman Mailer and Gore Vidal who he felt Kirkwood deserved just as much attention as. Russo: "When we finally started talking, I was very flattered by his attention and maybe he was flattered by mine." Though Russo doubts that he was the first professor to teach Kirkwood's work, he says, "I think some of the questions I raised about his texts were probably unique. I was looking more deeply. There's something called New Criticism which looks at motifs of text, so I was interpreting his texts in terms of not just what was happening in one book but consistently throughout his books. The character Boots shows up in [two] novels and many of the same concepts appear in all of his books."

Russo sometimes found getting information out of Kirkwood about his work rather difficult. "Talk about being coy," he says. "Every time I tried to pin him down on things he would squirm away. That may have been part of the amusement he had with me. I sometimes was amazed that he wanted to spend any time talking to me at all about his literature, but he did. I think the game was this sort of chess game with other people. He loved being-on-a-witness-stand kind of approach: could he outsmart the jury, could he outsmart the D.A.? He called me 'The D.A.' when I questioned him. That element of game-playing…works very well in fiction." Did Russo not find this annoying? "I thought it was right in character. He is Peter, he is Josh, so of course he's not going to tell us the complete truth. Because I don't think those characters are completely truthful. Yet, if you were to ask the average reader, they think these are the most openly honest books they've ever read."

Russo says that his students picked up readily on the sexual ambiguity in Kirkwood's characters. "I said to him once, 'The biggest question I get in my classes is, "Are you gay or bi-sexual?"' He said, 'No, no, no, no — what you need to say to anyone who asks if I'm gay, give them my address and tell them to come over to my apartment and they can find out for themselves.' I thought that was a wonderful answer."

Asked about writers whom he considers similar to Kirkwood, Russo comes up with an unexpected name: "Probably Ira Levin is the closest." Russo says the acclaimed author of tales of suspense, horror and intrigue like *A Kiss Before Dying*, *Rosemary's Baby*, *The Stepford Wives*, *Deathtrap*, *The Boys from Brazil* and *Sliver* was like Kirkwood because he was "a man who worked on novels, plays, screenplays, did all of the things Jim did. I think they certainly dealt with similar themes. They seemed to come out of that same feeling that they were renaissance men and that they could do every part of the North American culture. I don't think there are too many writers who have succeeded that way, or even tried."

Another project on which Kirkwood worked in this period was a stage musical entitled *Club Mardi Gras*, a collaboration with three-time Tony Award-winning Ron Field, who it was planned would be the project's choreographer and director.

Kirkwood explained, "It was Ron Field who came to me with the idea of investigating a specific world as material for a show. Alternately tired and elated from the happy rebound of *A Chorus Line*, I was most pessimistic that any idea for any musical would grab my interest for quite some time." Kirkwood's interest was piqued by an idea about a drag club — the titular Mardi Gras — whose glory days had been after the Second World War and which had now fallen on hard times because, "The one-time cosmopolitan night club audience no longer exists; the days of the Blue Angel, Ruban Bleu, Bon Soir, Mocambo, Ciro's are gone." (Kirkwood, of course, was listing some of the regular gigs of the Kirkwood & Goodman comedy team.) Kirkwood was excited about exploring "a milieu that has remained totally untouched, so far as the basis for a musical play." In the *Miami Herald* in January 1977, it was revealed that producer Zev Bufman had signed a contract with Fields and Kirkwood. The project was described therein as a "$750,000 musical" and it was stated that the three were planning to convene in San Francisco on February 1 for a tour of local drag shows, whereupon they would conduct five days of interviews. Bufman's proposed timetable involved spending the rest of the winter raising the budget "from sources within the entertainment industry, including movie studios, record firms and Broadway financiers." "This is partly an exposé on how these people became what society considers freaks," said Bufman. "How they got there, what they're going to do, how they will wind up. For some, life has hope and meaning, the play will suggest. For others, there will be nothing but despair." Ron Field later explained that he wanted to produce a show that tackled homosexuality and that he wanted a musical in which the songs would be organic. The drag club idea was his solution to this conundrum. "That put it into an area that was glamorous, entertaining, bitchy, sad, pathetic, relevant, informative," he said. "I went, 'Wait a minute, *wait a minute*! It's never been on the stage before! What is this world of homosexuals who, for two-thirds of their life, get dressed up as another sex? What pushed them into that? Are they living out a fantasy? Have they succumbed or are they on top of it? That's real interesting.'" Field also revealed that after approaching Kirkwood with the idea and beginning research with him at San Francisco drag club Finnochio's, he had realized while looking at the audience lining up to see the "freaks" inside that they were as fascinating as the show. He also asserted that part of the reason for the decline in attendances at drag clubs was that younger gay men considered female impersonators to be Uncle Toms in that they represented an old view of homosexuality. Kirkwood said, "He called me, and I got to thinking: 'What an odd bunch of people to deal with, what a strange profession they're in, and yet they're all really entertainers. What they want to do is entertain, no matter how they're doing it'…Well, it was my idea to make it a club that had been in existence for 35 years, and the club was going to close…I thought it could be a really very touching show and kind of moving, the last night of this club. What are these people going to do?…They are not the kind of people who can go and audition for *Carmelina* or any other regular musical."

In the *Miami Herald* article, Bufman talked of the musical going into rehearsals in October and opening in late November, playing in San Francisco and Los Angeles and then moving onto Broadway, "God willing." God may have been willing but Kirkwood wasn't, following a difference of opinion with Field. "Ron and I went to San Francisco, talked to the female impersonators, went to the clubs," he said. "And suddenly Ron got a different attitude toward the characters. In a way he wanted to wipe them out. I wanted people to empathize with their plight and suddenly we were at totally different poles. Ron felt very strongly that they should not be allowed to go on in this very tacky old profession that had fallen into disrepair. I thought that certainly some character in the show can have that idea and that approach but, as the creators, if we're going to put 25 or 30 people on the stage we want to wipe out, how are we going to make the audience care about them? I woke up one morning and thought, 'No, I can't go on with this. If we're at such disparate poles right now, if we feel so differently about the chemistry of this material, then I'd better withdraw'…So I called Ron and told him that I thought I shouldn't do the show, that I thought it was still a good idea, but I thought he was going to be in trouble if he held that view about the characters."

Kirkwood's withdrawal seems to have scuppered the project. He and Field, however, had done considerable work on it, with a draft of a first act — at least — having been completed. That first act opens with Steve Layton Jr. — an unusually nostalgic 24-year-old — walking onto the darkened stage of the Mardi Gras and reminiscing about the club and his life, helped by the offstage voices of people like his father and mother, lovers and childhood friends. In this sequence a man rings Steve in the past and talks about all the times they've had sex. After he has finished, the voice of Steve's father informs the caller that he must have wanted Steve Junior. Thus ends Layton's Jr.'s life at home.

We are then taken properly to Club Mardi Gras on its closing night. The owner has sold up and the dancers and drag artists are all waxing nostalgic as they prepare to make their bittersweet final performances.

The scenes alternate between drag queens performing their shtick — a performance within the play — and scenes in which they chat in the dressing rooms. In the script, the proposed original songs are "sketched in," Kirkwood giving direction as to what they should contain thematically. The theme of one of the original proposed songs would seem to be Kirkwood's own philosophy on life: that you should not dwell on your misfortune but try to improve your life, that if you're not having a good time it's your own fault and that if you're happy you make others happy. The theme of another is the history of female impersonation, a number intended to eventually employ the entire cast, bar one, and which, rather ambitiously, is supposed to take in the ancient Greeks and Romans, the Kabuki Theatre, Shakespeare, the Dancing Roys of Morocco, Julian Eltinge, Bert Savoy, Bert Lahr, Bobby Clark, Ray Bolger in *Charley's Aunt*, Danny La Rue, Milton Berle, Jack Benny, the Marx Brothers, Jack Lemmon and Tony Curtis in *Some Like It Hot*, Jonathan Winters, Johnny Carson, Flip Wilson and T.C. Jones. There are also intended to be songs from "real life," such as a parody of "Falling in Love Again," as well as songs done "straight," the latter category including "One," one of the more famous songs from *A Chorus Line*.

The Mardi Gras drag queens specialize in impersonating old-time movie and stage stars, such as Marlene Dietrich, Tallulah Bankhead (whose singular mannerisms, of course, Kirkwood knew something about) and Carol Channing (whom Kirkwood also knew). Kirkwood executes well routines based on obscene *double entendre* and filthy wisecracks. (One character says he wouldn't hurt a fly, unless it was open; two characters have an exchange about a Tampax stuck behind an ear which raises the alarming question of where the pencil thought to be there is.) He also adroitly depicts the drag artists' endless bitchiness and how it is leavened by self-deprecation. (On the latter score, the character Mickey comes out with a good and perceptive line when he notes that the irony of being a female impersonator is that no woman would be caught dead in their sort of outfits.)

However, genuine pathos — as opposed to shrill dramatics — is not in evidence until a quite moving speech by Bobby during the act he is being allowed to perform for old time's sake after a long absence from the Mardi Gras. He reveals that he got fired from the club after an incident where he had sex with a man who turned out to be an undercover cop in denial who — once the passion was over — promptly booked him. Act One closes with Bobby collapsing on stage, not long after claiming to the audience that he has taken some poison pills.

The personas of the drag queens when they are onstage at Club Mardi Gras are essentially no different to their depicted offstage personalities. This may be accurate but it also creates a problem. While the drag queens' self-deprecation is almost as endearing as it's meant to be, they are endlessly nasty. For instance, Mickey, after giving a grateful Bobby some M&Ms, says that he has had them up his ass all afternoon and that the commercial that claims they don't melt is correct. The latter (one hopes) joke is also representative of the distasteful humor running throughout, even if some of the gags are funny. Said humor takes a decidedly queasy turn when the character J. Heavon Jones starts telling his backstory from the Mardi Gras' stage, one that includes a childhood carnal relationship with his wheelchair-bound father. This section is truly nauseous and its jocular tone inappropriate. This is aside from the Too Much Information caveat, which also applies to the whole work. Yes, these people might have incredible drama in their lives and Kirkwood seems to have captured their world, vernacular and viewpoints well, but do we really want to know about them? In order to care about them we have to like them and one doesn't have to be John Simon to find their endless in-fighting tiresome, their perpetual false good spirits overbearing and their obsession with sex, or at least with talking about it, juvenile.

There is also from today's perspective a general feeling of over-familiarity about the milieu depicted. Though it might have broken new ground if produced at the time, documentaries, TV dramas and stage shows have now made drag queens' personality types and the flavor of their humor common knowledge and much of *Club Mardi Gras* therefore banal. One last problem is a recurring sense of cliché. For instance, the sole black "girl" (J Heavon Jones) is described by Kirkwood as — wait for it — "sassy."

One wonders about Kirkwood's state of mind when working on this project. Piazza suspects that his fascination with transvestites (which would reveal itself in other ways) stemmed from the fact that, "He admired anyone with an outrageous personality, he loved eccentricity, loved just bigger-than-life." However, if Kirkwood was shaken by critics thinking he was proselytizing for homosexuality with the 1975 play version of *P.S. Your Cat is Dead!*, how on earth did he think he was going to deal with what they made of this show? It's almost as though he was testing his own resolve by working on it. Perhaps this also helps explain why he pulled out of the project.

Five years later, the musical *La Cage Aux Follies* would cover very similar territory to great commercial and critical success. Kirkwood was in the running for the job of writing said show, though Paonessa says that not too much should be read into this. "Everybody was offered *La Cage Aux Follies*," he avows. "He was one of the first. And then it wound up being Arthur Laurents." Though Arthur Laurents was a long-time friend of Kirkwood — and though his credentials as writer of the books of *West Side Story* and *Gypsy* amongst famous others made him much better-qualified for the task — Jim Piazza reports that Kirkwood was none too happy at losing out on the gig: "He was very pissed off, very upset about that, and he told me there had been some fighting or something, words exchanged." Those "words exchanged" were not with Laurents himself. "No. Never," is Laurents' response when asked if Kirkwood tackled him on the issue, though he also says, "I never heard Jimmy's name mentioned," in the context of the show.

Perhaps this is an appropriate place to discuss Kirkwood's complicated relationship with Laurents. Though he liked and admired Laurents very much, the latter was a man who could go from pleasant to acerbic very easily and perhaps more importantly was a legend in a way Kirkwood could never be. "He was in awe of Arthur because he knew that Arthur was the more prolific and probably more talented and had a bigger name," says Piazza. "Jimmy was kind of neutered around Arthur…Arthur came to a rehearsal of *Chorus Line* with Stephen Sondheim and they sat there and giggled through the whole thing, very patronizingly. Jimmy was furious with him. Then when it opened and [was] a big hit and Arthur called for house seats, Jimmy was very put out." "Apocryphal," insists Laurents of the giggling allegation. However, he admits that he did have ambivalent feelings about the *A Chorus Line* preview he and composer Sondheim saw. He says, "We both thought that once they started in announcing that they were going to tell their stories where you could count how many there were, you thought, 'Well, I have to sit through that number of stories.' There's a song in *Camelot* that Alan Lerner wrote: 'If ever I should leave you, it wouldn't be in autumn.' So you know you're going to have to go through the four seasons, which is not a good idea to know. And here you had to go through the people. What was wonderful was the staging."

Laurents describes his relationship with Kirkwood as, "Very good friends." He also says he very much respected Kirkwood's art. "He fought very hard to be recognized as a serious writer and I think that he appreciated that I went out of my way to present him as that," he says. "Jimmy left me money in his will because I think I was the only one who publicly said he was a writer and pushed him as a writer." He declines to state whether he thinks Kirkwood was in the heavyweight or lightweight writing camps:

"I think that's not the way to examine it. The question is whether he was a truthful writer, and he was for the most part very truthful." However, Laurents adds, "There was also the giddy side of him…He gave a talk at a 72nd Street bar here — it's an intellectual center — and he asked me to introduce him because he felt that [if] I would present him so people would take him seriously. And he tried, but he came out and made jokes." Though he respected his books, Laurents felt Kirkwood's giddiness and his love of glamour meant he peaked with his debut: "When he was writing *There [Must] Be a Pony!* he was writing about things he really knew and it had an authenticity and a seriousness whether he liked it or not. When he began departing from what he actually knew, it then began to be good, facile and not really digging. And that was like that world he travelled in…I didn't travel in the world that Jimmy did. Out on the island, we would go over to his house sometimes but he always had to have a celebrity there." Referring to Sydney Biddle Barrows, briefly notorious in the seventies when exposed as a panderer to high-class clientele, Laurents says, "I remember one week it was Mayflower Madam. That was good enough. She was a celebrity."

By April 1977, Kirkwood had finished work on what he termed on its first page the "first draft" of the movie script of *Some Kind of Hero*, although one wonders what the script he had presented to Jerry Paonessa the previous year was if not that.

Paonessa had long been an admirer of his work and the two had a mutual friend but what eventually led them to hook up was Paonessa managing to get hold of an advance copy of the then-unpublished *Some Kind of Hero* in a not-quite-legal manner with a view to producing a film adaptation. Paonessa: "How it works is you go in and you just sneak it out of the agent's office or out of the Xerox place. It's often the way bestsellers are confiscated in America, way before they're published. They pay the Xerox guy ten bucks or twenty bucks, or you can get it snuck through the hallowed halls of the publishers. I read it in manuscript form and fell in love with it."

That Kirkwood was nearby watching over both the original stage production of *P.S. Your Cat is Dead!* and *A Chorus Line* provided an ideal opportunity to meet. The two saw *Cat* together, then, Paonessa says, "He said, 'You know, I have this new show opening and it has never been performed in front of an audience and it's for tomorrow night. Do you want to go?' I said, 'Sure.' I wanted that book badly so I decided that even if I hated it, I would lie. Of course, he brought me to an event which I will never, ever forget as long as I live and that was the first performance of *A Chorus Line*. It was an experience you can't describe. I was sort of flattered that he took me as opposed to Arthur but Arthur is much more of an archivist of Jimmy's life than he is in terms of understanding film or theatre or any of those, and I don't mean it in any pejorative way. Arthur was a great archivist but the problem with Jimmy's creative life is that the only other people who were around specifically was [Kirkwood's lawyer] Elliot Lefkowitz and these people never really were in love with Jimmy's work and his creativity. If you ask Arthur or Elisa [Lefkowitz, Elliot's daughter and executrix of Kirkwood's literary estate] or if Elliot were alive I guarantee — I don't mean to belittle them at all — they probably haven't read half of what he has written. And it's too bad, because in order to help plan the future, if you will, you need to know what the past is. By the way, the thing about *Some Kind of Hero* was that, when I flew in to see it and went crazy over it, about two weeks later the rest of the world saw it. I immediately wanted to negotiate pre-acquisition of the rights and ultimately got them. That started for Jimmy and me a very long creative team."

"It was about 140 pages, I believe," Paonessa says of the first version of the screenplay of *Hero*. "Jimmy is really good at the first adaptation because he gets the essence of the character and the plot and story really well, but then losing that forty pages is really tough. He did the same thing with *Good Times/Bad Times*...His very first draft was 140 pages and I loved both of the pieces, but we had to break our asses to hone it down to what I think eventually was 125 pages and we had a lot of arguments. I was trying to teach Jimmy what went on in Hollywood where it's different from the Dramatists Guild. [With] the Dramatists Guild the writer is always right and in a pinch the writer would be the one who would reign and that's not true of the Writers Guild. The Dramatists Guild supported the writer, but the Writers Guild really was more in favor of the director. So I explained a little bit of the ropes to him."

It would take many years and an absolute desecration of Kirkwood's original script before the green light for filming *Some Kind of Hero* was given. "We had the seven years of doom and gloom where it sat," says Paonessa. "I had set the picture up at Paramount. It was the very first deal that Michael Eisner and Barry Diller had made. They had taken over Paramount. This was the first project that was developed...[Kirkwood would say], 'Jerry, what's happening, how is it possible they've hit me with all this money, they've paid for the option. Why?' I would say, 'Jimmy, I don't know'...I found out later about three or four months after the movie was made. The reason that project took so long and was in limbo was that Barry Diller hated it and Michael Eisner loved it and nobody knew that there was somebody with a second agenda. So we sat there with our thumbs up our ass every week saying, 'Hey, what's happening to the movie?'"

Paonessa would become Kirkwood's mentor in Hollywood as Kirkwood turned his attention increasingly toward film. "Jimmy, as much as his mother and dad were in Hollywood, really didn't know very much about the movie business," says Paonessa. "It was still an enigma to people who were in the theatre, so I really led him through and taught him and was very honest with him as opposed to people saying, 'Oh, Jimmy, we love you.'" Though they had a long friendship in addition to their extensive professional partnership, Paonessa points out that contrary to rumor they weren't *that* close: "I never had sex with Jimmy. *Everybody* thought we had. First of all, it wasn't of any appeal to me, but if we had, it would have changed everything." Paonessa recollects Kirkwood asking him on several occasions to quit his job to be his manager. Paonessa always declined: "I told him that if I do [it] as a friend and a collaborator, you can't yell at me, you can't say no."

With that *Hero* script under his belt, Kirkwood lectured on writing on the QE II in June. Kirkwood was a trim figure for all of his life due to the tennis that he played just about every day. Recalls Beckenstein, "Jim would play tennis for four hours in the heat of the summer whenever he could find partners and always had a pro at one club or another to play with and take lessons from." However, Kirkwood, as he wrote his friend Andrew Morse, gained fourteen pounds on his first-class trip to "merry England." He exulted in said letter in the fact that "the great deluxe traveling and a good vacation" were obtained free because he lectured on the trip over and back. Despite that indication of base motives, lecturing was something he enjoyed doing. Recalls Beckenstein, "He also lectured at colleges, etc. He was signed with a couple of lecture bureaus. He was a wonderfully entertaining, eclectic speaker with a great sense of humor."

In August '77, Kirkwood was informing James Leo Herlihy, "There has suddenly pulled together a deal to actually film GT/BT. With that dear Jim Bradley who's had it on option for years. Anyhow — foreign money, no one else you know, unknown director, Cliff Robertson to act in it. Jane Alexander too, a few others, search is on for the two boys. Filming to start end of October. And here I am with one month to write the fuckin' screenplay. So, darling, that's what I'm attempting to do. I'm up to page 30 and will have it finished in some form or other by 20 Sept."

The Kirkwood screenplay of *Good Times/Bad Times* in his papers is undated. The story is set in 1961, i.e., after Kirkwood's Brewster Academy tenure but before the events in the novel. However, this is nothing like the extent of the changes the author has made to his story. The character of Mrs. Hoyt has a far bigger role than in the source material. Her brother, the school's sports coach, had recently hanged himself in the school gym, leading to her mental fragility and alcoholism. Her husband sees the consequent decline in the school's athletic program as intertwined with its broader decay, the main manifestation of which is falling rolls. We see a lot more of their troubled (and, unlike in the book, childless) marriage. It is Hoyt's despair at the school's condition that makes him so keen for Peter Kilburn to perform his soliloquy. As his job becomes under ever-greater threat, Hoyt is increasingly desperate, successively slapping Peter, Jordan and his wife in the face.

Homosexuality has been largely stripped from the story. The alcohol rubdown scene is far less sexual. Hoyt is presented as primarily interested in Peter Kilburn as the child he never had. This gives his disgust at finding Peter and Jordan in bed together a different quality. The kiss that Peter and Jordan share is not the full kiss on the lips of the book but a quick smacker on the cheek no more erotic than the celebrations on a sports field. Despite all this, though, Kirkwood seems unable to resist — in his usual style — planting a few clues to his sexuality: some deliberate vestiges of sensuality in the alcohol rubdown, Peter kissing a dead Jordan's forehead, two boys sneaking off together into the woods... The deadly climatic chase is not about lust, however, but the fact that the school's declining reputation doesn't need Peter running away on top of Jordan's demise. Though Hoyt does, as in the book, press his lips to Peter's face while asking if this was how Jordan did it, this seems more a sign of his erratic psychological condition than sexual desire and jealousy.

The title of the movie is given a different rationale to that in the book, where it comes partly from Peter musing on whether the good times will ever return after his current bad times: an inscription in a watch given to Jordan's grandfather by his grandmother reading, "Good times/bad times — long as we're together."

Kirkwood's script is competent enough, and in places he displays an acute cinematic awareness, such as his use of a montage of a dismal football match to demonstrate Hoyt's dismay at his school's condition. It's doubtful that the script would have made a great movie, though. Kirkwood's retention of the framing device from the book is unwise: the linear is far more important in film than it is in prose, where immersion in the protagonist's psyche can compensate for such plot-spoilers. The dialogue is often very pat. While the removal of Hoyt's predatory homosexuality might have pleased those who thought his character smeared gays as pedophiles, it actually damages the narrative. Without the horror of having someone bigger and stronger forcing himself on him, it removes a lot of the justification for Peter killing Hoyt.

Nineteen seventy-seven was the year that Kirkwood successfully ran for a seat on the council of the Dramatists Guild of America. Peter Stone, who was involved with the Guild's council at the time and became the organization's long-running president in 1981, recalled at one of Kirkwood's memorials that Kirkwood "recognized the perilous position of playwrights in an industry that was completely unionized from box office men and stagehands to actors and directors, everyone in fact but playwrights…He served there faithfully and strenuously until his death, attending every meeting when he wasn't out of town with a show and volunteering for any job that his fellow council members were reluctant to take, like mediating a symposium featuring the two heads of the Shubert Organization. Afraid that the questions from the audience, which consisted of 200 frustrated playwrights, might have turned hostile, there was a certain reticence among the other council members being part of such an unpredictable bloodsport. But Jimmy with his usual good spirits finally raised his hand and volunteered, or as he so articulately put it, 'What the fuck.'" Kirkwood so adored the Dramatists Guild that in his will he left the organization all of his future non-*A Chorus Line* earnings from plays, a somewhat lucrative behest. Beckenstein points out, "*Legends!*, *P.S.* and occasionally *UTBU* are always being optioned and performed somewhere, both in America and around the world."

In August '77, Kirkwood, Beckenstein, Kirkwood's current agent at William Morris Janet Roberts and Roberts' husband attended the Provincetown Playhouse to take in the Boston Repertory Company's production of *P.S. Your Cat is Dead!*, which was playing in Provincetown for the summer after six months in the company's home city. When they arrived, Kirkwood was told he had a message to call home. The curtain was held while he rang his house watcher to be told that his beloved Bobby Seale had been found dead on the front lawn. "We were in shock," says Beckenstein. "He was one of the healthiest, most active cats you could imagine." A bigger shock was awaiting them when they sat down to watch the play. In the first scene in *P.S. Your Cat is Dead!* Kate answers the phone in Jimmy Zoole's apartment and exclaims, "Oh, no, not his cat! Oh, Bobby Seale is dead!" "It was just an incredible, unbelievable moment," says Beckenstein. Janet Roberts, seated alongside Kirkwood, squeezed his hand, sometimes digging her nails in, whenever Bobby Seale's name was mentioned by the cast. Beckenstein: "He said afterward, 'If she did that one more time, I was going to slug her.'"

September 11, 1977, saw Guillermo Vilas defeat Jimmy Connors in the final of tennis' US Open. Vilas' second Grand Slam victory of the year went down well with Kirkwood on two counts. Firstly, for such an alternative and informal person, he was surprisingly conventional when it came to the on-court conduct of bad boys like Connors and John McEnroe (who had begun to make a name for himself that year). "We just didn't like that behavior, bad sportsmanship," says Homer Price, Kirkwood's fellow tennis enthusiast. Secondly: "Jimmy was in love with Vilas. He thought he was so gorgeous," reveals Price.

James Kirkwood and Arthur Beckenstein, life partners. JENNIFER GIRARD

Kirkwood's personalized celebrity Christmas cards were legendary. From top, he is seen with Elizabeth Taylor, Liberace and Carol Channing & Mary Martin. COURTESY OF ARTHUR BECKENSTEIN

The photograph used for a divine Kirkwood Christmas card, 1970. His mother — to whom this picture was sent — was not amused. ARTHUR BECKENSTEIN

The photograph used for a less sacrilegious but perhaps even more shocking Christmas card from 1969. ARTHUR BECKENSTEIN

With friend Gino Marino, who inspired his character Vito Antenucci.
COURTESY OF ARTHUR BECKENSTEIN

With old flame Elaine Stritch, 1983. She may have been the inspiration for Kate in P.S. Your Cat is Dead! ARTHUR BECKENSTEIN

With best friend and collaborator James Leo Herlihy, early 1970s. COURTESY OF ARTHUR BECKENSTEIN

Homer Price, friend and confidante. COURTESY OF ARTHUR BECKENSTEIN

With pet chipmunk Spike, early 1970s. Even Spike would, after a fashion, wind up in Kirkwood's fiction. ARTHUR BECKENSTEIN

Arthur Cormier, former POW whose experiences helped form Some Kind of Hero. COURTESY OF ARTHUR CORMIER

On The Merv Griffin Show, *mid-1970s.*

Kirkwood takes elaborate revenge on a critic.

With Michael Bennett, director of A Chorus Line, *mid-1970s.*
COURTESY OF ARTHUR BECKENSTEIN

SIXTEEN

On November 15, 1977, Kirkwood signed a contract for a pilot for a TV series to be called *Harold*.

The idea for *Harold* was developed by Kirkwood in collaboration with his old friend from *Valiant Lady* days, Patti Goldstein. "We were always goofing off on things," says Goldstein, "and it was one of those, 'Wouldn't it be a good idea if,' and I had this idea and Jimmy just howled and thought that was so funny and wonderful and that we should do it together." Their premise was that a struggling actor finds that a mutt named Harold foisted on him has the star potential that producers seem to think he himself is lacking. The deal for the program was brokered through agent Beryl Vertue of the Robert Stigwood Organization. The show actually got as far as the casting stage for the part of Harold. Of this, Beckenstein remembers, "about a dozen dogs all out of their cages at the same time misbehaving. About four had 'accidents' in the Paramount boardroom. [The] trainer said, 'This never happens.' All the dogs looked alike, like Benji or Sandy from *Annie*."

Kirkwood put together a script for a thirty-minute pilot, plus synopses for a further seven episodes (including a two-parter). Despite the canine casting call, the pilot was not actually filmed and the series never came into being. Goldstein: "I remember we had a couple of meetings with CBS and it was a go, or it almost was a go, and then suddenly the bottom fell out of it and I don't think either one of us ever understood quite why. It was just one of those things."

The pilot script for *Harold* is attributed to Kirkwood alone but with a credit indicating it was "created" by him and Goldstein. Kirkwood gives some of the characters intriguingly familiar names: the jobbing actor male protagonist is Josh like the character in *There Must Be a Pony!*, while his girlfriend (another mostly unemployed thespian) is named Muriel and nicknamed Moo-Moo, both like Kirkwood's ex-beau Bentley. Possibly also autobiographical is the reason Josh stymies Muriel's desire to get married: the fact that Josh's father and mother were themselves married and divorced multiple times. The pilot sees Josh unwillingly gifted a cute-looking cocker spaniel by a shifty Puerto Rican youth when out jogging one day. When he reluctantly allows it to accompany him to an audition for a play, it is spotted by the producers, who think it perfect for a canine role in the show. As well as the screen presence the play's producers identify, Harold has another gift in the form of an almost supernatural ability to understand human emotion. Josh's life now begins to revolve around Harold's successful career.

Kirkwood's first TV script is very conventional in the mode of seventies U.S. small-screen comedy. You can virtually hear the gales of canned laughter when Josh responds to Muriel pointing out that he equates marriage with prison with the limp line, "Isn't it funny that a judge sentences you to either one — or both?" The dissolves are creakingly predictable, such as the one where Josh says to the doe-eyed Harold, "I absolutely cannot have a dog. Have you got that straight?" followed naturally by a scene where Josh arrives back at his apartment with the pooch in tow. There's nothing laugh-out-loud — or even laugh-inwardly — funny here, although it's not without a corny, wholesome charm. It's certainly no worse than most American sitcoms of the time, which was an era well before the literate *Frasier* or the slightly daring and slightly alternative *Friends*. It's also mildly impressive that Kirkwood applies himself with such discipline to operating within these restrictive parameters. Nonetheless, it's an exercise beneath his talents and yet another fruitless scriptwriting diversion from his true, novel-based *métier*.

In either late 1977 or early 1978, Kirkwood ran into Vivian Matalon. He informed Matalon that in the forthcoming New York revival of *P.S. Your Cat is Dead!* he was intending to cut the scene with the three interlopers which the director had wanted excluded from its original Broadway production. "I said, 'I'm going to kill you,'" recalls Matalon. "He thought it didn't add anything to the play, which is what I told him in the first place." Paonessa: "He finally listened and took out those three characters, the trio as they were called, [who] really did not help the play at all." William Russo offers an alternative explanation for the decision: "He might have been taken aback that it became a cult gay favorite with the S&M crowd." Whether or not that latter analysis is correct, Beckenstein reveals of the previously published seven-character version, "Jim bought back all remaining copies…He did not want it done after it was rewritten."

Considering that the play had been dogged by misfortune — bad reviews, controversy, early closing and even murder — one would imagine that Kirkwood would by now want to move on. However, there seemed to be a lot of pride wrapped up in *P.S. Your Cat is Dead!* for the author. John Shearin, who would play Kate's date Fred Gable and understudy for Jimmy Zoole in the new production, says, "He loved the play quite a lot, he really did, and felt that it hadn't gotten a fair shot on Broadway. They felt that it was due to be done again and done in a way more consistent with what Jimmy's vision of it was." Nonetheless, this would not be a formal second chance on Broadway, it being a production enjoying that nebulous description applied to NY shows not technically playing in Manhattan's theatre district, "off-Broadway."

Vasili Bogazianos, who had understudied Vito in San Francisco and would play the role in the New York revival, makes an interesting observation when he says that perhaps Kirkwood's determination to continue mounting this play, and to bring it back to a locale where it had failed was influenced by his experience honing *A Chorus Line* over a long period of time. "*Chorus Line* was workshop forever, before it finally got to Broadway," he says. "You can make an argument that San Francisco was a workshop." Something perhaps supporting this idea is the revelation in an article on the 1978 production at a point where it was still in previews that "Kirkwood is leading discussions with the audiences after every Tuesday and Wednesday performance."

The play was being mounted by Terry Spiegel and Francine Haskell, associate producers on the original production. Though the director was officially the late Robert Nigro, Bogazianos recalls Kirkwood being in the driving seat. "It was clear that it was Jim's show," he says. "Jim was there at all the rehearsals. It is kind of unusual to have the author in residency the entire time. It did seem a little much, but he was very helpful. You could say, 'Did you mean this?' or 'Did you mean that?'" Did he feel almost that Jimmy was more in control than Nigro? "I'd have to say yes." Bogazianos also recalls Spiegel and Haskell attending rehearsals, adding, "The producers being there might have been a little weird, but they kept their distance." Beckenstein was also involved, designing some images projected in the production and a typographic logo intertwined with an image of Kirkwood's late kitty Bobby Seale taken from the original photo shoot he had done for the novel's back cover. The logo artwork won him a couple of awards and was used on the play's posters, tee-shirts and tote bags and on the 1972 paperback edition of the novel, as well as the published edition of the new version of the play.

Bogazianos had become friends with Kirkwood in San Francisco and had been encouraged by the writer to audition for the new NY production. He was certainly able to replicate Vito's Bronx accent and syntax: "I am Greek American and a Queens background, but obviously close enough to Vito. Most of my friends were Italian. It was pretty authentic.

I grew up speaking that way…The irony is I had to go back to it…I was nineteen or twenty years old and people started making fun of me and I started taking acting a little seriously and I thought perhaps I should have a more standard American speech."

Peter Simon was cast as Jimmy Zoole. There were some problems with the actress who took the role of Kate. Joan Wells was the first woman picked but was dispensed with before opening night. "She was with us for about three weeks and she was replaced by Claire Malis," says Bogazianos. "We the actors all thought [Wells] was doing a great job. They seemed really intent on getting somebody glamorous and Joan was a wonderful actress, but I don't know that you'd call her glamorous." Shearin also doesn't know why Wells was fired but was intrigued to be told by this author that Kate was possibly based on Elaine Stritch: "That makes really great sense in terms of the girl who was playing that part at first because she looked a lot like Elaine Stritch."

Both Bogazianos and Shearin say that "Bobby" Nigro was a good and likable director. Shearin adds, "The director was feeling a lot of heat from above. Now, whether that was from the producers or Jimmy or both I'm not sure, but I think it's safe to say that Jimmy was very determined that this was going to work and be right, and I think therein lies the key as to why they were having such difficulty with the woman. The part of the woman is maybe the least well-written, the least well-defined in the show, and they were just having a really tough time getting the right tone in the performance."

Aside from the dropping of the trio of interlopers, the changes to this version of *P.S. Your Cat is Dead!* are almost all minor, at least going by the commercially published version. The situation and setting is naturally the same as before. Kirkwood's stage directions this time dictate that slides of Vito's police fingerprint cards and mugshots be projected. Kirkwood has another attempt at creating a convincing reason for Zoole's failure to bring in the cops: he calls them but gets fed up of hanging on the line and events quickly turn so that it would not be wise for him to do so. Meanwhile, Vito has a playful chat with Kate on the phone before her re-entry. Vito attempts to dial — using his nose — a friend to try to secure his rescue. (Zoole stops him.) Unwisely, Kirkwood jettisons the scene where Kate walks in to find Zoole feeding Vito a cigarette, instead relying on the intrinsic bizarreness of her stumbling upon a bound and half-naked Vito to inspire laughter. Fred — for no plausible reason and with no discernible difference to the way the drama proceeds — persuades Kate to stay a little longer to chat with Zoole and Vito.

Bogazianos, who had seen the transition from the West Coast version first hand, says of the biggest change, "I got to say for my money, I kind of liked the guys coming in. It added an element of danger, and it was funny to see Vito talk his way out of that. I was sorry to see it go. I understood why they may have wanted to get rid of them but I would have opted to keep it in. I remember a line [when] Vito is basically trying to convince these guys that Jimmy and him already have a relationship and they got no business interfering and he is trying to tell them some of the stuff they do and he talks about that they have this great thing they do with Vicks Vaporub and a cantaloupe. You could see everybody in the audience going, 'Now how would you do that, how would that be working exactly?' I thought it was funny."

Kirkwood mitigates any damage the loss of the interlopers might do to the structure (the gratitude Zoole feels toward Vito for helping him escape their clutches originally smoothed over hostility between Zoole and Vito) by lessening the tension between Zoole and his captive, Zoole immediately and completely untying Vito when Kate and Fred depart. At the conclusion of this version of the play, Zoole decides to write a book about what has happened that evening. Memories are blurred as to what the last line of this production was. Bogazianos supplied this author with three different finales, but can't recall which was ultimately chosen. In one, Zoole concludes proceedings by saying, "Vito, you must really learn to take rejection as a sign of…rejection." Another has Vito simply saying, "Good night, Jimmy," while a third features the line "Eey, my pleasure," which is, more or less, the closer of the second published version.

In the beginning, Vito's appearance is again not a surprise to the audience. At the conclusion, the audience is not rooting for Vito in his offer to help Zoole out financially (which offer is slightly changed in detail) but is instead with Zoole in wanting to get rid of this tiresomely persistent intruder. The retained latter fault means that once more we have a play without a resolution (unless Zoole's determination to start a new book counts) and certainly without the emotional impact of the ending of the novel.

"I like the opening we had in the play," says Bogazianos regarding the issue of Vito's presence being known to the audience from the get-go, "but that's self-serving because I really as an actor loved doing it. You have a darkened stage and this guy sneaks around and you don't know what's going to happen and there were a couple of funny bits of business. He opens a cookie jar thinking there's going to be money or something in it and there's a cookie in there — 'Fuckin' cookie!' If I'm not mistaken, that bit was discovered in rehearsal with Jeff Druce and Milton Katselas [on the West Coast]. Jeff did that in rehearsals and Milton liked it and Jimmy put it in." Shearin feels there was a deficiency in the play compared to the novel: "Jimmy, I don't find him all that engaging. He comes across as kind of a wiseass instead of a guy who is genuinely conflicted about things and going through some very difficult adjustments in his life and personality and lifestyle."

There were no out-of-town tryouts before the play opened at the Promenade Theatre on February 1, 1978. There is unanimity that the play went down well with the public. Bogazianos: "We just caught on. People heard about us, word-of-mouth was good and we just started drawing really big audiences to the point where they moved the production downtown." Shearin says, "I think we were all surprised at how much the audience really loved it. We thought we had a nice little show but I don't think any of us were prepared for just the guffaws and huge enjoyment that the audience evidenced. The laughs really started coming hard once Vito got strapped down to the sink and I remember standing off-stage listening and thinking, 'Damn, this is great, they're really loving this,' and I must say it gave me a lot of confidence, because when I came on the audience was so into the experience that I don't know who couldn't have gotten laughs by the time I got on. I was playing the quintessential square, straight guy. We had a great time in that scene."

Recollections differ about the reviews, "They were mixed," says Bogazianos. "They were generally good for me, really mixed on the play and generally bad for Peter...The critics were not kind to our Jimmy Zoole. Really good actor. He'd been on a soap for a while and he was looking for this to be a step away from a soap and they were pretty cruel to him. John Simon was especially cruel." Shearin's memory is, "It actually did quite well with reviews. I was very pleased." The critics, of course, could be forgiven for a slightly tart response on the grounds that it was now second time around for a play (third if you count the West Coast version) on which they had already given their verdicts. "I don't think anybody brought up San Francisco but there was a lot of mention of the play having been done before," says Bogazianos. *New York* magazine went so far as to describe the revival as "an absurd and unnecessary act."

Just as their recollections about the reviews vary, so the memories of Shearin and Bogazianos are at odds on the subject of the atmosphere in the company following their publication. Shearin: "I got the feeling that everybody, all the producers and Jimmy, were feeling very good and sort of vindicated and that this had been worth doing." Conversely, Bogazianos says of Kirkwood, "He didn't seem real pleased. I think he still was a little stung that the reviews weren't better. Because he had worked on it and he had made all those adjustments and we tried all this different stuff in rehearsal. I think he thought he had done a really good job and unfortunately that point of view wasn't shared by everybody." He adds, "He didn't seem crushed."

Regardless of who is right on this point, one review in particular was significant, that of Clive Barnes, whose comments about proselytizing for homosexuality in his 1975 *New York Times* review had seemed to engender such panic in both the producers and Kirkwood personally. Vivian Matalon, director of that '75 production, says, "I saw Clive Barnes' review of the off-Broadway production and he said that it was not as good as the Broadway production but that it was probably a play whose time had come." Barnes did indeed say, "Perhaps it is simply a play whose time has come" in his review of the revival, although also pointed out that his original notice had been favorable. Either way, times were certainly changing: 1978 saw the publication of *Faggots* by Larry Kramer. This novel depicted the bathhouse-and-poppers lifestyle of many urban homosexuals in eye-watering and unapologetic detail. It made Kramer's name and became a bestseller. Although Kramer encountered hostility from both heterosexuals (the expected bigotries) and homosexuals (the perhaps less expected resistance of gays to the idea of showing their world warts-and-all), it was unquestionably a milestone for both the gay community and gay arts. It and the works it inspired would shortly make the type of circumspection about homosexuality to be found in Kirkwood's art seem ridiculously old-fashioned.

"It would have taken a kind of fiber Jimmy didn't have," Arthur Laurents says of the idea of Kirkwood's writing ceasing to be ambivalent on sexual matters. Even had Kirkwood possessed that allegedly absent fiber, Laurents doesn't feel he would know what to do with it. "It's one thing not to say, but when you do say, you can't just say," he offers. "You have to examine the whole sociological picture. That demands a kind of seriousness he didn't have. He didn't want to take the time."

Larry Kramer and Kirkwood were actually friends. Kramer knew of and admired Kirkwood's work long before they met. "I don't think I met him until I moved out to the Hamptons myself in 1971," Kramer says. "People didn't stay out there in the winter, so the few of us who did saw each other socially. Jimmy made me dinner lots of times and I would often spend the night because he lived so far out and on the bay, which was freezing, and we cuddled to keep each other warm…We made love a bunch of times, which I remember was very, very nice, but we were never lovers more than that. As I recall, he always seemed to have a significant other." Perhaps surprisingly, Kramer fiercely resists the idea that Kirkwood's failure to be anything like as frank in his fiction as he himself was in *Faggots* shows either a failure of nerve or dishonesty. "Times were different and he was if anything ahead of the crowd," he says. "A book with a gay leading character was not likely to get published by mainstream publishers. Jimmy had to figure out a way to get into his work what was dear to him, while still attracting the mainstream audiences and publishers. That was just a fact of life. *Faggots* could not have been published then. So he was like an underground treat for those of us who loved him, his writing, his inimitable style. Even by the time of *P.S. Your Cat is Dead!* it was touch-and-go getting a show like this on [Broadway], and it was more gay than his other work." Echoing Arthur Laurents' theory, Kramer says, "Also you have to remember he grew up in Hollywood where being gay was not anything you wanted known publicly or it would ruin your career." Kramer also says, "For many young gay readers and writers he was a pioneer because you could read him and know he was gay because of the sensibility of his style, and because there would always be a gay character in it. Nothing coy about that. You didn't see any other gay writers being so courageous. Sondheim still hasn't written a gay musical and look how many years ago was *Chorus Line*. Jimmy wrote more gay stuff than Jamie Herlihy…I don't know if he ever read *Faggots,* or what he thought of it… We lost touch, sort of, when I moved back into the city and he got caught up in the huge success of *Chorus Line*. Don't know why we never saw each other in the city really, because we had enjoyed each other so much in the country. Just life, I guess, and moving on."

P.S. Your Cat is Dead! would actually run in New York for close to a year. Ironically, part of the reason for its success, according to Shearin, was that it acquired a reputation as a gay-friendly show. "We had an enormous gay constituency," he says. "The audience was, if you looked out at the house any given night, a huge percentage of youngish white males. I guess I'm making certain assumptions but I think my assumptions were pretty accurate…I think that worked well for moving it to the Village, as well."

The relocation to which he refers occurred on May 26 when the show opened at the Circle in the Square theatre downtown. Asked if there had been an ultimate objective of getting the play back on Broadway proper, Bogazianos says, "I never heard any talk about that. There may have been. I just never heard any of it…My sense of it was that it worked better off-Broadway because it was more intimate and that intimacy with the audience helped the play succeed." Kirkwood himself didn't seem bothered by non-Broadway status, stating just before the Promenade opening, "It always belonged off-Broadway."

Feeling that he had done as much as he could with his role, Shearin declined to follow the play to its new venue. Bogazianos remained. The latter would see quite a few cast changes during the run. He estimates half a dozen different actors played Jimmy Zoole. "It's just a difficult role," he says. "Just striking a balance between being this whiny loser who depends on his aunt for his livelihood and you have to be believable as a handsome leading man and you have to be very funny and pretty good at physical comedy and you have to make the transition from this uptight guy, down on his luck saying goodbye to his girlfriend to being a bisexual author. It's a big leap."

Despite the length of its run, there is perhaps a metaphor to be extracted from the fact that the play came to an end by literally being evicted from the Circle in the Square. Theatre owner Theodore Mann wanted the venue for a new show, *I'm Getting My Act Together and Taking It on the Road*. Spiegel and Haskell even went to the state Supreme Court in Manhattan to prevent the show's eviction but lost when Mann's lawyers successfully argued that the show's box-office gross over four weeks did not justify it continuing.

Bogazianos, who strangely says he was unaware of the court case, recalls, "They just put up a notice and they said we're at the end of our run. We had a good run and nobody really questioned it because it's not that usual to have an off-Broadway show run that long." Bogazianos vaguely recalls the last show as being on New Year's Eve, but he seems to be confusing that with the day on which the play itself is set. The December 5, 1978, edition of *The New York Times* which reported the outcome of the court case stated that the play would close on December 10, "after 56 previews and 300 performances." "We were still drawing big houses so I'm sure they could have kept running," says Bogazianos. Of the last performance, he says, "I remember it just being a really raucous good time. We went out with a bang and we had a full house."

Kirkwood had arguably achieved some sort of moral victory by securing a second and quite lengthy New York run and in causing Clive Barnes to (sort of) recant. However, the show had not made it back to Broadway — which eventuality, whatever his claim of it not belonging there, Kirkwood would surely have loved — and its run had ended in semi-humiliation via the eviction. The January before the opening of the new version, Kirkwood had said of *Cat*, "I think that play is my purgatory. I seem to be there forever." Many a true word said in self-deprecation, some might aver. One is tempted to pick another metaphor from the fact that Kirkwood's insistence in pushing this show at the public instead of simply moving on to a new project occasioned a falling out between him and his old friend Liz Smith. "He wanted me to come downtown and see the show," she recalls. "I said, 'No, I've already seen it, I saw it the first time and I don't have time to come see it.' He got really mad at me and so we didn't speak for a little while." Perhaps less can be read into the fact that John Simon still couldn't be persuaded of *Cat*'s merits (little has ever made Simon recant), but had Kirkwood gone through all of this for another vituperative Simon slating, this one signed off with the line, "P.S. Your play is dead"?

Having said all of the above, it should be pointed out that the *Cat* play is a surprisingly lucrative and enduring part of the Kirkwood *oeuvre*. In 1980, its author was able to marvel/brag, "It's been done in South Africa, Argentina, Madrid, Chile, Peru. It's going to open in Japan next month. It's been done in Germany, Sweden, all over the world." Something else that injects a smidgeon of irony is that despite her disdain for the warmed-over *Cat*, Liz Smith would be responsible for Kirkwood resuscitating another of his old projects.

SEVENTEEN

Though Kirkwood had become immersed in play, movie and TV projects, he had not abandoned novels, at least not technically. Yet the original vintage of the one further example of prose fiction he produced in his lifetime is betrayed by the fact that the first draft of its manuscript bears the credit "Jim Kirkwood," with "Jim" crossed through and replaced with "James," presumably following the 1963 death of his father. (That Kirkwood told "Hymie" he began the book on the 1964 South African tour is puzzling, but perhaps he meant a new draft.)

Beckenstein remembers Liz Smith as being instrumental in Kirkwood's decision in the late seventies to pull *The Angels or Whoever* out of the bottom drawer. "She strongly believed in that book," Beckenstein says of Kirkwood's rejected second novel. (Bizarrely, Smith says she can remember nothing about this.) Kirkwood's Boswell may also have played a part in the story's resurrection. William Russo confesses, "Unfortunately, I think I'm one of those who was guilty. I had said to him earlier, 'You do these wonderful first-person narrations, you may need to do a third-person narration,' and that's what *Hit Me with a Rainbow* wound up being." The sixties drafts are in the third-person, but it's possible Kirkwood was partly motivated to resurrect the book because of Russo's comments. "And that kind of objective storytelling really wasn't his strength," Russo now admits. So why encourage him to write something in the third-person? "It's like doing a change-of-pace role as an actor. To show the dimensions of his talent it was important to show some other aspects of his writing ability. So doing a third-person novel was a good idea. I'm not sure that was the one I would have picked, or the subject he could have done it on. That showed that he was interested in his literary reputation, it showed how much he wanted to please literary critics and be a legitimate figure on the American literary scene." Jerry Paonessa, meanwhile, says he takes "great pride" in having come up with the new title for *The Angels or Whoever*: "He was sitting in my office at United Artists one afternoon and I said, 'I've got it!' It was the last line of his book." Despite his pride, Paonessa admits he was never convinced of the literary merits of *Hit Me with a Rainbow*.

If Kirkwood's assumption was that in the decade-and-a-half since first writing *The Angels or Whoever* his skills had developed sufficiently for him to be able to turn the material into something substantial, his assumption was wrong, something that Paonessa apprehended when he read the new manuscript and Nick Ellison, Kirkwood's editor at publishers Delacourt, discovered to his dismay when he took receipt of it. "It was warmed-over Kirkwood," says Paonessa. "I never understood it. It didn't have that Kirkwood voice, that Kirkwood tone." Ellison was faced with a very different proposition to that of *Some Kind of Hero*, the book he had been proud to help publish at his previous place of employment, Crowell. Ellison had the dilemma of telling someone who was not just a client but a friend that substantial revision was needed. "You make the changes that can be made and you do them with rigor and you risk your friendship and you speak your mind because you're a professional and so is he," Ellison says. "You degrade yourself if you don't. There was no way you could change the fundamental nature of that hero, so I had to accept that on the one hand, and on the other hand get as many changes as I could having to do with pacing and other elements." He admits, "It was not easy because he was not lashed to the fear of destitution or poverty… He also believed in what he'd written…Remember, he was trying to do the best he could. It's not as if he made a conscious decision to write a lighter book." There was another consideration/problem that worked against fundamental improvement: "He was friends with Ross Claiborne also, who was head of Delacourt."

"I don't think I thought it was Jimmy's best but I suspect my thinking was that maybe the next one will be another *Good Times/Bad Times*," says Claiborne. "It wasn't a great book, no question about it. I was buying Jimmy." He was also buying a previously rejected novel, but wasn't informed of this. Claiborne: "I found that out later. I wasn't too pleased." Does he feel he was misled? "Well, it's happened before." However, Claiborne does point out, "I read the manuscript before we bought it. I'd never buy a book without [reading it] unless it was an extremely well-known writer [or] a three-book contract, something like that. I liked it well enough to publish it. The only thing I do remember is Jimmy almost insisted that Arthur do the jacket for the book. Neither the Art Director nor I were pleased, but I acquiesced."

Ellison says, "We hadn't paid that much money. I knew we'd make money on the book and that this was where Jimmy was in his life and it wasn't as if everybody could pop out a masterpiece every time. He still had great books in him, but he was so accustomed because of his fame and the vast amounts of money that were coming in that he could get away with being facile or a bit glib, using charm that was more style over substance.

I wanted him to get closer to the wellspring of what created *Good Times/ Bad Times*, *P.S. Your Cat is Dead!* and some scenes in *Some Kind of Hero*, but he was not capable of that at that point in his life. He'd had five years of screwing around and drinking and having fun and that's the best I could get out of him at that point. And he knew and we talked about it. It mirrored some of the softness that had occurred in his life and one too many parties. He had to get back to his roots…" Ellison's analysis is not technically undermined by the fact that he too was unaware that *Hit Me with a Rainbow* was a resuscitated old work, particularly considering his comment, "I said some of these things to him. He didn't take it so well, but he finally acknowledged it."

Beckenstein says in Kirkwood's defense, "Jimmy did go to parties and premieres, but he was in jeans and a sweatshirt every day at his typewriter. He never took a vacation. Aside from some traveling related to writing projects or lectures, I only remember one real vacation, to Africa in 1984. He partied on weekends, but he worked every day. He pushed and promoted his own projects, not waiting or relying on agents who didn't always fight as hard as he wanted them to." Jerry Paonessa, who collaborated on scripts with Kirkwood, recalls Kirkwood as a "very hard worker. My God, I never saw anybody so dedicated. He really worked us very, very hard and when we were planning on accomplishing Act One by Friday night — God damn it, we did it."

However, effort is of no worth if it is directed the wrong way. When it is considered that not only was *Hit Me with a Rainbow* essentially an old work, but that the book on which Kirkwood was working up to his death about his father also originated in the sixties, it leads one to the conclusion that post-1975 Kirkwood never really recovered his previous motivation to write novels. Alternatively, it could mean something worse: taken in conjunction with the way that he would spend much of the rest of his life revisiting and rewriting other previous works (the three productions of *P.S. Your Cat Is Dead!* being merely the start of this pattern), it might indicate an inspirational well-spring that was completely drained. Jim Piazza says, "He used to say that he loved writing novels because he had complete control and didn't have to collaborate with anyone, didn't have to rely on anyone else. He always said he was going to go back to writing a novel, but then didn't. I think he had worked through all of his ideas and didn't have any more."

Despite the fact that its gestation period had been a cumulative fifteen years or so, in an undated letter from probably late 1979, Kirkwood felt compelled to turn to James Leo Herlihy for help with finishing *Hit Me with a Rainbow*. He wrote, "I am struggling with the end of this Angel-less book and I need a page from you — from which I just might crib the whole thing or parts — about expecting miracles. Maggie, the lady, has finally decided she just will not cack [sic]. Die. Croak. She has decided she is going to expect a miracle and she has to talk for a page or so about miracles. The nature of them. The why's of them, the why-not's and the goddam fact that she is just not ready to go now. I know you can whack out a page of yummy thoughts that will inspire me. And also that I can goddam well use. That's it, baby. Do it and please have it ready by next Wednesday when I will arrive out there." (Later on in the same letter, Kirkwood says, "I'm thinking of using EXPECT A MIRACLE FOR MY TITLE. I wanted to use JUST ONE FUCKING MIRACLE, PLEASE! But they say bookstores won't stock the fucker. Shit. If you come up with a better title I'll use it, I will.") It's ironic that Kirkwood was asking Herlihy to literally write some of *Rainbow*, for it was Herlihy who had pointed out to Kirkwood that the reason *The Angels or Whoever* was rejected was probably because it lacked his distinctive personal voice. Kirkwood seems to have got the assistance he wished. In another undated letter from the same period, Kirkwood appears to be referring to *Rainbow* again when he says to Herlihy, "Here's the m.s. You'll recognize the end particularly. Tee-hee."

While *Rainbow* was wending its troubled path toward the publication schedules, Kirkwood was continuing to work on *Murder at the Vanities*, a musical on which he had embarked not long after a meeting with composer and sometime author Donald Oliver in the fall of 1979. The path of this project would be even more troubled than that of *Rainbow*.

In 1979, Oliver was conducting research at the Library of Congress for *The Greatest Revue Sketches*, published in 1982 by Avon Books. "In doing the research I read the script of a 1933/34 musical show called *Murder at the Vanities*, produced by Earl Carroll," Oliver recalls. Earl Carroll was notorious for the bawdiness of his annual Broadway Vanities productions in what were censorious times. In October 1979, Oliver went to the Library of Congress to check out copyrights and found that rights to *Murder at the Vanities* were available. The idea occurred to him to remake the 1933/34 stage show (as opposed to the 1934 movie).

Oliver is keen to point out that the reason he wanted to hire Kirkwood for the *Vanities* project was not the one that had made him so in-demand in recent years — his success with *A Chorus Line* — but because he was a fan of his previous work. He was introduced to the Kirkwood *oeuvre* in 1975 via the *P.S. Your Cat is Dead!* novel. From there he went on to consume all his other work: "I identified and empathized with his characters, with his way of writing, with his phrasing, with his breathing. I don't think I'd ever before or since been so enthralled with a writer's style. I had to know him after reading the book." Oliver found Kirkwood in the phone book. "I called Jimmy up and just said, 'I've just read your book. I thought it was absolutely fantastic,'" he recalls. The two met at the opening night of the first stage play of *Cat*, whereupon Oliver told him that *UTBU* (which he had loved) would make a great musical and suggested they collaborate on it. Oliver: "He goes, 'Okay! Let's *make* it into a musical — why not?' and that was it, just in this very outgoing, gregarious style that he had of being friendly and open to people and entertaining any wild suggestion that anybody would present."

The next time Oliver met Kirkwood, it would also lead to him proposing a joint venture in which Kirkwood would provide the libretto and he the music, but this suggestion was something more than a whim. That it resulted in something more than a half-serious display of enthusiasm from the author is quite remarkable, because come the fall of 1979 when this second meeting took place, the success of *A Chorus Line* had ensured that Kirkwood was massively in demand in this area. "I called up Jimmy after I got back from the Library of Congress and I said, 'I have an idea for a musical for you,'" says Oliver. "He said, 'Oh, everybody wants me to write musicals — what idea do you have?' Like sort of defiant, but comically defiant. That's the way Jimmy was. I said, 'Well, it's a murder mystery set backstage at the Earl Carroll Vanities in the 1930s,' and he goes, 'When can we meet?' He was instantly taken with the idea." The meeting with Kirkwood was productive in another area. Following it, Oliver came upon the "Buck and Bobby" sketch Kirkwood & Goodman had devised for the *Dance Me a Song* show and decided to use it in *The Greatest Revue Sketches*. "I was glad to put the sketch in because (a) it was still amusing, and (b) it helped fill out the book with writers who might be more familiar to 1980s readers," says Oliver.

Kirkwood began working on *Vanities* almost immediately. "It's another show-business tale, this one involving four backstage murders on opening night [at] a New York theatre during the Depression," Kirkwood would tell a journalist in 1981. "It's all show girls and glamour and lavish sets and feathers." Oliver: "I think what appealed to him is that it wasn't the same boy-meets-girl, boy-loses-girl, boy-gets-girl formulaic musical. This was something that was offbeat. *Chorus Line* was an offbeat show and he used to say that the total freshness of the concept appealed to him very much."

Oliver would collaborate with young lyricist David Spencer on the show's compositions. "I felt that we would have to do something quickly to prove to the man who wrote *Chorus Line* why David and I were the right songwriters for the show," Oliver says. "So without even the beginnings of a script we wrote a song called 'Pep Talk' (aka 'It's What She Would Have Wanted') to musicalize the beat we knew would have to be in the show no matter what the rest of the story turned out to be: the moment when the producer convinces the cast to perform despite the death of the first character, a fellow cast member." (When Oliver refers to cast, he means the cast of the Vanities show at which the murder takes place — this concept revolving around a show within a show, just like, coincidentally, *Club Mardi Gras* had.) Spencer demurs from this recollection slightly, saying, "A few songs were written before Jimmy's involvement, by way of exploring the material and having something to demonstrate what we were up to."

The other part of the creative team was director Bill Gile, who was on board before Kirkwood. Gile and Kirkwood constituted two "names," something commercially important insofar as the two composers were unknowns. Oliver: "Bill and I were very good friends. He had just been nominated for a Tony Award as Best Director of a Musical the same season as *Chorus Line* for *Very Good Eddie*." It being the case that there is not much for a director to actually physically direct at such an early stage, what was the rationale for engaging his services then? Oliver: "That time was the pinnacle of the director *auteur*. That was very much a thing to do: to have a director there to guide a show from inception to production. A director's involvement at this point in the proceedings can ensure that everyone goes in the same direction." Spencer (who says "Bill was not *officially* a part of it for one or two months") initially resisted the notion of Gile. "I hadn't liked his work," he says. Spencer also opines, "It was also too early to have had a director on board. Ideally we should have thoroughly tested out the writing collaboration first, up to and including producing a significant body of work on the piece." Any misgivings Spencer felt about Gile or the project as a whole were pushed to the side by the significant plus factors: "I was working on (I thought) a Broadway bound-show, I had adored Kirkwood's books as a teenager and college student, he and Bill Gile had credentials, Don had connections and it was all too seductive for an ambitious kid to see through."

Running parallel with the writing process was the quest to find backers for the production. "It was assumed that Jimmy and Jimmy's agent would take the lead in trying to get it produced," explains Oliver. It was a quest that would be as onerous and frustrating as the attempt to assemble a script. The two things may have been related, although for Oliver there was an additional factor involved. *Murder at the Vanities* was conceived as a return to a style of musical that had latterly been unfashionable. "This from the outset was a huge lavish ten-million dollar [show]" says Oliver. "Which at that time was just beyond the top dollar. We knew this would be [a] horrendously expensive show to produce. It had to be lavish by its standards. Now, we were just coming out of the austere era from the seventies when musicals stripped themselves down, when films stripped themselves down to two guitars and a rhythm section. Broadway at the end of the sixties, at the end of what's now called the Golden Era, was trying also to bring contemporary songs or contemporary sounds into the theatre. And shows had stripped themselves down to no scenery with minimal characters. There was a huge depression going on in New York at that time, too." Oliver feels Kirkwood had had an accidental part in beginning to reverse that depression: "*Chorus Line* was a huge influence in the renaissance of Broadway, just as *Lion King* became later on in the second wave of the area's renovation. When *Chorus Line* opened, New York was pretty awful. The Broadway area was dirty, filthy, full of sex shops and very dangerous to walk in, especially late at night when shows ended. *Chorus Line* was such a hit and brought so many people into the area that it forced the area to clean itself up." Nonetheless, the prevailing trend was not extravagance. Oliver: "When I was proposing a multi-million-dollar musical, at that time it was like: 'Whoa.'" The Shakespeare Festival had done very well out of Kirkwood and the other people who had written *A Chorus Line*. Did Oliver and Co. ever think of approaching them with *Vanities*? Oliver: "No, this was a patently commercial enterprise. *Chorus Line* was experimental. The Shakespeare Festival was doing things that were more *avant garde*-feeling…"

Despite the above, optimism and enthusiasm were in the air over the project. Because both Oliver and Spencer were not the men of means that Kirkwood and (to a lesser extent) Gile were, they had to keep up day-jobs while *Murder at the Vanities* was taking shape. Working on spec was something Oliver was happy to do because of the enormous carrot that appeared to be dangling before him. "When I first started with this, Biff Liff, Jimmy's agent at William Morris, took a meeting with me," he says. "Biff — a great man with vast experience in the theatre — said to me, 'You'll be a millionaire within a year, because this is the greatest idea for a show I've heard in years.' He was absolutely sincere. People were very excited about the idea then."

Oliver took work as a music copyist. Spencer, meanwhile, was holding down a clerical job. Even though his job was part-time, Spencer was finding that *Vanities* was requiring more attention than he could give it. "Here's where the sweetest side of Jimmy came into play," Spencer says. "Jim suggested I quit the job and he'd pay me what I had been earning. 'If we get a production, it's a loan,' he said. 'If not, all bets are off.' The money was a drop in the bucket to him, but as a gesture of faith and goodwill, it bespoke enormous generosity. In retrospect, it's a gesture I ought to have declined, because there are hierarchical strings attached to such gifts, even if they're not intended. But I must say, too, I have no memory of Jimmy specifically or implicitly ever holding it over my head. Though at some point, several months in, I began to feel very funny about the arrangement; and so in a private story meeting between the two of us, I quietly suggested to Jimmy that it was time for him to stop, that I'd be okay... Another sweet story about Jimmy: he bought us all gifts, once: expensive, clear, heavy-duty Lucite clipboards with our functions engraved in the plate, mine saying "LYRICIST"...I still have it and cherish it."

The early days of the attempts to mold the script were intensive, partly because, despite what might be assumed to be the contrary, the team was really starting from scratch. Oliver: "I had the original 1933 play script and a copy of the movie. We felt those plots were not stage-worthy in 1979/80. We jettisoned everything. One of the main reasons is that Earl Carroll didn't appear on stage in either one. He was an offstage presence. That was all okay while he was alive in 1933 and 1934, but we all believed that in 1979 to have a producer offstage and people calling him and going, 'Hey, this is what's going on, boss,' would have been cheap and not dramatic. So we made Earl Carroll the main character. He was not only the producer, blending fact and fiction, but he would also have to function as the detective; he would have to solve the problem at his own show." Spencer: "Earl Carroll was a dynamic figure to contemplate and it was terrific to think of him with all his other responsibilities having to become a detective too. And we were trying for a kind of hybrid, to overlay a contemporary sensibility upon a period novelty." The team also to some degree drew upon *The Body Merchant*, a 1976 biography of Earl Carroll by entertainer Ken Murray, who had once been a Vanities comic. Spencer: "It's a book you need to take with a grain of salt. In doing research, Don interviewed Murray and asked him about portions of the book which seemed uncorroborated elsewhere. According to Don, Murray cheerfully admitted that if he hadn't known something, he just made it up."

At one of their "many, many, many meetings" (Oliver), Kirkwood introduced the team to the what-if concept that had stood him and his collaborators in such good stead on *A Chorus Line*. "We operated in an enormously important milieu which is a No Shame Environment," explains Oliver. "Anybody could propose anything. If it's a great idea, you talk about it. If it's a sucky idea then you throw it out, but you don't feel the person speaking is an idiot because he proposed something that's not workable. Ideas beget other ideas. You know: 'What if the murderer was an alien from outer space?' If somebody proposed something that idiotic, you say, 'No,' but then, 'Oh, you know what — but maybe it's a foreigner,' and you go from there." When it is suggested that it sounds like he and Spencer were contributing just as much to the plot development as Kirkwood, Oliver says, "Without question."

Gile remembers the creative meetings as merry affairs. "When one of us came up with something [that] was really terrific, it was: 'I knew that, that was my idea first, I was just waiting for somebody else to-' and it was a joke. I don't ever remember not having a wonderful time at these meetings. Yes, they were very strong, very tough and all that, but we just had a wonderful time." Oliver recalls the "happy, funny, laughing" atmosphere being partly due to the pleasure he took in the company of the man of whom he had once been merely a fan but who was now a friend: "I loved Jimmy to death. I would walk through fire for him. I miss him to this day as a friend. He was a great person."

Following its unusually intensive editing/rewriting, *Hit Me with a Rainbow* reached the stores in March 1980. The book is dedicated to "Peggy Hillmer with love," Peggy Tufford's new married name. (The protagonist is also revealed to have an Aunt Peg.) Kirkwood explained of the title, "It means hit me with some of the goodies of life. We all know that we're going to get the bad news under the door, so hit me with a rainbow." Kirkwood was subsequently tickled when by coincidence a *Hagar the Horrible* comic strip depicted the titular Viking helping his dazed, hapless sidekick Eddie off the ground and marveling, "I never heard of anyone being hit by a rainbow!!" At one point, Kirkwood used this strip as a letterhead.

"That was terrible," says Bill Gile of the book. "It was awful." That someone who says of Kirkwood that he was "a wonderful person" and who cries when he speaks of him, can be so scathing about *Rainbow* is a measure of just how bad the novel is and what a fall from Kirkwood's previous heights it constituted.

The novel actually gets off to a good start. There is a familiar enjoyable playful Kirkwoodian tone in the opening pages, which focus on Kelly McDermott and his application for promotion in the publishing house at which he is an editor. There is even a passage or two of strikingly good writing, although there are early warning signs of what is to come via some notably bad dialogue: McDermott's would-be girlfriend says to him, "Some nights when we'd have a couple of drinks or a smoke, you'd get that delicate one inch off the ground and I'd see something bubbling up in you, right back there behind your eyes and I'd think: tonight he might just explode in a shower of words. But it never happened…" The suspicion that this indicates an author who now operates in such a rarefied atmosphere that he has lost touch with the way ordinary people speak is proven erroneous by that florid speech's presence in sixties drafts of *The Angels or Whoever*. This type of preposterously eloquent dialogue occurs again and again during the book. As does an obsession with luxury, Kirkwood taking inordinate length to describe vistas of plushness. (McDermott is Kirkwood's first protagonist who is truly well-off from the get-go.) Another motif is slightly cartoonish behavior such as the Tom & Jerry-esque passage in chapter six wherein a female secretary jumps up on a chair when McDermott says there are mice in the office.

Above all, what keeps cropping up is evidence of Kirkwood's unfamiliarity with writing in the third-person. Speaking at the time of the book's release, he said, "It's the first time I've attempted to write in the third person. It was difficult but I tried to do it in the close third person, so I had that compulsion of telling a story, because I think if I'm anything as a novelist I'm a storyteller." He fails in that stated objective. As with many novels written in the he-did-this, he-did-that style, the point-of-view switches between characters. However, Kirkwood allows the switches to become lurches, him sometimes disorientatingly going back and forth between characters in the same paragraph. On occasion one is not even sure who is telling the story or making a particular observation. Due to these shifting — and uncertain — points of view, the "voice" that gave such strength to his previous works is absent.

McDermott is a man who is incapable of having sexual intercourse due to some hinted-at but initially unspecified childhood trauma. The same trauma is the root cause of his stutter. Personal frustrations are added to by professional ones when McDermott quits his job after his desired promotion goes — he feels unfairly — to another worker. He subsequently visits a nightclub where to his amazement he is picked up by the famous actress (retired) Maggie Banner, a woman who is considerably older than his 27 years. Outside the nightclub, he gets into an altercation with Banner's childish lover, the former opera star Raffaello Tucci, after he accidentally knocks him to the ground. He is whisked away by Banner who, knowing of Raffaello's insane jealousy and his Mafia family, fears for his safety. From there, a chase across the country ensues, with the pair — accompanied by Banner's wiseacre bodyguard Stosh and Amazonian nurse Flora — trying to lay low from Raffaello, who is determined to get Banner back whether Banner is willing or not. There is a lot of hurly-burly — and Banner's entourage makes for something of a potentially intriguing madhouse — but it all feels like much ado about nothing. Additionally, we don't care about the characters. With his spiteful observations, including derogatory comments and thoughts about people's appearances, McDermott is considerably less likable than Kirkwood's previous protagonists. The author is clearly enamored of Maggie Banner, but most readers don't share his background and therefore his soft spot for eccentric, matriarchal movie stars. (As well as Muriel Bentley and Ava Gardner as previously mentioned, another candidate for the person on whom Banner is based is Tallulah Bankhead, who at one point Banner reminds McDermott of.) Raffaello (to whose point of view we are also treated) is a brute, even if his erratic temperament causes spasms of shame at his own behavior. Banner, Flora and Stosh are also tiresome in their endless sniggering about sex.

Any drama is undermined by ridiculous plot developments (at one point Banner disguises herself as a frumpish secretary to gauge McDermott's real feelings about his situation), the implausibly "literary" quality of the characters' speech and internal dialogue (Banner says to McDermott in a line even Barbara Cartland might have been too embarrassed to publish, "…by the time he undressed, desire had completely dissolved my virgin fears"), the utterly uninvolving nature of what they do and where they go (we are supposed to be impressed by the alternate gaudiness and poverty of Mexico, but the travelogue is boring) and the endlessly jarring switches of points of view without even the courtesy of a paragraph break.

During their travels, McDermott reveals (in the ornate dialogue that afflicts the book so much) to an attentive (actually, gossip-hungry) Banner the source of his sexual inadequacy: the fact that he killed his very pious but secretly sexually depraved father. To have had any hope of interesting the reader, Kirkwood should, rather than have McDermott recount these events to Banner, have presented them as flashbacks intercut with present-day conversation. Or else just wrote halfway believable dialogue. It's astonishing that the feel for the colloquial that has hitherto been one of Kirkwood's chief strengths is not just rarely discerned but has been replaced by something so diametrically opposed in quality. Only Stosh's dialogue rings in any way true.

There is the usual combination of frankness and denial about Kirkwood's sexuality. McDermott had "tried men. A man. Why not?" He had allowed himself to be picked up at the YMCA by "Gary" but does not experience a "really serious twinge…" This just seems another way by which Kirkwood can slip in some homosexuality, but keep his character unsullied by it. There is more trail-leaving in the form of the character of Stosh. The latter is reminiscent of Vito from *P.S. Your Cat is Dead!* on several counts: he talks in a New York vernacular (although is Polish where Vito was Italian), has aspirations in the stand-up comedy field, is a mixture of unworldly and streetwise and is bisexual. There is an interesting passage where McDermott observes that Banner seems *au fait* with Stosh's sexual tastes: "He was made uncomfortable by Maggie's open discussion of Stosh's proclivities. It made her too coolly wise, too knowing. It was slightly off-putting." Once again, Kirkwood's own terror of his true sexuality being known by the wider world seems to be surfacing. The book's sex scenes, incidentally (all hetero), are atrocious. McDermott becomes potent when he discovers that Banner is dying of an incurable disease and her fear and vulnerability turn him on. Leaving aside the vaguely disturbing cause of his tumescence, what follows is a you-wish scene where McDermott quickly climaxes and is then straightway able to produce another erection as though he is Superman or a time traveler who has picked up some supplies of the not-yet-invented Viagra. Meanwhile, a seven-page section of chapter 35 in which Banner and McDermott enjoy congress half-submerged in water is quite possibly the most mind-numbingly boring sex scene ever written. It is compounded by following shortly after a passage which could well win a competition to find literature's most ludicrous dialogue. Banner asks McDermott how much he loves her:

> *"Enough to black out all of Rhode Island and — start World War Five!"*
> *"Come now," she said, "let's keep a tight head on reality here!"*
> *"I swear it, may Mickey Mouse drop dead on his fifty-first birthday."*
> *"Then, for God's sake, take a shower with me!"*

The novel's climax constitutes a scene in which Raffaello catches up with the runaway quartet and makes a half-hearted and drunken attempt to shoot Banner and McDermott with a rifle, before realizing in a flash of understanding (and indeed a flash of good writing) what an unkempt loser he has descended into and fleeing.

Typical of its overall maladroit writing, the book ends on a line that doesn't seem to make sense. Marveling at the love she and McDermott have found, Banner says, "…everything else is pure…rainbows and hot fudge sundaes.…Nevertheless, Lord — hit me with a rainbow."

Notwithstanding its actual, original vintage, it is highly appropriate that *Hit Me with a Rainbow* appeared in 1980. The book is as glitzy, mindless and empty as were the eighties. One of the few autobiographical touches is when McDermott thinks to himself of his problematic life, "You keep your sense of humor finely honed; you live off it, because if you don't have humor, you don't have a chance." Though Kirkwood had written compellingly before on subjects of which he cannot have had first-hand knowledge, one does wonder whether the fact that this is the first Kirkwood novel not rooted to a large extent in autobiography accounts for its shallowness and unconvincing nature. Though *Pony!* and *Hero* have their *longueurs*, *Rainbow* is the first Kirkwood book that you really have to force yourself to read. It is simply groan-inducingly lackluster. Its tediousness and spectacularly bad writing become even more astonishing in light of Nick Ellison's demands for editing: it is incredible that this is a several-times revised and therefore *improved* book.

"I think he was disappointed in the reception of that book," says Homer Price, "because he thought it was a very good book. I didn't particularly like it." Beckenstein: "I don't think he thought it was his greatest work, but he liked it. It was one of his children." Yet his remark to Andrew Morse upon presenting him with a copy indicates that Kirkwood was probably aware of its shortcomings. "He told me before he even gave it to me that I wasn't going to like it," recalls Morse. "He said, 'It's different than everything else.'" Morse, in fact, did not like it and gave Kirkwood some notes as to why he was disappointed: "I wrote, 'Third-person, triteness, campiness, monologues.'" Kirkwood then wrote an amused inscription in Morse's copy of the book: "To Andrew, without whose aid, help, support and inspiration this book could never have been written."

A review of *Rainbow* in the *Los Angeles Times* summed up the general disappointment, and this despite being far too kind. "James Kirkwood… has made a literary career out of placing kooky but benign characters in outlandish but ultimately believable situations," wrote Miles Beller. "Past Kirkwood efforts like *P.S. Your Cat Is Dead* and *There Must Be a Pony!* did possess offbeat charm, peopled by off center characters negotiating their way through bizarre circumstances. *Hit Me with a Rainbow*, however, suggests the writer has relied too heavily on his stock-in-trade, producing a stilted and contrived work…*Rainbow* is not without merit — there are patches of clever dialogue and one or two engaging plot twists — but the book is too artificial to evoke any heartfelt responses." It may even have been a blessing that *Rainbow* — despite the fact that Kirkwood's name was now far bigger than when he had last published a novel — did not garner a review in *The New York Times*. David Spencer feels Kirkwood's false obituary prank of '75 had backfired on him: "Don and I were convinced it was why the *Times* completely ignored *Hit Me with a Rainbow* when it was published."

Asked if he got the feeling that Kirkwood genuinely thought that *Hit Me with a Rainbow* was a worthwhile book, William Russo says, "I certainly didn't hear him run down any of his own works. I think he thought it was going to be a very interesting commercial book, I think he thought it would be sold to the movies, that there were a number of older actresses who'd probably want to do it. He always had that kind of commercial appeal. You mention the obsession on age — I think his other obsession was making money. He was not averse to having a popular hit and doing well. That, too, I think worked against him in academic circles."

Whether or not Kirkwood believed in *Rainbow*, he was certainly happy to hawk it. Russo accompanied the author on a publicity tour for the book — one of only two occasions on which he met the man with whom he prodigiously corresponded — and was impressed by his slickness, and would become increasingly so as he learned more about his upbringing. "One would think that there would be all kinds of socialization problems," he says, "but he was very down-to-earth and I was amazed observing him at how he handled people. Maybe it was part of his performing background, but he was so socially adept, he instantly put people at ease. He was marvelous, he was amusing and I could see why people just thought the world of him." On his publicity tour, Kirkwood was just as disingenuous with the media about the book's vintage as he had been with his publisher, coming out in interviews with lines like, "I've never really written a love story. It's something very new as far as my writing."

The book did have some fans, even if they seemed restricted to — *quelle surprise* — older female movie stars. Marlene Dietrich sent a handwritten letter from her Paris home reading,

> *Dear Sir,*
> *Thanks a million for writing the 'Rainbow.' If you could send me Stosh it would make me happy. I really cried laughing — a rare event in this lousy world.*
> *Love + kisses.*

Though he had never met the now 78-year-old contemporary of his mother, Kirkwood replied to her, and not simply because he did to all of his fan letters. That the actress' name had a *cachet* for him was revealed as far back as his 1968 *Esquire* article on Clay Shaw when he said, *vis a vis* Herlihy's invitation to dinner, "I'd even said to a weekend guest and old friend, author James Leo Herlihy, that I wouldn't come into town if Marlene Dietrich asked me to an intimate supper for G. Garbo — with De Gaulle serving." "Jim corresponded with her for a while after that," Beckenstein says of Dietrich and her fan letter. "He wanted to go and see her but she was being a recluse and was seeing no one."

The other notable fan of an ostensibly friendless book was actress Natalie Wood, who optioned it for the screen. "She wanted to start playing older women," reveals Paonessa. "I worked extensively with Natalie Wood on that. Jimmy started writing the script and we got to a certain point where it just wasn't working and then we switched the option from *Hit Me with a Rainbow* to *There Must Be a Pony!*" Benjamin Morrison reveals, "One of the things Jim told me was that if I wrote a book, the most important thing I could do was sell it to the movies. Natalie Wood had the option for *Hit Me with a Rainbow* for more than a year and Jim told me that the Wagners [Wood was married to actor Robert Wagner] got in touch with him at some point asking if they could have the option on it for another year, but would it be okay with him if they didn't pay him anything for that 'cause times were tight and they were having a hard time and his answer was no, that he would not agree to do that."

It may have been the interest from Wood that led Donald Oliver and David Spencer to write what Oliver describes as a "bright, bouncy and rhythmic" theme song for *Hit Me with a Rainbow*." Spencer: "I think some movie guys were looking at the book and we were hoping to write the movie song, which Jimmy would have played for them in due course. The song was specifically drawn from events in the book, but did not refer to those events specifically, so it could function as a stand-alone pop song. As I recall it was pretty good." Oliver remembers them writing the song, "As a present for the publication." He adds, "I can't say that I pushed terribly hard to get it released, but we were joking at the time that it was the best song that Jack Jones never recorded and I got it to him and he wasn't interested in it and I didn't pursue it beyond that."

Natalie Wood was killed in a boating accident in November 1981. Paonessa: "Jimmy and I were both freaked out. I would have her over at our house every Wednesday and in the middle of this she died. It was

[a] very, very difficult thing to get through." Particularly for Kirkwood, for whom death was such a frequent visitor. Or does that make it easier?

Though Kirkwood would live another nine years after its publication, *Hit Me with a Rainbow* was the last book he would see published. "After *Hit Me with a Rainbow*, there was never talk about another book," says Gile. He offers a reason for this: "Writing a novel is a very, very lonely experience. If he was working on theatre things, it was always in collaboration. He loved the collaboration, he loved being able to have a social connection, whether it was giving a dinner after a work session or going out after a work session. He was an incredible social animal."

Not only does this theory chime with Kirkwood's comments about his love of the camaraderie of the theatre experience mentioned previously, but it is given credence by the fact that at this juncture Kirkwood began looking once again for work in the profession that he had previously given the impression of partially despising: acting. It was in 1980 that Kirkwood performed a bit part (as himself) in *Oh God! Part II*, the sequel to the movie in which George Burns played the great creator. He appeared in a cameo as a master of ceremonies in the Joan Crawford biopic *Mommie Dearest* (1981). In a 1984 interview, Kirkwood said, "I do about ten or twelve university lectures a year and that's a lot like performing…What I really liked about the profession was the camaraderie it involved. You really have to be alone to write, without distractions. But I think my gregarious side is ready to be aired." His signing with an acting agency in around 1984 may be what led to his somewhat meatier role as a Civil War captain in the horror flick *The Supernaturals* (1986). More than two decades after his previous appearance in *Divorce Court*, Kirkwood turned up on the show again, which was now in color. He played a waspish writer named Terrence Mack, a witness for the male half of the divorcing couple. He also hosted a pilot for the Showtime network. *Broadway Beat* was a putative magazine program about the Great White Way. "Jim Kirkwood" (as the announcer bills him) is quite good, certainly photogenic and confident, if a little intense and sometimes naïve with some of his hand movements. He began distributing résumés that focused not on his writing credits, but his acting history. "Jimmy would put his résumé in a butcher shop window," says Paonessa, laughing. "Again, it's 'more.' That's all he wanted was more. He was sort of crazy but we loved him." In one of said résumés (dating from after *The Supernaturals*), Kirkwood baldly stated of himself, "He misses acting. He would probably accept almost any reasonable acting job offered, short of understudying the German shepherd. If interested, please contact him immediately." He probably wasn't joking. The generic title of *The Supernaturals* says a lot about this slow-moving, clumsily directed and completely unmenacing horror variant of *Southern Comfort*, while *Mommie Dearest* is universally recognized as an all-time low in cinema history.

The George A Romero movie *Monkey Shines* (1988) carries a thank you to Kirkwood in its end credits. Explains Paonessa, who produced it, "He had a nice part at the beginning. A very short part, but it was like his trademark. He always wanted to be in a movie, any movie…Because of time, we had to cut him out…and I forgot to tell him. Oh, he was so furious he didn't talk to me for three weeks."

Mommie Dearest, incidentally, was a film for which Kirkwood had been asked to write the script. He had some firm ideas about how the movie should proceed. Rather than focus on the grievances of Crawford's unloved children as the book it was based upon did, he felt it should be "a picture about a compulsive woman in a compulsive business…I would have opened the picture on the day she left MGM. She packed her station wagon, cleaned out her dressing room and just left, all by herself. No goodbye lunch, no nothing. Just a lonely middle-aged woman who had once been the queen of the lot driving out alone, being treated as a has-been." In the end, Kirkwood turned the scriptwriting offer down. "I backed out because it was just too much work," he later explained. "I would have had to research a lot of things, which I loathe, and then on top of that I found out that [Crawford's daughter] Christina Crawford and her husband are coproducing the picture and that made me very leery." As for his acting role in this picture, Benjamin Morrison offers, "Jim was a ham. It would have been said as a self-deprecating joke at the time, but he really did tell me that when he turned down doing the script for *Mommie Dearest*, [he asked] 'Could you find a role for me?' And then they were sort of cornered into coming up with something that he could do. He was a ham and he admitted to being a ham."

One really doesn't want to belabor the point about Kirkwood's declining productivity in the field of novel writing, but that he would return to acting in preference to making certain that his "daddy book" would see publication before his life was out really is extraordinary. Comments that he made about it publicly indicate that Kirkwood felt it was almost an obligation to his father's memory to write a bookend to what might be termed his "mama book," *There Must Be a Pony!* As he himself would publicly and privately admit, his novel about his father was psychologically rather awkward for Kirkwood. One wonders whether all of this non-writing activity was, even if partially and subliminally, a way of taking refuge from that obligation.

EIGHTEEN

In May 1980, Kirkwood and Beckenstein embarked on a trans-Atlantic crossing on the *SS Norway*.

Kirkwood was once again engaged in lecturing work. During the trip, Joan Thompson looked up her sibling. Recalls Beckenstein, "Suddenly there was this call from a half-sister I'd never heard of who was in trouble and needed money. I wondered how she found him. It was bizarre." Perhaps more bizarre is that Kirkwood had never mentioned his half-sister to the man with whom he'd been sharing his life for a dozen years.

By David Spencer's estimation, it was probably in May 1980 that the work weekends at Kirkwood's East Hampton house that would be a feature of the *Vanities* creative process started. "He was possibly the most wonderful host one could ever imagine," says Bill Gile. "Everyone had their own room, there was a house boy and while I was there he made sure that I had a car of my own. He was absolutely fabulous. He told this about himself: Jimmy would talk to the wall if it had an ear painted on it. He was filled with wonderful stories and he told them beautifully…I would bring chicks there and the people had no business being there, but I would bring 'em because I knew that I was going to be there for a weekend without a fuck-buddy. Jimmy would be annoyed with me and he would glare at me, but he was unbelievably kind to these men I would bring."

At this stage in his life, Kirkwood was able to afford to be a compassionate and gracious host. Though always generous previously with his time and attention, the psychological legacy of his financially insecure childhood had hitherto ensured a certain reputation for miserliness. "Before that he was very tight with a dollar and that's because our father didn't have shit," recalls his brother. "He had social security and that was about it. Lee Goodman said that to me once: he's so tight, he squeaks when he walks." Kirkwood could make an exception, even pre-*A Chorus Line*, for family. He loaned money to his half-brother to buy a house when he was getting married for the second time. T. Michael Kirkwood: "He loaned me a couple of thousand dollars and as soon as we got the house and got our money straightened out, I paid him back and he sent the check back and said, 'Thank you very much for paying me back' and he made some smart crack like, 'I don't take money from my younger brother.'

He was generous in that way." Some people spoken to for this book suggest that Joan tapped Kirkwood for money too many times and that Kirkwood eventually tired of this, but his sister doesn't betray a memory in that direction. Asked if she felt Kirkwood was there for her if she needed financial assistance, she says, "Oh yes, definitely...I asked him for money I think twice. Not a huge amount. It was instant." Though Kirkwood refused to finance his brother's onetime ambitions to follow him and their father into the acting profession, T. Michael thinks the reasons are not related to meanness. Recalls their mutual half-sister, "Jimmy told me once that Terry, as he was then, was disappointed because Jimmy didn't try to do more for him as far as getting him into show business. Said he waited too long — I think he was nearly thirty then — and apparently Jimmy felt that's something you need to see to when you're very young." "He said, 'You're not serious enough about it,'" offers T. Michael. "I didn't understand it at the time but I do understand it [now]. You've got to be able to sleep in your car if need be and I wasn't willing to do that." Eventually, with offspring to support through college, T. Michael abandoned his thespian ambitions and moved into theatre management.

Kirkwood's wallet loosened as *A Chorus Line* poured forth its torrential revenue stream. Bill Gile avows, "He'd pick up the tab, again and again. You would have to slap it out of his hand. He literally fought you for the ticket or he would pay before you got in. If you would try to pay, they would say, 'It's paid.'" Beckenstein recalls, "After *A Chorus Line*, he was extremely generous with people, always grabbing the check. And people took advantage of his generosity. That was fine, but it really bugged me when people didn't offer to pay their way."

Yet the fact that a skinflint streak remained is hinted at by the fact that when asked if his brother changed after *A Chorus Line*'s success, T. Michael gives the somewhat ambivalent answer, "Well, maybe to some extent." It's also illustrated by other behavior of Kirkwood's. "He gave Ron, Lee and myself Cartier Tank watches," Beckenstein recalls. "I wore my new watch on our voyage on the *Norway*. I never said anything about the watch to anyone, but the wife of the entertainment director noticed it the first night and made a big fuss about it, saying she always wanted a Cartier Tank watch. When we got back to New York, my watch stopped working a week later. I took it to a watch [repairer] and the jeweler looked at me, smirked and said the watch was worth five dollars, not worth fixing." Beckenstein puts up a defense for Kirkwood: "Jimmy never pretended to buy it from Cartier, and at least I enjoyed it for our trip." Jim Piazza — who knew him intimately from 1983 onwards — says Kirkwood refused to shell out the modest amount required to replace his tennis shoes, with dire consequences. "He wore these awful cheap tennis shoes and they were going to ruin, they were just like sneakers," Piazza says. "His feet were horrible, they were just destroyed. He had dead nails." Kirkwood was also averse to the extra cost that went with brand names. "Jimmy was a very heavy drinker, a lot of vodka," says Piazza, "and he used to get the worst, cheapest vodka. I said, 'Jimmy, would you please get a bottle of Absolut, this is ridiculous.' So he'd get a bottle of Absolut for us, but for company out came the cheap stuff. He just couldn't do it." Piazza adds, "If there was free champagne despite his gout, he would show up, and he would say, 'Is this all they have?' Then he'd get sick the next day, but he would drink it because it was free. He loved a free party. In fact, friends used to yell at him because he didn't reciprocate." Piazza also says, "He was a kleptomaniac. He was always stealing stuff…I remember once he was telling me he was supposed to be interviewed on a radio show. I think it was Jack O'Brien's show, and they had him in the waiting room too long for his liking and he decided to just walk out, but he couldn't just walk out, he had to take something. So he took the big glass ashtray that was on the waiting room table…I have lost a pair of shoes, a bathing suit. My friend's pen went back and forth. He would steal it from him and I would steal it back from Jimmy and give it back to him, Jimmy would steal it the next time he was there. He had to *have*."

Quite the most bizarre manifestation of Kirkwood's intermittent stinginess came in the last couple of years of his life, by which point he and Piazza were lovers. (Piazza: "Lover days for sure. Friendship only goes so far!") "Jimmy had read an ad for this masturbation machine that had all sorts of speeds and vibrating calibrations," says Piazza. "You turned it on, stuck your dick in the leather-padded opening and chose from among at least a dozen stimulations. So it finally arrives at the Hamptons house. And Jimmy being Jimmy couldn't buy a new one, no. He had friends in LA who 'owed him' (whatever that meant) and they were repaying him with a free machine. Like new, they said. Okay, so trouble all ready, I can smell it. So it's mid-afternoon and Jimmy can't wait to try it and he insists I help him out with this. His eyesight isn't great and he can't see all the buttons so — okay, sure I'll help. He drops his drawers, gets lubed up and I turn on the machine which doesn't seem to be doing much but displaying a red light. I flip all the switches and [there's] a little sound here and there. Jimmy works himself up to an erection and gets himself lodged in the opening — an awkward position at best. But we've had a cocktail or two so we're dealing with it. And he starts yelling, 'I don't feel anything! Put it on high!' So I'm desperately hitting all the buttons. And nothing. Finally, I smell smoke and sure enough puffs of smoke billow out the back of this damn thing. Sounds like burning wire from the engine. And the machine is getting hotter and Jimmy's dick is stuck in the hole! He's screaming now and I can't stop laughing, which only pisses him off. But I don't know what to do and I run over and unplug the thing from the wall. Jimmy finally pulls his dick out and that was the end of that little experiment. I think he may have given his gift-givers a piece of his mind. Put into the closet, never to be tried again."

As T. Michael mentions, part of the reason for this dichotomy in Kirkwood's behavior would seem to be the terror that he would lose his fortune the way that his father — as rich in his heyday as his son was now — had done. Speaking in 1982, Kirkwood told *The New York Times* that he had a terrible fear "that I'll end up without money, that the bank will fail, and I'll start sneaking into cafeterias and eating a full meal and giving the cashier a check for a piece of pie and a glass of milk." Piazza offers, "Jimmy, like so many suddenly rich people, was ever insecure about money. Having gone hungry as a kid, he always feared that might happen again. He once told me the story of his agent informing him that he'd made so much he never had to work again. Those words somehow sparked utter panic." Benjamin Morrison recalls, "We once had an interesting conversation about if either one of us ever gets rich what will we do, 'cause at that point I was talking about becoming a writer as opposed to newspaper man. He told all about how he would hire a yacht and fly everyone he knew to Greece and put them on the yacht and have an ongoing sort of gala party for a week or a month or something. The money was going to be spent in a grand fashion." Such dreams of largesse were replaced, Morrison feels, by something of a paranoia once Kirkwood did indeed get rich. He says, "Jim became increasingly withdrawn after the success of *Chorus Line*." Morrison recalls an incident from within a year of the 1985 death of Kirkwood's Aunt Peg when he called him in Key West. "I'd had the number forever and I was going to try to get together with him," he says. "The phone was answered and I heard [adopts fragile, feminine voice], 'Hellooo? Who? You wanna speak to who? Who is this?' Well, he was trying to do an imitation of his dead aunt's voice to try to add one more degree of separation for whoever the motherfucker was who was going to be on the other end of the telephone that he didn't want to talk to. And I said, 'Jim, I think you're trying to be your aunt and, maybe nobody told you, but she died.' He had trust issues with people. I think this is something tied to cocaine…Going to see him in Key West, he had a very small circle of people that he saw or had anything to do with. My first assumption was that he thought he was going to be exploited in some way, shape or form, by virtually anybody else. My guess is that I would not have been allowed into any of that at all, virtually speaking, if I hadn't been this sort of longtime friend who went back to salad days before there was success…He did not get the results he had, I think, fully expected from having somewhere between fame and recognition and a solid amount of money coming in." Morrison offers an additional possible reason for Kirkwood's alternating generosity and meanness. "I had an interesting conversation with Jed Mattes," he reveals, referring to one of Kirkwood's agents. "Jed said, 'Well, *Chorus Line* is a hard show to do and takes really serious talent and a hell of a lot of money. So it's not like Rodgers and Hammerstein writing *Oklahoma!*, which every high school in the universe can put on.' Jim did not have much of the sense that the money was going to always be there."

There was, of course, an upside to Kirkwood's carefulness with money: security. "Nick Dante ended up dying broke," says Piazza. "Jimmy said he spent all of his money on boys and drugs. When you're poor and you start getting checks for $5,000 a week, you don't think in terms of taxes, you don't think in terms of anything, you think, 'Oh, I'm rich.' Jimmy had luckily found his lawyer at the time who kind of put him on a short leash and put money away."

While Kirkwood and his colleagues were trying to get *Murder at the Vanities* into presentable shape, *A Chorus Line* was continuing to enthrall both Broadway crowds and audiences at the various productions now fanning out across the globe. In March 1981, Kirkwood even saw a condensed performance of *A Chorus Line* at the White House.

It was around this time that Kirkwood exhibited more private ambivalence about that show's success and its role in his career. Recalls Richard Seff, "A friend of mine, Jason Darrow, was on *The Merv Griffin Show* one day, and Jim Kirkwood was the other guest. They were talking in the Green Room at length before they got [on] the air. Jimmy was saying to him, 'Here I am on talk shows about a thing I spent three weeks [sic] of my life on.' Somehow that bothered him that he wasn't recognized as a writer. That struck me as odd. It didn't satisfy him." The other side of the coin was an outrageous exultation in the show's success. Recalls Arthur Laurents of Kirkwood's house, "The shower curtains had *Chorus Line*. It was almost a joke." Though it was Beckenstein who was responsible for this ("I was proud of seeing all these *Chorus Line* merchandising items in Bloomingdales after the show opened and couldn't wait to buy them. There were glasses and a tray too, along with beach towels"), Kirkwood clearly didn't blanch at Beckenstein's purchases. Additionally, he used an *A Chorus Line* letterhead on his correspondence for a period.

The summer of 1981 saw Kirkwood taking another acting role, although this was due more to necessity than his awakened interest in matters thespian. He appeared in *Surprise!*, his own one-act play staged at East Hampton's John Drew Theatre in celebration of the 50th anniversary of the East Hampton Cultural Center Guild Hall, in which the John Drew Theatre was located. The play was directed by Bill Gile. Gile explains that the project was "…a proposal by the man who was the then-producer named Tony Stimac. He put together the idea that they would do three one-act plays, focusing on people who lived in the community." The three plays — all given a two-week run — were *Surprise!*, starring Dina Merrill and (it was intended) Cliff Robertson, *The VIPs* written by Cliff Robertson and also starring Robertson and Merrill, and *A Need for Brussel Sprouts* written by Murray Schisgal and starring Anne Jackson and Eli Wallach. Gile: "Everybody had a house there. It was a community project that was to grow out of the community, but hopefully go on to become a Broadway show: three different authors, three different small casts. I used to joke about it because working there, you go to the parking lot and everybody had a Mercedes, every single one of the actors or anybody working on it. Eli Wallach and Anne Jackson's play did actually make it to Broadway. With any three plays you are only as good as the weakest link and which show was going to be the weakest link was always scary and it depended who you talked to which was the weakest link. Jimmy's was the first out of the shoot. His show always was well-received. It was a wonderful time. I remember it was a very happy time which is unusual in theatre, very unusual that the creative process is happy. It's happy but seldom without explosions…[Though Kirkwood] knew how he wanted it to be, he was not averse to changing anything if I asked. He was incredibly professional."

Surprise! is a play about a husband and wife who are drifting apart, but are perversely reunited when the wife's lover dies on top of her. Kirkwood took the husband role when Merrill's then-spouse Cliff Robertson begged off. How good an actor was Kirkwood in *Surprise!*? Gile: "He was fine. He was incredibly forceful, strong, on stage." In order to devote himself properly to *Surprise!*, Kirkwood had to give up a cameo he had negotiated in the movie of *Some Kind of Hero*, filming on which had finally begun. Gile considers this to his credit: "Dina was upset because we weren't getting much rehearsed and so he came back to the Hamptons. He was just wonderful."

Kirkwood may have been wonderful but the play was not. Jim and Fran are the married couple. The former brings home a man after — we learn — discovering a diary that details her husband's unfaithfulness. Her revenge one-night stand dies after she has achieved three orgasms — and he five. Shortly after Fran realizes the man — whose name she has not quite got round to finding out — has expired, her husband arrives home. Partly because she is so flustered, she blurts out that she has found the diary pages. Jim tells her he has broken up with his mistress, although rather than guilt his motivation seems to be the fact that he has been told he has a good chance of becoming a congressman. A couple of friends of theirs unexpectedly arrive to wish them a happy anniversary and they frantically try to think of ways to hide the body. Both this and their previous heart-to-heart engender a certain feeling of solidarity that has not characterized their marriage for a long time. The play closes with a slammed door causing the body to tumble from its hiding place.

It would be unfair to complain too much about a one-act play being shallow and unsatisfying. However, one can't help but conclude that *Surprise!* would feel insubstantial even if it were to last for hours. Spoiled people with bourgeois problems and grievances might conceivably make for powerful reading in the context of a novel in which an author can go into sufficient depth to make them sympathetic (although Kirkwood didn't make too good a fist of relationship-oriented subject matter in *Some Kind of Hero*), but in this context we are left with something of negligible emotional impact. As ever with Kirkwood's theatre work, there are at least a couple of snort-inducing one-liners, but is that the sum-total of achievement he anticipated at the beginning of the months of work that presumably went into it? Meanwhile, *Surprise!* hardly indicates a writer brimming with new ideas: its line "It still amazes me we get up in the morning, brush our teeth and dress ourselves without running around naked sniffing each other" is very similar to a line in *Pony!* ("Baby, we're all animals! Animals is what we are. It's a wonder we're not all running around bare-ass, sniffing at one another and peeing on everything in sight!," a variant of which also crops up in *Good Times/Bad Times* and its screenplay.)

The reviews were mixed. The *East Hampton Summer Sun* opined that *Surprise!* was the best of the three plays. The unnamed reviewer found Kirkwood's acting "a little flat" but went so far as to declare Merrill's performance "one of the best acting performances I've ever seen." S/he found the play a "hilarious comedy" and "written brilliantly." Kirkwood gave "deep insight" into the minds of the married couple. Conversely, Allan Wallach of *Newsday* found Kirkwood's acting acceptable enough ("the playwright, although not an accomplished actor, is agreeable as the husband who strays") but found the script seriously wanting: "At first, Kirkwood has the kind of grisly fun with the situation that Joe Orton's *Loot* had with an unwanted body. But *Surprise!* is a one joke play with a punchline that comes too early; the play doesn't have anywhere to go but downhill. Kirkwood's attempt to add fresh surprises only adds length."

David Spencer, who attended the play, says of Kirkwood's acting, "He seemed only moderately good as a performer. He had a certain degree of presence, but he neither lost himself in the few roles I saw him play, nor let his natural persona inform them in any notable way." Of the *Surprise!* venture, he says, "Bill agreed to direct it, solely as a political gesture. In private he would denigrate the play, which indeed was not very good."

In an interview given to the *Sarasota Herald Tribune* published in March 1981, Kirkwood said of *Murder at the Vanities*, "It's a hell of a lot of fun but it's driving us crazy too. There's lots of bloodletting on this collaboration, and we aren't even through the first act yet!"

That the collaborators were not yet through the first act more than a year after the start of the project was an indication of just how difficult was the task they had set themselves. As was the fact that the expected backers were simply not signing up, despite several producer auditions. Donald Oliver says, not necessarily of only this first year or so, "We did one for the Shuberts. We did one for the Nederlanders. We did one for Robert Fryer and Mike Nichols' first wife. We did two for Michael Bennett. We wanted to get a producer on board as soon as we had enough material to attract one." Fryer, producer of many shows including the original Broadway productions of *Wonderful Town*, *Chicago* and *Auntie Mame*, was a friend and onetime colleague of Oliver's and it was the latter who mentioned *Vanities* to him in casual conversation. "To my surprise he asked if we could present it to him," says Oliver. "When I told Jimmy about this, he was furious because (a) I had approached Bobby without consulting him first and (b) because of his stature in the industry he thought he should be the only one to approach producers. Elliot Lefkowitz called my lawyer to complain. My lawyer was stupefied. He said to Elliot, 'You're upset because Don piqued the interest of a first-class producer? You should be thrilled no matter who approached whom.'" In the end, Fryer was evidently not sufficiently impressed by what he saw/heard to take on the project. Oliver belatedly came to suspect an unspoken reason for

Kirkwood's fury: "When I originally talked to Bobby about the show, I had totally forgotten that Jimmy was fired from the original production of *Auntie Mame*…Maybe that was the reason he was so pissed-off at me. If Bobby *had* liked it enough, his history with Jimmy would not have mattered a whit, if he even remembered it at all. Jimmy, on the other hand, could still have been carrying around the hurt from the firing."

Though Oliver says of the job of acquiring of a producer, "It can take years, and many rejections," it was obvious that there was a problem. Though the songs sometimes presented difficulties — Kirkwood's correspondence files show that at one point his famous composer friend Stephen Sondheim provided "help/suggestions" regarding three parts of the score — it was the script that was the crux. Today, both Oliver and Spencer agree that the concept of the show had a fundamental, nonnegotiable fault. Spencer puts it like this: "Musicals tend to resist genres like mystery, and certainly whodunits, for the basic reason that they tend to be about characters with passionate needs, who want something transformative, and that requires singing from the heart. Which is almost impossible to do over the long haul of an evening when you're trafficking in multiple characters *withholding* information. In fact, the quest for information, *per se*, is, in itself, impossible to musicalize, because it offers few, if any, exploitable emotional handles that can sustain the length of a song." Oliver says, "A musical being static in nature was very experimental at that time as in plotless musicals like *Follies* and *Company* and even *Pacific Overtures* where there wasn't a propulsion of boy-meets-girl, boy-loses-girl, boy-gets-girl, and you're rooting for them to get together at the end." However, he admits that *Vanities* proved a piece of experimentation too far: "Here you needed to solve a crime. A murder mystery musical has so many built-in difficulties…I regret very few things in life, but I regret that the idea that I presented to Jimmy was 'a murder mystery musical set backstage at a girlie show in the 1930s.' Because that is an impossible thing to pull off. A murder mystery sounds like a great idea, but go write it. A murder mystery by its very nature is static. Someone has been murdered and your characters, in trying to solve the murder, have to re-construct what already happened. The forward movement to the piece is in a circular pattern, because you have to keep going over the facts and put things together and make it develop for the audience so that they understand pieces of what happened only as you go, whereas a musical needs to have a relentlessly forward propulsive structure."

At the time, though, it was assumed this problem could be overcome and in order to help the team — specifically Kirkwood — do this, the idea was floated to approach thriller writer Donald E. Westlake to come on board as a collaborator. Oliver estimates this occurred in 1981. "We weren't trying to bring in anybody to do anything but to help with the mystery element of the show," says Oliver. "The actual murder mystery plotting. Since Don Westlake was knocking out his books like Stephen King does, we thought that he would be a logical choice to go to. He lived in New York, he was very approachable. He wasn't involved in the theatre so we thought he wouldn't be a threat to Jimmy's ego." Westlake indicated he was willing to come on board. Oliver: "Then we broached the subject to Jimmy." Kirkwood responded in the negative to the suggestion of a writing collaborator. Oliver: "I think he felt he didn't need one. Jimmy felt that if we just kept going the way we were going we could manage it. I had to respect his feeling. I wouldn't have gone to Jimmy with the idea and risked even potentially hurting him if I didn't think it was a viable means to get us produced. I remember telling Jimmy it had nothing to do with his talent, it's the plotting of the murder mystery—not the dialogue, not the characters, not the quirkiness. He said, 'I don't think it's as bad as you think it is. I think that whatever is troubling you we could work through on our own.'" From the sound of it, Oliver doesn't feel that Kirkwood's ego was getting in the way: "Jimmy never had a problem rewriting, never had a problem throwing out things. He was a thorough professional in his attitude. He was never one to hold onto anything that he loved so much. It was all for the service of the show."

"We never really admitted it was un-writable," says Oliver. "We kept forcing it and you don't want to say it's not writable, you want to say if we do this better, if we do this differently, if we try it this way…We tried so many different ways. We wrote over fifty songs and there are probably lyrics for even more that were not set to music. Of varying quality, of course. We would write character songs for various characters that we would know wouldn't be in the show but we thought would inspire a character, inspire a dialogue, inspire action. So we tried varying approaches to getting this monster to move and it was still leaden. But I don't blame Jimmy for it. It's un-writable." Spencer, in contrast, does blame their librettist. "Jim simply couldn't write anything for it coherently," he says. "Draft after draft he was floundering to find a tone, a propulsive throughline, even a sensible beat-to-beat progression. He was brilliantly talented at writing a certain kind of thing, which was semi-autobiographical character pieces. He was not a writer with a mechanism for craft and structure to guide him. He didn't think that way; he couldn't talk in those terms. He was one of those writers who blasts it out in a white heat, without a lot of planning or outlining. A perfectly legitimate way to write, but it tends to work best with prose fiction, which doesn't have to be scrupulously neat. Musicals require assiduous, *conscious* attention to matters structural, and there Jim was hopeless. At one point I was meeting with him regularly to help him plot it. Since the challenge itself was so insoluble, it seems paradoxical to fault Jim for not being able to deliver, but even allowing for the troubled context, he was palpably in over his head." Spencer was also not happy about writing the superfluous songs: "Because Jim's work was so weak, the book rarely led the way, which ideally it must. Often I found myself writing songs first to give Jim inspiration and guidance." After writing two or three character sketch lyrics that he knew would never get into the show in order to provide Kirkwood raw material, Spencer refused to co-operate with that strategy any further.

Not that Spencer could fault Kirkwood's work ethic. "I remember how Jim labored to deliver something to earn his collaborators' enthusiasm on *Murder at the Vanities,*" he says. "He sensed — at times flat-out knew — he was disappointing us and he was unhappy about the process much of the time. I don't mean scowling-unpleasant unhappy, I mean within himself (though it did engender some tense and unpleasant moments). He was in a position to bail, but it seemed as if he himself was trying to hang onto an opportunity. I had the sense that he well knew *A Chorus Line* had been a gift, all his new straight plays were tanking, *Hit Me with a Rainbow* had proven well below his best, and he wanted to prove himself anew to his colleagues and to the industry." Oliver and Spencer's memories differ slightly on whether Kirkwood was willing to translate that work ethic to becoming conversant in writing styles with which he was not familiar. Oliver: "Whatever we would give Jimmy, he would read it. He would do his homework. He wanted it to be good. Jimmy really wanted this to work." Spencer feels this willingness was restricted to research material pertaining directly to the project, the period, etc., and says, "I'd recommend mysteries for him to read, movies for him to rent, just to get the feel, and he never did."

Spencer also feels that substance abuse was going on with Kirkwood and that this may have been partly why the writing did not seem to be progressing. "Jimmy did recreational drugs," he says. "Pot, poppers, things like that. I don't know how intense the use was, but I know it was regular. He would sometimes discuss what he perceived as their merits with Bill Gile. I gathered it was also a sexual stimulant for him. I can't help but think that drug use also affected Jim's ability to write at the top of his game."

Though Oliver admits relations between Spencer and Kirkwood were "absolutely cordial on the surface," he also says Kirkwood was "a little intimidated" by Spencer, "caused in no small part by David's forced role as the one who could help Jimmy plot the show." Spencer admits he was made slightly uncomfortable by the alien culture he found himself in. Although he says homosexuality "was never an issue between me and any homosexual who's ever been my friend," he reports a "discomfort" that came from "my being continually expected to play along with and endorse the campiness, the dishy backbiting…" Spencer also insists his misgivings about Kirkwood's abilities were confirmed by the opinions of others. At the height of his frustration, he broke internal confidence and took aside Ed Kleban — fellow lyricist and of course most famous for his lyrics for *A Chorus Line* — to, as he puts it, "get a reality check." Spencer: "This is pretty much word-for-word what he told me — and the reason I remember it so vividly is because it was a watershed moment to have confirmed that it wasn't just *me* and that someone successful without an axe to grind was validating my own perceptions and somewhat echoing my experiences: 'Jimmy was brought on to work with Nick Dante, but we realized early that Jimmy couldn't write it either. Really there were five book-writers on *A Chorus Line*, and Jimmy's contribution was the least of them. Jimmy worked in certain specifically prescribed areas, where it was felt he had some strength, and mostly that was the relationship between Cassie and Zach, which is generally considered to be the weakest part of the show.'" Though Kleban would seem to be in a minority amongst the *A Chorus Line* staff in allegedly thinking Kirkwood's contribution unimportant (and that the Cassie and Zach scenes were the musical's weak spot), Spencer says that his unease about Kirkwood's abilities was corroborated elsewhere. Expressing his concerns about Kirkwood being unable to produce acceptable work on *Murder at the Vanities* to his then-agent Charles Hunt by saying, "I mean, James Kirkwood. Who *knew* he couldn't write a musical book?," he found Hunt responding, "David, *everybody* knows!" Spencer adds, "The word had clearly been out for a long time." Spencer continues, "The thing you have to understand about Jimmy is that at heart he meant well, and people who didn't have to work with him collaboratively loved him. He was a terrific presence at parties, he was a wildly entertaining and dishy raconteur, and because of his novels especially he was perceived as being a genuine showbiz insider who was also a dazzling wit and a brilliant wordsmith. As indeed he could be — when he was in his element. But as an artist he worked purely off instinct and impulse. I think, on some level, he didn't understand why he had to keep doing real homework when he had already made it writing about the stuff he knew from life experience. When I knew him, the white-heat muse had burned itself out and he didn't have craft to fall back on. Which is not meant as criticism. A white-heat writer is what he was; you couldn't make him into something else. But he didn't understand that about himself.

"Jimmy claimed, deep into the process, that he had warned us, right up front, that plotting and mystery were not his *forte*, and claimed our response had been to assure him that we'd all manage to work through such limitations together. I have *absolutely* no memory of this…I would have lobbied for us finding another librettist, despite the *cachet* that we thought Jim's name brought to the table, and refused to go further." Oliver counters, "Jimmy did say early on, 'I don't have a clue how to write a murder mystery.' Which was the open invitation for all of us to sit around and plot it." Regardless of how admirable Kirkwood's honestly on that point was, if someone doesn't know how to write a murder mystery, why is he on board for a murder mystery? Oliver: "Yeah, um, good question. I wanted to work with him so much…I have been known to be ridiculously optimistic and even naïve at times, and my feeling was that I didn't think anybody knew how to write a musical murder mystery so we could do it just as well as anybody else could."

It should be pointed out that some thought that it was not Kirkwood who was the suspect part of the equation. Oliver remembers that at one stage Kirkwood was invited by an agent to dump his teammates for more illustrious composers. "Agents and people say all kinds of things," he notes. "Somebody said to him, 'You've won the Pulitzer Prize, you've written the biggest show in 25 years on Broadway and one of the biggest shows ever, what are you doing with these novices? If you ally yourself with Jerry Herman or Kander & Ebb it would be a lot easier to get the show produced.' Jimmy repeated the conversation to me. But Jimmy was very, very, very loyal and he would never hurt anybody intentionally, ever." Another thing that should be mentioned is that his letters reveal that Kirkwood did not like Spencer either as a person or a collaborator (in a letter to Stephen Sondheim, he described him as "intractable to work with").

Murder at the Vanities got its only public performance in Kirkwood's lifetime on May 5, 1982, at the Merkin Concert Hall. "Jimmy volunteered to do it as a favor for a friend, or maybe it was a social acquaintance; indeed, I believe it was the woman running the Bloomingdale House of Music," says Spencer. "She solicited, or Jim offered, the *Murder at the Vanities* reading to be a special feature of [a] Bloomingdale-sponsored concert series. I voiced strong objections to Bill and especially Don about doing it, because I thought the show was still a mess at the core, there would be nothing to learn from the effort, and there could be no practical outcome to the experience. In fact, I was concerned it had the potential to hurt. Not just the show, but Don and me as writers. But I let myself be persuaded by Don and Bill (who directed the presentation) that Jim needed the stroking to stay enthusiastic, and that it would have created all kinds of bad karma to say no, so I eventually gave in. I'm not entirely sure I could have prevented it happening without me in any event."

A videotape exists of this public reading of just under an hour-and-a-half which shows that it consisted of songs, dialogue and an announcer's linking narrative. Spencer says, "It was a very long first act. No second act and no revealing to the audience the solution to the mystery, which left people frustrated and wondering what the point of the exercise had been, and, believe me, I empathized. It went pretty much as I expected. Some of the songs went over okay, but the book wasn't working so nothing else could work optimally and you could feel when the audience stopped concentrating. And that's death. I remember feeling a little embarrassed, and glad when it was over."

Oliver recalls, "We had a very pregnant heroine, like eight months or something like that. Mary Bracken Phillips." The publicity flyer read, 'The role of Earl Carroll will be read by Mr. Kirkwood.' "Wankery," says Spencer. "Ego stroke of a former actor. He wasn't right for it, but I recall it was a respectable enough 'Author reads' kind of thing. It didn't add to the luster, though. Ideally, the role required a real, convincingly heterosexual leading man. At the time we were talking Kevin Kline, Hal Linden, Len Cariou, and while Jimmy was no one's idea of a mincer, he wouldn't fool anyone's gaydar either, certainly no woman's." Kirkwood also provided the linking narration, which he bookended with his customary jocularity. (His opening statement to the audience was, "Good evening, ladies and gentlemen. I'm an alcoholic.")

This performance is probably the reason for the existence of the one-act script in Kirkwood's papers. A full-length, two-act version in Oliver's files dates from 1982. Spencer says, "I can tell you that whatever you have is misleading and certainly not definitive. There was never a definitive draft. To use a word coined by James, the project was 'misbefucked' from the beginning and was in constant flux." The show takes place in the Earl Carroll Theatre in September 1933. The occasion is the opening night of the 11th edition of the Earl Carroll Vanities. Prohibition is just about to be repealed, as explained in a prologue which involves projecting an old RKO newsreel onto a curtain. It is also explained in this sequence that

Carroll has spent a year in prison for staging a show involving nude girls in tubs of champagne. We are then into familiar show-within-a-show territory for Kirkwood. In *Murder at the Vanities,* the audience is seeing parts of the same show witnessed by the proposed audience at the 1933 *Vanities.* Another similarity it has with *Club Mardi Gras* is that it features the backstage intrigues of the fictional show's cast, in this case a horny drummer, a diva, bitching showgirls and various others. The milieu of creative people and the window into their rehearsals also brings to mind *A Chorus Line.* Though the script includes full song lyrics instead of directions for songs like *Club Mardi Gras,* even the full '82 version has a first act that ends with a scene that describes a song rather than presents its lyric. Oliver: "The only song that David and I could never crack really was the end-of-the-first-act number when the second murder takes place. We created several drafts of musical sequences but we didn't ever have anything viable in this spot."

The play is quite amusing in places, with several one-liners that sing, especially in the bitchy repartee. The cynical and potty-mouthed performer Winnie is an engaging character. The dialogue is generally possessed of a vitality and verisimilitude, although magician Anton's East European vernacular is not consistently rendered. Unfortunately, proving that revision isn't always improvement, the hilarious scene from the show-within-the-show in the earlier one-act version where the character Bernie uses a machine that cures people of their ills by transferring them into the body of his assistant — causing the latter to incrementally pick up all manner of tics, including hiccups, sneezing and effeminacy — is reduced (even ridiculed) in the revised two-act configuration. (It's a matter of opinion as to whether an improvement is effected by the excision from the revised version of Sticks' jaw-dropping line, "If I could figure out how to furnish one, I'd live in it!" when told he is "cunt-happy.")

The full version, of course, gives us a *denouement,* one rendered in classic whodunit style with the detective (Carroll) eliminating in the presence of the survivors the innocent parties before unmasking the villain. This scene reveals detailed and fairly clever plotting, although the manner in which Carroll tricks the culprit into exposing herself is unpersuasive. Though the night's traumas have made Carroll realize that love is more important than show business, we are left at the end with an impression of a somewhat uninvolving scenario: few of the cast and crew of *Vanities* are as vulnerable as the boys and girls on the chorus line in Michael Bennett's show. Additionally, their characters are a little samey. The whole thing also seems a tad over-familiar. This is on paper, of course. On stage it would possibly have been a different matter, for the lyrics are very good and witty and indicate that the show would come to life and be an enjoyable — if hardly intellectual or substantial — night out.

The show came close to making it to the stage proper when the late David Merrick expressed interest by approaching the team himself. Merrick was a theatre legend who would ultimately produce over eighty plays and musicals on Broadway, including *Hello, Dolly!*, *Oliver!*, *Carnival*, *Look Back in Anger* and *Promises, Promises*. "David Merrick's interest came out of the blue," recalls Oliver. "*42nd Street* was running on Broadway at the time. Part of the scenery at the very end of the show were marquees of shows that were on Broadway in 1933, and one of the marquees was *Murder at the Vanities*…So David Merrick came up to Jimmy one night in some restaurant and said, 'Jimmy, I hear you're doing *Murder at the Vanities*. That's my show, you know, you've got to give that show to me, it's in my *42nd Street*, you've got to do it.'" Naturally, a reading was arranged for the enthusiastic living legend. It took place in either January or February 1983. Oliver: "We did a very full audition for Mr. Merrick. We did most of the songs linked by narration. You don't tell the jokes; you don't try and act out the dialogue. At this kind of presentation you may do sections of dialogue leading up to the songs, but your objective is just to make the show feel exciting and alive." The cast performing at this audition was chock full of familiar Broadway faces, David Cryer, Betsy Joslyn and Gary Krawford among them. Oliver notes, "When they took their seats, Mr. Merrick looked at the cast, turned to Biff Liff and asked, 'Is this playing somewhere?'" Spencer: "Biff Liff was very enthusiastic, gave me a big hug, pumped my hand after. He seemed very pleased." Within what Oliver estimates was weeks of their reading, Merrick suffered a debilitating stroke which put him out of action for quite a while. "I've always denied that our reading had anything to do with his stroke," says Oliver. "Jimmy used to joke he was found with a copy of our script in his hands."

The humor was, one suspects, grim. Having already experienced the sort of knockbacks that can make a creative team doubt their abilities or the validity of what they are trying to do, that the one occasion when a producer approached them rather than the other way around ended up with them having hope snatched away from under their noses must have made the *Vanities* team to some degree wonder if fate had decreed that this show was not going to happen. Perhaps it is this that made them go back to Michael Bennett.

Michael Bennett had, of course, done as well out of *A Chorus Line* as had Kirkwood, both financially and reputation-wise. Though he'd subsequently had mixed fortunes — the failure of *Ballroom* (1978) being followed by the success of *Dreamgirls* (1981) — his name had a *cachet* that would almost certainly have assured *Murder at the Vanities* a degree of success. Oliver: "The first time Michael turned it down, it was because he was getting ready to consider doing *Love Me or Leave Me* with Ann-Margret and Marvin Hamlisch and he didn't want to do two show-business musicals at the same time, or on top of each other…Jimmy said to me, 'Well, [Bennett's professional partner] Bob Avian wasn't hot on the score.' I accept that it's certainly a possibility, but since the score had received high praise from many Broadway professionals, this could have been a way of massaging Jimmy. My theory is that because they were still actively involved with one another as part of the *Chorus Line* creative team, Michael and Bob didn't want to tell Jimmy they didn't have confidence in the script." The second time the team auditioned *Vanities* for Bennett, after *Love Me or Leave Me* had been called off, the producer/ choreographer/director was expressing more than the passing interest he had previously and negotiations began taking place that Oliver says were, "The closest the show ever came to actually being produced."

The formal entrée of Bennett would have changed the chemistry of the *Vanities* collaborative process, perhaps profoundly. "We would have let him direct it in two seconds," says Oliver. "That was the idea. Bill was going to step aside." And the "very, very, very loyal" Kirkwood would have gone along with that? Oliver: "At this point? In a heartbeat. All of us would have. Even Bill did not want to stand in the way of the show getting done." Spencer's memories are different. He says, "Don subsequently reported to me Bill's fear that his days were numbered on the project, that Michael would muscle him out…and I believe that Don and I agreed to protect him, or try to. Though, ironically, we had no such compunctions about Jim. We knew he couldn't deliver a workable script, we suspected that *Bennett* knew — after *A Chorus Line* he *had* to — and the fantasy projection was that Bennett would bring in a better writer once he had signed on. But Bennett never followed through." For his part, Gile says, "It was a show that was written just as the economics of theatre was changing and we went from being a one-million-dollar production to eight million within a year-and-a-half, and I realized I would never be involved with it because to risk eight million on somebody who's, although I had successes, I had not anything that was millions…"

Bennett, according to Oliver, may not have been overly impressed with what was on the page so far, but recognized its potential. Oliver thinks it was probably this that led Bennett to insist on a clause in any contract he might sign which eventually scuppered the whole deal, although he emphasizes that he is just guessing: "It crashed and burned when Michael insisted that at any point in the show's development he could name himself a co-author on the show and get co-author's royalties. My supposition is that Michael was already feeling, 'If I have to bring in a co-author, I need to have points to give him'...If this was the case, it was a practical notion rather than an ego notion. When a producer or a director wants to bring in a co-author, nobody wants to give up any of their points. Or, it could have been that since on his previous shows Michael contributed so much to the story and structure, this time he wanted to be compensated for his authorial contributions. Either way, Jimmy was highly insulted and refused to negotiate further. It was a deal-breaker." From Beckenstein's recollections of Kirkwood's feelings about Bennett, Kirkwood may have felt he had good cause to take affront: "When *A Chorus Line* was happening it was the most wonderful collaboration between all of the creators. Afterward, when the success of it took shape, Michael began to take all the credit and not mention anybody else and it just infuriated Jimmy. He had a great sense of justice."

Though there was no formal declaration of giving up, Oliver remembers this latest knockback as the one that began to dilute energy and enthusiasm in the collaborative team. They lost their director in May 1983 when during a BMI Showcase party a drunk Gile insulted Spencer and a friend of his. The next day Spencer rang Oliver and told him he wasn't prepared to work with Gile any longer. The *Vanities* project staggered on a little longer, then dribbled to a halt. In late 1983, there was one last flicker of life when director-choreographer Joe Layton took an interest in it. "I liked Joe a lot," says Oliver. "He seemed *very* interested. He said he'd direct, choreograph *and* produce." Spencer: "[He] flew us — Jimmy, Don and me — out to Chicago, where he was directing at the time, to discuss it with him. It never progressed past that series of meetings. And I believe that was the last time I saw Jim."

"Please don't assume there was any kind of meeting at which Jimmy announced something like, 'Fellas, I can't keep hammering away at this. I've got to move on,'" says Oliver. "It wasn't like that at all. When someone professed interest there was always a 'waiting' period until their interest waned or atrophied. This 'waiting' period would stretch to around six months before we'd accept that the interest level was now at zero and we'd hatch a new strategy to get the show produced. By the time 1982-1983 rolled around, we, the collaborators, were all at a point of diminished enthusiasm and it was good for *all* of us to begin working on other things, not just Jimmy. I do remember a conversation where Jimmy told me he was going to work on other projects (i.e., *Legends!*) but since he was involved with other projects during the time we were doing *Vanities*, doing other projects didn't preclude his interest in, or time commitment to *Vanities*. By 1982-1983 we all just didn't know what else to do to get someone interested in the property who could move it towards production, with all that entailed. None of us had actively worked on it for a while by the time it became apparent that Joe wasn't going to do anything with the show, so *Vanities* became a victim of inertia. Our involvement petered out rather than stopped abruptly."

In 1990, the year after Kirkwood's death, Oliver and Spencer tried to revive the *Murder at the Vanities* concept. They re-approached Donald E. Westlake and asked him to be the librettist. Westlake started from scratch, using none of Kirkwood's book. The results were ultimately the same. "Donald was a master plotter and it was beyond him to plot this thing," says Oliver. Spencer says, "Westlake did his damndest — and it was *infinitely* better, lighter, more entertaining — but even he couldn't crack it sufficiently."

Jim Piazza has an interesting observation on the project relating to a feeling of his that Kirkwood deliberately tended to work in this period with people not as successful as he had now become. "I thought that Jimmy was not slumming exactly, but really, after *A Chorus Line* you expect a career to just soar and it just seemed that Jimmy was more caught up in working with unknowns," he says. "Given his personality and his demands, I could picture him burning bridges. I think he and Jerry Herman had had words, I think there was a yelling match there, I'm not sure after the *La Cage* thing…He was always brewing these things, he was mad at people. He may have been compelled to work with people that were just in awe of him, that he didn't know well and he could play the grand man, and kind of take over."

Asked how they look back now on *Murder at the Vanities*, Kirkwood's collaborators come out with wildly varying responses.

Gile: "As one of the happiest and most creative experience[s] I have ever had in my life. Fishermen talk about the one that got away. This is the one that got away. It's a wonderful show, it's absolutely wonderful and it's laying there dormant and should be at least published if not produced… His work on that was extraordinary."

Spencer: "The Kirkwood version: as a learning experience that went on far too long. The Westlake version: as a really noble try — but too late…I was thrown into the deep end of a very dysfunctional pool and had no idea how to deal with it…*Murder at the Vanities* was doomed almost at the inception."

Oliver: "I came to him with a murder mystery musical in which everything is subjugated to a plot which by its very nature fights a musical. It was a misbegotten idea."

NINETEEN

James Kirkwood's personalized Christmas cards were celebrated among his friends and acquaintances. Banal though this may sound, they were notable as yet another way this almost universally loved personality endeared himself to people. The end of 1981 saw Kirkwood devise a new celebrity cameo spin on his cards.

He and Beckenstein had earlier that year gone backstage at the Martin Beck Theatre on Broadway to see Kirkwood's old acquaintance Elizabeth Taylor, who was starring in a revival of *The Little Foxes*. Beckenstein took a photograph of the pair smiling for the camera. It went out that Yuletide on a card with the legend, "Happy Holidays" signed "The Kirkwoods." Liz Smith by now had an entertainment and showbiz gossip segment on NBC's news program *Live at Five*. She held the card up on her show and declared it the funniest Christmas card she had received. Beckenstein: "Terrence McNally had sent his mother a copy of the card and hadn't heard anything from her for a couple of weeks. When he talked to her, he said, 'Mother, did you get Jimmy's Christmas card I sent you?' She said, 'Yes.' He thought it was odd that here was Jimmy with the most famous woman in America and all she could say was 'Yes.' Elizabeth did have honey-colored hair for her part, but there was no mistaking that face. Terrence said, 'And what did you think? Did you recognize who he was with?' His mother said, 'Yes, wasn't it Arthur?'"

Beckenstein adds, "Another story about that card was they were late in being delivered. Jimmy always had Elliot, his lawyer, follow up on details and problems. They had a very close relationship. Elliot adored Jimmy and Jimmy thought the world of Elliot, who could be a bulldog and really fought for his clients." Elliot Lefkowitz, who had represented Elizabeth Taylor at one point, called the president of Kodak to complain that Taylor was very upset that she didn't have her copies of the cards yet. Beckenstein: "That evening, a vice-president of Kodak hand-delivered the cards to Jim's home."

The following year, Kirkwood and Beckenstein went backstage when Liberace was appearing at Radio City in a lavish Christmas show with the Radio City Rockettes. Beckenstein took a picture of Kirkwood with the famously gaudy and camp pianist. Again, the picture went out as a

Christmas card and again the legend — even more surreally this year — was "Happy Holidays" from "The Kirkwoods." Liz Smith thought that was even funnier than the Liz Taylor card and once again held it up on her show. "He managed to find people every year after that to be in his cards," Beckenstein says. Kirkwood's 1985 card featured him, Mary Martin and Carol Channing, the stars of his play *Legends!* Another card featured Kirkwood with Bernie Jacobs and Jerry Schoenfeld, the two men who ran American theatre's fabled Shubert Organization. In each case, everybody was presented as "family."

Beckenstein suspects that the Kirkwood wacky card tradition started back in the fifties in the *Valiant Lady* days. "There was a picture of him with a little baby and he was bending down 'cooing' this sweet baby," he explains. That the picture — whose baby was actually probably that of his character Mickey Emerson's dead lover Bonnie Withers — bore, as with his later cards, the legend "The Kirkwoods" created some confusion. Beckenstein recalls, "His mother was very annoyed at some of those cards, especially with the baby, when people kept responding to her how badly they felt that he was left with this adorable little baby and that they didn't even know he was married and what did happen to his wife?" Beckenstein continues, "He went on to send cards in the seventies, with whatever crazy scheme he could imagine. I was usually the photographer. An old house burned down and the only thing left amid all the ashes was a brick fireplace and mantle. He put a wreath on the fireplace along with candlesticks and sat curled up naked in front of the fireplace with a big scarf wrapped around his neck. You couldn't see anything, except his profile." The legend this time was "Merry Christmas from my house to yours." The following year, Kirkwood really got into the Christmas spirit — in one sense — with a "Christ" card. Terrence McNally recalls, "He had three stones in front of his house on the water on Three Mile Harbor and at high tide the stones were barely, barely covered so you could stand on them, but it looked like you were walking on water. It said, 'Merry Christmas' and there was Jimmy with a beard, which he had in those days, and full white biblical robes." Beckenstein: "It really did look like he was walking on water — this was in the early seventies, before computers and Photoshop…His mother and his first agent Phyllis Jackson were extremely upset, thinking it was in poor taste…I always thought the next year should have been the last picture on the roll where he fell backward off the rock."

Though his Christmas cards were amusing, they also seem like another way for Kirkwood to be playfully coy about his sexuality. Plenty of

Kirkwood's recipients would have been *au fait* with his relationship with Beckenstein, but the latter doesn't appear on any of them. Beckenstein is relaxed about it. "Whenever we were anyplace, although he might not have said 'My partner' [he said], 'This is Arthur' and made it be known that I was with him," he reasons. "He was kind of an independent spirit and his Christmas cards would go to a long list of people in the business who wouldn't know who I am."

There was a huge irony surrounding Kirkwood's Christmas cards. Beckenstein: "Jimmy hated Christmas. He always wanted to escape and be away for Christmas. The one time that we went on vacation, it was over Christmas and New Year's. He just didn't want to be involved." Though Beckenstein says of Kirkwood, "He enjoyed *making* a Christmas card," he explains, "He thought it was a big intrusion upon his life and work getting involved in Christmas cards and everybody that you were dealing with [was] tied up because of the Christmas holiday."

William Russo says of Kirkwood, "I suppose by today's standards you would call him a workaholic. He once said to me, 'My life is my work,' and I believed it because there was a period there in the early eighties where he was writing five or six screenplays in a year, constantly working. I was always amazed that he had time to talk to me or write to me or to do any of these social things because he was so productive. The act of working may have been something to blot out things he didn't want to think about."

Nineteen eighty-two was another busy year for Kirkwood. Unless it was successful in the blotting out Russo theorizes, all of his work was futile. Firstly, there was the ongoing desultory attention to the novel about his father. He said of *I Teach Flying* at a lecture that April, "It's a book that's very personal to me so I've just stopped working on it until I really could get a chunk of time and go off by myself and not just *fiddle* with it. And I hope to do that soon. Except I owe Paramount two rewrites on this screenplay."

"It was painful," Arthur Laurents says of *I Teach Flying*. "He didn't want to face what his father was or what his relationship with his father was. His mother — I met her with him–that was fine, they were very close and he loved her and she loved him and that was easy. The father was tough." Was Lila Lee any better as a parent? "No, she wasn't, but she didn't demand of him, and James Kirkwood [Sr.] did." Laurents was shown a version of *I Teach Flying*. Laurents: "I said to him, 'It's schizophrenic. Part of it is wonderfully serious, it's about your father, and the other part was kind of giddy. I think you should concentrate on your father' — and he concentrated on the other!…That could have been wonderful. There were a lot of pages. Three hundred and something. He got wobbly. I think he felt he wanted to make whatever is considered commercial, which really no one knows." Laurents was conscious of the drought of published Kirkwood work in the eighties. He says, "I did try to get him to do things with the novels and with the book about his father, but Jerry Paonessa adored him and was bad for him because anything Jimmy did was great, and that doesn't help."

In January '82, *Variety* reported that Kirkwood was collaborating with Paonessa on a film tentatively titled *Both Sides of the Park*. The script would eventually be retitled *East Side/West Side*. As with all Kirkwood film scripts (unless the rewritten *Some Kind of Hero* can be said to count), it would never make the jump to production.

The story was the idea of comic Alan King and his business partner Rupert Hitzig who together ran the production company King-Hitzig. It was this pair who were also trying to find backers for Kirkwood's dramatization of *Good Times/Bad Times*. They had seen a factual magazine article which they considered to have potential for a movie. "It was a real-life case," says Hitzig. "I don't think we optioned it from the [real] people. It was something in *People* magazine. A guy got exposed and he had two wives. I don't think it was on both sides of Central Park — we just made that up — but we thought about the comic aspect of a man not remembering the idiosyncrasies of which wife he's with that night and what would it be like if you had to eat two Thanksgiving dinners. Jimmy had a great sense of humor and he was a lovely man. He was around our office and we loved him as a writer and we thought it was a good project for him. I think that Jimmy was a very good screenwriter. I've been a script doctor all my life and I know that we worked fairly closely and Alan was a brilliant comic, so it was more collaborative than anything. We'd sit around and then he'd write it."

The script that exists in Kirkwood's files bears the credit "By James Kirkwood and Gerald S. Paonessa." Recalls Paonessa, "Dawn Steel was there at the time running the studio [Paramount] and he said, 'Look, I don't want to do this film alone, I want Jerry to do it with me and if you [don't] want Jerry then I'm not doing it.' So they said okay." A nice gesture, but Paonessa — who recalls the true-life story originating not with *People* magazine but the somewhat more upscale *New Yorker* — says of the subsequent collaborative process, "Oh, it was murder! What would happen is we would do a scene-by-scene treatment and sometimes I would go off and do the rough first draft, sometimes he would. In that particular case, I think he wrote the first draft. Unfortunately, we really didn't see eye-to-eye on the tone on the piece." Kirkwood had been impressed by the unusual combination of burlesque and black humor in the 1980 movie *Airplane!* Paonessa: "Jimmy thought it was the funniest movie he had ever seen in his life and he was right, but [consequently] he saw *East Side/West Side* as more of a slapstick comedy. I saw it much more like the film that came out around that time which was very sophisticated called *A Touch of Class* with Glenda Jackson and George Segal. He saw it more the other way and he had the Pulitzer Prize. So we went in, gave them the [screenplay], they went ballistic, they went crazy, they hated it. And I'll never forget Alan King say[ing], 'That wife, that woman, the shrew — she is so ugly I wouldn't want to fuck her with *your* dick'… Jimmy really was very upset, as was I, but in Hollywood that goes [on] all the time. They wanted us to do another draft and we said no and we got fired."

The plot — set in 1982 — is about a successful New York architect named Charlie Coulter who is still fond of Doris, his wife of twelve years, but also aware that the marriage has started to pall. He meets and falls in love with a vivacious and sassy young fitness instructor named Jody (the name of Paonessa's wife), yet he can't bring himself to split up with Doris. Matters are massively complicated when first Jody, then Doris, announces she is pregnant. Coulter starts living a double life, traveling back and forth between Jody's West Side apartment and his home with Doris on the East Side. In balancing his two families he is assisted by his secretary Ruth, who for some reason is "proud" of him for the deception he is maintaining. Ultimately and inevitably, the marital excreta hits the fan with the women finding out about each other's respective existence. On the way to this — underwhelming — denouement, we are "treated" to a lightweight, if largely good-natured, comedy completely lacking in laughs with the one exception of a scene set at La Papa Theatre in which a bewildered Coulter watches an utterly sick musical.

As well as the low laugh ratio, the script suffers from several other faults. One is the fundamental flaw with the premise. Though one acknowledges that this is nothing but a comedy, an audience still needs to empathize with a protagonist and — inoffensive tenderfoot though he is — Coulter is at bottom a man who is deceiving the person who is supposed to be his nearest and dearest. As well as his mistress. Things are not helped by a distasteful subplot about Coulter's chauffeur developing a hatred for black people after his wife deserts him for a basketball player. Nor for that matter by the smaller part of a German beauty parlor assistant who is rendered surprisingly Nazi-like considering that World War II had ended nearly four decades before. There is also an overwhelming sense of received technique. La Papa Theatre excepted, Kirkwood and Paonessa's tableaux and gags are ones you feel you've seen somewhere before, from misunderstandings caused by characters juggling simultaneous conversations in person and on the phone to the *matre d'* who drops his fawning manner and French accent to suddenly speak in contemptuous Brooklynese. This probably wouldn't matter if the tableaux and gags were high-quality, but the authors just don't have a knack for snappy, call-and-response movie comedy dialogue or for genuinely funny scene-making.

The script's changed title echoes that of *Good Times/Bad Times*. Though Paonessa maintains this is a coincidence, it is still unfortunate for the *Good Times/Bad Times* novel is a work of real resonance with, incidentally, more laughs in it, despite its grim subject matter. Jim Piazza, though, recalls Kirkwood having no illusions in this area. "He did give me *East Side/West Side* to read," he says. "Truly a hack job. He was taking Hollywood for a ride because he was getting a lot of money for stuff that he would just hack write, just really throw away and not rewrite...Jimmy walked away with a quarter of a million dollars for that." (Hitzig says that that figure is an over-estimate to the tune of around $200,000.) Amongst Kirkwood's East Hampton circle was celebrated playwright Edward Albee. "Edward Albee used to call him a hack," says Piazza. "I mean they were friends but he was always saying [that]." However, Piazza says that one is not to infer that it didn't bother Kirkwood that none of his original scripts made the screen. "I think he was very distressed by that," he says. "I think he was pissed off that he would go down historically as a co-author of *Chorus Line*...The idea of him sharing credit just killed him. He wanted really to be thought of as a much more important writer than that."

Kirkwood did his stake for a claim to be remembered as an important writer no good with *Witches* (aka *Witch Story*), another screenplay he completed in 1982.

"Jimmy and I loved horror movies and loved thrillers and that kind of stuff," says Paonessa. "Although he never wrote one, which is kind of interesting. I think we both came up with the idea about doing a project based on, not witches, but on a warlock and it started off being a very serious film, because what we wanted to do was another *Amityville Horror*, which was a very scary movie. I took him around to the various studios, but as we went through it and started outlining it, it became very comic." Paonessa says of the resultant *Witches* screenplay, "They liked it a *lot* at Paramount, but not enough to immediately commit ten-to-fifteen million dollars to it." Immediately or ever. In that, Paramount joined United Artists, about whose vacillation on the project Kirkwood wrote in a letter to Herlihy in approximately 1980: "I have just made a deal with U.A. for the WITCHES story — only there's one problem — I didn't want to par-ticularly [sic] do it and they farted around for so long I HAVE COMPLETELY FORGOTTEN WHAT WAS ORIGINALLY IN MIND. So…next time I see you I will have to pump your brains for ideas and try to tell you mine and probably pay you a fee to sit and listen and react to me for a day or two." Revealing a certain crushing of the spirit by Hollywood he also wrote, "I am not doing any of these under pressure. I'll fucking do them when I feel like it is my motto now. 'Cause when I'm dead and buried in the sod — ashes strewn around, there won't be any need for having to have gone thru pressure THEN, so I won't now." In another letter, he wrote, "Jerry Paonessa says that United Artists has given the GO AHEAD TO witch story…providing we can get a director and the right cast." He added, "I believe that just the way I believe my cock will grow longer if I pray." Kirkwood's ribald pessimism turned out to be justified. *Witches* never got made. The reason for the non-appearance would appear to be less than complicated: it wasn't very good.

The screenplay bears Kirkwood's name alone but Paonessa recalls it as a collaboration between them. (Judging by Kirkwood's comments above, Herlihy may warrant a credit too.) *Witches* is set in 1980 and features an ex-actor-turned-writer named James Courtland, known as "Jimmy" to his friends who is planning on writing a serious novel about his father. The script states that he is open, immediately likable and has a boyish grin. All very Jimmy Kirkwood so far, though Courtland being in his late thirties is a you-wish element. The differences begin with the fact that Courtland has recently struck big with a novel about witchcraft and is currently writing the screen adaptation of it. The novel is read by a real-life warlock named Colin McNair who, mistakenly believing that Courtland is interested in the occult, is anxious that Courtland ghostwrite his own autobiography. When Courtland declines, McNair sets out to persuade him to change his mind by putting a spell on him — and all sorts of hilarity doesn't ensue.

Witches doesn't have any deep pretensions. However, it fails even in its modest aim to be a lightweight comedy. Kirkwood's problem seems to be that he doesn't — at least with original material rather than scripts based on his own novels — have a screenwriter's sensibility, the ability to write specifically for that particular medium, to give each a scene a resonance — either comedic or dramatic — rather than to employ it as a mechanical device to move the (itself hardly engaging) story forward. Not that he is not aware of this necessity or doesn't *try*. The trouble is that his humorous exchanges and his sight gags — again — are almost painfully generic. The movie clichés that abound this time include an out-of-control speedboat that leaves a trail of devastation and profanities in its wake, noisy sex overheard by a tame elderly couple and an owl that shows eerie signs of being psychic by suddenly opening its eyes or turning its head upon the occurrence of incidents of significance both in its presence and not.

There was somewhat more comedy attending the failure of *Good Times/Bad Times* to — again — reach the screen, albeit bitter. Recalls Hitzig, "I got a phone call from California saying that Strom Thurmond Jr. was on the phone, wanted to talk to me about *Good Times/Bad Times*." Naturally, Hitzig took the call from the son of the very famous senator: "He said, 'I'm interested in backing up to six million dollars *Good Times/Bad Times* and I'm in Los Angeles but I will be coming in and staying with Betty Buckley.' So we said, 'Come on into town and come up to our offices'… Jimmy Kirkwood was there when we met and in walks this kid in a raincoat, a young kid about 27, and he started to talk to us and he said, 'There will be no problem at all getting the money together. I have a backer.'" Alan King and Hitzig checked the credit line, which seemed genuine, and rang the number for Betty Buckley provided to them by Thurmond Jr. Recalls Hitzig, "I actually invited him to my house. We did a lot of preparation. Alan and I took him to lunch on Thursday. He had dinner with us Wednesday. He had authorized me to take a $250,000 fee out of the six million dollars that he was going to put up for *Good Times/Bad Times*. I was going to shoot it at my school, Milton Academy. Jimmy was thrilled because I was working on the script with him. So Friday we were supposed to meet him before he went back to Los Angeles to cement the deal and we decided to meet in a bar at the Lexington Hotel. I had a production manager that had done a budget and was going to meet us there. He met me a little bit earlier than Strom Jr., was coming in and he said, 'I didn't trust this guy so I called the senator in Washington and said, "Tell the senator that we are calling from New York and that his son is going to be producing a movie in New York with Alan King and Rupert Hitzig," and the senator got on the line and he said, "I'm very glad my son is so precocious. He is eighteen months old!"' The kid walked in — I put the production manager over by the wall — and he sat down and I said, 'Tell me who you are and don't move because the man over there at the corner is the FBI and you're going to be under arrest unless you come clean.' And he started to cry and he said, 'I am not Strom Thurmond, my name is — I forget his name now — and I just wanted a chance to read for the part and I live in New Jersey and Betty Buckley was my friend Elizabeth.'"

And then there were other distractions. In August '82, *The New York Times* reported, "James Kirkwood...is set to make his movie directing debut with a thriller called *Crooked Tree*. It's about an Indian woman who's inhabited by the spirit of a medicine man and who — unconsciously — influences bears to attack people. The picture's producer, David Gentile, hopes to start shooting in upper Michigan next month. Mr. Kirkwood says it's only lately that being a director started to appeal to him."

Four months before, Kirkwood had been asked at a lecture if directing was an avenue he wanted to go down and replied, "Yes, I would. Now I would. I wish I had directed the movie of *Some Kind of Hero*. I never really wanted to have that responsibility. I think it's a terrific one and very difficult one to juggle and I never really wanted to be in that position of telling people what to do. But I like actors and I like working with them and now that I know the whole thing is a cosmic joke anyhow — which has just finally occurred to me in the last year or so — and it doesn't make any difference. I think nobody knows that much more than anybody else, almost, in this business. I really mean it. Of course, there are some geniuses, but the rest of the people, they're talented to a certain extent." He did allow, "It's not wise to try to direct your own material because I think you need that other eye. I would rather direct somebody else's." Even there, though, he added the caveat, "I could direct a production of *P.S. Your Cat is Dead!* now because I've seen it so often and it wouldn't make any difference. The play is what it is, whatever it is."

Crooked Tree was the first novel by a young Detroit writer named Robert C. Wilson. It had generated much publicity even before its 1980 publication when a number of major publishers bid for it after his agent made multiple submissions. Explains Wilson of his book, "The main character was an attorney who was from the Detroit area. *Crooked Tree* was a story that was set in northern Michigan in the woods and the central focus of the plot was the 'bearwalk.' Indians who lived in the area called the Ottawa believe that certain medicine [men] — shamen — could leave their bodies and inhabit the bodies of animals." The novel was quickly optioned for a motion picture production and no less a director than William Friedkin — famous for *The Exorcist* — was lined up to shoot it for Warner Brothers. After a delay on the part of Warner Brothers, Friedkin pulled out of the project. "James Kirkwood expressed an interest," says

Wilson. "James Kirkwood told me it was the best terror-suspense thriller he had ever read. Naturally, that's the kind of thing that a writer doesn't forget. He had provided a quote to the publisher or maybe it was to my agent back at the time, and they used that in the advertising…The plan was that Kirkwood would direct it and his studio would be Paramount." Wilson recalls David Gentile as in fact being the junior partner in the production team to Sidney Glazier.

Whatever Kirkwood's enthusiasm for the project, the switch from Friedkin — a famous and acclaimed director — to Kirkwood — who had never directed anything in his life — was on the surface absurd. Wilson says, "I remember talking about that, but he was with Paramount, they believed in him, they were willing to go forward with him and so was Glazier and so I never really had any reservations about it." Though Wilson never met Kirkwood, in their telephone discussions he found him to have helpful suggestions about how his story could be made more cinematic: "He had a very good mind for plot and story and everything." Kirkwood and Gentile favored pop singer-turned-actress Cher for the lead female role Janis Michelson following raves for her performance in the play *Welcome to the Five and Dime, Jimmy Dean, Jimmy Dean*. Wilson: "Cher was considering the role. She never committed to it, though. She was suddenly hot and had lots of offers."

Despite his and Kirkwood's mutual excitement over the project, it gradually dawned on Wilson that the movie was going to flounder just as the earlier Friedkin-Warners arrangement had. "It was a series of things," he recalls. "It was one delay after another. The reason for it not going forward as I understood at the time was because of the disagreements that Kirkwood had with Paramount." In fact, Wilson got the impression that previous problems between Kirkwood and Paramount lay behind his surprise move into direction: "In that way he would be able to establish himself with a good commercial film and be able to do his own things and not run into the kinds of problems that he apparently had with *Some Kind of Hero*." Though the latter project had finally made it to the screen in April 1982, four months before *The New York Times* story about *Crooked Tree*, it was in a severely traduced form. Wilson has a hunch that Kirkwood was particularly disappointed that none of the book's homosexuality made the transition. He says, "One of the most interesting things about the novel that wasn't in the movie was when the main character was in the prisoner of war camp and he was with another prisoner and they developed a relationship between themselves, and it was this natural relationship. For somebody like me who was not gay it was an eye-opening experience showing how that type of a relationship could grow and it was a wonderful piece of writing. I can't say he ever said that to me, but that was always what I had thought."

It would not be until four years to the month after his "first draft revised" version, dated April 1977, that a screenplay of *Some Kind of Hero* vaguely acceptable to Paramount Pictures was ready. This script — which itself has inserted pages with later dates in their headers — was credited to "Robert Boris and James Kirkwood" and was the one used for the movie. As Beckenstein notes, though, "This version of *Some Kind of Hero* was not a collaboration but a rewrite by the studio."

Ryan O'Neal had once been slated to take the leading man's role in *Some Kind of Hero*, but that fell through. Though O'Neal fit the "very good looking" description in the book of its protagonist Eddie Keller and his replacement in the role did not, it was not this about the casting that literally astonished and dismayed many who admired the book. Eddie Keller was portrayed by black comic and actor Richard Pryor. Explains Jerry Paonessa, "It sat there for seven years and nothing happened. I then had to leave my work on it because I had just been made a Vice President of United Artists. Right after that, Paramount realized that they had a pay-or-play deal with Richard Pryor. Richard Pryor was about to get a million dollars. That would be like ten, twenty million today. So they said, 'Well, look, take a look over these scripts'…So of all the scripts that Pryor read he decided that he would do *Some Kind of Hero* and doing that, of course, made it a 'go' picture, made it a very big deal. I couldn't do anything to help because I was at United Artists. They didn't want Jimmy to do the rewrite, they wanted somebody else." That Pryor received $1m for the picture is ironic in light of the fact that Christopher (*Superman*) Reeve reportedly turned down the role of Eddie Keller because the million dollars he wanted for playing it wasn't forthcoming. Kirkwood said of Reeve, "I thought he was all wrong for the part," but at the very least, Reeve was, like the original character, white.

Screenwriter and novelist William Goldman commented in *Adventures in the Screen Trade*, "If I had been offered James Kirkwood's novel *Some Kind of Hero* with the proviso that, oh yes, we're going to keep it just as it is with one teeny-weeny change — we're going to make the main character black so we can nab Richard Pryor — I couldn't have done it. Kirkwood is a fine writer and Pryor is a dazzling talent, but when commercial matters dictate a total subversion of the source material we are in, as the French say, deep shit."

"The studio thought I might be upset, since the character wasn't black in my book," Kirkwood said at the time. "But I'm very excited about it." He wrote Pryor a telegram of congratulations when the actor was cast and another when the movie was finished. In the latter, Kirkwood told Pryor he had "made a writer extremely happy" because of his "touching and funny" performance, signing off by wishing him "triple orgasms until you're 87."

Kirkwood was surely intelligent enough to appreciate that the mindset of the black Vietnam vet Pryor played theoretically involved a layer that was naturally wholly absent from his book, one perhaps best expressed by boxer Muhammad Ali when fighting the draft: "No Vietcong ever called me nigger." One is unfortunately driven to wonder whether Kirkwood accepted the Pryor decision with such equanimity because he had secured not only an executive producer credit but a bit part in the film (which in the end he had to sacrifice for *Surprise!* anyway). However, Paonessa says the reason for Kirkwood's equanimity was less sinister: "There's something so wonderful about Jimmy. [He said], 'Yeah, he's white and, yeah, he was black, [but] it's a *movie*! I always wanted to make a movie.'…He was the biggest movie fan in the world. The movies were magic to him."

Robert Boris took Kirkwood's actually rather good original script and made it much more of a comedy. Kirkwood said, "I originally wrote the screenplay and then when they got Richard Pryor he got someone to come in to change the dialogue so [it] would be more indigenous to a black man." Boris would also seem to have "Pryor-ized" said dialogue, that is, made many lines fit the star's delivery style. Paonessa confirms that he understands that this is indeed the case, commenting derisively, "He added a lot of, 'Hey motherfuck, hey dude, motherfucking dude, fuck, motherfuck.'" Though the story of the movie is largely the same as that of the novel, its tone then is profoundly dissimilar.

Although the producers manage to retain most of what was in the Vietnam portion in Kirkwood's original — including, unfortunately, a frequent absence of a sense of danger or misery — the POW camp scenes feel very compressed. When Eddie Keller is back in civilian life, completely new scenes are added in which he is accidentally caught up in a robbery at a bank that has just refused him a loan and in which he attempts a robbery and has to cry off when the teller notices he has wet himself. William Goldman's previously mentioned astute observation merely referred to the very idiocy of the principle of casting Pryor, not the results, which are even worse. The film is very light and superficial, the clear consequence of it having been rewritten around the permanently incredulous, eyes-on-stalks screen persona Pryor had already established in several movies. It is this screen persona which undermines what attempts there are at pathos. For instance, when Keller's wife tells him that there's someone else and then says she hasn't given him the worst news yet, Pryor crosses his eyes and mock-faints. Another example is the way that the lingerie store squirt gun stick-up culminates in Keller fleeing empty-handed, terror on his face, pursued by an elderly female shopkeeper wielding a stick.

The ending of the story is altered to enable the sort of climatic finale more expected in cinema than in novels. The book's conclusion, wherein Keller makes a canny, bloodless getaway from the Mafia men trying to double-cross him over the securities exchange, is replaced by a scene wherein he gets into a fist-fight with two of them in his hotel room. To some extent, this is a reasonable change, but the scene is utterly formulaic in its cartoon, almost slow-motion, violence, lacking only a tumble through a sugar-glass window to complete the set of Hollywood clichés. Keller is then driven off by the Fritzi Donovan character (Margot Kidder), who has a slightly bigger role than in the book, though is renamed Toni. The 97-minute film is insubstantial and almost perfunctory and the cuts/alterations engendered by the rewriting sometimes show.

Kirkwood's April 1977 screenplay is actually quite faithful to his book yet still manages to incorporate the kind of scene juxtapositions, tweaks in motivation and telescoping/conflation of incident necessary to create a more cinematic narrative. The aborted robbery of the woman with the elevated shoe (absent from the Pryor version) is moved forward in the chronology, placed before Keller's squirt gun stick-up, something that actually helps build the tension in the run-up to the store robbery. Keller only gets $137 from the stick-up, making the mugging which lands him the securities a real necessity. In being forced to condense the events, Kirkwood ends up improving or dispensing with the book's more unconvincing and embarrassing sections. The POW scenes are more effective, the unhappy reunion between Keller and his wife far more plausible and the meeting between Keller and his father less artificially confrontational. Meanwhile, the gay sex scene in the prison camp is believable and would have been revolutionary for such a film (though inconceivable for Pryor to be involved with), and the scenes with Keller's stroke-afflicted mother are moving. The lead-up to the squirt gun stick-up is very well written and naturalistic, capturing the nervousness, boredom and frustration of Keller as he seeks at length the right place to rob. Kirkwood continually impresses with his savviness about the different requirements of the film medium: apparently apprehending that the lack of the interior voice provided by a novel will result in Keller's sorrow over having to rob in the first place not being adequately communicated, he includes a scene where after having done his deal with the Mafioso he returns the money to the shop whose cash register he emptied. (Interestingly, he is chased out with a stick by the elderly female proprietor.) The script ends with a scene between Keller and Ginger, Vin's girlfriend, whose warmth and platonic nature was probably considered not conventional enough for a movie *denouement*. Kirkwood later said, "I had written a really marvelous ending for it and I think it would have picked the whole film up at the end and they not only wouldn't even do it, they wouldn't even give it to Richard Pryor to read."

Though it has a clunky scene or two and though Kirkwood doesn't communicate as well as he intends that Keller's pursuit of Vin's girlfriend Ginger is for non-sexual and sentimental purposes, it is a fine piece of work and would have made for a very good and unusually nuanced 'Nam movie. (We should note that Jerry Paonessa's hand may have been at work in the tight plotting, certainly judging by Kirkwood's talk in the Carole Hemingway radio interview of working with him in the editing process.) Of all the screenplays Kirkwood wrote, it is by far the best and the fact that it was rejected in favor of a comedy-drama-by-numbers rewritten almost precisely to iron out all those nuances may provide some explanation as to why he was never again able to come up with a movie script of such quality: why write well and realistically, Kirkwood may have been thinking, when Hollywood studios specifically didn't want that?

The April '77 Kirkwood screenplay is, incidentally, almost exactly the same number of pages as the '81 Boris-Kirkwood version, so running length presumably wasn't an additional element in the motive for the changes. Kirkwood's friend Andrew Morse says insult was added to the injury of Boris' rewrite: "Paramount tried to take his name off of the screenplay credits because that way they'd have [to] pay him less."

Some Kind of Hero is largely forgotten by cineastes today, but was actually very successful. In its first three weeks of release, it held down the number two spot in the chart of highest-grossest movies in the United States. It ended up the 30th highest-grossest movie in America that year (a position no doubt assisted by the commercial gravitational pull of Pryor's in-performance film *Richard Pryor Live on the Sunset Strip*, which finished 20th in the same chart). It can be argued that in bringing Kirkwood's writing to a mass audience (it even turns his book title into a disco theme tune), the movie of *Some Kind of Hero* does Kirkwood's writing a favor — but of what use is exposure if the people to whom the work is exposed will come away thinking that the author of the source material cannot be anything special?

Paonessa vigorously denies that Kirkwood's Hollywood enterprises were a wasteful distraction from his novel writing. "I would say that he was open to anything," he says. "It was all to do with Jimmy Kirkwood. *Anything* anybody would do of his, he would be happy with. That's what I loved about him. I don't think he decided at any point in his career that he was going to concentrate on one media more than the other. I think that whatever came along that looked great he would get involved. The focus was only Jimmy." Was it not dispiriting for Kirkwood to repeatedly work hard on projects that never reached fruition? Paonessa: "Yeah, but that's the way it goes out here. That's why they pay you tons and tons of money for screenplays that never get produced. Being dispirited is very quickly assuaged with a box of money. We were going to give Jimmy, I think, a quarter of a million dollars to write *Some Kind of Hero* and he had never written a screenplay before. I wanted that deal for him because I wanted him involved, but it's a very dispiriting business. The one thing he didn't do was to sit around and lollygag over it. If you asked him if he were happy, he would say, 'Absolutely. All I wanted was more.' That's Jimmy."

However, as previously touched on, it doesn't seem to have been quite as simple as Paonessa maintains. In July 1977, Kirkwood wrote to Herlihy, "I'm thinking Calif. is just never going to happen for me business-wise in the movies. So be it. Everything gets stalled isn't that interesting. Pony bought at Columbia. Nada. Good Tits Bad Tits Warners. Nada. Hero — Paramount. Nada. Poland My Poland — Fox. Nada. I think there might be a conspiracy against me." Neither the injection of jocularity nor the fact that *Some Kind of Hero* subsequently made it out of "development hell" prevented his disillusion mounting. In 1980, he revealed to Herlihy that he had turned down an offer from Natalie Wood to write the screenplay for the movie of *Hit Me with a Rainbow* that she was hoping to make and star in, "as I have been hurt toomuch [sic] and don't want no more thank you very much." Kirkwood had also been bemused to find out about the star system. In 1980, he said, "I was asked to do a screenplay a couple of years ago for Tatum O'Neal. She was eleven or twelve at the time and I heard that she had final approval. I thought, 'Oh dear. That's strange, for someone in his majority years to be writing a screenplay where a twelve-year-old kid has final say.'" By January 1989, he was fulminating on Hollywood to the *St Petersburg Times*, "I hate it. I hate what happens. They never do it the way you thought they were gonna do it. It always turns out to be bastardized. The romance and the honeymoon are terrific, but you turn in the script and they say, 'What's that? Take that scene out, change this here. The character can't say that.' You have no control, whereas in a play, you do. I love going to movies. But I would never write for them again unless I'm crawling in the gutter begging for scraps."

Kirkwood had finally realized that he was in a long and ignoble tradition of fine prose writers who have been courted by a Hollywood machine that chewed them up and then spat them out. He did not publicly express such sentiments about the theatre, partly no doubt because he more frequently managed the slightly easier task of getting his scripts produced in that medium, but if he was honest with himself he would have to admit that theatre opportunities that had opened up for him post-1975 had been as detrimental as the cinema offers: *Club Mardi Gras* and *Murder at the Vanities* had eaten up a huge amount of his time to no avail. *A Chorus Line* was the undoing of Kirkwood's art perhaps not because it made him convinced he was a playwright/screenwriter rather than a novelist, but because it made other people — at least for a honeymoon period — think he was. Had he not had all the offers of work from producers who imagined *A Chorus Line* proved he was capable of writing a stage or screen smash, he would not have had any option but to continue with what had previously given him the most financial and aesthetic success.

That his (original) screenplays tended to be comedic only compounded the matter, for his legendary — even forcibly acquired — penchant for humor in his own life simply did not translate to written light entertainment. In fact, the assertion of Patti Goldstein that her old friend was a performer, not a writer, to the core comes to mind here. Kirkwood humor — notwithstanding the laugh-out-loud elements of the novel version of *P.S. Your Cat is Dead!* — would seem to be dependent on Kirkwood's magnetic presence. David Spencer recalls with affection how funny Kirkwood could be in the flesh: "Jim was not a wit in the sense of Peter Stone or Larry Gelbart. He didn't traffic in that kind of lightning wordplay. But he was delightfully naughty and dishy. It wasn't so much the words that were funny, it was the delivery. And, of course, comedy is about timing."

August 1982 marked the return of Kirkwood to another past work when a new production of the stage version of *There Must Be a Pony!* opened at the John Drew Theatre in East Hampton. This version was one-act as opposed to 1962's three, shaving an hour off the original running time.

"The one-act version I asked him to do," says Paonessa. "I had three friends who were really terrific playwrights. What I wanted to do was produce an evening of one-acts. 'Three By Three' was the name of it, and I was going to produce it in Los Angeles and it was going to be *There Must Be a Pony!* reduced to one act and one of David Rabe's plays and one of Jerry Cash's." "It was too long and overwritten," Kirkwood said in '82 of the original stage version of *There Must Be a Pony!* "But I was younger then and more stubborn than I am now. I guess I needed to get away from it to find perspective. I guess twenty years is enough perspective. It's a leaner piece now and I've cut some of the over melodramatic moments." He said that the play was now a much more optimistic look at how a mother and son survive a crisis, and that that optimism might be just what Broadway needed these days.

"They were feeling out the territory," says Jack Sydow of the one-act production. "I think it was only scheduled to run a week. [He was hoping] he'd be able to get a producer or raise money, based on that." The director of *UTBU* and the man who directed Kirkwood in *Brigadoon* and *Call Me Madam* was not the director for this production (Anthony Stimac — the production impetus behind the triptych that included *Surprise!* — fulfilled that task) but took an acting role. "A friend of mine was on the board at the theatre in East Hampton and I called Jimmy and said, 'I'd love to do Merwin,'" says Sydow. "I was then teaching at the University of Washington and that was a summer production. He thought that would be terrific and he talked to the producers and I was hired to do that. I don't know why, because Merwin is described in the book as a short, dumpy man and I am six-foot-2½ and was then rather skinny."

Sydow wasn't surprised that Kirkwood should spend time revising the stage version of *There Must Be a Pony!* rather than work on something new "because it was his first book, and it had been a great success and he was very anxious to see if he could make it work. It hadn't worked with Myrna Loy and he thought with a different kind of actress…" Broadway legend Chita Rivera was originally cast as Rita Cydney and advertisements for the play appeared with her face and name. When Rivera was offered a rare movie role, she found herself torn. Kirkwood and the producers graciously released her from her obligations. For Sydow, the new version was doomed by the choice of Joan Hackett to replace Rivera. "They were so concerned in getting a name that they didn't get somebody that had the flamboyance that's needed for the character," Sydow says. Despite having built a name on stage with *Call Me By My Rightful Name* and in film with *Will Penny*, Hackett, Sydow felt, was not the magnetic figure required to convey the demeanor of a queen (if slightly past-it) of celluloid: "She was a Method actress and she was always in herself and she didn't have any sense of the star quality." There was another cinema-caused casting change. Donald Oliver points out, "Matthew Broderick was slated to play Josh. Then he got cast in his first film, *Max Dugan Returns*. Dean Devlin eventually played the role." Oliver and David Spencer, incidentally, provided an orchestrated song for the play. "If Love Were…" was not sung on the stage, but heard through a radio on the set, a blast from Rita's showbiz past sung by Hackett.

Sydow, of course, had once told Kirkwood to stick to his playwriting guns over the stage production of *P.S. Your Cat is Dead!* He now found Kirkwood reverting to over-indulgent type. "Joan Hackett was a wonderful actress, but she was very finicky and wanted a lot of little changes all the time and he kept accommodating her and accommodating her," he says. Though Kirkwood might not have been inclined to express his exasperation at Hackett, Sydow was. "I got really cranky with her," he recalls. "We were in a notes session. This is towards the end. It was probably after a dress rehearsal. There was some problem about her suitcase and how to handle the suitcase. She was sitting next to me. She said to the director, 'What if I have an impulse to do such and such?' and I said, 'Squelch it.' Everybody in the room screamed with laughter, because she was always having impulses. Even she laughed."

Finally, Kirkwood's solicitous façade cracked, providing an insight into a part of his psyche of which even an old pal like Sydow hadn't been aware. Sydow: "One thing I found out about Jimmy on that show is he approached all the productions that he worked on with great enthusiasm and was looking forward to everything being wonderful, then when things started to go wrong little by little he would make certain complaints, but not really strong enough until everything would build up in him and then he'd pop. It really got quite ugly sometimes." In this instance, the cause — and direction — of the popping was Hackett. Says Sydow, "He wrote a letter that really upset her, talking about how she had wrecked the play."

Kirkwood's letter read:

Dear Joan,

I don't want to be mean or destructive but I must be candid. Last night the first act was disastrous. There was garbage being strewn all over the stage. There were very few of your speeches delivered as they were either rewritten or written originally. I think I've been very easy, too easy, rewriting for your demands and then to still have the speeches massacred — is the final embarrassment.

> *When your talent comes through, as it does in most of the second act, it is rewarding to sit there and watch the play. I can no longer put myself through the torture of watching the first act, however. In fact, I think it is by far the wisest choice to abstain from seeing the play any more if you continue to give the performance you're giving in the first act.*
>
> *Rita is not a ditz, she is a woman somewhat screwed up and lost. She does have the capacity to love. She is not talking "cocktail party" talk, she is telling her son what happened, the results of an alliance with a charmer named Lance. That's her reality, she has to spill it out to someone.*
>
> *I don't feel the intense affection in the scenes with Ben, I don't feel the urgency of getting him to go away for the weekend, I don't feel her true renewed zest for life. It seems to be by the numbers.*
>
> *If you think this is cruel — you should try sitting out front and watching the play go down the drain. That's cruel. If you were so disdainful of playing this woman, why on earth did you agree to do it?*
>
> *You have a reputation for being difficult. You must know it. I now see it and understand where it came from. It is not based on rumors, it's based on fact. You are an attractive, interesting, talented, difficult lady and I cannot tell you how sad I am that our relationship has to come to a rather abrupt and depressing end. I am truly sorry.*

Kirkwood was clearly in such a blind rage when he bashed out the letter that he had forgotten the difference between scenes and acts, the latter of which his play had just one.

It may be a point in Hackett's defense that there was not much to be wrecked. As with the 1962 version, in the one-act revival the deceased Ben Nichols is found sprawled on the house's game-room couch rather than outside. Audaciously, though, the play doesn't show the discovery of Ben's body. Nor does it show the relationship between Ben, Rita and Josh, the action beginning with the point in the story wherein Rita is facing official questioning about the circumstances of the suicide. It also dispenses with the original ending that traced Rita's mental disintegration. Even the middle section that is left is condensed. Such is the précis and exposition consequently needed that an unusual degree of information is packed into the dialogue. Though some of the year-references are retained from the two-decades-old first version, paradoxically Kirkwood replaces a reference to *Captain Kangaroo* with one to *Sesame Street*. Josh finds the suicide note (there is just one) when he goes around retrieving money from his hidey-holes in preparation for a flight to Ohio after falling out with his mother, the newel-post being the last of three places he looks.

In some ways, this variant of the '62 original is a superior play. Certainly, the jettisoning of the empty party yap is a blessing, while Josh's habit of secreting money in the newel-post is cleverly seeded by Kirkwood. However, the pathos is fatally reduced by the concertinaing of events: as Ben is not seen, the effect on Rita and Josh of what he has done is commensurately less powerful, as is their relief and joy at the discovery of the newel-post apologia. Though Kirkwood's editing and shortening is very competent, it is to a purpose that feels ultimately indeterminate.

The New York Times found Hackett "quite wonderful" in spurts but "under-directed" and (interestingly) "over-indulged." The play itself was adjudged by the paper to be not in fact a play, complaining that "The most dramatic, comic and tender scenes…cry out for the camera" and that "it remains novelistic, relying on recounting of details, midscene narration (direct addresses to the audiences) and between-the-scenes sum-ups." Kirkwood's writing was "self-consciously clever and ceaselessly sentimental" and "the characters are types, not people." Its summation was that the work was "a misshapen and misplaced hybrid." Long Island newspaper *Newsday* said that "*Chorus Line*'s inventiveness is altogether missing…," finding the script "without the wit and grace and daring that would raise it above a barroom confessional." Like *The New York Times*, it had a problem with Kirkwood "telling us as in a novel, rather than showing us, as in a play." However, the reviewer noted the second act was less guilty of this sort of inappropriate exposition and theorized that this was because Kirkwood had been "rewriting right on up to opening night. At least one of the characters listed in the playbill never appears on stage due to successive rewriting."

The play appeared and disappeared without trace. Sydow's hardly overwhelming recollection of its staging is, "It went okay. I really don't have any concrete memories of the thing. I guess I was so upset with what was going on with the leading lady."

This was not the first time Kirkwood had returned to the *Pony* play. A two-act version of *There Must Be a Pony!* exists in his papers. Though it is undated, it would seem to have originated in the 1970s. In this one, the time is 1956. There are more monologues from Josh, to such an extent that some feel like post-modern asides to the audience. Ironically, they are less necessary here than in the one-act play, because they explain nothing that the action doesn't. A more valid form of exposition is provided by newscasts which serve to convey information about the death and the investigation. The dialogue is frequently significantly different to that in the other two stage versions of *Pony!* and often has an impressive vitality.

Though we see Ben, his overhead flip of Josh from the first, 1962, production is absent. Josh is not directly seen discovering his body. Rita attempts suicide by drowning, something that is hinted at in the three-act version. As with the one-act version, a bitter Josh turns slightly nasty before discovery of the notes (two of them this time) in the newel-post serves to exonerate Ben in his eyes. Though it has a slightly pat climax to the first act (Josh immediately deciding Ben is a "bastard" when Nichols' wife materializes), it is the best of Kirkwood's three *Pony!* play scripts. Ironic then that though it was taken on for representation by Esther Sherman of the William Morris agency, this two-act version was the only one that did not obtain a stage production.

On February 2 1983, Kirkwood attended a double birthday party for Lena Horne and Liz Smith at New York's trendy Studio 54 nightclub. There, Kirkwood met 35-year-old song lyricist, freelance journalist and budding playwright Jim Piazza, who would be a significant figure in his remaining years.

Piazza had long been a fan of Kirkwood's work, particularly *Good Times/Bad Times*, which, despite its ambivalence about homosexuality, Piazza had, like many gay young men, treasured as a book that proved he was not alone. Piazza: "A friend of mine who knew Jimmy said, 'There is someone here you've always wanted to meet, come over here.'" So I went over and Jimmy was wearing a, for some ungodly reason, fishing vest. He always dressed very out of character and he was with his friend David and they were on some kind of fabulous designer drug and in very good spirits. I said to him, 'God, I've always wanted to meet you and now that I have, on to the next one,' and he laughed. I was just trying to ingratiate myself. We became instant friends and by the end of that night he decided that we should write together. We just decided that we were of one mind."

One friend of Kirkwood's, who prefers not to be named, says of Piazza, "Jimmy was his ticket to a better life, and it didn't work out…Jimmy was very prone to sycophants. And Jim Piazza — to be vulgar — had his tongue way up Jimmy's ass. I mean, he was a shocker…He was so two-faced and such a sycophant, and Jimmy ate it up. We all were horrified, 'cause he was not nice. And Jimmy would put him up to putting people down. Arthur couldn't stand him, and neither could I."

"There were friends that he was getting bored with," Piazza says in his defense. "Jimmy would go through people and…I was the new thing. And there was never a shortage of people flattering Jimmy, ever, ever. He always had that. He always had young actors or young writers always [doing that].

Yes, that may have been true. I was obviously trying to impress him. We shared the same sense of humor and Jimmy saw me maybe a little bit like himself...so it was beyond just a younger writer flattering his way in. Jimmy felt that we had a very compatible view of the world and [we] found each other vastly amusing. Probably an old friend who may have been not being invited over so much might feel that, sure, but what are you going to do?"

Though friends and collaborators, Piazza reveals that he and Kirkwood only became lovers in February 1987. It was around the time they met, though, that Kirkwood and Arthur Beckenstein ceased being lovers. "My relationship with Jimmy changed at some point in the early eighties," says Beckenstein. "He was seeing someone else and wanted me to know. He decided the sexual part of our relationship was over. I still loved Jimmy and my life with him and he still loved me. I decided to continue living with him in East Hampton on weekends, but in the role of a best friend, biggest supporter. I still spent as much time in East Hampton as I always had. We still traveled together and I was his companion at all important social functions. In the following years, he saw a number of other people but our close relationship always remained constant. Looking back on the early years of our relationship, he once told me, 'If you ever see anyone else, I don't want to know.' At the time, I was shocked by what he said and thought, 'I'm not going to see anyone else.' So when he confessed to me, I knew he was serious."

Jim Piazza confirms — from direct knowledge — the suspicions of others mentioned in this book that Kirkwood was using drugs heavily at this juncture. "The early eighties, everybody discovered cocaine and there were a lot of people just gone," he says. "Drugs figured so prominently in our relationship and I think Arthur always kind of blamed me for somehow introducing him. I didn't have any money — it was Jimmy. Cocaine was the coin of the realm [at] that time. It was just there all the time. A friend of his had given him a gift of this thing that you could actually do it at a restaurant table and it looked like a salt shaker and had no after-effects, no telltale signs. We did cocaine everywhere there was to do it and all the time. [Someone involved in the theatre] had a lot of access to drugs and would give us just tons of it and we would spend many a night in Jimmy's apartment doling it out in containers and jars. It was a lot about drugs...We used to do these mushrooms he used to get from somebody out in the West Coast and he loved those mushrooms. They were hallucinogenic but mild. And we experimented early on with Ecstasy. We did a lot of Ecstasy together; we just thought it was the best. It's a whole other kind of drug, at least then it was. You were supposed to have great sex on it, but we ended up talking, constantly. Arthur was never in on that. Arthur never got high with us, ever, ever, ever." Beckenstein asserts, "Jimmy was *not* a cocaine addict. It was *not* an addiction. He did use coke recreationally, as did a lot of people in the eighties. He never used it when he was working and only used it socially when partying with friends. I never got into drugs, but it was very commonplace and available if you wanted to try it in those days." Whatever its level, Beckenstein was aware of the irony of Kirkwood's indulgence. In reference to the hard-drinking James Kirkwood Sr. and Lila Lee, Beckenstein says, "He didn't have a lot of tolerance for their abuse problem. And yet he had his own problems with recreational drugs."

Kirkwood himself said in a letter to Herlihy in August 1977, "I hardly ever smoke anymore and because of my hypertension I can't take speed to help me work so I snort a little coke and pretend that helps and I think it does." It's a sentence in which Kirkwood seems hardly able to muster the willpower to kid himself. In a 1984 appearance on Chicago Channel 11's *Kup's Show*, Kirkwood had this to say about cocaine: "The terrible thing is it's happening all over the country, it's not just Hollywood…I think cocaine's a killer…There's a great fallacy about cocaine. People say it's not addictive, but it is addictive. I have a lot of friends that are having terrible problems with it. Especially in this business, it makes people do things that they shouldn't do to get the money to support the habit. It's a brutal, brutal drug." Perhaps it was genuine lack of knowledge of Kirkwood's habits that explains why his fellow panelists did not raise an eyebrow at his reference to "friends."

Arthur Laurents says, "Jimmy was heavy into coke." Does that affect the quality of a writer's output? Laurents: "Oh, absolutely." Because of his knowledge of dependence through his lover Tom Hatcher, Laurents did not attempt to bring Kirkwood up on his drug use. "I learnt a lot from Tom with AA," he explains. "You can't twelve-step anyone, really. They have to do it themselves." Did Kirkwood want to? "No, he didn't. He loved his life."

"I think the writing was very affected by the drugs," says Piazza. "Until the end he was writing a book about his father and he just didn't finish it and the writing was not really Jimmy's standard. He read it out loud to us; he read a chapter or two. It was always sitting there and it just didn't seem to be going anywhere."

Beckenstein doesn't feel Kirkwood's craft was affected by drugs, saying, "It wasn't an addiction that kept him from working." Yet, as Piazza points out of cocaine, "If you're a writer it will affect you, but you'll still write." An important distinction. When Kirkwood met Piazza, Kirkwood had already embarked on a play that was originally titled *Star Wars* in reference to its subject matter of two feuding Hollywood actresses. Wiser legal minds prevailed and it was re-titled *Legends!* Around six months after meeting Piazza, and with *Legends!* far from finished, Kirkwood embarked on a play with him too, originally entitled *Anything at Eight* but eventually renamed *Stage-Stuck* after the mildly dyslexic Piazza tickled Kirkwood by misreading "stage-struck" on one of their East Hampton work weekends. "*Stage-Stuck* was a play about cocaine," says Piazza. "We wrote it high for the most part. I don't know if Jimmy used it when he was writing *Legends!* I wouldn't be surprised." Neither of these projects were anything like vintage Kirkwood.

Piazza thinks that drugs contributed to what he found to be Kirkwood's penchant for violence, which seems on some level to have still been as marked as it was thirty years before in the Kirkwood & Goodman days. "One night he just hauled off and just slapped me so hard," Piazza recalls. "I almost went flying off the chair. It was in front of friends of mine I had invited…He pretended it was a 'love tap' but it wasn't at all. The room stopped cold for a second and I was completely shocked and humiliated. I whispered to him that if he ever tried that again I'd come right back at him. I'm Sicilian, after all…And he used to hit this guy David. He was his boyfriend at the time…He used to hit him a *lot*…David would sometimes cry after being hit…Very cocaine behavior." Yet other things Piazza says would seem to indicate a far more deep-seated and sinister reason for these outbursts. "I always noticed how quick it would happen," he says. "No warning, really, just a sudden hand being raised. Almost uncontrolled. And not a good deal of apology on his part afterward. The inner demons at work, I suppose. There's something in Jimmy that was really kind of crazy. He took a lot of sadistic glee in certain things and he could be very volatile…I always think that his parents were so bizarre, his upbringing was so strange, that he was very damaged…We used to love to gamble on tennis. He hated paying up, but he would eventually, but one guy welched on him badly. He went to his house; I think he beat him up." Was Kirkwood a good scrapper? "He fought with that Irish intensity where it's just whatever you have: hands, fists, kick, whatever. I don't think he would think twice about picking a plate up and smashing it across the room if that's what was available."

Piazza says, "Jimmy was a tortured soul in a lot of ways." He recalls Elaine Stritch referring to Kirkwood as "Bobby Blamer." "He used to laugh at that," says Piazza. "He used to refer to himself as Bobby Blamer, because it was always somebody else's fault. It was always this one's fault he didn't get enough money. His phone calls were always yelling. If it was business, there was always a problem that was somebody's fault. He laughed a lot, but if he lost a tennis game it would be devastating."

As with so many Americans, Kirkwood tried to solve whatever issues he perceived himself as having via therapy, attending sessions for several years with celebrity shrink and author Mildred Newman. Piazza: "He used to call her all hours of the night and day: 'I just had this dream about a ship. What do you think?' She would always take his calls. Jimmy was no dummy. He was a very smart guy. He could write very honestly about himself and he could speak very honestly about himself. He had insight, but then he could cover it up just as quickly. I think therapy probably was enlightening." It was also sometimes humorous. "His session was right before Terrence McNally's and he used to ask Mildred if he could hide in the closet so he could overhear Terrence's therapy session," reveals Piazza. "She'd say, 'You get out of here.' So he would leave him notes under the pillow on the couch: 'I know you're crazy.'"

Piazza adds, "I think he did the best he could controlling his worst impulses. It meant so much to him to be adored." He also readily acknowledges that Kirkwood, in addition to his faults, had considerable attributes as a person. "He was amazing," he says. "He was the life of the party. He was very funny. I still hear his laugh now. I do hope that my discourse here is fair. I don't want to paint him as some monster. It's just that I knew him so fully, all the sides."

One side he saw was Kirkwood's vulnerability: "One night at the house I heard him creeping around the kitchen about three in the morning. He was sitting in there eating a pint of ice cream. I said, 'What are you doing?' He said, 'I'm so afraid of dying.' We just sat and talked for like a half-an-hour about that." This fear of mortality was expressed long before Kirkwood was afflicted by the illness that ultimately killed him so it seems it would be fair to assume that it stemmed from the same wellspring that made him fudge his age and which led him to hide his now balding pate. Piazza: "He used to get pissed off. He'd say, 'I'm not pretty anymore. My shoulders are too broad, my chest is too hairy. I was so pretty. Now look at me.' He'd get very down about that." "He certainly didn't want anybody to know he had a hairpiece," says Donald Oliver. "That was another one of his vanities." Piazza: "It covered fully, and I'm almost positive it was sewed onto, the scalp. I never, ever saw him without it and he showered with it on. It wasn't, of course, one of those things up for discussion or even humor." Piazza adds of the facial hair Kirkwood had been neatly trimming since the late sixties with a break of a few clean-shaven years in the mid-seventies, "I do remember once when he considered shaving his beard. Then Homer told him, 'You're too old!,' which stung. He never shaved it."

"I always thought he was doing it to keep me close to him," says Jim Piazza of *Stage-Stuck*, on which Piazza and Kirkwood began collaborating in 1983. "That his heart wasn't particularly in it, but he was having fun in the [process]."

Speaking in 1987 — three-and-a-half years after starting it, but with it still two years away from reaching a commercial stage — Kirkwood explained of *Stage-Stuck*, "It's kind of a far-out thing about what people will do to make a play a hit these days — which is almost anything. It starts out to be kind of a Sam Shepard kitchen drama, with a mother and father, two kids and an old grandmother. Then it starts escalating, because the 'money' people want bad language, then a disease, then some musical numbers. It explodes and grows until it's a total madhouse." Piazza later wrote of the play's genesis, "Despite the fortune he'd made on Broadway as co-author of *A Chorus Line*, Jimmy ached to lunch on the hand that fed him. He wanted to get even for all the slights he'd suffered, real or imagined, during his tumultuous career as an actor and playwright. And a vitriolic, no-holds-barred, naming-names send-up was the way he wanted to do it." Piazza's opinion is that Kirkwood's professional fury was not always righteous. "He was never at a loss for targets for his rage," he says. "Michael Bennett, Joe Papp, whoever was around. Stephen Sondheim. Anybody that he felt had crossed him or didn't treat him properly."

In the same 1987 interview mentioned above, Kirkwood said, "One's best work is often the most fun to do. I think my best book was *Good Times/Bad Times*, and that was the easiest book for me to write. It was like self-writing, it just came out. I had a terrific time. Every day I got up and thought, 'Oh God, I wonder what's gonna happen next?' If [*Stage-Stuck*] is as much fun for the audience as it was to write, it'll be terrific." Piazza is very pleased by Kirkwood's blissful recollection of the writing process. His own memories are, "Upstairs in his room in the Hamptons for the most part was where we wrote it. He had a study right next to his bedroom and we would sometimes work absolutely together or we would say, 'Okay, you take that scene, I'll take this scene, I'll meet you downstairs for lunch. I'll have Arthur make us lunch' — which Arthur was never pleased with! So I would go in the downstairs living room, Jimmy would be upstairs and then we'd meet over lunch and we would read what we had written to Arthur who would just sit there sometimes stone-faced and Jimmy would yell at him and say, 'Is this the funniest thing you ever heard?' And he said, 'Well, no'…It was just so bizarre, but we were having a good time. We would just crack each other up. We would just write and he would say, 'Okay, I have to do some coke but we're not doing any coke until I've finished this scene.' That was his reward."

Piazza doesn't seem to remember a time in the elongated writing process of *Stage-Stuck* when he felt he had to defer to the more experienced member of the duo. "We would fight," he says. "I think that's why he liked me. I really fought for what I thought was good. He'd say, 'A line isn't funny unless you have three things, it has to be bomp, bomp, bomp.' And I'd say, 'Well, sometimes, not always.' And I would write lines with just two and he would think they were funny and I'd say, 'It's two, not three.' Basically, we got a kick out of each other."

Even when the two wrote separate scenes, Piazza says each of them "dabbled" in the scenes the other had written, thus making it impossible to differentiate between their writing. "I always thought that was really half-and-half," he says.

On September 29, 1983, *A Chorus Line* officially became the longest-running play in Broadway history, taking the record from *Grease* with its 3,389th performance. A special celebratory show was arranged in which 330 dancers who had appeared in *A Chorus Line* since its opening at the Public took the stage, including the majority of the original company. "They spent $60,000 in support so that the stage wouldn't collapse into the basement," recalls Donna McKechnie. "[Bennett] had each number done by a different company, from a different part of the world."

Kirkwood wrote an article to mark the record-break for *Playbill* magazine in which he displayed none of the ambivalence about the show's position in his life that Seff and Piazza have noted. In it, he said, "How does all this feel? Absolutely terrific, amazing, unbelievable that nine years, which represents a certain chunk of one's life, has gone by with that light bulb marquee flashing around the front of the Shubert Theatre announcing *A Chorus Line* on the inside…How's it been, seeing it again and again with different casts in different theatres in different cities? I don't think there has ever been a time when, during the opening dance combinations, the tiny hairs on my arms and along my spine haven't stood erect in honor of the pure raw energy of the actor-dancers upholding the tradition and discipline of the theatre…God Bless the living theatre and a million thanks for the great luck to have been a part of *A Chorus Line*."

In the same article, Kirkwood surmised about what it would feel like when the show was no longer on Broadway. His conclusion — "A trifle ghostly, a void, a small sadness" — was something he would never have to experience. *A Chorus Line*'s Broadway run outlasted its co-librettist by just over one year, closing on April 28, 1990, after 6,137 performances. It was Joe Papp's decision to bring the curtain down. He said when he made the announcement in late February of that year that *A Chorus Line* had been losing $40,000 to $50,000 per week since the beginning of January and was projected to continue making losses. He had toyed with prolonging the show's life by moving it to a smaller Broadway theatre or taking it back to the Public, and rejected both ideas. "We're not *The Fantasticks*," he said in reference to a show that had been playing off-Broadway since 1960. He reasoned, "I thought, 'Why step back?' We would lose the glory... We're *A Chorus Line*. We're the symbol of Broadway."

The consequence of all this was that *A Chorus Line*'s record as longest-running Broadway show was overhauled by Andrew Lloyd Webber's *Cats* in 1997, something that caused no little anguish to Baayork Lee. "I was very, very sad," she says, "because I think they had *Cats limping* in, keeping it open and do you know I think they were giving tickets away just so that it would stay open, so they would break the record."

With Nicholas Dante his co-librettist on A Chorus Line, *mid-1970s.* COURTESY OF ARTHUR BECKENSTEIN

With Donna McKechnie, 'Cassie' in A Chorus Line. *The picture dates from a 1983 party to celebrate the show becoming the longest-running on Broadway.* ARTHUR BECKENSTEIN

On Cinema Showcase, *circa 1979.*

Talking to Jim Whaley, circa 1979.

Dear Sir—

Thanks a million for writing the "Rainbow".
If you could send me Stosh it could make me happy.
I really cried laughing — a rare event in this lousy world.
love + kisses
Marlene Dietrich

A fan letter from Marlene Dietrich, 1980.

William Russo, the professor who considered himself James Kirkwood's Boswell. COURTESY OF WILLIAM RUSSO

With friend, collaborator and supporter Jerry Paonessa. COURTESY OF ARTHUR BECKENSTEIN

Kirkwood loved tennis and pursued it all his life. COURTESY OF ARTHUR BECKENSTEIN

Richard Pryor in the movie adaptation of Some Kind of Hero.

With his collaborators on Murder at the Vanities, *David Spencer and Donald Oliver, early 1980s.* COURTESY OF DONALD OLIVER

With Elaine Stritch and friend Liz Smith, early 1980s. COURTESY OF ARTHUR BECKENSTEIN

Elizabeth Taylor effectively becomes Kirkwood's mother — with Robert Wagner effectively Reid Russell — in 1986 TV movie There Must Be a Pony!

In motion picture The Supernaturals, *1986.*

With Mary Martin (left) and Carol Channing on the 1986/87 Legends! *tour.* COURTESY OF ARTHUR BECKENSTEIN

Kirkwood and his final collaborator Jim Piazza flanking Esther Margolis and Bess Myerson at a fund-raiser at Kirkwood's East Hampton house, 1987. COURTESY OF JIM PIAZZA

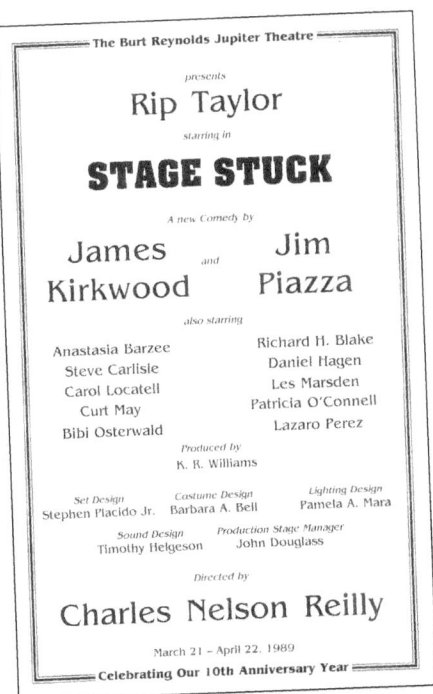

Program title for Stage-Stuck, *a Kirkwood play that few people saw, including (in its finished state) Kirkwood.* COURTESY OF JIM PIAZZA

Kirkwood with Andrew Morse, who set up the James Kirkwood Literary Prize. COURTESY OF ANDREW MORSE

May			1989				April **22**
S	M	T	W	T	F	S	112/253
	1	2	3	4	5	6	
7	8	9	10	11	12	13	Saturday
14	15	16	17	18	19	20	
21	22	23	24	25	26	27	
28	29	30	31				

7:00 A.M.		P.M. 12:00
7:15	*End of Run*	12:15
7:30		12:30
7:45		12:45
8:00		1:00
8:15		1:15
8:30		1:30
8:45		1:45
9:00		2:00
9:15		2:15
9:30		2:30
9:45		2:45
10:00		3:00
10:15		3:15
10:30		3:30
10:45		3:45
11:00		4:00
11:15		4:15
11:30		4:30
11:45		4:45

Sunday, April 23
113/252

Kirkwood's spooky final diary entry. ARTHUR BECKENSTEIN

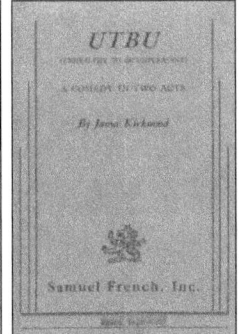

The oeuvre.

James Kirkwood, 1924-1989. COURTESY OF ARTHUR BECKENSTEIN

TWENTY

By January 1985, Kirkwood's infatuation with the IBM typewriter that had been partly responsible (in one story) for his career as a writer, and which had even prompted a poem by him entitled *Love Affair*, was over.

He had transferred his affections to the new technology of the word processor. Recalls T. Michael Kirkwood, "He just raved about it. He said, 'Oh my God — the time it saves!'" From hereon, though Kirkwood would sometimes write notes and possibly sections of works in longhand, Beckenstein's recollection is that his handwritten first drafts became a thing of history.

On January 19, 1985, Kirkwood wrote his first letter to Herlihy on his new toy, the squared, slick typeface an instantly noticeable contrast to the classic typewriter script in which all previous missives had been rendered. He said, "I simply had to write you a little letter to prove that I can, in fact, type on this word processor and also print it…" Kirkwood was clearly bowled over by the cutting-edge technology with which he was dealing: "All I have to do is press two keys and the entire mess will get slapped on paper and then off it goes to my dear Jamie."

Not that this prevented Kirkwood sending Herlihy a copy of his ode to his IBM Correcting Selectrix II. *Love Affair* may have been among the batch of what he described as "my poem-ettes" that Kirkwood dispatched to Herlihy on January 19, 1985. He explained of his verse to his old friend, "I'm going to keep on writing until I get better and better and eventually have enough for a small book, with either illustrations or fotos. Just a light, little amusing bookette, dontchaknow." The only published Kirkwood poem seems to be *Through the Province of the Poor to the Playground of the Rich*, printed in *The Bridgehampton Sun* on August 27, 1980. The work, which, like most of his poems, is blank verse, gently mocks the way the rich denizens of the Hamptons (of which he, of course, was one) for the way they imagine their problems compare to those of the low-waged and unemployed. It's summed up by the passage in which he describes himself as "…an ex-bleeding heart liberal/Now grown more acerbic with my age/And a snatch of smug affluence." It's more ambitious and serious in tone than most Kirkwood verse. His other, unpublished poems are indeed "light" and "little," as he described them, but he was also accurate in his "amusing" summary. He was no poet laureate but his verse brings a smile to the lips, particularly the pithy, whimsical *A Poem a Day Keeps the Doctor Away*.

On Friday, September 6, and Saturday, September 7, 1985, Avery Fisher Hall, New York played host to revival performances of the 1971 Stephen Sondheim/James Goldman musical *Follies*. Kirkwood attended the Friday performance. *Follies* overlapped in theme a little with *Murder at the Vanities* in that it dealt with the Ziegfeld Follies, revues similar to the contemporaneous Carroll Vanities, though less dirty. Kirkwood's old flame Elaine Stritch played Hattie Walker in the revival.

Kirkwood had decided to attend only at the last minute. Recalls Donald Oliver, "I invited Jimmy to go with me and he said, 'Oh, I'm in East Hampton, I don't want to come in, September in East Hampton's my favorite time.'" Kirkwood changed his mind and ended up attending as Oliver's date. Oliver: "After they found out that he was there, [record producer] Tom Shepherd asked him to do the liner notes for the record. Jimmy and I talked forever that night. We walked from the Lincoln Center to the restaurant where we were going to have dinner afterwards and I don't want to take credit for anything, but a lot of what he wrote in the liner notes was based on the conversations that we had. It was solidifying our own thoughts because it was a very emotional evening for those of us who loved *Follies* and loved musical theatre." Was Jimmy a big Sondheim fan? "I think he liked Steve in Steve's big songwriting mode. I don't think he would have liked the more modern, less song-y things."

Kirkwood's liner notes were effusive, despite the fact that he had reason to harbor some resentment toward Sondheim due to that giggling party he had — allegedly — made up with Arthur Laurents at an early run-through of *A Chorus Line*. "It was an evening with a built-in double whammy," wrote Kirkwood of the first night of the *Follies* mini-revival in reference to the fact that the musical was about a 1971 reunion of a forties Follies cast. He pointed out, "They in 1971, were looking back through a hazy gauze at a time of lush innocence…We, in the harsh reality of 1985 with Broadway being fed intravenously, were looking back at the relatively cushy good times of 1971." Kirkwood also wrote, "There are those who say Stephen Sondheim tends to back away from emotion, from anything that might be construed to be sentimental. That might be true at times, in some of his cooler, diamond-sharp works, but not in *Follies*. If so, why were there so many glistening eyes at intermission? Why, after a final standing ovation and then some, was such a dazed audience straggling out into the night?" As with Kirkwood's *Esquire* article on Clay

Shaw (however flawed by partisanship that was), one is struck here by the good writing, the affecting emotionality and the intelligent observations, making one wish that his journalistic legacy was not so meager. "Sondheim wrote back," reveals Jim Piazza. "He said, 'I blush.'"

As for Kirkwood's other musical tastes, Piazza says, "He loved his opera. He loved *La Traviata* and all that kind [of thing]. He loved the Italian composers, Italian opera. He had a gardener out in the Hamptons whose name was Mario and he'd open the window and say, '*Mar*-io, *Mar*-io!' Sing an aria to him. Toward the end, his favorite song he played over and over was called 'Where Do You Go When You Dream.' Anne Murray. He just loved that song. He loved [Andrew Lloyd Webber's] *Phantom of the Opera*, because it reminded him of Italian opera music. He loved a musical called *Chess*." At Kirkwood's Key West memorial, "Nessun Dorma" was sung. A highlight of the opera *Turandot* (beloved of Peter Kilburn in *Good Times/Bad Times*), Evan Rhodes said it was Kirkwood's favorite aria. Andrew Morse says of Kirkwood, "He mostly liked show tunes. In fact, we were driving out to East Hampton one time. 'Memory' from *Cats* came on and he turned to me and goes, 'Do you want to see me cry?' And he started crying, but not hysterically or anything. He was a very emotional kind of person. He was so touched by it."

In fall 1983, Kirkwood finished the first draft of *Legends!*

"Another ode to his mother," is how Piazza describes it. Beckenstein sees it slightly differently, as more of an ode to his mother's type of actress: "He knew those ladies and knew their lives and how tragic it could be and when they're a certain age and they're trying to find work, they can't. He just knew that world of Hollywood and liked writing about it."

The saga of *Legends!* is such a long and tortuous one that it seems best to discuss the contents and merits of the play here — with the proviso that the comments below refer to the published Samuel French edition of the play only. Because the author followed it on the road, constantly cutting and honing it, *Legends!* is surely the Kirkwood work that was changed and amended most — which is saying something for somebody so prone to revising his plays. Even so, there is a validity to reviewing the commercially available edition as the definitive version. Though what is on the page is not necessarily what most audiences saw on its journey across the United States — Kirkwood didn't include either the catfight climax or the subsequent musical finale of "Accentuate The Positive" in the Samuel French edition, the latter partly because it is unlikely that the two actors cast in the leading roles will always be versed in musical theatre — it is the way that Kirkwood (at least ultimately) felt the play should be presented.

Sylvia Glenn and Leatrice Monsée are both actresses, but are vastly different personalities. The former is profane and has had a career in which she has played forceful women, if not outright tramps, something reflected in her turbulent, several-times-married private life. The latter is renowned almost as an angelic figure, in senses both personal and professional (she played nuns, nurses and saints). She is also a few years older than Sylvia, though tries to keep this secret. What the two have in common is their loathing for one another and the fact that their careers are in the doldrums. Martin Klemmer is a legend in his own mind (he, without fail, introduces himself to people as "producer of the off-Broadway hit *Craps!*"). He hits upon the idea of a show that will exploit the public's knowledge of the feud between these two old-time movie stars, as well as the lingering public affection for them. He asks for a meeting with the pair, which Sylvia arranges at the apartment of a friend whose financial circumstances are visually more impressive than her own.

The opening scene features Klemmer hustling frantically on the telephone, trying to con theatre producer Bernie Jacobs, screen star Paul Newman and Sylvia and Leatrice into taking part in his new venture about two feuding actresses, which he has titled — why not? — *Star Wars*. The scene involves all sorts of lies, half-truths, misleading insinuation and imitations of bad telephonic connections to try to persuade the various parties to take part. It's actually quite funny, and indeed, whenever Klemmer is on the stage (page) the play is immediately more interesting, Kirkwood portraying his unapologetic sleaziness well, if a trifle cornily. Another Klemmer scene involves him making calls from a subway station to a hoped-for financier (who calls him back believing he is at the top showbusiness restaurant Sardi's) as well as to his own secretary, who informs him that both the main actor and his understudy in *Craps!* are drunk. As Klemmer simultaneously tries to convince the financier of the viability of *Star Wars* and attempts to get his secretary to devise a way to sober up the actors — at the same time having to find ways to explain away the sounds of trains and fire engines — a call comes in on an adjacent payphone which turns out to be from a distressed gentleman who imagines he has rung a suicide hotline. Klemmer — in his own brash, manic, mercenary way — tries to help the man out of his depression while maintaining his other two conversations. It's good stuff, even occasionally hilarious (when a fire siren sounds, Klemmer covers up by imitating a Sardi's *maître d'* telling a waiter, "Philipe, not so much flambé on ze crepes!")

Unfortunately, Klemmer is not on the stage nearly as often as two characters who though no more likable are far less interesting. Sylvia and Leatrice are the kind of egocentric movie matriarchs with whom Kirkwood had deep — if ambivalent — psychological connections. (The main one gets a name check: it is revealed Sylvia's daughter is named Lila.) However, their presence in Kirkwood's art had never been particularly successful and *Legends!* simply confirms why. Egotists prone to dramatics do not inspire empathy or sympathy — although one gets the impression that Kirkwood imagines that when they are women, they possess a certain outrageous charm. Especially black women: the play features an African-American maid called Aretha who Kirkwood doesn't actually describe as "sassy" in the character notes, but is cut from a certain clichéd feisty cloth. (Judging by Kirkwood's own comments in *Diary of a Mad Playwright*, his recounting of the staging of *Legends!*, the bantering relationship between the Aretha character and Sylvia was based on a maid — color unspecified — his mother once had. Kirkwood also had a black cleaning lady off-and-on for three decades named Aretha.)

There is a bit of silent comedy near the beginning involving Sylvia and Aretha as they — unaware of each other's presence — march about the borrowed apartment shifting things around and then back again when they mysteriously move, but it is similar to Marx Brothers sight gags only in its lack of sound, not funniness. Eventually, they discover each other and Sylvia tells Aretha about the imminent meeting with Klemmer. Aretha is surprised to find out how uneventful Sylvia's life is as Sylvia tells her of a routine which involves "…sitting at home watching *Dallas* or *Falcon's Crest* or *Dynasty*…and wondering what witch doctor Joan Collins goes to to keep looking like that!" The bitchiness between Sylvia and the shortly present Leatrice makes for a couple of good lines. (Regarding the uptight Leatrice's insistence on having a swear-box on her sets, Sylvia recalls a rumor that, "Ethel Merman came up to you once and said, 'I hear it costs a quarter every time you say a no-no. Well, babe, here's five bucks, go fuck yourself!'") However, another similar bit of bitchiness (on not speaking ill of the recently deceased: "They don't change just because they're dead, you know") falls flat for the Kirkwood devotee: he'd already used it in *Hit Me with a Rainbow*.

A stripper named Boom-Boom Johnson turns up. Unaware that the function for which he has been booked — a surprise party for Aretha's soon-to-be-married niece — has been cancelled, he does his thing for the three startled ladies. When a cop is called to the disturbance caused by the inevitably feuding Sylvia and Leatrice, he and Boom-Boom have a surreal conversation based on the cop's misunderstanding that Boom-Boom's employers, the Chippendales, have something to do with restoring furniture. It's amusing and suggestive enough that Benny Hill would have been proud, whatever that's worth. Also fairly funny is the way that Klemmer starts behaving when he is unsuspectingly fed a hashish-laced cake by the ladies (who are irritated that he is insinuating that he can get other actresses if they don't sign on his terms), even if his actions indicate that he has gone on an acid trip rather than gotten a little high.

It's impressive the way that Kirkwood can write with empathy and accuracy about women of a certain age, especially as his novels were usually what one might call "guys' books." However, verisimilitude does not necessarily make for interesting material. The interlude where Leatrice reveals she has undergone a mastectomy injects some welcome pathos, but this is about the only point in the otherwise snide and raucous proceedings where we don't want to see the back of the two women.

In *Diary of a Mad Playwright*, Kirkwood makes a comment about *Legends!* that unwittingly reveals its limitations: "We all felt it was a good show for the theatre-party people." The play's shortcomings clearly didn't matter to the crowds that flocked to see *Legends!* in 1986/87, but without two affection-generating icons like Carol Channing and Mary Martin being present in the flesh, the play feels quite slight. There is nothing profoundly wrong with it, but in terms of the amount of time and especially mental energy something so insubstantial took up in Kirkwood's life, the complaint can only be made yet again that one wishes he had spent that time writing novels.

David Spencer thinks it is those feelings of insubstantiality that were running through director Mike Nichols' head when in August 1984 he read Kirkwood's play at the author's request. The two were acquaintances and Nichols had once toyed with the idea of directing one of the stage versions of *P.S. Your Cat is Dead!* Kirkwood couldn't have given it to a bigger name to read: Nichols was famous for directing the films *The Graduate* and *Catch-22*, among others. Kirkwood recalled that Nichols rang him two days after receiving the script and told him he liked the play. He then suggested that the two leading ladies be played by drag queens on the grounds that "thirty percent of those ladies are the fantasies of their hairdressers." He also said the play lacked an important element: "screwing." Eventually, Nichols begged off because he had other commitments and didn't want to mess Kirkwood around for several months only to have to give him a "no." Kirkwood wrote all this in *Diary of a Mad Playwright* and seemed to take it at face value. David Spencer opines, "Nichols was deliberately presenting himself as an impossible choice. For whatever reason, he didn't want to say 'no' to Jimmy, so he made the conditions of his 'yes' so outrageous that *Jim* would have to decline. Not an unknown tactic. As a theatre man, Jimmy wasn't anywhere near as clever as Nichols, but I was flabbergasted that, as a guy who'd at least been around the block a few times, he didn't even *consider* that Nichols was shining him on." Gary Beach, who would play Martin Klemmer in the play and become friendly with Kirkwood, agrees with Spencer. "I don't think he was serious at all," he says of Nichols. "Probably not his cup of tea." Paonessa also agrees, and is not amused. "What Mike Nichols did was reprehensible," he says. "It was so heinous a manipulation — of course Mike is the mastermind of manipulation — that Jimmy didn't even get it."

Failing to procure Nichols was ostensibly a blow because having him on board would have made it far easier for Kirkwood to find producers for the play. In fact, he found them shortly afterwards "by chance, by serendipitous occurrence," him adding to this explanation, "In retrospect, by means of the devil himself." As suggested by David Spencer, some consider the good name Kirkwood had acquired in theatre circles through *A Chorus Line* to be erroneous. One friend, who prefers not to be named, says of Kirkwood co-writing *A Chorus Line*, "There wasn't a moment in the text of *A Chorus Line*, not a comma, that didn't filter through Michael Bennett. Jimmy was basically a hired-hand, as were all the collaborators. This one supplied this, that one supplied that, but it was Michael's overall vision putting the jigsaw puzzle pieces together. When any show is a major success there's a tendency to elevate all the people who worked on the show as if each person's contribution was equally responsible for the show's success. This works either for or against the person so elevated." In the case of *Legends!*, it so happened that this elevation worked *for* Kirkwood, because it brought him his financier.

In April 1984, Kirkwood was asked by Ahmet Ertegun — former songwriter and now president of Atlantic Records — and his business partner Kevin Eggers to write the book to a musical primarily based on the infamous myth-debunking biography *Elvis* by Albert Goldman. Presley was a subject of little interest to a lover of musicals and opera. Kirkwood told them that though he didn't dislike him or his work, he was no particular fan of nor had any great knowledge about Presley. That the prospective producers explained that they weren't worried by this gives an indication of the level of ego-gratifying attention to which Kirkwood was being subjected at this juncture in his life and how the fact that he'd co-written the most successful show in Broadway history could make people's natural common sense go haywire. Kirkwood read the Goldman book and liked it more than he thought he would. He intimated to Ertegun and Eggers that he was considering their proposal. By September, he was still considering and a slightly agitated Eggers rang Kirkwood to ask why he wouldn't sign up. Kirkwood explained that he was finishing *Legends!* and that his own play took precedence. Eggers asked to read *Legends!* Eggers liked it very much and requested permission to show it to Ertegun. Ertegun also enjoyed it and, without even trying, Kirkwood had producers for his play. (Bob Regester and Cheryl Crawford came in with Eggers and Ertegun.)

Gary Beach says that Kirkwood indicated to him that he had no interest in writing the Elvis musical. He says that both sides — Kirkwood and Eggers/Ertegun — were just using each other. This certainly seems to be partly borne out by Ertegun. "Kevin came to me to see if I could help him put on the Presley show, which I thought had some merit," says Ertegun. "I didn't know Mr. Kirkwood but Kevin told me that he thought he'd be great." Because Kirkwood had co-written the book of the most successful show in Broadway history? "Yeah, that's probably why he went to him, which is not necessarily the most intelligent thing, but on the other hand that was typical of Kevin. Then Kevin said to me that in order to get him to do that we've got to produce this other play... This whole thing was not my maneuver. It was done by Kevin Eggers." Of Eggers' comments on *Legends!*, Ertegun remembers, "He told me this play would have two big stars, it wouldn't cost anything and so forth." Asked what he thought when he read the *Legends!* script, Ertegun admits, "I wasn't crazy about it..."

Though each side may ultimately have been using the other, Kirkwood did at one point seem to have been taking the Elvis project seriously. He went to the extent of producing an eight-page document on 14"-long paper (i.e., a couple of inches longer than "letter-size") titled "ELVIS-- Rough scene by scene." (There are also seventeen pages of handwritten notes, but much of this seems to be *aide-mémoire* or material expanded upon in the typed pages.) Considering Goldman's scurrilous book was probably his main source of knowledge about Elvis, Kirkwood's ideas are surprisingly conventional and cornball. The odd profanity and hint of homosexual blackmail aside, Kirkwood is recounting the Elvis legend, not the Elvis story. The typed pages end with Presley's 1958 induction into the army, so Kirkwood had a way to go before he reached his 1977 death. Kirkwood's interspersed suggestions about where songs might go raises a problem that would possibly have been insurmountable for this mooted production. The whole idea of an Elvis musical with an original score is illogical: the necessary juxtaposition of famous Elvis numbers with new material would surely be jarring and puzzling. Ertegun says, "A couple of ideas that Mr. Kirkwood mentioned were I thought very good." Paonessa goes a lot further. "Quite frankly, the work that was done on Elvis was absolutely terrific," he says. "We did it in outline and I have got to tell you it's one of the best things he's ever done. Whether that outline is maybe on some scraps of paper, it was really, really good."

However, Paonessa acknowledges that Kirkwood only agreed to think about the Elvis project "because he was a little concerned about getting *Legends!* off the ground." From Paonessa's point of view, getting *Legends!* off the ground was proving difficult because it wasn't up to much. "I told Jimmy — I was being honest but he didn't want to hear it — it needed to be rewritten…Jimmy wanted everything prematurely. God knows he worked like a devil writing, but he wanted to see it go to the next stage quickly. Writing and rewriting, Jimmy didn't want to be bothered with it, unless he was like being hammered over the head by Michael Bennett. It was mildly funny, I guess, but if he had taken the time to take another couple of rewrites over a year, I think it could have been great. Great, great premise, terrific idea, but [not] in execution."

Whatever the play's shortcomings and their own misgivings, Eggers and Ertegun signed up to the project and the hunt began for cast and crew. According to notes found by Beckenstein, Kirkwood's wish-list was comprised of Glenda Jackson and Julie Harris, although in a letter Kirkwood said, "If I had my druthers I'd snatch Angela L. [presumably Lansbury] for Sylvia and Julie Harris for Leatrice…" (Eileen Heckart and Frances Sternhagen took the roles at an Actors Studio reading.) Though Jackson and Harris would have been very famous to moviegoers, the two actresses ultimately cast in the leading roles were just as famous to theatre lovers: Carol Channing (Sylvia) and Mary Martin (Leatrice). Since Kirkwood had first met her back in the stand-up days, Channing had become a somewhat over-the-top and clichéd figure, but there was no doubting her talent nor her box-office allure. Mary Martin also possessed a name that lived up to the title of the play, and it was no small coup Kirkwood secured by personally enticing her out of her almost decade-long retirement to star in his work. There was a connection between the three, one that illustrates just how hot was the Kirkwood & Goodman stand-up act with a certain crowd at a certain point in time: back in 1948, Martin had adopted young up-and-comer Channing as her protégée and insisted on taking her after curtain of their respective shows one night to see Kirkwood & Goodman at the Bon Soir.

Clifford Williams was hired as director, the Englishman who had been intended to direct the first play version of *P.S. Your Cat is Dead!* when the Robert Stigwood organization had it under option. Rehearsals started in the first week of December 1985, at which point the plan was to open in Texas — Mary Martin's home state — before moving, via LA, into New York.

No sooner were rehearsals underway than Kirkwood received some bad news. On December 10, his Aunt Peggy died in his Key West house. Though she had apparently gone peacefully — she was found sitting in a chair with a breakfast roll in her hand — losing his second mother was an emotional blow for Kirkwood, not helped by the fact that with all the problems with *Legends!* he felt that he couldn't abandon the show to fly down to Florida. Peggy's ashes were buried next to Lila Lee in Elyria.

The same week brought bad news of a different kind with the premiere of the movie version of *A Chorus Line*. The obvious hope for the film had been that it would follow in the footsteps of the likes of *West Side Story* and *The King and I* in triumphantly transferring the magic it had possessed for its live audiences to celluloid. The film, in fact, was a travesty of the stage show, something that no doubt gave Kirkwood further cause to "hate" Hollywood and its processes.

Kirkwood later said of the movie adaptation, "Michael Bennett was going to direct it and Nick and I were going to write it. It was going to be the whole team that did it on Broadway. Then Michael had a very bad experience with Universal on another film that he was going to direct before that and he just left a note on his desk one day at the studio and it said, 'Gone fishing.' He left California and walked out of *A Chorus Line*. I think because of that, the studio got angry at all of us although we didn't have anything to do with that." Donna McKechnie says of Bennett, "He had a great idea for the film. It was not a film of the stage audition. It was going to be a film audition for the film. In other words, it would be on a soundstage and not on a theatre stage."

The reason for not involving Kirkwood and Dante changed as the property switched hands (the film rights were sold from studio to studio down the years). In 1984, Kirkwood said, "It's that terrible old cliché: they say, 'Well, they're much too close to it.'" Kirkwood's film producer friend David Gentile confided to *Crooked Tree* author Robert C. Wilson that an agent representing Kirkwood who informed him he was too close to the material was simultaneously representing other parties agitating to write the screenplay. Kirkwood was so unhappy that he was thinking of switching agents over it. Of course, Kirkwood may have got it wrong,

Gentile (by no means considered a perennially reliable person) may have got it wrong and there is a certain danger here of a Chinese Whispers process. Whatever the truth, it was Arnold Schulman — whose credits included *Goodbye Columbus* and *Funny Girl* sequel *Funny Lady* — that was chosen to write the script. Those who thought that the inclusion of two new songs by Hamlisch & Kleban and the appointment of no less a director than Richard Attenborough — still basking in plaudits for *Gandhi* — were good harbingers were to be proved severely mistaken.

"If I were going to do it as [a] film, I would do it as a very tough, hard, biting almost documentary," Kirkwood told Jim Whaley several years before the film was completed. He also said, "It's a very tough property to turn into a movie and in a way I'm very relieved that I'm not going to do it because I don't have that burden then." The toughness of the task facing any adapter revolved around a few things. *A Chorus Line* is a far more concentrated piece of work than the likes of *West Side Story* and *The King and I*, being set in one place on one day. It is also a piece of work that by its very nature can't be "opened out." The small alterations to the story that we see in the film such as the flashbacks to when Cassie and Zach were in a relationship are really the maximum changes that could be made without destroying the very point of the work: to convey the tenseness of a focused audition process. Though a theatre musical allows a certain kind of fantasy that theoretically doesn't lend itself to a naturalistic medium like cinema (people bursting into song, accompanied by instrumentation that seems to exist in the ether), other movie musical adaptations had not found this a problem. However, the fact that cinema calls for small brush strokes more than extravagant paint splashes is telling in other ways here: it's interesting that the comments of the dancers during their monologues — those sarcastic or self-deprecating or bitchy lines that draw laughs in theatres — simply seem arch in the movie.

That said, there are faults in the film that can't be put down to the intrinsic difficulty of the switch between mediums. The music suffers from the film being made in the period it was. Despite the enduring toe-tapping nature of "One" and "Dance: Ten, Looks: Three" (the "tits 'n' ass" song), no composition no matter how good could emerge unscathed from the unlovely styles and production methods of the 1980s. The colossal drums, the gaseous synthesized percussion rolls and the puny, shrill (presumably synthesized) brass all do a disservice to Kleban and Hamlisch's art. Meanwhile, the casting seems casual. Michael Douglas is, as ever, impressive but his effortlessly powerful performance as Zach simply emphasizes the lack of charisma of almost all the other actors, among whom an all-American blandness prevails. Attenborough's direction of the dance routines is maladroit. Though the final "glitz" sequence is very good, never do the routines approach breathtaking.

Insanely, the climax of the stage play — the intricate interweaving and overlapping of three different songs — does not appear in the film. This is not quite compensated for by a clever twist not in the stage play: when Zach calls out the dancers' names, it is not, as they think, to offer them parts but to reject them. (This leads to a double twist: the mistakenly-called Diane had been crestfallen when she was told to get back in line.)

As important as she feels the Cassie and Zach "second act" — to which Kirkwood contributed so much — was to the original show, Donna McKechnie was dismayed that it became almost the centerpiece of the *A Chorus Line* movie. She says, "When she gets the job [in the stage show], you kind of felt, 'Well, will they get back together?,' but it's not about that so you can't have them care that much about it. They made that tremendous mistake in the writing in the film; because they really went for the romance and it was awful…It lost everything."

"He missed the whole point of the show," says Baayork Lee of Attenborough. "I mean, he gave 'What I Did for Love' to Cassie. When Diana sings that song she represents every single dancer that ever took a class or anybody in the theatre and what we do, and all of a sudden it became a love song."

The mediocrity of its film incarnation has had a fairly devastating effect on *A Chorus Line*: it has been denied posterity. TV programs devoted to great musicals, for instance, mention *A Chorus Line* fleetingly, if at all, because such is the nature of television that its first port of call is filmed evidence of greatness. In the case of *A Chorus Line*, unlike other stage shows that became movies like *West Side Story*, *The Sound of Music*, *Oliver!* et al., there is none. Coupled with the fact that the Original Cast Recording LP — recorded quickly and in the wake of a squabble about pay — is rather flat, it means that *A Chorus Line* is only surrounded by a glow for those who have seen it in the flesh.

Kirkwood later said that the experience of seeing the movie made him feel that those responsible for it were killing his children. He effectively distanced himself from the film when he allowed the biographical notes of the published version of *Legends!* to carry the tart line, "He is the co-author of the book of *A Chorus Line* (the Broadway musical, not the film)."

Kirkwood wasn't much happier the following year when a filmed version of his debut novel finally saw the light of day, more than a quarter-century after the movie rights had first been sold. His disappointment was centered less on the fact that it was only a TV movie than on issues of quality. *There Must Be a Pony!* was broadcast by the ABC network on October 5, 1986 — coincidentally almost exactly fifty years after the terrible events in Manhattan Beach that inspired the parent book. Robert Wagner played Ben Nichols. Wagner was a pretty big name, but the production's Rita Cydney was an actual legend. This may have been down to Kirkwood, who in '81 and '82 had vigorously solicited Elizabeth Taylor's participation in the play version by sending it to both her secretary and (along with *Hit Me with a Rainbow*) her agent. Taylor not only gave the leading character that star quality cited as requisite by Jack Sydow, but was, no doubt unbeknownst to the producers, poetically appropriate because she had been supposedly present when Kirkwood had his supposed Damascene conversion to writing in his hotel back in the late fifties. Unfortunately, the good news ended there.

It's possible that those who have never read Kirkwood's original book might consider the *Pony* TV movie to be quality drama, but it's doubtful. Even those not continually distracted by their knowledge that the book's plot is re-ordered will notice that ersatz quality that seems to go hand-in-hand with movies made for television, at least in that era: the banality of the dialogue, the frequent hamminess of the acting and, of course, the washed-out video rather than lush film tape. The absence of any attempt to capture a teenager's point of view sucks the kernel out of the story, creating a grand pointlessness. Oddly, there is a suggestion in the script that Josh might be homosexual that is not pursued.

"His play endings are very different from his book endings," William Russo says of *There Must Be a Pony!* "I suspect that after he wrote a half-dozen play versions of *There Must Be a Pony!* he hadn't read his own novel for years, and this is where I theorize that his memory was changing or he was being perhaps more honest or after his mother died he could be more forthright. Then, of course, there was the movie version, which I think he despised, which I thought was very faithful to the book." Russo finds the casting of Taylor intriguing: "I always thought she bore a very striking resemblance to Jim Kirkwood's mother, physically. She was an ideal choice to play the part."

The irony of all this is that Kirkwood's own screenplay for *There Must Be a Pony!* is no better. The screenplay is clearly one intended for a big screen production rather than television, judging by settings that would have been beyond the budgets of the American networks. It is undated but must be post-1975, before which point he had not tackled the screenplay format, unless the step outline of *Nothing but the Night* is counted. It starts promisingly, with Kirkwood setting the scene with a voiceover from Josh (fifteen here, as opposed to sixteen in the plays) and some intelligently-chosen vignettes from Rita and Josh's lives. Ben's implied reason for marrying his wife for money rather than love is better explained than in any of the play versions. However, a scene where Rita is literally impaled on a fire hydrant is ludicrous, the dialogue between Ben and Rita and Ben, Rita and Josh never sizzles the way the exchanges between Rita and Josh do and the scene wherein Mrs. Nichols confronts Rita is very clunky, both in drunken ramblings to herself which are embarrassingly transparent exposition and the instant conversion by Josh to the opinion that Ben is a bastard.

Though Kirkwood does his best to open out the story so as to take advantage of the multiplicity of settings afforded by the motion picture, there are some essential elements of the story that it becomes clear don't travel over to celluloid well. The main one is that ending: finding and reading a note is a passive act which though it makes a perfectly good *denouement* to a book — and to some extent a play, which is intrinsically cerebral — is almost antithetical to the proactive principles of the movie climax. The other main fault is the bland timbre. Although a note at the start of the screenplay insists that its 1954 period setting is not laid on thick, it's certainly laid on thick in the dialogue (which naturally replicates much of the stage versions' dialogue). Though to some extent, the dialogue feels period-correct, boasting several lesser-known phrases that have since fallen from use, it also feels period-correct in the sense of the type of language you would have expected to hear in film productions of the time rather than in real life. When Kirkwood began writing about the events in *There Must Be a Pony!* in the fifties, such were the mores of the era that it would have been if not so much unthinkable then certainly daring (with all the commercial and sociological drawbacks that went with that) to portray life, especially teen life, as-is. A few swearwords had crept into the stage productions of *Pony!* over the years but that and the frankness about Rita and Ben being physically intimate is the extent of Kirkwood's recasting of the story for a more permissive age here. It's quite possible that Kirkwood would not have been able to update the dialogue and events even had he desired to because — as semi-suggested by Russo — he now remembered them the way they were depicted in the novel rather than the way they happened. As a consequence, his screenplay feels as much like a script for a family viewing TV movie as the actual Elizabeth Taylor TV movie.

Kirkwood's endless journeys back to the events surrounding the death of Reid Russell via his novel, three stage versions and the screenplay — as well as public readings of the novel's Ben/Reid body discovery scene in lectures — would, incidentally, seem to provide some kind of counterbalance to the theories of those who suspect he may have had blood on his hands. Surely it would take a man with ice running through his veins to not feel debilitatingly daunted at psychologically revisiting the scene of his crime so frequently.

"I got a call from my agent that James Kirkwood had written this play and it's going to star Mary Martin and Carol Channing," recalls Gary Beach. "Not a musical. I thought, 'Oh, that'll be fun' — tour round the county for what at the time was going to be Dallas, Los Angeles and then to New York. Not until I joined the rehearsal period did I realize, 'No, that's not such a definite idea, Mary may not want to go to New York.' I think if I had been presented with a package of, 'Oh, you're going to tour every town you ever heard of for a year and possibly not come into New York,' I don't think I would have found that attractive."

Asked what he thought of the first version of the play that he read, Beach says, "I thought it was fun. I thought frankly, 'The idea of Mary Martin and Carol Channing doing those roles piques my interest'…The role that I was to play was fun. I opened the show and closed the show and that was basically it. I had a five-, six-minute scene at the beginning of the show, all alone, tiny set, center-stage, that set the play up."

Of Beach's Martin Klemmer character, Donald Oliver reveals, "The role of the producer in *Legends!* was based on me. Originally. Not as it ended up, because he ended up being rather hysterical and overdone, but as it started it was the fact that Jimmy used to say he admired me for my fearlessness. That was the impetus for the Gary Beach character, that he had the nerve to call one lady and say, 'She'll do it if you do it' and the other one to say, 'She'll do it if you do it,' which, of course, was a technique that was used many, many times in theatre."

Though he thought the play fun, as an experienced theatre man, Beach also knew that the out-of-town try-outs were necessary to address the play's transparent faults. "It definitely needed work," he says. This work would be postponed and compromised — perhaps fatally — by a problem that raised its head during rehearsals: Mary Martin was having severe trouble remembering her lines. "She had not been on a stage in a decade and had basically retired," says Beach. "I think she lost that little muscle." Martin was distraught and the production and writing team were panicked as it became increasingly obvious as the rehearsals continued that things were not improving much. Re-casting with Julie Andrews was raised by Channing (who would later completely redeem herself for this apparent disloyalty), hypnotism was suggested and finally — after considerable agonizing — it was agreed that Martin would take the stage wearing an earpiece that would enable her to receive secret prompts.

Trish Garland, who played Judy in the original production of *A Chorus Line*, was pleasantly amazed to find herself hired to choreograph the striptease routine of Boom-Boom Johnson. "They really decided just to make it a choreographed number, as opposed to someone just coming in," Garland recalls. "When Jimmy called me, I actually didn't consider myself a choreographer and I kept telling him, 'Why don't you call Wayne?' as in Wayne Cilento, or 'Thommie' as in Thommie Walsh, and he said, 'No, we want you.'" She adds of the decision to properly choreograph the number, "I think that wasn't just Jimmy's decision, that was Clifford." She says of her and Clifford Williams' attention to Boom-Boom's routine, "He and we worked on some music and it didn't work and then we got the piece that we finally ended up with and it was great." Garland is referring to the assertive Aretha Franklin recording "Respect." Garland: "It just became a showstopper. I don't think they expected that either, but it became that."

New Year's Day saw 1986 saw the 61-year-old Kirkwood confiding to James Leo Herlihy, "Methinks, between thee and me I am really, for the first time, feeling AGE, and I don't like it." He elucidated, "I hurted [sic] my wrist playing tennis three weeks ago, just a little twist, and it's still bad, I still can't play, and recently, one knee is doing what it did years ago. I'm praying it's just a very brief encore and not back onstage for a stay. Also second opinion surgeons want to operate on my hand but it's not really bothering me so I am loathe to lie down for them. So all in all, it's a pudding I'm in and what I should do is turn into pollyanna and think of all the good things and fuck the rest. But all I've been doing lately is to concentrate on the downers. I think I'd better get a whole shelf of positive-thinking books and dive into them. I seem to be negativizing myself and that's ridiculous." He had other things on his mind too: "Darling, in case you don't realize it, my royalties are not what they used to be the last TEN YEARS. I mean, I'm no longer flush."

Though he didn't mention *Legends!* in the letter, that, of course, also continued to be something of a "downer." A couple of days before the opening in Dallas saw a summit meeting with the author and the producers. One of those producers, Ahmet Ertegun, was referred to by Kirkwood throughout *Diary of a Mad Playwright* as the "Dread Turk." Kirkwood's disdain for him was illustrated by one point in the book wherein he wrote that a glance by him over at Ertegun "was not returned by anything that could be called human communication." Yet this disdain was by no means representative of the people with whom Ertegun worked. A legend in the popular music industry for his vision in setting up Atlantic Records and his good musical taste in the grittily-talented people he signed or nurtured, he did not conform to any template of a mercenary mogul. A litmus test of the regard in which he was held is provided by the fact that The Rolling Stones' Keith Richards — a man who does not suffer fools gladly — only ever had warm words to say about Ertegun. It would seem that Kirkwood had taken one of his legendary disproportionate and not-quite-rational dislikes.

One of Kirkwood's complaints about Ertegun was that while he had criticisms about the play and severe concerns about Martin's difficulties, he did not leaven them with any praise. "In my work, in show business, I'm very straightforward about what I think about things," says Ertegun in response. "If an amateur singer comes up and auditions for me, then you say, 'Oh very, very nice. You should continue.' You sort of encourage them, but you don't tell them they're terrible. But professionals, you have to tell them, because otherwise they waste your time and their time. You have to say what you believe. I can understand that he may have thought that he had a great work of art there, as many people do about whatever they create, but you have to face whatever other people think as well." He adds, "I never had any disagreement with Mr. Kirkwood, I liked him very much. Two or three people have written that we had run-ins and so forth. We may have had slight disagreements about how the play was going, but that's normal." (Ertegun had not read — or heard of –*Diary of a Mad Playwright* when he was interviewed for this book.)

"That got us open," says Beach of Mary Martin's earpiece. Said opening took place on January 7, 1986. "It wasn't by any means a perfect event, but it got us open and it got us from town to town to town and, oddly enough, some of the reviews were good," says Beach. Some were, but the most striking thing about the *Legends!* tour, which was to last for the whole of 1986, was the dichotomy of the packed theatres and rapturous receptions therein and the mainly lukewarm response of the critics. Was this strange? Beach: "Not really. One of our stage managers, maybe a little rudely, called it the dancing bears: it's not that they're that good at dancing; it's that they're bears and they're dancing — that's something in itself. I think that's what the ladies had. It's not that the play's good or if they're good — it's: 'Jesus Christ, that's Mary Martin and Carol Channing up there. They're legends.' That's what the play had going for it. I was still in my thirties and I met everybody I'd ever heard of. [They] came backstage to see those ladies. It was incredible." Ertegun agrees with Beach's assessment: "We were playing the hinterlands so with those two big names, of course, we did business. It had nothing to do with the play."

Of Martin's memory problems, Beach says, "That was hell for Jimmy because he wanted to work on the play, Clifford wanted to work on the play, Carol Channing definitely wanted to work on the play and everything was brought to a halt because Mary did not have that ability anymore. We actually left Los Angeles after our rehearsal period and got on a plane to go to Dallas and our leading lady didn't know her lines… [He] had to write for Carol and Annie-Joe and pages were hitting the ground that Mary was on. It's like, 'Take that out, she'll never learn this.' That's not the way a writer can work."

This only added to the burden of Clifford Williams, for problems connected to *Legends!* were by no means restricted to Mary Martin. Channing and Williams were destined never to gel. Beach: "Clifford had a pipe and Carol was rehearsing a scene [where] she would grab a crucifix off the mantelpiece, walk downstage center and deliver this speech straight out. She was talking to her dead husband. So Clifford said, 'Carol, the next time, sit down on the couch and just deliver it'… So the next day we get to that very portion and Clifford had his legs crossed and he was banging his pipe against the heel of his shoe. Carol went through the speech and she stopped and he looked up and he said, 'What's wrong?' She said, 'I did exactly what you told me and you weren't even watching.' And he said, 'I was listening. I don't have to look, I can hear.' And she said, 'Oh, then maybe you should direct radio'… That sort of drew the line in the sand. She's a very talented woman and I adored her, but she never really trusted Clifford and Clifford never really liked her. That was half the [main] cast and the other half of the cast was Mary who didn't know the lines." Referring to the woman who played Aretha, he adds, "Then we had Annie-Joe who was proving to be a little bit difficult. So he had his hands full. How do you direct that? These ladies all were very demanding."

However, Kirkwood friend and, of course, director himself Bill Gile thought that Williams was part of the problem, both in his paucity of credits and the fact that as a non-native he did not stay with the show permanently but jetted in and out. "The two women, the two legends, needed a director of such power and stature that they couldn't argue with him, couldn't negate his work," says Gile. "He also abandoned them. He should never have been hired if he wasn't going to stay with it. Well, of course, he saw the handwriting on the wall, that he probably felt he couldn't save it and abandoned it. I mean, I don't blame him, except he should never have been brought on." How did Kirkwood feel about Williams' work on *Legends!*? Gile: "He thought he did wonderful work and he was incredibly disappointed that he abandoned it. You don't abandon a piece like that and still keep your name on it." Did Gary Beach feel that Williams' presence should have been a permanent one? "At the time I did, but looking back what could he have done? If the star of your show doesn't know her lines, what good are you going to do?" But what about helping maintain cast camaraderie and morale, which can be integral to a show's success? Beach: "Most of the time after a show opens you don't see the director that often. I think we saw Clifford more often than we would have because Jimmy had to continue to write scenes." Gile adds of Williams (who he admits he never met), "He was being paid an extraordinary amount of money per week in royalties. He got two percent or more, maybe three, of the gross on sold-out houses."

Some problems at least proved relatively easy to fix. At the first preview in Dallas, the cast and Kirkwood were shocked that Klemmer's treatment of the two ladies seemed to cause things to end on a sour note. Beach recalls, "All through rehearsal my stuff had just been very successful and everything was landing and the jokes were there. We got in front of an audience of regular people who weren't particularly showbiz and I came across as a little Napoleon. Not funny, just taking advantage of these poor old ladies. So what had intended to be funny was not at all. Jimmy came to the dressing room after the show at that very first preview and he saw me sitting there and he says, 'Don't worry, we'll work on this. It'll be fine.' And I thought, 'Oh my God, I have to sign for a year of this?' The next morning the phone rings in my hotel. I wake up. It's Jimmy. At one point, Mary says, 'Mr. Klemmer — have a brownie.' Big laugh because they're hash brownies. And I say, 'No, thank you, I've just eaten.' [Kirkwood said], 'So what if you take one?' I said, 'Oh, my God, that'll be fantastic.' So we met that evening around 4:30, Mary and Carol, stage management, myself, Jimmy, Clifford. We didn't change one line. I sort of riffed and ad-libbed with movement and whatever and what had been a downer ended up with big applause as I left the show — and that night, too, in front of an audience, which is the good part. So just by doing that one little thing, he changed the whole complexion of the play. The ladies won, they'd made a fool out of me, they were getting together, they were going to do the play and I was an idiot. It just worked. That was the second performance."

The show played in Texas for nearly two weeks. "Jimmy flew me down to Texas to see *Legends!*" says Bill Gile. "It was awfully good. Here's the problem. There was a grotesque miscasting. There was a fat black maid in it and she was just a nightmare on stage and off. She wasn't funny. Being fat doesn't make them funny and she was really bad from almost the moment she walked on stage. The casting was absolutely dead-on except for this woman and she was a nightmare and she should have been fired. Why he didn't fire her, I don't know. I guess she actually got a good review so he would have had a hard time justifying it, but anyhow, she was really a monster and as many problems as they were having with Carol Channing at the time, I feel the real problem was this awful miscast maid. She was a dominant figure in the play, she was like on stage at least a third of the time, so it was hard to ignore her or work around her. While it may have been slight, with the right casting I think it would have gone somewhere." Annie-Joe Edwards certainly came in for some barbed comments from Kirkwood in *Diary of a Mad Playwright* regarding unreliable and diva-ish behavior. Beach defends her: "She was put into a strange position because she had this magnificent role and it kept getting smaller and smaller and smaller. Then, of course, we were going through a time in this country where all of a sudden a large black woman wearing a maid's costume was offensive to people and she had to fight that."

"I wished to God I had been given an opportunity to direct it, because as a director of some clout, some note, I think I could have saved it," Gile says. Of course, a show playing to capacity houses does not need saving, but he is referring to the potential of *Legends!* "coming in." For him, a major obstacle to *Legends!* making it to New York was Mary Martin's profit-decimating insistence on playing seven rather than the traditional eight performances per week. Gile describes this situation as "ridiculous" and says, "I think they would have brought it to Broadway if she hadn't that clause in the contract."

While in Dallas, Kirkwood took the opportunity to visit his half-sister, whom he embroiled in an incident that showed wealth had not obliterated his taste for risk. Recalls Joan, "We went to an upper-end restaurant. We were at the bar, then we were going to go to dinner. We had a drink or two and then, he said, 'C'mon.' We got up and he took my elbow and steered me toward the front door and we got outside and he said, 'Come on!' I said, 'What's the matter?' He said, 'I walked the check.' Now, he could well afford to pay it but something like that, he just got a kick out of it or something. I was mortified." Jerry Paonessa was in town with Kirkwood and Joan recalls, "When Jimmy took me up to the hotel room, he said, 'There is a roll-out bed and that's where he sleeps.' Didn't want me to think I guess that the other guy was gay." She feels this demonstrates that Kirkwood knew that she knew of his sexuality despite the fact of their never discussing it.

The show was in Los Angeles from January 23 to March 29. During this period in the sunny state, Jim Piazza flew in and Kirkwood worked with him on improving not only *Legends!* but *Stage-Stuck*. The latter had been put on the backburner lately. "There was a point where he just couldn't do it," says Piazza of *Stage-Stuck*. "He was doing *Legends!* and he had no time and kind of lost interest in the play, because *Legends!* was so sapping him of everything. I used to get very jealous. We were working on our play and he said, 'Oh, we're going to do this, we're going to do great' and then the *Legends!* thing would come up and he said, 'I promise as soon as I get this done, we'll do the other and we'll make sure that that one gets on.' We were just finishing up writing when the *Legends!* thing happened. He had me come out to Los Angeles to help him a little bit with that because Jimmy wasn't really that great with one-liners or jokes and that was kind of the thing that I did, because I had been a stand-up comic for a while. I knew my way around a punchline." Couldn't Kirkwood call on his own stand-up experience? Piazza: "Jimmy did 'bits'…Jimmy was funny with language, but he wasn't a joke kind of guy. He couldn't give you a zinger necessarily. He could in conversation, in that party kind of way, but on the page that was not really what he could do best."

Piazza says that the *Legends!* scene in which Klemmer juggles three telephone calls in a New York subway station, which would make its first appearance in Philadelphia in September, was a collaboration between he and Kirkwood. He also says he wrote several of the one-liners used in the play: "Some of the lines: 'So few women can carry off aluminum foil'; something about a dress. The bitchy things back and forth. I think I wrote about maybe seven or eight one-liners and then that scene with Gary. I don't remember exactly which 'cause they were so rushed. You would just write it in and that would be it." Piazza would not receive credit for his contributions nor would they be mentioned in *Diary of a Mad Playwright*, something that puts Kirkwood's occasions of fury over not receiving sufficient credit for his contribution to *A Chorus Line* into a different light. "I remember writing one-liners and I would see that onstage getting a laugh and I'd say, 'God,'" Piazza admits. Of *Diary of a Mad Playwright*, he says, "That was hurtful. I think I was in it once as 'Court Jester' and then once or twice he said, 'Oh my friend Jim came out to visit'…We were not lovers at that point when he wrote that, but I was much closer to him by far than that book would imply and there was a sense of being dismissed out of anxiety that there would be talk that I was doing more than I was.

But who am I at that point?" However, there was some compensation: "I think he was paying me $500 a week." Piazza also feels he contributed to the quality of *Diary of a Mad Playwright*, for the purpose of which book Kirkwood meticulously wrote up each day's events. "I helped him," he says. "I would read over the diary, his page notes every day, because he couldn't remember. He'd say, 'Did Mary really say that in rehearsal?'"

Of *Stage-Stuck*, Piazza says, "I kept rewriting it while Jimmy was on the road with *Legends!* and I was working with Sandra Lee…She posed questions to me, made some suggestions, some of which I took, others not." It was Lee — well known for her roles in *Hello, Dolly!* and others — who directed the first reading of *Stage-Stuck*. "It was just before *Legends!* got off the ground, few months before," says Piazza. The reading was at the legendary Actors Studio in NYC, where the likes of Brando and Monroe had done their time as students of Lee Strasberg. Says Piazza, "The place was jammed with celebs and the cast was star-studded." Among the stars in the cast were Ann Meara (Ben Stiller's mother), Carrie Nye (Dick Cavett's late wife), Chip Zien (one of the stars of *Into The Woods*), David Margulies, Carol Shelley and Julie Haggerty. Jerry Paonessa recalls that Kirkwood was delighted that director and screenwriter Joseph L. Mankiewicz (*All About Eve*) was in attendance. Piazza: "At that point, we had no backers. It was our first trial run."

Piazza recalls a day on the beach in LA when he showed Kirkwood some rewrites of *Stage-Stuck*. "A rare day off for him," he says. "We were in Santa Monica and he said, 'Give me the damn pages now.' He was very short with me, like he was going to be daddy-checking to see what I had done. I remember sitting on the dune being a wreck and I was chain-smoking. He was walking up and down on the beach looking at the rewrites and finally he came back after twenty minutes and said, 'Yeah, they're okay, all right,' and he threw them back at me. That was his way of saying, 'You did good,' but he could never say 'Great.' He wouldn't do that."

Los Angeles saw the jettisoning of the original ending of *Legends!* in which the two ladies fake a fight in order to get back in the limelight, the curtain descending as their mock battle conveniently attracts a battery of squad cars, yelling reporters and flashbulb-popping cameramen. In preference to this, Beach recalls, "They decided they should sing. By 'they,' I mean the producers. So they came up with 'Ac-cent-tchu-ate The Positive,' that old song, and they brought in [top arranger] Marc Shaiman to work on the number, they brought in Peter Gennaro — who was a major choreographer — to choreograph them. This is like overkill. But it seemed to work for our audience. They liked it. The critics questioned it." Possibly because of the incongruity of an old song grafted onto a new play? (It first appeared in the Bing Crosby movie *Here Come the Waves* in 1944.) Beach: "Exactly. And the music just came up out of nowhere and the lights on the stage went down and spotlights came up." For Ertegun, it was a step in the right direction, but only one. "What bothered me is that we had two great singing stars and we had no songs in it," he says. "It was presented as a straight play and nobody wanted to have any music in it. Nobody except the public. If I had had more time and been able to convince everyone, I think we could have had a hit show with two or three fun songs in it. It could have been a fun little musical." Gary Beach agrees with the proposition that the song finale was really a sop to audience members who knew Martin and Channing as musical stars, but disagrees with Ertegun's assessment that the play would have been stronger with more numbers: "I think that the piece itself, the way Jimmy wanted it to go, was a deeper piece than it ended up being. It didn't start out being the Broadway comedy it ended up being." Trish Garland: "They were trying anything possible to make it work and that was just one way that they were trying to save the show. Because the one musical number did really work and so could a second musical number really work? I don't think that was what the problem was with the show, but they were trying to figure it out…That's not what Jimmy had intended. That's why when they put in the strip number and they choreographed it, they didn't put on a choreography credit, because they didn't want people to think there was a number."

As well as requests for changes from the producers, Kirkwood also often found the cast proffering ideas. "I'm afraid everywhere he turned he got suggestions," says Beach. "To his credit he dealt with them beautifully. Only a few times did he go over the top a bit and [say], 'Oh, go fuck yourself'…He had a lot to be pissed off about a lot of the time. Chunks would just be taken out and no one would tell him. Or someone would say, 'I need a line here' and then two minutes later say, 'Well, what am I going to say?' It was difficult for him."

In Los Angeles much time and energy was wasted in a ludicrous and operatic *contretemps* over the set's sofa, which an outraged Channing insisted had been altered. "They had it re-covered and for some reason or other it felt higher," says Beach, "and so that became the point of the evening, that the reason the play wasn't working was because the couch was too high. It was like that all the time. There was always something wrong. Then there were times it was just so much fun I couldn't believe it. We hit a place called Sacramento, California. The play worked, the audiences poured in, they laughed, they screamed, they stood, they loved it. And then you go to a place like Kansas City, Missouri, where I'm not sure they had ever heard of Mary Martin and Carol Channing and it was just as dull as it could possibly be."

By now it was obvious that the original three-city itinerary was way off the mark. Beach: "All of a sudden they started booking this show because it was a huge deal to have these two ladies in a tour and you still had people who remembered them from *Peter Pan* and *Hello, Dolly!* and *South Pacific* and *Gentlemen Prefer Blondes*. They were big deals and Mary hadn't gone on stage in decades [sic]. People were making money."

The tour reached New Orleans on April 2 and stayed there through April 13. Benjamin Morrison took in the show in his hometown and wasn't impressed. "*Legends!* is not a good show," he says. "*Legends!* was a wonderful premise and had two leading ladies who — and none of this ever gets talked about — really don't have any business being on the stage together. They're radically different kinds of Hollywood or Broadway theatrical types. But those were the two ladies who he ended up with. One of the things a friend of mine told me after seeing the show — and he was very right about this — [is that] it's a show that everyone who thought about buying a ticket wanted to love. People really wanted to go in and have the time of their life. I have friends who still feel that way based on the fact that they were so charmed by the actresses and about getting to see them and see them together, and all that sort of stuff. But the strength of the writing isn't as good as it needs to be. There's a line in there that they're rattling off a list of actresses and they're dismissing them. One of the two ladies walking across the stage doing some business says something to the other lady of, 'Lana Turner — too pretty.' Well, that's not funny. It got a laugh because of the cadence of it, but it's just the kind of thing that he really needed to do something stronger with. Additionally, the idea of the wild and crazy walk-in. There's a wild and crazy walk-in in *P.S. Your Cat is Dead!* The S&M leather guy walks in to brighten up Act II or something. Well, that was perfectly fine and was perfectly wonderful. He does exactly the same thing in *Legends!*: the male stripper comes in just to brighten up and lighten up things and he's pushed out on stage and then he's pulled off the stage and in both cases neither set of people are particularly heard of 'til the curtain call."

Morrison's underwhelmed opinions presented a difficulty for him as someone who was both a professional critic and a friend of the author. "As a critic, I've been taught that you could never lie about what your opinion of things were," he says. "I really worked on the language of what to tell him after I'd seen *Legends!* It was really tough for me being in the audience. I would never have reviewed that. I would almost have lost my job." Morrison's verbal review to his old friend's face was an elliptical one. "Well, I said very nice things about it," he says. "The best things I could — 'Oh, it's such a pleasure to see all those people up there.' You know — what the fuck does that mean? And, 'You've really done some nice things.' That doesn't mean anything. 'I like the way you're combing your hair today' — that's about what that means. But I really worked hard on not damning with faint praise and on sounding very supportive. My sense was that he was used to having people talk around the faults in the play. I think he knew what was going on with the play. There were excuses, and they are real excuses, that Mary Martin could not remember lines, but I think the guy who wrote the earlier books would have had the ability to put that play together, even if he had to call up Carrie Fisher, or the equivalent of Carrie Fisher, to pump up some of the lines for him, and make the whole thing work. My guess is that because of drugs or whatever it might have been, he did not have that ability himself. And it may be that the talent never was there, or to that level, or to the level that it needed to be."

Morrison wasn't the only one of Kirkwood's friends dismayed by *Legends!* who was careful not to reveal the extent of his dismay. "It was a rough evening," Homer Price says of his own viewing, presumably in Florida, where he spent time. "I didn't like it at all. Jimmy said, 'What do you think?' I said, 'It's good, Jimmy.' [Laughs.] What was I going to say? 'I don't like it'? No, Jimmy did not like bad news." In the interests of balance, we should point out that not all of Kirkwood's friends disliked what they saw. "*Legends!* was really a charming play," insists Lomax Study, "and the cast was just perfect. Carol Channing and Mary Martin played against each other like you wouldn't believe."

Morrison's suspicions of a drug-related deterioration in Kirkwood's talent are interesting because they come not from intimate knowledge, as do Piazza's observations, but from simple hunch. "I never saw him have coke, I don't think we ever talked about it on the phone, I don't think we ever talked about it in person," he admits. "But he had that glazed-eye look that I would get from people who are on coke on a regular basis. You're looking straight in their eyes and they're not quite there." "I would say [it was] recreational," demurs Beach. "I spent quite a bit of time with him out on the road and I never remember thinking, "Oh my God, get it together man…'"

The tour moved onto San Antonio (April 15-April 20), San Francisco (April 23-June 1), San Diego (June 4-June 8) and Phoenix, Arizona

(June 11-June 15). It was in this period that a turning point for the play occurred. Though the earpiece had kept the show — and Martin — staggering on this far, when Martin began receiving taxi calls on the device, she decided enough was enough. "It was in Phoenix, Arizona," says Beach. "Other people name other cities but I remember exactly where it was. I got a call saying that Mary's going on tonight without the earpiece: 'We're going to rehearse at five o'clock' or something. That night I saw why she was Mary Martin, the star. She had the energy, she was fantastic and the show was just wonderful that night. She never put that thing in again. Then Jimmy could begin working on the play and really working on the characters and the relationships between the two ladies. I do think that the play we ended up with was far better than the one we started with, but that didn't start happening until six or seven months into the run because he had to write around Mary, not for her." "It got better and better," concedes Ertegun. "But it's a very slight play. There's no deep message in it. It was a good entertainment, but I think that with a bit of music it would have been a charming thing. Somehow everybody resisted that idea."

The tour then visited Sacramento, California (June 18-June 22), Portland, Oregon (June 25-July 2), Seattle, Washington (July 5-July 13), Kansas City (July 16-July 20) and Boston, Massachusetts (July 23-August 9). Kirkwood invited his old friend and sounding board Arthur Laurents to a matinée performance in the latter city on August 6. "He wanted me to take over the direction," claims Laurents. "The play was very much like Jimmy in an odd way. It was schizophrenic. Some of it was right out hilarious camp and then there was Mary Martin making a big speech about a mastectomy from no place. When I went up to Boston, Tom Hatcher came with me and he sat between me and Jimmy and he laughed up the whole thing. He knew me so well he knew what I thought of it, he knew it wasn't for me, and he maneuvered it so Jimmy understood, 'cause I never wanted to offend Jimmy." Kirkwood understood nothing judging by *Diary of a Mad Playwright* where he wrote that Laurents and Hatcher "were getting a kick out of it" and took Laurents' interval and after-show comments about the play being "fun, it's a romp!" and about Mary Martin being "honest and very truthful" as anything other than the polite circumnavigating of its quality they seem to be.

It was in Boston that *Legends!* — despite the script improvements and Martin's recovered facilities — became doomed. "Mary had a speech that Jimmy wrote," says Beach. "Jimmy loved the speech. I loved the speech. Mary delivered it beautifully." The speech was destined to go down well with an audience that Beach describes as "mostly older ladies." Beach explains, "It was a story that Mary told about her character Leatrice having a mastectomy. How she had moved to Paris, opened a restaurant, met a young man, he became her lover, she [discovered] cancer of the breast, had to have the breast removed and the young lover left her. She delivered that speech even when she was using the earpiece just beautifully and the audience loved it. This was the mid-eighties and that kind of thing wasn't talked about a whole lot then." Kevin Eggers, however, wasn't happy with its inclusion. "Kevin decided it was wrong," says Beach, "that it was a downer for the audience. I was sitting in the audience section of the Shubert Theater right next to Jimmy when Mary was presented with this: 'We're cutting this'…No one asked her or anything. She stood up and she gave a speech that was right out of *All About Eve*. It was, 'Never in my life, in a life in the theatre, have I been treated like this. I will not go into New York. I wish you luck if you want to go into New York but it will be without Mary Martin'…And she stormed offstage left…It was the last straw." He points out, "She never dropped it. She kept it in. And Jimmy wanted her to keep it in." Once it was announced that Martin was not renewing her contract, Channing declared that she would not renew hers on the grounds that she would not perform the play with anybody except Martin.

The play that was now a dead duck moved to Washington, D.C., playing there August 12 through August 31. It seems surprising that it wasn't until the tour reached this city that the Klemmer subway scene was rehearsed considering Piazza's clear memory of co-writing it back in LA five months before. Piazza: "What we worked on together was put in at varying points. Often, Jimmy would call me in NYC for input, so I wasn't always on hand to see how they fit into the play. We definitely did work on Martin's scenes while I was in LA. Jimmy was eager to expand Gary's role. He saw him as a life-blood of the play, a quick study and always good for a sustained laugh. In a constantly evolving production, as *Legends!* was, things are tossed out, put back in on a daily basis." Beach says of the subway scene, "We worked on it in the basement at the National Theatre in Washington — [Kirkwood] directed it — and we put it up in Philadelphia. It was really successful. It was great." *Legends!* played in Philadelphia, Pennsylvania, from September 3 to September 28.

The visit of the tour to Cleveland, Ohio, from October 1 to October 5, gave Kirkwood's friends and family from Elyria the opportunity to see his latest work. From there the tour moved to Chicago (October 8-October 26). Kirkwood's family history was intertwined with the Windy City, but not in a good way: his mother's distillery-owning father had been run out by Mafia types muscling in on his then-illegal business and of course his own father had been arrested there for his alleged crime of appearing in *Tobacco Road*. However, there was some good Chicago-related news for Kirkwood this year. October 7 was proclaimed James Kirkwood Day by city Mayor Harold Washington. A party was thrown at Suzy Wong's restaurant in honor of "his contributions to stage, screen, television and the literary world." *Legends!* then moved through St. Louis, Missouri (October 29-November 9) and Atlanta, Georgia (November 12-November 16). It was on November 16 that Kirkwood wrote a long, impassioned but typically humorous letter to Martin and Channing — carbon-copied to the rest of the cast and crew — pleading with them to change their minds about not renewing their contracts and likening the situation to two chefs who have been laboring over a banquet for a year flushing said banquet down the toilet because they are too bushed to proceed with the party. It was to no avail. Kirkwood was left so exhausted and distraught by the year he'd been through and by its sour *denouement* that, for the first time in living memory, he didn't bother preparing one of his much-loved custom-made Christmas cards.

From November 19 until the end of the tour on January 18, 1987, *Legends!* was in Florida, playing Orlando (November 19-November 23), St. Petersburg (November 26-November 30), Miami Beach (December 12-December 14), Fort Lauderdale (December 17-January 4) and Palm Beach (January 6-onwards). Though the hope that Martin (and hence Channing) could be persuaded to change her mind still persisted, the tour dissolved with things in an unresolved state. "I've been in the business over thirty years and still think of the closing day of *Legends!* in Palm Beach, Florida, as one of the saddest days," Beach laments. "All this was for nothing? We played to a packed house, cheered. Mike Nichols had flown in that day to see the show, for what reason who knows. They rolled a cake out on the stage at the end of the performance. Jimmy very sweetly announced that we had been touring for one year and Carol and Mary and I had not missed one performance. And he said we wanted to announce this afternoon that we're going to take just a few weeks off and then open at the La Fontaine Theatre in New York. And, of course, Mary and Carol went, 'No, no!' It was with humor that he did it, but I think he really had that hope that after all was said and done we'd come into New York…Jimmy felt, and I believe he was right, if the show had come in they probably would have had a nice season of people just trooping in to see those two ladies on stage together."

"He's an old friend of mine," Ertegun says of Nichols' presence. The latter would seem to have had a change of heart over the project. Ertegun says that Nichols was present, "to see if he had any ideas of what we could do and whether he thought it would work on Broadway…He quite liked it." Did Nichols seem enthusiastic about trying to get it to New York? Ertegun: "No. Because he didn't see what could be done with the play." Not necessarily attributing these thoughts to Nichols, Ertegun says, "There was a lot to be fixed but it was very hard to do because we had two ageing actresses who were not very pliable. They were the main reason why the show was a success, but at the same time we couldn't work with them as we could have worked with two young actresses."

Mary Martin said in a December 1986 *New York Times* article, "I love the road, I love going from city to city. But I'm 73. I don't want to push that too far." There was no mention of the dispute over the mastectomy speech scene, indicating that road weariness would have caused her to leave the production even had this issue not arisen. Beach: "I don't feel she felt she was doing her best work. I think she was tired. She said she was 72 — who knows how old she was. She was lonely a good deal of the time. She didn't see her family as much as she wanted to. I think all of that had a lot to do with it. Honestly, I think Jimmy and a lot of us held out through the closing in Palm Beach that maybe something'll happen. I know we talked on the phone after that: 'Hear anything?' And nothing was happening." In the December 1986 *New York Times* article, Channing was quoted as saying, "I went into the show because Mary wanted me in the show. I'll do whatever Mary wants to do."

The play, of course, could conceivably have been re-cast for a New York run. "By that time it had become national press for a while," says Beach. "It was like, 'No, you want those [actresses]'…They had become identified with the role and they had been reported on as feuding and all of this kind of stuff, so that's what the audience wanted to see. They did talk to Ann Miller for a while about replacing Mary but nothing came of that." Would he have gone along with that? "I think so, unless something else came along. I had a ball."

"I had a good time," Ertegun says of *Legends!* "I thought it was fun, it was a rewarding and instructive experience." However, asked whether if Martin had been persuaded to stay he would have been in favor of the show coming in, Ertegun says, "I don't think so." A possible explanation as to why is revealed when he says, "I doubt it," in response to the question of whether it would have withstood the harsher scrutiny of the New York critics. Kevin Eggers would seem to have been of a different opinion, even had the producers been unable to retain either Channing or Martin. The aforesaid 1986 *New York Times* article said, "Mr. Eggers insists that the producers are recruiting two replacements and that the show is definitely coming to Broadway next May. But he would not say who those replacements might be." In around 1989, Kirkwood told an interviewer that negotiations had begun for a London edition which could star Maggie Smith and Diana Rigg. "It would be different, more sophisticated," he said.

Neither Eggers' re-casting nor the British production ever materialized. Nor did the Elvis musical that had brought about the whole *Legends!* caravan in the first instance. "I lost interest in the Elvis project because all the leads that Kevin Eggers came up with were fine, but they turned out to be not there," says Ertegun. After his experience with *Legends!* would he have still have been in favor of Kirkwood writing the book? "Probably not." However, Ertegun says this is not because of disagreements over *Legends!* "I'm not sure he would have been the right person to write the Elvis Presley musical," he says. "I doubt that he would really get into the essence of the character of Elvis Presley."

It's difficult to categorize as another of Kirkwood's failed eighties projects a show that made it into production, played for a year to packed houses and grossed an estimated ten million dollars, with a twenty percent return. However, it's also difficult to characterize a work which obtained lukewarm reviews, caused discomfort to friends of the author who had to face him after seeing it, never fully paid back its investors and did not make it to Broadway as a success. On top of that is the stark fact that Kirkwood squandered an entire creative year continuously honing a play that was never going to be more than slight.

"The thing with Jimmy is that he would say how horrible it was, but he never talked about how much money he made from that," says Piazza. "He made a lot of money from that play." Additionally, Piazza says, "The reviews were horrible, they were always after Jimmy, but he was back in the news and going to all the right parties and blah, blah, blah." There was another benefit from the show: Kirkwood got a book out of it. He had regretted not keeping a journal when he was collaborating on *A Chorus Line* and didn't make the same mistake this time. Beach: "Sometimes — I would never have said this to him — I'd think while he was out working on the play he was really working on the book. 'Oh, this'll be good in the book.' He actually honestly and nicely told everybody, 'I'm writing a book about this, people,' and whether you believed him or not was up to you."

Whether *Legends!* can be categorized as a success, failure or something in between, it would be indisputably fair to characterize the next show on which Kirkwood worked as an utter disaster.

TWENTY-ONE

Two weeks after the end of the *Legends!* tour, Kirkwood lectured at the Florida Suncoast Writers Conference. While there he gave an interview to the local paper *St. Petersburg Times* that suggested that, to some extent, he had already put some distance between himself and *Legends!*

"'I look back on it now with a certain amount of loving horror," he said as though discussing events of the dim past. "I think it was a theatrical freak…I felt often that I took the brunt of criticism because critics or audiences don't know what goes on behind the scenes. You can't get out on stage and stamp your foot and say, 'Hey!,' and you can't give out interviews while the thing is running, because you destroy the ladies." Yet, Kirkwood made it clear that in terms of "loving horror" he was speaking of that particular production, not the play itself. Revealing that it was a smash in Argentina, he said, "I think it will have 'legs,' because there are always two ladies that are right for it." In an ominous comment for those who might have felt that he had already spent too much of his recent life revisiting and re-jigging his literary past, he added, "And I'm gonna do a lot of work on it."

Kirkwood stated in *Diary of a Mad Playwright* that in the summer of 1987 he had turned down a proposal to make a TV pilot for a series based on *Legends!* on the grounds that the deal was not all that good and that he'd already done his time in hell with the property. How then to explain the presence in Kirkwood's papers of a ten-page proposal for a *Legends!* television series that would have used the original play as the program's pilot? The four main characters would have been the same in a show that would have expanded the theme of the professional comeback of the two ladies to a revitalization of other areas of their lives. The women would not have gone into rehearsal for their play until the last episode of the first season. Kirkwood acknowledged in the proposal the similarity of his idea (at least in TV terms) to the then-successful *Golden Girls*. Whether it be because of this or some other reason, the show was never made.

Kirkwood mentioned in a letter to Herlihy in January 1986 the problems he was continuing to have with *I Teach Flying*, now two years shy of being two-decades-in-the-making: "I can't tell you how I'm resisting getting back into my daddy book. I just am. I would much rather lie abed and read. I keep sticking my toe in the water, reading over pages, starting to write little disconnected episodes and then I find an excuse. An ingrown toenail, or watering the garden or some such shit. This is not like me. So I am confused about WHAT THE REAL REASON IS." Whatever that elusive reason was, by '87 it would seem to have evaporated. Russo recalls Kirkwood feeling that year that he was on the home lap of *I Teach Flying*: "He kept telling me, 'Oh, I'm on page 120 of a book about my father,' 'I'm on page 190,' 'I'm on page 300.' The last time I heard from him he was way over 400 pages on that book." Russo feels one cannot necessarily read anything into the fact that by 1987 it had been nineteen years since he had begun it: "He was so busy. I was always amazed that he could finish anything with all of the interruptions. He was constantly stopping to do something else. There was a need to do this, a need to do that. But it seems to me in the last few years, he was really putting his attention into *I Teach Flying* and he told me he had made tremendous strides and I thought he was going to finish it very soon." This is borne out in a letter Kirkwood sent to Herlihy dated October 31, 1988, in which he said, "I'm on page 488 of my Daddy book, just spinning out googies after googie. Listen, I'm having fun, that's the main thing." It was a work that Russo remembers Kirkwood intimated would make up for his lack of productivity in novel writing in later years: "He was always dangling the carrot: 'I'm working on a novel, you're going to love this novel, I'm working on my daddy novel.' He kept telling me this was going to be my favorite...I always wonder how much that book would have enhanced his reputation. I think he thought it was going to be his best."

Not that Kirkwood was devoting himself exclusively to *Flying*. He had revealed to the *St. Petersburg Times* that he expected *Stage-Stuck* to go into rehearsal in the spring. Furthermore, he was going to direct it. "I just thought, 'Why not just jump in? What're they gonna do, kill me?'" he reasoned.

Initially, it seemed that producer Alexander Cohen — famous for his office above the Shubert Theatre — was going to finance *Stage-Stuck*. Piazza: "Jimmy had sent him a knight's helmet or something like that and a cape and a sword and said, 'You're the last of the knights in shining armor, you've got to do this play.' We met him in his office. That came close and then the stock market crash happened and everyone lost their money." Naturally, there was much despair in the writers' camp at their hopes being so upended by fate — and it certainly must have seemed like *déjà vu* to Kirkwood following the way *Murder at the Vanities* had lost its champion when David Merrick suffered a stroke. "We were getting a lot of turn-downs," admits Piazza. "The play was off the wall. Jimmy had marquee value but we weren't getting bites of anything that he thought was interesting enough to do, because he felt that he was on a certain level. He wasn't going to take some rep company somewhere in Arkansas…It just sat there for a long time. It dwelled." Another supporter materialized in the shape of one Joe Civita from Massachusetts who put up $50,000. Piazza: "The money went for options and initial 'line-production,' getting the play on its feet, as in staged readings, hiring actors, etc., to attract other investors." Piazza describes Civita as "a real character" and says, "That was his one-time investment in the arts. Never even read the play. Just liked us, admired Jimmy." When Civita also dropped out of the picture, the project was once again in hiatus.

In approximately the last quarter of 1988, however, the pair received two expressions of interest within an hour. One was from the Tennessee Williams Theatre in Florida and had been obtained by the previously mentioned David, Kirkwood's Key West boyfriend. The theatre was not proposing a hugely lucrative deal but was offering Kirkwood the chance to direct. Despite the directing opportunity, though, Kirkwood ultimately passed on it. Piazza: "I think Jimmy thought it was small potatoes. I thought that would have been a great place to do it. We would have had much more autonomy to do it down there and let the play begin to gel. I was excited about that. Jimmy was not." The second call was from director Charles Nelson Reilly, who wanted to put the play on at actor Burt Reynolds' theatre, also in Florida. This venue was that strange beast, a dinner theatre: the evening's entertainment followed a meal, which was served in the same room as the plays were staged. Reynolds actually seemed to be have been hooked by discussion in *Stage-Stuck* about a dinner theatre. "Wanted to do the play based on that monologue," is Piazza's impression. "Then we had the waiting period from then to them actually finding a slot and time to do it." Though a big budget was promised, according to Piazza, it may actually have been something no less banal than the identity of the theatre's owner that had swayed it for Kirkwood. "Jimmy was just star struck," says Piazza. "The idea of Burt Reynolds, that was great. He thought he'd be [talking] with Burt Reynolds." Piazza reveals that Reynolds had at some time in the past expressed interest in appearing in a movie version of *P.S. Your Cat is Dead!*

July 1987 brought the death of Michael Bennett, aged just 44. The cause was one that would cut down many, many friends and acquaintances of Kirkwood's in the coming years: Acquired Immune Deficiency Syndrome. Attending Bennett's memorial service, Kirkwood was dismayed that *A Chorus Line* was mentioned over and over, as though it were Bennett's only, as opposed to crowning, achievement. Beckenstein recalls, "Jimmy said, 'I really don't want any mention of *A Chorus Line* if there's a memorial service for me.' He wanted to be known as a writer for all of his work."

This is not to say that Kirkwood was incapable of being petulant if he felt his contribution to that show was not given enough credit, as illustrated by his behavior towards Joseph Papp on August 10, 1987, when the Shubert Theatre celebrated the 5,000th performance of *A Chorus Line*. Piazza says that Kirkwood was wont to tell him that his falling-out with Liz Smith over her declining to attend the *Cat* revival involved him grabbing her by the throat at a cocktail party and calling her a "lousy fucking dyke cunt!" and that an altercation with John Simon over his review of same production was one in which he grabbed Simon's tie and started to choke him with it. Beckenstein — who saw the confrontation with Simon — questions the veracity of both claims, but Piazza was a direct eyewitness to the Papp incident and other third parties confirm it did involve violence. Following the curtain, there was a party at the Palladium at which Papp gave a speech which he clearly felt in line with the fact that the evening had been dedicated to the memory of the recently-deceased Bennett. Though Kirkwood was happy for Bennett to be lauded, he objected to the rest of the show's creators, including Marvin Hamlisch, not receiving praise as well. Different versions of what then occurred were given to *Newsday* by the principals. Kirkwood claimed that he approached Papp's table and said, "Joe, I don't understand your behavior…Not mentioning the name of the creators is reprehensible, embarrassing and hurtful." According to Kirkwood, Papp looked up and replied, "Go fuck yourself." Kirkwood waited until Papp got to his feet and then pushed him down on the floor. "He got back up and we began sparring," said Kirkwood. "We cuffed each other a few times but no one was damaged." Papp responded that Kirkwood had come up to his table and made "scurrilous remarks." "Here I'd spent all day working and preparing this show," Papp said. "It was to honor Michael Bennett, it was in his memory. I wanted it all to go to Michael Bennett. There were many names I didn't mention — but that wasn't even the point. It was the way he came at me, his aggressive tone. He made a million dollars on this show, through my efforts. A man died doing this show. You'd think this would push his ego aside a bit, that he would be open and giving enough to understand the situation."

"It's *Rashomon* all over again, isn't it?" says Piazza, referring to the Japanese movie in which different people have conflicting memories of the same events. "The evening was to be a tribute to Michael Bennett. Papp said he would only be mentioning him. Instead, he mentioned one or two others involved in the production. Not Jimmy. At the banquet afterwards,

Jimmy was enraged about it and asked me what he should do. I suggested at some point he speak to Papp, maybe one of his fabulous letters. I didn't mean now, certainly, after an evening of cocktails. Jimmy jumped up from our table, stormed over to Papp and told him he was a prick for not mentioning him. Papp waved him off and continued eating…What's not commented in the paper is Papp's additional remark: 'I made you a millionaire — now fuck off!'…The skirmish moved onto the dance floor. Papp's son grabbed him, I pulled Jimmy off.…The dance floor was slippery and it was ludicrous. In a film, it would have been hilarious. [Australian entertainer] Peter Allen was sitting at our table and by the time we returned, he'd fled — it was all much too hot for him." Piazza adds, "It's important to remember that both of these guys were not well at this point in their lives."

Kirkwood had clearly made it up with Papp before March 1988, when he sent him a friendly letter referring to a correspondence of a few months previously in which they had discussed an all-black company of *A Chorus Line*, a measure the type of which Kirkwood felt was necessary to provide the show "a shot of adrenalin." Papp also attended Kirkwood's New York memorial — at least for a while. "Everybody liked him and he liked everybody except Joseph Papp," says Arthur Laurents. "I said that at his memorial and it got an enormous laugh and Joseph Papp walked out. Papp didn't recognize him as a writer…He wanted to be acknowledged and Joe Papp didn't and that's why he was angry at him." However, the argument could be made that at least Papp was honest about his dismissiveness of Kirkwood's contribution to *A Chorus Line*, which is more than can be said for Laurents. The latter asserts, "In the end it was Michael Bennett who did it all and Jimmy and Nick Dante were really serving what Michael Bennett wanted. He was the be-all-and-end-all…Nobody took him seriously as a librettist from that…Jimmy and Nick Dante were sort of glorified secretaries for Michael Bennett. Ed Kleban — I once said to him about my friend Jimmy Kirkwood. He said, 'Who's he?'" Yet asked if he ever said all of this to his friend's face, Laurents admits, "No, because it would have hurt him. Besides, I really think Jimmy knew. He was not a fool. He didn't want other people to say it — that's why he was so angry with Papp — but he knew."

"His act was shockingly villainous," says Benjamin Morrison of Kirkwood's behavior that night. "And totally self-centered." He also observes that when he heard about it, it struck him as "coke behavior."

It can't be denied that whatever the apparent dip in the quality of Kirkwood's art, there was no let-up in his productivity. This juncture saw him working on three projects: *Stage-Stuck*, *I Teach Flying* and *Diary of a Mad Playwright*.

His account of the *Legends!* tour was bought by Dutton. "I believe that Dutton was the sole bidder for the project," says Carole DeSanti, the then-young editor given the task of overseeing the project. "It wasn't an auction and I believe our early enthusiasm for it carried the day." What Dutton saw from Kirkwood, DeSanti recalls, was "a partial draft, a good chunk of pages that gave a very clear sense of what the book would be in tone and content." The enthusiasm was partly calculated. DeSanti candidly admits something that brings to mind Richard Kluger's memory that Simon & Schuster only agreed to publish *American Grotesque* because they were interested in whatever Kirkwood's next work of fiction transpired to be. "If anything, our hopes were more that we would have a foot in the door for Jimmy's next novel," she says. "There was quite a bit of affection and respect for Kirkwood's previous work in-house. Especially on the part of Dutton's publisher at the time, Richard Marek, who also had an interest in the theatre and its personalities and stories." DeSanti is not surprised that Dutton would be angling for Kirkwood's future novels despite the fact that his last one was a stinker. "We don't generally make the case in our industry that because a prior work may not have been as strong as earlier work, that we would never consider anything further from an author and that he or she has nothing more to offer," she reasons. "That kind of thinking is too critically high-handed. We try to keep an open mind until we actually read the writing in question and see what can be done with it. After all, there are many factors that go into the making of novels, the editorial process being one of them. As far as I recall, insofar as we'd heard of it, we thought that the next novel might be of interest. But really, there was no firm discussion of any of this whatsoever — our focus was really on getting *Diary* completed and published." Nor were Dutton put off by the fact that *Legends!* itself had not been a critical success. If anything, the opposite. DeSanti: "The whole idea of the book was a behind-the-scenes tale of what can go wrong in the theatre world. It wouldn't have been half as much fun if it had been some yawn of a success story, and certainly wouldn't have showcased Kirkwood's witty, mischievous, dark sensibility in the same way…which [was] what we all enjoyed about it."

Kirkwood had already decided on the final title when he signed terms with Dutton. It was either an allusion to *Diary of a Mad Old Man* by Jow Tanizaki or *Diary of a Mad Housewife* by Sue Kaufman (or both). "We thought it was catchy enough," says DeSanti, "Would speak to the theatre-readership always thought to be the core audience for the book and accurately described the book. We didn't consider changing it." One thing that was changed was Beckenstein's preliminary cover design featuring a strait-jacketed Kirkwood being pushed in a wheelchair by an orderly, despite a photo session having been conducted for a mock-up Beckenstein prepared. DeSanti offers, "Maybe he did intend it seriously or at least semi-seriously, but he certainly knew that it's not up to the author to come up with the jacket concept — that's the job of the publisher, and he was a seasoned professional in that regard. Also, he was enough of a realist to understand the publisher's point of view that the audience would want to see Martin and Channing on the jacket, and I believe he provided us with the photo that was used."

DeSanti brings to mind another Kluger comment on Kirkwood's previous work of non-fiction when, asked what she thought of the finished *Playwright* manuscript, she says it was "quite long and had to be cut." She adds, "I knew that Jimmy was going to be sensitive about that. Our main editorial struggle was around the issue that I wanted the *Diary* to be a more crafted document and felt that the book-as-artifact was just as 'valid' and important an enterprise as the play, not a kind of cathartic exercise for the author/playwright. I felt that some sections were self-indulgent and carried a shade too much bitterness. That tone at times made Jimmy less sympathetic to the reader than he both needed and deserved to be. I tried pretty hard to convince him that a more controlled, crafted piece of writing would be the playwright's/the writer's ultimate vindication. Of course, as an artist Jimmy basically agreed, but he was wrestling with his need to have his say, once and for all. We went back and forth about this and his agent, Jed Mattes, was an excellent diplomat/mediator, and we all compromised some in the end."

Kirkwood was anxious over one particular proposed cut, though his comments about it to Herlihy in a letter of September 9, 1988, were doubtlessly tongue-in-cheek to some extent: "The publishers and I are fighting over the word CUNT, which is used in the book several times. I cut one cunt but I insist on keeping the other two. One is a quote from Ann Miller — you remember little Annie — when she said, 'I saw the show and Mary was, well, all right, but what you need up on that stage is two cunts and with Carol and me you'd have a couple.' And the other use is when Clifford, walking me to the parking lot said, 'Isn't it amazing we ended up with four cunts in the cast?' Four asked I, who? Well, Clifford said, scratching his chin, 'There's Mary and Carol and Annie-Joe and — hmn...wait a minute I was sure there were four!' I will go all the way to the Supreme Court on this one. And I'm sure you'll be right behind me, PRODDING me on, as always." For the record, Kirkwood emerged triumphant from his "cunt" wars. In the same letter, Kirkwood described the manuscript he had submitted as, "the steaming turd of a book…" — but then he had used a similar phrase to describe the developing *A Chorus Line*.

DeSanti found her author not to be the kind to pull rank, although also not without a manipulative side. "Jimmy was always extraordinarily respectful, even though I was rather a junior person in the scheme of things," she says. "He knew that I engaged with the spirit of his book, and cared about it, and he listened to what I had to say. On one occasion, when I didn't get some chunk of the editing back to him by 5pm on the date I'd promised, he called in a rage and told me he'd given away first-row seats that night to *Phantom of the Opera* — at that time hard-to-get tickets — just so he could stay home and work on the editing. I was so aghast and upset that I was practically in tears — and then he burst out laughing and then scolded me and told me he was just trying to make a point! This was typical — he was mischievous and splenetic, generally wanting to have things his way and be in control (not unlike most authors in this), a bit dramatic and ultimately good-natured."

As if *Stage-Stuck, I Teach Flying* and *Diary of a Mad Playwright* was not enough to have on his professional plate, another idea for a project was percolating in Kirkwood's mind at this point. It involved a combination of writing and performing. Jerry Paonessa: "After *Stage-Stuck*, the next thing he was going to try to do, and had started working on already, was a one-man show. He was trying to put things together and thinking about what should go in. He was very excited about it. The funny thing is, [in] New York, every other show that opens is a one-man or a one-woman show these days and this really preceded it enormously." Paonessa recalls Kirkwood seeking and receiving advice from actress Phyllis Newman, who had recently done her own one-woman show.

Presumably, Kirkwood was still sticking to a writing timetable that had been prepared for him, free of charge, by Paonessa. The disparity between the number of projects on which the ever-ambitious Kirkwood wanted to work and the number of hours in the day was something that caused him so much anxiety that Paonessa decided to do something about it. Paonessa: "He said, 'I don't know how I'm going to do all this stuff, I have so much I want to do.' I said, 'You tell me what you want to accomplish and I will tell you how you're going to do it.'"

Though Piazza and Kirkwood were now lovers, this did not in any way mean that Arthur Beckenstein was no longer part of the picture — which itself did not mean that the resultant triangle was a harmonious one. "Arthur does not like me," admits Piazza. "We always referred to him as the First Wife." Piazza says he knew Beckenstein and Kirkwood's relationship was no longer a physical one, adding, "Jimmy had many affairs and Arthur never left. They would have these huge fights in the way that an old married couple would. Arthur would put up with all of Jimmy's boys. There were many of us came through. Some stayed for a year, some two years, some longer than that…Jimmy would be in bed with someone else and Arthur would be downstairs mowing the lawn, just *there*, and it just seemed very masochistic to me on Arthur's part…I don't think it was ritualistic. I don't think anyone put a hood on and got into a bullwhip costume. Arthur had a much more of a recessive personality and Jimmy ruled the house. It just seemed that everything was Jimmy's world and Arthur really just lived in Jimmy's world."

"I swear I had no idea Piazza and Jimmy were involved," says Beckenstein. "And Jimmy was more discrete than Piazza describes. If he had affairs, he did not flaunt them in my face." As for Kirkwood's relationship with Piazza, Beckenstein says, "The word 'lover' implies to me a more caring relationship. I think they were working together and they got stoned together. I might believe that they had sex." Piazza says, "I have never bragged that Jimmy and I were romantically involved. We adored one another and when it finally became sexual, it seemed entirely natural. Yes, he probably did keep it from Arthur because he needed him. Jimmy could be pragmatic in all things."

Piazza opines of Kirkwood and Beckenstein's relationship, "It's one of those very twisty long-term marriages that you see a lot in successful couples…[Arthur] adored Jimmy; just idolized him…Arthur enjoyed the spotlight with Jimmy. He liked being the husband or the wife or whatever he was and he felt that all the other boys were just passing through and bided his time. Jimmy would always say, 'Arthur, get a boyfriend. Just go out and meet people.' Arthur wouldn't have any of that…Arthur was always 'outside,' trimming the hedges while Jimmy was upstairs with his friends laughing and Arthur would be just kind of eavesdropping or listening. It was very odd, and Jimmy loved the drama of it. He loved creating situations like that. They shared the house, they had the garden together, they had the cats together, they had a life together in a way, they had a lot of mutual friends and they just shared a lot of memories. I think Arthur for Jimmy was always the once handsome boy that he fell in love with a long time before who he had known before *Chorus Line*." Piazza says Kirkwood's awe at the wealth of Beckenstein's family also worked to keep them together: "They would pull up their yacht in the harbor in the Hamptons. I went out there one day. We sailed out. It was just like something out of a movie." Additionally: "Jimmy wanted to, like, leap through the roof and Arthur was always pulling at his cuffs. I always thought that Jimmy kept Arthur for that reason. I think that Arthur was his nagging anchor, that Jimmy knew in a way if it wasn't there he might actually go through the roof."

Surely, though the various lovers of Kirkwood might be laughing at Arthur for his alleged uptightness, etc., the fact that Beckenstein was and always would be the permanent fixture meant that the joke was on them? Piazza: "That's certainly one way to look at it. Yes, Arthur was a constant so you could say he got the last laugh. But what kind of a laugh was it, really? Watching Jimmy die? And it's not as if Arthur were suddenly rich as the result. He already was. At the same time, he suffered Jimmy's wrath more than the passing parade."

As a man over sixty, James Kirkwood had naturally had a few health problems even despite his preternatural fitness. However, his ailments had hitherto been ones relatively easily containable via medication: high blood pressure, hypertension, gout (a logical condition given Kirkwood's penchant for fine living) and Karpel Tunnel Syndrome (a pinched nerve with some of the symptoms of gout). And if he was never quite able to give up cigarettes, to quote Beckenstein, "He wasn't a big smoker. He didn't buy cigarettes. If he was at a party and people were having drinks and smoking, he would bum a cigarette." However, at the tail-end of the eighties, Kirkwood was about to experience health problems that recourse to drugs could not fix.

Friends remember Kirkwood as merrily promiscuous. Nick Ellison, who is straight, says: "He would often joke about, 'Boy, this bed has seen some serious action.' He would kid me. He said, 'I can't have breakfast, I gotta take a Sitz Bath.' He once burst out laughing at breakfast in a diner and said, 'I had a dream that I was with Mike Dukakis.' (He was running for president). And I said, 'Jim, check please.'" Ron Plotkin — a gay man but never a lover of Kirkwood's — recalls, "He had those twinkly blue eyes and if he had a bead on you — watch out. I remember sitting in a room with some friends and he was looking around the room and I said, 'I know what you're thinking. I'm the only one in this room that you haven't been to bed with.' And he said, 'Oh, you little rat!' I said, 'I don't know whether I should be insulted or not.'"

But there was a downside to the fun. During the *Legends!* run, Bob Regester, one of its four producers, had been diagnosed with AIDS. He succumbed to it in October 1987, three months after Michael Bennett.

February 1988 was the month that Kirkwood's old lover, stand-up partner and friend Lee Goodman was also cut down by the disease.

By this point, Ronald Plotkin was no longer Goodman's partner, but the two were still close friends. "They thought he had leukemia because it was early — 1980," he recalls. "So [we] went through the whole thing of having our masks and everything when we went in and then he kind of rallied and they said, 'No, that's not what it was.' They didn't have the tests for HIV at the time so they didn't indicate any of that until just before he died in '88. It was in '86 when he called me and I happened to be in London at the time visiting with friends of ours and he told me that he got the word. At that time they didn't have a lot of the cocktails or anything. He just couldn't believe it. The day that he died, I called him and he said, 'I'm really seriously ill,' so I said, 'I'll be right there.' By the time I got there he was dead."

Plotkin called Kirkwood to tell him the tragic news: "I said, 'We've lost Lee.' And he said, 'Where did you lose him?' I said, 'No, he's passed away.' It was just something I had difficulty dealing with. I couldn't say the word 'dead' or 'died' and I went for months without doing that and he was very supportive because I had to take care of everything. In August of '88 I had a heart attack and after I got out of the hospital, Jim said, 'I want you to come out to the house.' So we went out to the house together and I said something about Lee passing, the loss of Lee. He said, 'You've got to say that he died.' I couldn't. I finally did and I felt a weight lifted because he said, 'It's not that you don't care about him and don't miss him, but it's something you have to face up to.' He had also arranged for the memorial service we had for Lee at Chita's restaurant and he gave this absolutely lovely speech." Kirkwood knew that his half-sister remembered Goodman fondly from the forties and fifties (she had even stayed with Goodman on one occasion) and took the trouble to ring Joan to inform her of his death. Joan feels that it was the only time that Kirkwood ever got close to discussing his sexuality with her. She recalls, "I said, 'What happened?' and he said, 'Guess.'"

Kirkwood's knowledge of the effects of AIDS went back further than the deaths of Bennett, Regester and Goodman. His brother T. Michael had a gay younger brother named Tony. Explains T. Michael, "My mother had remarried, so he was no relation to Jimmy." James Kirkwood and Tony became friends. T. Michael: "I hadn't seen Tony in almost a year. I remember asking after Tony one day, and there was a silence – that deadly silence. I asked if he had AIDS. [The disease] must have been around awhile for me to have guessed such a thing." Tony died in November

1984. Kirkwood met a Canadian former partner of Tony's named Nick. "Nick — I don't remember when — but he started to develop AIDS," says T. Michael. "Jimmy offered him a job in New York. Jimmy helped him out and I thought that was so terrific. Finally, when it started getting so bad, he went back to Canada [where] you don't have to pay out billions of dollars to get an aspirin or some fucking thing."

Kirkwood had known death quite intimately in his life, but what occurred from the mid-1980s onwards with AIDS was a veritable holocaust for which not even he could have prepared. At a time when the so-called AIDS drugs cocktail had not been formulated and when HIV-positive was a condition that constituted a death sentence, the gay community was being decimated. The dread of the ailment cropped up in Kirkwood's correspondence with Herlihy. For instance, this passage from a letter dated September 9, 1988, in which he refers to a Key West friend: "John Fisher is losing weight and is being very brave but he's scared shitless and we're going through that whole thing and I hate it, hate it, hate it. But there's nothing to do but go through it." In a letter to Herlihy of October 31, 1988, Kirkwood's reluctance to even mention the disease's title may be self-parody, but only just: "Chuck, incidentally, has IT but is doing great, feeling great, and testing very good now. He is the healthiest one with IT that I know."

"We were going to memorial services every fucking day, sometimes three a day," recalls Bill Gile of the gay community in the worst stages of the AIDS epidemic. "The amount of time it took, if you were conscientious, if you were a friend, to live through that part of the AIDS epidemic…I did it all. Jimmy did it. We'd find each other at the memorial services of friends we didn't even know we had in common, let alone the number of people who were passing through *Chorus Line* who were dying…Everyone in my address book died. By the time I was copying my address book down again, I got to the 'K' page, I had to start again because everybody on the new K page was dead — and I put them in a few days ago. I actually stopped keeping track of people's numbers at that point."

Though Kirkwood was still a far from "out" gay (Piazza: "Towards the end of his life, the last couple of years, there was a gay calendar that came out, gay history, and he was included and he was *furious*"), he didn't flinch from involvement in the anti-AIDS cause. Gile: "He was very supportive of the gay movement. He gave, huge generosity to the AIDS movement." "He was very available to benefits," says Piazza. "Gave a very powerful speech at a fundraiser at Palladium in which he read from Edgar Allan Poe then spoke of his own losses. Lee was either dying or had just died at that point…He went into this real angry thing about AIDS. Jimmy was that way. He would take illness personally. He would almost give it a face: fuck death, fuck AIDS, how dare you do this to us. I didn't sense that he was scared for himself. It didn't seem that way…It may have entered his mind. He didn't have sores; he didn't have anything like that. He would eat anybody under the table. He drank, oftentimes to excess. He didn't have any of the outward signs of someone in the full-blown state of AIDS at that time at all." However, Kirkwood's cousin Lila has an impressionistic memory that all was not well for a considerable period before his death. "I didn't see him the last few years of his life because he was so ill and he really didn't want to see people," she says. "We were going to see him in Florida one time and he said, 'Oh, I feel so rotten, I'd rather just talk to you on the phone.'"

Like all gay men, at that point in history Kirkwood would have been subject to much whispering and rumor-mongering if he did not look well. In an age when ignorance about AIDS and its causes was prevalent even among the gay community, this could be more than a little unpleasant. As Benjamin Morrison notes, "People were scared to kiss then. Straight women would lean over and shake my hand during that period, 'cause they didn't want to kiss a gay man on the mouth. We were crazy. We didn't have any knowledge. So we blamed the government. Why not?" Piazza: "AIDS was not only fearful but inexplicable. The atmosphere was full of rumor, innuendo and those who were afflicted early on suffered essentially from a Scarlet Letter of Kaposi." Nick Ellison recalls Kirkwood looking cadaverous at this point in time and being concerned about his health. So was Benjamin Morrison, but his feelings were diffused and confused by his (correct) suspicion that Kirkwood was a cokehead. "One of the things cocaine does, and one of the things AIDS does to people, is make them skinny," says Morrison. "I just had a sense that he looked bad, and my recollection is that I even sort of hoped, 'Well, maybe it's just the cocaine, rather than being AIDS.'" "People thought I had AIDS then, too," says Piazza, "and I didn't. I just was coked-up. We were just cadavers. I'm almost positive that would be why Jimmy looked that way." The emotional toll taken by *Legends!* had also not helped matters. Piazza: "He was so over-exhausted from that play and probably doing a lot of drugs, lot of Valium for sure, cocaine when he could get it, pot a lot, and drinking heavily."

Yet, even Piazza had moments of doubt. At one point, he, *vis a vis* Kirkwood's insecurity about his fading looks, suggested plastic surgery. "I said, 'Jimmy, why don't you get some face work done? Why don't you get a lift and do your eyes?'" he recalls. "He said, 'If only I could but I can't.' And that's the first time I ever thought that he had a condition, something that [meant] he couldn't have surgery. It was doctor's orders or something like that. It was odd that he said he couldn't have it...Jimmy may have been sick for a longer time than it first appeared because he used to do so many pills and medications and I never really questioned what they were. I wondered in the back of mind if he had AIDS at that point. I never really knew."

Andrew Morse recalls discussing AIDS with Kirkwood at some point after Goodman's death. Says Morse, "He'd spoken to his doctor about should he get tested and his doctor just said to him 'Well, there's really nothing that we can do for it, so why bother knowing something bad?'"

"You can say I don't like condoms," Kirkwood himself said in a magazine interview circa 1989, although this was only as a characteristic fob-off to a question about the nature of his sexuality. He did, however, have a comment to make about the AIDS epidemic: "If Gore Vidal had written a book about this ten years ago, no one would have believed it. They would have said, 'You've gone too far.'"

Despite the carnage going on around him, Kirkwood — amazingly — doesn't seem to have changed his own promiscuous lifestyle in the second half of the eighties, either by reducing the number of his partners or by practicing safe sex. Says Gile of such attitudes, "The huge wave had passed. We didn't think it was preventable at all, and this whole thing about safe sex didn't happen for a long time after that." Piazza, who actually became Kirkwood's lover "fully" — as opposed to the previous "tentatively" — in the same month that Goodman died, disagrees, pointing out that he himself knew enough to insist on condoms. Though he says he and Kirkwood were "intimate for quite some time, safely so, but still intimate," he doesn't necessarily think the safely part applied to all Kirkwood's lovers at this juncture. "Jimmy, being of his generation, hated the idea of safe sex," he says. "My feeling is that if Jimmy could get away with unsafe sex with someone, he would. Not the case with me, as I was adamant. But others might not have been so demanding, especially if they were somewhat in awe of him." Piazza does add, "There were, of course, many of Jimmy's sex partners who died but to say he was the transmitter would be slanderous and without any basis in fact." Piazza explains of the times, "People were in denial in a great way. For me, the seventies was this extraordinary liberating time, when it was bathhouses and it was open sex and it was sex was another way of saying hello and everybody was fucking everybody. It almost became a political action. It was just this great big party, just this explosive party of freedom…There was a point where it was almost scary. It was a little too free and I always worried in the back of my mind that something bad could happen. Bad things did happen. People would get beaten up or almost murdered in these sex places in the parks or whatever, certain people were always getting syphilis or VD. And when this came along, I think people knew that something was very wrong. Most of us thought we had it and were just too scared to be tested. It took me two years before I actually got a test. Larry Kramer was certainly shouting the warnings out early enough. I think probably by '83 or '84 it was really, really known. I remember there was a boy that worked as Jimmy's house boy in the Hamptons and I think they were probably having sex and he died of AIDS. A very sweet kid, can't remember his name. So it was all around us. Whole dinner parties I remember — people probably all gone by now." As for Kirkwood, Piazza says, "I think there was that thing in him that was very defiant even in the face of all that."

Arthur Laurents was not surprised that Kirkwood exposed himself to danger against his better knowledge. "Everyone thinks he's invincible," he reasons. "It doesn't have to do with intelligence; it has to do with human fallibility. You think everyone else but you." Larry Kramer says of Kirkwood, "That he died from AIDS, even while being aware of it, could be said about almost everyone who did die from it, then and now. Our tragedy."

Terrence McNally suspected there was something amiss with Kirkwood's health at the end of 1988. He recalls, "He loved Christmas enormously and when he called me from Key West and he said he wasn't coming to New York for Christmas, I told my partner. Right away he said, 'I think he's sick. Something's wrong. He would never miss Christmas.' He loved Rockefeller Centre, St. Patrick's Cathedral, the lights, the stores. He was the original 'Christmas is my favorite time of the year' person." Leaving aside the curious disparity between Beckenstein's and McNally's impressions of what Kirkwood felt about the Yuletide season, Beckenstein noticed something was wrong at around this time too. "Jimmy got sick in January of '89," is Beckenstein's recollection. "He had just come back from Key West. He was lecturing down there."

It would seem that Key West was where Kirkwood had contracted the disease that would hasten the end of his life. The artistic and — even more so — gay communities had mushroomed since Kirkwood had first bought property in the locale. Recalls Ross Claiborne, "When I came down here in the eighties, it was a known fact that there were nine Pulitzer-Prize-winning writers living here, at least wintering here." Though heterosexual writers were resident, there was a significant overlap between the writing and gay communities, with Truman Capote, James Leo Herlihy, Dotson Raider, Evan Rhodes, Terrence McNally, Tennessee Williams and others either frequently or permanently present. "Jimmy loved it down here," says Claiborne. "Jimmy had a very active sexual life down here, as did most people." It was a life that for the most part excluded Kirkwood's significant other. Claiborne: "Jimmy staked out the Keys as his territory. I never saw Arthur down here. I know he has been, but I never saw him down here." Claiborne recalls a friend of Kirkwood's named John who was "blonde and good-looking, young…He was a fellow tennis player…We knew that John had AIDS and I always assumed that Jimmy got it from John." Claiborne is referring to John Fisher, the person whom Kirkwood wrote Herlihy in September '88 was being very brave but scared shitless about the weight he was losing. "John Fisher I knew very well," says Piazza. "He died of AIDS. He was a writer, children's books, or editor or publisher. He was a sweet guy. They played tennis and they were lovers for quite a while down in Key West."

"He was in Key West most of that fall before he died," recalls Homer Price. "He looked very bad when I was down there in late January…I was worried about him even then. I didn't know what was going on; I didn't know how serious it was…The library had a lecture series of authors. I went to this lecture at the library in Key West and he strode out on that stage looking like a million dollars with a spring in his step. He was a real actor and he gave a wonderful lecture. I think that was his last public appearance."

Kirkwood got back to the Hamptons before Price. Kirkwood and Piazza were scheduled to depart to Jupiter, the strangely named area in Florida in which Burt Reynolds' theatre was located, on Saturday, February 25. Piazza ended up going to Jupiter alone after a traumatic incident the previous Sunday. On that day, he and Kirkwood had gone to see *I Could Go on Lip-Synching* at Theatre Off Park. After going backstage and sharing stories about Tallulah Bankhead with John Epperson, star of the show, they repaired to the bar. Suddenly, Kirkwood complained of a backache so searing that he decided to go back to his Manhattan apartment. Piazza dropped him off, then went home. He received a call from Kirkwood around seven the next morning. Piazza: "He said, 'I have had a stroke, I think, and I'm a little blind.'" Piazza rushed around to Kirkwood's apartment. Upon his arrival, it was to be met by the sight of the right side of Kirkwood's face drooped and paralyzed. "He couldn't talk, and in a way because he was talking funny, my first reaction was to laugh," says Piazza. "I thought he was pulling a prank with me when I walked in because he was talking out of the side of his mouth and then I realized that he'd had partial stroke and it was just so scary." Piazza was struck by the terrified look in his friend's eyes.

"It was snowing, it was like a blizzard, and I had to get him downstairs and into a cab and to a hospital across town and it was just horrible," says Piazza. "He was scared to death." A further indignity for Kirkwood was that the hospital forms required him to give his age. Even in the midst of his pain and fright, Kirkwood couldn't bring himself to divulge the fact that he was 64. Piazza: "I had to fill out his forms and I said, 'Jimmy, how old are you, really?' He said, '59, goddamn it.'"

There followed an uneasy two days in which Kirkwood was subjected to EKGs, CAT scans and spinal taps in order to find out the source of the malaise. The doctors and medical staff appeared increasingly puzzled as Kirkwood, barely able to move, was in ever-increasing pain. Finally, it was discovered that Kirkwood had a tumor near his spine. Surgery, it was said, would be necessary. Though Kirkwood was able to leave the hospital, flying to Florida to help supervise the journey of his new play from paper to stage was naturally out of the question. As was postponing its opening: casting and set design had been arranged, contracts signed and tickets sold. "I just felt so bad," says Piazza. "He said, 'You have to go, you have to do this for both of us, it's the play we wrote together, you have to go down there.' I was scared to death…I thought we were going to Florida together and Jimmy [would] probably be going out to dinner with Burt and charming everybody and we would get the play on and it would be great fun. The idea of going down alone totally unprepared for these characters…I mean, these were old veteran troopers."

Piazza's fears were realized when he arrived in Jupiter: "Charles Nelson Reilly [was] charming, but not a stranger to the bottle and kind of wooing me, trying to win me over so that I would write the play the way he wanted it done, and then the cast kind of wooing me in their individual way wanting to get their parts up and that. I was at a loss. I couldn't call Jimmy and I didn't know what I was doing." Bibi Osterwald, signed to play the character Bucky Bumpurs, introduced herself to Piazza and explained that she had taken the role because of Kirkwood, with whom she went way back. After asking when Kirkwood was coming, she explained that he had promised her a "complete rewrite" and demanded, "Two solid laughs in the first act. Two solid laughs in the second. And no long speeches."

At first, Kirkwood seemed to genuinely believe that at some point he would be coming to Florida to help Piazza with rewrites. "His paralysis worked out better, his face got better and he was a little optimistic," says

Piazza. In the meantime, Piazza had to attend to reworking the script. "I was being pressured by Burt and by Charles to rewrite," he says. Despite his supine position and weakened state, Kirkwood was exerting a considerable amount of pressure on Piazza as well via the telephone: "Jimmy kept saying, 'Don't change a word of mine' and I had to. I was lying to him on the phone saying, 'Oh, nothing has changed and they love every word' and rewriting as I went because I was in the real world. He said, 'Are people asking about me?' and 'I said, 'Oh, absolutely' and he said, 'Does Burt ask about me?' I said, 'Oh, definitely.' And, of course, Burt hadn't. So I got a get-well card and I couldn't get Burt to sign it so I forged his name on it. I felt so bad and he was thrilled that Burt Reynolds had [sent it]. It was just an awful, awful period and I knew he was sick up here and I wanted to be up here and I couldn't. It was my first experience and it was very overwhelming for me with this movie star crazy guy and oh please. It was weird. I still get anxiety when I think about it."

Added to the anxiety was conflict with Beckenstein. Says the latter of Kirkwood, "His mind was on what was happening in Jupiter. He wondered how it was going and he wanted to be there." "Arthur would call me and say, 'You're not to call Jimmy with any bad news, he can't be upset,'" says Piazza. "Jimmy would call and say, 'So what's going on? Tell me.' So I said, 'Arthur said not to.' And he said, 'Fuck Arthur.' Even at the end it was like that. That was the triangle we always had. Arthur thinking that I was somehow a bad influence on Jimmy and trying to keep me at bay."

"I went to see him and he was in bad shape," says Homer Price of Kirkwood. "The next morning Arthur called me and I went over and we took him to the hospital and that was the beginning of the end. He never really was even ambulatory, I think, or maybe barely, after that." "He was complaining about pains in his neck and his shoulder," explains Beckenstein. "Jim was in so much pain he could not walk. I remember the head of the neurology department telling Jim that he had Lyme disease and he would be better on Monday. I knew it wasn't Lyme disease, because he had been tested for that. I think he was admitted [to] New York Hospital at that time. I remember Jim having his sense of humor even when he was in such bad shape. He was trying to win over the nurses; it was his way of getting through…They put him in a neck brace. They thought it was a tennis injury or spinal injury."

"The last times I went to see him, he was in the hospital and he said to me he'd injured his hand playing tennis," recalls Laurents. "And, believe it or not, I believed him. And then I went to see him and he had this great roaring scar down his back and I thought, 'Something's very wrong here.' I forget his explanation, but I was scared that he was in a bad place. He lived recklessly."

Stage-Stuck is yet another — third by this author's reckoning, fourth if you count *A Chorus Line*, which only looks at the auditions — Kirkwood project that is a show about staging a show. Like all the previous ones except *A Chorus Line*, it drips with theatre references that most critics but few of the wider general public would understand. It's also, like most of the others, a depiction of bitchy, in-fighting, vainglorious people who, though they are the butt of many of the jokes, dismay with their un-personableness.

Stage-Stuck opens in the home of an outrageously clichéd Deep South white trash family who are amazed to find that one of their member, who had gone to Hollywood and become a diva, has returned to the fold. It's not until well into the scene when a character looks into the wings and asks for his line that we realize this is the rehearsal for a play. This play-within-a-play, *In the Absence of August*, is a translation of a French production that has been brought over to the States by the ambitious but misguided producer Moe Shaugnessey. Though the cast discuss possible replacements for their drama queen cokehead director Peter Poll, this is the only thing that does not happen in a vain attempt to improve *In the Absence of August*, which sees the cynical introduction of ludicrously gratuitous foul language, violence, a shipwreck, a train collision, a dive bomber crash, sex and musical farting. The determination to outrage by the producer of the fictional play is matched by an apparent resolve by the writers of the real one along similar lines. For instance, the character Raoul — whose struggles with English are additionally hindered by his lisp — seems designed to cock a snook at PC depictions of both Latinos *and* gays. Though the humor is often genuinely funny, it is also consciously outrageous and tiresomely cold-eyed about human foibles, written to provoke the sort of screaming laughter that is slightly contrived and which results when people give in against their better judgment to being tickled by the unmentionable inflections of existence. There is also lots of score-settling by Kirkwood. Michael Bennett, Bob Fosse and Mike Nichols all come in for criticism over their alleged avariciousness, while Mary Martin gets it in the neck for the prim reluctance to swear on stage that Kirkwood encountered during the *Legends!* tour. Theatre critics are also the target of abuse. Some of the dialogue is good and some awful, but this author is at liberty to reproduce neither variety because Kirkwood literary executrix Elisa Lefkowitz requested that only published material be extracted herein.

Leaving aside the tone, there is structural incompetence, such as a clumsy moment when the *In the Absence of August* cast realize that the reason the play is so bad is because it has been translated from the French by a man who barely understands that language. This fundamental plot development is conveyed in a fleeting collective cast gesture just when an explicitly stated revelation and discussion is called for. Ultimately, the cast of *In the Absence of August* are besieged, making pompous speeches about the validity of live drama to disgruntled theatregoers who literally want to lynch them. Though the audiences of *Stage-Stuck* might not have been thinking quite the same way, they would have been cognizant of the fact that they had witnessed an essentially shallow, vulgar and spiteful play. Its authors commit a last, fatal mistake in making its finale a parody of the glitzy rendition of "One" that closes *A Chorus Line*, unwisely putting the audience in mind of Kirkwood glories that are receding ever farther into the past.

"It was sort of a nasty humor," says Beckenstein. "His involvement in *Stage-Stuck* was unfortunate. That was a wasted period of time. Anybody that read that play was very disappointed by it. I wish he'd put that energy into finishing the novel." Jerry Paonessa took in the aforementioned reading of *Stage-Stuck* at the Actors Studio. "It was a bitter experience for me," says the man whom Arthur Laurents has accused in this text of uncritical adoration of Kirkwood's output. "I really hated the play and he got angry at me for hating it. Oh, it was awful. It was all the things that Jimmy was not and that Jim Piazza brought out in Jimmy: mean-spirited, nasty, bad taste. It wasn't funny. Jimmy loved Jim Piazza. He thought he was the funniest human being alive." Piazza can at least plead innocence when it comes to the Raoul character. He explains, "Quite honestly, that was Jimmy's invention which I didn't really like a lot, but then we had this actor in Florida who really took to it and he really did it. We'd hoped in the end it was more endearing. I felt probably a little bit cringy about that and I think Jimmy loved that because his generation, that was more part of the humor, that campy kind of thing." Piazza adds that the snide references to Michael Bennett in *Stage-Stuck* were down to the fact that "he thought that Michael betrayed him. They were supposed to work on another project together and never did. [Presumably *Murder at the Vanities*.] And he said that Michael would be seductive. He claimed Nick Dante was in love with Michael Bennett like crazy and Michael kind of played on that to get the best out of him and then he dumped him when

[*A Chorus Line*] opened." Piazza also says, "He always blamed Michael Bennett for some kind of a downer on the first preview night with an audience for *Chorus Line*: Jimmy was in the other room out of it and he always blamed Michael for spoiling the evening for him." (Presumably *A Chorus Line*'s formal opening night.)

Once he had gotten over his initial terror, Piazza found that he was enjoying himself in Florida. He recalls, "Jimmy said, 'Tell them I'll be down soon,' and I said, 'Oh, he's coming down next week,' or 'He's coming down the week after that,' and pretty soon it was clear that he was not coming down and then there was a point where I was delighted that he wasn't coming down, because I had finally gotten control of the play I thought, and I was earning my respect down there. I was doing the work and I was very engaged and I knew if Jimmy came down he was going to take over, so it was like the protégé feeling his oats. Then I was lying to him on the phone saying we hadn't changed a word and he knew I was lying and it was this back-and-forth thing, but I think at that point Jimmy was so ill that it didn't really matter. He was just going through the motions."

As well as the eccentricities of Reilly, Piazza had to contend with the behavior of Rip Taylor. Cast in the role of Moe Shaughnessy, Taylor was a Vegas lounge act comedian hoping for a legitimate stage career. Piazza claims the authors had misgivings about him when he rang, pre-production, to ask if his character had to be quite so "Jewish" and had vetoed his casting — only to be one-upped by Taylor who contacted Burt Reynolds directly and got himself put back in the play. "I was having to write jokes for him because he was a jokester," says Piazza, "so I was doing monologues for him that weren't in the original play."

On opening night, March 23, Kirkwood's agent Esther Sherman approached Piazza: "She said, 'I just have one thing to ask you.' I said, 'What?' She said, 'Should I have the chicken or the fish?' I couldn't believe that's all she cared about." Piazza later wrote that he watched the opening night "with horrified fascination." Part of this was down to the fact that opening night also served as the first technical run-through. Piazza learnt that Taylor had reached an agreement with Reynolds whereby his own one-man Vegas show would replace *Stage-Stuck* at the theatre should the play close early, thus creating a potential conflict of interest. Piazza was naturally not happy about this, or the fact that Taylor's machinations seemed to leave him too busy to learn his lines, which he ended up taping to bits of the stage furniture. This latter maneuver proved futile when Taylor found come opening night that he couldn't read them in the dark.

Furthermore, "He was stepping out of character to do his bits," says Piazza. The latter does, though, have some good things to say about Taylor: "He was a trouper, he really did give it what he could...I did get him to take off his hairpiece. He had never appeared bald before."

The second night was even more of a disaster. A gas leak in the dinner theatre's kitchen caused the evacuation of the whole venue and the cancellation of the second act. "They couldn't leave," says Piazza of the audience gathered in the parking lot. "They were afraid that if someone started their engine it would ignite and they were just sitting there. I was so exhausted and a wreck. The cast saw me in tears and nobody was at all sympathetic because it was like the Titanic."

As the run continued, the reviews came in. "They weren't terrible," says Piazza. "They said 'Kirkwood and Piazza fail on this that and the other' and I think *Variety* was fair and said, 'It's still a work in progress.' They weren't devastating, because it was too local. They're not going to come down that hard on a dinner theatre production." Worse reaction came from the audiences. Some members of what was a retirees community were disgusted by the language they heard. "Unbelievable," recalls Piazza. "The people were fleeing in intermission."

In the second week of the show's run, Piazza's anxiety was massively ratcheted up by Reilly. "Charles Nelson Reilly, who could be such a bitch, was floating the theory that Jimmy was dying of AIDS, which was not very fun to hear on my end," recalls Piazza. "In fact, he had told me one morning that Jimmy had died. I freaked out and I called New York and, in fact, Jimmy was not dead. Charles was very strange." Piazza found this sort of behavior not untypical of older homosexuals: "They were about the same age and, that whole generation of gay men, they were friends and yet they had this kind of competitive thing and [were] closet-ey a lot. It was interesting."

Despite all the problems, a sense of solidarity was building up among the company as Piazza continued to try to make good the script's deficits. "I think towards the end of the run of *Stage-Stuck*, as bad as it was, it was really getting to that point where it was working because it was a real, wild, crazy satire that needs time to cook," says Piazza. "The actors were really getting into it, we were getting great physical sight-gag laughs, we were getting a lot of stuff which was fun." Piazza noticed that the audience reception was becoming warmer and that people suddenly did not seem too embarrassed to come backstage. Just when hope was springing, however, Reynolds pulled the plug. The rumor Piazza heard was that he had noticed some walk-outs during the first act on the occasion he came to see the show and had been shaken by hate mail received from disgruntled attendees. *Stage-Stuck* closed on April 2 after just eleven days, three weeks earlier than planned. It was the theatre's first-ever cancellation of a running show in its decade-long history. The theatre's producer, Ken Williams, claimed that it was actually costing more to close the show in scrapping the set and souvenir items and paying off the actors than it would cost to keep it running. "What we want to do is make sure we have the faith and trust of the audience for the future," he explained. Considering what subsequently happened to the theatre, Williams and Reynolds would seem to have failed in that objective. Says Piazza of Reynolds, "From the grapevine I heard that he blamed the bankruptcy of the theatre on us."

Piazza called Kirkwood with the bad news. "He said, 'Fuck 'em, are you okay?'" recalls Piazza. "I thought it was so touching and I thought that was kind of really in the end what our relationship was about. It was more than the play." After the final night's performance, Piazza packed his bags and headed to Fort Lauderdale to housesit for friends. "He wanted to remain in my mind as handsome, sexy, capable," says Piazza. "I was Jimmy's last 'fling' and when he insisted I not come back to NY I felt that to mean he didn't want me to see him wasting away." The final communication — or near-communication — between Kirkwood and Piazza occurred while the latter was still in his friends' Fort Lauderdale home a week to ten days before Kirkwood's death. "They had this old answering machine," says Piazza. "Jimmy had the number and he called me up in this very halting voice. Before I could get to the machine to pick up the phone I realized he was saying goodbye to me. My finger was in the air and I wanted to pick up the phone and part of me couldn't. He was halfway through this very touching message that he was leaving me, saying goodbye, he was dying. I stood there and I listened to this whole thing. I was just sobbing, I was just crying so hard, and then the phone went off. I didn't speak. It always haunts me, that moment."

"Everybody died," says Bill Gile of the eighties AIDS epidemic. "Not high fatality. Everybody. It was a hundred percent death."

This, of course, is not quite true. (Gile himself survived to 2011.) However, that 100% fatality rate is fairly accurate for those gay cast and crew members of *A Chorus Line*. Bobby Tufford: "In *Chorus Line*, everyone in that was homosexual and they all died of AIDS, unfortunately. I'm not trying to be critical, you understand." Lest anyone thinks this is small-town mentality, the ultra-cosmopolitan figure of Liz Smith concurs: "So many people from *A Chorus Line,* they had such a fantastic success that it was almost like they were handed their own deaths on a plate because they were all sleeping with each other and taking drugs and having a ball and nobody knew about AIDS — or not everybody did — and so they ended up, all of them, dying. It was out of just exuberant ignorance." Now Kirkwood was added to that list.

"At the time, in the eighties, if anyone was ill, the first thing you thought was, they have AIDS," says Beckenstein. "I was furious when I heard about people who had no idea what was wrong with Jimmy starting rumors that he had AIDS. Specifically, I heard that Charles Nelson Reilly was telling people that he had AIDS." Fair enough, except that Reilly and his ilk were correct. "It really wasn't until the end of February that he found out that he was HIV-positive," says Beckenstein. "He didn't know his HIV status. I know 'cause I remember being in the doctor's office and the doctor telling him in front of me and then looking at Jimmy and saying, 'Oh, I shouldn't have said anything. I should have told you in private.'" The Bell's Palsy by which Kirkwood had been stricken before Piazza left for Florida and which had been improving suddenly became the least of his problems. Beckenstein: "He became paralyzed maybe a month before he died…He was diagnosed with a very lethal type of cancer and had a large, tumor embedded under an area of the spine that made it impossible to operate…That was what was causing the pain…I was with him most of the time he was sick, when he was in bad shape. I took a leave of absence from my job to be with him…He had a wonderful full-time nurse at home and there was another nurse who came in to stay during the night…Jim Piazza would call to talk to him and I would ask Jim Piazza to tell white lies to him and tell him it's going great. We knew Jimmy was dying and I wanted him to have good news. I'm sure he knew how bad things were, but he was fighting with every ounce of his strength, as long as the doctors gave him hope."

Because Kirkwood was HIV-positive, the assumption for many was that the cancer had taken a grip because his immune system had been shredded. Yet, Paonessa, who was around Kirkwood a lot in the final weeks, says, "He and I never, ever mentioned the word AIDS. Never. He had cancer. I talked to every one of his doctors. I guarantee you he never had the conversation." Jim Piazza offers, "When he was in the hospital, in those days they would put something on the door to indicate this person had AIDS and he didn't have one. I asked his lawyer after he died and his lawyer was very, very coy about it. No one ever said for sure Jimmy had AIDS. I assume that he probably did. I thought that maybe he had enough power or enough pull or enough money where he wouldn't have to be marked in that way. His lawyer said, 'Oh, believe me, they're coming out of the woodwork now that he's dead saying that this happened to them because of Jimmy.' I think he was being very protective of Jimmy's finances to avoid one of those Rock Hudson lawsuits [from] people who were having sex with him and he was unprotected." Beckenstein offers, "The cancer caused his death — no doubt made worse by his compromised immune system."

Of course, had Kirkwood been content to restrict his sexual activities to Beckenstein, who loved him beyond reproach, he would not have ended up in this terrible situation. However, the man who patiently put up with Kirkwood's foibles for two decades declines to criticize him. Asked if he was angry at Kirkwood's disloyalty and its consequences, Beckenstein merely says, "It made me sad." As to whether he was surprised that Kirkwood should expose himself to the dangers of the disease that had taken the lives of so many of their friends, he says — again not quite answering — "Jimmy liked to live life to the hilt. Nobody knows how you acquire an HIV status, how it happened." Does he have any reason to believe that Kirkwood acquired an HIV-positive status by ways that were not related to sexual activity? "No." Did Kirkwood ever express regret that he'd ended up in this position? "He was very upset. It's kind of a personal question. I don't know that he was kicking himself. You can't change your life and history and what happened." Though Arthur Laurents says, "I like Arthur enormously," he says of the issue of whether Beckenstein became angry over Kirkwood's self-inflicted predicament, "The trouble with Arthur is he'd never get angry at anything. He just doesn't have the balls."

Paonessa says, "I kept saying, 'How long does the man have?' They were not going to tell me, because then it becomes a self-fulfilling prophesy. If you tell a man he's got a year, he's got a year. But one doctor that I talked to said that he knew six months before. Jimmy knew." Paonessa adds of Kirkwood, "He said something very, very strange. He said, 'Do you think that I brought this on myself?' Because he was desperate to pull Mary and Carol. I mean this is like the dream of a lifetime, to have the two of them on Broadway. He meant did he create his own cancer by trying to get this production mounted with Carol and Mary." Jim Piazza says, "That *Legends!* tour took a lot out of him. It was more than he could really deal with — the pressure."

In *Diary of a Mad Playwright*, Kirkwood related his traumatic visit to Bob Regester in hospital in August 1986 just after the producer had been given the news that he was HIV-positive: "What do you say to someone who has just been told this? You say, 'Of course you can lick it, they're working on all sorts of cures and drugs and…so much is a positive mental state.' But the words have a hollow ring." Ironically, Kirkwood was now intoning such platitudes to himself. Though his great intelligence prohibited too much self-deception, eternal optimism had got him through much trauma and heartache in his life hitherto and it was perfectly natural that he should take the attitude that he could almost will himself better. Beckenstein says that despite Kirkwood's paralysis and need for round-the-clock nursing, "His mind was very sharp and his sense of humor was intact…He was just trying everything and fighting and open to anything to beat this cancer that he had."

This attitude caused some considerable distress to Homer Price. "Jimmy really didn't want to face the fact that he was going to die," he says. "He said to me two weeks before he died, 'I'm not going to die, am I? I'm not going to die? All I really want is another five years.' Oh God. I went outside the hospital room and cried when I saw him one day. He was working with physical therapy and I knew it wasn't going to do any good. I was very upset because the doctor was not telling him the truth either and Arthur wasn't telling him the truth." Price called James Leo Herlihy: "I said, 'Jamie, I'm so upset, I don't know what to do. I want to tell Jimmy that he's not going to get better so he can have a week or two or a month of kind of relaxing and not concentrating on trying to get better and coming to grips with what's happening and think about the wonderful moments in his life.' Jamie said, 'Well, Homer, that's maybe what you want to do, but has he asked the doctor what's going on?' I said, 'I don't think so.' And [he] said, 'Well, there you have it…' I thought, 'Jamie's got a view here that's the right one. Jimmy [is] a very forthright person and he doesn't want to know.'"

As he had throughout his life, Kirkwood in this period exhibited a certain reticence, even shame, about his sexuality. "He had AIDS and he was trying to keep it from people, even close people," says Price. "He never even opened up to me and I was really one of his very closest friends, especially towards the end…Arthur was hiding it from everybody." "Jimmy was very open about his life, but this was something he didn't want to share," says Beckenstein, who admits he was surprised by Kirkwood's determination to keep his AIDS secret. "I think he just suddenly didn't want it in the news that he died of AIDS." He adds, "AIDS and HIV status was something that people didn't own up to publicly in the eighties…The mayor of New York (Koch) and the president (Reagan) during those years, treated gay people like lepers. Unless you lived through it, it is hard to imagine…When it was divulged that Rock Hudson died of AIDS [1985], it was shocking. There was a stigma attached, the public feared and shunned anyone with AIDS. It was a mysterious plague we knew very little about."

"He was home, but he was in excruciating pain and in the end had to go back to hospital," recalls Paonessa. "He asked me to come. In excruciating pain, he turned to me and he said, as if I was Cecil B. DeMille, 'You know, darling, having the twins was easier than this,' and then he said, 'Tell Mr. DeMille that I'm ready for my cocoa'…In the face of all that pain, here was a man who just innately was humorous and funny." There was an almost surreal *contretemps* between Kirkwood and Beckenstein. Paonessa: "You have to understand the nature of the relationship between Arthur and Jimmy, which was very finicky. Jimmy again doubled over in pain: 'Arthur, I want some lemon sherbet. I am fucking dying here, Arthur, get me a fucking sherbet.' And Arthur was concerned about him having his lettuce, having his salad." Kirkwood would remain in hospital until April 21, the day before his death.

One of the few glimmers of pleasure Kirkwood was able to obtain during this bleak period was via the cover endorsements that were coming in for *Diary of a Mad Playwright*. Upon the book's publication later that year, its jacket would be plastered with raves from luminaries like Arthur Laurents, Mary Rodgers, Peter Stone, Garson Kanin and Ira Levin. Furthermore, these were not the usual platitudes he had always been able to expect from his pals even when the product of which they were expressing their supposed enjoyment was execrable (*Hit Me with a Rainbow* carried gushing endorsements from James Leo Herlihy and Liz Smith), but articulated what would seem to be genuine admiration for as solid a piece of book journalism as *American Grotesque* had been flawed. "I was bringing quotes over to him every day," Beckenstein said in the week after his death. "He got great pleasure from that." Though Beckenstein also said Kirkwood regretted that he would not live to see the book in print, it must have done his ego some good that at the end of his life he had succeeded in helping to reestablish a fading reputation.

"I had been in Florida and I came back the night that he was dying," says Piazza. "And Arthur basically said you can't come over. I was *persona non grata* at that point…Arthur could deal with a host of Jimmy's lovers, but my relationship was far more than that." In fact, though Beckenstein may have disliked him, and notwithstanding the fact that he was "excluded" from Kirkwood's memorial, Piazza was being treated no differently than anyone else in Kirkwood's circle bar Paonessa. Whether it was a disinclination to run the risk of his sexuality and/or AIDS coming up or a fear of people seeing his deteriorating looks or both, Kirkwood spent the last weeks of his life avoiding friends and family who wanted to see him. "In the end he refused to see anyone but me and Arthur," says Paonessa. "His friends — some life-long — were hurt by this." Beckenstein: "He only wanted to see people who were positive and supporting [in] the end. He just didn't want the bad news, a tear or a glum face. Throughout his life, he always said, 'Just give me the good news.'" T. Michael Kirkwood: "I never knew how sick Jimmy was. He didn't want to tell people, or tell me anyway. I knew things weren't good. We hadn't talked back and forth in a long time and one of the last things he wrote me was, 'Well, are you getting laid? I know I'm not.'" Bill Gile: "I actually didn't know how ill he was until [mutual friend] Jay Lowman called me and then said, 'Don't ask to see him because he's so ill, he can hardly do it'…One thing I do know that he said: 'I would give everything I owned for one hour without this pain.' That was a quote that came back to me." A taste of the bewilderment that many must have felt at Kirkwood's self-imposed isolation is provided by Donald Oliver, who says, "I talked to him when he was ill, but it even took me a while to find out that he was ill. Are you getting any kind of sense that he pulled away from people toward the end? I would hate to think right now that it was only because of me that I didn't meet with him. Because I did like him so much."

By the time of that inaccessible end, Kirkwood was no longer fooling himself. The turning point was his doctors coming clean with him about his prospects. Beckenstein: "As soon as they told him there was no hope, he gave up. This was a day or two before he died. They just gave him medication for the pain and he said he wanted to go home."

Paonessa recalled a certain peace of mind as Kirkwood's life ebbed away on April 20 at New York Hospital, as relayed at Kirkwood's Shubert Theatre memorial: "He said, 'Can you come over? I really want to talk to you.' I came over. He said, 'Listen baby, I know what a lot of you have known for a very long time.' That was that the cancer that he had was incurable. He said, 'I want to be home. I don't want to be in this hospital.' We had a conversation that lasted about two hours. If anybody ever asked Jimmy Kirkwood what he wanted out of life, he would say, 'I only want one thing — more.' I always got the feeling he was never satisfied, but this one day, these two hours in that hospital, we covered everything. All the rotten things that had happened, all the great things that had happened. We just recounted all [the] things in his life and for the first time I saw that he was really satisfied. We talked about spirituality. He's a very, very spiritual guy. Both being fallen Catholics, we kind of had gotten away from that form of spirituality but he really realized that there was something bigger.

He said, 'It's time to get rid of this old shell. Get rid of the body and let's just continue with the spirit' and it was great to hear him say that. As we went over all the accomplishments, I really saw that he was satisfied. He said, 'I only have one regret.'" Said regret was his failure to finish *I Teach Flying*, the novel about his father he had begun writing 21 years before.

Paonessa now says, "That was the most important [thing]. That was his great unfinished work…On his deathbed, Jimmy dictated the last section of the unfinished book to me and made me promise him that I would see that it was published…I said, 'Look, we don't have much time, would you tell me how you want the story to go between now and the next 100 pages (which, if he'd written it, would have been 400 pages), and tell me what happens…Jimmy dictated to me the story, structure and character development as he wanted it to be." At the time, Paonessa had not read the manuscript of *I Teach Flying* so didn't understand much of what his friend was saying, but faithfully scribbled everything down.

Paonessa related the events following this at the Shubert Theatre memorial: "Then Arthur came in. Jimmy kept nodding off. He was very clear, he was very lucid, he was on medication, but he was bright-eyed — those bright blue eyes — he couldn't have been clearer. Nodded off a little bit and Arthur and I sat with him and Arthur said, 'He told me how he wanted to go. He said he wanted to fall asleep holding my hand.' Then Jimmy got up, he saw Arthur, he smiled and he said, 'Well, guys, I don't know whether it's going to be tonight or tomorrow but it's gonna be soon.' He knew, but he was happy about it. Then he would nod off again. He got up and he looked at me and he said, 'Did I go yet?' I said, 'What, are you crazy? You think I'm going to go with you? Friendship is one thing, but that's really asking too much.' He said, 'No, it isn't!' He nodded off again and slept very peacefully that night. Arthur and I went home. The next morning, according to his wishes, we got him home." Home meant Kirkwood's city apartment, because his Hamptons house was a hundred miles away in an area with no specialized health care.

Kirkwood died on April 21, four hours after leaving hospital for the second time in as many days, holding Beckenstein's hand as he had wished. Kirkwood was dead past the point where Beckenstein thought he was still alive. "I didn't realize it was my pulse I was feeling," says Beckenstein. Eerily, this scenario was very similar to a proposed scene for *I Teach Flying* that Kirkwood had dictated to Paonessa.

Laurents recalls, "When he was in the hospital…he said, 'If I can't walk when I get out, I don't want to live.' He came out in a wheelchair." Piazza: "He committed suicide. The story that I heard was that Jimmy could have had a bit more time but that he would have been confined to a wheelchair. Knowing Jimmy, he said, 'That means I can never play tennis again. I'd rather be dead.' I think he opted to go out early on his own speed. He didn't want to end up a basket case. I wasn't there, but I'm assuming that's what he did…If he was going to be drooling and sitting in a wheelchair and watching the world go by, I think he would have been horrified. I don't think he was the kind of person to just be happy to be alive. He had to be an active player. Jimmy wasn't a watcher."

T. Michael Kirkwood recalls, "I was managing a little theatre. I don't get home 'til twelve, one o'clock, something. I had two messages on my machine. One was from Arthur, who I'd never talked to over the phone before in my life, and one was from my sister Joan, who I'd never met before in my entire life. All it said was, 'Call me no matter what time it is.' Well, I knew, of course, right then that Jimmy had to have passed away. I had no knowledge of it coming or that he was that ill or anything else. So I called Arthur and he told me and then I called Joan and talked to Joan for about — God — two hours." Joan Kirkwood, as with so many other friends and family, had been kept out of the loop. She says, "I never knew he was sick." She attended Kirkwood's Shubert Theatre New York memorial service on June 1, 1989 (there was another memorial in Key West on May 3 the same year at the Tennessee Williams Fine Arts Theatre), where she met Terry/Michael Kirkwood for the first time. From what both Joan and T. Michael say, they didn't particularly find that they liked each other, although that may be chiefly down to the fact that T. Michael adored his father and Joan — clearly bitter about his failure to maintain contact — has less worshipful feelings. It was also the first time Joan had met Arthur Beckenstein. Though she had never discussed it with her half-brother, she took the opportunity to ask Beckenstein about Kirkwood's sexuality and had the nature of his relationship with Beckenstein confirmed for the first time.

Homer Price recalls Beckenstein sticking to the line that Kirkwood being HIV-positive was not to be mentioned: "Even after Jimmy died. What was it he said Jimmy died of? What the hell was it? Some kind of cancer, leukemia? I can't remember now what we were supposed to say. At any rate, Arthur said, 'You know you mustn't tell anybody that Jimmy had AIDS'…And I flew up at Arthur and said, 'Don't you tell me what to tell people. I'm not going to bruit it about, but if good friends of Jimmy ask me, of course, I'm going to tell them.' Oh, I was so annoyed at Arthur. Arthur is as stubborn as can be sometimes. I love him and he is a dear, dear sweet person, but…" T. Michael: "When they said he'd passed, they never said he died of AIDS. Liz Smith had a big article about, 'This has been a terrible year, we've lost so many good artist[ic] people to AIDS' and she listed a flock of people along with Jimmy. And I said, 'Well [that] confirms it.' I mean, I suspected it anyway. Arthur was even pissed because somebody said at the memorial house they had no idea how old Jimmy was and 'he always claims he was younger.' Arthur was very upset about this. I said, 'Arthur, get over it, Jimmy's dead, what the hell are you trying to protect his age for?' It was kind of bizarre." Beckenstein says, "I kept his secret for many years, but there have been so many reports, lists of people who died from the disease, documentaries naming him…that I finally admitted the truth. If he were here today, I think he would be more honest about it." Beckenstein did make an exception at the time with Kirkwood's half-sister. Recalls Joan, "When Arthur called me to tell me that Jimmy died, he told me he had — what did he tell me — viral meningitis? I don't know what he said, but he said something. I called Arthur, it wasn't too long after that, and I said, 'I want to know the truth.' And that's when he said."

The Guardian in the UK printed a James Kirkwood obituary by W.J. Weatherby headed "The Longest Run." Weatherby wrote, "When he died, he was stated to be only 58, although he said not long ago he was 64." This was by no means the only Kirkwood obituary to point out that he was not born in the year he had for so long led people to assume he was. Though Weatherby doesn't state whether he admitted to his true age in public or in private, either would indicate Kirkwood was getting more relaxed about revealing his vintage.

In addition to the moment of his passing mirroring a proposed scene for *I Teach Flying* that he had just dictated, there were a couple of other eerie things surrounding Kirkwood's death. In his appointment book, on the page for April 22 — the day after his passing — he had written "End of run." This was clearly a reference to the originally scheduled final performance of *Stage-Stuck*, but even so it can't help but seem slightly spooky. Spookier still was the fact that the April 22 edition of *The New York Times* not only carried an obituary for Kirkwood but on the same page a notice marking the passing of one James Knot, which just happened to be the name of the playwright character in *Stage-Stuck*.

TWENTY-TWO

Just before he passed away, Kirkwood left a remembrance in the form of checks made out to a long list of fixtures of his life, including his cleaning woman. In addition, he drew up a will. Aside from the Dramatists Guild bequest, James Kirkwood left his estate to a trust comprised of ten relatives and friends. As beneficiaries die, the pot is redistributed among the remainder of the legatees.

Diary of a Mad Playwright — published in September 1989 — was well-received. Excepting his Samuel French-published plays *P.S. Your Cat is Dead!* and *Legends!* and the script of *A Chorus Line*, it remains one of only two Kirkwood works in print in his native country, the other being the novel *P.S. Your Cat is Dead!*

Carole DeSanti says Dutton did not know that the author would not live to see the book on the stands until "a very late stage in the process." She adds, "There was no discussion of his health and no indication on his part that he was ill in our interactions up to the very last. He always played the role of the consummate professional writer and while I knew that he wasn't entirely well, I had no idea how sick he really was." Had Dutton known beforehand that the author would not be around to promote the book, would that have changed their decision to purchase it? "Probably not," DeSanti says. "It was a kinder, gentler time in publishing and our acquisition was based on what the book was, our realistic expectations for it and our respect for Kirkwood as a writer." Asked how the book did commercially, DeSanti says, "Sales were pretty quiet, as I remember, but, also, Dutton was going through a reorganization itself at the time. The whole publishing and editorial staff was let go in 1989, and there was quite a bit of chaos as the titles were absorbed into the parent company. We were all in a state of upheaval and this tragedy was a part of it all. But, in business terms, we had always seen the book as a targeted piece of non-fiction, not a general-audience title. We thought that it would sell to theatre-buffs and Kirkwood fans and perhaps some others based on the behind-the-scenes stories and I think our projections were accurate. Of course, if Jimmy had been able to go on the road and charm his audiences as he did all of us, something more might conceivably have happened — these things aren't entirely predictable. But we published it as a good piece of documentary theatre-writing with some great, well-told, one-of-a-kind stories."

Kirkwood writes in a diary format, though these are clearly not verbatim journal notes but accounts shaped and revised for purposes of good reading. We are quickly apprised of the fact that we are in a world somewhat different to the normal one. In detailing in *Diary of a Mad Playwright* the in-fighting between *Legends!* producers, writers and cast in fine detail, Kirkwood must have realized even as he wrote of them that these were issues and rarefied conditions whose significance was ludicrously magnified when dealt with in this manner and might even be absurd to people outside the cosseted and often well-paid theatre milieu who had somewhat more substantial problems with which to contend. Adding to the sense of claustrophobia, he continually makes references to theatre people, especially actresses, whose names are clearly supposed to impress us but which, in fact, are only resonant for his generation: by definition, dedicated theatre actors don't leave an enduring legacy like cinema stars, however renowned in their heyday.

On the other hand, the book, as the saying goes, is what it is.

Diary of a Mad Playwright moves too quickly into the production process, with the creative and conceptual sweat involved in dreaming up and writing the play dispensed with in the two-page introduction. Conversely, the early chapters detailing the acquiring of backers and the casting move at a snail's pace and come dangerously close to boring. The interest level picks up when Larry Hagman — Mary Martin's son but far better known to the modern public than his mother via his role as J.R. in TV's *Dallas* — makes a cameo appearance. The first moment of pathos is provided by Carol Channing's entreaty to Kirkwood not to make a script cut that might undermine her character with an explanation that involves her own loveless childhood.

It is the snowballing catastrophes, though, that really give the narrative momentum: Kirkwood having to cede some of his royalties to accommodate the reduced potential profit engendered by Martin refusing to perform more than seven times a week; Carol Channing's early attempt to get Martin replaced by Julie Andrews; Channing's hysterical reaction to criticism; Annie-Joe Edwards replacing Kirkwood's lines with her own, missing performances and allegedly sulking through some of the shows for which she did turn up; Ertegun being in Kirkwood's eyes "a complete downer"; Eggers attempting rewrites and engaging in brinkmanship over script and cast changes; the *Waiting-for-Godot* quality of the promised appearance of Mike Nichols whom Kirkwood is endlessly being told by

Eggers that Ertegun is going to bring to a performance with a view to directing; Kirkwood threatening to take his name off the play in protest at imposed script changes; Martin receiving taxi dispatch calls in her earpiece; promoters in Portland flitting after paying off some debts with the advance and then declaring bankruptcy; Kirkwood agreeing to further cuts in royalties as profits prove mysteriously elusive even as house records are broken; Carol Channing's husband/manager demanding a written apology be delivered from Arthur Laurents after the playwright makes some innocuous comments about Channing's performance at a Boston matinée performance; Channing correcting Martin onstage when she fluffs her lines; Channing and Martin arguing onstage; Martin deciding a line that has been getting laughs is inappropriate and peremptorily declaring she is dropping it…

At one point Kirkwood reports that he is horrified to learn that Channing has repeated a private comment of his to Martin. "The evening taught me one thing…don't say a word if you don't want it eventually broadcast or in print," he laments. This is something of a cheek, for this book is the very soul of indiscretion: throughout, Kirkwood is repeating private conversations that most concerned can't have known would be heard outside of the room in which they took place. Though Kirkwood says "bless her" about the way Carol Channing, for all her diva-esque stunts, went out of her way to give due credit to Kirkwood's writing in interviews, no similar credit is extended by Kirkwood to Jim Piazza for his contributions to the play. Instead, Piazza receives merely an acknowledgment of being "friend and court jester" in the long roll-call at the start of the book and the disingenuous mini-pen portrait "not all that silent when it comes to good suggestions" in the book's text. Elsewhere, though, more of the good side of Kirkwood shines through. Though he mercilessly details the prima donna behavior of the actresses, he does note his own sulks and flouncy exits. Upon the occasion of the bad news about his Aunt Peggy, he also acknowledges his irrationally angry response to death.

Though the prose is always light and easy to read, in a book of this kind the writing has to be employed to serve the events. Correspondingly, it's unclear how much credit can be extended to Kirkwood for the entertainment value. For instance, when Kirkwood is assigned the task of auditioning a succession of male strippers for the role of Boom-Boom Johnson and bears witness to one of them having his finale of flinging his G-string skywards undermined by it getting caught on an overhead light, necessitating a call-out for a janitor, it would doubtless be funny however well or badly Kirkwood related it. Nonetheless, despite this and the lack of scope for lyrical text, Kirkwood does manage to throw in the odd wonderful line in his singular voice, such as his summary of his reaction to the stripper auditioning process: "I didn't know whether to laugh, cry, blush, shit, or go blind."

Ultimately, *Diary of a Mad Playwright* is a book about the wrong project. Kirkwood effectively admits early on that he wrote it because he failed to keep a diary of the genesis of *A Chorus Line* ("fool that I was"). The problems and the arguments that attended the *Legends!* tour are collectively certainly a story, and it could be argued one intrinsically more dramatic than the success tale of *A Chorus Line*. However, as the latest he-saids, she-saids in what went wrong and why with this mediocre work roll around, it's difficult to suppress the sentiment, "Who cares?"

Incidentally, *Diary of a Mad Playwright* is the Kirkwood book that best communicates his personality: vivacious, flirtatious, hard-working, occasionally petulant and absolutely suffused with theatre culture. It was dedicated to, "everyone who has ever written a play, and especially to anyone who might be thinking about writing one."

The book carried an effusive foreword from Terrence McNally, dated May 28, 1989, in which the playwright talked of his deceased friend in the present tense. Arthur Laurents proffered an encomium that stated that the book was "as endearingly outrageous as he is." However, Laurents has a problem with the title. "He wasn't a mad playwright," he says. "A mad playwright is like Gogol. It's a nice title, but he wasn't there. He was a cautious playwright. He was a would-be commercial playwright."

A package of *Legends!* and *Diary of a Mad Playwright* was optioned by Disney at one point. Gary Beach: "Years ago, Disney purchased the rights to the book and the play for a project for Bette Midler and the idea was that she would play the Carol Channing role. It would be onstage and offstage. When I heard about it I said, 'I want to audition for the role of Jimmy.' Nothing ever came of it." "She would have made an incredibly phenomenal film, I believe," says Bill Gile of Midler, "because she had Jimmy talking or narrating a film about the play. You could take the best scenes from the play and do them and then do all the off-stage stuff. It's a great film waiting to be done."

Another project featuring Kirkwood as a character that did not quite reach fruition was *Greetings from Neptune*. A 2001 play by Jim Piazza, it sought to make sense of his relationship with Kirkwood while at the same time satirizing the already almost beyond-parody events leading up to and during the production of *Stage-Stuck*. Piazza explains, "That relationship with Jimmy has always, not gotten in the way, but I wanted to in a way encapsulate it. I wanted to present Jimmy once again. I wanted to tell his story. I didn't know if anybody else was going to tell his story. As a writer, you just [use] whatever you have. Very few relationships in life come with a beginning, middle and an end very clearly like that. It's almost cinematic, our relationship." Though *Greetings from Neptune* never obtained a formal production, there were a series of what Piazza terms high-profile readings with varying casts directed by Justin Ross, who had been in the company of a production of *A Chorus Line*. It was at Ross' instigation that the actor who played Kirkwood (here called Mickey Driscoll) was none other than Robert LuPone, the original Zach in *A Chorus Line*. Kelly Bishop (*A Chorus Line*'s original Sheila) also featured.

Kirkwood appeared in the self-published novel *Mal Tempo and Friends* (2001) by William Russo. The titular character is an immortal whose supposed meetings with various celebrities and major figures throughout history give Russo the excuse to write profiles of them, one such person being Kirkwood. "I first started writing that as a kind of a joke well before he died," says Russo. "We were out on the book tour for *Hit Me with a Rainbow* and we were coming home from some dreary 2am TV interview and I was driving him. I told him I was writing this book about a mythical character. Quite frankly he had met everyone and I told him who Mel Tempo was and he said, 'Oh, I've met him, too!' So I thought that gave me *carte blanche*. I told him that it was a character who met everybody who was famous in history and was not a lucky charm and he said that's why he thought he had met him. He did not think he was a lucky person."

The *P.S. Your Cat is Dead!* novel was brought back into print to capitalize on the 2003 theatrical release of the movie of the book, directed by and starring (as Jimmy Zoole) Steve Guttenberg. Guttenberg's take on *P.S. Your Cat is Dead!* — he co-wrote the script with Jeff Korn — is one that uses elements of both the novel and the play(s). It also introduces completely new elements and makes some quite fundamental changes. Perhaps the most striking change is that the burglar character is turned from an Italian-American into a Mexican-American, which necessitates a change of name: Vito Antenucci becomes Eddie (as in Eduardo) Tesoro (played by Lombardo Boyar). Vito's distinctive lingo therefore gets jettisoned. This isn't the sacrilege it might at first appear to be. Pinpoint-accurate as it was for the time, Vito's vernacular would be archaic for a modern audience. Even Zoole in the original book makes reference to how old-fashioned Zito's turn-of-phrase is already becoming ("*no one* says 'youse' any more"). However, it can't be denied that in losing the rough-hewn poetry of his vernacular, Vito/Eddie loses a lot of his charm. Other changes are that the film is set not in New York but LA. (The apartment actually looks quite luxurious but apparently that was unintentional — the stains on the furniture didn't show up as much as expected on screen.) Fred Gable becomes a rather stiff black man (well-acted by Tom Wright).

Zoole's discovery of Eddie/Vito (who, as in the play, the audience knows is in the apartment) is perhaps more realistically depicted than in the source(s): Zoole sees his legs under his bed and, after getting over his bewilderment, in almost silent fury forces him to come out. Additionally, the way Jimmy finds out his cat has passed away (Zoole gets on the phone to the vet to assure himself that the jeering Eddie is lying, but then sees Kate's Post-It note communicating this information) is actually moving, more so than in the novel/play, and gives more reason for the work to take its title from the feline death, summing up as it does the disappointments of Zoole's life. The story is opened out a little: we see Zoole walking the streets, up on his roof, at acting jobs, visiting Aunt Claire and going to the supermarket.

Wright is not alone in his fine acting. Eddie's fear at his predicament particularly impresses, as does Zoole's anger (the way Guttenberg wordlessly throws wine into the face of Boyar — to whom at this point he has yet to speak — conveys real menace and smoldering fury), even if the grimacing set of Guttenberg's face is often remarkably miserable, as though he is constantly on the verge of tears. The appearance of the three interlopers (all men this time) is truly unsettling, not necessarily because of the loud rock soundtrack that accompanies their entrance, but because of great casting and acting: a sleazier trio one never saw. To top off their menace, they actually bind Zoole. The film additionally has a very agreeable jazzy soundtrack supplied by Dean Grinsfelder.

Where Guttenberg's movie falls down is with bad editing and the inability to resolve the problem Kirkwood encountered in the play (but not the book): finding a good ending. Evidence of clumsy cutting appears at the close of the scene where Kate comes back to find Zoole feeding the bound Eddie a cigarette. The bang-arama-thons/"We been making it since last August 22" stuff from the novel/plays was clearly filmed but cut out because, though we don't see it, there is a reference to it when Kate and Fred leave. This is insanity — not only will the reference bewilder the viewer, but those severed pieces of dialogue were among the funniest of the original work.

The film begins to sag following the departure of the interlopers and eventually fades to a whimper. Zoole gives Eddie the twenty-years-in the-wrong-job speech, telling him the notion of his misdirected career had occurred to him when he had been tied up. It's a strange thing to think when one is in danger of being raped. That would not be too jarring in itself, but some more maladroit editing ruins the ending and finally prevents the film from achieving worthiness. Zoole and Eddie shake hands and the latter departs. Later, an exhausted Zoole goes up onto his roof to look at the sunrise. Zoole appears. Initially, Zoole is stony-faced but as the two sit there wordlessly looking at each other, Zoole gives a small smile. The end. It's an utterly inadequate close. The alternate ending shown on the DVD release of the movie is little better. This one features the same scene, but fleshes it out a little with Eddie offering to pay the rent, cook and clean for Zoole while Zoole writes his novel. It remains unconvincing even leaving aside the issue of how a loser like Eddie is going to find the money to keep a roof over their heads. The problem is the same one that afflicted all versions of the play: the rapport between the two hasn't been plausibly established the way that it is in the novel. The easiest way to do that would have been to have Eddie/Vito — as in the novel — feeling remorse about destroying Zoole's manuscript because having been lovers with a writer he understood how devastating that would be. Though the film script incorporates, unlike the play, the fact that Vito had a literary lover, this route is spurned.

This failure at the very death of the film is a shame, for Guttenberg's version of *Cat* is easily the most serious and heartfelt attempt at capturing the true nature of a Kirkwood book to reach either large or small screen.

Two thousand and four saw the announcement that two Kirkwood-related works were scheduled for a Broadway appearance. One was fairly predictable: a revival of *A Chorus Line*. The other was not predictable at all: a revival of *Legends!*, even if the latter play's perception as a flop is, as with *P.S. Your Cat is Dead!*, belied by its productions in various languages across the globe down the years. An English-language revival was the idea of producer Ben Sprecher after he had been approached by Joan Collins, who wanted to return to the stage. Sprecher looked at many stageworks before deciding that a revival of *Legends!* would be the ideal vehicle. (Ironically, when *Legends!* was first touring, Sprecher was the manager of the Theatre De Lys, the off-Broadway venue that the ladies end up being offered by Martin Klemmer after he has led them to believe they would be playing one of the most prestigious theatres on Broadway. Far more ironically, of course, Collins is mentioned in the original *Legends!* script.)

The new *Legends!* went out on the road in September 2006 starting in Toronto, with the aim of it coming in to Broadway — something that the original had never managed to do — in May 2007. Sprecher lucked out on the actress who agreed to play Leatrice: Linda Evans. Collins and Evans were certainly legends to eighties TV audiences and furthermore names inextricably linked with each other through playing adversaries in the glitzy soap opera *Dynasty*. Beckenstein feels that Kirkwood himself would have been pleased by that casting. So does William Russo, who says, "I remember saying to him in '86, 'Jim, you know, whatever they're saying about the play in twenty years, it's a perfect concept for somebody like Joan Collins and Linda Evans to do on stage.' He said, 'Do you think so?' I was kind of taken aback when I saw they're doing a tour. He would love that."

A Chorus Line made its return to Broadway in October 2006, reviewing in September. Original dancer Baayork Lee was asked to be choreographer and original choreographer Bob Avian took on direction duties, thus retaining a thread to the original production despite the new producers, cast and location (the Shubert Theatre was unavailable, necessitating a move to the Gerald Schoenfeld Theatre).

While the new *A Chorus Line* ran until August 2008, *Legends!* once again failed to come in. Some who saw it on tour got more entertainment from reports of the genuine feuding going on between the two women playing the fictional feuding actresses than from the show itself. Collins' public allegation that Evans was too rough in the fight scene, causing her physical injury, was met with the jaw-dropping, you-couldn't-make-it-up response from Evans' manager, "Joan Collins is the biggest fucking sack of shit. She's the single most unprofessional actress working in Hollywood." One gets the feeling that Kirkwood would have loved *that*.

May 2007 saw the publication of the first full-length book about James Kirkwood in the shape of William Russo's self-published *Riding James Kirkwood's Pony*. It was not so much a biography as an examination of Kirkwood's different explorations of the death of Reid Russell via his versions of *There Must Be a Pony!* in multiple media. As Kirkwood's self-appointed Boswell, as well as a correspondent with his best friend James Leo Herlihy, Russo was in a good position to conduct such an investigation. Frustratingly, though, he fails to comprehensibly moor his suppositions to events and confidences, while his theories about Kirkwood building walls of alibi in his work seem inchoate where they are not simply unconvincing. The reader is left uncomfortably aware where Russo isn't that Kirkwood's reported comment to his Boswell that he is "as mad as a March hare" may not have been the joke it was taken as. For this reader, Russo's theorizing is brought further into question by his claim in his acknowledgements that he conducted "several interviews" with me. In fact, I granted Russo no interviews, but rather interviewed him once for this work, during the course of which I relayed him information that he has deployed in *Riding James Kirkwood's Pony*, by whose publication I was surprised (and indeed trumped).

In March 2009, there finally occurred a New York staging of *Legends!* — albeit a one-off performance — courtesy of John Epperson aka Lypsinka. Epperson is a drag queen by profession and had always been intrigued by the section of *Diary of a Mad Playwright* relating how Mike Nichols suggested the play be performed by men dressed as women. Epperson called his staging an "adaption" of Kirkwood's play: aside from the new element of drag, the ending was different and the pop culture references updated. Whoopi Goldberg was due to play Aretha but had to pull out through illness. Epperson took his adaptation to Washington in 2010. Jim Piazza saw the New York performance. "I was disappointed," he says. "I was very touched in the beginning. I know John pretty well. I think Jimmy would have smacked him upside the head if he had seen some of the things that he was rearranging in the script." Beckenstein finds himself in a rare moment of agreement with Piazza, saying Kirkwood would have been "upset" by the changes made, adjudging them "way too extensive" (even if "in the spirit of Jimmy's humor") and causing *Legends!* to become a completely different play. He does add, though, that it was a "more fun, lively and entertaining show" than either the Channing/Martin or Collins/Evans versions.

The last dangling thread of Kirkwood's writing career remains *I Teach Flying*. "That book was really important to him," says Paonessa. "I think that he was trying to exorcise a ghost and trying to make a reconciliation. He used to call it a serious book." Kirkwood had tried to prepare his brother for any pain the book's eventual publication might cause him. "He didn't tell me much about it," says T. Michael. "What he did tell me was, 'Look — don't be upset about this because it's fiction, I'm just using what I know between a father and a son and yadda yadda.'"

I Teach Flying's first-person point of view is that of Kevin Tierney, son of old-time movie stars Colin Tierney and Nerissa Nevins, who is writing from the perspective of what appears to be late middle age. Kevin's narration begins at the point that his father kills his mother and younger brother, something that we are told in the second sentence occurred when he was eight years old and his father 61. A lapel-grabber of an opener to be sure, even if part of the motivation for it seems to be to make Kirkwood's real-life mother as conveniently absent from the narrative as his father was from *There Must Be a Pony!*

Things aren't as sinister as they seem: mother and child had accidentally fallen to their deaths down a steep exterior stairwell in foggy conditions, even if they were at the time fleeing the maniacal temper of the father. Naturally, a scandal ensues. The writing is okay here, the dramatic incidents (including a funeral at which the father is wretched with guilt and physically sick) convincing enough without quite having great verisimilitude. Real-life movie industry people appear at the funeral and such figures pepper the narrative, including actors Douglas Fairbanks, James Cagney and Dolores Del Rio, Mary Pickford's brother Jack and director Mickey Neilan.

Kevin is whisked off to live with an aunt and uncle in Corain, Ohio (located, we are informed, not far from Elyria). In further dislocation of the purely autobiographical, Kevin's Aunt Augusta is not the sunny soul that Kirkwood's Aunt Peggy was but instead a rather stern and humorless figure — even though Kevin grows fond of her — while twinkle-eyed Uncle Frank is rendered sympathetically. Kevin's assimilation into Corain (so gray compared to sunny California) is fairly intriguing, although his playmates Sydney and Roxy never quite seem real (particularly their too-poetic, too-tidy dialogue) and in the former's obsession with pubic hair and the latter's cross-eyed precocity are slightly distasteful in their freakishness. Kevin is afflicted by a slight stammer and though this prevents him being called upon to recite much in class, he does well at school by developing a quasi-photographic memory, something that seems to confirm the memories of many in this book about the author's true-life ability for above-average information retention, even though the stutter (shared by *Rainbow*'s Kelly McDermott) seems fictional, with nobody remembering Kirkwood either having that problem or referring to having been so afflicted.

Though everything thus far is a quite enjoyable read, *I Teach Flying* really comes alive when Kevin's father re-enters his life as the production of *Tobacco Road* in which he is appearing as Jeeter Lester comes to nearby Cleveland when Kevin is eleven. Kirkwood vividly evokes his own father's loud, larger-than-life personality, as well as the celebrity status that stage actors enjoyed in the era before television. (On a similar theme, he also convincingly portrays the mores of the age.) As in real life, Tierney Sr. alternates between adoring and ignoring his son. Kirkwood's strength with such autobiographical material is a contrast to the soap opera death of Kevin's playmate Roxy in an accident.

The visit to Cleveland sees Kevin sharing a hotel suite with his father, which enables him to spy on Tierney Sr. having sex with an endless succession of female colleagues and seeing just how massive is his engorged penis. Though this may be autobiographical, it's rendered at inordinate length:

Kirkwood really likes the dirty stuff. (A Kirkwood sketch from sometime after 1975 spends 5½ pages depicting a man chatting up a woman in a bar in order to deliver a punch line about a "pussy" that is "as big as my hat.")

Kevin and his father subsequently live together in a house in Martha's Vineyard and the closeness of father and son is touchingly conveyed. While there, Kevin starts to attach weights to his penis with the aim of making it as big as his father's after noticing natives in a jungle movie lengthening their ear lobes with metals, rocks, etc. The details of this are bizarre where they are not wince-making and one can't help but feel that these passages are a little irresponsible insofar as some people might be attempted to try a procedure that risks causing medical damage, especially as Kirkwood depicts it as achieving Kevin's objective.

While in Martha's Vineyard, Tierney Sr. meets and falls in love with an Olympic swimmer named Camilla Berg several decades his junior. Kevin is also very fond of her. However, the prospects of her becoming his stepmother are dashed by tragedy: a swim in bad weather leaves Camilla drowned and Tierney Sr. fighting for his life. The newspapers have a field day with a man whose partners seem to be doomed. Suspicion briefly falls upon Colin Tierney and though the suspicions are allayed, it adversely affects his film career.

Kevin returns to Corain. Eventually his father, after a period of understandable self-pity, falls in love with another vivacious young woman several decades his junior — Dee-Dee — and one by whom Kevin is also smitten, both as a woman and a potential stepmother. Tierney Sr. and Dee-Dee wed, with Dee-Dee already pregnant. Any scandal Tierney Sr.'s cradle-snatching causes is rendered kids' stuff when shortly after their marriage their car is rammed at an intersection by a driver who has skipped a red light. Father and son are badly injured, but Dee-Dee and unborn child are left dead. The specter of a jinx afflicting any woman who comes within Tierney Sr.'s orbit is naturally raised again by the newspapers, but a devastated, battle-weary Colin Tierney is naturally more concerned by his loss. This is all skillfully rendered, the unusually high quotient of tragedy and misfortune in one life not coming across as implausible — and one assumes this would be so even for those unaware of the unlikely degree of trauma in the author's own childhood and adolescence.

A recuperating Kevin is sent to a Catholic boarding school in Los Angeles. In this section, Kirkwood uses the alleged attack on a nun by his real-life St. John's Military Academy schoolmate Buddy, although frankly produces a vignette of surprisingly little power from such material. At this school also, the fourteen-year-old Kevin is the willing subject of the sexual attentions of a monsignor and of the physical education instructor and his wife. The sections which give the book its awkward title occur here. They are dream sequences in which the teenaged Kevin literally teaches people from a stage how to fly. The first of the two sequences in which he does this is, it has to be said, rather boring, partly because dream sequences do not have material consequences.

 Kevin returns to Corain to finish high school because his uncle has had a stroke and his aunt needs help. While there, an actress files a paternity suit against Kevin's father, the unexpected upshot of which is that Colin Tierney marries her. They have a son, Terry, whom they start bringing up on Argyle Avenue, Kirkwood Sr.'s real-life residence in Hollywood. Kevin moves in with them after his graduation. We are treated to well-written versions of incidents from Kirkwood's life at this juncture as well as ones that are presumably fictional. The former includes Kevin being chased out of the apartment by a father so furious that he can't be bothered closing the bathrobe that is exposing his massive member to anybody who cares to look (and many who don't) and Kevin applying for and gaining employment at Grauman's Chinese Theatre, where such events as the world premiere of *Mrs. Miniver* occur. Considering that Kevin obtaining work as a gigolo seems to have no antecedent in Kirkwood's own life, its authenticity is impressive. Kevin's clients include a middle-aged fat man with glasses who wants not sex but to be told he is a "pretty peacock," an ancient English dame who masturbates while Kevin is given oral sex by his madam and a spoiled young starlet named Merilee Moon who is kept locked up by her parents and maid lest her nymphomaniac tendencies destroy her squeaky-clean image. Though this gives Kirkwood an excuse to indulge in writing about sex — something which frankly he was never good at, despite his apparent gleaming-eyed enthusiasm for it — it makes for absorbing reading. Tierney Sr.'s fortunes, meanwhile, have taken another bad turn. His wife has left him — abandoning Terry in the process — and he is facing ruin because of his financial adviser's bad decisions. Said financial adviser commits suicide after an altercation between the two, leading to more hostile media attention.

 Kirkwood's manuscript ends at a point where Kevin is just about to surprise his father by using his gigolo earnings to buy him a house on Tierney Drive, a street named after him on property that he once owned.

 Though the existing manuscript runs to 600 double-spaced typed pages (around 200,000 words, which depending on typeface- and page-size would translate to between 400-500 pages in a commercially published book), it still feels so far from being finished that it seems clear it would have ended up as Kirkwood's grand statement if it had been. Something else leading to that conclusion is the surprising honesty of the book. For instance, there is for once an absence of coyness about Kirkwood's/the narrator's homosexual urges. In later years Kirkwood took to wearing what could be mistaken for a wedding ring, but here there is no "disguise": Kevin relates his sexual encounters with the Christ lookalike monsignor at his school with no caveats or apology or even any agonizing about what this means about his sexuality or psychological make-up. Similar matter-of-factness attends the book's timeline. Although Kirkwood had always been realistic enough to know that he couldn't keep his vintage a complete secret (for instance, he said to the Elyria *Chronicle-Telegram* in April 1978, "I used to lie about my age, but the *Chronicle-Telegram* keeps printing, 'Kirkwood, a 1942 graduate of EHS'"), there is a difference between admitting it in selected and — in a pre-Internet era — inaccessible areas of the media and forthrightness in what would have been a nationally distributed book. Though Kirkwood renders Kevin as a baby born in the winter of 1925, this is only six months adrift of his own birth date. There seems no reason to assume that Kirkwood would have tampered with the chronology before publication, not least because it would have posed too many problems with the real-life events he incorporates, like the beginning of World War II. It would seem that Kirkwood was finally learning to relax about giving away both his sexuality and his age in his writing. Because of this, the book almost has the flavor of a valediction. Though it is difficult to square this perception with the fact that it was two decades in the writing — Kirkwood would have had no intimation of mortality for most of the time he was plotting and writing it — one can't completely escape the sense of it being the last testament of a man who no longer had anything to lose.

With such an incomplete manuscript, it is difficult to evaluate the position of *Flying* in Kirkwood's canon unless we use the crude (or should that be: only valid?) yardstick: the readability of what there is. The quality and — especially — tone of the writing reinforces the conviction that *Hit Me with a Rainbow* was an aberration. From the get-go, this *feels* like a James Kirkwood novel: informal, easy-rolling, first-person, mostly exuberant, conversational and sensitive. This author would place it in terms of enjoyment provided below *P.S. Your Cat Is Dead!*, *Good Times/ Bad Times* and *Some Kind of Hero* but above *There Must Be a Pony!* and *Hit Me with a Rainbow*. It certainly deserves publication (hopefully with a less ungainly title; a simple change to *The Flying Teacher* would be a big improvement). The fact that Kirkwood first put aside this novel to cover the Clay Shaw trial and did it last to collaborate with Jim Piazza is something of a tragedy considering how virtually worthless were *American Grotesque* and *Stage-Struck*.

In the plan for the completion of *I Teach Flying* dictated by Kirkwood to Paonessa at New York Hospital on April 20, 1989, Kirkwood said, "The main thing to accomplish is that Kevin secures a future for his father which he hopes will compensate for all the shit dumped on his father." This is clearly the novel-as-wish-fulfillment, Kirkwood desiring to create an alternate reality where his dad did not end up living an old age that was, to use Lomax Study's phrase, "a misery." The way Kirkwood dictated that this outcome be achieved was thus: A mugging incident has made the father increasingly ill, eventually confining him to bed. Kevin tells his father and Terry about buying the house for them all in Laurel Canyon but though they move into it, Kevin has to continue his "callboy" activities because the outright purchase of the house has depleted most of his savings and Tierney Sr. is not able to provide for himself and his younger son. As Kevin continues hooking, he encounters a Tyrone Power-type actor with a small penis. Kevin treats him well and eventually the actor falls in love with him. Meanwhile, Kevin continues as the client of Merilee Moon. It transpires that Miss Moon has a brain tumor and is known by her parents to be dying, thus explaining why they have tolerated her outrageous behavior. When she passes, Merilee leaves Kevin $50,000, a rather significant sum in the 1940s. However, this isn't the preamble to a corny Hollywood-style ending: Colin Tierney also dies. Kevin walks into the room to find Terry holding his hand, under the impression he is merely asleep.

Kirkwood also outlined to Paonessa a couple of scenes/story components which he felt should be integrated: a warm scene between father and son, perhaps when Colin Tierney is engaged in one of his kitchen-demolishing bread-making sessions, and a reference to the fact that Colin Tierney always travels with a steamer trunk filled with mementoes from his life.

Kirkwood told Paonessa that the novel required approximately 100 additional typewritten pages. This would bring it up to 700 pages in manuscript form (around 235,000 words). He also had one other request: that James Leo Herlihy be asked to complete the novel. Kirkwood and Herlihy's friendship had remained strong right to the very end. "They were so bonded," says Piazza. "They had a very special relationship that was very private to them. I think he idolized Jim Herlihy in a way. Jim

[Herlihy] was a very handsome guy, very intense, really; psychic in a way and when I met him he was working with people with AIDS. I think he was supplying them with marijuana and was helping people to die. There was always one or two people in the house that were in the final stages of AIDS. I think Jimmy really admired him for that. He was like a Mother Teresa and I think he was just so astonished that anybody could do that, be so altruistic…In his house in Los Angeles, we were there for dinner and, it was an odd evening because Jimmy was kind of almost thinking about giving me to Jim Herlihy as a gift. I had no idea what he was doing and then he was about to leave and he said, 'Well, do you want to stay here?' And I said, 'Why would I stay here?' It just completely threw me off and I realized what it was. It was these two old friends who were kind of sharing their boys."

A Kirkwood/Herlihy novel was at once, and remains, an intriguing idea. It was perfectly, poetically appropriate: the two were friends, contemporaries, onetime lovers, onetime collaborators and among the greatest writers of their generation. (They had also both lost their way as writers, if for wildly different reasons.) One might assume that if anything were to pull Herlihy out of his premature retirement from writing, even temporarily, it might be the sentimental act of fulfilling the deathbed wish of his friend. Paonessa reported in the document in which he typed up his notes about Kirkwood's intended ending, "I have reviewed these notes with Mr. Herlihy at great length."

"Jamie read the thing and said he didn't want to do it," says Homer Price, friend of both men. "He didn't want to touch it. I don't think he told me the reason. I was disappointed because I thought he would be ideal." Beckenstein says, "Jamie Herlihy said it wasn't quite a novel, it was sort of between a memoir and a novel. He didn't want to take on that job." Following Herlihy's 1993 suicide, his reasons became moot. However, comments by William Russo — who corresponded with but never met Herlihy — suggest it may have been an emotional rather than an aesthetic reason. Additionally, from comments in Herlihy's letters to him, Russo believes that Herlihy killed himself because he was "unnerved" by Kirkwood's death. "I do think that there was a very close tie there," says Russo.

Arthur Beckenstein: "Arthur Laurents, Evan Rhodes and James Leo Herlihy told me after he passed away that the manuscript needed a lot of work. Arthur Laurents having heard some of *Flying* while Jim was alive and healthy told him it was some of his best writing. Arthur was not one to be generous with praise." Nonetheless, Laurents — like Rhodes and

Herlihy had done — declined to finish the book. Says Laurents, "After he died, Arthur brought me this unpublished novel and he said to me, 'I'd like to publish it. See if you think it's publishable.' I read it and I said, 'No, it isn't.' He was searching for where he was, but he hadn't found it…The culture moves on and what was acceptable in the sixties isn't acceptable in the seventies and so forth, and he had not moved on with it. People knew more and they wanted more." Beckenstein: "Arthur Laurents thought it needed too much work and it might become somebody else's book if someone else were to finish it."

Paonessa doesn't blame any of the three. "It wasn't very good," he says. "And it wasn't very finished. Think of yourself being approached to finish somebody's work who was a good friend and has a reputation. It's not an easy subject, the whole idea of finishing someone else's novel." Laurents says, "I don't understand this thing of having someone else finish the book. It's yours, or isn't. Otherwise, it's something to make money or what. It isn't as though he had something burning that he wanted to say."

Andrew Morse, the only other person whom Beckenstein allowed to read *Flying*, opines, "It's 600 pages and out of the 600 pages I thought certainly there were at least a couple of hundred pages, especially the scene where the father's in the bathrobe flying after him. I thought there were some very, very compelling scenes. It was uneven and there were some problems with it, but if he had had enough time to write another draft of it, or even a third or fourth draft, he could have made a really excellent novel out of it. I really did enjoy it. I told Arthur, 'Somebody who knows what the fuck they're doing writing-wise should get a hold of this and extract the stuff that's the most straightforward or whatever and do something with it 'cause it's great.'"

Morse adds of Kirkwood, "He talked to me about that flying dream a lot. He had that a lot. I'm surprised that it didn't occupy a larger space in that manuscript. Sometimes I talked to him before he went to sleep late at night and I'd say, 'Have your flying dream.'" For the record, dream experts and psychiatrists seem to concur that flying in dreams is a symbol of the dreamer's confidence and ability to soar above problems (at least if no problems are encountered in flight). In Kirkwood's case, the recurring nature of this theme in his night-time visions suggests that he felt that way about himself on a permanent basis, rather than it being related to him having overcome a specific recent obstacle. The fact that he saw himself teaching other people this physical feat/state of mind, of course, adds an extra dimension, suggesting that he felt a mission to let the rest of humanity in on the secret to his happiness. Some, of course, have doubts about the self-therapy function of dreams and raise the question of why our sleeping thoughts don't explicitly instruct us what our problems or feelings are rather than rely on us to decode symbolism that is often far from straightforward. However, the fact that he consulted Mildred Newman so assiduously about his dreams suggests, for what it's worth, that Kirkwood would probably have gravitated towards the interpretation of those who buy into dream symbolism on this matter, even if he gave no particular indication in *I Teach Flying* of intending the dream sequences as anything other than woozy interlude.

The book still tugs at Paonessa's conscience. "I have a lot of anxiety over it, even though the attorney and Arthur have said not to be," he says. "I made him a promise on his deathbed. I feel really negligent, but life is not over yet. We'll see what happens."

Following his death, Andrew Morse hit upon the idea of a writing prize to help celebrate Kirkwood's talent and keep his memory alive. It was poetic that Morse should inaugurate it, for though he was Kirkwood's friend, he had started out as merely a fan. Morse discovered Kirkwood when he was at boarding school in the 1970s. "I was sure that this girl Julia who had very distinctive red hair had said to me, '*Good Times/Bad Times* is a great book' and it turned out — I asked her later — that she'd never even heard of *Good Times/Bad Times*," he says. "She was such a distinctive-looking girl that it kind of makes me wonder about the whole thing. It's sort of like cosmic. I don't mean to sound completely cracked. I got a copy of *Good Times/Bad Times* and read it, thought it was terrific and so then I bought pretty much all the rest of his books that I could find. *P.S. Your Cat is Dead!* was playing in Boston at the time and if you wanted to be an usher you could see the show for free, so I saw the show like two or three or four times just because I thought it was incredibly funny." Morse subsequently went to see *A Chorus Line* in New York and recalls that it "knocked me out." Morse: "I finally just thought, 'Fuck, I got to write this guy a fan letter.' I can't think of anybody that I've written a fan letter to. 'I'm in boarding school and he went to boarding school. I'll write him a note.' So I wrote him a note and said something like, 'I realize you're totally famous, but I just wanted to let you know how much I love your work' and all that kind of stuff. It couldn't have been more than two weeks later, I get a letter back on *Chorus Line* stationery and it's from James Kirkwood say[ing], 'You get a whole bunch of medals for having read four of my books and seeing both *P.S. Your Cat is Dead!* and *A Chorus Line*.'"

So began a friendship lasting the rest of Kirkwood's life. Morse: "We just would make each other laugh. He was a great friend. There was a lot of disparity in our ages, but that didn't seem to mean anything. He had a very youthful outlook on life and he was just a riot. If you were really feeling down or something, he'd say something that would just crack you up. You very rarely are fortunate enough to meet people that exceed the real deal, especially when they're writers. So often you read a book and then you meet the author and they turn out to be a jerk or an anti-social type or whatever, and that's kind of why they're an author. Because Jimmy was an actor for so many years before he became a writer, he had a real charm."

Morse reasoned of the literary prize in Kirkwood's name, "Well, what better place than to have a prize at UCLA adult extension where he first got going as a writer? I figured you could give [it to] a writing student. The teachers could submit [what] they thought was good, a couple of professors there could judge it and then I'd fund it like for 500 bucks or whatever and every year that would take place. Initially, I didn't think I would be doing it all myself. I spoke to Jimmy Herlihy. He was not very into it at all. I remember him saying something like, 'My dear boy, have you mistaken people's reluctance to be involved with it for polite disinterest?' or something like that and it really pissed me off." Morse found Arthur Beckenstein far more amenable: "Arthur was very, very in favor of it. He thought it was a great idea and he contributed to it and a number of different friends of mine contributed to it, just because they loved his books. By and large, I'm the one who set up the whole thing and I paid for it. Originally, I set up an account and then I realized that the interest from the account was going to be nowhere near enough to do it, so I just cut checks every year for everybody."

The prize was inaugurated in 1991 and has been running — bar a gap in 1995 — ever since. In addition to the cash prize, each year Morse trawls the Internet for copies of *There Must Be a Pony!*, which he decided — being the work Kirkwood submitted in part as his project at the UCLA writing class — should also be given to the first-prize winners. Initially, there was a single winner of the James Kirkwood Literary Prize, but in 2002 it was decided to award first, second and third prizes of $500, $300 and $200. (Originally, the winning story also appeared in a literary magazine called *West/Word*, now defunct.) In the early days, Morse and Kirkwood's agent Jed Mattes read through all the submissions and Mattes chose the winner. Following Mattes' death in 2003, Morse felt uncomfortable at the idea that he — a professional musician rather than a writer — be the one to choose the winner, so a compromise was reached whereby the submissions are read through by the extension program's staff and Morse is asked to rank the three entries sent to him.

"Every fall I make the trip out to LA and there's this little luncheon at the faculty center," says Morse. "You have the writers and then their boyfriends or girlfriends or whoever and a family member and the professors that are professor of the student who's won, as well as a number of other people that work in the writer's program. [Head of the Writers' Program] Linda Venis says a couple of words and then I say a few words about Jimmy and then talk about the stories. Then the writers can say something. It's a nice thing for a fledgling writer to put on their résumé: winner of the James Kirkwood Award."

Initially, the award was for a writer whose work had achieved literary excellence in the spirit of Kirkwood's own work but Morse admits that the practicalities of simply finding excellence *per se* in a writing class have meant that the definition "gets looser and looser." He says, "What you are really hoping for is something that has some warmth, some humor, a beginning, a middle and an end. I always like a little bit of craziness. There was one story a couple of years ago that was by far the best story of the entire lot." Referring to 2003 prize winner "Fledgling" by Andy Hunter, he says, "The narrator was a sort of down-and-out guy, a young guy, and he tried to rescue this bird and the woman at the animal shelter where he bought it was just so abrupt and obnoxious that he decided at the last second that he wasn't going to give her the bird and so he was running away, holding this little bird and the lady was kind of running after him. All these dogs are barking, because she had a bunch of dogs. It was just a very great, very Kirkwoodian type of scene, completely out of control, crazy, yet incredibly humorous."

Though the intention of the prize with regard to Kirkwood is, Morse says, "a way of keeping him around in a kind of abstract way," he has been very pleasantly surprised to find that to some extent that objective hasn't been necessary. "You'd be stunned by the number of people who've received the award who have actually read books of Jimmy's," he says. "A lot of them will go, '*P.S. Your Cat is Dead!* was one of my favorite books' or '*There Must Be a Pony!*, I remember reading that when I was in 8th grade.' It's just so sweet."

EPILOGUE

JAMES KIRKWOOD: SOME STRAY QUOTES

James Kirkwood: "There is possibly nothing that can equal the excitement of feeling the waves of response from a theatre audience…You rarely have the pleasure of witnessing a reader enjoying your novel. But a stage performance is ephemeral; once it's given it vanishes into the air. A book is eminently tangible."

Jim Piazza: "My mother instinctively did not approve of my relationship with Jimmy. I was out in California visiting her. He called and my mother picked up and he was being charming with her and she wasn't buying it. My mother was a very Italian mother and afterwards she said, 'Who is this, how old is he?' I said, 'Well, you know who his mother was?' She said, 'Who?' She almost died, because when she was a kid she won a lookalike contest to his mother, so when she found out Jimmy was the son of her idol then it was fine. Jimmy loved that story because his mother became the star of the show again rather than him. He delighted in that."

Jack Sydow: "Jimmy once said to me, 'Oh, there is nothing to writing, Jack, go ahead and write. All you have to do is be a good liar.'"

James Kirkwood: "Usually something kicks off an idea, something that's happened to me or someone I know. I take that idea and then go on to imagine it heightened thematically or dramatically. I like being able to work with events that are based in reality; it's a way to get rid of your emotional angst, get rid of your anger or whatever else you've been carting around for years."

Elaine Stritch: "There was an actress named Galina Talva who played opposite Jimmy in *Call Me Madam* and she was the little princess in Lichtenburg. She had one of the funniest cues to go into a song that I've ever heard in my life and I couldn't look at Jimmy Kirkwood on the stage whilst he said it. She came onto the stage as the princess to do the Ocarina Dance. The cue was, 'I love my people. The fair is open.' And then she sang this awful song: 'Dance to the Music of the Ocarina.' Twenty years passed and I was living in London. My husband and I met Jimmy in the Savoy Bar. I looked up and there was Jimmy Kirkwood and he said, 'I love my people. The fair is open!' and that's full projecting, all over the bar. I laughed for a week. Twenty years and I hadn't seen him! He was adorable."

Nick Ellison: "James Kirkwood and a few other writers of his ilk were so skillful in using what I think of as a velvet fist school of writing. Of writing with a lightness of touch and an inherently exquisite sense of prose poetry almost, a rhythm to each sentence, and like a classic British mystery that just reads like cutting through butter. A lot of critics missed Jim because of that and instead of seeing it as an aspect of his genius they saw it as, 'Oh, I'm supposed to work harder if it's literary.'"

James Kirkwood: "I always make the main character me. It's always easier to write that way."

Jack Sydow: "Jimmy had so many friends, and lots of them I never met… Jimmy knew everybody."

Jim Piazza: "He didn't like telling old stories because it dated him, but one night after pressuring him he walked me through this wonderful fantasy tour of New York that he knew as a young man. He said, 'That place there was a bar,' 'Dorothy Kilgallen always had a met stool there,' and he would point to a dry cleaner and say, 'That was a jazz club' and, 'That's where I lived there.' It was a wonderful, wonderful memory walk."

James Kirkwood: "I like to be in the dark when I write, when I'm getting into my mind, which is certainly dark."

Arthur Beckenstein: "I do remember on one social occasion in the seventies, an exchange between Edward Albee and Jimmy about *Good Times/ Bad Times*…Edward said the book was intellectual. Jimmy disagreed and said, 'It is not an intellectual book. I am not an intellectual, I never went to college. I'm a storyteller.'"

James Kirkwood: "Writing, to me, is telling a good story, it's entertaining people. It does not have, *per se*, to have a quote message unquote. It can and should say something about the human condition, about our life on this planet and how we live it. But I believe it should be done in the terms of the characters and what they do, how they feel and the story you tell involving them. Then, after reading the story and after having been involved with the characters, you can look back and say, Oh, I see, the author was saying something about life in general, something bigger more all-encompassing than merely the story of Dick and Jane…Writing about ideas or ideals on their own is big trouble."

Terrence McNally: "He was always good for a laugh. The kind of thing Jimmy would do would be outrageous. I was on a panel with him once and we went around the room saying, 'I'm Terrence McNally,' 'I'm Edward Albee,' 'I'm Arthur Laurents,' and it got to Jimmy, he says, 'I'm Lana Turner'…There was a pause and then everyone laughed hilariously. It was a very stuffy seminar on the state of the American theatre and he absolutely broke the ice. Another time we were talking to the critics' convention and they wanted three playwrights to talk to them and air our side of it, why we think we're sometimes not appreciated, that their reviews aren't very helpful, blah, blah, blah. We're sitting behind a table on the stage and the critics are out in the audience and we're introduced. It was me, Jimmy and I think maybe Arthur Laurents. Jimmy put a gun out in front. Said, 'All right–let's talk'…He was a life force. When he was in the room he was the most noticeable person in it. He was a show-off, not in a pejorative [way], but you just noticed him. He was larger-than-life and he was very colorful. People liked him. I certainly never heard anybody say, 'I can't stand Jimmy Kirkwood,' 'I don't like him' or 'He's dull' or 'He's a bastard.'"

William Russo: "Kirkwood had his finger on a pulse and I think his work is still extremely readable. He can handle such deep philosophical concepts as The Big Joker in the Sky and do it in a conversational sense. His books being out of print shows he's not appreciated, but that happened to Herman Melville — he was out of print for thirty or forty years. The problem for Jim was that he did not have an academic cadre of supporters who were touting his work. In American publishing if you're dead, you're dead. Once you die and you're not able to go out on a book tour, once you're not there to go out and do these sound bites and sell the book, you disappear, you fade away, and the tragedy is that Jim Kirkwood was made for the sound bite."

T. Michael Kirkwood: "I said, 'Maybe I'll write something,' and he said, 'Even if you're going to fictionalize everything, stick to something you know. Don't try to make up how you went mountain climbing if you've never climbed a mountain before.'"

James Kirkwood: "Writing is also an act of blind faith. You can't know when you sit down to attempt to write anything you're going to accomplish it. You must believe that somehow inspiration will come…We inspire ourselves by sitting down in relative quiet and concentrating and allowing our minds to open up and investigate the ideas we might have…"

Bill Gile: "Bloomington, Indiana, is one tiny town with a huge university and the major thoroughfare is called Kirkwood Avenue. I set the kids a project: nobody's getting any recommendations until I get one of those signs to take back. So that drunken night we crawled up on each other's shoulders and pulled down the street sign saying Kirkwood Avenue, which I brought back to Jimmy. He said it was, 'My favorite possession ever, ever, ever.' He loved surprises like that. Little tiny, valueless toys, things that could be given him that let him know you were thinking of him."

James Kirkwood: "I opened the cover of my last book just to look at my credits. There they all were: novels, non-fiction, plays. I thought, 'Well, if you've done all that, then you *must* be a writer.'"

Arthur Beckenstein: "I think he wanted success more than money. Success and recognition."

Terrence McNally: "People will still say out of the blue, 'God, I miss Jimmy'… When people say 'Jimmy,' they don't have to say 'Jimmy Kirkwood' — and it's a pretty common name. But he was Jimmy and people still miss him and I can't think of many people that you can say over fifteen years after they've left, 'Oh God, I miss Jimmy' and everyone knows who he means and agrees with his sentiment. He was really a very beloved person. He was not a sweetie pie. He could be very difficult and cruel and bitchy. But they really liked his spirit. He was a real character."

James Kirkwood: "I'm terrified of death. Not the process of dying — we're all doing that — but the moment of death, what happens afterward. It scares the hell out of me, the never-ever-again aspect of it all…I think it's a lot of that Catholic upbringing. I still have terrible panics about it."

Jim Piazza: "He had a great sense of energy and charisma but I don't think Jimmy was ever truly really happy. There was one time when he said, 'I want to show you something that makes me really happy.' We went to Sardi's bar about five or six o'clock at night. It was getting dark early as we were sitting there across the street [from] the Shubert Theatre and the neon sign started to go round with his name. That thrilled him."

William Russo: "I asked him once, 'Are you ever going to write an autobiography?' Which was sort of a loaded question because, in essence, everything he wrote was autobiography. He said no, he wasn't ready to ring that bell yet, but he would at some point. Then I said, 'Well, how about a biography?' and he became livid about biographies. I think it had something to do with control. At the time Tennessee Williams had died and I think what I raised was the biography written by Dotson Raider, who knew both Jim and Tennessee Williams. He was livid about that book. He said, 'Friends don't do that, friends don't write those kind of biographies,' and I just thought it was [a] curious thing for him to say, since he was so publicly honest, it seemed, about things. I mean, what did he have to hide? Which is why I'm a little surprised that you're writing a biography. He didn't really want one, and are you going to be printing things he would have been angry about? I guess so."

James Kirkwood: "I think writing is a mystical act. One of the miracles of it all is that you're never quite certain where your thoughts or characters came from. At the end of a day I look back on the pages in wonderment, often thinking, 'My God, I don't even remember thinking *that* thought or imagining *that* character.' I write out of blind faith and the more I do it, the more I realize much of it comes from the subconscious. Writing can be joyous, uplifting, painful and torturous, all in one day. And I absolutely love it."

FINIS

SELECTED BIBLIOGRAPHY

BOOKS BY JAMES KIRKWOOD

There Must Be A Pony! (as Jim Kirkwood); Little, Brown; 1960

UTBU: Unhealthy to be Unpleasant: A comedy in two acts; Samuel French; 1966

Good Times/Bad Times; Simon and Schuster; 1968

American Grotesque; Simon and Schuster; 1970

P.S. Your Cat is Dead!; Stein and Day; 1972

Some Kind of Hero; Thomas Y. Crowell; 1975

P.S. Your Cat is Dead! A comedy in two acts; Samuel French; 1976

P.S. Your Cat is Dead! A comedy in two acts; Samuel French; 1979

Hit Me with a Rainbow; Delacorte Press; 1980

Legends!: A play; Samuel French; 1987

Diary of a Mad Playwright; E P Dutton; 1989

American Grotesque (revised paperback); HarperPerennial; 1992

A Chorus Line: The Complete Book of the Musical (with Michael Bennett; Nicholas Dante; Edward Kleban; Marvin Hamlisch); Applause; 2000

UNPUBLISHED WORKS BY JAMES KIRKWOOD

The Angels or Whoever (novel); circa 1960s

Club Mardi Gras (stage musical; Act I); circa 1977

"ELVIS — Rough scene by scene" (stage musical; partial outline); circa mid-1980s

Good Times/Bad Times (screenplay); Not dated

Harold (TV pilot and episode synopses); circa 1977

I Teach Flying (novel); 1968-1989

"In Favor of Candor" (six-page dramatic sketch); Not dated

Legends! (proposal for TV series); circa late-1980s

"Life with My Movie Star Mother" (text of presentation); 1974

"My Father" (monologue); Not dated

Murder at the Vanities (stage musical; Act I); circa early 1980s

Murder at the Vanities (stage musical; Full version); 1982

Nothing but the Night (step outline for screenplay); circa late 1950s

P.S. Your Cat is Dead! (play); circa 1973

Poland, My Poland (screenplay); 1976

"Ron Field and James Kirkwood Present a Concept for a New Musical Play" (Proposal for *Club Mardi Gras*) (Not dated)

Some Kind of Hero (screenplay); 1977

Surprise! (play); circa 1981

There Must Be a Pony! (screenplay); Not dated

There Must Be a Pony! (play; three-act version); 1962

There Must Be a Pony! (play; two-act version); circa 1970s

There Must Be a Pony! (play; one-act version); circa 1982

Witches (screenplay); 1982

Poems, various; circa 1980s

Comedy sketches, various (with Lee Goodman); 1940s-1950s

The Marriage Habit (play) (with Edwin Duerr); circa 1957

The Boys on the Hill (step outline for stage musical) (with Evan Rhodes); circa 1968

Some Kind of Hero (screenplay) (with Robert Boris); 1981

East Side/West Side (screenplay) (with Gerald S. Paonessa); circa 1982

Stage-Stuck (play) (with Jim Piazza); 1989

MAGAZINE FEATURES BY JAMES KIRKWOOD

Esquire 1968; "SO HERE YOU ARE CLAY SHAW..." (as printed in *American Grotesque*)

Playbill 1969; "That Uncertain Path"

Playbill 1972; "Changing Muses in Midstream"

Playbill 1983; "Not in my Wildest Dreams..."

Dramatist's Guild Quarterly 1980; "The Librettist: Indispensible, Stylish, Sometimes Forgotten" (Panel discussion among Arthur Laurents, Michael Stewart, Alan Jay Lerner, Joseph Stein and Kirkwood)

MAGAZINES EDITED BY JAMES KIRKWOOD

AM; three issues; 1945

LINER NOTES BY JAMES KIRKWOOD

Follies in Concert; 1985

POEM BY JAMES KIRKWOOD

"Through the Province of the Poor to the Playground of the Rich"; *The Bridgehampton Sun;* 1980

OTHER BOOKS

Alan J. Pakula: His Films and His Life; Jared Brown; Back Stage; 2005

Let Justice Be Done; William Davy; Jordan; 1999

Destiny Betrayed; James Dieugenio; Sheridan Square; 1992

I'm Owen Harrison Harding; James Whitfield Ellison; Doubleday; 1955

What They Did for Love; Denny Martin Flinn; Bantam; 1989

On the Trail of the Assassins; Jim Garrison; Penguin; 1992

Intimate Nights: The Golden Age of New York Cabaret; James Gavin; Grove Weidenfeld; 1991

Adventures in the Screen Trade; William Goldman; Futura; 1985

All Fall Down; James Leo Herlihy; Penguin; 1962

Midnight Cowboy; James Leo Herlihy; Panther; 1970

Season of the Witch; James Leo Herlihy; Simon and Schuster; 1971

Sal Mineo: His Life, Murder, and Mystery; H. Paul Jeffers; Carroll & Graf; 2000

A Cast of Killers: The Twentieth Anniversary Edition; Sidney D. Kirkpatrick; BookSurge; 2007

A Separate Peace; John Knowles; Bantam; 1959

Myrna Loy: Being and Becoming; Myrna Loy/James Kotsilibas-Davis; Knopf; 1987

A Chorus Line and the Musicals of Michael Bennett; Ken Mandelbaum; St Martin's Press; 1989

Shockproof Sydney Skate; Marijane Meaker; Perennial; 2002

A Farewell to Justice; Joan Mellen; Potomac; 2005

Jim Garrison: His Life and Times; Joan Mellen; JFK Lancer; 2008

Greatest Revue Sketches; Donald Oliver; Avon; 1982

Mal Tempo & Friends; William Russo; Xlibris Corporation; 2001

Riding James Kirkwood's Pony; William Russo; Xlibris Corporation; 2007

The Catcher in the Rye; J. D. Salinger; Penguin; 1972

The Play Goes On: A Memoir; Neil Simon; Simon and Schuster; 2002

The Longest Line; Gary Stevens/Alan George; Applause; 2000

JFK: The Book of the Film; Oliver Stone/Zachary Sklar; Applause; 2000

On the Line; Robert Viagas/Baayork Lee/Thommie Walsh; William Morrow & Co; 1990

OTHER UNPUBLISHED WORKS

All My Lovers are Dead (partial and unpublished autobiography); Lila Lee; 1973

In the Shadow of a Star (partial and unpublished autobiography); Peggy Tufford Hillmer; 1970

Greetings from Neptune (play); Jim Piazza; 2001

CORRESPONDENCE

Correspondence between James Kirkwood Sr. and Lila Lee and James Kirkwood; 1928

Correspondence between James Kirkwood and James Leo Herlihy; 1960s-1980s

Letters from James Kirkwood to various parties, including Bob Cromling, Carol Channing & Mary Martin, Jim Garrison, Joan Hackett, "Hymie," Phyllis Jackson, Marvin Hamlisch, James Kirkwood Sr., Lila Lee, Little, Brown, Nancy Martin, Andrew Morse, Joseph Papp,

Richard Pryor, William Russo, Stephen Sondheim, Elizabeth Taylor, Sidney Wasserman, Douglas Watt; 1950s-1980s

Letters to Kirkwood from various parties, including Marlene Dietrich, Phyllis Jackson, Lila Lee, Rosalind Russell, Clay Shaw, Liz Smith, Harold Washington; 1960s-1980s

MISCELLANEOUS

School records and reports on James Kirkwood; 1930s-1940s

Yearbooks for Brewster Academy, Elyria High School and Hewlett School; early 1940s

Coast Guard records on James Kirkwood; 1940s

Notes to himself by Kirkwood about arrest on drug possession; 1968

James Kirkwood résumés; 1950s-1980s

Lecture notes; Not dated

Lila Lee medical history summary; 1973

James Kirkwood's ideas and plan for the completion of *I Teach Flying* as dictated to Jerry Paonessa; 1989

AUDIO AND VISUAL RECORDED SOURCES

Motion picture: *To Be or Not to Be*; 1942

Motion picture: *Some Kind of Hero*; 1982

Motion picture: *The Supernaturals*; 1986

Television: *Valiant Lady*; various episodes; late-1950s

Television: *Divorce Court*; circa late-1950s

Television: *Lamp Unto My Feet*: "Something for Bernice"; 1955

Television: *This is Your Life*: "Lila Lee"; 1957

Television: *Merv Griffin Show*; circa mid-1970s

Television: Pia Lindstrom interviews James Kirkwood; circa late 1970s

Television: *Joe Franklin Show*; 1979

Television: *Kup's Show*; circa 1979

Television: *Cinema Showcase*; circa 1979/80

Television: *Broadway Beat* (pilot); circa 1980s

Television: *Divorce Court*; circa 1980s

Television: Interview with Kirkwood by Frank Romano; Unknown program; circa 1980s

Television: *Dick Cavett Show*; 1980

Television: *Joe Franklin Show*; 1980

Television: *Kup's Show*; 1984

Television: *There Must be a Pony!* (TV movie); 1986

Television: Interview with Kirkwood by "Brett"; Unknown program; circa late-1980s

Radio and television: Kirkwood & Goodman (various segments from radio and TV, incl WOR, *Hold That Camera* and *Garry Moore Show*); 1950s

Radio: James Kirkwood radio interview; Unknown program, New Orleans; 1969

Radio: *Carole Hemingway Show*; 1976

Radio: *Roy Leonard Show*; 1978

Video tape: James Kirkwood and Peggy Hillmer, back deck conversation, East Hampton; 1982

Video tape: Reading: *Murder at the Vanities*, Merkin Concert Hall; 1982

Video tape: Commencement address: Genesee Community College, New York; 1988

Video tape: James Kirkwood Key West memorial; 1989

Video tape: James Kirkwood New York memorial; 1989

Audio tape: James Kirkwood and father; conversation at unknown location; circa late-1950s

Audio tape: Lecture: Northern Illinois University; 1980

Audio tape: Lecture: Lincoln Center; 1982

MAGAZINE FEATURES ON JAMES KIRKWOOD

Radio-TV Mirror 1954; "JIMMY KIRKWOOD His Love Story"

Library Journal June 1960 (feature on writers whose first works were appearing that season)

Equity October 1963; "An Interview JIM KIRKWOOD"

After Dark February 1972; "Good Times Getting Better"

Mandate November 1975; "Meet James Kirkwood P.S. Your brilliance is showing!"

Voice August 1990; "Guess Who's Coming to Dinner Theater" (by Jim Piazza)

ADDITIONAL PERIODICAL FEATURES ON JAMES KIRKWOOD

Advocate, The, June 15, 1977 ("A Little Drag Music")

Backstage, November 12, 1982 ("Collaboration is Key Factor in Musical Theatre Productions")

Chicago Daily Tribune, August 23, 1924 ("Lila Lee, Film Star, Becomes Mother Of Girl")

Chronicle-Telegram, The, February 5, 1960, ("The Genesis of a Novel")

Cleveland Plain Dealer, 1938 ("Stage Reunites Father and Son")

Daily News, August 11, 1982 ("Two murder-comedies about to hit Broadway")

East Hampton Star, July 22, 1971 ("THE STAR TALKS TO: James Kirkwood about His Work")

Hamptons Newspaper/Magazine, August 30, 1984 ("James Kirkwood: Writing that blends catharsis and craft")

Joplin Globe, December 16 1948

Los Angeles Times Calendar, December 31, 1972 ("James Kirkwood, Student, Makes Good")

Los Angeles Times, The 1936 (Coverage of investigation into Reid Russell death)

Los Angeles Times, The, February 22, 1976, ("P.S.: Who in This Room is Named Kirkwood?")

Miami Herald, The, January 20, 1977 ("'Drag Queen' Musical Readied by Bufman")

New York Herald Tribune, The, September 21, 1960 ("An Actor Finds Happiness in Writing")

New York Times, The August 13, 1982, ("Actor turned writer turns into director")

New York Times, The, December 9, 1986, ("'Legends' turns a Profit Without Broadway")

New York Times, The, March 4, 1990 ("Curtains for A Chorus Line and for a Stage of City History")

New York Times, The, October 7, 1973, "Publisher Wears Two Hats"

Paterson News, March 13, 1975 "Great Write Way for Kirkwood"

Plain Dealer, 1980 ("KIRKWOOD")

San Francisco Chronicle, August 13, 1987 ("Fists Fly at Party for 5,000th 'Chorus Line'")

San Francisco Chronicle, 1936 (Coverage of investigation into Reid Russell death)

Sarasota Herald-Tribune, March 16, 1981 ("A Classic Play–And The Man Who Helped Create It")

Theatre Week, March 12, 1990 ("How to Remember Broadway's Baby")

Unknown magazine, circa 1989, ("A Cat & Pony Lines & Legends!")

Unknown newspaper, 1978 ("Kirkwood's 'Cat' slinks Into Town")

Unknown newspaper, early 1980s ("'Chorus Line' A Special Show For Kirkwood")

Unknown newspapers, 1968 (Reports of Kirkwood's arrest for drug possession)

Variety, January 20, 1982 ("Kirkwood pens 'murder' tuner; Phyllis Diller set to topline")

Various newspapers, 1920s and 1930s, Coverage of separation, divorce and custody arrangements of James Kirkwood Sr. and Lila Lee

Various newspapers, April 1989, James Kirkwood obituaries

Wisconsin State Journal, The, May 12 1948

WEBSITES

http://www.ibdb.com
http://www.jfklancer.com
http://www.newspaperarchive.com
http://www.wikipedia.org

Many newspapers, periodicals, TV and radio shows and websites were of additional use but their listing here would be impracticable. I have endeavoured to mention them in the main text. Apologies to any inadvertently omitted.

INDEX

Accused 121, 157
Ace, Goodman 204, 205, 314
Aerial Gunner 68-69, 85
After Dark 47, 122, 231, 271, 279, 311
Aldrich Family 95, 118
Albee, Edward 310, 428, 552, 553
All My Lovers are Dead 17, 19, 23-24, 25, 30, 33, 34, 40, 41, 128, 178, 282
American Grotesque 15, 54, 223, 236-257, 259, 270, 283, 315, 324, 504, 525, 544
Andrews, Julie 481, 532
Attenborough, Richard 477, 478
Auntie Mame 135-138, 140, 149, 408, 409
Austin, Lyn 203, 204

Ballard, Kaye 92, 181, 275
Bankhead, Tallulah 128-132, 135, 136, 137, 149, 166, *192*, 275, 350, 393, 514
Barnes, Clive 308, 377, 379
Beach, Gary 473, 474, 481, 483, 484, 485, 486, 488, 489, 490, 491, 492-493, 494, 495, 496, 534
Beach, Mildred 52, 53, 55, 216
Beckenstein, Arthur 20, 21, 22, 42, 53, 54, 60, 62, 67, 88, 115, 117, 131-132, 145, 147, 148, 168, 198, 201, 202, 210, 213, 218, 219, 231, 256, 259-265, 266, 267, 268, 270, 271, 273, 282, 283, 297, 298, 303, 313, 314, 328-329, 342, 343, 346, 355, 357-358, *361*, 371, 372, 383, 385, 395, 397, 401, 402, 405-406, 418, 423-424, 425, 433, 444-445, 467, 469, 475, 501-502, 504-505, 506-508, 513, 516, 518, 522, 523, 524-526, 527, 528, 529, 538, 539, 545, 546, 548, 552, 554
Bennett, Michael 11, 283-284, 287-303, 305, 313, 314-315, 328, 340, *369*, 408, 415, 416-418, 448, 449, 473, 475, 476, 501, 502, 503, 508, 509, 517, 518-519
Bentley, Muriel 116-117, 118-119, *190*, 371, 393
Bertrand, Clay 222, 239, 244, 246, 248
Bishop, Kelly 296, 301, 314, 535

Blood and Sand 16, 17
Bogazianos, Vasili 373-374, 375-377, 378-379
Bolton, Whitney 134, 143, 155
Book World 11, 12, 323
Boris, Robert 433, 434, 436
Boys on the Hill, The 217, 218-219, 284
Brando, Marlon 185, 488
Brigadoon 173-174, 439
Brooks, Mel 133, 342
Buckley, Betty 430, 431
Bufman, Zev 348-349
Bullock, Ned 53, 54, 57, 60, 70, 88, 216

Call Me Madam 181-182, 439, 551-552
Capote, Truman 250, 251, 514
Carroll, Earl 386, 387, 390, 414-415, 468
Carson, Johnny 130, 350
Catcher in the Rye, The 150, 159, 162, 167, 224, 226, 229, 230, 231, 345
Chaney, Sr., Lon 16, 24
Channing, Carol 305, 350, *362*, 424, *460*, 472, 475, 481-484, 486, 489, 490, 491, 493, 494, 495, 496, 505, 523, 532, 533, 534, 539
Chaplin, Charlie 16, 17
Chicago Tribune, The 12, 19, 134, 323
Chorus Line, A 11-12, 220, 284, 287-303, 305, 312-317, 324, 326, 328-329, 334, 340, 343, 345, 346, 348, 350, 352, 353-354, 357, *369*, 373, 378, 386, 387, 388, 389, 390, 401, 402, 404, 405-406, 411, 412, 415, 416, 417, 418, 419, 428, 438, 442, 448, 449-450, *453*, 468, 473, 476, 477-478, 482, 487, 496, 501-503, 506, 507, 510, 517, 518, 519, 521-522, 531, 534, 535, 537, 538, 547
Cirker, Ira 111-112, 114-115, 123, 124, 125
Claiborne, Ross 268, 384, 513-514
Club Mardi Gras 347-352, 388, 415, 438
Coleman, Nancy 111, 112, 127, *190*, 198
Collins, Joan 471, 537, 538, 539
Cormier, Arthur 280-281, 317, 319, 324, *368*

Cosmopolitan 12, 229, 324
Coward, Noël 85, 224, 305
Crawford, Joan 157, 199, 398, 399
Cromling, Bob 61, 69, 136, 137, 138, 139, 143, 269
Crooked Tree 431-433, 476

Dance Me a Song 90, 387
Dante, Nicholas 11, 288, 290, 292, 293-294, 295-296, 297-298, 300, 313, 314, 315, 340, 405, 412, *453*, 476, 503, 518-519
Davidson, Marjorie 67, 79-80
DeMille, Cecil B., 16, 525
DeSanti, Carole 504, 505, 506, 531
Desmond, John 88, 95, 111, 113-114, 115, 116, 119-121, 123-124, 125-126, 130, 138, 143, 165, 201, 203, 282
Diary of a Mad Playwright 41, 201, 471, 472, 482, 483, 486, 487, 488, 492, 499, 503, 506, 523, 525, 531-534, 539
Dick Cavett Show, The 31, 49, 71, 326
Dietrich, Marlene 21, 350, 396-397, *455*
Divorce Court 124, 275, 398
Donahue, Nancy 198, 199
Druce, Jeff 336, 377, 338, 339, 376
Duerr, Edwin 132-133, 134
Dullea, Keir 307, 337
Dynasty 471, 538

East Side/West Side 426,-428
Edwards, Annie-Joe 484, 486, 505, 532
Edwards, Gus 16, 17
Eggers, Kevin 41, 473, 474, 475, 493, 495, 496, 532, 533
Eggler, Bruce 236, 252, 256
Ellison, Harlan 324, 326
Ellison, Nick 150, 232, 277, 316-317, 328-329, 384-385, 395, 508, 511, 552
Elvis 473-476, 496
Equity 122, 123, 145, 171, 180, 181
Ertegun, Ahmet 473, 474, 475, 482-483, 484, 489, 492, 495, 496, 532, 533
Esquire 54, 220, 222, 223, 232, 237, 238, 241, 242, 397, 468-469
Evans, Linda 538, 539

Farrow, John 23-24, 263
Ferrie, David 239, 243, 244, 245, 246, 247, 248, 249, 255, 257

Field, Ron 348, 349
Fisher, John 510, 514
Follies 128, 287, 409, 468
Fonville, Harold 85-86, 182
Fosse, Bib 90, 517
Foxworth, Robert 336, 337

Garbo, Greta 126, 397
Gardner, Ava 117, 393
Garland, Trish 292, 297, 300-301, 482, 489
Garrison, Jim 221, 232, 236, 237, 238, 239, 240, 241, 242, 244, 246, 247, 248, 249, 250, 251, 252, 253, 254, 255, 256, 257
Gavin, James 85, 86, 87, 90, 91, 96
Gentile, David 431, 432, 476-477
Gile, Bill 262, 283, 388, 389, 391, 398, 401, 402, 406-407, 411, 417, 418, 419, 484-486, 510, 512, 521, 526, 534, 554
Goldman, Albert 473-474
Goldman, William 433, 434
Goldstein, Patti 88, 125, 157, 262, 371
Goodman, Lee 42, 85-97, 115, 119, 121, 128, 138, 146, 147, 172, 182, *189*, 198, 217, 275, 278-279, 302, 303, 317, 348, 387, 401, 446, 475, 509, 512
Good Times/Bad Times 22, 24, 43, 52-58, 94, 160, 213-217, 219, 221, 224, 226-232, 235, 237-238, 240, 260, 293, 318, 324, 331-334, 354-357, 384, 385, 407, 426, 428, 430, 443, 448, 469, 543, 547, 552
Granger, Farley 174-175
Greenall Jr., Walter G. 53, 54, 58, *106*, 216
Greetings from Neptune 534, 535
Guttenberg, Steve 535, 536, 537

Hackett, Joan 439-442
Hamilton, Margaret 202, 205
Hamlisch, Marvin 292, 295, 296, 297, 298, 300, 340, 417, 477, 502
Hamula, Esther 49, 50-51, 52, 60, 61, 62, 63, 80, 83-84, *108*, *109*, 269-270, 344
Harold 371-372
Haskell, Francine 373, 379
Hatcher, Tom 492, 445
Helms, Peter 175-176, 177
Hemingway, Carole 344, 436

Herlihy, James Leo 17, 166-167, 197-198, 201-204, 208-210, 213, 217, 221, 224, 236, 241, 242, 253, 334-335, 340, 355, *366*, 378, 385-386, 397, 429, 437, 445, 467, 482, 499-500, 505, 510, 514, 524, 525, 538, 544-546, 548
Herman, Jerry 413, 419
Hitchcock, Alfred 126, 146, 157, 174
Hit Me with a Rainbow 12, 97, 117, 210, 215, 346, 383-386, 391-398, 411, 437, 471, 479, 525, 535, 543
Hitzig, Rupert 426, 428, 430
Hollywood Canteen 69, 85
Hoopes, Matt 55, 331, 332-334

I Teach Flying 48, 68, 69, 88, 219, 232, 425, 499, 500, 503, 506, 527, 529, 539-547

Jacobs, Bernard 315, 424, 470
Jackson, Glenda 427, 475
Jackson, Phyllis 155, 156, 161, 273, 326, 424
JFK 238, 242, 253, 255, 256
Jolson, Al 20, 22
Junior Miss 58, 59

Katselas, Milton 256, 307, 334-335, 337, 338, 339, 340, 376
Kennedy, John F. 182, 221, 223, 238, 239, 243, 245, 248, 249, 251, 255, 256
Kennedy, Robert 177, 240
Kenwith, Herbert 124, 125
Kilburn, Terry 17, 152-153, 154-155, 216-217, 322, 328
King, Alan 426, 427, 430
Kirkwood, Sr., James 15-19, 21-25, 28, 29, 30, 31, 33, 40, 43, 47, 48, 50, 51-52, 67-68, 69, 70-71, 79-80, 81, 85, *99*, *101*, *102*, 119-121, 122, 128, 139, 143, 148, 152, 162, 168-169, 182-185, *191*, 197, 199, 219, 224, 225, 232, 263, 267-268, 270, 279, 297, 383, 385, 399, 401, 402, 404, 425-426, 429, 445, 494, 500, 527, 528, 539, 540, 542
Kirkwood, T. Michael 18, 67-68, 79-80, 82, 120, 121, 122, 169, 182-183, 184-185, *188*, 199, 220, 267, 311-312, 339, 401-402, 404, 467, 509, 510, 526, 528-529, 539, 553
Kirsch, Robert R. 132, 152-155, 167, 172, 211, 323
Kleban, Edward 292, 293, 295, 296, 298, 300, 301, 340, 412, 477, 503

Kluger, Richard 235, 237, 240, 273, 504, 505
Kramer, Anne 152, 153
Kramer, Larry 377-378, 513

La Cage Aux Follies 351, 352, 419
Lamp Unto My Feet 119-121, 125, *191*, 275
Laurents, Arthur 89, 116, 262, 263, 266, 267, 268, 293, 352-353, 377, 378, 405, 425-426, 445, 468, 492, 503, 513, 516, 518, 523, 525, 527, 533, 534, 545-546, 553
Lee, Baayork 21, 291, 294, 297, 298, 450, 478, 538
Lee, Lila 15, 16-17, 18, 19-28, 29, 30, 31, 33-36, 38-43, 47, 48, 49, 50, 58-59, 63, 67, 68, 71, 72, 76, 79, 81, 82, 83, 84, 86, *99*, *100*, *101*, *102*, *104*, *105*, 111, 115, 119, 120-121, 128, 129, 138-139, 145, 148, 149, 151, 152, 155, 161-162, 164, 169, 177, 179-180, 183, *191*, *193*, *195*, 197, 198, 200-201, 205, 213, 224, 263, 268, 281-283, 297, 315, 355, 397, 423, 424, 425, 445, 469, 471, 476, 479, 539, 551
Lefkowitz, Elisa 354, 518
Lefkowitz, Elliot 354, 408, 423
Legends! 12, 41, 357, 419, 424, 446, *460*, 469-473, 474, 475-476, 478, 481-486, 487-497, 499, 504-506, 508, 511, 517, 523, 531, 532-534, 537-538, 539
Leonard, John 248, 249
Leonard, Roy 280, 338-339, 341
Liberace *362*, 423
Library Journal 166, 229
Los Angeles Examiner 35-36, 40, 167
Los Angeles Times 33, 34, 37, 38, 39, 47, 132, 146, 147, 152, 153, 167, 228, 250, 324, 395
Loy, Myrna 175-178, 179, 439
LuPone, Robert 313, 535

Mailer, Norman 265, 346
Mandate 56, 310, 311, 336
Mandelbaum, Ken 293, 328
Marriage Habit, The 132, 133, 134
Martin, Mary *362*, 424, *460*, 472, 475, 476, 481-482, 483-484, 486, 489, 490, 491, 492-493, 494, 495-496, 505, 517, 523, 532, 533, 539
Martin, Nancy 57, 58, 97, *107*
Mason, Marsha 313-314
Matalon, Vivian 271, 305-306, 307-308, 309, 310, 311, 337, 372, 377

Mattes, Jed 405, 505, 548
McKechnie, Donna 287-300, 301, 312-317, 449, *453*, 476, 478
McNally, Terrence 147, 157, 220, 251, 268, 310, 423, 424, 447, 513, 514, 534, 553, 554
Mellen, Joan 236-237, 244
Merrick, David 416, 500
Merrill, Dina 355, 406-407
Midler, Bette 322, 534
Midnight Cowboy 201, 208, 209, 277
Miller, Ann 495, 505
Mineo, Sal 307, 337-340
Mommie Dearest 157, 398, 399
Morison, Patricia 143, 144
Morris, Gouverneur 30, 31, 33, 34-35, 37, 38, 39, 41, 47, 52
Morrison, Benjamin 56, 209, 220-221, 235-236, 238, 239, 240, 241, 250, 253, 255-256, 257, 259, 265, 266, 397, 399, 404-405, 490-491, 503, 511
Morris, Ruth 30, 31, 33, 34-35, 36, 37, 38, 39, 40, 41, 47, *104*
Morse, Andrew 262, 355, 395, 436, *461*, 469, 512, 546, 547-549
Mulligan, Robert 231-232
Murder at the Vanities 181, 386, 389, 405-420, 438, *458*, 468, 500, 518
Murphy, John E. 81, 83, 115, 198
Murphy, Mary 198, 224
Musante, Tony 307, 309

Never Too Late 198, 200, 275
New York Times 59, 67, 81, 133, 167, 206, 207, 229, 248, 249, 278, 287, 308, 324, 325, 326, 377, 379, 396, 404, 431, 432, 442, 495, 496, 529
Nichols, Lila Lee 20, 21, 24, 26, 27, 31, 50, 52, 59-60, 62, 63, 70, *107*, 165, 267, 326-327
Nichols, Mike 408, 472, 473, 494, 495, 517, 532, 539
Nigro, Robert 373, 374
Nothing but the Night 132, 134, 135, 479

Oliver, Donald 386-389, 390-391, 397, 408, 409, 410, 411, 412, 413, 414, 415, 416, 417, 418, 419, 420, 440, 447, *458*, 468, 481, 526
Oswald, Lee Harvey 221, 222, 223, 239, 244, 245, 246, 248, 249, 255, 257

Pakula, Alan 161, 171, 178
Paonessa, Jerry 23, 209, 241, 250, 327, 342, 344, 351-352, 353-355, 372, 383-384, 385, 397-398, 399, 426-429, 433, 434, 436-437, 439, *456*, 473, 475, 486, 488, 506, 518, 522, 523, 525-527, 539, 544, 545, 546, 547
Papp, Joseph 42, 289, 290, 291, 301, 316, 448, 450, 502-503
Pearson, Anne 111, 127
Peine, Jack R. 25, 49
Piazza, Jim 20, 21, 42, 43, 48, 68, 115, 128, 209, 217, 230, 263, 264, 266, 267, 268, 270, 343, 351, 352, 385, 402-404, 405, 419, 428, 443-444, 445-449, *450*, 469, 487-488, 491, 493, 496, 500-502, 503, 506-508, 510-513, 514-516, 518-521, 522, 523, 525, 527-528, 533, 534-535, 539, 544-545, 551, 552, 554-555
Pickford, Mary 16, 18, 21, 183-184, 540
Playbill 48, 138, 143, 144, 145, 231, 449
Playboy 232, 236, 278
Plotkin, Ronald 85, 86, 87-88, 89, 90, 91-92, 94, 95, 96, 97, 116-117, 139, 145-146, 147, 151, 172, 173, 198, 279, 302-303, 317, 327, 508, 509
Poland My Poland 341-342, 437
Powers, Beatrice 24, 67
Price, Homer 17, 62, 129, 147, 197, 201, 204, 208, 221, 250, 253, 256, 262, 270, 296-297, 303, 315, 327, 358, *366*, 395, 491, 514, 516, 524, 528, 545
P.S. Your Cat is Dead! 11, 97, 140, 172, 198, 226, 251, 270-278, 279, 283, 293, 303, 305-312, 317, 324, 334-340, 351, 353, 357-358, *365*, 372-380, 385, 386, 394, 395, 431, 438, 440, 472, 476, 490, 501, 531, 535-537, 543, 547, 549
Pryor, Richard 433-435, 436, *457*

Randall, Tony 202, 203, 204, 205, 206, 208
Raye, Martha 181-182
Reed, Lydia 111, 127
Reed, Rex 277, 311
Regester, Bob 474, 508, 509, 523
Reilly, Charles Nelson 501, 515, 516, 519, 520, 522
Reynolds, Burt 501, 514, 516, 519, 520, 521
Rhodes, Evan 17, 18, 33, 41, 205, 217-218, 240, 282, 469, 514, 545

Riding James Kirkwood's Pony 43-44, 538-539
Ritter, Thelma 202, 203
Roberts, Donald 53, 57, 58
Robertson, Cliff 355, 406-407
Rope 126, 135, 174
Russell, Reid 30-31, 33, 34-43, 47, 49, 53, 60, 88, 134, 139, 146, 149, 158, 163, 297, 480-481, 538
Russell, Rosalind 136-138, 179
Russell, Victoria 33, 34, 28, 38, 39, 41
Russo, Perry 244, 245, 246, 247, 250-251
Russo, William 18, 36, 42-44, 49, 53-57, 69, 76, 88, 97, 135, 146, 147, 150, 166, 202, 230-231, 266, 277, 328, 346-347, 372, 383, 396, 425, *456*, 479, 480, 500, 535, 538-539, 545, 553, 555
Ruth, Ralph 60, 61, 269

Salinger, J D 150, 162, 167, 229
San Francisco Chronicle 35, 37, 38
Schirmer Jr., Gus 128, 129-130
Seff, Richard 89, 92, 95, 96, 116, 123, 130, 138, 202, 262, 272, 315, 405, 449
Separate Peace, A 226, 231, 232, 331, 345
Shaw, Clay 54, *195*, 221-223, 232, 235, 236-239, 241-257, 279, 397, 468-469, 544
Shearin, John 372, 374, 376, 378, 379
Simon, John 309-310, 351, 376, 380, 502
Simon, Neil 314-315, 335
Sinatra, Frank 117, 123
Sklar, Zachary 238, 242, 251, 252, 253, 254, 255, 256-257
Smith, David 331-332, 333-334
Smith, Liz 88, 91, 92, 262, 297, 380, 383, 423, 424, 443, *458*, 502, 521-522, 525, 529
Sokolov, Raymond A. 324-325, 326, 327
Some Kind of Hero 11, 12, 55, 82, 88, 119, 259, 263, 316, 317-328, 340, 343-344, 353, 354-355, *368*, 384, 385, 406, 407, 426, 431, 432-438, *457*, 543
Sondheim, Stephen 287, 352, 378, 409, 413, 448, 468, 469
Spencer, David 387, 388, 389, 390, 391, 396, 397, 401, 408, 409, 410, 411, 412, 413, 414, 416, 417, 418, 419, 438, 440, *458*, 472-473
Spiegel, Terry 305, 373, 379
Sprecher, Ben 537, 538
Stage-Struck 446-449, 487, 488, 500, 501, 503, 506, 517-521, 529, 534, 544

Stimac, Anthony 406, 439
Stone, Oliver 238, 242, 255, 256
Stone, Peter 357, 438, 525
Stritch, Elaine 115-116, 271, *365*, 374, 446, *458*, 468, 551-552
Study, Lomax 19, 23, 70-76, 81, 93-94, 145, 161, 182, 183-184, 200, 491, 544
Supernaturals, The 398-399, 459
Surprise! 406-408, 434, 439
Sutton, Dolores 89, 112, 114, 117, 123, 124, 125, 127, 135, 265
Swanson, Gloria 20, 21, 72
Sydow, Jack 20, 89, 116, 172, 173-175, 179, 181-183, 203-205, 206, 208, 265, 284, 305, 306, 327, 439-440, 442, 479, 551, 552

Taylor, Elizabeth 145, *362*, 423, 424, *459*, 479, 480
Taylor, Rip 519-520
Teenagers Unlimited 91, 275
There Must Be a Pony! 12, 15, 22, 30-31, 41, 43, 44, 49, 52, 97, 132, 134, 144-146, 149-156, 158-169, 171-172, 174, 175-180, 184, 185, 199-200, 202, 206, 210, 214-215, 216, 224, 235, 237, 251, 273, 297, 324, 353, 371, 395, 397, 399, 407, 437, 438-443, *459*, 478-481, 538, 539, 543, 548, 549
This Is Your Life 138-139, *193*
Thompson, Joan 24, 67, 79, 85, 86, 87, 88, 116, 121, 124, 155, 183, 185, 200, 267-268, 401-402, 486-487, 509, 528, 529
Timmons, Stuart 236, 237
Tobacco Road 51, 70, 494, 540
To Be or Not To Be 341-342
Today Show, The 83, 339
To Kill a Mockingbird 178, 185, 231
Tufford, Bobby 18, 20, 21, 26, 27, 48, 49-50, 58, 60, 62, 63, 69, 70, 269, 283, 521
Tufford, Leonard 25, 27, 28, 50
Tufford, Peggy 16, 21, 25-26, 28, 51, 61, *103*, 155, *195*, 283, 391, 404, 476, 533, 540

Unholy Three, The 16, 24
UTBU 162, 201, 202-208, 209, 210, 272, 314, 357, 387, 439

Variety 93, 130, 325, 426, 520
Valentino, Rudolph 16, 17

Valiant Lady 95, 111-115, 119, 121, 122-125, 126, 127-128, 130, 131, 135, 136, 137, 138, 140, 145, 157, 165, 174, *190*, 198, 201, 262, 265, 275, 282, 371, 424
Vidal, Gore 224, 346, 512

Wagner, Robert 397, *459*, 479
Walker, Nancy 203-204
Wasserman, Sidney 26-29, 49, 60, 62, 63, 172, 197, 223, 269, 282
Webb, Alan 202, 203, 204, 205, 206
Welcome Darlings 130-132, 135, 143, 166, *192*, 275

Westlake, Donald E. 410, 419-420
Whaley, Jim 150, 230, 302, 341, *454*, 477
Williams, Clifford 305, 476, 482, 484, 485
Williams, Tennessee 224, 240, 283, 310, 337, 501, 514, 528, 555
Wilson, Robert C. 431-432, 476
Witches 428-430
Wonderful Town 118, 181, 275, 408
Wood, Natalie 397-398, 437
Woods, Donald 175-176

You Can't Live Forever 68, 85

Bear Manor Media

Classic Cinema.
Timeless TV.
Retro Radio.

WWW.BEARMANORMEDIA.COM

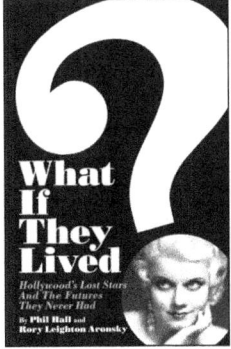

www.ingramcontent.com/pod-product-compliance
Lightning Source LLC
Chambersburg PA
CBHW071932240426
43668CB00038B/1222